NATIVE AMERICANS INFORMATION DIRECTORY

Highlights

The *Native Americans Information Directory (NAID)* is a comprehensive guide to resources for and about the indigenous peoples of the United States and Canada, including:

- Indians
- Eskimos
- Aleuts

- Metis
- Inuits
- Hawaiians

Identifies Wide Variety of Resources

NAID provides current, detailed information on a wide range of print and "live" resources concerned with Native American life and culture, including:

- Tribes & Native Communities
- Organizations
- Museum & Library Collections
- Government Agencies & Programs
- Research Centers
- Education Programs
- Studies Programs
- Publications and Publishers
- Broadcast Media
- Videos
- Scholarships, Fellowships, & Loans

Detailed Information in a Convenient Arrangement

The first edition of *NAID* offers a convenient one-stop source of information. It consists of two parts:

Descriptive Listings — *NAID's* more than 4,500 entries are organized into sections by group of native peoples. Within each section, listings are arranged into categories by type of information resource. Each listing typically contains descriptive information and complete contact data, including addresses, telephone, toll-free, and fax numbers, and personal names.

Master Name and Keyword Index — provides a single alphabetical arrangement of all resources mentioned within the descriptive listings, including former and alternate names.

ISSN 1063-9632

NATIVE AMERICANS INFORMATION DIRECTORY

First Edition

A Guide to Organizations, Agencies, Institutions,
Programs, Publications, Services, and Other
Resources Concerned with the Indigenous Peoples
of the United States and Canada, including:

- American Indians
- Alaska Natives
- Native Hawaiians
- Aboriginal Canadians

Julia C. Furtaw, Editor

Kimberly Burton Faulkner, Associate Editor

 **Gale Research Inc.** • DETROIT • LONDON

124414

Amy Lucas, *Senior Editor*
Julia C. Furtaw, *Editor*
Kimberly Burton Faulkner, *Associate Editor*
Julie Anne Bilenchi, *Assistant Editor*

Aided by:
Susan Bartos, Sandra Doran, Christine Mathews

Victoria B. Cariappa, *Research Manager*
Maureen Richards, *Research Supervisor*
Mary Beth McElmeel and Tamara C. Nott, *Editorial Associates*
Andrea B. Ghorai, Daniel J. Jankowski, Julie K. Karmazin, Robert S. Lazich,
and Donna Melnychenko, *Editorial Assistants*

Mary Beth Trimper, *Production Manager*
Mary Winterhalter, *Production Assistant*

Benita Spight, *Data Entry Supervisor*
Gwendolyn Tucker, *Data Entry Group Leader*
Virgil L. Burton III, *Data Entry Associate*

Cynthia Baldwin, *Art Director*
Mary Krzewinski, *Graphic Designer*
C.J. Jonik, Keyliner

Theresa Rocklin, *Supervisor of Editorial Programming Services*
Timothy Richardson, *Computer Programmer*

The paper used in this publication meets the minimum requirements of AmericanNational Standard for Information Sciences—Permanence Paper for PrintedLibrary Materials, ANSI Z39.48-1984. ∞™

This book is printed on recycled paper that meets Environmental Protection Agency Standards. ♲

ISSN 1063-9632
ISBN 0-8103-8854-5

Printed in the United States of America

Published simultaneously in the United Kingdom
by Gale Research International Limited
(An affiliated company of Gale Research Inc.)

Contents

Aboriginal Canadians
Including Indians, Inuits, and Metis

General Resources on Native Americans

Acknowledgments

The editor would like to extend sincere thanks to the following members of the *Native Americans Information Directory* Advisory Board for reviewing the scope, coverage, content, and arrangement of this volume:

- Naomi Caldwell-Wood, President, American Indian Library Association
- Elizabeth Pa Martin, attorney of Hawaiian native ancestry; Executive Director, Native Hawaiian Advisory Council and President, Hui Na'auao
- Dr. James H. May, Vice Provost for Information Resources, California State University, Chico; member, United Keetoowah Band of Indians and the White House Conference on Indian Education

Thanks are also due to the many national and local organizations, government officials, and reference librarians throughout the U.S. and Canada who kindly provided information for inclusion or recommended resources for use in compiling the directory.

Introduction

Ethnic minorities represent an increasingly important segment of the population in the United States and Canada. In recent years, there has been a renewed interest in the rich and diverse heritage of Native Americans—the indigenous peoples of the United States and Canada. Although Indians, Eskimos, Aleuts, Metis, Inuits, and Native Hawaiians represent less than 1% of the total population in these countries, students, tourists, government agencies, journalists, historians, and other researchers often need information on political, economic, social, or educational issues relating to Native Americans.

The first edition of *Native Americans Information Directory (NAID)* meets the need for information on all aspects of Native American life and culture. *NAID* provides libraries, schools, businesses, organizations, and individuals with the most up-to-date information on a wide variety of organizations, agencies, institutions, programs, publications, services, and other resources concerned with the native peoples of the United States and Canada, including:

- Tribes & Native Communities
- National Organizations
- Regional, State, & Local Organizations
- Government Agencies
- Museum Collections
- Library Collections
- Research Centers
- Education Services
- Studies Programs

- Scholarships, Fellowships, & Loans
- Directories
- Journals and Magazines
- Newsletters
- Newspapers
- Publishers
- Radio Stations
- Videos

Compiled with the Help of Native American Experts

NAID comprises more than 4,500 listings of resources that provide information on a broad range of topics relating to the Native American community, including culture, heritage, education, social concerns, politics, and employment.

The process used to determine the scope, coverage, content, and arrangement of these listings was guided by an advisory board of prominent Native Americans.

NAID's broad geographic scope, comprehensive coverage, and convenient single volume format eliminates the need to consult multiple, often hard- to-locate specialized sources.

Covers All the Indigenous Peoples of the United States and Canada

NAID's coverage encompasses native groups whose origins are in the aboriginal peoples of the United States and Canada, including:

American Indians (Navajo, Cherokee, Ute, Seminole, Sioux, Chippewa, and other federally recognized tribes)
Alaska Natives (Indians, Eskimos, and Aleuts)
Aboriginal Canadians (Indians, Metis, and Inuits)
Native Hawaiians (Descendents of aboriginal inhabitants of the Hawaiian Islands)

Convenient Arrangement and Thorough Indexing Speed Access to Information Resources

NAID consists of a main body of descriptive listings and a Master Name and Keyword Index.

The **Descriptive Listings** are organized into sections by group of native peoples, as listed on the

"Contents" pages, providing an overview of all resources specifically relating to these groups. A section covering information resources on minorities in general that include Native Americans is also included. The entries in each section are arranged by type of information resource.

Listings typically provide complete contact and descriptive data, enabling the user to easily determine relevant resources and then contact organizations by telephone or mail for further information.

The **Master Name and Keyword Index** speeds access to the descriptive entries through its single alphabetic listing of the organizations, agencies, institutions, programs, publications, services, and other resources included in *NAID*. Citations for significant keywords appearing in organization names and publication titles, and to former/alternate names mentioned within the descriptive listings, are also included.

For more information on the content, arrangement, and indexing of *NAID,* consult the "User's Guide" following this Introduction.

Method of Compilation

NAID was compiled from a wide variety of information sources. Relevant entries were carefully selected from other Gale Research Inc. directories, government publications, and lists and directories supplied by numerous national and local organizations. Telephone inquiries were also employed to gather data and/ or verify information.

Comments Welcome

We encourage users to bring new or unlisted organizations to our attention. Every effort will be made to cover them in subsequent editions of the Directory. Comments and suggestions for improving the *Directory* are also welcome. Please contact:

Native Americans Information Directory
Gale Research Inc.
835 Penobscot Bldg.
Detroit, MI 48226-4094
Telephone: (313)961-2242
Toll-Free: 800-347-GALE
FAX: (313)961-6815

Julia C. Furtaw

User's Guide

The *Native Americans Information Directory (NAID)* consists of:

- Descriptive Listings
- Master Name and Keyword Index

Each part is fully described below.

Descriptive Listings

The Descriptive Listings are organized into five sections:

American Indians
Alaska Natives
Aboriginal Canadians
Native Hawaiians
General Resources

The first four sections contain information resources targeted specifically to each group of native peoples; the final section covers resources addressing the needs and concerns of Indians, Eskimos, Metis, Inuits, and Native Hawaiians in general.

Each section contains up to 15 categories of information sources, as described below; categories appear in the order listed. Entries within each section are grouped by category, then listed alphabetically either by name or title, or state or province. Entries are numbered sequentially, beginning with the first entry in the first section. All resources listed are included in each relevant section, providing a complete selection of information resources pertinent to each ethnic group.

Categories of Information Resources

▶ Tribal Communities

- **Scope:** Federally recognized tribes, bands, and tribal communities in the United States and Canada.
- **Entries include:** Tribe, band, or tribal community name, address, telephone, toll-free, and fax numbers, and name of contact. U.S. entries also include the Bureau of Indian Affairs agency and office with which they are affiliated.
- **Arrangement:** Alphabetical by state or province, then alphabetical by city names within state or province, and alphabetical by tribe, band, or tribal community names within cities.
- **Source:** U.S. government documents and original research.
- **Indexed by:** Tribe, band, or tribal community name, significant keywords, and geographic designations within organization names.

▶ National Organizations

- **Scope:** Primarily nonprofit membership organizations in the U.S. and Canada, including social, philanthropic, cultural, professional, and business groups concerned with Indians, Eskimos, Metis, Inuits, and Native Hawaiians, or these minorities in general.
- **Entries include:** Organization name, address, telephone, fax, and toll- free numbers, name of contact, and a brief description of the organization's purpose and activities.
- **Arrangement:** Alphabetical by organization name.
- **Source:** *Encyclopedia of Associations, Volume 1, National Organizations of the U.S.,* 27th Edition and *International Organizations,* 26th Edition (published by Gale Research Inc.); supplemented by original research.
- **Indexed by:** Organization name and significant keywords.

▶ **Regional, State/Provincial, and Local Organizations**

- **Scope:** Regional, state, provincial, and local organizations, including affiliates of selected national organizations; cultural, social, philanthropic, professional, and business groups; and social service agencies concerned with Native Americans or minorities in general. (For further information on local affiliates of national organizations, also consult the "National Organizations" category.)
- **Entries include:** Organization name, address, telephone, toll-free, and fax numbers, and name of contact. Some entries also include a brief description of the group's purpose and activities.
- **Arrangement:** Alphabetical by state or province, then alphabetical by city names within state or province, and alphabetical by organization names within cities.
- **Source:** Original research.
- **Indexed by:** Organization name and significant keywords, including geographic designations within organization names.

▶ **Federal Government Agencies**

- **Scope:** Units of the federal government in the U.S. and Canada concerned specifically with Indians, Eskimos, Metis, Inuits, and Native Hawaiians, or with civil rights, affirmative action, equal employment opportunity, and other areas of interest to the Native American community.
- **Entries include:** Agency or unit name, address, telephone, toll-free, and fax numbers, and name of contact.
- **Arrangement:** Alphabetical by agency name.
- **Source:** *United States Government Manual* and original research.
- **Indexed by:** Parent agency and specific unit names, as well as significant keywords within names.

▶ **Federal Domestic Assistance Programs**

- **Scope:** U.S. federally funded programs, projects, services, and activities that provide assistance or benefits to the Native American community in such areas as minority business assistance, civil rights, and education.
- **Entries include:** Sponsoring federal agency name, program name, address, telephone, toll-free, and fax numbers, name of contact, and a brief program description. *Catalog of Federal Domestic Assistance* numbers are also included for easy cross-reference to complete *Catalog* listings.
- **Arrangement:** Alphabetical by agency and program name.
- **Source:** *Catalog of Federal Domestic Assistance.*
- **Indexed by:** Parent agency name, program name, and significant keywords within names.

▶ **State/Provincial, and Local Government Agencies**

- **Scope:** State, province, and local government agencies concerned specifically with Indian, Eskimo, Metis, Inuit, and Native Hawaiian affairs or with general areas such as equal employment, fair housing, civil rights, and minority business development.
- **Entries include:** Agency name, address, telephone, toll-free, and fax numbers, and name of contact.
- **Arrangement:** Alphabetical by state or province, then alphabetical by agency names within state or province.
- **Source:** Original research.
- **Indexed by:** Parent agency and specific unit names, and geographic designations and significant keywords within agency names.

▶ **Library Collections**

- **Scope:** Libraries with special collections about or of particular interest to Native Americans, including educational, historical, and cultural archives.
- **Entries include:** Parent organization name, library name, address, telephone, toll-free, and fax numbers, name of contact, and a general description of collections and holdings.
- **Arrangement:** Alphabetical by parent organization name.
- **Source:** *Directory of Special Libraries and Information Centers,* 16th Edition (published by Gale Research Inc.); supplemented by original research.
- **Indexed by:** Sponsoring organization and library names and significant keywords within names.

► **Museum Collections**

- **Scope:** Museums, galleries, exhibits, and other collections featuring Native American culture and artists.
- **Entries include:** Organization name, address, and telephone, toll-free, and fax numbers. Most entries also include a brief description of collections and holdings.
- **Arrangement:** Alphabetical by state, then alphabetical by organization names within state.
- **Source:** Original research.
- **Indexed by:** Organization name, significant keywords, and geographic designations within organization names.

► **Research Centers**

- **Scope:** Research centers operated by universities and other nonprofit organizations studying Native American life, history, and culture, including topics such as education, archaeology, and law.
- **Entries include:** Sponsoring institution name, research center name, address, telephone, toll-free, and fax numbers, name of contact, and a brief description of activities, facilities, and services.
- **Arrangement:** Alphabetical by institution and/or research center name.
- **Source:** *Research Centers Directory,* 17th Edition (published by Gale Research Inc.)
- **Indexed by:** Institution and research center name and significant keywords within names.

► **Education Programs and Services**

- **Scope:** Elementary schools, high schools, and community colleges that are operated by and for Indians, Eskimos, Metis, and Inuits (although funding may be through sources other than the tribe or band itself). Also includes Indian-controlled Head Start programs in the U.S. and educational programs and schools operated in the state of Hawaii for Hawaiian natives.
- **Entries include:** Program, school, or college name, address, telephone, toll-free, and fax numbers, name of contact, and grade ranges for each school.
- **Arrangement:** Alphabetical by state or province within the following three categories: Head Start Programs; Schools; Community Colleges and alphabetical by program, school, or college name within each category.
- **Source:** Original research.
- **Indexed by:** Program, school, or college name and significant keywords.

► **Studies Programs**

- **Scope:** Colleges and universities that offer formal Native studies programs.
- **Entries include:** Institution name, program name, address, telephone, toll-free, and fax numbers, and name of contact.
- **Arrangement:** Alphabetical by institution name within the following three categories: Two-Year Programs; Four-Year Programs; and Graduate Programs.
- **Source:** Original research.
- **Indexed by:** Institution and program names.

► **Scholarships, Fellowships, and Loans**

- **Scope:** Financial aid resources for all levels and areas of post-secondary education, including law, engineering, journalism, and the health professions.
- **Entries include:** Scholarship name and sponsoring institution, address, telephone, toll-free, and fax numbers, contact name, and a brief description of award and eligibility requirements.
- **Arrangement:** Alphabetical by scholarship name.
- **Source:** *Scholarships, Fellowships and Loans,* 9th Edition (published by Gale Research Inc.)
- **Indexed by:** Scholarship name and significant keywords appearing within the scholarship name.

► **Print and Broadcast Media**

- **Scope:** Directories, journals, magazines, newsletters, and newspapers that focus on Native Americans or minorities in general, covering a wide variety of topics such as culture, heritage, family, health, and education; Indian-controlled public radio stations in the U.S.; and radio stations with music, information, and entertainment programming aimed wholly or partially at the Native American community.

- **Entries include:** Publication and publisher names or station call letters, address, telephone, toll-free, and fax numbers, and a brief description, including either publication scope, frequency, and other details, or station frequency and programming information.
- **Arrangement:** Alphabetical by publication title or station call letters within the following five categories: Directories; Journals and Magazines; Newsletters; Newspapers; and Radio Stations.
- **Source:** *Gale Directory of Publications and Broadcast Media,* 125th Edition (formerly *Ayer Directory of Publications); Newsletters in Print,* 6th Edition; *Directories in Print,* 10th Edition (all published by Gale Research Inc.); supplemented by original research.
- **Indexed by:** Publication title or station call letters and significant keywords within titles.

▶ **Publishers**

- **Scope:** Large and small firms that publish books by and about Native Americans, as well as books on topics of interest to Native Americans.
- **Entries include:** Publisher name, address, telephone, toll-free, and fax numbers, names of officials, and a brief description of publishing activity.
- **Arrangement:** Alphabetical by publisher name.
- **Source:** *Publishers Directory,* 13th Edition (published by Gale Research Inc.).
- **Indexed by:** Publisher name.

▶ **Videos**

- **Scope:** Educational and general interest videos focusing on the Native American community, including those covering culture, heritage, and history.
- **Entries include:** Video title, distributor name, address, telephone, toll- free, and fax numbers, program description, release date, run time, format, and acquisition availability.
- **Arrangement:** Alphabetical by video title.
- **Source:** *Video Source Book,* 13th Edition (published by Gale Research Inc.) and supplemented by original research.
- **Indexed by:** Video title and significant keywords within titles.

Master Name and Keyword Index

The alphabetical Master Name and Keyword Index provides access to all entries included in *NAID,* as well as to former or alternate names that appear within entry text. The index also provides access to entries via citations to all significant subject keywords appearing in an entry name. Broad terms such as "Indian" and "Education" are used as subject keywords along with more specific terms, such as "Cherokee" and "Metis."

Index references are to entry numbers rather than page numbers. Entry numbers appear in the index in **boldface** type if the reference is to a main entry, and in lightface if the reference is to a program or former or alternate name included within the text of the cited entry.

If several entries have the same parent organization, as is the case with many of the government groups listed in *NAID,* related units are indexed individually by name and are also listed under the name of the parent organization. The names of all federal government organizations are indexed under "U.S." or "Canada."

NATIVE AMERICANS INFORMATION DIRECTORY

American Indians

Tribal Communities

Alabama

★1★
Poarch Band of Creek Indians
Rte. 3, Box 243-A
Atmore, AL 36502
Eddie Tullis, Chm.
Ph: (205)368-9136
Fax: (205)368-4502

BIA Area Office: Eastern. **BIA Agency:** Choctaw.

Arizona

★2★
Yavapai-Apache Community Council
PO Box 1188
Camp Verde, AZ 86322
Theodore Smith Sr., Pres.
Ph: (602)567-3649

BIA Area Office: Phoenix. **BIA Agency:** Truxton Canon.

★3★
Mohave-Apache Community Council (Fort McDowell)
PO Box 17779
Fountain Hills, AZ 85268
David King, Pres.
Ph: (602)990-0995
Fax: (602)837-1630

BIA Area Office: Phoenix. **BIA Agency:** Salt River.

★4★
Kaibab Paiute Tribal Council
Tribal Affairs Bldg.
HC65 Box 2
Fredonia, AZ 86022
Gloria Bulletts, Chm.
Ph: (602)643-7245

BIA Area Office: Phoenix. **BIA Agency:** So. Paiute.

★5★
Hopi Tribe
Tribal Council
PO Box 123
Kykotsmovi, AZ 86039
Vernon Masayesva, Chm.
Ph: (602)734-2445

BIA Area Office: Phoenix. **BIA Agency:** Hopi.

★6★
Ak Chin Indian Community Council
Rte. 2, Box 27
Maricopa, AZ 85239
Delia Carlisle, Chm.
Ph: (602)568-2227

BIA Area Office: Phoenix. **BIA Agency:** Pima.

★7★
Colorado River Indian Tribes
Tribal Council
Rte. 1, Box 23-B
Parker, AZ 85344
Daniel Eddy Jr., Chm.
Ph: (602)669-9211
Fax: (602)669-5675

BIA Area Office: Phoenix. **BIA Agency:** Colorado River.

★8★
Tonto Apache Tribal Council
Tonto Reservation No. 30
Payson, AZ 85541
Louise C. Lopez, Chm.
Ph: (602)474-5000

BIA Area Office: Phoenix. **BIA Agency:** Truxton Canon.

★9★
Hualapai Tribe
Tribal Council
PO Box 168
Peach Springs, AZ 86434
Earl Havaton, Chm.
Ph: (602)769-2216

BIA Area Office: Phoenix. **BIA Agency:** Truxton Canon.

★10★
Yavapai-Prescott Board of Directors
530 E. Merritt St.
Prescott, AZ 86301-2038
Patricia McGee, Pres.
Ph: (602)445-8790
Fax: (602)778-9445

BIA Area Office: Phoenix. **BIA Agency:** Truxton Canon.

★11★
Gila River Indian Community Council
PO Box 97
Sacaton, AZ 85247
Thomas R. White Jr., Gov.
Ph: (602)562-3311
Fax: (602)562-3422

BIA Area Office: Phoenix.

★12★
San Carlos Tribal Council
PO Box 0   Ph: (602)475-2361
San Carlos, AZ 85550   Fax: (602)475-2566
Buck Kitcheyan, Chm.
BIA Area Office: Phoenix. **BIA Agency:** San Carlos.

★13★
Salt River Pima-Maricopa Indian Community Council
Rte. 1, Box 216   Ph: (602)941-7277
Scottsdale, AZ 85256   Fax: (602)945-3698
Ivan Makil, Pres.
BIA Area Office: Phoenix. **BIA Agency:** Salt River.

★14★
Tohono O'Odham Nation
Tribal Council
PO Box 837
Sells, AZ 85634   Ph: (602)383-2221
Josiah Moore, Chm.
BIA Area Office: Phoenix. **BIA Agency:** Papago.

★15★
Cocopah Tribal Council
Bin G
Somerton, AZ 85350   Ph: (602)627-2102
Dale Phillips, Chm.
BIA Area Office: Phoenix. **BIA Agency:** Ft. Yuma.

★16★
Havasupai Tribal Council
PO Box 10
Supai, AZ 86435   Ph: (602)448-2961
Don Watahomigie, Chm.
BIA Area Office: Phoenix. **BIA Agency:** Truxton Conon.

★17★
San Juan Southern Paiute Council
PO Box 2656
Tuba City, AZ 86045   Ph: (602)283-4583
Evelyn James, Pres.
BIA Area Office: Phoenix. **BIA Agency:** So. Paiute.

★18★
Pascua Yaqui Tribal Council
7474 S. Camino de Oeste
Tucson, AZ 85746   Ph: (602)883-2838
Arcadio Gastelum, Chm.
BIA Area Office: Phoenix. **BIA Agency:** Salt River.

★19★
White Mountain Apache Tribe
Tribal Council
PO Box 700   Ph: (602)338-4346
Whiteriver, AZ 85941   Fax: (602)338-4778
Ronnie Lupe, Chm.
BIA Area Office: Phoenix. **BIA Agency:** Ft. Apache.

★20★
Navajo Nation Council
PO Box 308   Ph: (602)871-6352
Window Rock, AZ 86515   Fax: (602)871-4025
Petersen Zah, Pres.
BIA Area Office: Navajo. **BIA Agency:** Navajo.

★21★
Quechan Tribal Council
PO Box 1352   Ph: (619)572-0213
Yuma, AZ 85364   Fax: (619)572-2102
Fritz Brown, Pres.
BIA Area Office: Phoenix. **BIA Agency:** Ft. Yuma.

——————— **California** ———————

★22★
Viejas Tribal Council
PO Box 908
Alpine, CA 92001   Ph: (619)445-3810
Anthony Pico, Chr.
BIA Area Office: Sacramento. **BIA Agency:** So. Calif.

★23★
Alturas Rancheria
PO Box 1035
Alturas, CA 96101   Ph: (916)233-5571
Norma Jean Garcia, Chr.
BIA Area Office: Sacramento. **BIA Agency:** No. Calif.

★24★
Cahuilla Band of Mission Indians
PO Box 860
Anza, CA 92306   Ph: (714)763-5549
Lois Candelaria, Spokesperson
BIA Area Office: Sacramento. **BIA Agency:** So. Calif.

★25★
Ramona Band of Cahuilla Indians
PO Box 26
Anza, CA 92306
Anne Hamilton, Rep.
BIA Area Office: Sacramento. **BIA Agency:** So. Calif.

★26★
Big Sandy Rancheria
PO Box 337
Auberry, CA 93602   Ph: (209)855-4003
Thane V. Baty, Chr.
BIA Area Office: Sacramento. **BIA Agency:** Cent. Calif.

★27★
Morongo Band of Mission Indians
11581 Potrero Rd.   Ph: (714)849-4697
Banning, CA 92220   Fax: (714)849-4425
Adalaide Presley, Chr.
BIA Area Office: Sacramento. **BIA Agency:** So. Calif.

★28★
Benton Paiute Reservation
Star Rte. 4, Box 56-A
Benton, CA 93512   Ph: (619)933-2321
Rose Marie Bahe, Chr.
BIA Area Office: Sacramento. **BIA Agency:** Cent. Calif.

★29★
Big Pine Reservation
PO Box 700   Ph: (619)938-2121
Big Pine, CA 93513   Fax: (619)938-2942
Velma Jones, Chr.
BIA Area Office: Sacramento. **BIA Agency:** Cent. Calif.

★30★
Bishop Indian Tribal Council
PO Box 548
Bishop, CA 93514   Ph: (619)873-3584
Jess R. Paco, Chr.
BIA Area Office: Sacramento. **BIA Agency:** Cent. Calif.

★31★
Blue Lake Rancheria
PO Box 428
Blue Lake, CA 95525   Ph: (707)668-5101
Sylvia Daniels, Chr.
BIA Area Office: Sacramento. **BIA Agency:** No. Calif.

★32★
Manzanita General Council
PO Box 1302
Boulevard, CA 92005   Ph: (619)478-5028
Frances Shaw, Chr.

BIA Area Office: Sacramento. **BIA Agency:** So. Calif.

★33★
Bridgeport Indian Colony
PO Box 37
Bridgeport, CA 93517
Art Sam, Chr.

BIA Area Office: Sacramento. **BIA Agency:** Cent. Calif.

★34★
Rumsey Rancheria
PO Box 18
Brooks, CA 95606   Ph: (916)796-3400
Philip Knight, Chr.

BIA Area Office: Sacramento. **BIA Agency:** Cent. Calif.

★35★
Pit River Tribal Council
PO Drawer 1570
Burney, CA 96013   Ph: (916)335-5421
Rodney Lego, Chr.

BIA Area Office: Sacramento. **BIA Agency:** No. Calif.

★36★
Campo Band of Mission Indians
1779 Campo Truck Trail   Ph: (619)478-9046
Campo, CA 92006   Fax: (619)478-5818
Ralph Goff, Chr.

BIA Area Office: Sacramento. **BIA Agency:** So. Calif.

★37★
Cedarville Rancheria
PO Box 126
Cedarville, CA 96104   Ph: (916)279-2270
Andrew Phoenix, Chr.

BIA Area Office: Sacramento. **BIA Agency:** No. Calif.

★38★
Chemehuevi Tribal Council
PO Box 1976
Chemehuevi Valley, CA 92363   Ph: (619)858-4531
Christine Walker, Chm.

BIA Area Office: Phoenix. **BIA Agency:** Colorado River.

★39★
Cortina Rancheria
PO Box 7470
Citrus Heights, CA 95621-7470   Ph: (916)726-7118
Mary Norton, Chr.

BIA Area Office: Sacramento. **BIA Agency:** Cent. Calif.

★40★
Elem Indian Colony of Pomo Indians
Sulphur Bank Rancheria
PO Box 618
Clearlake Oaks, CA 95423
Delbert L. Thomas Jr., Chr.

BIA Area Office: Sacramento. **BIA Agency:** Cent. Calif.

★41★
Cloverdale Rancheria
285 Santana Dr.
Cloverdale, CA 95424   Ph: (707)894-5773
John Santana, Rep.

BIA Area Office: Sacramento. **BIA Agency:** Cent. Calif.

★42★
Picayune Rancheria
PO Box 708   Ph: (209)683-6633
Coarsegold, CA 93614   Fax: (209)683-6633
Jane Wyatt, Chr.

BIA Area Office: Sacramento. **BIA Agency:** Cent. Calif.

★43★
Colusa Rancheria
PO Box 8
Colusa, CA 95932   Ph: (916)458-8231
Delbert Benjamin, Chr.

BIA Area Office: Sacramento. **BIA Agency:** Cent. Calif.

★44★
Round Valley Reservation
PO Box 448
Covelo, CA 95428   Ph: (707)983-6126
Gaylan Azbill, Pres.

BIA Area Office: Sacramento. **BIA Agency:** Cent. Calif.

★45★
Elk Valley Rancheria
PO Box 1042
Crescent City, CA 95531   Ph: (707)464-4680
John Green, Vice Chairperson

BIA Area Office: Sacramento. **BIA Agency:** No. Calif.

★46★
Timbisha Shoshone Tribe
PO Box 206   Ph: (619)786-2374
Death Valley, CA 92328   Fax: (619)786-2344
Angie Boland, Contact

BIA Area Office: Sacramento. **BIA Agency:** Cent. Calif.

★47★
Sycuan Business Committee
5459 Dehesa Rd.
El Cajon, CA 92021   Ph: (619)445-2613
Anna Sandoval, Spokesperson

BIA Area Office: Sacramento. **BIA Agency:** So. Calif.

★48★
Grindstone Rancheria
PO Box 63
Elk Creek, CA 95939   Ph: (916)968-5116
Frank Burrows, Chr.

BIA Area Office: Sacramento. **BIA Agency:** Cent. Calif.

★49★
Jamul Indian Village
461 Las Brisas
Escondido, CA 92027   Ph: (614)480-9888
Raymond Hunter, Chr.

BIA Area Office: Sacramento. **BIA Agency:** So. Calif.

★50★
Quartz Valley Indian Reservation
PO Box 737
Etna, CA 96027   Ph: (916)467-3307
Betty Hall, Chr.

BIA Area Office: Sacramento. **BIA Agency:** No. Calif.

★51★
Rohnerville Rancheria
PO Box 108
Eureka, CA 95502   Ph: (707)443-6150
Aileen Bowie, Chr.

BIA Area Office: Sacramento. **BIA Agency:** No. Calif.

★52★
Yurok Indian Reservation
Yurok Transition Team
517 3rd St., Ste. 21   Ph: (707)444-0433
Eureka, CA 95501   Free: 800-848-8765
BIA Area Office: Sacramento. **BIA Agency:** No. Calif.

★53★
Big Valley Rancheria
PO Box 153
Finley, CA 95453
Manuel Gomez, Chr.
BIA Area Office: Sacramento. **BIA Agency:** Cent. Calif.

★54★
Fort Bidwell Community Council
PO Box 127
Fort Bidwell, CA 96112   Ph: (916)279-6310
Ralph De Garmo, Chr.
BIA Area Office: Sacramento. **BIA Agency:** No. Calif.

★55★
Table Mountain Rancheria
PO Box 243
Friant, CA 93626   Ph: (209)822-2125
Lewis Barnes, Chr.
BIA Area Office: Sacramento. **BIA Agency:** Cent. Calif.

★56★
Dry Creek Rancheria
PO Box 607
Geyserville, CA 95441   Ph: (707)431-8232
Stanley Cordova, Chr.
BIA Area Office: Sacramento. **BIA Agency:** Cent. Calif.

★57★
Karuk Tribe of California
PO Box 1016
Happy Camp, CA 96039   Ph: (916)493-5305
Alvis Johnson, Chr.
BIA Area Office: Sacramento. **BIA Agency:** No. Calif.

★58★
Santa Rosa Reservation
325 N. Western Ave.
Hemet, CA 92343   Ph: (619)741-5211
Anthony Largo, Spokesperson
BIA Area Office: Sacramento. **BIA Agency:** So. Calif.

★59★
San Manuel Band of Mission Indians
5438 N. Victoria Ave.
Highland, CA 92346   Ph: (714)862-8509
Henry Duro, Chr.
BIA Area Office: Sacramento. **BIA Agency:** So. Calif.

★60★
Hoopa Valley Indian Rancheria
PO Box 1348
Hoopa, CA 95546   Ph: (916)625-4211
Dale Risling, Chr.
BIA Area Office: Sacramento. **BIA Agency:** No. Calif.

★61★
Hopland Reservation
PO Box 610   Ph: (707)744-1647
Hopland, CA 95449   Fax: (707)744-1506
Donald Ray, Chr.
BIA Area Office: Sacramento. **BIA Agency:** Cent. Calif.

★62★
Fort Independence Reservation
PO Box 67
Independence, CA 93526   Ph: (619)878-2126
Vernon Miller, Chr.
BIA Area Office: Sacramento. **BIA Agency:** Cent. Calif.

★63★
Cabazon Indians of California
84-245 Indio Spring Dr.
Indio, CA 92201   Ph: (619)342-2593
John A. James, Chr.
BIA Area Office: Sacramento. **BIA Agency:** So. Calif.

★64★
Buena Vista Rancheria
4650 Calmine Rd.
Ione, CA 95640
Lucille Lucero, Rep.
BIA Area Office: Sacramento. **BIA Agency:** Cent. Calif.

★65★
Jackson Rancheria
1600 Bingo Way
Jackson, CA 95642
Margaret Dalton, Chr.
BIA Area Office: Sacramento. **BIA Agency:** Cent. Calif.

★66★
Chicken Ranch Rancheria
PO Box 1699
Jamestown, CA 95327   Ph: (209)984-3057
Loren Mathieson, Chr.
BIA Area Office: Sacramento. **BIA Agency:** Cent. Calif.

★67★
Coast Indian Community of the Resighini Rancheria
PO Box 529
Klamath, CA 95548   Ph: (707)482-2431
Vlayn McCovey, Pres.
BIA Area Office: Sacramento. **BIA Agency:** No. Calif.

★68★
Barona General Business Committee
1095 Barona Rd.
Lakeside, CA 92040   Ph: (619)443-6612
Clifford M. LaChappa Sr., Chr.
BIA Area Office: Sacramento. **BIA Agency:** So. Calif.

★69★
La Posta Band of Mission Indians
1064 Barona Rd.
Lakeside, CA 92040   Ph: (619)561-2924
Gwendolyn Parada, Chr.
BIA Area Office: Sacramento. **BIA Agency:** So. Calif.

★70★
Laytonville Rancheria
PO Box 48
Laytonville, CA 95454
Bert Sloan Jr., Chr.
BIA Area Office: Sacramento. **BIA Agency:** Cent. Calif.

★71★
Santa Rosa Rancheria
16835 Alkali Dr.   Ph: (209)924-1278
Lemoore, CA 93245   Fax: (209)924-8949
Clarence Atwell Jr., Chr.
BIA Area Office: Sacramento. **BIA Agency:** Cent. Calif.

★72★
Table Bluff Rancheria
PO Box 519   Ph: (707)733-5055
Loleta, CA 95551   Fax: (707)733-5601
Albert James, Chr.
BIA Area Office: Sacramento. **BIA Agency:** No. Calif.

★73★
Lone Pine Reservation
Star Rte. 1-1101 S. Main St.
Lone Pine, CA 93545   Ph: (619)876-5414
Sandra Jefferson Yonge, Chr.
BIA Area Office: Sacramento. **BIA Agency:** Cent. Calif.

★74★
Woodfords Community Council
96 Washoe Blvd.
Markleeville, CA 96120   Ph: (916)694-2170
Kevin Jones, Chm.
BIA Area Office: Phoenix. **BIA Agency:** W. Nevada.

★75★
Middletown Rancheria
PO Box 292
Middletown, CA 95461
Larry Simon, Chr.
BIA Area Office: Sacramento. **BIA Agency:** Cent. Calif.

★76★
Fort Mohave Tribal Council
500 Merriman Ave.
Needles, CA 92363   Ph: (619)326-4591
Nora Garcia, Chm.
BIA Area Office: Phoenix. **BIA Agency:** Colorado River.

★77★
Robinson Rancheria
PO Box 1119   Ph: (707)275-0527
Nice, CA 95464   Fax: (707)275-9132
Curtis F. Anderson Jr., Chr.
BIA Area Office: Sacramento. **BIA Agency:** Cent. Calif.

★78★
North Fork Rancheria
PO Box 120
North Fork, CA 93643
Juanita Williams, Spokesperson
BIA Area Office: Sacramento. **BIA Agency:** Cent. Calif.

★79★
Berry Creek Rancheria
1779 Mitchell Ave.
Oroville, CA 95966   Ph: (916)534-3859
Gus Martin Sr., Chr.
BIA Area Office: Sacramento. **BIA Agency:** No. Calif.

★80★
Mooretown Rancheria
PO Box 1842   Ph: (916)533-3625
Oroville, CA 95965   Fax: (916)533-1531
Jessie M. Gilkey, Chr.
BIA Area Office: Sacramento. **BIA Agency:** Cent. Calif.

★81★
Pala Band of Mission Indians
PO Box 43   Ph: (619)742-3784
Pala, CA 92059   Fax: (619)742-1411
Robert Smith, Chr.
BIA Area Office: Sacramento. **BIA Agency:** So. Calif.

★82★
Agua Caliente Tribal Council
960 E. Tahquitz Way, No. 106
Palm Springs, CA 92262   Ph: (619)325-5673
Richard M. Milanovich, Chr.
BIA Area Office: Sacramento. **BIA Agency:** Palm Springs.

★83★
Twenty Nine Palms Band of Mission Indians
c/o Glen Calac
1150 E. Palm Canyon Dr., No. 75
Palm Springs, CA 92262   Ph: (619)322-7481
June Mike, Chr.
BIA Area Office: Sacramento. **BIA Agency:** So. Calif.

★84★
Pauma Band of Mission Indians
PO Box 86   Ph: (619)742-1289
Pauma Valley, CA 92061   Fax: (619)742-1932
Florence Lofton, Chr.
BIA Area Office: Sacramento. **BIA Agency:** So. Calif.

★85★
Cuyapaipe Band of Mission Indians
4390 La Posta Trucktrail
Pine Valley, CA 92062   Ph: (619)478-5289
Tony J. Pinto, Chr.
BIA Area Office: Sacramento. **BIA Agency:** So. Calif.

★86★
Manchester/Point Arena Rancheria
PO Box 623
Point Arena, CA 95468   Ph: (707)882-2788
Harry N. Pinola, Chr.
BIA Area Office: Sacramento. **BIA Agency:** Cent. Calif.

★87★
Tule River Reservation
PO Box 589   Ph: (209)781-4271
Porterville, CA 93258   Fax: (209)781-4610
Nicola Larsen, Chr.
BIA Area Office: Sacramento. **BIA Agency:** Cent. Calif.

★88★
Inaja and Cosmit Band of Mission Indians
715 B St., No. 5
Ramona, CA 92065
Rebecca Contreras, Chr.
BIA Area Office: Sacramento. **BIA Agency:** So. Calif.

★89★
Greenville Rancheria
1304 E St., Ste. 106
Redding, CA 96001
Percy Tejada, Chr.
BIA Area Office: Sacramento. **BIA Agency:** Cent. Calif.

★90★
Redding Rancheria
1786 California St.
Redding, CA 96001   Ph: (916)241-1871
Barbara Murphy, Chr.
BIA Area Office: Sacramento. **BIA Agency:** No. Calif.

★91★
Coyote Valley Reservation
PO Box 39   Ph: (707)485-8723
Redwood Valley, CA 95470-0039   Fax: (707)468-5615
Doris Renick, Chr.
BIA Area Office: Sacramento. **BIA Agency:** Cent. Calif.

★92★
Redwood Valley Rancheria
PO Box 499
Redwood Valley, CA 95470   Ph: (707)485-0361
Rita Hoel, Chr.
BIA Area Office: Sacramento. **BIA Agency:** Cent. Calif.

★93★
Upper Lake Rancheria
PO Box 245272
Sacramento, CA 95820   Ph: (916)371-5637
Phyllis Harden, Vice Chairperson
BIA Area Office: Sacramento. **BIA Agency:** Cent. Calif.

★94★
Soboba Band of Mission Indians
PO Box 487
San Jacinto, CA 92383   Ph: (714)654-2765
Robert J. Salgado, Chr.
BIA Area Office: Sacramento. **BIA Agency:** So. Calif.

★95★
Santa Ynez Band of Mission Indians
PO Box 517
Santa Ynez, CA 93460   Ph: (805)688-7997
David Dominguez, Chr.
BIA Area Office: Sacramento. **BIA Agency:** So. Calif.

★96★
Mesa Grande Band of Mission Indians
PO Box 270
Santa Ysabel, CA 92070   Ph: (619)782-3835
Delmar Nejo, Chr.
BIA Area Office: Sacramento. **BIA Agency:** So. Calif.

★97★
Santa Ysabel Band of Mission Indians
PO Box 130
Santa Ysabel, CA 92070   Ph: (619)765-0845
James Ponchetti, Acting Chairman
BIA Area Office: Sacramento. **BIA Agency:** So. Calif.

★98★
Shingle Springs Rancheria
PO Box 1340
Shingle Springs, CA 95682   Ph: (916)676-8010
Elsie Shilin, Chr.
BIA Area Office: Sacramento. **BIA Agency:** Cent. Calif.

★99★
Smith River Rancheria
PO Box 239
Smith River, CA 95567   Ph: (707)487-9255
William H. Richards Sr., Chr.
BIA Area Office: Sacramento. **BIA Agency:** No. Calif.

★100★
Stewarts Point Rancheria
PO Box 54
Stewarts Point, CA 95480
Leslie Marrufo Jr., Chr.
BIA Area Office: Sacramento. **BIA Agency:** Cent. Calif.

★101★
Susanville Rancheria
PO Drawer U
Susanville, CA 96130   Ph: (916)257-6264
Aaron Dixon, Chr.
BIA Area Office: Sacramento. **BIA Agency:** No. Calif.

★102★
Winnemucca Colony Council
2700 Sunkist
Susanville, CA 96130   Ph: (916)257-7093
Glenn Wasson, Chm.
BIA Area Office: Phoenix. **BIA Agency:** W. Nevada.

★103★
Pechanga Band of Mission Indians
PO Box 1477   Ph: (714)676-2768
Temecula, CA 92390   Fax: (714)699-6983
Jennie Miranda, Spokesperson
BIA Area Office: Sacramento. **BIA Agency:** So. Calif.

★104★
Torres-Martinez Band of Mission Indians
66-725 Martinez Rd.
Thermal, CA 92274   Ph: (619)397-0300
Helen Jose, Chr.
BIA Area Office: Sacramento. **BIA Agency:** So. Calif.

★105★
Cold Springs Rancheria
PO Box 209
Tollhouse, CA 93667   Ph: (209)855-2326
Frank J. Lee, Chr.
BIA Area Office: Sacramento. **BIA Agency:** Cent. Calif.

★106★
Big Lagoon Rancheria
PO Drawer 3060
Trinidad, CA 95570   Ph: (707)826-2079
Virgil Moorehead, Chr.
BIA Area Office: Sacramento. **BIA Agency:** No. Calif.

★107★
Trinidad Rancheria
PO Box 630
Trinidad, CA 95570   Ph: (707)677-0211
Carol Ervin, Chr.
BIA Area Office: Sacramento. **BIA Agency:** No. Calif.

★108★
Tuolumne Me-wuk Rancheria
19595 Miwuk St.
Tuolumne, CA 95379   Ph: (209)928-3475
Sonny Hendricks, Chr.
BIA Area Office: Sacramento. **BIA Agency:** Cent. Calif.

★109★
Pinoleville Rancheria
367 N. State St., Ste. 204
Ukiah, CA 95482   Ph: (707)463-1454
Marie Pollock, Chr.
BIA Area Office: Sacramento. **BIA Agency:** Cent. Calif.

★110★
Sherwood Valley Rancheria
2141 S. State St.
Ukiah, CA 95482   Ph: (707)468-1337
Mike Knight, Chr.
BIA Area Office: Sacramento. **BIA Agency:** Cent. Calif.

★111★
La Jolla Band of Mission Indians
Star Rte., Box 158
Valley Center, CA 92082   Ph: (619)742-3771
Doris J. Magante, Chr.
BIA Area Office: Sacramento. **BIA Agency:** So. Calif.

★112★
Rincon Band of Mission Indians
PO Box 68   Ph: (619)749-1051
Valley Center, CA 92082   Fax: (619)749-8901
Edward Arviso, Chr.
BIA Area Office: Sacramento. **BIA Agency:** So. Calif.

★113★
San Pasqual General Council
PO Box 365
Valley Center, CA 92082   Ph: (619)749-3200
Diana Martinez, Chr.
BIA Area Office: Sacramento. **BIA Agency:** So. Calif.

★114★
Los Coyotes Band of Mission Indians
PO Box 86
Warner Springs, CA 92086   Ph: (619)782-3269
Banning Taylor, Spokesman
BIA Area Office: Sacramento. **BIA Agency:** So. Calif.

★115★
Potter Valley Rancheria
PO Box 2273
West Sacramento, CA 95619   Ph: (916)372-3428
Shirley Laiwa, Rep.
BIA Area Office: Sacramento. **BIA Agency:** Cent. Calif.

—————— **Colorado** ——————

★116★
Southern Ute Tribal Council
PO Box 737
Ignacio, CO 81137   Ph: (303)563-4525
Leonard C. Burch, Chr.
BIA Area Office: Albuquerque. **BIA Agency:** Southern Ute.

★117★
Ute Mountain Ute Tribe
Tribal Council
General Delivery
Towaoc, CO 81344   Ph: (303)565-3751
Judy Knight-Frank, Chr.
BIA Area Office: Albuquerque. **BIA Agency:** Ute Mountain.

—————— **Connecticut** ——————

★118★
Mashantucket Pequot Tribe
PO Box 160   Ph: (203)536-2681
Ledyard, CT 06339   Fax: (203)572-0421
Richard A. Hayward, Chr.
BIA Area Office: Eastern. **BIA Agency:** Eastern.

—————— **Florida** ——————

★119★
Seminole Tribe
6073 Stirling Rd.   Ph: (305)584-0400
Hollywood, FL 33024   Fax: (305)581-8917
James Billie, Chr.
BIA Area Office: Eastern. **BIA Agency:** Seminole.

★120★
Miccosukee Business Committee
PO Box 440021, Tamiami Sta.   Ph: (305)223-8380
Miami, FL 33144   Fax: (305)223-1011
Billy Cypress, Chr.
BIA Area Office: Eastern. **BIA Agency:** Eastern.

—————— **Idaho** ——————

★121★
Kootenai Tribal Council
PO Box 1269   Ph: (208)267-3519
Bonners Ferry, ID 83805   Fax: (208)267-2762
Velma Bahe, Chm.
BIA Area Office: Portland. **BIA Agency:** No. Idaho.

★122★
Fort Hall Business Council
PO Box 306   Ph: (208)238-3700
Fort Hall, ID 83203   Fax: (208)237-0796
Keslay Edmo, Chm.
BIA Area Office: Portland. **BIA Agency:** Ft. Hall.

★123★
Northwestern Band of Shoshone Nation
PO Box 145   Ph: (208)785-7302
Fort Hall, ID 83203-0145   Fax: (208)237-0797
Leonard M. Alex, Chm.
BIA Area Office: Portland. **BIA Agency:** Ft. Hall.

★124★
Nez Perce Tribal Executive Committee
PO Box 305   Ph: (208)843-2253
Lapwai, ID 83540   Fax: (208)843-2036
Charles Hayes, Chm.
BIA Area Office: Portland. **BIA Agency:** No. Idaho.

★125★
Coeur D'Alene Tribal Council
Plummer, ID 83851   Ph: (208)274-3100
                              Fax: (208)274-3010
Ernest Stensgar, Chm.
BIA Area Office: Portland. **BIA Agency:** No. Idaho.

—————— **Iowa** ——————

★126★
Sac and Fox Tribal Council
Rte. 2, Box 56C   Ph: (515)484-4678
Tama, IA 52339   Fax: (515)484-5218
Louis Mitchell, Chm.
BIA Area Office: Minneaplis. **BIA Agency:** Sac and Fox.

—————— **Kansas** ——————

★127★
Kickapoo Tribe of Kansas
Tribal Council
Rte. 1, Box 157A
Horton, KS 66349   Ph: (913)486-2131
Steve Cadue, Chr.
BIA Area Office: Anadarko. **BIA Agency:** Horton.

★128★
Prairie Band Potawatomi Tribal Council
PO Box 97
Mayetta, KS 66509   Ph: (913)966-2255
George Wahquahboshkuk, Chr.
BIA Area Office: Anadarko. **BIA Agency:** Horton.

★129★
Sac and Fox of Missouri Tribal Council
RR 1, Box 60
Reserve, KS 66434-9723   Ph: (913)742-7471
Sandra Keo, Chr.
BIA Area Office: Anadarko. **BIA Agency:** Horton.

★130★
Iowa of Kansas Executive Committee
Rte.1, Box 58A
White Cloud, KS 66094   Ph: (913)595-3258
Leon Campbell, Chr.
BIA Area Office: Anadarko. **BIA Agency:** Horton.

Louisiana

★131★
Chitimacha Tribe
PO Box 661   Ph: (318)923-4973
Charenton, LA 70523   Fax: (318)923-7791
Ralph Darden, Chr.
BIA Area Office: Eastern. **BIA Agency:** Eastern.

★132★
Coushatta Tribe
PO Box 818   Ph: (318)584-2261
Elton, LA 70532   Fax: (318)584-2998
Lovelin Poncho, Chr.
BIA Area Office: Eastern. **BIA Agency:** Eastern.

★133★
Tunica-Biloxi Indian Tribe
PO Box 311   Ph: (318)253-9767
Mansura, LA 71351   Fax: (318)253-9791
Earl Barbry Sr., Chm.
BIA Area Office: Eastern. **BIA Agency:** Eastern.

Maine

★134★
Houlton Band of Maliseet Indians
Bell Rd.
PO Box 748   Ph: (207)532-4273
Houlton, ME 04730   Fax: (207)532-2660
Clair Sabattis, Chr.
BIA Area Office: Eastern. **BIA Agency:** Eastern.

★135★
Penobscot Nation
Community Building - Indian Island   Ph: (207)827-7776
Old Town, ME 04468   Fax: (207)827-6042
James Sappier, Gov.
BIA Area Office: Eastern. **BIA Agency:** Eastern.

★136★
Passamaquoddy Tribe of Maine
Pleasant Point Reservation
PO Box 343   Ph: (207)853-2551
Perry, ME 04667   Fax: (207)853-6039
Melvin Francis, Gov.
BIA Area Office: Eastern. **BIA Agency:** Eastern.

★137★
Passamaquoddy Tribe of Maine
Indian Township Reservation
PO Box 301   Ph: (207)796-2301
Princeton, ME 04668   Fax: (207)796-5256
Robert Newell, Gov.
BIA Area Office: Eastern. **BIA Agency:** Eastern.

Massachusetts

★138★
Wampanoag Tribal Council of Gay Head
State Rd., RFD Box 137   Ph: (508)645-9265
Gay Head, MA 02535   Fax: (508)645-3790
Donald A. Widdiss, Pres.
BIA Area Office: Eastern. **BIA Agency:** Eastern.

Michigan

★139★
Keweenaw Bay Tribal Council
Center Bldg.
Rte.1, Box 45   Ph: (906)353-6623
Baraga, MI 49908   Fax: (906)353-7450
Frederick Dakota, Chm.
BIA Area Office: Minneapolis. **BIA Agency:** Michigan.

★140★
Bay Mills Executive Council
Rte. 1   Ph: (906)248-3241
Brimley, MI 49715   Fax: (906)248-3283
Jeff Parker, Chm.
BIA Area Office: Minneapolis. **BIA Agency:** Michigan.

★141★
Saginaw Chippewa Tribal Council
7070 E. Broadway Rd.   Ph: (517)772-5700
Mt. Pleasant, MI 48858   Fax: (517)772-3508
Timothy J. Davis, Chief
BIA Area Office: Minneapolis. **BIA Agency:** Michigan.

★142★
Sault Ste. Marie Chippewa Tribal Council
206 Greenough St.   Ph: (906)635-6050
Sault Ste. Marie, MI 49783   Fax: (906)635-0741
Bernard Bouschor, Pres.
BIA Area Office: Minneapolis. **BIA Agency:** Michigan.

★143★
Grand Traverse Band of Ottawa and Chippewa Tribes Tribal Council
Rte. 1, Box 135   Ph: (616)271-3538
Suttons Bay, MI 49682   Fax: (616)271-4230
Joseph C. Raphael, Chm.
BIA Area Office: Minneapolis. **BIA Agency:** Michigan.

★144★
Lac Vieux Desert Band of Chippewa Indians
PO Box 446   Ph: (906)358-4577
Watersmeet, MI 49969   Fax: (906)358-4785
John McGeshick, Chm.
BIA Area Office: Minneapolis. **BIA Agency:** Michigan.

★145★
Hannahville Indian Community Council
N14911 Hannahville Blvd. Rd.   Ph: (906)466-2342
Wilson, MI 49896-9728   Fax: (906)466-2418
Kenneth Meshiguad, Chm.
BIA Area Office: Minneapolis. **BIA Agency:** Michigan.

Minnesota

★146★
Northwest Angle No. 33 Band
Angle Inlet, MN 56711
Ken Sandy, Chief
Ph: (807)733-2200

★147★
Leech Lake Reservation Business Committee
Rte.3, Box 100
Cass Lake, MN 56633
Daniel Brown, Chm.
Ph: (218)335-2207
Fax: (218)335-8309

BIA Area Office: Minneapolis. **BIA Agency:** Minnesota.

★148★
Minnesota Chippewa Tribal Executive Committee
Box 217C
Cass Lake, MN 56633
Darrell Wadena, Pres.
Ph: (218)335-2252
Fax: (218)335-6562

BIA Area Office: Minneapolis. **BIA Agency:** Minnesota.

★149★
Fond du Lac Reservation Business Committee
105 University Rd.
Cloquet, MN 55720
Robert Peacock, Chm.
Ph: (218)879-4593
Fax: (218)897-4164

BIA Area Office: Minneapolis. **BIA Agency:** Minnesota.

★150★
Grand Portage Reservation Business Committee
PO Box 428
Grand Portage, MN 55605
James Hendrickson, Chm.
Ph: (218)475-2279
Fax: (218)475-2284

BIA Area Office: Minneapolis. **BIA Agency:** Minnesota.

★151★
Upper Sioux Board of Trustees
PO Box 147
Granite Falls, MN 56241
Dean Blue, Chm.
Ph: (612)564-2360

BIA Area Office: Minneapolis. **BIA Agency:** MN/Sioux.

★152★
Lower Sioux Indian Community Council
RR 1, Box 308
Morton, MN 56270
David Larsen, Pres.
Ph: (507)697-6185

BIA Area Office: Minneapolis. **BIA Agency:** Minn./Soiux.

★153★
Nett Lake Reservation Business Committee (Bois Forte)
PO Box 16
Nett Lake, MN 55772
Eugene Boshey Sr., Chm.
Ph: (218)757-3261
Fax: (218)757-3312

BIA Area Office: Minneapolis. **BIA Agency:** Minnesota.

★154★
Mille Lacs Reservation Business Committee
Star Rte.
Onamia, MN 56359
Arthur Gahbow, Chm.
Ph: (612)532-4181
Fax: (612)532-4209

BIA Area Office: Minneapolis. **BIA Agency:** Minnesota.

★155★
Shakopee Sioux Community Council
2330 Sioux Tr., NW
Prior Lake, MN 55372
Leonard Prescott, Chm.
Ph: (612)445-8900
Fax: (612)445-5906

BIA Area Office: Minneapolis. **BIA Agency:** MN/Sioux.

★156★
Red Lake Reservation Tribal Council
PO Box 550
Red Lake, MN 56671
Gerald Brun, Chm.
Ph: (218)679-3341
Fax: (218)679-3378

BIA Area Office: Minneapolis. **BIA Agency:** Red Lake.

★157★
Prairie Island Community Council (Minnesota Mdewakanton Sioux)
5750 Sturgeon Lake Rd.
Welch, MN 55089
Dale Childs, Pres.
Ph: (612)388-8889
Fax: (612)388-1576

BIA Area Office: Minneapolis. **BIA Agency:** Minn./Sioux.

★158★
White Earth Band of Chippewa Reservation Business Committee
PO Box 418
White Earth, MN 56591
Darrell Wadena, Chm.
Ph: (218)983-3285
Fax: (218)983-3641

BIA Area Office: Minneapolis. **BIA Agency:** Minnesota.

Mississippi

★159★
Mississippi Band of Choctaw Indians
PO Box 6010 - Choctaw Branch
Philadelphia, MS 39350
Phillip Martin, Tribal Chief
Ph: (601)656-5251
Fax: (601)656-1992

BIA Area Office: Eastern. **BIA Agency:** Choctaw.

Missouri

★160★
Eastern Shawnee Tribe of Oklahoma
PO Box 350
Seneca, MO 64865
George J. Captain, Chief
Ph: (918)666-2435

BIA Area Office: Muskogee. **BIA Agency:** Miami.

Montana

★161★
Chippewa-Cree Business Committee
Rocky Boy Rte.
PO Box 544
Box Elder, MT 59521
Rocky M. Stump Sr., Chr.
Ph: (406)395-4282
Fax: (406)395-4497

BIA Area Office: Billings. **BIA Agency:** Rocky Boy's.

★162★
Blackfeet Tribal Business Council
PO Box 850
Browning, MT 59417
Earl Old Person, Chr.
Ph: (406)338-7521
Fax: (406)338-7530

BIA Area Office: Billings. **BIA Agency:** Blackfeet.

★163★
Crow Tribal Council
Box 159
Crow Agency, MT 59022
Clara Nomee, Chr.
Ph: (406)638-2303
Fax: (406)638-2638

BIA Area Office: Billings. **BIA Agency:** Crow.

★164★
Fort Belknap Indian Community Council
PO Box 249   Ph: (406)353-2205
Harlem, MT 59526   Fax: (406)353-2797
Donovan Archambault, Pres.
BIA Area Office: Billings. **BIA Agency:** Ft. Belknap.

★165★
Northern Cheyenne Tribal Council
PO Box 128   Ph: (406)477-8283
Lame Deer, MT 59043   Fax: (406)477-6210
Edwin Dahle, Pres.
BIA Area Office: Billings. **BIA Agency:** No. Cheyenne.

★166★
Confederated Salish and Kootenai Tribes
Tribal Council
Box 278   Ph: (406)675-2700
Pablo, MT 59855   Fax: (406)675-2806
Michael T. Pablo, Chm.
BIA Area Office: Portland. **BIA Agency:** Flathead.

★167★
Fort Peck Tribal Executive Board
PO Box 1027   Ph: (406)768-5155
Poplar, MT 59255   Fax: (406)768-5478
Lawrence D. Wetsit, Chr.
BIA Area Office: Billings. **BIA Agency:** Ft. Peck.

─────────────── **Nebraska** ───────────────

★168★
Omaha Tribal Council
PO Box 368   Ph: (402)837-5391
Macy, NE 68039   Fax: (402)878-2943
Doran L. Morris Sr., Chr.
BIA Area Office: Aberdeen. **BIA Agency:** Winnebago.

★169★
Santee Sioux Tribal Council
Rte. 2   Ph: (402)857-3302
Niobrara, NE 68760   Fax: (402)857-3307
Daniel Denney Sr., Chr.
BIA Area Office: Aberdeen. **BIA Agency:** Winnebago.

★170★
Winnebago Tribe of Nebraska
Tribal Council
Winnebago, NE 68071   Ph: (402)878-2272
                                    Fax: (402)878-2963
Gerben Earth, Chr.
BIA Area Office: Aberdeen. **BIA Agency:** Winnebago.

─────────────── **Nevada** ───────────────

★171★
Yomba Tribal Council
Rte. 1, Box 24   Ph: (702)964-2463
Austin, NV 89310   Fax: (702)964-2443
Levi Hooper, Chm.
BIA Area Office: Phoenix. **BIA Agency:** W. Nevada.

★172★
Battle Mountain Band Council
35 Mountain View Dr., No. 138-13
Battle Mountain, NV 89820   Ph: (702)635-2004
Glen Holley, Chm.
BIA Area Office: Phoenix. **BIA Agency:** Ea. Nevada.

★173★
Carson Colony Community Council
652 Oneida St.
Carson City, NV 89703   Ph: (702)883-6431
Hal Malone, Chm.
BIA Area Office: Phoenix. **BIA Agency:** W. Nevada.

★174★
Stewart Community Council
5258 Snyder Ave.
Carson City, NV 89701   Ph: (702)885-9115
Darrell Kizer, Chm.
BIA Area Office: Phoenix. **BIA Agency:** W. Nevada.

★175★
Duckwater Shoshone Tribal Council
PO Box 68   Ph: (702)863-0227
Duckwater, NV 89314   Fax: (702)863-0301
Jerry Millett, Chm.
BIA Area Office: Phoenix. **BIA Agency:** Ea. Nevada.

★176★
Elko Band Council
PO Box 748
Elko, NV 89801   Ph: (702)738-8889
Davis Gonzales, Chm.
BIA Area Office: Phoenix. **BIA Agency:** Ea. Nevada.

★177★
Tribal Council of the Te-Moak Western Shoshone
Indians of Nevada
525 Sunset St.
Elko, NV 89801   Ph: (702)738-9251
Anthony Tom, Chm.
BIA Area Office: Phoenix. **BIA Agency:** Ea. Nevada.

★178★
Ely Colony Council
16 Shoshone Circle
Ely, NV 89301   Ph: (702)289-3013
Jerry Charles, Chm.
BIA Area Office: Phoenix. **BIA Agency:** Ea. Nevada.

★179★
Fallon Business Council
8955 Mission Rd.   Ph: (702)423-6075
Fallon, NV 89406   Fax: (702)423-5202
Merlin Dixon, Chm.
BIA Area Office: Phoenix. **BIA Agency:** W. Nevada.

★180★
Dresslerville Community Council
1585 Watasheamu Rd.
Gardnerville, NV 89410   Ph: (702)838-6431
Romaine Smokey Jr., Chm.
BIA Area Office: Phoenix. **BIA Agency:** W. Nevada.

★181★
Washoe Tribal Council
Rte. 2, 919 Hwy. 395 S.
Gardnerville, NV 89410   Ph: (702)265-4191
A. Brian Wallace, Chm.
BIA Area Office: Phoenix. **BIA Agency:** W. Nevada.

★182★
Las Vegas Colony Council
1 Paiute Dr.   Ph: (702)386-3926
Las Vegas, NV 89106   Fax: (702)383-4019
Alfreda Mitre, Chm.
BIA Area Office: Phoenix. **BIA Agency:** So. Paiute.

★183★
South Fork Band Council
Box B-13
Lee, NV 89829   Ph: (702)744-4273
Gordon Healy, Chm.
BIA Area Office: Phoenix. **BIA Agency:** Ea. Nevada.

★184★
Lovelock Tribal Council
Box 878
Lovelock, NV 89419   Ph: (702)273-7861
Alfred Happy, Chm.
BIA Area Office: Phoenix. **BIA Agency:** W. Nevada.

★185★
Fort McDermitt Tribal Council
PO Box 457
McDermitt, NV 89421   Ph: (702)532-8259
Glen Abel, Acting Chairman
BIA Area Office: Phoenix. **BIA Agency:** W. Nevada.

★186★
Moapa Business Council
PO Box 56
Moapa, NV 89025   Ph: (702)865-2787
Leroy Anderson, Chm.
BIA Area Office: Phoenix. **BIA Agency:** So. Paiute F.S.

★187★
Pyramid Lake Paiute Tribal Council
PO Box 256   Ph: (702)574-0140
Nixon, NV 89424   Fax: (702)786-8232
Elwood Lowery, Chm.
BIA Area Office: Phoenix. **BIA Agency:** W. Nevada.

★188★
Shoshone Paiute Business Council
PO Box 219   Ph: (702)757-3161
Owyhee, NV 89832   Fax: (702)757-2219
James Paiva, Chm.
BIA Area Office: Phoenix. **BIA Agency:** So. Paiute.

★189★
Reno-Sparks Indian Council
98 Colony Rd.
Reno, NV 89502   Ph: (702)329-2936
Robert Shaw, Chm.
BIA Area Office: Phoenix. **BIA Agency:** W. Nevada.

★190★
Walker River Paiute Tribal Council
PO Box 220   Ph: (702)773-2306
Schurz, NV 89427   Fax: (702)773-2985
Anita Collins, Chm.
BIA Area Office: Phoenix. **BIA Agency:** W. Nevada.

★191★
Wells Indian Colony and Council
PO Box 809
Wells, NV 89835   Ph: (702)752-3045
BIA Area Office: Phoenix. **BIA Agency:** Ea. Nevada.

★192★
Summit Lake Paiute Council
PO Box 1958
Winnemucca, NV 89445   Ph: (702)623-5151
Robyn Burdette, Chm.
BIA Area Office: Phoenix. **BIA Agency:** W. Nevada.

★193★
Yerington Paiute Tribal Council
171 Campbell Ln.   Ph: (702)463-3301
Yerington, NV 89447   Fax: (702)463-2416
Gloria J. Brunette, Chm.
BIA Area Office: Phoenix. **BIA Agency:** W. Nevada.

——————— **New Mexico** ———————

★194★
Pueblo of Acoma
PO Box 309
Acomita, NM 87034   Ph: (505)552-6604
Reginald Pasqual, Gov.
BIA Area Office: Albuquerque. **BIA Agency:** So. Pueblos.

★195★
Pueblo of Sandia
PO Box 6008
Bernalillo, NM 87004   Ph: (505)867-3317
Manuel Montoya, Gov.
BIA Area Office: Albuquerque. **BIA Agency:** So. Pueblos.

★196★
Pueblo of Santa Ana
PO Box 37
Bernalillo, NM 87004   Ph: (505)867-3301
Lawrence Montoya Sr., Gov.
BIA Area Office: Albuquerque. **BIA Agency:** So. Pueblos.

★197★
Pueblo of Cochiti
PO Box 70
Cochiti, NM 87041   Ph: (505)465-2244
Cedric Chavez, Gov.
BIA Area Office: Albuquerque. **BIA Agency:** So. Pueblos.

★198★
Jicarilla Apache Tribal Council
PO Box 147
Dulce, NM 87528   Ph: (505)759-3242
Levi Pesata, Pres.
BIA Area Office: Albuquerque. **BIA Agency:** Jicarilla.

★199★
Pueblo of Santa Clara
PO Box 580
Espanola, NM 87532   Ph: (505)753-7316
Walter Dasheno, Gov.
BIA Area Office: Albuquerque. **BIA Agency:** No. Pueblos.

★200★
Pueblo of Isleta
PO Box 317
Isleta, NM 87002   Ph: (505)869-3111
Alex Lucero, Gov.
BIA Area Office: Albuquerque. **BIA Agency:** So. Pueblos.

★201★
Pueblo of Jemez
PO Box 78
Jemez Pueblo, NM 87024   Ph: (505)834-7359
Jose R. Toledo, Gov.
BIA Area Office: Albuquerque. **BIA Agency:** So. Pueblos.

★202★
Pueblo of Laguna
PO Box 194
Laguna, NM 87026   Ph: (505)552-6654
Harry D. Early, Gov.
BIA Area Office: Albuquerque. **BIA Agency:** Laguna.

★203★
Mescalero Apache Tribal Council
PO Box 176
Mescalero, NM 87340   Ph: (505)671-4495
Wendell Chino, Pres.
BIA Area Office: Albuquerque. **BIA Agency:** Mescalero.

★204★
Pueblo of Picuris
PO Box 127
Penasco, NM 87553   Ph: (505)587-2519
Joe Quanchello, Gov.
BIA Area Office: Albuquerque. **BIA Agency:** No. Pueblos.

★205★
Ramah Navajo Chapter
Rte. 2, Box 13
Ramah, NM 87321   Ph: (505)775-3383
Martha Garcia, Pres.
BIA Area Office: Alburque. **BIA Agency:** Ramah/Navajo.

★206★
Pueblo of San Felipe
PO Box A
San Felipe Pueblo, NM 87001   Ph: (505)867-3381
Frank Tenorio, Gov.
BIA Area Office: Albuquerque. **BIA Agency:** So. Pueblos.

★207★
Pueblo of San Juan
PO Box 1099
San Juan Pueblo, NM 87566   Ph: (505)852-4400
Wilfred Garcia, Gov.
BIA Area Office: Albuquerque. **BIA Agency:** No. Pueblos.

★208★
Pueblo of Zia
General Delivery
San Ysidro, NM 87053   Ph: (505)867-3304
Earl Gachupin, Gov.
BIA Area Office: Albuquerque. **BIA Agency:** So. Pueblos.

★209★
Pueblo of Nambe
Rte. 1, Box 117-BB
Santa Fe, NM 87501   Ph: (505)455-2036
Tony B. Vigil, Gov.
BIA Area Office: Albuquerque. **BIA Agency:** No. Pueblos.

★210★
Pueblo of Pojoaque
Rte. 11, Box 71
Santa Fe, NM 87501   Ph: (505)455-2278
Jacob Viarrial, Gov.
BIA Area Office: Albuquerque. **BIA Agency:** No. Pueblos.

★211★
Pueblo of San Ildefonso
Rte. 5, Box 315-A
Santa Fe, NM 87501   Ph: (505)455-2273
Dennis Martinez, Gov.
BIA Area Office: Albuquerque. **BIA Agency:** No. Pueblos.

★212★
Pueblo of Tesuque
Rte. 11, Box 1
Santa Fe, NM 87501   Ph: (505)983-2667
J. Marvin Herrera, Gov.
BIA Area Office: Albuquerque. **BIA Agency:** No. Pueblos.

★213★
Pueblo of Santo Domingo
PO Box 99
Santo Domingo Pueblo, NM 87052   Ph: (505)465-2214
Ramon Garcia, Gov.
BIA Area Office: Albuquerque. **BIA Agency:** So. Pueblos.

★214★
Pueblo of Taos
PO Box 1846   Ph: (505)758-9593
Taos, NM 87571   Fax: (505)758-8831
Jimmy Cordova, Gov.
BIA Area Office: Albuquerque. **BIA Agency:** No. Pueblos.

★215★
Pueblo of Zuni
PO Box 339
Zuni, NM 87327   Ph: (505)782-4481
Robert Lewis, Gov.
BIA Area Office: Albuquerque. **BIA Agency:** Zuni.

—————— **New York** ——————

★216★
Tonawanda Band of Senecas
Council of Chiefs
7027 Meadville Rd.   Ph: (716)542-9942
Basom, NY 14013   Fax: (716)542-9692
Bernie Parker, Chief
BIA Area Office: Eastern. **BIA Agency:** NY Liaison Office.

★217★
St. Regis Mohawk Council Chiefs
Akwesasne Community Building   Ph: (518)358-2272
Hogansburg, NY 13655   Fax: (518)358-3203
L. David Jacobs, Head Chief
BIA Area Office: Eastern. **BIA Agency:** NY Liaison Office.

★218★
Tuscarora Nation
5616 Walmore Rd.
Lewiston, NY 14092   Ph: (716)297-4990
Arnold Hewitt, Chief
BIA Area Office: Eastern. **BIA Agency:** NY Liaison Office.

★219★
Onondaga Nation
PO Box 319B
Nedrow, NY 13120   Ph: (315)469-8507
Leon Shenandoah, Head Chief
BIA Area Office: Eastern. **BIA Agency:** NY Liaison Office.

★220★
Oneida Nation of New York
West Rd.
PO Box 1   Ph: (315)697-8251
Oneida, NY 13421   Fax: (315)697-8259
Richard Raymond
Chrisjohn Halbritter, Tribal Leader
BIA Area Office: Eastern. **BIA Agency:** NY Liaison Office.

★221★
Seneca Nation of Indians
PO Box 231
Salamanca, NY 14081
Calvin John, Pres.
Ph: (716)945-1790
Fax: (716)945-3917
BIA Area Office: Eastern. **BIA Agency:** NY Liaison Office.

★222★
Cayuga Nation
PO Box 11
Versailles, NY 14168
James Leaffe, Chief
Ph: (716)532-4847
Fax: (716)532-5417
BIA Area Office: Eastern. **BIA Agency:** NY Liaison Office.

─────── **North Carolina** ───────

★223★
Eastern Band of Cherokee Indians
PO Box 455
Cherokee, NC 28719
Jonathan L. Taylor, Principal Chief
Ph: (704)497-2771
Fax: (704)497-2952
BIA Area Office: Eastern. **BIA Agency:** Cherokee.

─────── **North Dakota** ───────

★224★
Turtle Mountain Band of Chippewa
Tribal Council
Belcourt, ND 58316
Twila Martin-Kekahbah, Chr.
Ph: (701)477-6451
Fax: (701)477-6835
BIA Area Office: Aberdeen. **BIA Agency:** Turtle Mt.

★225★
Devils Lake Sioux Tribal Council
Sioux Community Center
Fort Totten, ND 58335
Peter Belgarde Jr., Chr.
Ph: (701)766-4221
Fax: (701)766-4854
BIA Area Office: Aberdeen. **BIA Agency:** Fort Totten.

★226★
Standing Rock Sioux Tribal Council
Fort Yates, ND 58538
Charles W. Murphy, Chr.
Ph: (701)854-7231
Fax: (701)854-7299
BIA Area Office: Aberdeen. **BIA Agency:** Standing Rock.

★227★
Three Affiliated Tribes Business Council
PO Box 220
New Town, ND 58763
Wilbur D. Wilkison, Chr.
Ph: (701)627-4781
Fax: (701)627-3805
BIA Area Office: Aberdeen. **BIA Agency:** Ft. Berthold.

─────── **Oklahoma** ───────

★228★
Chickasaw Nation of Oklahoma
PO Box 1548
Ada, OK 74820
Bill Anoatubby, Gov.
Ph: (405)436-2603
Fax: (405)436-4287
BIA Area Office: Muskogee. **BIA Agency:** Chickasaw.

★229★
Apache Business Committee
PO Box 1220
Anadarko, OK 73005
Amos Pewenofkit Sr., Vice Chairman
Ph: (405)247-9493
BIA Area Office: Anadarko. **BIA Agency:** Anadarko.

★230★
Delaware Executive Committee
PO Box 825
Anadarko, OK 73005
Michael Hunter, Vice President
Ph: (405)247-2448
BIA Area Office: Anadarko. **BIA Agency:** Anadarko.

★231★
Wichita Executive Committee
PO Box 729
Anadarko, OK 73005
Gary McAdams, Acting Pres.
Ph: (405)247-2425
BIA Area Office: Anadarko. **BIA Agency:** Anadarko.

★232★
Fort Sill Apache Business Committee
Rte. 2, Box 121
Apache, OK 73006
Mildred Cleghorn, Chr.
Ph: (405)588-2298
BIA Area Office: Anadarko. **BIA Agency:** Anadarko.

★233★
Caddo Tribe
Tribal Council
PO Box 487
Binger, OK 73009
Leonard Williams, Chr.
Ph: (405)656-2344
BIA Area Office: Anadarko. **BIA Agency:** Anadarko.

★234★
Kiowa Business Committee
PO Box 369
Carnegie, OK 73015
Joseph Goombi, Chr.
Ph: (405)654-2300
BIA Area Office: Anadarko. **BIA Agency:** Anadarko.

★235★
Cheyenne-Arapaho Business Committee
PO Box 38
Concho, OK 73022
Juanita L. Learned, Chr.
Ph: (405)262-0345
BIA Area Office: Anadarko. **BIA Agency:** Concho.

★236★
Choctaw Nation of Oklahoma
16th and Locust St.
PO Drawer 1210
Durant, OK 74701
Hollis E. Roberts, Chief
Ph: (405)924-8280
Fax: (405)924-1100
BIA Area Office: Muskogee. **BIA Agency:** Talhina.

★237★
Alabama-Quassarte Tribal Town
PO Box 404
Eufaula, OK 74432
Kenneth L. Tiger, Chief
Ph: (405)452-3262
BIA Area Office: Muskogee. **BIA Agency:** Okmulgee.

★238★
Kaw Business Committee
Drawer 50
Kaw City, OK 74641
Wanda Stone, Chr.
Ph: (405)269-2552
Fax: (405)269-2301
BIA Area Office: Anadarko. **BIA Agency:** Pawnee.

★239★
Comanche Tribal Business Committee
HC 32, Box 1720
Lawton, OK 73502   Ph: (405)492-4988
Wallace Coffey, Chr.
BIA Area Office: Anadarko. **BIA Agency:** Anadarko.

★240★
Kickapoo Tribe of Oklahoma
Business Committee
PO Box 70
McLoud, OK 74851   Ph: (405)964-2075
Riacardo Salazar, Chr.
BIA Area Office: Anadarko. **BIA Agency:** Shawnee.

★241★
Miami Tribe of Oklahoma
PO Box 636
Miami, OK 74355   Ph: (918)542-1445
Floyd Leonard, Chief
BIA Area Office: Muskogee. **BIA Agency:** Miami.

★242★
Oodoc Tribe of Oklahoma
PO Box 939
Miami, OK 74354   Ph: (918)542-1190
Bill G. Follis, Chief
BIA Area Office: Muskogee. **BIA Agency:** Miami.

★243★
Ottawa Tribe of Oklahoma
PO Box 110
Miami, OK 74355   Ph: (918)540-1536
Charles Dawes, Chief
BIA Area Office: Muskogee. **BIA Agency:** Miami.

★244★
Peoria Indian Tribe of Oklahoma
PO Box 1527
Miami, OK 74355   Ph: (918)540-2535
Louis E. Myers, Chief
BIA Area Office: Muskogee. **BIA Agency:** Miami.

★245★
Seneca-Cayuga Tribe of Oklahoma
PO Box 1283
Miami, OK 74355   Ph: (918)542-6609
Terry L. Whitetree, Chief
BIA Area Office: Muskogee. **BIA Agency:** Miami.

★246★
Kialegee Tribal Town
Rte. 3, Box 18-C
Okemah, OK 74859   Ph: (405)452-3262
Johnny Billy, Tribal Town King
BIA Area Office: Muskogee. **BIA Agency:** Okmulgee.

★247★
Thlopthlocco Tribal Town
Box 706   Ph: (918)623-2620
Okemah, OK 74859   Fax: (918)623-2404
Charlie McGertt, Town King
BIA Area Office: Muskogee. **BIA Agency:** Okmulgee.

★248★
Creek Nation of Oklahoma
PO Box 580   Ph: (918)756-8700
Okmulgee, OK 74447   Fax: (918)756-3340
Claude A. Cox, Principal Chief
BIA Area Office: Muskogee. **BIA Agency:** Okmulgee.

★249★
Osage Tribe of Indians
Tribal Administration Bldg.   Ph: (918)287-4622
Pawhuska, OK 74056   Fax: (918)287-1229
Charles O. Tillman Jr., Principal Chief
BIA Area Office: Muskogee. **BIA Agency:** Osage.

★250★
Pawnee Business Council
PO Box 470
Pawnee, OK 74058   Ph: (918)762-3624
Robert L. Chapman, Pres.
BIA Area Office: Anadarko. **BIA Agency:** Pawnee.

★251★
Iowa of Oklahoma Business Committee
Iowa Veterans Hall
PO Box 190
Perkins, OK 74059   Ph: (405)547-2403
Howard Springer, Chr.
BIA Area Office: Anadarko. **BIA Agency:** Shawnee.

★252★
Ponca Business Committee
PO Box 2, White Eagle
Ponca City, OK 74601   Ph: (405)762-8104
Kinsel V. Lieb, Chr.
BIA Area Office: Anadarko. **BIA Agency:** Pawnee.

★253★
Quapaw Tribal Business Committee
PO Box 765   Ph: (918)542-1853
Quapaw, OK 74363   Fax: (918)542-1559
Willis H. Matthews Jr., Chm.
BIA Area Office: Muskogee. **BIA Agency:** Miami.

★254★
Otoe-Missouria Tribal Council
PO Box 68
Red Rock, OK 74651   Ph: (405)723-4434
Della C. Warrior, Chr.
BIA Area Office: Anadarko. **BIA Agency:** Pawnee.

★255★
Absentee-Shawnee Executive Committee
2025 S. Gordon Cooper Dr.
Shawnee, OK 74801-9381   Ph: (405)275-4030
John Edwards, Gov.
BIA Area Office: Anadarko. **BIA Agency:** Shawnee.

★256★
Citizen Band Potawatomi Business Committee
1901 S. Gordon Cooper Dr.
Shawnee, OK 74801   Ph: (405)275-3121
John A. Barrett, Chr.
BIA Area Office: Anadarko. **BIA Agency:** Shawnee.

★257★
Sac and Fox of Oklahoma Business Committee
Rte. 2, Box 246
Stroud, OK 74079   Ph: (918)968-3526
Elmer Manatowa Jr., Principal Chief
BIA Area Office: Anadarko. **BIA Agency:** Shawnee.

★258★
Cherokee Nation of Oklahoma
PO Box 948   Ph: (918)456-0671
Tahlequah, OK 74465   Fax: (918)456-6485
Wilma Mankiller, Principal Chief
BIA Area Office: Muskogee. **BIA Agency:** Tahlequah.

★259★
United Keetoowah Band of Cherokee Indians
2450 S. Muskogee Ave.
Tahlequah, OK 74464   Ph: (918)456-5491
John Hair, Chief
BIA Area Office: Muskogee. **BIA Agency:** Muskogee Area.

★260★
Tonkawa Business Committee
PO Box 70
Tonkawa, OK 74653   Ph: (405)628-2561
Virginia Combrink, Pres.
BIA Area Office: Anadarko. **BIA Agency:** Pawnee.

★261★
Seminole Nation of Oklahoma
PO Box 1498   Ph: (405)257-6287
Wewoka, OK 74884   Fax: (405)257-6748
Jerry Haney, Principal Chief
BIA Area Office: Muskogee. **BIA Agency:** Wewoka.

★262★
Wyandotte Tribe of Oklahoma
PO Box 250   Ph: (918)678-2297
Wyandotte, OK 74370   Fax: (918)678-2944
Leaford Bearskin, Chief
BIA Area Office: Muskogee. **BIA Agency:** Miami.

Oregon

★263★
Burns-Paiute General Council
HC 71, 100 Pasigo St.   Ph: (503)573-2088
Burns, OR 97720   Fax: (503)573-2323
Larry Richards, Chm.
BIA Area Office: Portland. **BIA Agency:** Warm Springs.

★264★
Klamath General Council
Box 436   Ph: (503)783-2219
Chiloquin, OR 97624   Fax: (503)783-2029
Elwood Miller Jr., Chm.
BIA Area Office: Portland. **BIA Agency:** Warm Springs.

★265★
**Confederated Tribes of Coos Lower Umpqua and
  Suislaw Indians**
455 S. 4th St.   Ph: (503)267-5454
Coos Bay, OR 97420   Fax: (503)269-1647
Stephen Brainard, Chm.
BIA Area Office: Portland. **BIA Agency:** Siletz.

★266★
Coquille Indian Tribe
250 Hull St.   Ph: (503)888-4274
Coos Bay, OR 97420   Fax: (503)888-5799
James Metcalf, Chm.
BIA Area Office: Portland. **BIA Agency:** Siletz.

★267★
**Confederated Tribes of the Grande Ronde Tribal
  Council**
PO Box 38   Ph: (503)879-5215
Grande Ronde, OR 97347   Fax: (503)879-5964
Mark Mercier, Chm.
BIA Area Office: Portland. **BIA Agency:** Siletz.

★268★
Umatilla Board of Trustees
PO Box 638   Ph: (503)276-3165
Pendelton, OR 97801   Fax: (503)276-9060
Elwood H. Patawa, Chr.
BIA Area Office: Portland. **BIA Agency:** Umatilla.

★269★
Cow Creek Band of Umpqua Indians
649 W. Harrison   Ph: (503)672-9405
Roseburg, OR 97470   Fax: (503)673-0432
Sue Shaffer, Chm.
BIA Area Office: Portland. **BIA Agency:** Siletz.

★270★
Siletz Tribal Council
PO Box 549   Ph: (503)444-2513
Siletz, OR 97380   Fax: (503)444-2307
Delores Pigsley, Chm.
BIA Area Office: Portland. **BIA Agency:** Siletz.

★271★
Warm Springs Tribal Council
PO Box C   Ph: (503)553-1161
Warm Springs, OR 97761   Fax: (503)553-1294
Zane Jackson Sr., Chr.
BIA Area Office: Portland. **BIA Agency:** Warm Springs.

Rhode Island

★272★
Narragansett Indian Tribe
PO Box 268   Ph: (401)364-1100
Charleston, RI 02813   Fax: (401)364-1104
George H. Hopkins, Chief Sachem
BIA Area Office: Eastern. **BIA Agency:** Eastern.

South Dakota

★273★
Cheyenne River Sioux Tribal Council
PO Box 590   Ph: (605)964-4155
Eagle Butte, SD 57625   Fax: (605)964-4151
Gregg Bourland, Chairman
BIA Area Office: Aberdeen. **BIA Agency:** Cheyenne River.

★274★
Flandreau Santee Sioux Executive Committee
Flandreau Field Office
PO Box 283
Flandreau, SD 57028   Ph: (605)997-3891
Lee A. Taylor, Pres.
BIA Area Office: Aberdeen. **BIA Agency:** Aberdeen.

★275★
**Crow Creek Sioux Tribe
Tribal Council**
PO Box 658   Ph: (605)245-2221
Fort Thompson, SD 57339   Fax: (605)245-2216
Nelson Baline Jr., Chr.
BIA Area Office: Aberdeen. **BIA Agency:** Crow Creek

★276★
Ponca Tribal Council
Ponca Tribe of Nebraska
Lake Andes, SD 57356   Ph: (605)487-7796
Gloria Chytka, Acting Chr.
BIA Area Office: Aberdeen.

★277★
Lower Brule Sioux Tribal Council
Lower Brule, SD 57548   Ph: (605)473-5561
Michael Jandreau, Chr.   Fax: (605)473-5491

BIA Area Office: Aberdeen.

★278★
Yankton Sioux Tribal Business and Claims Committee
Box 248   Ph: (605)384-3641
Marty, SD 57361   Fax: (605)384-5706
Stephen Cournoyer Jr., Chr.
BIA Area Office: Aberdeen. **BIA Agency:** Yankton.

★279★
Oglala Sioux Tribal Council
Pine Ridge, SD 57770   Ph: (605)867-5821
                                         Fax: (605)867-5582
BIA Area Office: Aberdeen. **BIA Agency:** Pine Ridge.

★280★
Rosebud Sioux Tribal Council
Rosebud, SD 57570   Ph: (605)747-2381
Ralph Moran, Pres.   Fax: (605)747-2243

BIA Area Office: Aberdeen. **BIA Agency:** Rosebud.

★281★
Sisseton-Wahpeton Sioux Tribal Council
Agency Village
Rte. 2   Ph: (605)698-3911
Sisseton, SD 57262   Fax: (605)698-3708
Russell Hawkins, Chr.
BIA Area Office: Aberdeen. **BIA Agency:** Sisseton.

──────────── **Texas** ────────────

★282★
Kickapoo Traditional Tribe of Texas
PO Box 972   Ph: (512)773-2105
Eagle Pass, TX 78853   Fax: (512)757-9228
Raul Garza, Chr.
BIA Area Office: Anadarko. **BIA Agency:** Anadarko Area.

★283★
Ysleta del Sur Pueblo
PO Box 17579, Ysleta Sta.   Ph: (915)859-7913
El Paso, TX 79917   Fax: (915)859-2988
Raymond D. Apodaca, Gov.
BIA Area Office: Albuquerque. **BIA Agency:** So. Pueblos.

★284★
Alabama-Coushatta Tribe of Texas
Rte. 3, Box 659
Livingston, TX 77351   Ph: (409)563-4391
Perry Williams, Chr.
BIA Area Office: Anadarko. **BIA Agency:** Anadarko.

──────────── **Utah** ────────────

★285★
Tribal Council of Paiute Indian Tribe of Utah
600 N. 100 E. Paiute Dr.
Cedar City, UT 84720   Ph: (801)586-1111
Geneal Anderson, Chm.
BIA Area Office: Phoenix. **BIA Agency:** So. Paiute F.S.

★286★
Skull Valley Executive Committee
c/o Unitah and Ouray Agency
PO Box 130   Ph: (801)722-2406
Fort Duchesne, UT 84026   Fax: (801)722-2374
Lawrence Bear, Chm.
BIA Area Office: Phoenix. **BIA Agency:** Unitah and Ouray.

★287★
Uintah and Ouray Tribal Business Committee
PO Box 130
Fort Duchesne, UT 84026   Ph: (801)722-5141
Luke Duncan, Chm.
BIA Area Office: Phoenix. **BIA Agency:** Unitah and Ouray.

★288★
Goshute Business Council
PO Box 6104   Ph: (801)234-1138
Ibapah, UT 84034   Fax: (801)234-1136
Harlin Pete, Chm.
BIA Area Office: Phoenix. **BIA Agency:** Ea. Nevada.

──────────── **Washington** ────────────

★289★
Stillaquamish Board of Directors
3439 Stoluckquamish Ln.   Ph: (206)652-7362
Arlington, WA 98223   Fax: (206)435-2204
Gail Greger, Chm.

★290★
Muckleshoot Tribal Council
39015 172nd St., SE   Ph: (206)939-3311
Auburn, WA 98002   Fax: (206)939-5311
Virginia Cross, Chm.
BIA Area Office: Portland. **BIA Agency:** Puget Sound.

★291★
Lummi Business Council
2616 Kwina Rd.   Ph: (206)734-8180
Bellingham, WA 98226-9298   Fax: (206)384-4737
Samuel M. Cagey, Chm.
BIA Area Office: Portland. **BIA Agency:** Puget Sound.

★292★
Sauk-Suiattle Tribal Council
5318 Chief Brown Ln.   Ph: (206)435-8366
Darrington, WA 98241   Fax: (206)436-1511
J. Lawrence Joseph, Chm.
BIA Area Office: Portland. **BIA Agency:** Puget Sound.

★293★
Nooksack Tribal Council
PO Box 157   Ph: (206)592-5176
Deming, WA 98244   Fax: (206)592-5753
Hubert Williams, Chm.
BIA Area Office: Portland. **BIA Agency:** Puget Sound.

★294★
Hoh Tribal Business Council
HC 80, Box 917   Ph: (206)374-6582
Forks, WA 98331   Fax: (206)374-6549
Mary K. Leitka, Chm.
BIA Area Office: Portland. **BIA Agency:** Olympic Peninsula.

★295★
Port Gamble Community Council
PO Box 280   Ph: (206)297-2646
Kingston, WA 98346   Fax: (206)287-3413
Gerald J. Jones, Chm.
BIA Area Office: Portland. **BIA Agency:** Puget Sound.

★296★
Swinomish Indian Tribal Community
PO Box 817
Ph: (206)466-3163
LaConner, WA 98257
Fax: (206)466-4047
Robert Joe Sr., Chr.
BIA Area Office: Portland. **BIA Agency:** Puget Sound.

★297★
Quileute Tribal Council
PO Box 279
Ph: (206)374-6163
LaFush, WA 98350
Fax: (206)374-8250
James R. Jamie, Chm.
BIA Area Office: Portland. **BIA Agency:** Olympic Peninsula.

★298★
Tulalip Board of Directors
6700 Totem Beach Rd.
Ph: (206)653-4585
Marysville, WA 98270
Fax: (206)653-3054
Stanley Jones Sr., Chr.
BIA Area Office: Portland. **BIA Agency:** Puget Sound.

★299★
Makah Tribal Council
PO Box 115
Ph: (206)645-2201
Neah Bay, WA 98357
Fax: (206)645-2323
Vivian C. Lawrence, Chm.
BIA Area Office: Portland. **BIA Agency:** Olympic Peninsula.

★300★
Colville Business Committee
PO Box 150
Ph: (509)634-4711
Nespelem, WA 99155
Fax: (509)634-4116
Jude C. Stensgar, Chm.
BIA Area Office: Portland. **BIA Agency:** Colville.

★301★
Chehalis Business Council
PO Box 536
Ph: (206)273-5911
Oakville, WA 98568
Fax: (206)273-5914
Percy Youckton, Chm.
BIA Area Office: Portland. **BIA Agency:** Olympic Peninsula.

★302★
Nisqually Indian Community Council
4820 She-Nah-Num Dr., SE
Ph: (206)456-5221
Olympia, WA 98503
Fax: (206)438-2375
Dorian Sanchez, Chm.
BIA Area Office: Portland. **BIA Agency:** Puget Sound.

★303★
Lower Elwha Community Council
1666 Lower Elwha Rd.
Ph: (206)452-8471
Port Angeles, WA 98362
Fax: (206)452-4848
Carla J. Elofson, Chm.
BIA Area Office: Portland. **BIA Agency:** Olympic Peninsula.

★304★
Upper Skagit Tribal Council
2284 Community Plaza
Ph: (206)856-5501
Sedro Woolley, WA 98284
Fax: (206)856-2712
Floyd Williams, Chr.
BIA Area Office: Portland. **BIA Agency:** Puget Sound.

★305★
Jamestown Band of Klallam Indians
305 Old Blyn Hwy.
Ph: (206)683-1109
Sequim, WA 98382
Fax: (206)683-4366
William Ron Allen, Chm.
BIA Area Office: Portland. **BIA Agency:** Olympic Peninsula.

★306★
Skokomish Tribal Council
80 Tribal Center Rd.
Ph: (206)426-4232
Shelton, WA 98584
Fax: (206)877-5148
Denny Hurtado, Chm.
BIA Area Office: Portland. **BIA Agency:** Olympic Peninsula.

★307★
Squaxin Island Tribal Council
SE 70, Squaxin Ln.
Ph: (206)426-9781
Shelton, WA 98584
Fax: (206)426-3971
David Lopeman, Chm.
BIA Area Office: Portland. **BIA Agency:** Olympic Peninsula.

★308★
Suquamish Tribal Council
PO Box 498
Ph: (206)598-3311
Suquamish, WA 98392
Fax: (206)598-4666
Georgia C. George, Chr.
BIA Area Office: Portland. **BIA Agency:** Puget Sound.

★309★
Puyallup Tribal Council
2002 E. 28th St.
Ph: (206)597-6200
Tacoma, WA 98404
Fax: (206)848-7341
Roleen Hargrove, Chm.
BIA Area Office: Portland. **BIA Agency:** Puget Sound.

★310★
Quinault Business Committee
PO Box 189
Ph: (206)276-8211
Taholah, WA 98587
Fax: (206)276-4682
Joseph DeLaCruz, Pres.
BIA Area Office: Portland. **BIA Agency:** Olympic Peninsula.

★311★
Shoalwater Bay Tribal Council
PO Box 130
Ph: (206)267-6766
Tokeland, WA 98590
Fax: (206)267-6778
Douglas M. Davis, Chm.
BIA Area Office: Portland. **BIA Agency:** Olympic Peninsula.

★312★
Yakima Tribe
Tribal Council
PO Box 151
Ph: (509)865-5121
Toppenish, WA 98948
Fax: (509)865-5528
Levi George, Chr.
BIA Area Office: Portland. **BIA Agency:** Yakima.

★313★
Kalispel Business Committee
Box 39
Ph: (509)445-1147
Usk, WA 99180
Fax: (509)455-1705
Glen Nenema, Chm.
BIA Area Office: Portland. **BIA Agency:** Spokane.

★314★
Spokane Business Council
PO Box 100
Wellpinit, WA 99040
Ph: (509)258-4581
Bruce Winne, Chm.
BIA Area Office: Portland. **B \ Agency:** Spokane.

————————— **Wisconsin** —————————

★315★
Red Cliff Tribal Council
PO Box 529   Ph: (715)779-5805
Bayfield, WI 54814   Fax: (715)779-3151
Patricia DePerry, Chm.
BIA Area Office: Minneapolis. **BIA Agency:** Great Lakes.

★316★
Stockbridge-Munsee Tribal Council
Rte. 1   Ph: (715)793-4111
Bowler, WI 54416   Fax: (715)793-4299
Reginald C. Miller, Pres.
BIA Area Office: Minneapolis. **BIA Agency:** Great Lakes.

★317★
Forest County Potawatomi Executive Council
PO Box 346   Ph: (715)487-2903
Crandon, WI 54520   Fax: (715)478-5280
Hartford Shegonee, Chm.
BIA Area Office: Minneapolis. **BIA Agency:** Great Lakes.

★318★
Sokaogon Chippewa Tribal Council
Rte. 1, Box 625   Ph: (715)478-2604
Crandon, WI 54520   Fax: (715)478-5275
Ray McGeshick, Chm.
BIA Area Office: Minneapolis. **BIA Agency:** Great Lakes.

★319★
Lac Courte Oreilles Governing Board
Rte. 2, Box 2700   Ph: (715)634-8934
Hayward, WI 54843   Fax: (715)634-4797
Gaiashkibos, Chm.
BIA Area Office: Minneapolis. **BIA Agency:** Great Lakes.

★320★
St. Croix Council
PO Box 287   Ph: (715)349-2195
Hertel, WI 54845   Fax: (715)349-5768
Donald Saros, Pres.
BIA Area Office: Minneapolis. **BIA Agency:** Great Lakes.

★321★
Menominee Indian Tribe of Wisconsin
PO Box 397   Ph: (715)799-5100
Keshena, WI 54135   Fax: (715)799-3802
Ben Miller, Chm.
BIA Area Office: Minneapolis. **BIA Agency:** Menominee.

★322★
Lac du Flambeau Tribal Council
PO Box 67   Ph: (715)588-3303
Lac du Flambeau, WI 54538   Fax: (715)588-7930
Michael W. Allen Sr., Pres.
BIA Area Office: Minneapolis. **BIA Agency:** Great Lakes.

★323★
Bad River Tribal Council
PO Box 39   Ph: (715)682-4212
Odanah, WI 54861   Fax: (715)682-6679
Donald Moore Sr., Chm.
BIA Area Office: Minneapolis. **BIA Agency:** Great Lakes.

★324★
Oneida Tribal Business Committee
PO Box 365   Ph: (414)869-2772
Oneida, WI 54155-0365   Fax: (414)869-2194
Richard G. Hill, Chm.
BIA Area Office: Minneapolis. **BIA Agency:** Great lakes.

★325★
Wisconsin Winnebago Business Committee
PO Box 311   Ph: (608)372-4147
Tomah, WI 54660   Fax: (608)372-3561
Gordon Thunder, Chm.
BIA Area Office: Minneapolis. **BIA Agency:** Great Lakes.

————————— **Wyoming** —————————

★326★
Arapahoe Business Council
PO Box 217   Ph: (307)332-6120
Fort Washakie, WY 82514   Fax: (307)332-3055
Virginia Sutter, Chr.
BIA Area Office: Billings. **BIA Agency:** Wind River.

★327★
Shoshone Business Council
PO Box 217   Ph: (307)332-3532
Fort Washakie, WY 82514   Fax: (307)332-3055
Alfred Ward, Chr.
BIA Area Office: Billings. **BIA Agency:** Wind River.

National Organizations

★328★
All Indian Pueblo Council (AIPC)
PO Box 3256
Albuquerque, NM 87190   Ph: (505)881-1992
James Hena, Chm.
Description: Indian tribes. Serves as advocate on behalf of 19 Pueblo Indian tribes on education, health, social, and economic issues; lobbies on those issues before state and national legislatures. Activities are centered in New Mexico. Operates boarding school, Indian Pueblo Cultural Center, museum, and theater in Albuquerque, NM. Maintains Business Development Center; operates 618 volume library and archival collection. Offers placement service and charitable program; conducts children's services; bestows awards. **Founded:** 1598. **Members:** 19. **State Groups:** 40. **Publications:** *Governors 19 Indian Pueblos*, annual. Directory. • Also publishes pamphlet and brochure.

★329★
American Indian Archaeological Institute (AIAI)
38 Curtis Rd.
PO Box 1260   Ph: (203)868-0518
Washington Green, CT 06793-0260   Fax: (203)868-1649
Susan F. Payne, Dir.
Description: Individuals, families, libraries, and institutions. To discover, preserve, and interpret information about Native Americans of the northeastern woodlands area of the U.S., including their migration, survival patterns, cultural changes, and beliefs; to enhance appreciation for their cultures and achievements. Conducts archaeological surveys and excavations. Provides indoor and outdoor exhibits covering 12,000 years of North American prehistory, history, and contemporary native themes. Maintains quarter-mile Quinnetukut Habitat Trail and Indian Encampment with three wigwams and longhouses; conducts field trips. Sponsors archaeological training sessions, teacher workshops, craft workshops, summer youth programs, symposia, lectures, and film festivals. Maintains 2000 volume library and Museum Center for the Study of the Past and Present. **Founded:** 1971. **Members:** 1350. **Publications:** *Artifacts*, 4/year. Magazine. • Also publishes museum catalogs and educational resource pamphlets. **Formerly:** (1975) Shepaug Valley Archaeological Society.

★330★
American Indian College Fund (AICF)
217 E. 85th St., Ste. 201　　　　Ph: (212)988-4155
New York, NY 10028　　　　　　Free: 800-776-3863
David Archambault, Exec.Dir.　　Fax: (212)734-5118

Description: Raises funds to support tribally-controlled colleges. Administrative costs are underwritten by grants, allowing all individual donations to go to the colleges for the benefit of Native American students. **Founded:** 1989.

★331★
American Indian Council of Architects and Engineers (AICAE)
11675 SW 66th Ave.　　　　　Ph: (503)639-4914
Portland, OR 97223　　　　　Fax: (503)620-2743
Frederick G. Cooper, Pres.

Description: American Indian-owned architectural and engineering firms. Seeks to: enhance the role and improve the professional skills of American Indians in architecture and engineering; encourage American Indians to pursue careers in these fields. Represents interests of members at the national level. **Founded:** 1976. **Members:** 30. **Publications:** *AICAE Directory*, annual. ° *AICAE Newsletter*, semiannual.

★332★
American Indian Culture Research Center (AICRC)
Box 98
Blue Cloud Abbey
Marvin, SD 57251　　　　　　Ph: (605)432-5528
Rev. Stanislaus Maudlin OSB, Exec.Dir.

Description: Corporation that supports Indian leaders and Indian educators in their ambitions for rebuilding the Indian community. Aids in teaching the non-Indian public about the culture and philosophy of the Indian. Serves as a resource for guidance and funding in Indian self-help programs. Has compiled an oral history and a photographic collection. Conducts workshops and seminars; compiles statistics. Maintains speakers' bureau, 8000 volume library, and small museum. **Founded:** 1967. **State Groups:** 2. **Publications:** Distributes films, books, records, and tapes.

★333★
American Indian Development Association (AIDA)
PO Box 2793
Bellingham, WA 98227

Description: Purposes are to: assist American Indians and Indian organizations in developing resources in harmony with their culture; provide technical assistance, land energy, and water resource evaluation, and program development and funding assistance in both private and federal sectors. AIDA is currently unable to respond to new inquiries for assistance, and is involved with current projects only on a volunteer basis. **Founded:** 1973.

★334★
American Indian Graduate Center (AIGC)
4520 Montgomery Blvd., NE, Ste. 1-B
Alburquerque, NM 87109　　　　Ph: (505)881-4584
Lorraine P. Edmo, Dir.

Description: Provides scholarship and fellowship assistance for Native American students from federally recognized tribes at the graduate and professional school levels. Encourages colleges and universities to cooperate with financial assistance for those Native American students receiving its grants. **Founded:** 1969. **Publications:** *American Indian Graduate Record*, semiannual. **Formerly:** (1989) American Indian Scholarships.

★335★
American Indian Health Care Association (AIHCA)
245 E. 6th St., Ste. 499
Saint Paul, MN 55101　　　　　Ph: (612)293-0233
Michael Arfsten, Exec.Dir.

Description: Urban Indian health programs; staff and support persons from member programs and other concerned persons. Develops and assists in the implementation of improved management techniques for urban Indian health care centers including quality community education programs and quality health care delivery systems responsive to community needs. Provides training, technical assistance, health care delivery management, research, and evaluation for Indian health programs and organizations. Bestows Healthy Tradition awards and recognition for Indian health care achievements within and outside programs of urban Indian health care. Compiles statistics on health services provided by programs of clinical, and fiscal training and information exchange; maintains library and speakers' bureau. **Founded:** 1975. **Members:** 37. **Regional Groups:** 9. **State Groups:** 35. **Local Groups:** 37. **Publications:** *Native AIDS Briefs*, quarterly. Newsletter. ° *Native Newsbriefs*, quarterly. Newsletter. ° *Summary Program Publication*, annual. ° Also publishes *Health Promotion and Disease Prevention Bibliography*, AIDS brochures and posters, reports, and monographs.

★336★
American Indian Heritage Foundation (AIHF)
6051 Arlington Blvd.
Falls Church, VA 22044　　　　Ph: (202)463-4267
Dr. Wil Rose, CEO

Description: Tribal members and individual donors. Purpose is to inform and educate non-Indians concerning the culture and heritage of the American Indian. Seeks to respond to the spiritual and physical needs of American Indians and to inspire Indian youth. Sponsors food and clothing distribution program. Presents cultural concerts for children. Bestows cash awards and medals to outstanding Indian youth in seven categories; provides scholarships and camp grants. Operates speakers' bureau and museum; maintains 250 volume library. Sponsors American Indian Heritage Month and Seminars; also sponsors annual National Indian Awards Night, Miss Indian U.S.A. Pageant, and semiannual children's show. **Founded:** 1973. **Members:** 260,000. **State Groups:** 19. **Publications:** *Pathfinder Newsletter*, quarterly. ° *Project Letter*, monthly. ° *Tsa-La-Gi Columns*, quarterly. Newsletter. ° Also publishes brochure.

★337★
American Indian Higher Education Consortium (AIHEC)
513 Capitol Court NE. Ste. 100　　Ph: (202)544-9289
Washington, DC 20002　　　　　Fax: (202)544-4084
Georgianna Tiger, Exec.Dir.

Description: Organization of tribally controlled colleges in the U.S. and Canada. Seeks to encourage and foster the improvement of native post-secondary education and the development of the culture, traditions, and languages, of Native Americans. **Founded:** 1972. **Members:** 28. **Publications:** *Tribal College Journal*.

★338★
American Indian Historical Society (AIHS)
1493 Masonic Ave.
San Francisco, CA 94117　　　　Ph: (415)626-5235
Jeanette Henry Costo, Exec.Sec.

Description: American Indians, tribal groups, and others supporting the society's educational and cultural programs. Sponsors classes, forums, and lectures on the history of American Indians. Programs include: evaluation and correction of textbooks as they depict the role of the Indian in American history; preparation of materials supporting rights of the Indian. Founded the Indian Historian Press to publish educational books and periodicals for the general reader and the educational community. Maintains library. **Founded:** 1964. **Members:** 1962. **Publications:** *The Indian Historian*, annual. ° *Wassaja* (newspaper), periodic. ° Also publishes books.

★339★
American Indian Law Alliance (AILA)
488 7th Ave., Ste. 5K
New York, NY 10018　　　　　Ph: (212)268-1347
Remarks: Further information unavailable at this time.

★340★
American Indian Law Center (AILC)
PO Box 4456, Sta. A
Albuquerque, NM 87196　　　　Ph: (505)277-5462
Phillip Sam Deloria, Exec.Dir.

Description: Located at the University of New Mexico School of Law, funded primarily by government and foundation contracts and grants, and from contracts with Indian tribes and Indian organizations. Purpose is to render services, primarily research and training, of a broad legal and governmental nature. The demands of society on Indian tribal governments as well as their own entry into many areas of property rights and civil rights open many new frontiers in Indian law. The center and its staff of Indian law school graduates and attorneys constitute a major resource in assisting the tribes, as well as private and public agencies, in research of basic Indian law. Assists tribes in making legal decisions when assistance is necessary. Serves on a cooperative basis with other related programs in Indian affairs. Helped found and currently provides staff support to the Commission on State-Tribal Relations, a group of elected tribal, state, and municipal officials interested in cooperative intergovernmental relations on Indian reservations. Provides individualized training programs for tribal judges and tribal prosecutors in addition to others tailored to the needs of tribal communities. Offers Pre-Law Summer Institute for American Indians who have been accepted into or who indicate an interest in attending a law school. Provides assistance to Alaskan natives. Sponsors seminars; maintains library and audiovisual materials. **Founded:** 1967. **State Groups:** 12. **Publications:** *American Indian Law Newsletter*, bimonthly. Newsletter covering policy and legislation at the national, regional, state, local, and tribal government levels. • Also publishes manuals for tribal judges and prosecutors and on Indian criminal court procedures and other law-related areas.

★341★
American Indian Liberation Crusade (AILC)
4009 S. Halldale Ave.
Los Angeles, CA 90062   Ph: (213)299-1810
Henry E. Hedrick, Pres.

Description: Presents radio broadcasts (the American Indian Hour) publicizing the physical and spiritual needs of American Indians and appeals for funds. Supports missionaries on American Indian fields; sponsors summer Bible camps, Bible schools for children, and other charitable programs; provides emergency relief. **Founded:** 1952. **Members:** 4000. **Regional Groups:** 1. **State Groups:** 5. **Publications:** *Indian Crusader*, quarterly. Newsletter covering programs, ministries, and projects of the association.

★342★
American Indian Library Association (AILA)
c/o Amer. Library Assn.
50 E. Huron St.
Chicago, IL 60611
Naomi Caldwell Wood, Pres.

Description: Individuals and institutions interested in promoting the development, maintenance, and improvement of libraries, library systems, and cultural information services on reservations and in communities of Native Americans and Native Alaskans. Develops and encourages adoption of standards for Indian libraries; provides technical assistance to Indian tribes on establishing and maintaining archives systems. Works to enhance the capibilities of libraries to assist Indians who are writing tribal histories and to perpetuate knowledge of Indian language, history, legal rights, and culture. Seeks support for the establishment of networks for exchange of information among Indian tribes. Communicates the needs of Indian libraries to legislators and the library community. Coordinates development of courses, workshops, institutes, and internships on Indian library services. **Founded:** 1979. **Publications:** *American Indian Libraries Newsletter*, periodic.

★343★
American Indian Lore Association (AILA)
960 Walhonding Ave.
Logan, OH 43138   Ph: (614)385-7136
Leland L. Conner, Chief

Description: Students and patrons of the Indian arts, crafts, and history. Presents Catlin Peace Pipe Award annually. **Founded:** 1957.

★344★
American Indian Movement (AIM)
710 Clayton St., Apt. 1
San Francisco, CA 94117   Ph: (415)566-0251
Antonio Gonzales, Dir.

Description: Primary objective is to encourage self-determination among American Indians and to establish international recognition of American Indian treaty rights. Membership limited to American

Indians. Founded Heart of the Earth Survival School, which enrolls 600 students in preschool to adult programs. Maintains historical archives. Offers charitable, educational, and children's services; maintains speakers' bureau; conducts research; compiles statistics. **Founded:** 1968. **Members:** 5000. **Publications:** *Survival News*, quarterly.

★345★
American Indian Refugees (AIR)
Description: Descendants of American Indian refugees; Indians who are nonreservation and nontribal. To acquire land for a "tribal-communal" way of life and to revive the traditional Indian attachment with the land as a vital part of Indian existence. Attempts to help Indians gain economic self-sustenance by encouraging self-confidence, control over their own affairs, and total control over their potential. Develops Indian talent by providing special education for those showing specific talents. Programs include an agricultural project in improvement of livestock, an educational program in socialism of Indians, and a program on prevention of cruelty to children and concern for animals. Sponsors competitions in the areas of agriculture and animal husbandry. Maintains 300 volume library. **Founded:** 1974. **Members:** 3. **State Groups:** 2. **Publications:** *Smoke Signal Express*, annual. **Formerly:** (1980) True People of the Western Hemisphere. Address unknown.

★346★
American Indian Registry for the Performing Arts (AIRPA)
1717 N. Highland, Ste. 614
Los Angeles, CA 90028   Ph: (213)962-6574
Yvonne Paradise, Exec.Dir.

Description: American Indian performers (172) and technical personnel in the entertainment field (43). Objective is to establish and develop a registry of American Indians seeking employment in the entertainment industry. Promotes participation by American Indians in the entertainment industry; opposes stereotypical portrayals of American Indians. Disseminates information to members on subjects pertaining to the industry and other fields. Conducts performance and technical skills training courses to enhance members' talents and marketability. Offers casting assistance. Assists in development of Tribal Film Commissions. Sponsors seminars and workshops. **Founded:** 1983. **Members:** 215. **State Groups:** 3. **Publications:** *AIRPA Newsletter*, monthly. • *American Indian Talent Directory*, annual. • Also publishes *Entertainment Guide to American Indian Productions*.

★347★
American Indian Research and Development (AIRD)
2424 Springer Dr., Ste. 200   Ph: (405)364-0656
Norman, OK 73069   Fax: (405)364-5464
Stuart A. Tonemah, Pres.

Description: Educational service organization which seeks to improve the quality of education for gifted and talented Native American students. Provides training and tecnichal assistance to local and state education agencies, tribes, and other Native American organizations. Offers summer programs on leadership, creativity, and tribal cultural assessment. Conducts research, develops curriculum and teaching materials. Maintains speakers' bureau; sponsors competitions; compiles statistics. **Founded:** 1982. **Publications:** *American Indian Gifted and Talented Assessment Model*, *Centering Optimum Youth Opportunities Toward Exellence Catalog*, and *Elementary American Indian Gifted and Talented Assessment Model*.

★348★
American Indian Science and Education Center
1085 14th St., Ste. 1506
Boulder, CO 80302   Ph: (303)492-8658
Norbert S. Hill, Exec. Officer

Description: Provides training and educational opportunities to American Indian college students and tribal leaders. Sponsors internships nationwide and specially designed workshops. Conducts research and community-affiliated programs for people interested in health, natural resources, and other areas of need in Indian country. Sponsors competitive scholarships for outstanding American Indian college students. Maintains library of 1500 volumes on Indian-related issues and education. **Founded:** 1960. **Publications:** *Journal*, biennial. **Formerly:** (1980) United Scholarship Service for American Indian Students (also known as United Scholarship Service); (1988) National Center for American Indian Alternative Education. Presently inactive.

★349★
American Indian Science and Engineering Society (AISES)

1085 14th St., Ste. 1506   Ph: (303)492-8658
Boulder, CO 80302   Fax: (303)492-7090
Norbert S. Hill Jr., Exec.Dir.

Description: American Indian and non-Indian students and professionals in science, technology, and engineering fields; corporations representing energy, mining, aerospace, electronic, and computer fields. Seeks to motivate and encourage students to pursue graduate studies in science, engineering, and technology. Sponsors science fairs in grade schools, teacher training workshops, and student chapters in colleges. Offers scholarships. Adult members serve as role models, advisers, and mentors for students. Bestows awards. **Founded:** 1977. **Members:** 1400. **Publications:** *AISES Newsletter*, quarterly. Includes calendar of events and employment opportunities. • *Annual Report*. • *Science Education Newsletter*, quarterly. • *Winds of Change*, quarterly. • Also publishes *Indian Biographies*.

★350★
American Native Press Research Association (ANPRA)

University of Arkansas at Little Rock
Dept. of English
2801 S. University Ave.
Little Rock, AR 72204   Ph: (501)569-3160
Johnye E. Strickland, Corr.Sec.-Treas.

Description: Membership includes contributors to the American Indian and Alaska Native Periodicals Project, nonprofit educational and cultural institutions, and individuals interested in the study of the American native press. Purposes are to: promote and foster academic research concerning the American native press, those involved in it, and American native periodical literature as a whole; disseminate research results; refine methodologies for discussing the American native press. **Founded:** 1984. **Members:** 70.

★351★
Americans for Indian Opportunity (AIO)

3508 Garfield St. NW
Washington, DC 20007   Ph: (202)338-8809
LaDonna Harris, Exec.Dir.

Description: Promotes economic self-sufficiency for American Indian tribes and individuals, and political self-government for members of American Indian tribes. Seeks to: help American Indians, Eskimos, and Aleuts establish self-help programs at the local level; improve communications among Native Americans and with non-Indians; educate the public on the achievements and current needs of Native Americans. Supports projects in education, health, housing, job development, and training opportunities for Indian young people. Assists in establishing local centers with similar goals. Monitors federal agencies to ensure the fair and proper administration of Indian programs and to obtain federal programs and grants of benefit to Indians on a local or national scale. Conducts research; bestows awards; compiles statistics. Maintains speakers' bureau. Holds seminars. **Founded:** 1970. **State Groups:** 7. **Publications:** *Red Alert*, periodic. • Also publishes *You Don't Have to Be Poor to Be Indian* and other resource information.

★352★
ARROW, Incorporated

1000 Connecticut Ave., NW, Ste. 1206
Washington, DC 20036   Ph: (202)296-0685
Robert LaFollette Bennett, Pres.

Description: Dedicated to the advancement of the American Indian. Seeks to help the American Indian achieve a better educational, cultural, and economic standard and provide needy individuals with health care. ARROW stands for Americans for Restitution and Righting of Old Wrongs. Works to improve tribal law and justice. Provides programs on drug and child abuse prevention. Offers direct aid and scholarships. **Founded:** 1949. **Members:** 2250. **State Groups:** 4. **Publications:** *American Indian Courtline*, periodic (in conjunction with National American Indian Court Clerks Association).

Includes *Directory of Indian Court Clerks and Administrators.* • *Americans for the Restitution and Righting of Old Wrongs*, annual. • Also publishes *Adolescence - A Tough Time for Indian Youth, Protecting Youth From Alcohol and Substance Abuse: What Can We Do?, Positive Self Esteem Can Protect Native American Youth*, and *Strong Tribal Identity Can Protect Native American Youth* (handbooks). **Formerly:** (1953) National Congress of American Indian Fund.

★353★
Associated Committee of Friends on Indian Affairs (ACFIA)

Box 1661
Richmond, IN 47375   Ph: (317)962-9169
Harold V. Smuck, Contact

Description: Missionary project of the Religious Society of Friends (Quakers). Work is concentrated in Indian Centers in Alabama, Iowa, and Oklahoma. **Founded:** 1869. **Publications:** *Indian Progress*, 3/year.

★354★
Association on American Indian Affairs (AAIA)

245 5th Ave.
New York, NY 10016   Ph: (212)689-8720
Gary Niles Kimble, Exec.Dir.

Description: Provides legal and technical assistance to Indian tribes throughout the U.S. in health, education, economic development, resource utilization, family defense, and the administration of justice. Maintains American Indian Fund. **Founded:** 1923. **Members:** 40,000. **State Groups:** 12. **Publications:** *Indian Affairs*, 4/year. Newsletter. • Also publishes books. **Formerly:** (1946) American Association on Indian Affairs.

★355★
Association of American Indian Physicians (AAIP)

Bldg. D
10015 S. Pennsylvania
Oklahoma City, OK 73159   Ph: (405)692-1202
Terry Hunter, Exec.Dir.

Description: Physicians (M.D. or D.O.) of American Indian descent. Encourages American Indians to enter the health professions. Provides a forum for the interchange of ideas and information of mutual interest to physicians of Indian descent. Establishes contacts with government agencies to provide consultation and other expert opinion regarding health care of American Indians and Alaskan Natives; receives contracts and grant monies and other forms of assistance from these sources. Supports and encourages all other agencies and organizations, Indian and non-Indian, working to improve health conditions of American Indians and Alaskan Natives. Locates scholarship funds for Indian professional students; provides counseling assistance; preserves American Indian culture. Conducts seminars for students interested in health careers and for counselors in government and other schools where American Indian children are taught. **Founded:** 1971. **Members:** 152. **Publications:** *Newsletter*, quarterly. • Also publishes *American Indian Health Careers Handbook*.

★356★
Association of Community Tribal Schools (ACTS)

c/o Dr. Roger Bordeaux
616 4th Ave., W.
Sisseton, SD 57262-1349   Ph: (605)698-3112
Dr. Roger Bordeaux, Exec.Dir.

Description: American Indian-controlled schools organized under the Indian Self-Determination and Educational Assistance Act and Tribally Controlled Schools Act; American Indian schools seeking status under these acts; interested individuals and organizations. Advocates Indian self-determination and Indian-controlled schools; provides technical assistance in making self-determination contracts; offers school board training assistance. **Founded:** 1982. **Members:** 30. **Regional Groups:** 2. **Publications:** *Newsletter*, monthly. • Plans to publish directory. **Formerly:** (1987) Association of Contract Tribal Schools.

★357★
Bureau of Catholic Indian Missions (BCIM)
2021 H St. NW   Ph: (202)331-8542
Washington, DC 20006   Fax: (202)331-8544
Rev.Msgr. Paul A. Lenz, Exec.Dir.

Description: Purpose is to conduct religious, charitable, and educational activities at American Indian and Eskimo missions. Maintains speakers' bureau; conducts research programs. **Founded:** 1874. **Publications:** *Bureau of Catholic Indian Missions-Newsletter*, monthly. • *Bureau of Catholic Indian Missions-Quarterly*.

★358★
Cherokee National Historical Society (CNHS)
PO Box 515
Tahlequah, OK 74465   Ph: (918)456-6007
Marilyn G. Moss, Exec.Dir.

Description: Persons and organizations interested in preserving the history and tradition of the Cherokee Indian Nation. Seeks to interest the public in Cherokee history. Plans to mark locations of historic significance to the Cherokees, including graves of officials and other prominent persons of the Nation. Sponsors educational, charitable, and benevolent activities for Cherokees and their descendants. Operates Cherokee Heritage Center, which includes the Cherokee National Museum, Cherokee Arboretum and Herb Garden (including trees and plants used traditionally by Cherokees for food, fiber, and medicines), and Cherokee National Archives of documents, papers, books, and other materials on Cherokee history and development. Maintains a "living" Indian Village, circa 1700-50 and a Rural Cherokee Museum Village, circa 1875-90; annually presents The Trail of Tears, an outdoor epic symphonic drama relating to Cherokee history in the southern highlands and the Southwest; sponsors annual Trail of Tears Indian art show; conducts a lecture series on Cherokee history and culture. Maintains Cherokee Hall of Fame for persons of Cherokee descent who have made distinguished contributions to the nation; also maintains the Ho-Chee-Nee Trail of Tears Memorial Chapel. Plans to restore a number of both pre- and post-Civil War historic Cherokee Nation buildings in the area of the old Cherokee Nation in the Southwest. **Founded:** 1963. **Members:** 900. **State Groups:** 15. **Publications:** *The Columns*, 4/year. Newsletter. • *Trail of Tears Drama Program*, annual. Includes theater company bibliographical information and description of programs at the Cherokee Heritage Center; also features color prints of Indian art.

★359★
Coalition for Indian Education (CIA)
3620 Wyoming Blvd. NE, Ste. 206
Albuquerque, NM 87111   Ph: (505)275-9788
Dean Chavers, V.Pres.

Description: Native American educators and others working to ensure that education, health, and other programs for Native Americans are effective and outstanding in their performance. Conducts lobbying and research activities. Offers informational services, training, and technical assistance. Maintains library, speakers' bureau, and placement service. Sponsors competitions; bestows awards. **Founded:** 1987. **Members:** 500. **State Groups:** 1. **Local Groups:** 50. **Publications:** *CIE Newsletter*, 3/year. Includes updates on federal legislation and association activities; also includes classified. • Also publishes *The Indian Dropout - An Annotated Bibliography*.

★360★
Concerned American Indian Parents (CAIP)
CUHCC Clinic
2016 16th Ave., S.
Minneapolis, MN 55404   Ph: (612)627-6888
Fred Veilleux, Contact

Description: Serves as a network for American Indian parents and others interested in abolishing symbols that are degrading to American Indians, such as the Redskins and Indians logos adopted by sports teams in the U.S. Seeks to make the future easier for American Indian children by educating the public about the racial messages inherent in such symbols. **Founded:** 1987. **Publications:** none.

★361★
Continental Confederation of Adopted Indians (CCAI)
960 Walhonding Ave.
Logan, OH 43138   Ph: (614)385-7136
Leland L. Conner, Chief

Description: Non-Indians who have been presented with honorary tribal chieftainship, an official Indian name, or recipients of any other Indian-oriented awards. Persons so honored include Wayne Newton, Reginald Laubin, and Ann Miller. Membership also open to blooded Indians. Maintains Indian Lore Hall of Fame. Bestows Annual National Catlin Peace Pipe Achievement Award. Maintains speakers' bureau. **Founded:** 1950. **Members:** 150. **Publications:** *Bulletin*, bimonthly.

★362★
Council of Energy Resource Tribes (CERT)
1999 Broadway, Ste. 2600
Denver, CO 80202   Ph: (303)297-2378
A. David Lester, Exec.Dir.

Description: American Indian tribes owning energy resources. Promotes the general welfare of members through the protection, conservation, control, and prudent management of their oil, coal, natural gas, uranium, geothermal, oil shale, and other resources. Provides on-site technical assistance to tribes in all aspects of energy resource management, economic development, and environmental protection. Conducts programs aimed at enhancing tribal planning and management capacities. Sponsors workshops. **Founded:** 1975. **Members:** 44. **State Groups:** 30.

★363★
Council for Indian Education (CIE)
517 Rimrock Rd.
Billings, MT 59102   Ph: (406)252-7451
Dr. Hap Gilliland, Pres.

Description: Individuals interested in improving and securing higher standards of education for American Indian children. Promotes quality children's literature on Indian culture. Publishes books about American Indian life, past and present, for use in reading programs. Conducts in-service education of teachers working on Indian reservations. **Founded:** 1970. **Members:** 100. **State Groups:** 1. **Publications:** Children's books and teacher training textbooks. **Formerly:** (1982) Montana Council for Indian Education.

★364★
Council for Native American Indians (CNAIP)
280 Broadway, Ste. 316
New York, NY 10007   Ph: (212)732-0485
Walter S. James Jr., Exec.Dir.

Description: Individuals interested in the holistic philosophies and teachings of the earlier indigenous groups of North and Central America. Conducts research on the social, economic, and political relationships between the indigenous groups and the 16th century settlers in New York City and Long Island, NY areas. Conducts educational series for children that teaches concepts of discipline through the methods and techniques of the ancient peoples. Sponsors charitable programs; compiles statistics. **Founded:** 1974. **Members:** 843. **Publications:** *Newsletter*, periodic. • Also publishes *Earth Walk and Four Directions for Peace* and *Medicine Lodge*.

★365★
Crazy Horse Memorial Foundation (CHMF)
The Black Hills
Ave. of the Chiefs
Crazy Horse, SD 57730-9506   Ph: (605)673-4681
Ruth Ziolkowski, Bd.Chm.

Description: Seeks completion of the memorial to North American Indians begun by sculptor Korczak Ziolkowski (1908-82). (This memorial is to be a statue, 563 feet high and 641 feet long, depicting the Sioux leader Crazy Horse astride his pony and pointing to the lands of his people. Ziolkowski's wife and children are continuing work on the statue, which is being carved from Thunderhead Mountain in South Dakota.) Maintains museum of art and artifacts of Indian tribes from many areas of the United States, a museum-studio of American and European antiques, art objects, marble, bronze, and mahogany sculpture. Operates library of 15,000 volumes on Indian culture, heritage, arts, crafts, and history. Offers scholarships to Native Americans. Plans to establish a university and medical center for Native Americans. **Founded:** 1948. **Members:** 23. **State Groups:** 6. **Publications:** *Crazy Horse Progress*, quarterly. Newsletter. • Has also published *Korczak: Storyteller in Stone* (biography), *Crazy Horse and Korczak*, and *Korczak, Saga of Sitting Bull's Bones*, and *Crazy Horse Memorial 40th Anniversary Booklet*.

★366★
Creek Indian Memorial Association (CIMA)
Creek Council House Museum
Town Sq.
Okmulgee, OK 74447   Ph: (918)756-2324
Tommy A. Steinsiek, Curator

Description: Operates museum of Creek Indian culture containing displays of Indian artifacts, archaeology artifacts, Indian murals, and paintings. Maintains library of approximately 200 books, including Creek readers, dictionaries, documents, and newspapers. Conducts fundraising activities. **Founded:** 1923. **Members:** 113. **State Groups:** 3. **Publications:** Booklets and leaflets on Creek history and legend. **Formerly:** (1923) Indian Historical Society.

★367★
Dakota Women of All Red Nations (DWARN)
c/o Lorelei DeCora
PO Box 423
Rosebud, SD 57570
Lorelei DeCora, Chair

Description: Grass roots organization of American Indian women seeking to advance the Native American movement. Is establishing local chapters to work on issues of concern such as sterilization abuse and women's health, adoption and foster-care abuse, community education, political imprisonment, legal and juvenile justice problems, and problems caused by energy resource development by multinational corporations on Indian land. Supports leadership roles for American Indian women. **Founded:** 1978. **Publications:** Reports on health problems of American Indian women. **Formerly:** (1985) Women of All Red Nations.

★368★
Fans Against Indian Racism (FAIR)

Description: Sports fans who feel that the Washington Redskins football team name is racially insulting to native Americans. Activities have included sending an airplane over a Redskins' game trailing a banner reading "Make Washington America's Team. Change The Name." Address unknown.

★369★
First Nations Development Institute (FNDI)
69 Kelley Rd.
Falmouth, VA 22405   Ph: (703)371-5615
Rebecca Adamson, Pres.

Description: Aims to help tribes achieve self-sufficiency; promotes economic development and commercial enterprises of reservation-based Indian tribes through technical assistance and workshops. Maintains research and data bank. **Founded:** 1980. **State Groups:** 30. **Publications:** *First Nations Business Alert*, quarterly. Looseleaf newsletter providing business news about and of interest to tribes. • Also publishes resource documents and brochures. **Formerly:** (1991) First Nations Financial Project.

★370★
Five Civilized Tribes Foundation (FCTF)
c/o Chickasaw Nation
PO Box 1548
Ada, OK 74820   Ph: (405)436-2603
Gov. Overton James, Chm.

Description: The Cherokee, Choctaw, Chickasaw, Creek, and Seminole Indian Nations of Oklahoma. FCTF is a grant-funded organization which provides coordination to tribal activities and programs, including social programs, industrial development, and administrative activities. Provides representation for the five tribes at the national level. Presently inactive. **Founded:** 1974. **Members:** 5. **Regional Groups:** 3.

★371★
Gathering of Nations (GN)
PO Box 75102, Sta. 14
Albuquerque, NM 87120-1269   Ph: (505)836-2810
Derek Mathews, Dir.

Description: Native Americans. Promotes the expression of Native American culture and religion, including Native American song and dance. Sponsors periodic song, dance, and Miss Indian World competitions; bestows awards. **Founded:** 1984.

★372★
Indian Arts and Crafts Association (IACA)
122 La Veta Dr. NE, Ste. B
Albuquerque, NM 87108   Ph: (505)265-9149
Helen Skredergards, Exec.Dir.

Description: Indian craftspeople and artists, museums, dealers, collectors, and others. To promote, preserve, protect, and enhance the understanding of authentic American Indian arts and crafts. Sets code of ethics for members. Conducts consumer education seminars, meetings, and display programs; works with related government groups. Sponsors competitions; bestows awards; operates speakers' bureau. **Founded:** 1974. **Members:** 695. **State Groups:** 2. **Publications:** *Indian Arts and Crafts Association–Directory*, annual. • *Indian Arts and Crafts Association–Newsletter*, monthly. • Also publishes brochures.

★373★
Indian Heritage Council (IHC)
Henry St.
Box 2302
Morristown, TN 37816   Ph: (615)581-5714
Louis Hooban, CEO

Description: American Indians and interested others. Promotes and supports Indian endeavors. Seeks a deeper understanding between Indians and non-Indians of the cultural, educational, spiritual, and historical aspects of Native Americans. Conducts research and educational programs. Sponsors charitable events. Operates speakers' bureau. **Founded:** 1988. **Local Groups:** 6. **Publications:** *Newsletter*, quarterly. Reports actions taken on behalf of Indian causes and promotions. • Also publishes *Great American Indian Bible*.

★374★
Indian Law Resource Center (ILRC)
508 Stuart
Helena, MT 59601   Ph: (406)449-2006
Robert T. Coulter, Exec. Dir.

Description: A legal, educational, counseling, and research service for American Indians and other Indians in the Western Hemisphere. Works to enable Indian people to survive as distinct peoples with unique cultures. Combats discrimination and injustice in the law and in public policy. Engages in human rights advocacy and environmental protection on behalf of Indians in the U.N. and U.S. courts; holds consultative status as a nongovernmental organization with the U.N. Economic and Social Council; offers free legal help. Conducts research and educational programs. **Founded:** 1978. **State Groups:** 8. **Publications:** *Annual Report*. • *Indian Rights-Human Rights* (handbook), articles, reports, and reprints.

★375★
Indian Rights Association (IRA)
c/o Janney Montgomery
1601 Market St.
Philadelphia, PA 19103   Ph: (215)665-4523
Janney Montgomery, Contact

Description: Individuals interested in protection of the legal and human rights of American Indians and promotion of their welfare. Maintains first-hand knowledge of conditions in Indian communities; keeps in touch with governmental Indian affairs; monitors and reports on judicial and legislative activities involving Indian concerns; acts as a clearinghouse for appeals of all sorts for aid to Indians and for information on all phases of Indian affairs. Sponsors prominent artists and speakers in programs introducing local communities to Native American cultures. Maintains archives and library of 1200 texts and journals. **Founded:** 1882. **Members:** 1000. **State Groups:**

3. **Publications:** *Indian Truth*, bimonthly. • Also publishes pamphlets and American Indian Lands and Communities (map).

★376★
Indian Youth of America (IYA)
609 Badgerow Bldg.
PO Box 2786
Sioux City, IA 51106   Ph: (712)252-3230
Patricia Trudell Gordon, Exec.Dir.

Description: Native American organization dedicated to improving the lives of Indian children. Works to provide opportunities and experiences that will aid Indian youth in their educational, career, cultural, and personal growth. Maintains an Indian Child Welfare Program, which attempts to prevent the distressful effects brought on by the breakup of Indian families. Goals of the program are: to inform families, social service agencies, and courts about the rights of Indian people under the Indian Child Welfare Act; to provide referral services to social service agencies in locating tribes and suitable placement for Indian children; to counsel Indian children and their parents and recruit Indian foster homes for Indian children. Sponsors a cultural enrichment project, a summer camp program, an after school Indian youth program, and an annual Christmas party for Indian children. Conducts career awareness placement service, parenting classes, and athletic clinics; maintains resource center. **Founded:** 1978. **Members:** 7. **State Groups:** 5. **Publications:** *Indian Youth of America–Newsletter*, quarterly. Includes works by Native American authors, calendar of events, and educational, camping, and career opportunities listings. • Also publishes brochure. • Also publishes brochure.

★377★
Indians Into Medicine (INMED)
University of North Dakota
School of Medicine
501 N. Columbia Rd.
Grand Forks, ND 58203   Ph: (701)777-3037
Gary D. Farris, Dir.

Description: Support program for American Indian students. Seeks to: increase the awareness of and interest in healthcare professions among young American Indians; recruit and enroll American Indians in healthcare education programs; place American health professionals in service to Indian communities. Coordinates financial and personal support for students in healthcare curricula. Provides referral and counseling services. Maintains 2000 volume library of medical textbooks. **Founded:** 1973. **State Groups:** 10. **Publications:** *Serpent, Staff and Drum* , quarterly. Newsletter. • Also publishes program information and motivational materials.

★378★
Indigenous Communications Association (ICA)
PO Box 748
Hogansburg, NY 13655   Ph: (518)358-4185
Ray Cook, Dir.

Description: Native American owned and/or operated radio stations in the U.S. Plans to develop the Native American Public Radio Satellite Network in conjuction with the Native American Public Broadcasting Consortium (see separate entry) to provide programming to native-controlled public radio stations.

★379★
Indigenous People's Network (IPN)
226 Blackman Hill Rd.
Berkshire, NY 13736
John Mohawk, Co-Dir.

Description: Indigenous, human rights, and energy-conscious organizations. Provides communications services and information to people in remote areas that have little access to public media; disseminates information on threats to the existence of indigenous people; seeks to raise the consciousness of people in North America and Western Europe. Activities include: documentation missions; indigenous refugee project, which assists Mayan refugees fleeing the war areas of Central America; the Indigenous People's Radio Network, which features taped interviews with indigenous leaders and community elders. Maintains speakers' bureau. **Founded:** 1983. **Members:** 70. **Regional Groups:** 25. **State Groups:** 4. **Publications:** *Congressional Indian Report*, weekly. • *Federal Register and Environmental Report*, weekly. • *IPN Weekly Report*. • Also publishes *Native Peoples in Struggle* (book).

★380★
Indigenous Women's Network (IWN)
PO Box 174
Lake Elmo, MN 55042   Ph: (612)770-3861
Winona LaDuke, Chair

Description: Individuals seeking to increase visibility of the indigenous women of the Western Hemisphere. Encourages the resolution of contemporary problems through traditional values. Opearates speakers' bureau; sponsors educational programs; conducts research. **Founded:** 1989. **Members:** 300. **Publications:** *Indigenous Woman*, semiannual. Magazine.

★381★
Institute of American Indian Arts (IAIA)
PO Box 20007
Santa Fe, NM 87504   Ph: (505)988-6463
Kathryn Harris Tijerina, Pres.

Description: Federally chartered private institution. Offers learning opportunities in the arts and crafts to Native American youth (Indian, Eskimo, or Aleut). Emphasis is placed upon Indian traditions as the basis for creative expression in fine arts including painting, sculpture, museum studies, creative writing, printmaking, photography, communications, design, and dance, as well as training in metal crafts, jewelry, ceramics, textiles, and various traditional crafts. Students are encouraged to identify with their heritage and to be aware of themselves as members of a race rich in architecture, the fine arts, music, pageantry, and the humanities. All programs are based on elements of the Native American cultural heritage that emphasize differences between Native American and non-Native American cultures. Sponsors Indian arts-oriented junior college offering Associate of Fine Arts degrees in various fields as well as seminars, an exhibition program, and traveling exhibits. Maintains extensive library, museum, and biographical archives. Provides placement service. **Founded:** 1962. **State Groups:** 10. **Publications:** *Faculty Handbook*, annual. • *School Catalog*, annual. • *Student Handbook*, annual. **Formerly:** (1962) Sante Fe Indian School.

★382★
Institute for the Development of Indian Law (IDIL)
c/o K. Kirke Kickingbird
Oklahoma City University
School of Law
2501 N. Blackwelder
Oklahoma City, OK 73106   Ph: (405)521-5188
K. Kirke Kickingbird, Exec.Dir.

Description: Public interest law firm that functions as a research training center on federal Indian law. The institute places special emphasis on three areas: Indian sovereignty; encouragement of Indian self-confidence and self-government; clarification of historical and legal foundations of modern Indian rights. Activities include: research and analysis; training and technical assistance; dissemination of educational materials relating to federal Indian law, Indian Treaties, curriculum and community development, and other subjects. Maintains library of 1500 volumes on law. Conducts educational programs for Indians and non-Indians. Holds seminars on federal Indian law, taxation, and the role of Indians in the development of the U.S. constitution. **Founded:** 1971. **State Groups:** 5. **Publications:** *American Indian Journal*, quarterly. • *Annual Publications Catalogue*. • *Publications and Materials List*, semiannual. • Also publishes *The Indians and the U.S. Constitution* (book, brochure, and videotape); makes available films, videotapes, and filmstrips.

★383★
Institute for the Study of Traditional American Indian Arts (ISTAIA)
PO Box 66124
Portland, OR 97266   Ph: (503)233-8131
John M. Gogol, Pres.

Description: Native American artists and craftspeople, anthropologists, museum personnel, researchers, and collectors of Native American art. Promotes traditional Native American arts through publications, lectures, and seminars. Conducts research.

Founded: 1982. **Publications:** *American Indian Basketry and Other Native Arts*, quarterly. Magazine.

★384★
Inter-Tribal Indian Ceremonial Association (ITIC)
Box 1
Church Rock, NM 87311 Ph: (505)863-3896
Laurance D. Linford, Exec.Dir.

Description: An official agency of the state of New Mexico. Members are Indian people, businessmen, dealers in Indian arts and crafts, and individuals interested in the annual Inter-Tribal Indian Ceremonial sponsored by the association each summer "to extol virtues and beauty of traditional Indian culture." The six-day program includes Indian dances, sports, arts and crafts, rituals, and a rodeo. Conducts correspondence and other activities in connection with legislation affecting Indian arts and crafts. Sponsors competition; bestows awards; conducts specialized education and children's services; maintains biographical archives, a small mailing library, and Red Rock Park as a museum. Plans to operate hall of fame. **Founded:** 1921. **Members:** 350. **State Groups:** 3. **Publications:** Educational materials on Indian crafts; also produces color slides of Indian ceremonies.

★385★
International Indian Treaty Council (IITC)
710 Clayton St., No. 1
San Francisco, CA 94117 Ph: (415)566-0251
Antonio Gonzales, EXO

Description: Organization of 98 traditional Indian governments formed to draw attention to Indian problems and Indian rights, largely through the efforts of the American Indian Movement (see separate entry). Maintains NGO status with the United Nations; makes regular presentations to the U.N. Commission on Human Rights; cosponsored a conference in Geneva, Switzerland in 1981 on Indigenous People and the Land. Cooperates with other human rights organizations; maintains a research and documentation center in South Dakota and an American Indian Treaty Council Information Center in New York, New York. **Founded:** 1974. **State Groups:** 5. **Publications:** *Treaty Council News*, quarterly.

★386★
Marquette League for Catholic Indian Missions (MLCIM)
1011 First Ave.
New York, NY 10022
Rev. Thomas A. Modugno, Dir.

Description: Provides financial support for the material welfare of Catholic Indian missions in the United States. **Founded:** 1904.

★387★
NAIM Ministries (NAIM)
PO Box 151
Point Roberts, WA 98281 Ph: (604)946-1227
William Lottis, Gen.Dir.

Description: Professionals, such as teachers and engineers, who also have some theological training. Objective is to establish indigenous Native American churches in urban centers and on reservations. Conducts economic, educational, social, and rehabilitation programs. Offers alcohol treatment and cross-cultural communication seminars. **Founded:** 1949. **Members:** 120. **State Groups:** 94. **Publications:** *Dear Team*, monthly. • *Infocus*, quarterly. Newsletter reporting on new staff, new ministries, and association activities. **Formerly:** (1986) Marine Medical Mission; North America Indian Mission.

★388★
National American Indian Court Clerks Association (NAICCA)
1000 Connecticut St. NW, Ste. 1206
Washington, DC 20036 Ph: (202)296-0685
E. Thomas Colosimo, Sec.-Treas.

Description: American Indian court clerks and administrators. Works to: improve the efficiency and provide for the upgrading of the American Indian court system through research, professional advancement, and continuing education programs; provide support services for all court officers at a professional level; maintain and improve the integrity and capability of the American Indian court system in providing equal protection to all persons before Indian courts. Seeks to elevate the status of court clerks and administrators through training and continuing education programs. **Founded:** 1980. **Members:** 290. **Publications:** *Courtline*, semiannual. Newsletter.

★389★
National American Indian Court Judges Association (NAICJA)
1000 Connecticut Ave. NW, Ste. 1206
Washington, DC 20036 Ph: (202)296-0685
Judge Elbridge Coochise, Pres.

Description: American Indian court judges. Seeks to improve the American Indian court system throughout the United States by furthering knowledge and understanding of it, and maintaining its integrity in providing equal protection to all persons. Offers periodic training sessions on criminal law and family law/child welfare. Conducts research and continuing education programs. **Founded:** 1968. **Members:** 256. **Publications:** *Indian Courts Newsletter*, periodic.

★390★
National American Indian Housing Council (NAIHC)
122 C St., NW, Ste. 280 Ph: (202)783-2667
Washington, DC 20001 Fax: (202)347-1785
Virginia E. Spencer, Exec.Dir.

Description: American Indian tribal housing authorities. Works with the U.S. Department of Housing and Urban Development to provide training and technical assistance to members. **Founded:** 1974. **Members:** 172. **Publications:** *Newsletter*, monthly.

★391★
National Center for American Indian Enterprise Development (NCAIED)
953 E. Juanita Ave.
Mesa, AZ 85204 Ph: (602)831-7524
Steven L. A. Stallings, Pres.

Description: To promote business and economic development among American Indians and tribes. Offers business training services to American Indians who own or plan to start businesses in fields including manufacturing, service, construction, retailing, and wholesaling. Assists Indians and tribes in: developing management abilities; assessing operating costs; preparing finance proposals; obtaining financing, bonding, and insurance; controlling the business through effective accounting and information systems; negotiating contracts, leases, and purchases; planning for future business growth. Provides services such as feasibility studies, site/location analysis, loan packaging, and promotion and fundraising campaigns. Sponsors Management Institute: Training for Indian Managers; conducts youth entrepreneurship programs and business and pre-business workshops; sponsors training and business success seminars. Operates the UIDA Group Inc., a development company. Maintains hall of fame and charitable program; bestows awards; compiles statistics. **Founded:** 1969. **Members:** 150. **Regional Groups:** 3. **Publications:** *Directory of American Indian Businesses*, annual. • *Indian Business and Management*, quarterly. **Formerly:** (1989) United Indian Development Association.

★392★
National Congress of American Indians (NCAI)
900 Pennsylvania Ave. SE
Washington, DC 20003 Ph: (202)546-9404

Description: Tribes representing 600,000 Indians (155) and individuals (2000). Seeks to: protect, conserve, and develop Indian natural and human resources; serve legislative interests of Indian tribes; improve health, education, and economic conditions. Administers NCAI Fund for educational and charitable purposes. Conducts research on Indian problems as a service to Indian tribes. Offers training seminars. Bestows congressional awards; compiles statistics. NCAI claims to be the oldest and largest national membership organization of American Indians and Alaskan natives. **Founded:** 1944. **Members:** 2155. **State Groups:** 15. **Publications:** *Annual Conference Report*. • *Sentinel*, periodic. Bulletin providing information on political and legislative news. Includes survey results, calendar of events, and federal register notices.

★393★
National Council of BIA Educators (NCBIAE)
6001 Marble NE, Ste. 10
Albuquerque, NM 87110   Ph: (505)266-6638
Fannie Bahe, Exec. Officer

Description: Professional educators employed in federal schools operated by the Bureau of Indian Affairs. To protect the rights and interests of teachers in Indian education; to promote quality educational opportunities for Indian students. Maintains speakers' bureau. **Founded:** 1967. **Members:** 150.

★394★
National Indian Athletic Association (NIAA)

Description: Organizes, coordinates and sponsors athletic, artistic and cultural events at local, state, regional, and national levels. Compiles statistics. **Founded:** 1973. **Members:** 6000. **Formerly:** (1982) National Indian Activities Association. Address unknown.

★395★
National Indian Council on Aging (NICOA)
6400 Uptown Blvd. NE
City Centre, Ste. 510-W
Albuquerque, NM 87110   Ph: (505)888-3302
Dave Baldridge, Exec.Dir.

Description: Native Americans. Seeks to bring about improved, comprehensive services to the Indian and Alaskan native elderly. Objectives are: to act as a focal point for the articulation of the needs of the Indian elderly; to disseminate information on Indian aging programs; to provide technical assistance and training opportunities to tribal organizations in the development of their programs. Conducts research on the needs of Indian elderly. **Founded:** 1976. **Members:** 300. **State Groups:** 8. **Publications:** *Elder Voices*, quarterly. * Also publishes proceedings, reports, and monographs. Write to request publication list.

★396★
National Indian Counselors Association (NICA)
Wilson Hall, Rm. 104
Washington State Univ.
Pullman, WA 99164-4012   Ph: (509)335-8676
Dora K. Thompson, Pres.

Description: Native American counselors concerned with improving the counseling of Native Americans. Exchanges ideas, identifies problems, and promotes educational and counseling growth and leadership. Makes recommendations for improved policies in educating Native Americans. Conducts networking among Native American counselors and workshops related to counseling Native Americans. Maintains data base. **Founded:** 1980. **Members:** 100.

★397★
National Indian Education Association (NIEA)
1819 H St. NW, Ste. 800
Washington, DC 20006   Ph: (202)835-3001
Donna Rhodes, Pres.

Description: American Indians; associate members are non-Indians. Advocates educational programs to improve the social and economic well-being of American Indians and Alaskan natives. Represents diversity of geographic and tribal backgrounds. Focuses on exchange of ideas, techniques, and research methods among the participants in Indian/native education. **Founded:** 1970. **Members:** 2000. **State Groups:** 1. **Publications:** quarterly. *Indian Education Newsletter*, 4/year.

★398★
National Indian Health Board (NIHB)
1385 S. Colorado Blvd. Ste. A-708
Denver, CO 80222   Ph: (303)759-3075
Levi Mestegh, Exec.Dir.

Description: Indians of all tribes and natives of Alaskan villages. Advocates the improvement of health conditions which directly or indirectly affect American Indians and Alaskan Natives. Seeks to inform the public of the health condition of Native Americans; represents Indians and their interests. Conducts seminars and workshops on health subjects. Provides technical assistance to members and Indian organizations. Bestows awards to nominated individuals who have made significant contributions in the Indian health field. **Founded:** 1969. **Members:** 12. **Regional Groups:** 12. **State Groups:** 6. **Publications:** *Conference Report*, annual. * *NIHB Health Reporter*, bimonthly. * Also publishes special reports on health issues and produces audiotapes.

★399★
National Indian Social Workers Association (NISWA)
PO Box 27463
Albuquerque, NM 87125
Mary Kihega, Sec.-Treas.

Description: Advocates for the rights of American Indians and Alaska Natives in social services areas. Provides training and technical assistance to tribal and nontribal organizations in subjects including counseling, program development, and planning and administration. Encourages publication of articles and books which clearly depict characteristics of American Indian and Alaska Native life; encourages American Indian and Alaska Native students to enter the field of social work. Holds seminars on Indian child welfare. Conducts survey research on major advocacy issues; sponsors competitions; bestows Indian Social Worker of the Year Award. Maintains speakers' bureau; compiles statistics. **Founded:** 1970. **Members:** 200. **Regional Groups:** 7. **Publications:** *National Indian Social Workers Association–The Association*, periodic. Newsletter; includes calendar of events and news of members, research, and awards. **Formerly:** (1981) Association of American Indian Social Workers; (1984) Association of American Indian and Alaskan Native Social Workers. Presently inactive.

★400★
National Indian Traders Association
3575 S. Fox
Englewood, CO 80110   Ph: (303)762-6579
Dr. Moto, Pres.

Description: Promotes Native American and Native Alaskan-produced arts and crafts. Provides a clearinghouse and consultation. **Founded:** 1981. **Publications:** *National Indian Arts and Crafts Directory*, biannual.

★401★
National Indian Training and Research Center (NITRC)
2121 S. Mill Ave., Ste. 216
Tempe, AZ 85282   Ph: (602)967-9484
Francis McKinley, Exec.Dir.

Description: To involve American Indians in leadership and professional roles in training and research projects for the social and economic betterment of Indian people. Believes that American Indians must have a free hand in determining their destiny and identity; therefore the planning and implementation of programs must be done primarily by Indians. Seeks to orient and train professionals working with American Indians so that they might better understand and appreciate the American Indian's life and culture. Conducts model and demonstration training programs to develop methodologies, curricula, and educational materials that provide the American Indian with a more meaningful and relevant education. Sponsors research and development for prototype programs and to increase information and knowledge about the American Indian, specifically in the field of education. Provides services in evaluation, program development, proposal writing, surveys, technical assistance, and training. Maintains 1000 volume library. **Founded:** 1969. **State Groups:** 3. **Publications:** *Introducing Public School Finance to Native Americans* (book).

★402★
National Indian Youth Council (NIYC)
318 Elm St. SE
Albuquerque, NM 87102   Ph: (505)247-2251
Cheryl J. Mann, Exec.Dir.

Description: Aims to: protect Indian natural resources; protect Indian religious freedom and other tribal and individual civil liberties; protect and enhance treaty rights and federal government's trust relationship and responsibilities; improve Indian health and education; preserve the Indian family unit and community. Operates educational and employment programs and sponsors action-related research projects. Compiles statistics on the Indian electorate. **Founded:** 1961. **Members:** 46,000. **Publications:** *Americans Before Columbus*, bimonthly. * *Indian Elected Officials Directory*, biennial. *

Indian Elected Officials Directory, biennial. • *Indian Voter Survey Reports*, periodic. Describes political attitudes of Native Americans living on reservations.

★403★
National Native American AIDS Task Force
c/o Indian Health Council
PO Box 406
Pauma Valley, CA 92061
Tom Lidot, Exec.Dir.   Ph: (619)749-1410

★404★
National Native American Chamber of Commerce (NNACC)
225 Valencia St.
San Francisco, CA 94103
Chockie Cottier, Contact

Description: Supports the development of regional and local chambers of commerce for Native Americans. Advocates business related education for Native American youth and businesspeople. **Founded:** 1985. **Regional Groups:** 12. **Local Groups:** 50. **Publications:** Information packet containing sample bylaws and advocacy instructions for individuals wishing to organize a chapter.

★405★
National Native American Cooperative (NNAC)
PO Box 1000
San Carlos, AZ 85550-1000
Fred Synder, Exec. Officer   Ph: (602)230-3399

Description: Native American artists and craftsmen, cultural presenters, dance groups, and individuals interested in preserving American Indian crafts, culture, and traditional education. Provides incentives to Native Americans to encourage the preservation of their culture; offers assistance marketing American Indian crafts and locating material that is difficult to find. Supplies referral information on public health, education, career counseling, scholarships and funding sources, marketing, models, and dance. Sponsors crafts and cultural demonstrations. Conducts powwows and exhibitions. Is currently developing a North American Indian Trade and Information Center. Sponsors competitions; compiles statistics; operates speakers' bureau. Maintains museum, biographical archives, and 30,000 volume library. **Founded:** 1969. **Members:** 2700. **Publications:** *Native American Directory*, quinquennial. Lists organizations, events, and tribal offices and reserves. • Also makes available copies of material related to Native American crafts.

★406★
National Tribal Chairman's Association (NTCA)
818 18th St., NW, Ste. 840
Washington, DC 20006
Raymond Field, Exec.Dir.   Ph: (202)293-0031

Description: Federally recognized tribes and their leaders. Provides a united front for elected Indian leaders to consult with government officials; assists Indian groups in obtaining full rights from federal agencies; monitors federal programs that affect Indians. **Founded:** 1971. **Members:** 182. **State Groups:** 5. **Publications:** *List of Tribes and Tribal Leaders*, quarterly. • *Newsbrief*, periodic.

★407★
National Urban Indian Council (NUIC)
10068 University Station
Denver, CO 80210
Gregory W. Frazier, Chief Exec.   Ph: (303)750-2695

Description: According to the council, more than 50% of the American Indians and Alaska Natives in the U.S. now reside off their reservations. Because of this transition and the resulting problems that have arisen, the council was formed to serve as a coalition through which urban-based American Indian and Alaskan Native groups could communicate among themselves and with the public for mutual support and sharing of information. Compiles statistics; bestows awards; operates speakers' bureau and private personnel placement service. Conducts research; maintains 200 volume library. **Founded:** 1977. **Members:** 500. **Regional Groups:** 10. **Local Groups:** 150. **Publications:** *American Indian Review*, quarterly. • *Bulletin*, 9-10/year. • Also publishes *Source Document, American Indians*, and *Alaska Natives*.

★408★
National Women of Color Association
University of Wisconsin, La Crosse
Department of Women's Studies
336 N. Hall
La Crosse, WI 54601   Ph: (608)785-8357
Sondra O'Neil, Contact

Description: Fellowship of women of color, particularly (but not exclusively) Native American, African American, Asian American, and Latin American women. Shares research on minority women and provides public education on various subjects, including women and health, politics, and community organizing. **Publications:** *Women of Color Newsletter*.

★409★
Nations Ministries (NM)
Box 70
Honobia, OK 74549   Ph: (918)755-4570
Riley Donica, Dir.

Description: Individuals and churches conducting evangelical Christian ministry on American Indian reservations in the U.S. Bestows awards; maintains speakers' bureau. **Founded:** 1983. **State Groups:** 6. **Publications:** *Indian Nations News*, bimonthly.

★410★
Native American Community Board (NACB)
PO Box 572
Lake Andes, SD 57356-0572   Ph: (605)487-7072
Charon Asetoyer, Dir.

Description: Works toward the educational, social, and economic advancement of American Indians. Maintains Native American Women Health Education Resource Center, which provides selfhelp programs and workshops on issues such as fetal alcohol syndrome, AIDS awareness, family planning, domestic abuse and crisis, reproductive rights, and child development. Conducts adult education classes; offers support services to Native Americans seeking employment and educational opportunities. Conducts charitable programs; offers children's services; maintains speakers' bureau and placement service. Compiles statistics. Is concerned with treaty and environmental issues involving Native Americans. **Founded:** 1984. **Publications:** *Wicozanni-Wowapi*, quarterly. Newsletter. • Also publishes brochures and pamphlets.

★411★
Native American Educational Services College (NAESC)
2838 W. Peterson
Chicago, IL 60659   Ph: (312)761-5000
Faith Smith, Pres.

Description: An educational program accredited by the Commission on Institutions of Higher Education of the North Central Association of Colleges and Schools. Offers a B.A. degree to students at institutions in four American Indian communities (2 urban, 2 reservations). Maintains 5000 volume library on historical and contemporary American Indian topics. **Founded:** 1974. **Publications:** *College Catalog*, biennial. Directory. • *NAES-Rule*, quarterly. **Formerly:** Native American Educational Service.

★412★
Native American Journalists Association (NAJA)
Campus Box 287
Boulder, CO 80309   Ph: (303)492-7397
Paul DeMain, Pres.   Fax: (303)492-0585

★413★
Native American Law Students Association (NALSA)
Indian Law Clinic
Univ. of Montana Law School
Missoula, MT 59806   Ph: (406)243-6480
Magel Bird, Pres.

Description: American Indian or Native Alaskan law students. Promotes unity, communication, and cooperation among Native American law students; seeks to provide financial aid and summer employment opportunities such as tutorial programs, research projects, and curriculum development in American Indian law; offers a forum for discussion of legal problems relating to law affecting American Indians. Maintains speakers' bureau of students in the field of American Indian law. Operates no library; however, members have access to the extensive American Indian law collection at the University of New Mexico. **Founded:** 1970. **Members:** 160. **Regional Groups:** 6. **Local Groups:** 14. **Publications:** *Newsletter*, periodic. **Formerly:** (1990) American Indian Law Students Association.

★414★
Native American Policy Network (NAPN)
Barry University
11300 2nd Ave. NE
Miami, FL 33161   Ph: (305)899-3473
Prof. Michael E. Melody, Editor

Description: Academicians; Indian and political leaders; policymakers. Objective is to foster research in all areas of Native American policy. Organizes panels and seminars at the annual conventions of the American Political Science Association and Western Social Science Association. **Founded:** 1979. **Members:** 400. **Publications:** *NAPN Directory*, periodic. • *NAPN Newsletter*, 3/year.

★415★
Native American Program, Commission for Multicultural Ministries of ELCA (NAPCMM-ECL)
8765 W. Higgens Rd.
Chicago, IL 60631   Ph: (312)380-2838

Description: A program of the Evangelical Lutheran Church in America. Maintains a nine member board of American Indians and Alaskan natives. Acts as advocate and consultant to Lutheran churches on behalf of the needs of Indian communities. Supports American Indian and Alaskan native rights in ways consistent with Christian faith and life. **Founded:** 1987.

★416★
Native American Public Broadcasting Consortium (NAPBC)
PO Box 83111   Ph: (402)472-3522
Lincoln, NE 68501   Fax: (402)472-1785
Frank Blythe, Exec.Dir.

Description: Public television stations, schools, community groups, and tribal organizations promoting the production and distribution of high-quality programming by, for, and about Native Americans for public television and educational institutions. Objectives are to: catalog Indian programming; develop an efficient distribution system of Native American programming to public telecommunications and nonbroadcasting entities; encourage, recruit, and train Native Americans in public broadcasting; serve as a national resource and liasion for the Native American community and public broadcasting stations with regard to Native American programming. Sponsors fundraising proposal writing workshops. Maintains library of videotapes, films, and radio programs. Makes available job reference file listing Native Americans in the media. Plans to develop the Native American Public Radio Satellite Network in conjunction with the Indigenous Communications Association (see separate entry). **Founded:** 1977. **Members:** 65. **Publications:** *In-House Newsletter*, monthly. • Also publishes *Who Watches Public Television* and fact sheets.

★417★
Native American Rights Fund (NARF)
1506 Broadway
Boulder, CO 80302   Ph: (303)447-8760
John E. Echohawk, Dir.

Description: Represents Indian individuals and tribes in legal matters of national significance. Provides legal counsel in the protection of Indian lands and resources. Areas of concern are: tribal existence; protection of tribal resources; human rights, including educational matters and religious freedom; accountability of federal, state, and tribal governments; Indian law development. Serves as National Indian Law Support Center to legal service programs. Maintains National Indian Law Library, a repository for Indian legal materials and resources, containing 5000 files of Indian law cases, studies, and hearings. **Founded:** 1970. **State Groups:** 44. **Publications:** *Indian Law Support Center Reporter*, monthly. Newsletter providing local legal services attorneys with information on developments in

the area of Indian law. Includes summaries of recent court decisions in Indian country, Federal Register highlights, and new publications and materials. • *Legal Review*, semiannual. Newsletter covering NARF's involvement in Indian legal issues. • *National Indian Law Library Catalogue*, supplemented quarterly. • Also publishes index to *Indian Claims Commission Decisions*.

★418★
Native Americans for a Clean Environment (NACE)
PO Box 1671
Tahlequah, OK 74465   Ph: (918)458-4322
Vickie McCullough, Exec.Dir.

Description: Individuals devoted to halting contamination of the environment by nuclear waste and to promoting forms of energy production that are safer than nuclear power. Seeks to educate the public on safe disposal methods and the advantages of using renewable energy sources. Provides speakers for lectures on the nuclear industry, food irradiation, and uranium mining. Maintains library. **Founded:** 1985. **Members:** 500. **Publications:** *NACE News*, quarterly. Newsletter. • Also publishes *Raffinate* (brochure).

★419★
North American Indian Museums Association (NAIMA)
c/o National Museum of the American
    Indian
Broadway at 115th St.
New York, NY 10032
George H.J. Abrams, Chairperson

Description: Indian and Native American cultural centers and tribal museums, and museum professionals; affiliate members are native studies organizations, historical societies, and Indian community colleges. Goals are: to preserve and perpetuate the traditional cultures, history, and art of Native Americans through museums; to foster recognition of the diversity of tribal identities; to advocate the preservation and protection of the cultural resources and cultural integrity of Indian tribes. Assists tribal elders and religious leaders in instructing Indian children to respect their traditional culture. Coordinates development of member museums; provides technical assistance and training. Sponsors national and regional workshops, internships, and museum research. Presently inactive. **Founded:** 1979. **Members:** 50. **Regional Groups:** 10. **State Groups:** 1. **Publications:** *Directory of Indian Museums*, annual. • *Newsletter*, periodic.

★420★
North American Indian Women's Association (NAIWA)
9602 Maestor's Ln.
Gaithersburg, MD 20879   Ph: (301)330-0397
Ann French, Contact

Description: Women, 18 years and older, who are members of federally recognized tribes. Seeks to foster the general well-being of Indian people through unity of purpose. Promotes inter-tribal communication, awareness of the Native American culture, betterment of family life, health, and education, and strengthening of communication among Native Americans. **Founded:** 1970. **Regional Groups:** 6. **Local Groups:** 19. **Publications:** Brochure.

★421★
Order of the Indian Wars (OIW)
PO Box 7401   Ph: (501)225-3996
Little Rock, AR 72217   Fax: (501)225-5167
Jerry L. Russel, Chm.

Description: Professional and informal historians interested in the study of the frontier conflicts between Native Americans and the white settlers and among Indian tribes during the early settlement of the United States. Seeks to protect and preserve historic sites related to those wars. Believes citizens' groups must become more involved in historic preservation, or much of history will be irretrievably lost in the name of "progress." Conducts symposia. **Founded:** 1979. **Members:** 650. **Publications:** *Communique*, monthly.

★422★

Organization of North American Indian Students (ONAIS)
Northern Michigan University
Box 26, University Center
Marquette, MI 49855   Ph: (906)227-2138
Karen Moses, Exec. Officer

Description: University students of American Indian ancestry and other interested students. Encourages pride and identity in Indian culture and tradition; establishes communications among the native communities; promotes scholarship among Indian students attending institutions of higher learning. Sponsors basket weaving seminars, powwows, social and cultural gatherings, and annual Indian Awareness Week. **Founded:** 1971. **Members:** 40.

★423★

The Seventh Generation Fund for Indian Development (SGF)
PO Box 10
Forestville, CA 95436   Ph: (707)887-1559
Chris Peters, Exec.Dir.

Description: Indian tribes and organizations. Provides seed grants and technical assistance in order to increase self-reliance in Indian communities and decrease government dependency. Aims to: reclaim and live on aboriginal lands; protect tribal lands and natural resources; redevelop self-sufficient communities through food production, appropriate technologies, and alternative energy use; restore traditional indigenous forms of political organization or to modify existing governments along traditional lines. Supports and promotes the spiritual, cultural, and physical well-being of the Native family. Reports on such subjects as Native American rights, Indian family life, and judicial issues and cases affecting American Indians. Maintains small library on appropriate technologies, fundraising, and resource materials. The fund's title is drawn from the Hau de no sau nee (Six Nations) principle of considering the impact upon the seventh generation in the decision-making process. **Founded:** 1977. **State Groups:** 2. **Publications:** *Annual Report.* **Formerly:** (1984) Tribal Sovereignty Program.

★424★

Smoki People (SP)
PO Box 123
Prescott, AZ 86302   Ph: (602)445-1230
Michael E. Kennelly, Chief

Description: Local business and professional people (non-Indian) united to perpetuate by authentic, artistic reproduction the age-old ceremonials and dances of Indian tribes of North and South America. Members reconstruct these rituals and costumes by careful historical research. Maintains 600 volume library of Indian and Pre-Columbian Western Hemisphere subjects, and a museum. **Founded:** 1921. **Members:** 1600. **Publications:** *Smoki Ceremonials and Snake Dance,* annual.

★425★

Society for Advancement of Chicanos and Native Americans in Science (SACNAS)
c/o Frank Talamantes
Sinsheimer Labs
University of California
Santa Cruz, CA 95064   Ph: (408)459-4272
Dr. Frank Talamantes, Exec. Officer

Description: College professors, science professionals, undergraduate and graduate science students, and high school science teachers. Seeks to increase the participation of Hispanics and Native Americans in the sciences. Conducts high school science teaching workshops, student workshops, and technichal symposia. Bestows awards; operates speakers' bureau. **Founded:** 1973. **Members:** 500. **Publications:** *SACNAS Newsletter,* quarterly.

★426★

Survival of American Indians Association (SAIA)
7803-A Samurai Dr., SE
Olympia, WA 98503
Hank Adams, Dir.

Description: Indians and interested individuals. Provides public education on Indian rights and tribal government reform action.

Supports independent Indian education institutions. Maintains speakers' bureau. **Founded:** 1964. **Members:** 500. **Regional Groups:** 3. **State Groups:** 5. **Publications:** *The Renegade: A Strategy Journal of Indian Opinion,* periodic.

★427★

Survival International, U.S.A. (SIUSA)
2121 Decatur Pl. NW
Washington, DC 20008   Ph: (202)265-1077
Mary George Hardman, Exec.Dir.

Description: Individuals concerned with the rights of tribal peoples. Supports tribal groups in their efforts towards self-determination; helps them protect their lands, environment, and way of life. **Founded:** 1979. **Members:** 1100. **State Groups:** 3. **Publications:** *Survival International News,* semiannual. • Also publishes document series; distributes other publications concerning human rights of indigenous peoples.

★428★

Tekakwitha Conference National Center (TCNC)
PO Box 6759
Great Falls, MT 59406   Ph: (406)727-0147
Fred A. Buckles Jr., Exec.Dir.

Description: Catholic missionaries among American Indians; Eskimo and American Indian deacons and laypersons involved in ministry. Develops Catholic evangelization in the areas of Native American ministry, catechesis, liturgy, family life, evangelical liberation, ecumenical cooperation, and urban ministry, spirituality, and theology. Provides a forum for the exchange of ideas among Catholic Native Americans, Eskimos, and missionaries. Encourages development of Native American ministry by Indian people and attempts to assure Native American representation in the decision-making bodies of the church. Maintains 2000 volume library on scripture, theology, liturgy, religion, and Native Americans. **Founded:** 1939. **Members:** 12,000. **Regional Groups:** 3. **State Groups:** 6. **Publications:** *Cross and Feather News,* quarterly. Provides cultural, governmental, and spiritual information for Native Americans and Eskimos. Also includes book reviews, employment opportunities, and obituaries.

★429★

Thunderbird American Indian Dancers (TAID)
c/o Louis Mofsie
McBurney YMCA
215 W. 23rd St.
New York, NY 10011   Ph: (201)587-9633
Louis Mofsie, Dir.

Description: Indians and non-Indians who raise money for the Thunderbird Indian Scholarship Fund for Indian Students. Offers cultural classes in crafts, singing, dancing, and language. Sponsors Indian studies program for Indian youngsters. **Founded:** 1956. **Members:** 30.

★430★

United Indians of All Tribes Foundation (UIATF)
Daybreak Star Arts Center
Discovery Park
PO Box 99100
Seattle, WA 98199   Ph: (206)285-4425
Bernie Whitebear, Exec.Dir.

Description: Promotes the interests of Native Americans. Helps to develop and expand Native American economic self-sufficiency, education, and arts. Sponsors National Indian Cultural-Educational Center which houses a variety of ongoing programs such as model educational programs, community educational services, technical assistance, adult career education, and employment assistance. Operates Daybreak Star Press. Maintains 300 volume library, media center, museum, and Native American dinner theatre; conducts cultural symposia and rotating art exhibits. **Founded:** 1970. **Members:** 13. **State Groups:** 60. **Publications:** *Daybreak Star,* monthly. Magazine. • Has also developed Native American curriculum materials for public schools.

★431★
United Native Americans (UNA)
2434 Faria Ave.
Pinole, CA 94564   Ph: (415)758-8160
Lehman L. Brightman, Dir.

Description: Indians and interested non-Indians. Purposes are to: promote the general welfare of Americans; establish educational scholarships; find employment; provide legal aid, housing, food, lodging, and counseling for Indians. Aided in establishing Native American studies program at University of California at Berkeley. Maintains speakers' bureau. Sells historical posters of Indians. **Founded:** 1968. **Members:** 12,000. **Local Groups:** 18. **Publications:** *Warpath*, monthly.

★432★
United South and Eastern Tribes (USET)
1101 Kermit Dr., Ste. 302
Nashville, TN 37217   Ph: (615)361-8700
Lionel John, Exec.Dir.

Description: Alliance of 19 Indian tribes: Alabama-Coushatta Tribe of Texas; Eastern Band of Cherokee Indians; Chitimacha Tribe of Louisiana; Mississippi Band of Choctaw Indians; Coushatta Tribe of Louisiana; Poarch Band of Creek Indians; Houlton Band of Maliseet Indians; Mashantucket Pequot Indians of Connecticut; Miccosukee Tribe of Indians; Narrangansett Indian Tribe; Passamaquoddy Tribe-Indian Township; Passamaquoddy Tribe-Pleasant Point; Penobscot Indian Nation; St. Regis Mohawk; Seminole Tribe of Florida; Seneca Nation of Indians; Tunica-Biloxi Tribe of Louisiana; Wampanoag Tribal Council of Gay Head; Oneida Nation of New York. Promotes "strength in unity" of American Indian tribes and assists tribes in dealing with relevant issues. Fosters better understanding with other races. **Founded:** 1969. **Formerly:** (1969) United Southeast Tribes; (1978) United Southeastern Tribes.

★433★
Vietnam Era Veterans Inter-Tribal Association
    (VEVITA)
Mathew Kauley, Exec.Dir.   Ph: (405)273-6790

Description: American Indian veterans representing 200 tribes who served in Vietnam or who served in the armed forces during the Vietnam era (1959-1975). Purposes are: to promote a positive image of the Indian Vietnam veteran; to remember fellow servicemen who died in the war and in the years following; to offer Indian veterans a united voice in veteran affairs. Fosters exchange of information on problems related to Vietnam, such as agent orange, post-traumatic stress disorder, and discharge upgrades. Seeks to provide the means for Indian veterans to express pride in their warrior status. Presents gold star shawls to families of men killed in action in Vietnam. Bestows annual award to person conducting research on American Indian Vietnam era veterans. Sponsors Gourd Clan and Honor/Color Guard; operates Vietnam Era Veterans Inter-Tribal Association Auxiliary. Sponsors workshops and seminars. Compiles statistics; sponsors competitions; maintains hall of fame and museum. **Founded:** 1981. **Members:** 1000. **Regional Groups:** 1. **Local Groups:** 14. **Publications:** *Membership List*, periodic. • *Redsmoke Veterans News*, quarterly. Newsletter providing information on member activities, veterans affairs, and new members. Also includes poetry. • *Souvenir Pow-Wow Program*, annual. • *Veteran Small Business Directory*, annual. • Also publishes papers.

Regional, State/Provincial, & Local Organizations

─────────── **Alabama** ───────────

★434★
Alabama Indian Small Business Association
PO Box 1347   Ph: (205)539-0959
Huntsville, AL 35804   Fax: (205)533-9037
W. Diane Weston, Pres.

─────────── **Arizona** ───────────

★435★
Native American Business Coalition
6025 N. Smokerise   Ph: (602)526-0035
Flagstaff, AZ 86004   Fax: (602)526-2383
Bruce Yazzie, Pres.

★436★
Native Americans for Community Action, Inc.
Flagstaff Indian Center
2717 N. Steves Rd., Ste. 11   Ph: (602)526-2968
Flagstaff, AZ 86004   Fax: (602)526-0708
Rick Tewa, Exec.Dir.

★437★
Native American Finance Officers Association
PO Box 170   Ph: (602)729-6218
Fort Defiance, AZ 86504   Fax: (602)729-2135
Marlene Lynch, Pres.

★438★
Navajo Nation Business Association
PO Box 1217   Ph: (602)697-3534
Kayena, AZ 86033   Fax: (602)697-3464
Richard Mike, Pres.

★439★
Arizona Indian Business Development Center
953 E. Juanita St.
Mesa, AZ 85204   Ph: (602)831-7524

★440★
Affiliation of Arizona Indian Centers, Inc.
1515 E. Osborn Rd., Annex   Ph: (602)279-0618
Phoenix, AZ 85014   Fax: (602)279-0699
Joy Hanley, Exec.Dir.

★441★
Inter-Tribal Council of Arizona
4205 N. 7th Ave., Ste. 200   Ph: (602)248-0071
Phoenix, AZ 85013   Fax: (602)248-0080
John Lewis, Exec.Dir.

★442★
Phoenix Indian Center
2601 N. 3rd St, Ste. 100   Ph: (602)263-1017
Phoenix, AZ 85004   Fax: (602)263-7822
Bill Thorn Jr., Exec.Dir.

★443★
Urban Indian Health Project
1427 N. 3rd St., Ste. 100
Phoenix, AZ 85004   Ph: (602)263-8094
Erma Mundy, Exec.Dir.

★444★
Arizona Indian Business Development Center
2070 E. Southern Ave.
Tempe, AZ 85282   Ph: (602)945-2635

★445★
Traditional Indian Alliance
2925 S. 12th Ave.   Ph: (602)882-0555
Tucson, AZ 85713   Fax: (602)623-6529
Trudy Narum, Exec.Dir.

★446★
Tucson Indian Center
PO Box 2307   Ph: (602)884-7131
Tucson, AZ 85701   Fax: (602)884-0240
Guillermo Quiroga, Exec.Dir.

───────── Arkansas ─────────

★447★
American Indian Center of Arkansas
2 Van Circle, Ste. 2
Little Rock, AR 72207   Ph: (501)666-9032
Paul S. Austin, Dir.

───────── California ─────────

★448★
American Indian Center of Central California
PO Box 607   Ph: (209)855-2705
Auberry, CA 93602   Fax: (209)855-2695
Orie Medicinebull, Exec.Dir.

★449★
American Indian Council of Central California
2441 G St.   Ph: (805)327-2207
Bakersfield, CA 93303   Fax: (805)327-4533
Shirley Mantaghi, Dir.

★450★
American Indian Free Clinic
9500 Artesia Blvd.   Ph: (310)920-7227
Bellflower, CA 90706   Fax: (310)920-5677
Joan Freeman, Exec.Dir.

★451★
Inyo Child Care Services
Rte. 3, Box B-75
Bishop, CA 93514   Ph: (619)872-3911
Yvonne Deming, Dir.

★452★
Southern California Indian Center
500 E. Carson Plaza Dr., Ste. 101
Carson, CA 90746   Ph: (213)329-9595

★453★
Southern California Indian Center
5900 Eastern Ave., Ste. 104
Commerce, CA 90040   Ph: (213)728-8844
John Castillo, Exec.Dir.

★454★
Chapa-De Indian Education Center
PO Box 847   Ph: (916)621-7788
El Dorado, CA 95623   Fax: (916)621-7790
Peggy Ickef, Dir.

★455★
California Indian Business Development Center
9650 Flair Dr., Ste. 303
El Monte, CA 91731-3008   Ph: (818)442-3701

★456★
Indian Action Council of Northwestern California
PO Box 1287
Eureka, CA 95501   Ph: (707)443-8401
June Chilton, Dir.

★457★
United Indian Lodge
1116 9th St.
Eureka, CA 95501   Ph: (707)445-3071
Jim Kiogima, Exec.Dir.

★458★
Ya-Ka-Ama
6215 Eastside Rd.   Ph: (707)887-1541
Forestville, CA 95436   Fax: (707)887-1585
Joseph Ulmer, Dir.

★459★
Turtle Lodge
610 W. McKinley Ave.
Fresno, CA 93728   Ph: (209)445-2691
Vincent Harvier, Dir.
Formerly: Comprehensive Indian Rehabilitation Program.

★460★
Southern California Indian Center
12755 Brookhurst St.   Ph: (714)530-0221
Garden Grove, CA 92640   Fax: (714)636-4226
John Castillo, Dir.

★461★
Southern California Indian Center
2500 Wilshire Blvd.   Ph: (213)387-5772
Los Angeles, CA 90057   Fax: (213)387-9061
John Castillo, Exec.Dir.

★462★
United American Indian Involvement
118 Winston St.
Los Angeles, CA 90013   Ph: (213)625-2565
David Rambeaux, Dir.

★463★
American Indians in Business
1320 Webster St.   Ph: (510)763-3410
Oakland, CA 94612   Fax: (510)763-3646
Ray Brown, Chairman

★464★
Intertribal Friendship House
523 E. 14th St.   Ph: (510)452-1235
Oakland, CA 94606   Fax: (510)452-1234
Jim Lamenpi, Exec.Dir.

★465★
Native American Health Center
3124 E. 14th St.   Ph: (510)261-0524
Oakland, CA 94601   Fax: (510)261-6438
Martin Waukazoo, Exec.Dir.

★466★
Urban Indian Child Resource Center
390 Euclid Ave.   Ph: (510)832-2386
Oakland, CA 94610   Fax: (510)208-1866
Anne Alton, Dir.

★467★
American Indian Education Center
PO Box 40
Pala, CA 92059   Ph: (619)742-1121
Naida Garcia, Contact

★468★
Jurupa Mountains Cultural Center
7621 Granite Hill Dr.
Riverside, CA 92509   Ph: (714)685-5818
Ruth Kirkby, Exec.Dir.

★469★
Capital Area Indian Resources, Inc.
2949 Fulton Ave.   Ph: (916)491-9190
Sacramento, CA 95821   Fax: (916)971-9199
Cindy LaMarr, Exec.Dir.
Formerly: United American Indian Education Center.

★470★
Inter-Tribal Council of California
2025 P St.   Ph: (916)447-2033
Sacramento, CA 95814   Fax: (916)447-6949
Toni Thompson, Dir.

★471★
National Indian Contractors Association
1600 H St., Ste. C   Ph: (916)442-3079
Sacramento, CA 95814   Fax: (916)446-8825
Ben Shaneego, Pres.

★472★
Sacramento Urban Indian Health Project
801 Broadway   Ph: (916)441-0918
Sacramento, CA 95818   Fax: (916)441-1261
Beth Ninke, Dir.

★473★
San Diego American Indian Health Clinic
2561 1st Ave.   Ph: (619)234-2158
San Diego, CA 92103   Fax: (619)234-0206
Ellen Cayous, Dir.
Formerly: American Indian Medical Clinic.

★474★
American Indian Friendship House
80 Julian Ave.   Ph: (415)431-6323
San Francisco, CA 94103   Fax: (415)861-7507
Helen Waukazoo, Dir.

★475★
Indian Center of San Jose, Inc.
919 Alameda
San Jose, CA 95127   Ph: (408)971-9622
Jennifer Patel, Exec.Dir.

★476★
Mendocino County Indian Center
1621 Talmadge Rd.
Ukiah, CA 95482   Ph: (707)468-9269
Pam Mitchell, Dir.

———————— **Colorado** ————————

★477★
Denver Indian Center
4407 Morrison Rd.   Ph: (303)937-0401
Denver, CO 80219   Fax: (303)936-2699
John Emhoolha, Contact
Formerly: Denver Native Americans United, Inc.

★478★
Denver Indian Health Board
1739 Vine St.   Ph: (303)320-3974
Denver, CO 80206   Fax: (303)320-1576
John H. Compton, Exec.Dir.

★479★
Eagle Lodge—American Indian Alcoholism
  Rehabilitation Program
1264 Race St.
Denver, CO 80206   Ph: (303)393-7773
Pat Cheney, Exec.Dir.

★480★
Western American Indian Chamber of Commerce
c/o Native Resources
908 Main   Ph: (303)665-3476
Louisville, CO 80027   Fax: (303)665-3476
Ben Sherman, Pres.

———————— **Connecticut** ————————

★481★
American Indians for Development, Inc.
29 W. Main St.
PO Box 117   Ph: (203)238-4009
Meriden, CT 06450   Fax: (203)634-8975
Kenneth Attocknie, Exec.Dir.

———————— **Hawaii** ————————

★482★
American Indian Service Corporation
American Indian Center
1405 N. King St., Ste. 302
Honolulu, HI 96817   Ph: (808)847-2511

———————— **Illinois** ————————

★483★
American Indian Center
1630 W. Wilson   Ph: (312)275-5871
Chicago, IL 60640   Fax: (312)275-5874
Hank Bonga, Dir.

★484★
American Indian Health Service
838 W. Irving Park Rd.   Ph: (312)883-9100
Chicago, IL 60613   Fax: (312)883-0005
Paul Allen, Exec.Dir.

★485★
St. Augustine Center for American Indians
4512 N. Sheridan Blvd.   Ph: (312)784-1050
Chicago, IL 60640   Fax: (312)784-1450
Arlene Williams, Contact

———————— **Kansas** ————————

★486★
Haskell Indian Alcohol Education and Prevention
  Program
PO Box 864, Jayhawk Sta.   Ph: (913)843-3751
Lawrence, KS 66044   Fax: (913)843-8815

★487★
Indian Center of Lawrence
1423 Haskell St.
PO Box 1016
Lawrence, KS 66044   Ph: (913)841-7202
Charlene Johnson, Exec.Dir.

★488★
Mid-American All-Indian Center
650 N. Seneca
Wichita, KS 67203   Ph: (316)262-5221
Jerry Aday, Dir.

─────────── **Maine** ───────────

★489★
Central Maine Indian Association, Inc.
PO Box 2280
Bangor, ME 04401   Ph: (207)942-2926
Terry Polchies, Exec.Dir.

─────────── **Maryland** ───────────

★490★
Baltimore American Indian Center
113 S. Broadway
Baltimore, MD 21231   Ph: (301)675-3535
Barry Richardson, Exec.Dir.

─────────── **Massachusetts** ───────────

★491★
Boston Indian Council, Inc.
105 S. Huntington Ave.
Jamaica Plain, MA 02130   Ph: (617)232-0343
JoAnne Dunn, Exec.Dir.

─────────── **Michigan** ───────────

★492★
Detroit American Indian Health Center
4400 Livernois   Ph: (313)895-7859
Detroit, MI 48210   Fax: (313)895-7019
Maria Harrison, Admin.

★493★
North American Indian Association of Detroit, Inc.
22720 Plymouth Rd.   Ph: (313)535-2966
Detroit, MI 48239   Fax: (313)533-1080
Irene Lowry, Dir.

★494★
Urban Indian Affairs
1200 6th Ave., 8th Fl., Ste. 700
Detroit, MI 48052   Ph: (313)256-1633
Thelma Henry-Shipman, Contact

★495★
Native American Business Council Inc.
8720 Dixie Hwy.   Ph: (313)725-1990
Fair Haven, MI 48023   Fax: (313)725-5320
Ernie Young, Pres.

★496★
Genessee Valley Indian Association
124 W. 1st St.
Flint, MI 48502   Ph: (313)239-6621
Ron Douglas, Exec.Dir.
Also Known As: Genessee Indian Center.

★497★
Grand Rapids Inter-Tribal Council
45 Lexington NW   Ph: (616)774-8331
Grand Rapids, MI 49504   Fax: (616)774-2810
Wag Wheller, Exec.Dir.

★498★
American Indian Services
75 Victor St.
Highland Park, MI 48203   Ph: (313)865-2601
Harry Command, Dir.

★499★
Michigan Indian Child Welfare Agency
348 Davis Ct.
PO Box 1526
Kincheloe, MI 49788   Fax: (906)495-2295
LeAnne E. Silvey, Exec.Dir.

★500★
Lansing North American Indian Center
1235 Center St.
Lansing, MI 48906   Ph: (517)487-5409
Joan Spalding, Exec.Dir.

★501★
Saginaw Inter-Tribal Association, Inc.
3239 Christy Way
PO Box 7005
Saginaw, MI 48603   Ph: (517)792-4610
Victoria G. Miller, Exec.Dir.

★502★
Inter-Tribal Council of Michigan
405 E. Easterday Ave.   Ph: (906)632-6896
Sault Ste. Marie, MI 49783   Fax: (906)632-1810
Sharon Teeple, Contact

★503★
Native American Business Council of Michigan Inc.
PO Box 861
Warren, MI 48090   Ph: (313)756-1350
Description: Mentoring program for Native Americans owning or
starting businesses.

★504★
Southeastern Michigan Indians
PO Box 861
Warren, MI 48090   Ph: (313)756-1350
Nancy Ragsdale, Exec.Dir.

─────────── **Minnesota** ───────────

★505★
Minnesota Indian Business Development Center
3045 Farr Ave.
Cass Lake, MN 56633   Ph: (218)335-8583

★506★
American Indian Services
735 E. Franklin
Minneapolis, MN 55404   Ph: (612)871-2175

★507★
Indian Family Services
1305 E. 24th St.   Ph: (612)348-5788
Minneapolis, MN 55404   Fax: (612)348-4124
Doreen Day, Exec.Dir.

★508★
Minneapolis American Indian Center
1530 E. Franklin Ave.   Ph: (612)871-4555
Minneapolis, MN 55404   Fax: (612)871-6878
Francis Fairbanks, Exec.Dir.

★509★
Minnesota Indian Chamber of Commerce
1433 Franklin Ave., No. 3C   Ph: (612)871-2157
Minneapolis, MN 55404   Fax: (612)871-0021
Les King, Pres.

★510★
Juel Franks Chemical Dependency Services
806 N. Albert St.
Saint Paul, MN 55104   Ph: (612)644-6204
Marvin Hanks, Exec.Dir.
Description: Offers programs aimed at Native Americans.

★511★
South St. Paul Indian Education
727 Capitol Sq. Bldg.
550 Cedar St.   Ph: (612)296-6458
Saint Paul, MN 55101   Fax: (612)297-7895
Dr. Will Antell, Mngr.

─────────── **Missouri** ───────────

★512★
Heart of America Indian Center
1340 E. Admiral Blvd.   Ph: (816)421-7608
Kansas City, MO 64124   Fax: (816)421-6493
Chad Ellis, Exec.Dir.

★513★
American Indian Center
4115 Connecticut St.
Saint Louis, MO 63116   Ph: (314)773-3316
Evelyne Voelker, Exec.Dir.

★514★
Southwest Missouri Indian Center
2422 W. Division   Ph: (417)869-9550
Springfield, MO 65802   Fax: (417)869-0922
Mike Fields, Exec.Dir.

─────────── **Montana** ───────────

★515★
Anaconda Indian Alliance
Health Program
506 E. Park
PO Box 1108
Anaconda, MT 59711   Ph: (406)563-3459
Carolyn Brock, Exec.Dir.

★516★
Butte Indian Alcohol Program
Metal Banks Bldg., Ste. 309
Butte, MT 59701   Ph: (406)782-0461

★517★
North American Indian Alliance
100 E. Galena
PO Box 285   Ph: (406)723-4361
Butte, MT 59701   Fax: (406)782-4708
Lloyd Baron, Exec.Dir.

★518★
Native American Center Health Program
700 10th St.S.
PO Box 2612
Great Falls, MT 59403
Robert Pariseian, Exec.Dir.
Formerly: Great Falls Indian Education Center.

★519★
Helena Indian Alliance
Leo Pocha Memorial Health Clinic
436 N. Jackson
Helena, MT 59601   Ph: (406)442-9334
Francis Delguard, Exec.Dir.

★520★
Montana Indian Manufacturers Network
PO Box 6043   Ph: (406)443-5350
Helena, MT 59604   Fax: (406)443-5351
Leonard Smith, Dir.

★521★
Montana United Indian Association
PO Box 6043
Helena, MT 59604   Fax: (406)443-5351
George Hinkle, Contact

★522★
Missoula Indian Alcohol and Drug Service
2110 South Ave. W.
PO Box 4001
Missoula, MT 59806   Ph: (406)721-2700
Bill Houchin, Exec.Dir.

★523★
Missoula Indian Center
2228 S. Ave., W.
Missoula, MT 59801-6502

★524★
Native American Services Agency
Urban Indian Health Clinic
2228 South Ave.
Missoula, MT 59801   Fax: (406)329-3398
Bill Walls, Exec.Dir.

─────────── **Nebraska** ───────────

★525★
Lincoln Indian Center
1100 Military Rd.   Ph: (402)438-5231
Lincoln, NE 68508   Fax: (402)423-5236
Sidney Beane, Exec.Dir.

★526★
Nebraska Indian Education Association (NIEA)
Native American Community Development
  of Omaha, Inc.
2451 St.Mary St.
Omaha, NE 68105   Ph: (402)341-8471
Violet Fickel, Exec.Dir.

★527★
Nebraska Inter-Tribal Development Corporation
RR 1, Box 66A   Ph: (402)878-2242
Winnebago, NE 68071   Fax: (402)878-2504
Frank LaMere, Exec.Dir.

─────────── **Nevada** ───────────

★528★
Western Shoshone National Council
PO Box 68
Duckwater, NV 89314   Ph: (702)863-0227

★529★
Las Vegas Indian Center
2300 W. Bonanza Rd.   Ph: (702)647-5842
Las Vegas, NV 89106   Fax: (702)647-2647
Richard W. Arnold, Exec.Dir.

★530★
The Seventh Generation Fund for Indian Development Program for Native Women, Families and Youth
Box 72
Nixon, NV 89424   Ph: (702)574-0157
Debra Harry, Field Rep.

★531★
Inter-Tribal Council of Nevada
PO Box 7440   Ph: (702)355-0600
Reno, NV 89510   Fax: (702)355-0648
Daryl Crawford, Exec.Dir.

★532★
Nevada Urban Indians
401 W. 2nd St., Rm. 101   Ph: (702)329-2573
Reno, NV 89503   Fax: (702)329-2040

─────────── **New Mexico** ───────────

★533★
Native American Transportation Association
100 Eubank NE, Ste. D   Ph: (505)275-0933
Albuquerque, NM 87112   Fax: (505)294-2201
Edward Hall, Contact

★534★
New Mexico Indian Business Development Center
PO Box 3256
3939 San Pedro, NE
Albuquerque, NM 87190-3256   Ph: (505)889-9092

★535★
Five Sandoval Indian Pueblos, Inc.
PO Box 580   Ph: (505)867-3351
Bernalillo, NM 87004   Fax: (505)867-3514

★536★
Farmington Intertribal Indian Organization
100 W. Elm
PO Box 2322
Farmington, NM 87401   Ph: (505)327-6296
Velma Yazzie, Exec.Dir.

★537★
Native American Industrial Trade Association
PO Box B   Ph: (505)552-6041
Laguna, NM 87026   Fax: (505)552-9265
Ronald J. Solimon, Pres.

★538★
Indian Resource Development (IRD)
New Mexico State University
Box 30001, Dept. 3IRD   Ph: (505)646-1347
Las Cruces, NM 88003   Fax: (505)646-5975
Lance Lujan, Dir.

★539★
Eight Northern Pueblos, Inc.
PO Box 969   Ph: (505)852-4265
San Juan Pueblo, NM 87566   Fax: (505)852-4835
Herman Agoyo, Exec.Dir.

─────────── **New York** ───────────

★540★
The American Indian Community House
404 Lafayette St., 2nd Fl.
New York, NY 10003

★541★
North American Indian Club
PO Box 851
Syracuse, NY 13201   Ph: (315)476-7425

─────────── **North Carolina** ───────────

★542★
Cherokee Indian Business Development Center
165 French Broad Ave.
Asheville, NC 28801   Ph: (704)252-2516

★543★
Metrolina Native American Association
2601-A E. 7th St.
Charlotte, NC 28204   Ph: (704)331-4818
Gene Petiet, Exec.Dir.

★544★
Cherokee Indian Business Development Center
Alquoni Rd., Box 1200
Cherokee, NC 28719   Ph: (704)497-9335

★545★
Qualla Indian Boundary
PO Box 1178
Cherokee, NC 28719   Ph: (704)497-9416
Robin Schaeffer, Dir.

★546★
Cumberland County Association of Indian People
102 Indian Dr.   Ph: (919)483-8442
Fayetteville, NC 28301   Fax: (919)483-8742
Gladys Hunt, Dir.

★547★
Guilford Native American Association
400 Prescott
PO Box 5623   Ph: (919)273-8686
Greensboro, NC 27403   Fax: (919)272-2925
Ruth Revels, Exec.Dir.

★548★
North Carolina Indian Business Association
325 N. Salisbury St.   Ph: (919)733-5998
Raleigh, NC 27603   Fax: (919)733-9571
Wanda Burns-Ramsey, Pres.

North Dakota

★549★
North Dakota Indian Business Development Center
3315 University Dr.
Bismarck, ND 58501-7596   Ph: (701)255-3225

★550★
United Tribes Education Training Center
3315 S. Airport Rd.
Bismarck, ND 58501   Ph: (701)255-3285

Ohio

★551★
North American Indian Cultural Center
1062 Triplett Blvd.   Ph: (216)724-1280
Akron, OH 44306   Fax: (216)724-9298
Clark Hosick, Exec.Dir.

★552★
Cleveland American Indian Center
5500-02 Loraine Ave.
Cleveland, OH 44102   Ph: (216)961-3490
Jerome WarCloud, Exec.Dir.

★553★
Native American Indian Center
1862 Persons
Columbus, OH 43207   Ph: (614)443-6120
Selma Walker, Exec.Dir.

Oklahoma

★554★
Four Tribes Tribal Employment Rights Office
PO Box 1193   Ph: (405)247-9711
Anadarko, OK 73005   Fax: (405)247-2005
Jeff Foster, Contact

★555★
Oklahoma Indian Arts and Crafts Cooperative
PO Box 966
Anadarko, OK 73005   Ph: (405)247-3486
Laverna Capes, Manager

★556★
Inter-Tribal Council of Northeast Oklahoma
PO Box 1308   Ph: (918)540-2508
Miami, OK 74354   Fax: (918)540-2500
Donald Walker, Exec.Dir.

★557★
Oklahomans for Indian Opportunity
3001 S. Berry Rd., No. B   Ph: (405)329-3737
Norman, OK 73072   Fax: (405)329-8488
Iola Hayden, Exec.Dir.

★558★
Indian Healthcare Resource Center
915 S. Cincinnati
Box 184   Ph: (918)582-7225
Tulsa, OK 74119   Fax: (918)582-6405
Carmalita Skeeter, Exec.Dir.

★559★
Oklahoma Indian Business Development Center
5727 Garnett, Ste. H
Tulsa, OK 74146   Ph: (918)250-5950

Oregon

★560★
Oregon Indian Education Association
Eugene Office
720 Nantucket
Eugene, OR 97404   Ph: (503)888-4584
Twila Souers, Pres.

★561★
Research and Development for Indian Education
Northwest Regional Educational Laboratory
720 Nantucket   Ph: (503)888-4584
Eugene, OR 97404   Free: 800-547-6339
Twila Souers, Contact

★562★
Organization of the Forgotten American
PO Box 1257   Ph: (503)882-4441
Klamath Falls, OR 97601   Fax: (503)882-4442
Leonard Norris, Dir.

★563★
Native American Rehabilitation Association of the Northwest
1438 SE Division
Portland, OR 97202   Ph: (503)231-2641
Leon Stiffarm, Exec.Dir.

★564★
Northwest Indian Child Welfare
Portland State University
RR 1, PO Box 751   Ph: (503)725-3038
Portland, OR 97207   Fax: (503)725-4180
Terry L. Cross, Contact

★565★
United Indian Women
5632 NW Willbridge Ave.
Portland, OR 97210   Ph: (503)236-6154
Dorothy Ackerman, Contact

★566★
Chemawa Alcoholism Education Center
3760 Chemawa Rd. NE   Ph: (503)399-5942
Salem, OR 97305   Fax: (503)399-5973
John Spence, Prog.Dir.

★567★
Oregon Indian Education Association
Salem Office
1053 Koala, N.
Salem, OR 97303   Ph: (503)399-5942

Pennsylvania

★568★
United American Indians of the Delaware Valley
225 Chestnut St.
Philadelphia, PA 19106   Ph: (215)574-9020
Susan Heidi, Exec.Dir.

★569★
Council of Three Rivers American Indian Center, Inc.
200 Charles St.   Ph: (412)782-4457
Pittsburgh, PA 15238   Fax: (412)767-4808
Russell Sims, Exec.Dir.

Rhode Island

★570★
Rhode Island Indian Council, Inc.
444 Friendship St.   Ph: (401)331-4440
Providence, RI 02907   Fax: (401)331-4494
Christopher Camacho, Exec.Dir.

South Carolina

★571★
South Carolina Council on Native Americans
4801 Colonial Dr.
PO Box 21916   Ph: (803)754-7711
Columbia, SC 29221   Fax: (803)786-3647
Murphy Woods, Exec.Dir.

South Dakota

★572★
South Dakota Indian Education Association
Box 62
Batesland, SD 57716   Ph: (605)288-1804
Chris Bordeaux, Contact

★573★
South Dakota Urban Indian Health, Inc.
122 E. Dakota
Pierre, SD 57501   Ph: (605)224-8841

★574★
Sioux San Alcoholism Program
3200 Canyon Lake Dr.
Rapid City, SD 57701   Ph: (605)342-8925

★575★
American Indian Service Center
100 W. 6th St., No. 102
Sioux Falls, SD 57102   Ph: (605)334-4060
Rae Burnett, Exec.Dir.

Texas

★576★
American Indian Chamber of Commerce
PO Box 153409   Ph: (817)429-1866
Irving, TX 75015   Fax: (817)332-5103
Gene Bloomfield, Pres.

Utah

★577★
Utah Navajo Development Council
27 South 100 East
Blanding, UT 84511   Ph: (801)678-2285
Herbert Clah, Exec.Dir.

★578★
Indian Alcoholism Counseling and Recovery House Program
PO Box 1500
Salt Lake City, UT 84101   Ph: (801)328-8515

Virginia

★579★
Mattaponi-Pamunkey-Monacan JTPA Consortium
Mattaponi Indian Reservation
PO Box 360
King William, VA 23086-9734   Ph: (804)769-4767
Ann Richardson, Dir.

Washington

★580★
Washington State Indian Education Association
c/o Colville Confederated Tribes
PO Box 150   Ph: (509)634-4711
Nespelem, WA 99155   Fax: (509)634-8799
Gloria Adkins, Dir. of Higher Ed.

★581★
Seattle Indian Alcoholism Program
1421 Minor Ave.
Seattle, WA 98101   Ph: (206)296-7650
Marsha Wood, Dir.

★582★
Seattle Indian Health Board
611 12th Ave., S.
PO Box 3364
Seattle, WA 98114   Ph: (206)324-9360
Ralph Forguera, Dir.

★583★
United Indians of All Tribes Foundation
PO Box 99100   Ph: (206)285-4425
Seattle, WA 98199   Fax: (206)285-4427

★584★
Kitsap County Indian Center
9361 Bay Shore Dr. NW
Silverdale, WA 98383   Ph: (206)692-7460
Rose Walking Eagle, Dir.

★585★
American Indian Community Center
E. 905 3rd Ave.
Spokane, WA 99202   Ph: (509)535-0886
Sophie Tonasket, Exec.Dir.

★586★
Spokane Urban Indian Health Services
E. 905 3rd Ave.   Ph: (509)535-0868
Spokane, WA 99202   Fax: (509)535-3230
Leonard Hendricks, Dir.

Wisconsin

★587★
United Amerindian Health Center
PO Box 2248
Green Bay, WI 54306   Ph: (414)437-2161

★588★
Wisconsin Indian Education Association
PO Box 397   Ph: (715)799-5110
Keshena, WI 54135   Fax: (715)799-4525
Virginia Nuske, Sec.

★589★
American Indian Council on Alcoholism
2240 W. National Ave.   Ph: (414)671-2200
Milwaukee, WI 53205   Fax: (414)671-4570
Shirley Lafleur, Dir.

★590★
Milwaukee Indian Health Board and Center
930 N. 27th St.   Ph: (414)931-8111
Milwaukee, WI 53208   Fax: (414)931-0443
Jackie Schellinger, Dir.

★591★
Native American Center
University of Wisconsin at Stevens Point
Students Services Bldg., Rm. 206   Ph: (715)346-3828
Stevens Point, WI 54481   Fax: (715)346-2561
Dr. Ben Shkwegnaabi, Dir.

★592★
Wisconsin Indian Resource Council
University of Wisconsin at Stevens Point
Student Services Bldg., Rm. 018
Stevens Point, WI 54481   Ph: (715)346-2746
Idell Duffy, Dir.

─────────── **Wyoming** ───────────

★593★
Thunderchild
VA Hospital Bldg. 24   Ph: (307)672-3484
Sheridan, WY 82801   Fax: (307)672-0571

Federal Government Agencies

★594★
Indian Education Technical Assistance Center I
ORBIS Associates
1411 K St. NW, Ste. 200   Ph: (202)628-4444
Washington, DC 20005   Free: 800-621-2998
Gwen Shunatona, Dir.

Territory Includes: The District of Columbia, Arkansas, Louisiana, and Missouri.

★595★
Indian Education Technical Assistance Center V
2424 S. Springer Dr., Ste. 200   Ph: (405)360-1163
Norman, OK 73069   Free: 800-451-2191
Mary Ann Brittan, Dir.

Territory Includes: Oklahoma and Texas.

★596★
North Central Indian Education Technical Assistance Center II
3315 University Dr.   Ph: (701)258-0437
Bismarck, ND 58504   Free: 800-437-8054
Phil Baird, Dir.

Territory Includes: Iowa, Kansas, Minnesota, Nebraska, North Dakota, South Dakota, and Wisconsin.

★597★
Northwest Indian Education Technical Assistance Center III
School of Education
Gonzaga University   Ph: (509)328-4220
Spokane, WA 99258-0001   Free: 800-533-2554
Raymond Reyes, Dir.

Territory Includes: Colorado, Idaho, Montana, Oregon, Utah, Washington, and Wyoming.

★598★
Southwest Indian Education Technical Assistance Center IV
2121 S. Mill Ave., Ste. 216   Ph: (602)967-9428
Tempe, AZ 85282   Free: 800-528-6425
Shirley Hendricks, Dir.

Territory Includes: Arizona, California, Nevada, and New Mexico.

★599★
U.S. Department of Agriculture
Marketing and Inspection Services
Budget and Accounting Division
Native American and Asian Pacific Program
S. Agricultural Bldg.
Independence Ave. between 12th & 14th
   Sts.
Washington, DC 20250   Ph: (202)720-6312
Ardahila G. Short, Man.

★600★
U.S. Department of Education
Assistant Secretary for Elementary and Secondary Education
Office of Indian Education
400 Maryland Ave. SW
Washington, DC 20202   Ph: (202)401-1887
John W. Tippeconnic III, Dir.

★601★
U.S. Department of Health and Human Services
Administration for Children and Families
Administration for Native Americans
Hubert H. Humphrey Bldg.
200 Independence Ave. SW
Washington, DC 20201   Ph: (202)245-7776
S. Timothy Wapato, Commissioner

★602★
U.S. Department of Health and Human Services
Office of State and Community Programs
Office for American Indian, Alaskan Native and Native Hawaiian Programs
330 Independence Ave. SW
Washington, DC 20201   Ph: (202)619-2957

★603★
U.S. Department of Health and Human Services
Public Health Service
Indian Health Service
Parklawn Bldg.
5600 Fishers Ln.
Rockville, MD 20857   Ph: (301)443-1083
Everett R. Rhoades, Dir.

★604★
U.S. Department of Health and Human Services
Public Health Service
Indian Health Service
Office of Environmental Health and Engineering
Parklawn Bldg.
5600 Fishers Ln.
Rockville, MD 20857   Ph: (301)443-1247
Bill F. Pearson, Assoc.Dir.

★605★
U.S. Department of Health and Human Services
Public Health Service
Indian Health Service
Office of Health Program Research and Development
7900 S.J.J. Stock Rd.   Ph: (602)670-6600
Tucson, AZ 85746   Fax: (602)670-6158
Eleanore Robertson, Assoc.Dir.

★606★
U.S. Department of Health and Human Services
Public Health Service
Indian Health Service
Office of Health Programs
Parklawn Bldg.
5600 Fishers Ln.
Rockville, MD 20857   Ph: (301)443-1058
Phillip L. Smith, Assoc.Dir.

★607★
U.S. Department of Health and Human Services
Public Health Service
Indian Health Service
Office of Information Resources Management
Parklawn Bldg.
5600 Fishers Ln.
Rockville, MD 20857   Ph: (301)443-0750
Jack N. Markowitz, Assoc.Dir.

★608★
U.S. Department of Health and Human Services
Public Health Service
Indian Health Service
Office of Planning, Evaluation and Legislation
Parklawn Bldg.
5600 Fishers Ln.
Rockville, MD 20857   Ph: (301)443-4245
Luana L. Reyes, Assoc.Dir.

★609★
U.S. Department of Health and Human Services
Public Health Service
Indian Health Service
Office of Tribal Activities
Parklawn Bldg.
5600 Fishers Ln.
Rockville, MD 20857   Ph: (301)443-1104
Douglas Black, Assoc.Dir.

★610★
U.S. Department of Housing and Urban Development
Office of Indian and Alaska Native Programs
451 7th St. SW
Washington, DC 20410   Ph: (202)708-0420

★611★
U.S. Department of the Interior
Bureau of Indian Affairs
1849 C St. NW   Ph: (202)208-7163
Washington, DC 20240   Fax: (202)208-6334
Eddie F. Brown, Asst.Sec.

★612★
U.S. Department of the Interior
Bureau of Indian Affairs
Aberdeen Area Office
115 4th Ave. SE   Ph: (605)226-7261
Aberdeen, SD 57401   Fax: (605)226-7446
Jerry L. Jaeger, Dir.
Territory Includes: Nebraska, North Dakota, and South Dakota.

★613★
U.S. Department of the Interior
Bureau of Indian Affairs
Albuquerque Area Office
615 1st St. NW
PO Box 26567   Ph: (505)766-3171
Albuquerque, NM 87125-6567   Fax: (505)766-1964
Sidney L. Mills, Dir.
Territory Includes: Colorado and New Mexico.

★614★
U.S. Department of the Interior
Bureau of Indian Affairs
Anadarko Area Office
WCD Office Complex
PO Box 368   Ph: (405)247-6673
Anadarko, OK 75003   Fax: (405)247-7233
L.W. Collier Jr., Dir.
Territory Includes: Kansas and western Oklahoma.

★615★
U.S. Department of the Interior
Bureau of Indian Affairs
Billings Area Office
316 N. 26th St.   Ph: (406)657-6315
Billings, MT 58101   Fax: (406)657-6559
Richard Whitesell, Dir.
Territory Includes: Montana and Wyoming.

★616★
U.S. Department of the Interior
Bureau of Indian Affairs
Eastern Area Office
Virginia Sq. Plaza Bldg., Ste. 260
3701 N. Fairfax Dr.   Ph: (703)235-2571
Arlington, VA 22203   Fax: (703)235-8610
Billie D. Ott, Dir.
Territory Includes: Alabama, Connecticut, Florida, Louisiana, Maine, Massachusetts, Mississippi, New York, North Carolina, and Rhode Island.

★617★
U.S. Department of the Interior
Bureau of Indian Affairs
Juneau Area Office
9109 Mendenhall Mall Rd., Ste. 5
PO Box 3-8000   Ph: (907)586-7177
Juneau, AK 99802-1219   Fax: (907)586-7169
Niles Cesar, Dir.
Territory Includes: Alaska.

★618★
U.S. Department of the Interior
Bureau of Indian Affairs
Minneapolis Area Office
331 S. 2nd Ave.   Ph: (612)373-1000
Minneapolis, MN 55401   Fax: (612)373-1186
Earl Barlow, Dir.
Territory Includes: Iowa, Michigan, Minnesota, and Wisconsin.

★619★
U.S. Department of the Interior
Bureau of Indian Affairs
Muskogee Area Office
Old Federal Bldg.
5th & W. Okmulgee St.   Ph: (918)687-2296
Muskogee, OK 74401   Fax: (918)687-2571
Merritt E. Youngdeer, Dir.
Territory Includes: Eastern Oklahoma.

★620★
U.S. Department of the Interior
Bureau of Indian Affairs
Navajo Area Office
301 W. Hill
PO Box 1060   Ph: (505)863-8314
Gallup, NM 87301   Fax: (505)863-8245
Walter R. Mills, Dir.
Territory Includes: Navajo residents of New Mexico, Arizona, and Utah.

★621★
U.S. Department of the Interior
Bureau of Indian Affairs
Office of Indian Education Programs
1849 C St. NW   Ph: (202)208-6123
Washington, DC 20240   Fax: (202)208-3312
Edward F. Parisian, Dir.

★622★
U.S. Department of the Interior
Bureau of Indian Affairs
Office of Tribal Services
1849 C St. NW
Washington, DC 20240   Ph: (202)208-3463
Ronal Eden, Dir.

★623★
U.S. Department of the Interior
Bureau of Indian Affairs
Office of Trust and Economic Development
1849 C St. NW
Washington, DC 20240   Ph: (202)208-5831
Patrick A. Hayes, Dir.

★624★
U.S. Department of the Interior
Bureau of Indian Affairs
Phoenix Area Office
1 N. 1st St.   Ph: (602)379-6600
Phoenix, AZ 85001-0010   Fax: (602)379-4413
Wilson Barber Jr., Dir.
Territory Includes: Arizona (not including northern Arizona).

★625★
U.S. Department of the Interior
Bureau of Indian Affairs
Portland Area Office
911 NE 11th Ave.   Ph: (503)231-6702
Portland, OR 97232-4169   Fax: (503)231-2201
Stanley M. Speaks, Dir.
Territory Includes: Idaho, Oregon, and Washington.

★626★
U.S. Department of the Interior
Bureau of Indian Affairs
Sacramento Area Office
2800 Cottage Way   Ph: (916)978-4691
Sacramento, CA 95825   Fax: (916)978-4695
Ronald Jaeger, Dir.
Territory Includes: California.

★627★
U.S. Department of the Interior
Indian Arts and Crafts Board
1849 C St. NW
Washington, DC 20240   Ph: (202)208-3773
Lloyd Kiva New, Chairman

★628★
U.S. Department of the Interior
Office of the Solicitor
Indian Affairs Division
1849 C St. NW
Washington, DC 20240   Ph: (202)208-3401
Charles B. Hughes, Assoc.Solicitor

★629★
U.S. Department of the Interior
Policy, Management and Budget
Board of Indian Appeals
Ballston Tower No. 3
4015 Wilson Blvd.
Arlington, VA 22217   Ph: (703)235-3816
Judge Kathryn A. Lynn, Chief

★630★
U.S. Executive Office of the President
Office of Management and Budget
Indian Education
725 17th St. NW
Washington, DC 20503   Ph: (202)395-5880
Cynthia Brown, Specialist

★631★
U.S. Executive Office of the President
Office of Management and Budget
Indian Employment and Training Programs
725 17th St. NW
Washington, DC 20503   Ph: (202)395-3262
Maureen Walsh, Specialist

★632★
U.S. Executive Office of the President
Office of Management and Budget
Indian Health
725 17th St. NW
Washington, DC 20503   Ph: (202)395-4926
Bill Dorotinsky, Specialist

★633★
U.S. Executive Office of the President
Office of Management and Budget
Indian Programs
725 17th St. NW
Washington, DC 20503   Ph: (202)395-4993

Federal Domestic Assistance Programs

★634★
U.S. Department of Agriculture
Farmers Home Administration
Indian Tribes and Tribal Corporation Loans
Independence Ave. between 12th & 14th
  Sts.
Washington, DC 20250   Ph: (202)382-1490
Catalog Number: 10.421. **Objectives:** To enable federally recognized Indian tribes and tribal corporations to acquire land within tribal reservations and Alaskan communities. **Applicant Eligibility:** Limited to any Indian tribe recognized by the Secretary of the Interior or tribal corporation established pursuant to the Indian Reorganization Act which does not have adequate uncommitted funds to acquire lands within the tribe's reservation or in a community in Alaska incorporated by the Secretary of the Interior pursuant to the Indian Reorganization Act. Must be unable to obtain

sufficient credit elsewhere at reasonable rates and terms and must be able to show reasonable prospects of success as determined by an acceptable repayment plan and a satisfactory management plan for the land being acquired. **Types of Assistance:** Direct Loans; Guaranteed/Insured Loans. **Beneficiary Eligibility:** American Indian Tribe or tribal corporation recognized by the Secretary of the Interior.

★635★
U.S. Department of Commerce
Minority Business Development Agency
American Indian Program
14th & Constitution Ave. NW
Washington, DC 20230   Ph: (202)377-5770
Mr. Bharat Bhargava, Asst.Dir.

Catalog Number: 11.801. **Objectives:** To provide business development service to American Indians interested in entering, expanding, or improving their efforts in the marketplace. To help American Indian business development centers and American Indian business consultants to provide a wide range of services to American Indian clients, from initial consultation to the identification and resolution of specific business problems. **Applicant Eligibility:** MBDA selects applicants of American Indian origin only. Eligible applicants of American Indian origin may include individuals, nonprofit firms, and American Indian tribes. **Types of Assistance:** Project Grants (Cooperative Agreements). **Beneficiary Eligibility:** American Indians will benefit. Award recipients must provide assistance to American Indians interested in starting a business.

★636★
U.S. Department of Education
Office of Assistant Secretary for Educational
  Research and Improvement
Library Services for Indian Tribes and Hawaiian
  Natives
555 New Jersey Ave. NW
Washington, DC 20208-5517   Ph: (202)219-1323
Beth Fine, Program Officer

Catalog Number: 84.163. **Objectives:** Includes providing incentives for the establishment and expansion of tribal library programs for Hawaiian natives. **Applicant Eligibility:** Federally recognized Indian tribes and organizations that primarily serve Hawaiian Natives that are recognized by the Governor of the state of Hawaii may apply. Only Indian tribes and Hawaiian Native organizations that have received a basic grant are eligible to apply for special projects awards. **Types of Assistance:** Project grants (discretionary). **Beneficiary Eligibility:** Members of Indian tribes and Hawaiian Natives will benefit.

★637★
U.S. Department of Education
Office of the Assistant Secretary for Elementary and
  Secondary Education
Office of Indian Education
Indian Education Act—Fellowships for Students
400 Maryland Ave. SW
Washington, DC 20202   Ph: (202)401-1902
Dr. John Derby, Branch Chief, Indian Fellowship Program

Catalog Number: 84.087. **Objectives:** To enable Indian students to pursue a course of study leading to a postbaccalaureate degree in medicine, psychology, clinical psychology, law, education, and related fields; or an undergraduate or graduate degree in natural resources, business administration, engineering and related fields. **Applicant Eligibility:** An American Indian who is an enrolled member of a federally and State recognized tribe, and is in attendance, or who has been accepted for admission, as a full-time graduate or undergraduate student in an eligible field of study at an accredited institution as a degree candidate may apply. An applicant must not have obtained a terminal graduate or postbaccalaureate degree. **Types of Assistance:** Project Grants (Fellowships). **Beneficiary Eligibility:** Same as applicant eligibility.

★638★
U.S. Department of Education
Office of the Assistant Secretary for Elementary and
  Secondary Education
Office of Indian Education
Indian Education Act—Subpart 1
400 Maryland Ave. SW
Washington, DC 20202   Ph: (202)401-1902
Cathie Martin, Contact

Catalog Number: 84.060. **Objectives:** To develop and carry out supplementary elementary and secondary school programs designed to meet the special educational and culturally related academic needs of Indian children, for example to: (1) Improve academic performance, (2) reduce school dropout rates and improve attendance, and (3) integrate the value of cultural education into the school curriculum for Indian children. **Applicant Eligibility:** Local educational agencies (LEAs) that enroll at least 10 Indian children or in which Indians constitute at least 50 percent of the total enrollment. These requirements do not apply to LEAs serving Indian children in Alaska, California, and Oklahoma or located on, or in proximity to, an Indian reservation. An Indian tribe that operates a school in accordance to standards established by the Bureau of Indian Affairs according to Public Law 93-638 is deemed to be an LEA for the purposes of this program. Schools operated by the Bureau of Indian Affairs (BIA), Department of the Interior, are eligible only if funds are available in accordance with Section 5312(b)(3) of the Act. **Types of Assistance:** Formula Grants; Project Grants. **Beneficiary Eligibility:** Eligible Indian children enrolled in eligible local educational agencies, tribal schools, and BIA schools.

★639★
U.S. Department of Education
Office of the Assistant Secretary for Elementary and
  Secondary Education
Office of Indian Education
Indian Education Act—Subpart 1, Non-LEAs: Grants to
  Indian Controlled Schools
400 Maryland Ave. SW
Washington, DC 20202   Ph: (202)401-1902
Cathie Martin, Branch Chief

Catalog Number: 84.072. **Objectives:** To provide financial assistance to Indian-controlled schools to develop and implement cultural enrichment programs for elementary and secondary schools that are designed to meet the special educational needs of Indian children. The schools must be located on or near a reservation and must be governed by an Indian tribe or tribally sanctioned organization. **Applicant Eligibility:** An Indian tribe or Indian organization, or an LEA that will have been an LEA for not more than three years at the beginning of the proposed project period is eligible if it operates a school for Indian children that is located on or near a reservation. However, the requirement that a school be located on or near a reservation does not apply to any school serving Indian children in Alaska, California, or Oklahoma. **Types of Assistance:** Project Grants. **Beneficiary Eligibility:** Indian children enrolled in eligible schools will benefit.

★640★
U.S. Department of Education
Office of the Assistant Secretary for Elementary and
  Secondary Education
Office of Indian Education
Indian Education Act—Subpart 2
400 Maryland Ave. SW
Washington, DC 20202   Ph: (202)401-1902
Cathie Martin, Branch Chief

Catalog Number: 84.061. **Objectives:** To plan, develop, and implement programs and projects for the improvement of educational opportunities for Indian children, programs that serve gifted and talented Indian students, prepare and improve qualifications of persons serving Indian students in educational personnel positions, encourage Indian students to acquire a higher education, and reduce the incidence of dropping out of school among elementary and secondary school students. **Applicant Eligibility:** Eligible applicants include: State and local educational agencies, federally supported elementary and secondary schools for Indian children, Indian tribes, Indian organizations, Indian institutions, and consortia of higher education institutions, LEAs, SEAs, Indian tribes and Indian organizations. **Types of Assistance:** Project Grants. **Beneficiary Eligibility:** State and local educational agencies, institutions of higher education and Indian children will benefit.

★641★
U.S. Department of Education
Office of the Assistant Secretary for Elementary and
  Secondary Education
Office of Indian Education
Indian Education—Subpart 3, Adult Education
400 Maryland Ave. SW
Washington, DC 20202   Ph: (202)401-1902
Cathie Martin, Branch Chief

Catalog Number: 84.062. **Objectives:** To plan, develop, and implement programs for Indian adults to decrease the rate of illiteracy, increase the mastery of basic skills, increase the number who earn high school equivalency diplomas, and encourage the development of programs using cultured instruction for Indian adults. **Applicant Eligibility:** State and local educational agencies, Indian tribes, Indian institutions, and Indian organizations may apply. **Types of Assistance:** Project Grants. **Beneficiary Eligibility:** Indian adults will benefit.

★642★
U.S. Department of Education
Office of the Assistant Secretary for Vocational and
  Adult Education
Division of National Programs
Vocational Education—Indian and Hawaiian Natives
Washington, DC 20202-7242   Ph: (202)732-2380
Kate Homberg, Hawaiian Natives Prog.

Catalog Number: 84.101. **Objectives:** To make grants and contracts with Indian tribes or tribal organizations and to organizations primarily serving and representing Hawaiian Natives to plan, conduct, and administer programs or portions of programs authorized byu and consistent with the Carl D. Perkins Vocational Education Act. **Applicant Eligibility:** (1) A tribal organization or an Indian tribe which is eligible to contract with the Secretary of the Interior for the administration of programs under the Indian Self-Determination and Education Assistance Act of 1975 or under the Act of April 16, 1934. (2) Any organization primarily serving and representing Hawaiian Natives which is recognized by the Governor of Hawaii. **Types of Assistance:** Project Grants (Cooperative Agreements); Project Grants (Contracts). **Beneficiary Eligibility:** Federally recognized Indian tribes and Hawaiian Natives will benefit.

★643★
U.S. Department of Health and Human Services
Administration on Aging
American Indian, Alaskan Native, & Native Hawaiian
  Programs
Special Programs for the Aging, Title VI—Part B
  Grants to Native Hawaiians
330 Independence Ave. SW
Washington, DC 20201   Ph: (202)619-2957

Catalog Number: 93.655. **Objectives:** To promote the delivery of supportive services, including nutrition services to older Indians, Alaskan Natives, and Native Hawaiians. Services are comparable to services provided under Title III of the Older Americans Act of 1965, as amended. **Applicant Eligibility:** Includes public or nonprofit organizations which serve Native Hawaiian Elders, which represent at least 50 Indians or Hawaiians 60 years of age or older. Applicants must document that they have or will have the ability to deliver social and nutrition services. **Types of Assistance:** Project grants. **Beneficiary Eligibility:** Indians or Native Hawaiians who are 60 years of age and older, and in the case of nutrition, their spouses.

★644★
U.S. Department of Health and Human Services
Administration for Children and Families
Job Opportunities and Basic Skills Training
370 L'Enfant Promenade SW, 5th Fl.
Washington, DC 20447   Ph: (202)252-4950

Catalog Number: 93.021. **Objectives:** To assure that needy families with children and obtain the education, training, and employment that will help them avoid long-term welfare dependency. In addition, to enable needy individuals to participate in the program under Part F of the Social Security Act, each State agency must provide payment or reimbursement for such transportation and other work-related expenses as is necessary to enable such participation. Child care must be guaranteed if necessary to enable participation in Job Opportunity and Basic Skills Training (JOBS) or work activity. **Applicant Eligibility:** The United States, the Territories, including the Commonwealth of Puerto Rico, the Virgin Islands, Guam and American Samoa, and the federally recognized Indian Tribes and Alaska Native Organizations. **Types of Assistance:** Formula Grants. **Beneficiary Eligibility:** Welfare recipients and approved applicants, specifically those receiving Aid to Families with Dependent Children (AFDC) benefits or AFDC/Unemployed Parents benefits.

★645★
U.S. Department of Health and Human Services
Public Health Service
Indian Health Service
2101 E. Jefferson Blvd., Ste. 603
Rockville, MD 20852   Ph: (301)443-5204
Kay Carpentier, Grants Management Contact

Catalog Number: 93.905. **Objectives:** To conduct research and developmental activities in areas of Indian health care which further the performance of health responsibilities of the Indian Health Service. **Applicant Eligibility:** There are two groups of eligible applicants: (1) Federally recognized Indian tribes and tribal organizations which are contracting with the Indian Health Service under the authority of the Indian Self-Determination and Education Assistance Act; and (2) Indian Health Service components, including Service units and area offices. **Beneficiary Eligibility:** American Indian Tribes and Alaska Natives.

★646★
U.S. Department of Health and Human Services
Public Health Service
Indian Health Service
Health Management Development Program
2101 E. Jefferson Blvd., Ste. 603
Rockville, MD 20857   Ph: (301)443-5204
B. Bowman, Contact

Catalog Number: 93.228. **Objectives:** To improve the quality of the health of American Indians and Native Alaskans by providing a full range of curative, preventive and rehabilitative health services; and to increase the capability of American Indians and Native Alaskans to manage their own health programs. **Applicant Eligibility:** Federally-recognized tribes and tribal organizations. **Types of Assistance:** Project Grants. **Beneficiary Eligibility:** Individuals who are members of an eligible applicant tribe, band, group, or village and who may be regarded as within the scope of the Indian health and medical service program and who are regarded as an Indian by the community in which he lives as evidenced by such factors as tribal membership, enrollment, residence on tax exempt land, ownership of restricted property, active participation in tribal affairs or other relevant factors in keeping with general Bureau of Indian Affairs practices in the jurisdiction.

★647★
U.S. Department of Health and Human Services
Public Health Service
Indian Health Service
Health Professions Preparatory Scholarship Program
  for Indians
12300 Twinbrook Pkwy., Ste. 100
Rockville, MD 20852   Ph: (301)443-6197
Wes Picciotti, Contact

Catalog Number: 93.971. **Objectives:** To make scholarships to Indians for the purpose of completing compensatory pre-professional education to enable the recipient to qualify for enrollment or re-enrollment in a health professions school. **Applicant Eligibility:** Scholarship awards are made to individuals of American Indian or Native Alaskan descent, who have successfully completed high school education or high school equivalency and who have been accepted for enrollment in a compensatory, pre-professional general education course or curriculum. **Types of Assistance:** Project Grants. **Beneficiary Eligibility:** Individuals of American Indian or Native Alaskan descent.

★648★
U.S. Department of Health and Human Services
Public Health Service
Indian Health Service
Health Professions Recruitment Program for Indians
12300 Twinbrook Pkwy., Ste. 100
Rockville, MD 20852   Ph: (301)443-6197
Kay Carpenter, Grants Management Officer

Catalog Number: 93.970. **Objectives:** To identify Indians with a potential for education or training in the health professions, and to encourage and assist them to enroll in health or allied health professional schools. **Applicant Eligibility:** Public or private nonprofit health or educational entities or Indian tribes or tribal organizations as specifically provided in legislative authority. **Types of Assistance:** Project Grants. **Beneficiary Eligibility:** Preference is given to applicants in the following order of priority: (1) Indian tribes; (2) tribal organizations; (3) urban Indian organizations and other Indian health organizations; or (4) other public or nonprofit health or educational entities.

★649★
U.S. Department of Health and Human Services
Public Health Service
Indian Health Service
Health Professions Scholarship Program
200 Independence Ave. SW
Washington, DC 20201   Ph: (202)245-0146
Barbara N. Rosenberg, Grants Management Officer

Catalog Number: 93.972. **Objectives:** To promote service delivery improvement through research studies, and application of knowledge. **Applicant Eligibility:** Individuals of American Indian or Native Alaskan descent are given priority. Applicants for new awards: (1) must be accepted by an accredited U.S. educational institution for a full-time course of study leading to a degree in medicine, osteopathy, dentistry, or other participating health profession which is deemed necessary by the Indian Health Service; (2) be eligible for or hold an appointment as a Commissioned Officer in the Regular or Reserve Corps of the Public Health Service; or (3) be eligible for civilian service in the Indian Health Service. **Types of Assistance:** Project Grants.

★650★
U.S. Department of Health and Human Services
Public Health Service
Indian Health Service
Indian Health Service Loan Repayment Program
12300 Twinbrook Pkwy., Ste. 100   Ph: (301)443-4242
Rockville, MD 20852   Free: 800-962-2817
Charles Yepa, Contact

Catalog Number: 93.164. **Objectives:** To help insure an adequate supply of trained health professionals for Indian Health Service (IHS) facilities by providing for the repayment of educational loans for participants who agree (by written contract) to serve an applicable period of time in such a site; individuals who have conflicting service obligations may not participate in this program until those obligations are satisfied. The minimum period of participation is 2 years. Maximum program benefit is $25,000 per year. **Applicant Eligibility:** Eligible applicants must: (1) be individuals who (a) are enrolled as full-time students in the final year of a course of study or program leading to a degree in allopathic or osteopathic medicine, denistry or other health profession in a State; (b) are enrolled in an approved graduate training program in allopathic or osteopathic medicine, dentistry or other health profession; or (c) have a degree in allopathic or osteopathic medicine, dentistry or other health profession and have completed an approved graduate training program and have a current and valid license to practice such health profession in a State; (2) be eligible for appointment as a commissioned officer in the regular or reserve corps if the Public Health Service; be eligible for selection for civilian service in the IHS; or be an employee of a tribal health program or urban Indian Health Program funded under Title V of Public Law 94-437 and its amendments; (3) submit an application to participate in the Loan Repayment Program; and (4) sign and submit to the Secretary for Health and Human Services, at the time of such applicaiotn, a written contract agreeing to accept repayment of educational loans and to serve for the applicable period of service in a Retention/Recruitment Site as determined by the Secretary. **Types of Assistance:** Project Grants. **Beneficiary Eligibility:** Health

professionals who have unpaid educational loans will benefit from this program.

★651★
U.S. Department of Health and Human Services
Public Health Service
Indian Health Service
Research and Demonstration Projects for Indian Health
5600 Fishers Ln.
Rockville, MD 20852   Ph: (301)443-5204
Douglas Black, Contact

Catalog Number: 93.933. **Objectives:** To promote improved health care among American Indians and Alaska Natives through research studies, and demonstration projects. **Applicant Eligibility:** Federally recognized Indian tribes; tribal organizations; nonprofit intertribal organizations; nonprofit urban Indian organizations contracting with the Indian Health Service under Title V of the Indian Health Care Improvement Act; public or private nonprofit health and education entities; and State and local government health agencies. **Types of Assistance:** Project Grants. **Beneficiary Eligibility:** American Indians/Alaska Natives will be the ultimate beneficiaries of the funded projects either directly or indirectly depending upon the nature of the project. For example, those individuals who participate in research studies and receive services will be direct beneficiaries while those impacted by policy changes resulting from analyses of Indian health care issues will be indirect beneficiaries.

★652★
U.S. Department of Housing and Urban Development
Community Planning and Development
Indian Community Development Block Program
451 7th St. SW
Washington, DC 20410   Ph: (202)708-1322

Catalog Number: 14.223. **Objectives:** To provide assistance to Indian Tribes and Alaskan Native Villages in the development of viable Indian communities. **Applicant Eligibility:** Any Indian tribe, band, group, or nation, including Alaskan Indians, Aleuts, and Eskimos, and any Alaskan Native Village which is eligible for assistance under the Indian Self-Determination and Education Assistance Act. **Types of Assistance:** Project Grants. **Beneficiary Eligibility:** Indian tribes and Alaskan Native Villages as defined above.

★653★
U.S. Department of Housing and Urban Development
Public and Indian Housing
Washington, DC 20410   Ph: (202)755-0950

Catalog Number: 14.850. **Objectives:** To provide and operate cost-effective, decent, safe and sanitary dwellings for lower income families through an authorized local Public Housing Agency (PHA) or Indian Housing Authority (IHA). **Applicant Eligibility:** Public Housing Agencies and Indian Housing Authorities established in accordance with State or Tribal law are eligible. Other lower income families may be served under certain limited cirumstances. **Types of Assistance:** Direct Payments for Specified Use. **Beneficiary Eligibility:** Lower inocme families. ''Families'' include individuals who are 62 years old or older, disabled , or handicapped, or the remaining member of a tenant family.

★654★
U.S. Department of Housing and Urban Development
Public and Indian Housing
Comprehensive Improvment Assistance Program
Washington, DC 20413   Ph: (202)708-0950

Catalog Number: 14.852. **Applicant Eligibility:** Public Housing Agencies (PHAs) and Indian Housing Authorities (IHAs) operating PHA/IHA owned low income housing projects under an existing Annual Contributions Contract (ACC). **Types of Assistance:** Direct Loans; Project Grants; Direct Payments for Specified Use. **Beneficiary Eligibility:** The tenants of the modernized project are the ultimate beneficiaries.

★655★
U.S. Department of the Interior
Bureau of Indian Affairs
Indian Social Services—Child Welfare Assistance
18th & C Sts. NW
Washington, DC 20245   Ph: (202)208-2649
Sue Settles, Contact

Catalog Number: 15.103. **Objectives:** To provide foster home care and appropriate instiuttional care for dependent, neglected, and handicapped Indian children in need of protection residing on or near reservations, including those children living in jurisdictions under the BIA in Alaska and Oklahoma, when these services are not available from State or local public agencies. **Applicant Eligibility:** Dependent, neglected, and handicapped Indian children in need of protection whose families live on or near Indian reservations or in jurisdictions under the Bureau of Indian Affairs in Alaska and Oklahoma, and who are not elgible for similar Federal, State, or county funded programs. Applications may be made by a parent, guardian or person having custody of the child, or by court referral. **Types of Assistance:** Direct Payments for Specified Use. **Beneficiary Eligibility:** American Indian individuals/families.

★656★
U.S. Department of the Interior
Bureau of Indian Affairs
Indian Social Services—General Assistance
18th & C Sts. NW
Washington, DC 20245   Ph: (202)208-2649
Deborah Maddox, Contact

Catalog Number: 15.113. **Objectives:** To provide assistance for living needs to needy Indians on or near reservations, including those Indians living in jurisdictions under the Bureau of Indian Affairs in Oklahoma, when such assistance is not available from State or local public agencies. **Applicant Eligibility:** Needy Indians living on or near Indian reservations or in jurisdictions under the Bureau of Indains Affairs in Oklahoma. **Types of Assistance:** Unrestricted Direct Payments. **Beneficiary Eligibility:** Same as applicant eligibility.

★657★
U.S. Department of the Interior
Bureau of Indian Affairs
Office of Indian Education Programs
Higher Education Grant Program
18th & C Sts. NW
Washington, DC 20245   Ph: (202)208-4871
Dr. Reginald Rodriguez, Contact

Catalog Number: 15.114. **Objectives:** To provide finanical aid to eligible Indian students to enable them to attended accredited institutions of higher education. **Applicant Eligibility:** Must be a member of an Indian tribe or Alaska Native Village being served by the Bureau, be enrolled or accepted for enrollment in an accredited college, and have financial need as determined by the institution's financial aid office. **Types of Assistance:** Project Grants. **Beneficiary Eligibility:** Same as applicant eligibility.

★658★
U.S. Department of the Interior
Bureau of Indian Affairs
Office of Indian Education Programs
Indian Education—Assistance to Schools
18th & C Sts. NW
Washington, DC 20240   Ph: (202)208-4190
William Mehojah, Contact

Catalog Number: 15.130. **Objectives:** To provide supplemental education programs for eligible Indian students attending public schools. **Applicant Eligibility:** Tribal organizations, Indian Corporations, school districts or States which have eligible Indian children attending public school districts and have established Indian Education Committees to approve supplementary programs beneficial to Indian students. **Types of Assistance:** Direct Payments for Specified Use. **Beneficiary Eligibility:** Children who are enrolled members of a federally recognized Indian tribe or are at least one-fourth degree of Indian blood descent, who are between the age of 3 and grade 12. Priority is given to those residing on or near Indian reservations.

★659★
U.S. Department of the Interior
Bureau of Indian Affairs
Office of Indian Services
Indian Child Welfare Act—Title II Grants
1951 Constitution Ave.
Washington, DC 20245   Ph: (202)343-6434
Sue Settles, Contact

Catalog Number: 15.144. **Objectives:** To promote the stability and security of Indian tribes and families by the establishment of minimum Federal standards for the removal of Indian children from their families and the placment of such children in foster or adoptive homes and providing assistance to Indian tribes in the oepration of child and family service programs. **Applicant Eligibility:** The governing body of any tribe or tribes, or any Indian organization, including multi-service centers, may apply individually or as a consortium for a grant. **Types of Assistance:** Project Grants. **Beneficiary Eligibility:** Same as applicant eligibility.

★660★
U.S. Department of the Interior
Bureau of Indian Affairs
Office of Indian Services
Self Determination Grants—Indian Tribal Governments
1849 C St. NW
Washington, DC 20240   Ph: (202)208-5727
D. Homer, Div.Chief

Catalog Number: 15.142. **Objectives:** To aid Indian Tribes to exercise self-determination in accord with Public Law 93-638. **Applicant Eligibility:** Governing body of any federally recognized Indian tribe. **Types of Assistance:** Project Grants (Contracts); Advisory Services and Counseling; Provision of Specialized Services; Training. **Beneficiary Eligibility:** Federally recognized Indian tribe.

★661★
U.S. Department of the Interior
Bureau of Indian Affairs
Office of Indian Services
Training and Technical Assistance—Indian Tribal Governments
1849 C Sts. NW
Washington, DC 20240   Ph: (202)208-5727
D. Homer, Div.Chief

Catalog Number: 15.143. **Objectives:** To provide financial assistance to tribal governments so that they can improve their capacity to: (1) plan, conduct and administer Federal programs with special emphasis on improving their ability to contract; and (2) put special emphasis on strengthening and improving tribal governments with respect to their fiscal and managerial capabilities. This special program emphasis is intended to complement the Aid to Tribal Government Program. **Applicant Eligibility:** Only governing bodies of federally recognized Indian tribes are eligible to apply for self-determination grants. **Types of Assistance:** Project Grants. **Beneficiary Eligibility:** Federally recognized Indian tribes.

★662★
U.S. Department of the Interior
Bureau of Indian Affairs
Office of Tribal Services
Indian Employment Assistance
18th & C Sts. NW
Washington, DC 20240   Ph: (202)208-2570
Dean Poleahla, Contact

Catalog Number: 15.108. **Objectives:** To provide eligible American Indians vocational training and employment opportunities. **Applicant Eligibility:** Each individual American Indian applicant must be a member of a Federally recognized tribe, band, or group of Indians, whose residence is on or near an Indian reservation under the jurisdiction of the Bureau of Indian Affairs; or a descendant of one-fourth degree or more Indian blood of an enrolled member. The applicant must also be in need of financial assistance. **Types of Assistance:** Direct Payment for Specified Use. **Beneficiary Eligibility:** Same as applicant eligibility.

★663★
U.S. Department of the Interior
Bureau of Indian Affairs
Office of Tribal Services
Indian Housing Assistance
1849 C St. NW
Washington, DC 20240   Ph: (202)208-5427
A. Ronald Thurman, Contact

Catalog Number: 15.141. **Objectives:** To use the Indian Housing Improvement Program (HIP) and Bureau of Indian Affairs resources to substantially eliminate substandard Indian housing. This effort is combined with the Department of Health and Human Services. **Applicant Eligibility:** Indians in need of of financial assistance who meet the eligibility criteria of the HIP regulations (25 CFR, Subchapter K, Part 256). **Types of Assistance:** Project Grants (Contracts); Dissemination of Techinical Information. **Beneficiary Eligibility:** Same as applicant eligibility.

★664★
U.S. Department of the Interior
Bureau of Indian Affairs
Trust and Economic Development
Indian Business Development Program
18th & C Sts. NW
Washington, DC 20240   Ph: (202)208-3662

Catalog Number: 15.145. **Objectives:** To provide seed money to attract financing from other sources for developing Indian owned businesses; to improve Indian reservation economies by providing employment and goods and services where they are now deficient. **Applicant Eligibility:** Federally recognized Indian tribes and their members are eligible for grants when the business enterprise receiving the grant benefits a Federal Indian reservation. **Types of Assistance:** Project Grants; Direct Payments for Specified Use. **Beneficiary Eligibility:** Same as applicant eligibility.

★665★
U.S. Department of the Interior
Bureau of Indian Affairs
Trust and Economic Development
Indian Loans—Claims Assistance
18th & C Sts. NW
Washington, DC 20240   Ph: (202)208-5324
R.K. Nephew, Contact

Objectives: To enable Indian tribes or identifiable groups of Indians without available funds to obtain expert assistance in preparation and processing of claims pending before the U.S. Court of Claims. **Applicant Eligibility:** An Indian organization must have one or more pending claims of nature and in a stage of prosecution requiring the services of expert witnesses. **Types of Assistance:** Direct Loans. **Beneficiary Eligibility:** Same as applicant eligibility.

★666★
U.S. Department of the Interior
Bureau of Indian Affairs
Trust and Economic Development
Indian Loans—Economic Development
18th & C Sts. NW
Washington, DC 20240   Ph: (202)208-5324
R.K. Nephew, Contact

Catalog Number: 15.124. **Objectives:** To provide assistance to Indians, Alaska Natives, tribes, and Indian organizations to obtain financing from private and governmental sources which serve other citizens. When otherwise unavailable, financial assistance through the Bureau is provided eligible applicants for any purpose that will promote the economic development of a Federal Indian reservation. **Applicant Eligibility:** Indians, Alaska Natives, tribes, and Indian organizations. Individual applicants must be a member of a federally recognized tribe. Organizational applicants must have a form of organization satisfactory to the Assistant Secretary for Indian Affairs. **Types of Assistance:** Direct Loans; Guaranteed/Insured Loans; Provisions of Specialized Services. **Beneficiary Eligibility:** Same as applicant eligibility.

★667★
U.S. Department of the Interior
Indian Arts and Crafts Board
Indian Arts and Crafts Development
1849 C St. NW
Washington, DC 20240   Ph: (202)208-3773

Catalog Number: 15.850. **Objectives:** To encourage and promote the development of American Indian arts and crafts. **Applicant Eligibility:** Native Americans, Indian, Eskimo, and Aleut individuals and organizations, federally recognized Indian tribal governments, State and local governments, and nonprofit organizations. **Types of Assistance:** Use of Property, Facilities, and Equipment; Advisory Services and Counseling; Investigation of Complaints. **Beneficiary Eligibility:** Same as applicant eligibility.

★668★
U.S. Department of Justice
Office for Victims of Crime
Office of Justice Programs
Children's Justice Act for Native American Indian Tribes
633 Indiana Ave. NW
Washington, DC 20531   Ph: (202)514-6444
Marti Speights, Dir.

Catalog Number: 16.583. **Objectives:** Fifteen percent of the first $4.5 million of funds from the Crime Victims Fund that are transferred to the Department of Health and Human Services as part of the Children's Justice Act are to be statutorily reserved by the Office for Victims of Crime (OVC) to make grants for the purpose of assisting Native American Indian tribes in developing, establishing, and operating programs designed to improve the handling of child abuse cases, particularly cases of child sexual abuse, in a manner which limits additional trauma to the child victim and improves the investigation and prosecution of cases of child abuse. **Applicant Eligibility:** Federally recognized Indian tribal governments and nonprofit organizations that provide services to Native Americans. Specific criteria will vary depending on the grant. **Types of Assistance:** Project Grants; Direct Payments for Specified Use. **Beneficiary Eligibility:** Native American youth who are victims of child abuse and/or child sexual assault.

★669★
U.S. Department of Labor
Employment and Training Administration
Division of Indian and Native American Programs
Native American Employment and Training Programs
200 Constitution Ave. NW
Washington, DC 20210   Ph: (202)535-0500
Paul Mayrand, Contact

Catalog Number: 17.251. **Objectives:** To afford job training to Native Americans facing serious barriers to employment, who are in special need of such training to obtain productive employment. To reduce the economic disadvantages among Indians and others of Native American descent and to advance the economic and social development of such people. **Applicant Eligibility:** Indian tribes, bands or groups, Alaska Native villages or groups, and Hawaiian Native communities meeting the eligibility criteria, public bodies or private nonprofit agencies selected by the Secretary. Tribes, bands and groups may also form consortia in order to qualify for designation as a grantee. An independently eligible grantee shall be an Indian or Native American entity which has: (1) An identifiable Native American resident population of at least 1,000 individuals (for new grantees) within its designated service area, and (2) the capability to administer Indian and Native American employment and training programs. **Types of Assistance:** Formula Grants. **Beneficiary Eligibility:** Members of State or federally recognized Indian tribes, bands and other individuals of Native American descent, such as, but not limited to, the Kalamaths in Oregon, Micmac and Miliseet in Maine, the Lumbees in North Carolina and South Carolina, Indians variously descibed as terminated or landless, Eskimos and Aleuts in Alaska, and Hawaiian Natives. ("Hawaiian Native" means an individual any of whose ancestors were natives prior to 1778 of the area which now comprises the State of Hawaii.) Applicants must also be economically disadvantaged, unemployed, or underemployed. A Native American grantee may apply in some cases enroll participants who are not economically disadvantaged, unemployed, or underemployed in upgrading and retraining programs.

★670★
U.S. Equal Employment Opportunity Commission
Employment Discrimination Project Grants—Indian
   Tribes
1801 L St. NW
Washington, DC 20507   Ph: (202)663-4866
Catalog Number: 30.009. **Objectives:** To insure the protection of employment rights of Indians working on reservations. **Applicant Eligibility:** Any-land based Native American Tribe that has a tribal employment rights office established under an ordinance passed by the tribal council. **Types of Assistance:** Project Grants (Contracts). **Beneficiary Eligibility:** Native Americans employed or seeking employment on or near reservations with Tribal Employment Rights office having contracts.

State/Provincial & Local Government Agencies

Alabama

★671★
Alabama Indian Affairs Commission
339 Dexter Ave., Ste. 113
Montgomery, AL 36130   Ph: (205)242-2831

Arizona

★672★
Arizona Department of Education Services
Indian Education
1535 W. Jefferson
Phoenix, AZ 85007   Ph: (602)542-4391
Katie Stevens-Begaye, Contact

★673★
Arizona Indian Affairs Commission
1645 W. Jefferson, Rm. 127
Phoenix, AZ 85007   Ph: (602)542-3123
Hariette Toro, Chairperson

★674★
U.S. Department of the Interior
Bureau of Indian Affairs
Chinle Agency
PO Box 711
Chinle, AZ 86503

★675★
U.S. Department of the Interior
Bureau of Indian Affairs
Colorado River Agency
Rte. 1, Box 9-C
Parker, AZ 85344   Ph: (602)669-6121

★676★
U.S. Department of the Interior
Bureau of Indian Affairs
Fort Apache Agency
Whiteriver, AZ 85941   Ph: (602)338-4364

★677★
U.S. Department of the Interior
Bureau of Indian Affairs
Fort Definance Agency
PO Box 619
Fort Definance, AZ 86504

★678★
U.S. Department of the Interior
Bureau of Indian Affairs
Fort Yuma Agency
PO Box 1591
Yuma, AZ 85364   Ph: (602)572-0248

★679★
U.S. Department of the Interior
Bureau of Indian Affairs
Hopi Agency
Keams Canyon, AZ 86034

★680★
U.S. Department of the Interior
Bureau of Indian Affairs
Papago Agency
Sells, AZ 85634   Ph: (602)383-7286

★681★
U.S. Department of the Interior
Bureau of Indian Affairs
Pima Agency
Sacaton, AZ 85247   Ph: (602)562-3326

★682★
U.S. Department of the Interior
Bureau of Indian Affairs
Salt River Agency
Rte. 2
PO Box 117
Scottsdale, AZ 85256   Ph: (602)241-2842

★683★
U.S. Department of the Interior
Bureau of Indian Affairs
San Carlos Agency
San Carlos, AZ 85550   Ph: (602)475-2321

★684★
U.S. Department of the Interior
Bureau of Indian Affairs
Truxton Canyon Agency
Valentine, AZ 86437   Ph: (602)769-2286

★685★
U.S. Department of the Interior
Bureau of Indian Affairs
Western Navajo Agency
PO Box 127
Tuba City, AZ 86045

California

★686★
California Education Department
American Indian Education Office
PO Box 944272
Sacramento, CA 94244-2720   Ph: (916)322-9744

★687★
California Native American Heritage Commission
915 Capitol Mall, Rm. 288
Sacramento, CA 95814   Ph: (916)653-4082
Larry Myers, Exec.Sec.

★688★
U.S. Department of the Interior
Bureau of Indian Affairs
Central California Affairs
1800 Tribute Rd.
Box 15740
Sacramento, CA 95813-0770
Ph: (916)978-4337
Fax: (916)978-5589

★689★
U.S. Department of the Interior
Bureau of Indian Affairs
Hoopa Agency
PO Box 367
Hoopa, CA 95546
Ph: (916)246-5141
Fax: (916)246-5167

★690★
U.S. Department of the Interior
Bureau of Indian Affairs
Palm Springs Field Office
PO Box 2245
Palm Springs, CA 92262
Ph: (619)322-3086

★691★
U.S. Department of the Interior
Bureau of Indian Affairs
Southern California Agency
5750 Division St., Ste. 201
Riverside, CA 92506
Ph: (714)276-6624
Fax: (714)276-6641

─────── **Colorado** ───────

★692★
Colorado Commission on Indian Affairs
130 State Capitol Bldg.
Denver, CO 80203
Mary Jo Dennis, Contact
Ph: (303)866-3027

★693★
U.S. Department of the Interior
Bureau of Indian Affairs
Southern Ute Agency
PO Box 315
Ignacio, CO 81137
Ph: (303)563-4511
Fax: (303)565-9321

★694★
U.S. Department of the Interior
Bureau of Indian Affairs
Ute Mountain Ute Agency
Towaoc, CO 81334
Ph: (303)565-8471
Fax: (303)565-8906

─────── **Connecticut** ───────

★695★
Connecticut Department of Environmental Protection
Connecticut Indian Affairs Council
165 Capitol Ave., Rm. 240
Hartford, CT 06106

─────── **Florida** ───────

★696★
Florida Indian Affairs Council
521 E. College Ave.
Tallahassee, FL 32301
Joe A. Quetone, Exec.Dir.
Ph: (904)488-0730

★697★
U.S. Department of the Interior
Bureau of Indian Affairs
Miccosukee Agency
PO Box 44021
Tamiami Station, FL 33144
Ph: (703)235-2571
Fax: (703)235-8610

★698★
U.S. Department of the Interior
Bureau of Indian Affairs
Seminole Agency
6075 Stirling Rd.
Hollywood, FL 33024
Ph: (305)581-7050
Fax: (305)792-7340

─────── **Idaho** ───────

★699★
Idaho Education Department
Adult Education and Indian Education
Len B. Jordan Bldg.
650 W. State St.
Boise, ID 83720
Shirley Spencer, Contact
Ph: (208)334-2187

★700★
U.S. Department of the Interior
Bureau of Indian Affairs
Northern Idaho Agency
PO Drawer 277
Lapwai, ID 83540
Ph: (208)843-2300
Fax: (208)843-7142

─────── **Iowa** ───────

★701★
U.S. Department of the Interior
Bureau of Indian Affairs
Sac & Fox Area Field Office
Tama, IA 52339
Ph: (515)484-4041
Fax: (515)484-6518

─────── **Kansas** ───────

★702★
U.S. Department of the Interior
Bureau of Indian Affairs
Horton Agency
PO Box 31
Horton, KS 66439
Ph: (913)486-2161
Fax: (913)486-2515

─────── **Louisiana** ───────

★703★
Louisiana Indian Affairs Office
PO Box 94005
Baton Rouge, LA 70804-9005
Ph: (504)342-9796

─────── **Maryland** ───────

★704★
Maryland Indian Affairs Commisssion
100 Community Pl.
Crownsville, MD 21032-2023
Patricia King, Dir.
Ph: (410)514-7600

─────────── Massachusetts ───────────

★705★
Massachusetts Indian Affairs
100 Cambridge St., Rm. 1404
Boston, MA 02202   Ph: (617)727-6966
John Peters, Contact

─────────── Michigan ───────────

★706★
Michigan Indian Affairs Commission
611 W. Ottawa St., 3rd Fl.
Lansing, MI 48933   Ph: (517)373-0654
Betty Kienitz, Dir.

★707★
U.S. Department of the Interior
Bureau of Indian Affairs
Federal Square Office Plaza
Box 884   Ph: (906)632-6809
Sault Ste. Marie, MI 49783   Fax: (906)632-0689

─────────── Minnesota ───────────

★708★
Minnesota Education Department
Indian Education Section
Capitol Sq. Bldg.
550 Cedar St.
Saint Paul, MN 55101   Ph: (612)296-6458
Will Antell, Contact

★709★
Minnesota Indian Affairs Council
1819 Bemidji Ave.
Bemidji, MN 56601   Ph: (218)755-3825
Roger Head, Exec.Dir.

★710★
U.S. Department of the Interior
Bureau of Indian Affairs
Minnesota Agency
R.R. 2 - F C 200   Ph: (218)335-6913
Cass Lake, MN 56633   Fax: (218)335-2819

★711★
U.S. Department of the Interior
Bureau of Indian Affairs
Minnesota Sioux Area Field Office
2330 Sioux Trail, NW   Ph: (612)349-3597
Prior Lake, MN 55372   Fax: (612)349-3365

★712★
U.S. Department of the Interior
Bureau of Indian Affairs
Red Lake Agency
Red Lake, MN 56671   Ph: (218)679-3361
    Fax: (218)679-3378

─────────── Mississippi ───────────

★713★
U.S. Department of the Interior
Bureau of Indian Affairs
Choctaw Agency
421 Powell   Ph: (601)656-1521
Philadelphia, MS 39350   Fax: (601)656-2350

─────────── Montana ───────────

★714★
Montana Commerce Department
Indian Affairs
1424 9th Ave.
Helena, MT 59260   Ph: (406)444-3702
Kathleen Fleury, Coord.

★715★
Montana Governor's Office of Indian Affairs
1424 9th Ave.
Helena, MT 59620   Ph: (406)444-3702

★716★
U.S. Department of the Interior
Bureau of Indian Affairs
Blackfeet Agency
Browning, MT 59417   Ph: (406)338-7544
    Fax: (406)338-7716

★717★
U.S. Department of the Interior
Bureau of Indian Affairs
Crow Agency
Crow Agency, MT 59022   Ph: (406)638-2672
    Fax: (406)638-2380

★718★
U.S. Department of the Interior
Bureau of Indian Affairs
Flathead Agency
PO Box A
Ronan, MT 59864

★719★
U.S. Department of the Interior
Bureau of Indian Affairs
Fort Belknap Agency
PO Box 80   Ph: (406)353-2901
Harlem, MT 59526   Fax: (406)353-2886

★720★
U.S. Department of the Interior
Bureau of Indian Affairs
Fort Peck Agency
PO Box 637   Ph: (406)768-5312
Poplar, MT 59255   Fax: (406)768-3405

★721★
U.S. Department of the Interior
Bureau of Indian Affairs
Northern Cheyenne Agency
Lame Deer, MT 59043   Ph: (406)477-8242
    Fax: (406)477-6636

★722★
U.S. Department of the Interior
Bureau of Indian Affairs
Rocky Boy's Agency
Box Elder, MT 59521   Ph: (406)395-4476
    Fax: (406)395-4382

─────────── Nebraska ───────────

★723★
Nebraska Commission on Indian Affairs
PO Box 94981, State Capitol
Lincoln, NE 68509   Ph: (402)471-3475

★724★
U.S. Department of the Interior
Bureau of Indian Affairs
Winnebago Agency
Winnebago, NE 68071
Ph: (402)878-2201
Fax: (402)878-2943

─────────── **Nevada** ───────────

★725★
Nevada Indian Commission
3100 Mill St., Ste. 206
Reno, NV 89502
Gerald W. Allen, Dir.
Ph: (702)688-1347
Fax: (702)688-1113

★726★
U.S. Department of the Interior
Bureau of Indian Affairs
Eastern Neveda Agency
Elko, NV 89801
Ph: (702)738-5165

★727★
U.S. Department of the Interior
Bureau of Indian Affairs
Western Nevada Agency
1300 S. Curry St.
Carson City, NV 89701
Ph: (702)887-3500

─────────── **New Mexico** ───────────

★728★
New Mexico Education Department
Indian Education Unit
Education Bldg.
300 Don Gaspar
Santa Fe, NM 87501-2786
Nancy Martine Alonzo, Contact
Ph: (505)827-6679

★729★
New Mexico Indian Affairs Office
La Villa Rivera Bldg.
228 E. Palace Ave.
Sante Fe, NM 87501
Regis Pecos, Exec.Dir.
Ph: (505)827-6440

★730★
New Mexico Senate Standing Committee
Indian Affairs
State Capitol
Santa Fe, NM 87503
John Pinto, Democrat
Ph: (505)986-4314

★731★
New Mexico State Tribal Relations Committee
PO Box 4456, Sta. A
Albuquerque, NM 87196
Ph: (505)277-5462

★732★
U.S. Department of the Interior
Bureau of Indian Affairs
Eastern Navajo Agency
PO Box 328
Crownpoint, NM 87313

★733★
U.S. Department of the Interior
Bureau of Indian Affairs
Jicarilla Agency
Dulce, NM 87528
Ph: (505)759-3651
Fax: (505)759-3005

★734★
U.S. Department of the Interior
Bureau of Indian Affairs
Laguna Agency
PO Box 1448
Laguna, NM 87026
Ph: (505)243-4467
Fax: (505)552-7497

★735★
U.S. Department of the Interior
Bureau of Indian Affairs
Mescalero Agency
Mescalero, NM 88340
Ph: (505)671-4421
Fax: (505)671-4601

★736★
U.S. Department of the Interior
Bureau of Indian Affairs
Northern Pueblos Agency
Box 849
Federal PO Building
Santa Fe, NM 87501
Ph: (505)753-1400
Fax: (505)753-1404

★737★
U.S. Department of the Interior
Bureau of Indian Affairs
Ramah-Navajo Agency
Ramah, NM 87321

★738★
U.S. Department of the Interior
Bureau of Indian Affairs
Shiprock Agency
PO Box 966
Shiprock, NM 87420

★739★
U.S. Department of the Interior
Bureau of Indian Affairs
Southern Pueblos Agency
PO Box 1667
Albuquerque, NM 87103
Ph: (505)766-3021

★740★
U.S. Department of the Interior
Bureau of Indian Affairs
Zuni Agency
PO Box 338
Zuni, NM 87327
Ph: (505)782-4453
Fax: (505)782-5715

─────────── **New York** ───────────

★741★
New York Education Department
Native American Education Unit
471 Education Bldg. Annex
Albany, NY 12234
Ph: (518)474-7611

★742★
New York State Department of Indian Affairs
40 N. Pearl St.
Albany, NY 12243

★743★
U.S. Department of the Interior
Bureau of Indian Affairs
New York Liaison Office
Federal Building
100 S. Clinton St.
Syracuse, NY 13202
Ph: (315)423-5476
Fax: (315)423-5577

─────── North Carolina ───────

★744★
North Carolina Advisory Council on Indian Education
c/o Hope County Schools Asst.
  Superintendent
PO Box 468
Halifax, NC 27839-0468   Ph: (919)583-5111
Ralph Evans, Chairman

★745★
North Carolina Indian Affairs Commission
227 E. Edenton St.
Box 27647
Raleigh, NC 27611   Ph: (919)733-5998
A. Bruce Jones, Exec.Dir.

★746★
U.S. Department of the Interior
Bureau of Indian Affairs
Cherokee Agency
Cherokee, NC 28719   Ph: (704)497-9131
                      Fax: (704)497-6715

─────── North Dakota ───────

★747★
North Dakota Indian Affairs Commission
600 E. Boulevard
Bismark, ND 58505   Ph: (701)224-2428
Deborah A. Painte, Exec.Dir.

★748★
U.S. Department of the Interior
Bureau of Indian Affairs
Cheyenne River Agencu
Box 325   Ph: (605)964-6611
Eagle Butte, ND 57625   Fax: (605)964-4060

★749★
U.S. Department of the Interior
Bureau of Indian Affairs
Fort Berthold Agency
New Town, ND 58763   Ph: (701)627-4707
                      Fax: (701)627-3601

★750★
U.S. Department of the Interior
Bureau of Indian Affairs
Fort Totten Agency
Fort Totten, ND 58335   Ph: (701)766-4545
                      Fax: (701)766-4854

★751★
U.S. Department of the Interior
Bureau of Indian Affairs
Standing Rock Agency
Fort Yates, ND 58538   Ph: (701)854-3433
                      Fax: (701)854-7543

★752★
U.S. Department of the Interior
Bureau of Indian Affairs
Turtle Mountain Agency
Belcourt, ND 58316   Ph: (701)477-3191
                      Fax: (701)477-6628

─────── Oklahoma ───────

★753★
Oklahoma Education Department
Indian Education Section
2500 N. Lincoln Blvd.
Oklahoma City, OK 73105   Ph: (405)521-3311
Ron West, Contact

★754★
Oklahoma Historical Society
Indian Archives
2100 N. Lincoln
Oklahoma City, OK 73105-4997   Ph: (405)521-2491
William Weige, Contact

★755★
Oklahoma Indian Affairs Commission
4010 N. Lincoln Blvd., Ste. 200
Oklahoma City, OK 73105   Ph: (405)521-3828
Claude Cox, Chairperson

★756★
U.S. Department of the Interior
Bureau of Indian Affairs
Anadarko Agency
PO Box 309   Ph: (405)247-6673
Anadarko, OK 73005   Fax: (405)247-7314

★757★
U.S. Department of the Interior
Bureau of Indian Affairs
Ardmore Agency
PO Box 997
Ardmore, OK 73401

★758★
U.S. Department of the Interior
Bureau of Indian Affairs
Concho Agency
Concho, OK 73022   Ph: (405)262-7481
                      Fax: (405)262-3140

★759★
U.S. Department of the Interior
Bureau of Indian Affairs
Miami Agency
PO Box 391   Ph: (918)542-3396
Miami, OK 74354   Fax: (918)542-7202

★760★
U.S. Department of the Interior
Bureau of Indian Affairs
Osage Agency
Pawhuska, OK 74056   Ph: (918)287-2481
                      Fax: (918)542-1229

★761★
U.S. Department of the Interior
Bureau of Indian Affairs
Pawnee Agency
PO Box 440   Ph: (918)762-2585
Pawnee, OK 74058   Fax: (918)762-3201

★762★
U.S. Department of the Interior
Bureau of Indian Affairs
Tahlequah Agency
PO Box 828   Ph: (918)456-6146
Tahlequah, OK 74465   Fax: (918)458-0329

★763★
U.S. Department of the Interior
Bureau of Indian Affairs
Talihina Agency
PO Box Drawer II   Ph: (918)567-2207
Talihina, OK 74571   Fax: (918)567-2061

★764★
U.S. Department of the Interior
Bureau of Indian Affairs
Wewoka Agency
PO Box 1060   Ph: (405)257-6257
Wewoka, OK 74884   Fax: (405)257-6748

─────────── Oregon ───────────

★765★
Oregon Commission on Indian Services
454 State Capitol
Salem, OR 97310   Ph: (503)378-5481
Kathy Gorospe, Dir.

★766★
U.S. Department of the Interior
Bureau of Indian Affairs
Siletz Agency
PO Box 539   Ph: (503)444-2679
Siletz, OR 97380   Fax: (503)444-2513

★767★
U.S. Department of the Interior
Bureau of Indian Affairs
Umatilla Agency
PO Box 520   Ph: (503)276-3811
Pendleton, OR 97801   Fax: (503)276-3811

★768★
U.S. Department of the Interior
Bureau of Indian Affairs
Warm Springs Agency
Warm Springs, OR 97761   Ph: (503)553-2411
    Fax: (503)420-1426

─────────── South Dakota ───────────

★769★
South Dakota Education and Cultural Affairs
   Department
Indian Education
700 Governors Dr.
Pierre, SD 57501-3369   Ph: (605)773-4670

★770★
South Dakota Indian Affairs Office
Public Safety Bldg., 3rd Fl.
Pierre, SD 57501   Ph: (605)773-3415
Francis WhiteBird, Coord.

★771★
U.S. Department of the Interior
Bureau of Indian Affairs
Lower Brule Agency
Lower Brule, SD 57548   Ph: (605)473-5512
    Fax: (605)473-5491

★772★
U.S. Department of the Interior
Bureau of Indian Affairs
Pine Ridge Agency
Pine Ridge, SD 57770   Ph: (605)867-5121
    Fax: (605)867-1141

★773★
U.S. Department of the Interior
Bureau of Indian Affairs
Rosebud Agency
Rosebud, SD 57570   Ph: (605)747-2224
    Fax: (605)747-2805

★774★
U.S. Department of the Interior
Bureau of Indian Affairs
Sisseton Agency
Sisseton, SD 57262   Ph: (605)698-7676
    Fax: (605)698-7784

★775★
U.S. Department of the Interior
Bureau of Indian Affairs
Yankton Agency
Wagner, SD 57380   Ph: (605)384-3651
    Fax: (605)384-5706

─────────── Utah ───────────

★776★
U.S. Department of the Interior
Bureau of Indian Affairs
Uintah & Ouray Agency
Fort Duchesne, UT 84026   Ph: (801)722-2406

★777★
Utah Indian Affairs Division
324 S. State St.
Salt Lake City, UT 84111   Ph: (801)538-8700
Wil Numkena, Dir.

─────────── Virginia ───────────

★778★
Virginia Department of Human Resources
Indian Affairs Coordinator
9th St. Office Bldg., Rm. 622
Richmond, VA 23219

─────────── Washington ───────────

★779★
U.S. Department of the Interior
Bureau of Indian Affairs
Colville Agency
PO Box 111-0111   Ph: (509)634-4901
Nespelem, WA 99155   Fax: (509)439-9449

★780★
U.S. Department of the Interior
Bureau of Indian Affairs
Olympic Peninsula Agency
Box 120
Post Office Bldg.   Ph: (206)533-9100
Hoquiam, WA 98550   Fax: (206)390-9141

★781★
U.S. Department of the Interior
Bureau of Indian Affairs
Puget Sound Agency
3006 Colby St.
Federal Building   Ph: (206)258-2651
Everett, WA 98201   Fax: (206)258-1254

★782★
U.S. Department of the Interior
Bureau of Indian Affairs
Seattle Support Center
PO Box 80947
Seattle, WA 98108

★783★
U.S. Department of the Interior
Bureau of Indian Affairs
Spokane Agency
PO Box 389   Ph: (509)258-4561
Wellpinit, WA 99040   Fax: (509)258-4562

★784★
U.S. Department of the Interior
Bureau of Indian Affairs
Yakima Agency
PO Box 632   Ph: (509)865-2255
Toppenish, WA 98948   Fax: (509)446-8198

★785★
Washington Indian Affairs
Legislative Bldg.
Olympia, WA 98504   Ph: (206)753-2411
Michele Aguilar, Contact

───────── **Wisconsin** ─────────

★786★
U.S. Department of the Interior
Bureau of Indian Affairs
Great Lakes Agency
Ashland, WI 54806   Ph: (715)682-4527
                               Fax: (715)682-8897

───────── **Wyoming** ─────────

★787★
U.S. Department of the Interior
Bureau of Indian Affairs
Wind River Agency
Fort Washakie, WY 82514   Ph: (307)322-7810
                               Fax: (307)332-4578

Library Collections

★788★
Akwesasne Library Cultural Center
RR 1, Box 14C
Hogansburg, NY 13655   Ph: (518)358-2240
Carol White, Dir.

Special Collections: American Indian collection (1900 items).
Holdings: AV programs; pamphlets; framed pictures.

★789★
Allen County Historical Society
Elizabeth M. MacDonell Memorial Library
620 W. Market St.
Lima, OH 45801-4604   Ph: (419)222-9426
Anna B. Selfridge, Cur., Archv. & Mss.

Subjects: Local history and genealogy, Ohio history, railroading,
American Indians. **Special Collections:** John H. Keller Railroad
Collection; Interurban and Street Railway Collection; Lima
Locomotive Works Collection; Railroad Labor History Collection (30
cubic feet). **Holdings:** 8271 books; 585 bound periodical volumes;
Lima, Ohio newspapers, 1840s to present; Lima directories, 1876 to
present; 1938 reels of microfilm of newspapers and census records.
Remarks: Library is part of Allen County Museum.

★790★
Amarillo Public Library
Local History Collection
413 E. 4th
Box 2171   Ph: (806)378-3054
Amarillo, TX 79189-2171   Fax: (806)378-4245
Mary Kay Snell, Dir., Lib.Serv.

Subjects: Southwestern history, Indian tribes and customs, religion.
Special Collections: Bush/FitzSimon Collection of Books on the
Southwest; John L. McCarty Papers (4030). **Holdings:** 5078 books;
765 unbound periodicals; 219 maps.

★791★
American Indian Archaeological Institute
Library
38 Curtis Rd.
Box 1260   Ph: (203)868-0518
Washington Green, CT 06793-0260 Fax: (203)868-1649
Dr. Russell G. Handsman, Dir. of Res.

Subjects: Prehistoric and historic American archeology; American
Indian literature, history, crafts; ethnobotany. **Holdings:** 2000 books.

★792★
American Indian Bible College
Dorothy Cummings Memorial Library
10020 N. 15th Ave.
Phoenix, AZ 85021-2199   Ph: (602)944-3335
John S. Rose, Dir.

Subjects: Biblical studies, Native Americans. **Special Collections:**
Native American collection. **Holdings:** 14,000 books; 625 microfiche;
780 audio cassettes.

★793★
American Indian Research Project
Library
17 Dakota Hall
University of South Dakota
Vermillion, SD 57069   Ph: (605)677-5208
Dr. Herbert T. Hoover, Dir.

Subjects: South Dakota and Indian history. **Special Collections:**
Jurrens Collection of Native American music (36 tapes); South
Dakota Folk Music (22 tapes). **Holdings:** 5000 audiotapes.
Remarks: Alternate telephone number(s): (605)677-5011.

★794★
Angel Mounds State Historic Site
Library
8215 Pollack Ave.
Evansville, IN 47715   Ph: (812)853-3956
Rebecca Harris, Cur.

Subjects: Native Americans, Mississippian Indians, nature, Indiana
history. **Holdings:** 100.

★795★
Arizona Historical Society
Library
949 E. 2nd St.
Tucson, AZ 85719   Ph: (602)628-5774
Margaret S. Bret-Harte, Hd.Libn.

Subjects: Southwestern Americana - Arizona territorial and state government, mining, Mexican history, Spanish North American colonial history, military history, ranching, Southwestern Indians. **Special Collections:** W.J. Holliday books and manuscripts (6113 items); Charles B. Gatewood military collection; Byron Cummings ethnological and archaeological collection; Frederick S. Dellenbaugh Colorado River collection; Aguiar Collection of early 19th century Mexican documents; Carl Hayden biographical files of 1854-1864 Arizonans; Will C. Barnes ranching and forestry papers; manuscript collections (1120). **Holdings:** 50,000 books; 5000 bound periodical volumes; 10,000 pamphlets; 5000 maps; 250,000 photographs; 1000 manuscripts; 750 linear feet of documents.

★796★
Arizona State Parks
Homolovi Ruins State Park Library
523 W. 2nd St.
Winslow, AZ 86047   Ph: (602)289-4106
Karen Berggren, Pk.Mgr.

Subjects: Anasazi culture; prehistory of Southwestern United States; Hopi, Navajo, and other Northern Arizona Indian cultures; history of Northern Arizona. **Special Collections:** Development documents of Homolovi Ruins State Park. **Holdings:** 200 books; 50 other cataloged items.

★797★
Arkansas State University
Museum
Library/Archives
Box 490   Ph: (501)972-2074
State University, AR 72467   Fax: (501)972-5706
Joanna Davis, Cur.

Subjects: History - Indian, American military, Arkansas, United States, European; old textbooks; religion; children's rare books; minerals and fossils. **Special Collections:** Rare newspapers, 1750-1960 (1500); sheet music, 1840-1950 (1050 pieces); Sharp County, Arkansas Courthouse Ledgers. **Holdings:** 5000 books; 6500 other cataloged items.

★798★
Augustana College
Center for Western Studies
P.O. Box 727
Sioux Falls, SD 57197   Ph: (605)336-4007
Arthur R. Huseboe, Exec.Dir.

Subjects: Upper Great Plains history and literature, American literature, Plains Indians history, South Dakota history, Sioux Falls history. **Holdings:** 30,000 books and bound periodical volumes; 1500 linear feet of manuscript, photograph, and artifact collections.

★799★
Bacone College
Library
Special Collections
East Shawnee
Muskogee, OK 74403   Ph: (918)683-4581
Frances A. Donelson, Libn.

Subjects: North American Indians, nursing, radiologic technology, religion. **Holdings:** 31,000 books; 4746 bound periodical volumes; 10 drawers of microfiche; 2 cabinets of microfilm; 20 video cassettes.

★800★
Bethel College
Mennonite Library and Archives
300 E. 27th   Ph: (316)283-2500
North Newton, KS 67117-9989   Fax: (316)284-5286
Dale R. Schrag, Dir. of Libs.

Special Collections: Includes H.R. Voth Manuscript and Photograph Collection on Hopi Indians; Rodolphe Petter manuscript collection on Cheyenne Indians. **Holdings:** 25,300 books; 3200 bound periodical volumes; 1000 reels of microfilm; 1000 audiotapes; 150 maps.

★801★
Bishop Baraga Association
Archives
444 S. 4th St.
Box 550   Ph: (906)225-1141
Marquette, MI 49855   Fax: (906)225-0437
Regis Walling, Archv.

Subjects: Bishop Frederic Baraga, Native Americans, Catholic Church, United States history. **Special Collections:** Baraga Collection (books, diaries, letters, 1830-1868); microfilm of the Office of Indian Affairs, early 1800s. **Holdings:** 1003 books; microfilm.

★802★
Bitter Root Valley Historical Society
Ravalli County Museum
Miles Romney Memorial Library
Old Court House
205 Bedford Ave.
Hamilton, MT 59840   Ph: (406)363-3338
Helen Ann Bibler, Dir.

Subjects: Pioneer and Indian history. **Special Collections:** Indian Collection; Granville Stuart Collection; Western News Files, 1890-1977; Ravalli Republican Files, 1899 to present; Northwest Tribune Files, 1906-1950; Stevensville Register Files, 1906-1914; western history (two private libraries). **Holdings:** 500 books.

★803★
Black Hills State University
E.Y. Berry Library-Learning Center
Special Collections
1200 University   Ph: (605)642-6833
Spearfish, SD 57799-9511   Fax: (605)642-6298
Dora Ann Jones, Spec.Coll.Libn.

Subjects: Local and regional history, biography, Dakota Indians, western industry, transportation, North American Indians. **Special Collections:** E.Y. Berry Collection (manuscripts, photographs, color slides, tape recordings, and films, all dealing with his 20 years of service in the U.S. House of Representatives, 1951-1971); Black Hills State University Archives; Leland D. Case Library for Western Historical Studies; Library of American Civilization (microfiche); Wagner-Camp Collection (microcard); Cox Library (microfilm). **Holdings:** 12,392 volumes; 918 manuscript boxes; 54 VF drawers; 85 drawers of maps and photographs; 12,888 titles on 14,548 microforms.

★804★
Bridgeton Free Public Library
Special Collections
150 E. Commerce St.
Bridgeton, NJ 08302-2684   Ph: (609)451-2620
Patricia W. McCulley, Lib.Dir.

Subjects: Cumberland County history, local genealogy, Woodland Indians. **Holdings:** 2000 volumes, including newspapers, 1881 to present, bound and on microfilm; 20,000 Indian artifacts, 10,000 B.C. to circa 1700 A.D., collected within a 30-mile radius of the library.

★805★
Brown & Bain, P.A.
Library
2901 N. Central   Ph: (602)351-8039
Phoenix, AZ 85012-2788   Fax: (602)351-8516
Ellen Hepner, Libn.

Subjects: Law. **Special Collections:** Antitrust law; American Indian law; computer/technology law; trade secrets. **Holdings:** 30,000 volumes.

★806★
Buffalo Bill Historical Center
McCracken Research Library
Box 1000   Ph: (307)587-4771
Cody, WY 82414   Fax: (307)587-5714
Christina K. Stopka, Libn./Archv.

Subjects: Western American history and art, Indians of North America, firearms. **Special Collections:** William F. Cody Collection; Valley Ranch manuscript collection; Charles Belden Photo Collection; Mercaldo Photo Archives of Western subjects; photographs of noted Indians, military leaders, Indian campaigns. **Holdings:** 15,000 volumes; 30 volumes of press clippings; motion picture films; 616 reels of microfilm and 7000 books in the Yale Western Americana microfilm collection; 4000 slides; vertical files of gallery, museum, artist files, subject files.

★807★
Burlington County Lyceum of History and Natural Science
307 High St.   Ph: (609)267-7111
Mt. Holly, NJ 08060   Fax: (609)267-7495
C. Jackson Caldwell, Lib.Dir.

Subjects: Local history, American Indians. **Special Collections:** Bridgetown Library Collection; Nathan Dunn Collection; Henry Shinn Collection; Levis Collection; Judge William Slaughter Collection of the American Indian; Robert Mills' original plans for Mount Holly's landmark jail; Robert Mills' narrative on penal system revision. **Holdings:** 445 books; 1500 pamphlets, pictures, genealogical records, manuscripts, photographs, 1765 Library Charter. **Remarks:** Holdings listed are for the historical collection only. Maintained by Mount Holly Public Library and Langstaff Foundation.

★808★
The Cayuga Museum
Library
203 Genesee St.
Auburn, NY 13021   Ph: (315)253-8051
Peter L. Gabak, Dir.

Subjects: Central New York Indian and Cayuga County history, early sound motion pictures. **Special Collections:** General John S. Clark Collection of Indian history; Auburn Theological Seminary; Civil War; Case Film Research Laboratory materials; Cayuga County Historical Society collections and archives (1876-1973). **Holdings:** 3000 books; bound periodical volumes.

★809★
Charles Cook Theological School
Mary Mildred McCarthy Library
708 S. Lindon Ln.
Tempe, AZ 85281   Ph: (602)968-9354
Mark Thomas, Libn.

Subjects: Religion, Native Americans. **Special Collections:** Fey Collection (100 books); Indian Collection (1500 books); archives. **Holdings:** 11,000 books; 8 VF drawers.

★810★
Cherokee National Historical Society, Inc.
Cherokee National Archives
Box 515
TSA-LA-GI
Tahlequah, OK 74465   Ph: (918)456-6007
Tom Mooney, Archv.

Subjects: Cherokee history. **Special Collections:** W.W. Keeler (Principal Chief of Cherokees) papers; Cherokee National Executive Committee minutes, 1948 (origin) to 1970 (disbandment); Cherokee

Nation papers, 1969-1975; Earl Boyd Pierce (Counsel General of the Cherokee Nation) papers, 1928-1983; manuscript collections. **Holdings:** 3000 books; 500 bound periodical volumes; 100 reels of microfilm; 5 VF drawers of pamphlets; 7 VF drawers of papers and committee minutes.

★811★
Children's Museum of Indianapolis
Rauh Memorial Library
3000 N. Meridian St.
Box 3000   Ph: (317)924-5431
Indianapolis, IN 46206   Fax: (317)921-4019
Gregg Jackson, Libn./Archv.

Subjects: American history, American Indians, antiques, folk art, Indiana history, dolls, toys, museum studies, science, world cultures, education theory. **Special Collections:** Children's books (300). **Holdings:** 6000 books; 200 bound periodical volumes; 500 vertical file materials.

★812★
Church of Jesus Christ of Latter-Day Saints
Safford-Thatcher Stakes
Family History Center
1803 S. 8th Ave.
Safford, AZ 85546   Ph: (602)428-3194
Lorin W. Moffett, Dir.

Subjects: Genealogy. **Special Collections:** Indian Tribes (pamphlets); World Conference, 1969 (18 volumes); World Conference, 1981 (13 volumes); Genealogical Society Series (12 volumes). **Holdings:** 5000 books; 1087 bound periodical volumes; 3000 films; microfiche for genealogical research.

★813★
Colorado Springs Fine Arts Center
Reference Library and Taylor Museum Library
30 W. Dale St.
Colorado Springs, CO 80903   Ph: (719)634-5581
Roderick Dew, Libn.

Subjects: Art history, drawing, painting, sculpture, crafts, architecture, photography, graphic arts and printing, anthropology of the Southwest, museums and private collections. **Special Collections:** Santos; Indians of the Southwest; Latin American folk and Colonial art. **Holdings:** 27,000 books; 950 bound periodical volumes; 12 shelves of biographical files; 20 shelves of museum publications.

★814★
County of Los Angeles Public Library
American Indian Resource Center
Huntington Park Library
6518 Miles Ave.   Ph: (213)583-1461
Huntington Park, CA 90255   Fax: (213)587-2061
Tom Lippert, Libn.

Subjects: Indians of North America, including Southwest, Plains, Woodlands, and California Indians - history, tribal cultural histories, fine arts, religion, literature, laws and treaties. **Special Collections:** Federal Census Records (1880-1940); Current Events Files (652 subject headings; 12 VF drawers); Information and Referral File. **Holdings:** 9000 books; 35 16mm films; 65 titles in microform; 68 video cassettes; 400 audio cassettes; 300 federal and state documents.

★815★
Cranford Historical Society
Museum Library
124 N. Union Ave.
Cranford, NJ 07016   Ph: (908)276-0082
Patricia Pavlak, Cur.

Subjects: Local history, Indian artifacts, paintings. **Special Collections:** Harrison Huster Indian Collection; Victorian Parlor; early agricultural and household implements; Canton export china. **Holdings:** Books; pictures; clippings; articles; maps; oral history tapes; scrapbooks.

★816★
Crazy Horse Memorial Foundation
Library
University of North America
Avenue of the Chiefs
Crazy Horse, SD 57730-9998   Ph: (605)673-4681
Jessie Y. Sundstrom, Libn.

Subjects: American Indians, art. **Holdings:** 14,000 books.

★817★
Creek Indian Memorial Association
Creek Council House Museum
Library
Town Square
106 W. 6th St.
Okmulgee, OK 74447   Ph: (918)756-2324
Tommy A. Steinsick, Dir.

Subjects: Oklahoma history, Creek Indian history and culture. **Holdings:** 200 books; 60 bound periodical volumes; 2 VF drawers of clippings and biography notes; 150 documents and records of the Creek Nation.

★818★
Denver Art Museum
Frederic H. Douglas Library of Anthropology and Art
100 W. 14th Ave. Pkwy.   Ph: (303)640-1613
Denver, CO 80204   Fax: (303)640-5513
Margaret Goodrich, Libn.

Subjects: American Indians, African and Oceanic art, anthropology, primitive art. **Special Collections:** American Indians. **Holdings:** 6000 volumes; 144 linear feet of clippings; 840 linear feet of journals, serials, and monographs; U.S. government documents from the 19th and early 20th centuries.

★819★
Detroit Public Library
History and Travel Department
5201 Woodward Ave.
Detroit, MI 48202   Ph: (313)833-1445
James Tong, Chf.

Subjects: Political and social history, archeology, American Indians, geography, travel, biography. **Special Collections:** Map Collection (250,000 sheet maps; 4000 atlases). **Holdings:** 214,000 volumes; 92 VF drawers of travel pamphlets; 10 VF drawers of map publishers catalogs; 44 VF drawers; 8 Biography clippings.

★820★
Douglas County Museum
Lavola Bakken Memorial Library
Box 1550
Roseburg, OR 97470   Ph: (503)440-4507
Frederick R. Reenstjerna, Res.Libn.

Subjects: Douglas County history, Umpqua Indians, logging, sawmills and grist mills, marine history, mining, development of area towns, railroads, agriculture. **Special Collections:** Herbarium collection of Douglas County. **Holdings:** 2000 books; 200 vertical files of letters, diaries, manuscripts, census, cemetery records; 400 oral histories; 175 genealogies.

★821★
Dull Knife Memorial College
Dr. John Woodenlegs Memorial Library
Box 98
Lame Deer, MT 59043-0098   Ph: (406)477-8293
Joni A. Williams, Lib.Dir.

Subjects: Cheyenne history, sociology, psychology, human services. **Special Collections:** Cheyenne Collection (65 oral histories). **Holdings:** 10,000 books.

★822★
Earlham College
Quaker Collection
Lilly Library   Ph: (317)983-1511
Richmond, IN 47374   Fax: (317)983-1304
Thomas Hamm, Archv.

Subjects: Society of Friends (Quakers); Earlham College. **Special Collections:** Indian Affairs; collections of Chas. F. Coffin, Allen Jay, Barnabas C. Hobbs, Thomas E. Jones, David M. Edwards, William C. Dennis, Landrum Bolling, Josiah Parker, Elbert Russell, Marcus Mote, Clifford Crump, Esther Griffin White, Harlow Lindley; Earlham College Historical Collection; Willard Heiss; Homer L. Morris; Eli & Mahalah Jay; Joseph Moore; Indiana Yearly Meeting of Friends. **Holdings:** 12,000 books; 550 bound periodical volumes; 5000 pamphlets, manuscripts, photographs; 60 volumes of printed and bound theses; 250 audio cassettes; 1200 volumes of Quaker genealogy.

★823★
Edinboro University of Pennsylvania
Baron-Forness Library
Edinboro, PA 16444   Ph: (814)732-2780
          Fax: (814)732-2883
Barbara Grippe, Act.Dir.

Subjects: Art, history, literature. **Special Collections:** Southeast Asia; Erie Indians. **Holdings:** 323,619 books; 82,889 bound periodical volumes; 21,511 federal, state, U.N. documents; 1.2 million microforms.

★824★
ERIC Clearinghouse on Rural Education and Small Schools
Library
1031 Quarrier St.
Box 1348   Free: 800-624-9120
Charleston, WV 25325   Fax: (304)347-0487

Subjects: Education - rural, small schools, Mexican American, American Indian, Alaska Native, migrant, outdoor. **Holdings:** 300,000 documents on ERIC microfiche. **Also Known As:** CRESS.

★825★
Essex County Historical Society
Brewster Library
Court St.
Elizabethtown, NY 12932   Ph: (518)873-6466

Subjects: Adirondack history, folklore, literature; Indians of North America; Northern New York guidebooks; Essex County, New York. **Holdings:** 3038 books; 91 bound periodical volumes; 5000 pamphlets; 24 VF drawers of ephemera; 350 manuscripts; 32 reels of microfilm; 78 newspaper titles; 350 maps; 162 microforms and AV programs; 34 drawers of cemetery records.

★826★
The Farm Community
Farm School Library
Special Collections
50 The Farm
Summertown, TN 38483   Ph: (615)964-2325
Mary Ellen Bowe

Subjects: Classics, Native American lore, alternative energy, art, music, dance, world studies, history. **Holdings:** 3000 books; 100 maps.

★827★
Field Museum of Natural History
Webber Resource Center: Native Cultures of the Americas
Roosevelt Rd. & Lakeshore Dr.
Chicago, IL 60605   Ph: (312)922-9410
Alexia Trzyna, Div.Hd.

Subjects: Native North and South American culture and history; archaeology; contemporary Native American issues. **Special Collections:** Department of Anthropology archival photograph collection (6 albums); artifacts. **Holdings:** 1000 books; 35 periodical titles; 86 videotapes; 23 audiotapes; 45 maps; 140 teacher resources; activity boxes.

★828★
Fillmore County Historical Society
Historical Center
R.R. 1
Box 81 D
Fountain, MN 55935   Ph: (507)268-4449
Jerry Henke, Exec.Dir.
Subjects: History - Southeastern Minnesota, Southeastern Minnesota immigrants, agrarian history, agrarian machinery, Native American, rural lifestyles. **Special Collections:** Matthew Bue Photography Collection (5000 original glass negatives and photographs documenting life in Southeastern Minnesota, 1915-1950); Senator M. Anderson Collection (notes and documents on Minnesota government, 1927-1963). **Holdings:** 3700 books; 2200 bound periodical volumes; 1100 documents; 2800 nonbook items; 67 manuscripts.

★829★
Flint Institute of Arts
Library
1120 E. Kearsley St.
Flint, MI 48503   Ph: (313)234-1695
Christopher Young, Cur.
Subjects: Art - North American Indian, African, decorative, Oriental, contemporary; glass paperweights; painting; sculpture; photography. **Holdings:** 3500 books; catalogs of museums' collections; exhibition catalogs; prints; drawings.

★830★
Fort Lewis College
Center of Southwest Studies
Fort Lewis College Library   Ph: (303)247-7456
Durango, CO 81301   Fax: (303)247-7588
Richard N. Ellis, Dir.
Subjects: Southwestern U.S. history, American Indians, railroads, mining, energy, water. **Special Collections:** Spanish exploration and colonization; Indians of the Southwest; records of geological surveys; mining; military; newspapers; narrow gauge railroads; politics and government. **Holdings:** 9800 books; 500 bound periodical volumes; 2000 reels of microfilm; maps and photographs; manuscripts; college archives; personal papers; artifacts.

★831★
Frank Phillips Foundation, Inc.
Woolaroc Museum
Library
Rte. 3
Bartlesville, OK 74003   Ph: (918)336-0307
Linda Stone Laws, Cur. of Art
Subjects: Native American culture, art, early Americana, weaponry, natural history, history. **Holdings:** 800 books.

★832★
Free Library of Philadelphia
Social Science & History Department
Logan Square   Ph: (215)686-5396
Philadelphia, PA 19103   Fax: (215)563-3628
William Handley, Hd.
Subjects: History, biography, social sciences, books and printing, law, travels and geography, archeology, anthropology, bibliography, sports and games. **Special Collections:** American Indians (Wilberforce Eames); chess (Charles Willing); Confederate imprints (Simon Gratz); Regional Foundation Collection. **Holdings:** 167,500 volumes; 47,500 pamphlets; 19 VF drawers of clippings; 370 boxes of microcards; 4000 annual reports.

★833★
Fresno County Free Library
Special Collections
2420 Mariposa St.   Ph: (209)488-3209
Fresno, CA 93721   Fax: (209)488-1971
John K. Kallenberg, Libn.
Subjects: Fresno County - local history, architecture; American Indians - Mono, Miwok, Yokut. **Special Collections:** William Saroyan Collection (15,500 books, 432 periodicals, 4 linear feet of manuscripts, photographs); Leo Politi Collection; architectural photographs; Local History Collection (15 linear feet of oral history manuscripts, vertical files of ephemera, biographical sketches, broadsides, maps, pamphlets); Ta-Kwa-Teu-Nee-Ya-Y Collection (200 books). **Holdings:** 122 bound periodical volumes; 15 linear feet of archival materials; 15,000 microfiche; Fresno newspapers on microfilm (1840 to present).

★834★
Frontier Gateway Museum
Library
Belle Prairie Frontage Rd.
Box 1181
Glendive, MT 59330
Louise Cross, Cur.
Subjects: Homesteading in Montana, Indians of eastern Montana, prehistoric fossils, ranching, rural education, early businesses. **Special Collections:** Senator George McCone collection (40 items); M.E. Sutton Memorial Indian display (156 items); fossil collection. **Holdings:** 430 books; 290 unbound research items; 60 maps; 7 VF drawers of pictures; 14 VF drawers of clippings.

★835★
Fruitlands Museums
Library
102 Prospect Hill Rd.
Harvard, MA 01451   Ph: (508)456-3924
Maggie Stier, Cur.
Subjects: American Indians, 19th century American paintings, Transcendentalist history, Shaker history. **Special Collections:** Shaker and Transcendentalist manuscripts. **Holdings:** 5000 books, bound periodical volumes, and manuscripts; 200 unbound reports.

★836★
Fulton County Historical Society
Library
Rte. 3, Box 89
Rochester, IN 46975   Ph: (219)223-4436
Shirley Willard, Pres.
Subjects: Local history and genealogy, Elmo Lincoln (first movie Tarzan), Potawatomi Indians. **Special Collections:** Trail of Death removal of Potawatomi Indians from Indiana to Kansas in 1838; 40 volumes of newspapers, 1862-1921. **Holdings:** 4000 books; 15 file cabinets of clippings; 5 file cabinets of documents; 4 films; 25 rooms of archival materials.

★837★
Gallup Indian Medical Center
Medical Library
E. Nizhoni Blvd.
Box 1337
Gallup, NM 87301   Ph: (505)722-1119
Patricia V. Bradley, Med.Libn.
Subjects: Medicine, nursing, surgery, dentistry. **Special Collections:** Navajo Indian health. **Holdings:** 2000 books. **Remarks:** Maintained by U.S. Public Health Service - Navajo Area Indian Health Service.

★838★
Glassboro State College
Savitz Library
Stewart Room
Glassboro, NJ 08028
Ph: (609)863-6303
Clara M. Kirner, Spec.Coll.Libn.
Fax: (609)863-6313

Subjects: New Jersey history, early religious history, genealogy, Indians of North America, Revolutionary War, War of 1812, Grinnell Arctic expedition.

★839★
Grindstone Bluff Museum
Library
Box 7965
Shreveport, LA 71107
Ph: (318)425-5646
J. Ashley Sibley, Jr., Dir.

Subjects: Archeology, anthropology, regional American Indians, arts and crafts, geology, physical geography, nature. **Special Collections:** Caddo Indians; Arkansas-Louisiana-Texas archeological society journals (20 file drawers). **Holdings:** 5700 books; 2000 bound periodical volumes; 50 maps; 2500 slides; 50 original tape recordings; 2000 sound recordings.

★840★
Hartwick College
Stevens-German Library
Special Collections
Oneonta, NY 13820
Ph: (607)431-4440
Robert E. Danford, Dir.
Fax: (607)431-4457

Subjects: Indians of North America, especially Eastern Woodland Indians. **Special Collections:** Yager Collection of Rare Books; Congressman James Hanley papers concerned with Native Americans (2 cubic feet); Hatrwick Seminary records (40 cubic feet); Judge William Cooper papers (15 cubic feet); Willard E. Yager Manuscript Collection (15 cubic feet); John Christopher Hartwick Library (290 Files). **Holdings:** 6200 books; 200 bound periodical volumes; 200 folders of clippings; 1000 reels of microfilm; 3000 microfiche.

★841★
Heard Museum
Library and Archives
22 E. Monte Vista Rd.
Ph: (602)252-8840
Phoenix, AZ 85004-1480
Fax: (602)252-9757
Mario Nick Klimiades, Libn./Archv.

Subjects: American Indians, Native American art, ethnology, material culture, archeology, primitive art, Southwest travel, history, and exploration. **Special Collections:** Native American Artists Resource Collection (information on 8200 Native American artists); Fred Harvey Company papers and photographs. **Holdings:** 40,000 volumes; 300 films and videotapes; 10,000 photographs; slides; pamphlet file; clippings; museum archives; sound recordings; manuscripts.

★842★
Held-Poage Memorial Home & Research Library
603 W. Perkins St.
Ukiah, CA 95482-4726
Ph: (707)462-6969
Lila J. Lee, Libn.

Subjects: History - Mendocino County, California, U.S., Civil War; Pomo and other Indians. **Special Collections:** Writings of Edith Van Allen Murphey, Dr. John Whiz Hudson, Helen Carpenter. **Holdings:** 5000 books; 15,000 negatives; photographs; maps; bound county records; clippings; genealogies. **Remarks:** Maintained by Mendocino County Historical Society.

★843★
Hoard Historical Museum
Library
407 Merchant Ave.
Fort Atkinson, WI 53538
Ph: (414)563-7769
Helmut Knies, Cur.

Subjects: Black Hawk War, 1800-1840; local Indians and history; birds; quilts; furniture. **Special Collections:** Rare books on Black Hawk War, local history, and regional birds; Indian artifacts, 7000 B.C. to present; National Dairy Shrine Museum. **Holdings:** 5108 books; 4813 local pictures.

★844★
Huntington Free Library
Museum of the American Indian
Library
9 Westchester Sq.
Bronx, NY 10461
Ph: (212)829-7770
Mary B. Davis, Libn.

Subjects: Archeology and ethnology of Indians of the Western Hemisphere; linguistics; anthropology; history; current affairs. **Special Collections:** American Indian newspapers. **Holdings:** 17,000 volumes; 100 VF drawers; 50 manuscripts. **Remarks:** Museum also maintains archives.

★845★
Illinois State Historical Library
Old State Capitol
Springfield, IL 62701
Ph: (217)782-4836
Janice A. Petterchak, Hd.

Subjects: Illinois history, Lincolniana, Civil War history, Midwest Americana, Mormon history, Indian history, genealogy. **Special Collections:** Abraham Lincoln Collection (1425 manuscripts; 8000 books and pamphlets); Picture and Print Collection (250,000). **Holdings:** 166,000 volumes; 9 million manuscripts; 70,000 reels of newspapers on microfilm; 2000 maps; 3500 broadsides. **Remarks:** Maintained by Illinois (State) Historic Preservation Agency.

★846★
Indian and Colonial Research Center, Inc.
Eva Butler Library
Box 525
Old Mystic, CT 06372
Ph: (203)536-9771
Kathleen Greenhalgh, Libn.

Subjects: Indians, genealogy, colonial history. **Special Collections:** Elmer Waite collection of glass plate negatives of the area; rare American school books, 1700-1850 (300). **Holdings:** 2000 books; 954 manuscripts; 90 maps and atlases; 2000 early American notebooks; 69 boxes of bulletins and pamphlets; 2000 photographs. **Remarks:** Also maintains a museum.

★847★
Indian Temple Mound Museum
Library
139 Miracle Strip Pkwy.
PO Box 4009
Fort Walton Beach, FL 32548
Ph: (904)243-6521
Steve Tuthill, Musm.Dir.

Subjects: Archaeology and prehistoric people, anthropology, Native Americans, museum management, archaeological sites, Florida history. **Holdings:** 3500 books; 500 bound periodical volumes; 1500 slides and photographs.

★848★
Institute of American Indian and Alaska Native Culture and Arts Development
Library
College of Santa Fe Campus
St. Michael's Dr.
Box 20007
Ph: (505)988-6670
Santa Fe, NM 87504
Fax: (505)988-6446
Mary Young, Dir. of Libs.

Subjects: American Indian culture, history and technique of American Indian fine arts. **Special Collections:** Exhibition catalogs. **Holdings:** 18,000 books; 8 file drawers of archival materials; 9000 art slides; 4000 Indian slides; 24 file drawers of art catalogs; 27,826 Smithsonian Indian photographs; 8 file drawers of Indian newspapers; 60 tapes, 88 cassettes and 585 phonograph records of Indian music recordings; Indian newspapers. **Remarks:** Institute is not affiliated with the College of Santa Fe.

★849★
J.B. Speed Art Museum
Library
2035 S. 3rd St.   Ph: (502)636-2893
Louisville, KY 40208   Fax: (502)636-2899
Mary Jane Benedict, Libn.

Subjects: Art, decorative arts, architecture, archeology, film, photography. **Special Collections:** J.B. Speed's Lincoln Collection; Weygold Indian collection. **Holdings:** 14,285 books and bound periodical volumes; 54 VF drawers.

★850★
John Carter Brown Library
Box 1894   Ph: (401)863-2725
Providence, RI 02912   Fax: (401)863-3700
Norman Fiering, Dir./Libn.

Subjects: Discovery and exploration of North and South America to 1820; comparative colonization of the Americas, including Spain, Portugal, England, France, and Holland; impact of the new world on the old world, 1493-1800; history - maritime, science, printing. **Special Collections:** Braziliana; Caribbeana; maritime history; American Indian linguistics (books; manuscripts); history of cartography (2000 books); American Revolution (15,000 items); Arnold-Green papers (132 linear feet)- Bartlett papers (15 linear feet); Brown papers (681 linear feet); History of printing in the Americas (through 1820). **Holdings:** 55,000 volumes; 3000 bound periodical volumes; 1200 maps; 350 bound volumes of codices; 36 linear feet of manuscripts.

★851★
Joslyn Art Museum
Art Reference Library
2200 Dodge St.   Ph: (402)342-3300
Omaha, NE 68102   Fax: (402)342-2376

Subjects: American and European art, with emphasis on 19th and 20th centuries; Western and Native American art and history. **Special Collections:** Joslyn Museum history files. **Holdings:** 20,000 books; 3000 bound periodical volumes; 100 VF drawers on artists and museums; 500 bound bulletins and annual reports; 20,000 slides; 700 art reproductions.

★852★
Kankakee County Historical Society
Library
8th Ave. at Water St.
Kankakee, IL 60901   Ph: (815)932-5279
Carol A. Shidler, Dir.

Subjects: County and state history, Civil War. **Special Collections:** Indian artifact collection; photograph collection (6000); French-Canadian artifacts; newspaper collection, 1853-1987. **Holdings:** 4000 books; genealogies; city directories; manuscripts; documents; clippings; Civil War volumes.

★853★
Kansas Heritage Center
Library
Box 1275
Dodge City, KS 67801   Ph: (316)227-1616
Jeanie Covalt, Res.Libn.

Subjects: Frontier and pioneer life, Kansas, the West, Indians of North America, cowboys, cattle trade, transportation, agricultural history, folklore. **Special Collections:** Historical collections from the states of Kansas, Oklahoma, Arizona, Missouri, Colorado, and New Mexico. **Holdings:** 10,000 volumes; clippings; pamphlets; microfilm; filmstrips; slides; tapes and phonograph records; 16mm films; videotapes.

★854★
Kansas State Historical Society
Library
Historical Research Center
120 W. 10th St.   Ph: (913)296-3251
Topeka, KS 66612-1291   Fax: (913)296-1005
David A. Haury, Act.Dir.

Subjects: Kansas history, local history of other states, genealogy, American Indians, the West, American biography, Civil War. **Special Collections:** Kansas (20,974 books; 129,432 pamphlets); genealogy and local history (18,262 books; 7225 pamphlets); American Indians and the West (4721 books; 2115 pamphlets). **Holdings:** 132,973 books; 25,651 bound periodical volumes; 74,086 bound volumes of Kansas newspapers; 12,373 bound volumes of out-of-state newspapers; 1977 volumes of clippings; 51,706 reels of microfilm; 194 titles on microcard.

★855★
Kendall College
Library
Special Collections
2408 Orrington Ave.   Ph: (708)866-1322
Evanston, IL 60201   Fax: (312)866-1320
Iva M. Freeman, Dir.

Special Collections: North American Collection (Indian museum); Culinary Collection. **Holdings:** 30,000 books.

★856★
Kendall College
Mitchell Indian Museum
Library
2408 Orrington Ave.   Ph: (708)866-1395
Evanston, IL 60201   Fax: (708)866-1320
Jane T. Edwards, Dir./Cur.

Subjects: Native Americans - history, anthropology, art, literature, ethnography. **Special Collections:** Jesuit relations; Bureau of Ethnology reports. **Holdings:** 1100 books; 14 AV programs.

★857★
Kent Historical Society
Library
R.D. 1
Box 321
Kent, CT 06757   Ph: (203)927-3055
Emily Hopson, Info.Dir.

Subjects: Local history, settlement, development; Scaticook Indians; iron industry; genealogy. **Special Collections:** Collection of the works of George Lawrence Nelson (paintings and lithographs); photographs of early Kent (1000). **Holdings:** 20 VF drawers; ledgers.

★858★
Klamath County Museum
Research Library
1451 Main St.
Klamath Falls, OR 97601   Ph: (503)883-4208
Patsy H. McMillan, Musm.Dir.

Subjects: Oregon and local history, Modoc and Klamath Indians, Modoc Indian War. **Special Collections:** Modoc Indian War collection; oral history collection. **Holdings:** 1500 books; photo/document archives; microfilm.

★859★
Lake County Historical Society
Library
Box 1011
Lakeport, CA 95453   Ph: (707)279-4466
Norma Wright, Pres.

Subjects: Lake County Historical Society and Genealogical Society, mid-1800s to present; Pomo Indian history and culture; early pioneers. **Holdings:** 2200 photographs; 8200 manuscript pages; genealogical data; oral history tapes.

★860★
Lake Superior State University
Kenneth J. Shouldice Library
Michigan & Marine Collections
Sault Ste. Marie, MI 49783   Ph: (906)635-2402
Dr. Frederick A. Michels, Dir.   Fax: (906)635-2193

Subjects: History of Michigan's Upper Peninsula; Indians of Michigan's Upper Peninsula; local history of Sault Ste. Marie, Michigan. **Special Collections:** Special editions and sources of Longfellow's "Hiawatha"; Marine-Laker Collection. **Holdings:** 1400 books; Sault Evening News on microfilm; 16 VF drawers of pamphlets concerned with local and area history.

★861★
Landmark Conservators
Cabots Old Indian Pueblo Museum
Library
67-616 E. Desert View Ave.   Ph: (619)329-7610
Desert Hot Springs, CA 92240   Fax: (619)329-1956
Colbert H. Eyraud, Pres./Cur.

Subjects: Indians, history, art, earthquake and geothermal data, weather logs, business. **Special Collections:** City Council and Planning Commission agenda and actions, 1968-1985; Desert Sentinel newspaper, 1946-1981 (microfilm); Earthquake Watch newsletter, 1980-1982; photographs of Wintun Culture Indians in northern California (from original 1901 glass plates). **Holdings:** 3500 books; 50 bound periodical volumes; 20 VF drawers of clippings; 4 boxes of old newspapers; 1500 78rpm records; 100 Edison cylinders.

★862★
Lehigh County Historical Society
Scott Andrew Trexler II Memorial Library
Old Court House
5th & Hamilton Sts.
Box 1548
Allentown, PA 18105   Ph: (215)435-1072
June B. Griffiths, Libn./Archv.

Subjects: Pennsylvania and Lehigh County history, genealogy. **Special Collections:** Allentown Newspapers, 1810-1916; family genealogies; photographs; Civil War; Allentown imprints; native Indians. **Holdings:** 8000 books; 200 newspaper volumes; 2000 pamphlets; 200 manuscripts, archives, records of local families and businesses; deeds; maps; church records.

★863★
Lewis County Historical Museum
Library
599 NW Front St.
Chehalis, WA 98532   Ph: (206)748-0831
Brenda A. O'Connor, Dir.

Subjects: History of Lewis County, Chehalis Indians, genealogy. **Special Collections:** Includes Chehalis Indian Archival Files. **Holdings:** 12,000 photographs; 400 oral history cassette tapes; 36 feet of archival papers and newspaper clippings; 3 feet of family histories; 200 maps.

★864★
Lompoc Museum Associates, Inc.
Research Library
200 S. H St.
Lompoc, CA 93436   Ph: (805)736-3888
Dr. Roy A. Salls, Dir., Cur. of Anthropology

Subjects: Chumash Indians, Indians of Southern California, Lompoc natural history, Lompoc history, archeology. **Special Collections:** Manuscripts; historical photographs. **Holdings:** 1500 books; 4 VF drawers; 150 maps; 350 slides.

★865★
Los Angeles Public Library
History and Genealogy Department
630 W. 5th St.   Ph: (213)612-3314
Los Angeles, CA 90071   Fax: (213)612-0529
Jane Nowak, Dept.Mgr.

Subjects: History, travel, biography, Californiana, genealogy, local history, heraldry, newspapers. **Special Collections:** Genealogy (38,000 volumes); Californiana (20,000 items); maps and atlases; American Indians; World Wars I and II; travel; Security Pacific Bank historic photograph collection; Herald Examiner Newspaper and Photograph Morgues. **Holdings:** 290,000 volumes; 91,000 maps; 2.7 million photographs; 800 historical specimen newspapers; 25,000 reels of microfilm of newspapers; U.S. city directories; census records. **Remarks:** Library located at 433 S. Spring St., Los Angeles, CA 90013.

★866★
Lutheran Bible Institute of Seattle
Library
Providence Heights
Issaquah, WA 98027   Ph: (206)392-0400
Irene A. Hausken, Hd.Libn.

Subjects: Bible; theology - doctrinal, moral, pastoral, devotional; religion and philosophy; Christian church; missions; psychology; social sciences; Christian education; youth work; gerontology; Pacific Northwest Indians. **Holdings:** 27,000 books; 143 bound periodical volumes; 550 books on microfilm; 465 audio cassettes; 95 videotapes; 27 kits; 12 VF drawers.

★867★
Malki Museum
Archives
11-795 Fields Rd.
Morongo Indian Reservation
Banning, CA 92220   Ph: (714)849-7289
Katherine Saubel, Pres.

Subjects: Indians of southern California. **Special Collections:** Indian basketry, artifacts. **Holdings:** Manuscripts; photographs; oral history tapes; field notes from various anthropologists including John Peabody Harrington.

★868★
Marathon County Historical Museum
Library
403 McIndoe St.
Wausau, WI 54401   Ph: (715)848-6143
Mary Jane Hettinga, Libn.

Subjects: State and county history, antiques, logging, Indian lore. **Special Collections:** Books published by Van Vechten and Ellis at the Philosopher Press in Wausau (20 volumes); John D. Mylrea Journals (15); James Colby photographs (5500 glass negatives); D.C. Everest personal papers. **Holdings:** 7000 books; 6000 maps and photographs; 80 manuscripts; 26 VF drawers of clippings.

★869★
Maricopa County Law Library
East Court Bldg., 2nd Fl.
101 W. Jefferson St.   Ph: (602)262-3461
Phoenix, AZ 85003   Fax: (602)262-3677
Elizabeth Kelley Schneider, Dir.

Subjects: Law and allied subjects, professional responsibility, law office management. **Special Collections:** Native American law; tax and labor law. **Holdings:** 145,000 volumes.

★870★
Marin Museum of the American Indian
Library
Box 864
Novato, CA 94948   Ph: (415)897-4064
Janet Larson, Adm.Off.

Subjects: Indians of the San Francisco Bay area, California, and North America; ethnobotany; Native American arts; anthropology. **Holdings:** Figures not available. **Remarks:** Library located at 2200 Novato Blvd., Novato, CA 94947.

★871★
Marquette University
Department of Special Collections and University Archives
Manuscript Collections Memorial Library
Memorial Library
1415 W. Wisconsin Ave.   Ph: (414)288-7256
Milwaukee, WI 53233   Fax: (414)288-5324
Charles B. Elston, Hd.

Subjects: Catholic social thought and action, Catholic Indian ministry, Marquette University history, Jesuits and Jesuit institutions, recent U.S. political history, Catholic religious formation and vocation ministries. **Special Collections:** Includes Catholic Conference for Interracial Justice Collection, 1956 to present (200 feet); Project Equality, Inc. Collection, 1971 to present (45 feet); Bureau of Catholic Indian Missions Records, 1852 to present (300 feet); Holy Rosary Mission Records, 1852 to present (22 feet); St. Francis Mission Records, 1878 to present (23 feet); Siggenauk Center Records, 1974 to present (6 feet); Kisenanito Center Collection, 1976-1987 (3 feet). **Holdings:** 12,000 volumes; 3000 bound periodical volumes; 8600 cubic feet of archives and manuscripts; 450 reels of microfilm; 4050 feet of manuscript collections relating primarily to Catholic social action and the history of Jesuits and Jesuit institutions, 1865 to present; 4150 cubic feet of Marquette University Archives, 1881 to present; 400 cubic feet of Catholic Indian mission records, 1852 to present.

★872★
Martin County Historical Society, Inc.
Pioneer Museum
Library
304 E. Blue Earth Ave.
Fairmont, MN 56031   Ph: (507)235-5178
Helen Simon, Cur.

Subjects: American Indians, Civil War, Minnesota history. **Special Collections:** Local newspaper file, 1874 to present (bound volumes of city and county papers). **Holdings:** 612 bound periodical volumes; 476 reels of microfilm of Martin County newspapers.

★873★
Metropolitan Museum of Art
Robert Goldwater Library
1000 Fifth Ave.   Ph: (212)570-3707
New York, NY 10028-0198   Fax: (212)570-3879

Subjects: Archeology; art - African, Latin American, Indians of North America, Oceania. **Special Collections:** Photograph Study Collection (160,000 art object and field photographs). **Holdings:** 35,000 volumes.

★874★
Millicent Rogers Museum
Library
Box A   Ph: (505)758-2462
Taos, NM 87571   Fax: (505)758-7551
Patrick Hoolihan, Assoc.Dir.

Subjects: Indians of North America, local history, fine arts, museology, anthropology. **Special Collections:** Registry of Hispanic artists in New Mexico (109 artists). **Holdings:** 2000 books; 81 subject classification files.

★875★
Minneapolis Public Library & Information Center
Special Collections Department
300 Nicollet Mall
Minneapolis, MN 55401-1992   Ph: (612)372-6648
Edward R. Kukla, Dept.Hd.

Special Collections: Includes Minneapolis Athenaeum Collections (North American Indians, Spencer Natural History, Early American Exploration and Travel, Heffelfinger Aesop's and Others' Fables, History of Books and Printing; 5000 volumes).

★876★
Minnesota Historical Society
Fort Snelling Branch Library
Fort Snelling History Center   Ph: (612)726-1171
Saint Paul, MN 55111   Fax: (612)297-1357
Libby Tweedale

Subjects: History - Minnesota, regional, military; American Indians; American and regional archeology; 19th century America. **Holdings:** 6000 volumes; 1500 other cataloged items.

★877★
Minnesota Historical Society
Special Libraries
690 Cedar St.
Saint Paul, MN 55101   Ph: (612)296-2489
Patricia C. Harpole, Chf., Ref.Libs.

Subjects: Minnesota, transportation, agriculture, arts, commerce, family life, industry, Indians. **Special Collections:** Hubert H. Humphrey Photograph Collection (25,000); Norton & Peel Commercial Photograph Collection (75,000); St. Paul and Minneapolis newspaper negatives (1 million). **Holdings:** 250,000 photographs; 2000 art works; 2000 films, tapes, videotapes; 2000 35mm slides; 25,000 maps; 3000 posters.

★878★
Minot State University
Memorial Library
Minot, ND 58701   Ph: (701)857-3200
Larry Greenwood, Lib.Dir.   Fax: (701)839-6933

Special Collections: North Dakota Collection; Indians of the North Central States; North Dakota government documents; U.S. government documents selective depository.

★879★
Missouri Historical Society
Archives
Jefferson Memorial Bldg.
Forest Park   Ph: (314)746-5410
Saint Louis, MO 63112   Fax: (314)746-4548
Peter Michel, Dir. of Lib. & Archv.

Subjects: St. Louis history and culture, Missouri, Mississippi Valley, American West. **Special Collections:** Papers, journals, field notes of William Clark from his expedition with Meriwether Lewis; Louisiana Territory documents; papers of Thomas Jefferson; French and Spanish colonial administration; western exploration; North American Plains Indians; French settlement; German immigrants; Mexican and Civil Wars; business and commerce in the Missouri area; Women's Suffrage Movement; William Torrey Harris (founder of the St. Louis Philosophical Society); Charles Lindbergh; Russian Revolution; American fur trade. **Holdings:** 6000 linear feet of archival materials.

★880★
Missouri Historical Society
Library
225 S. Skinker Blvd.
Saint Louis, MO 63105   Ph: (314)746-4500
Peter Michel, Dir. of Lib. & Archv.

Subjects: History - St. Louis, Missouri, Western United States, Missouri and Mississippi Rivers; fur trade; biography; genealogy; theater; music; Thomas Jefferson; early Mississippi travel; steamboats; Lewis and Clark expedition; American Indians. **Special Collections:** Western Americana; 16th century maps; music collection; early national newspapers; theater collection; scrapbook collection; 1904 World's Fair; Missouri Gazette collection (complete file). **Holdings:** 70,000 book, pamphlet, and periodical titles; 2000 bound newspaper volumes; 2500 maps.

★881★
Monroe County Library System
General George Armstrong Custer Collection
3700 S. Custer   Ph: (313)241-5277
Monroe, MI 48161   Fax: (313)241-4722
Carl Katafiasz, Spec.Coll.Coord.

Subjects: General George A. Custer, Battle of Little Big Horn, American Indians, Indian wars, the West, Civil War. **Special Collections:** Custer Collection; Dr. Lawrence A. Frost Collection of Custeriana. **Holdings:** 4000 books; 18 bound periodical volumes; 1600 unbound periodicals; 163 newspapers; 110 books on microfilm; 5380 slides; 35 maps; 100 pictures; 150 pamphlets; 23 original manuscripts; 35 AV programs; 170 microfiche; 60 cassettes.

★882★
Montana Historical Society
Library/Archives
225 N. Roberts   Ph: (406)444-2681
Helena, MT 59620   Fax: (406)444-2696
Robert M. Clark, Hd., Lib. & Archv.Div.

Subjects: Lewis and Clark Expedition; George Armstrong Custer; Charles M. Russell; military history of the Montana Indians; Montana biography/genealogy; mining; cattle and range; homesteading. **Special Collections:** T.C. Power papers; Senator Lee Metcalf papers; Thomas Teakle Collection of books and L.A. Huffman photographs on western cattle and range subjects (2300 books and periodicals; 1100 photographs); F.J. and Jack Ellis Haynes Northern Pacific Railroad and Yellowstone National Park Photograph Collection; Anaconda Copper Mining Company papers; state government archives (5500 cubic feet). **Holdings:** 50,000 books; 5000 bound periodical volumes; 50,000 state publications; 6500 cubic feet of private papers; 200,000 photographs; 14,000 reels of microfilm of Montana and other newspapers; 16,000 maps; 4000 broadsides and ephemera.

★883★
Montclair Art Museum
Le Brun Library
3 S. Mountain Ave.   Ph: (201)746-5555
Montclair, NJ 07042-1747   Fax: (201)746-9118
Edith A. Rights, Libn.

Subjects: American and American Indian art, Chinese snuff bottles. **Special Collections:** Bookplates collection (6000). **Holdings:** 12,500 books; 3500 bound periodical volumes; museum bulletins and catalogs of exhibitions; posters; 125 VF drawers of clippings, pictures, pamphlets; 17,000 slides; 50 tapes of museum programs and lectures.

★884★
Museum of the Cherokee Indian
Archives
US 441 North-Drama Rd.
Box 1599
Cherokee, NC 28719   Ph: (704)497-3481
JoAnn Orr, Archv.

Subjects: Cherokee history. **Special Collections:** A Guide to Cherokee Documents in Foreign Archives (microfilm). **Holdings:** 15,000 books; manuscripts.

★885★
Museum of New Mexico
Photo Archives
Box 2087
Santa Fe, NM 87504   Ph: (505)827-6472
Arthur L. Olivas, Photo.Archv.

Subjects: Includes history of New Mexico and the West, Indians, anthropology, archeology, and ethnology. **Special Collections:** History of photography; photographs by William Henry Jackson, Ben Wittick, John K. Hillers, Edward S. Curtis, T. Harmon Parkhurst, J.R. Riddle, H.F. Robinson, Henry D. Tefft, Ralph H. Anderson, Nathaniel Frucht, J.C. Burge, Ferenz Fedor, Wyatt Davis, George L. Beam George C. Bennett, H.H. Bennett, Wesley Bradfield, Charles F. Lummis, Tyler Dingee, Philip E. Harroun, Harold Kellogg, Royal A. Prentice, Henry A. Schmidt, J.S. Wooley, Jesse L. Nusbaum, D.B. Chase, Timothy O'Sullivan, Nicholas Brown, Emerson A. Plunkett, Edward A. Kemp, Christian G. Kaadt, James N. Furlong, Kilburn Bros., George T. Miller, William H. Brown, Edward A. Troutman, A. Frank Randall, Aaron B. Craycraft, O.C. Hinman, W.E. Hook, Matilda Coxe Stevenson,Carols Vierra, C.B. Waite, Augustin V. Casasola, George W. James, B.H. Gurnsey, Keystone View Co., Joseph E. Smith; international publications. **Holdings:** 2500 volumes; 225,000 photographic prints; 150,000 negatives; 75,000 color transparencies (35mm and 5x7); black/white photographs (35mm and 11x14); film and glass negatives; postcards; stereographs; photographs of artwork and graphics; photographs of collection objects in Palace of the Governors, Fine Arts Museum, Museum of Indian Arts and Culture, Museum of International Folk Art.

★886★
Museum of Northern Arizona
Harold S. Colton Memorial Library
Rte. 4, Box 720   Ph: (602)774-5211
Flagstaff, AZ 86001   Fax: (602)779-1527
Dorothy A. House, Libn.

Subjects: American Southwest - archeology, geology, paleontology, ethnology, natural history, history, art. **Special Collections:** Southwestern archeology; Navajo and Hopi Indians; geology of the Colorado Plateau. **Holdings:** 23,500 books; 400 periodical titles; 25,900 pamphlets; map and manuscript collections.

★887★
Museum of Western Colorado
Archives
248 S. 4th St.
Grand Junction, CO 81501   Ph: (303)242-0971
Judy Prosser-Armstrong, Archv./Reg.

Subjects: History - western Colorado, Mesa County, Grand Junction; anthropology of southwestern Indians; Colorado railroad history; paleontology. **Special Collections:** Wilson Rockwell Collection of Western Colorado History (300 items); Al Look Collection; Moore Family Collection of Frank Dean plate glass negatives (600); Palisade Library Collection (230 items); Warren Kiefer Railroad Collection (1300 items); Don Winslow Collection of Comic Art (113 items); Mesa County oral history collection (1700 items); institutional archives. **Holdings:** 3000 books; 800 collections of manuscripts and documents; 12,000 photographs and negatives; 200 maps.

★888★
Museums of the City of Mobile
Museum Reference Library
355 Government St.
Mobile, AL 36602   Ph: (205)434-7651
Caldwell Delaney, Musm.Dir.

Subjects: Mobile and Gulf Coast history, Civil War, American art, Indian culture, fire service. **Special Collections:** Julian Lee Rayford Folklore Collection; Mary Fenollosa Collection; negatives (6000); riverboat waybills (250 items). **Holdings:** 3000 books; 50 bound periodical volumes; 200 pamphlets; 300 historic newspapers; 300 Volunteer Fire Company records; 1400 colonial and Confederate manuscript documents; 2000 historic mercantile invoices.

★889★
Muskegon County Museum
Library
430 W. Clay Ave.
Muskegon, MI 49440   Ph: (616)722-0278
John McGarry, Dir.

Subjects: Muskegon County history, Woodland Indians, lumbering, natural history, Michigan history, museum operations. **Special Collections:** Charles Yates Collection of Historical Photographs of Muskegon (2000 photographs; corresponding newspaper articles and manuscripts); Willard Gebhart collection of landscape design. **Holdings:** 2000 books; 7000 photographs.

★890★
National Archives & Records Administration
National Archives
Pacific Sierra Region
1000 Commodore Dr.   Ph: (415)876-9009
San Bruno, CA 94066   Fax: (415)876-0920
Waverly B. Lowell, Dir.

Subjects: Archival records of the Federal Government in Nevada (except Clark County), Northern California, Hawaii, the Pacific Ocean areas. **Special Collections:** Records of the government of American Samoa; records of the Bureau of Indian Affairs, California and Nevada; Chinese immigration records; records of naval shipyards at Pearl Harbor, HI, and Mare Island, CA; records relating to World War II industry, labor, housing, and racial discrimination in employment; records of Federal district courts in Northern California, Hawaii, and Nevada, and of the U.S. Court of Appeals for the Ninth Circuit; records relating to scientific anf technical research in agriculture, aviation, civil and military engineering, fisheries, forestry, high-energy physics, river basins, and waterways; records relating to maritime history; records relating to migratory labor. **Holdings:** 32,000 cubic feet of original records; 31,000 reels of microfilm.

★891★
National Archives & Records Administration
National Archives
Southwest Region
501 Felix at Hemphill, Bldg. 1
Box 6216
Fort Worth, TX 76115   Ph: (817)334-5525
Kent Carter, Dir., Archv.Br.

Subjects: Inactive records of U.S. government agencies in Texas, Oklahoma, Arkansas, New Mexico, Louisiana. **Special Collections:** U.S. census reports, 1790-1910; index to Civil War records; passenger records from various ports; Bureau of Indian Affairs records from the state of Oklahoma. **Holdings:** 56,000 cubic feet of records; 40,000 reels of microfilm.

★892★
National Archives & Records Administration
Still Picture Branch
8th St. and Pennsylvania Ave., N.W.
NNSP-18N
Washington, DC 20408   Ph: (202)501-5455
Elizabeth L. Hill, Chf.

Subjects: AV materials; still photography; posters; United States - history, politics, government. **Special Collections:** Includes historical photographs from such agencies as: Indian affairs; Anta rtic exploration. **Holdings:** 7 million archival photographs from U.S. Federal Government agencies which document American and world cultural, social, environmental, economic, technological, political history of a nong overnmental nature as well as activities of military and civilian governmental agencies; historical photographs of precursors of contemporary governmental activity.

★893★
National Society, Daughters of the American
  Revolution
Library
1776 D St., N.W.   Ph: (202)879-3229
Washington, DC 20006-5392   Fax: (202)879-3252
Eric G. Grundset, Lib.Dir.

Subjects: Genealogy, U.S. local history, U.S. history, American Indian history, American women's history. **Special Collections:** Genealogies; United States, state, county, local histories; published rosters of Revolutionary War soldiers; published vital records; cemetery inscriptions; Bible records; transcripts of various county records (such as wills), compiled by the Genealogical Records Committees of DAR; published archives of some of the thirteen original states; abstracts of some Revolutionary War pension files; American Indian history, genealogy, culture; U.S. City Directory Collection, 20th century. **Holdings:** 110,000 books; 10,000 bound periodical volumes; 250,000 files of manuscript material, genealogical records, pamphlets.

★894★
Native American Center for the Living Arts
Library
25 Rainbow Blvd.
Niagara Falls, NY 14303   Ph: (716)284-2427
Elwood Green, Musm.Dir./Coll.Cur.

Subjects: Native American history and education; art of North, Central, and South America; museology. **Special Collections:** Smithsonian Institution Bureau of American Ethnology Reports (30 volumes); educational resources (50 titles); native periodicals. **Holdings:** 800 books; 200 bound periodical volumes; 65 newsprint periodicals; 5000 slides; 2500 newspaper clippings; 30 native music and oral history tapes; 5 films; 15 videotapes. **Remarks:** The center's Education Department resources are included in the library holdings.

★895★
Native American Educational Services College
Central Library and Resource Center
2838 W. Peterson   Ph: (312)761-5000
Chicago, IL 60659   Fax: (312)761-3808
Anne Valdez, Libn.

Subjects: Indian community development, education, human services, history, culture and religion, government and Indian law, economic development. **Special Collections:** Sol Tax Collection; Armin Beck Special Collection. **Holdings:** 5000 books; 500 pamphlets; 1000 articles; studies; papers; 37 linear feet archives. **Also Known As:** NAES College.

★896★
Native American Rights Fund
National Indian Law Library
1522 Broadway
Boulder, CO 80302-6296   Ph: (303)447-8760
Deana J. Harragarra Waters, Law Libn.

Subjects: Federal Indian law, U.S. government-Indian relations, Indians. **Special Collections:** Indian Legal Materials and Resources (5000 documents). **Holdings:** 7500 books; 35 bound periodical volumes.

★897★
Navajo Nation Library System
Drawer K   Ph: (602)871-6376
Window Rock, AZ 86515   Fax: (602)871-7304
Irving Nelson, Mgr.

Subjects: Navajos, Indians of the Southwest, Indians of North America, archeology, Arizona history. **Special Collections:** Navajo History; Native American Research Library; J.L. Correll Collection (30 filing cabinets); Navajo Times (80 acid-free boxes). **Holdings:** 22,000 books; 1000 manuscripts; 60 films; 250 tape recordings; microfilm. **Remarks:** Maintains two branch libraries in Window Rock, AZ, and one branch library in Navajo, NM.

★898★
Nebraska State Historical Society
Department of Reference Services
Library
1500 R St.
Box 82554
Lincoln, NE 68501   Ph: (402)471-4751
Amdrea I. Paul, Dir., Ref.Serv.   Fax: (402)471-3100

Subjects: Nebraska history, Indians of the Great Plains, archeology, Great Plains history, genealogy. **Holdings:** 80,000 volumes; 563 sets of Sanborn Fire Insurance maps of Nebraska; 2000 maps and 400 atlases relating to Nebraska, 1854 to present; 2500 photographs in Solomon D. Butcher Photograph Collection of Sod Houses; 465 photographs in John A. Anderson Photograph Collection of Brule Sioux; 247,000 other photographs; Nebraska state government publications repository, 1905 to present; 15,000 volumes of genealogical materials.

★899★
Nebraska State Historical Society
Fort Robinson Museum
Research Library
Box 304
Crawford, NE 69339   Ph: (308)665-2852
Tom Buecker, Cur.

Subjects: Nebraska history. **Holdings:** Fort Robinson records on microfilm; Red Cloud and Spotted Tail Agency records; diaries and interview manuscripts; newspapers of Crawford and Chadron, Nebraska.

★900★
Nebraska State Historical Society
John G. Neihardt Center
Research Library
Elm and Washington Sts.
Box 344
Bancroft, NE 68004   Ph: (402)648-3388
Lori Utecht, Cur.

Subjects: John G. Neihardt; American Indian culture and religion; Missouri River; fur trade; Nebraska and Plains history. **Special Collections:** First editions, essays, and reviews of works by John Neihardt (1 VF drawer); Bancroft Blade, June 21, 1904 to August 9, 1907 (2 reels of microfilm). **Holdings:** 202 books; 74 bound periodical volumes; 100 audiotapes and transcripts; 1 VF drawer of pamphlets and photographs; 3 dissertations; clipping files.

★901★
Nelson-Atkins Museum of Art
Slide Library
4525 Oak St.
Kansas City, MO 64111-1873   Ph: (816)561-4000
Jan McKenna, Slide Libn.

Subjects: Oriental, Occidental, and Native art - architecture, sculpture, bronzes, painting, ceramics, decorative arts, furniture, textiles. **Holdings:** 70,000 slides.

★902★
Nevada Historical Society
Library
1650 N. Virginia St.
Reno, NV 89503-1799   Ph: (702)688-1190
Peter L. Bandurraga, Dir.

Subjects: Nevada history, mining, Indians, and agriculture. **Holdings:** 10,000 books; 5000 bound periodical volumes; 3000 manuscript collections; 3500 reels of microfilm; 100,000 photographs; 20,000 maps.

★903★
Northeastern Oklahoma State University
John Vaughan Library/LRC
Special Collections and Archives
Tahlequah, OK 74464   Ph: (918)456-5511
Bela Foltin, Dean   Fax: (918)458-2197

Special Collections: Cherokee Indian Collection (589 volumes); E. Edmondson Papers (240 boxes); Government Document Depository (332,000). **Holdings:** 9565 books; 480 bound periodical volumes; 5172 microfiche; 1752 reels of microfilm.

★904★
Northeastern University
Libraries
Special Collections
360 Huntington Ave.
Boston, MA 02115   Ph: (617)437-2350
Alan R. Benenfeld, Dean

Special Collections: Louise Hall Tharp-Horace Mann Collection; Irish Studies Collection; North American Indian Collection; Glen Grey-Casa Loma Orchestra Collection.

★905★
Northern Arizona University
Cline Library
Special Collections and Archives Department
Box 6022   Ph: (602)523-5551
Flagstaff, AZ 86011   Fax: (602)523-3770
Randall R. Butler, Spec.Coll. & Archv.Coord.

Subjects: Arizona, Southwestern U.S., Colorado River and Plateau, Grand Canyon, Elbert Hubbard (Roycroft Press), Navajo and Hopi Indians. **Special Collections:** Includes Alexander and Dorothea Lieghton Collection, 1940 (Navajo field mat erials in anthropology); Apachean Language Collection, including Chiricahua dia lects (over 300 cassettes). **Holdings:** 31,000 books; 1900 bound periodical volumes; 2334 linear feet of manuscripts, records, and archival materials; 3500 pamphlets; 551 oral history tapes; 1 million photographs; 4344 reels of microfilm; 3545 regional historical maps.

★906★
Northern Indiana Historical Society
Frederick Elbel Library
808 W. Washington   Ph: (219)284-9664
South Bend, IN 46601   Fax: (219)284-9059
Kathleen Stiso Mullins, Exec.Musm.Dir.

Subjects: Native American history and language; Indiana history; French, Indian, English, and American occupations of Saint Joseph River Valley region; pioneer life; Schuyler Colfax. **Special Collections:** Oliver Chilled Plow Co. Records; Oliver Family personal papers, diaries, photographs. **Holdings:** 7500 books; 1500 pamphlets; 20,000 photographs; bound newspapers, 1831-1964; 300 boxes of archival manuscripts, dissertations, documents; clipping files; oral history tapes; videotapes.

★907★
Northwestern Oklahoma State University
Library
Alva, OK 73717   Ph: (405)327-1700
Ray D. Lau, Lib.Dir.

Subjects: Education, arts and sciences, Oklahoma and local history, library science. **Special Collections:** William J. Mellor Collection of Indian artifacts, paintings, sculpture, stereoptican and slides, rare books (1000 items); Children's Literature Collection. **Holdings:** 125,000 volumes; 110,000 government publications; 300,000 items on microfiche.

★908★
Oakland Public Library
American Indian Library Project
Dimond Branch Library
3565 Fruitvale Ave.   Ph: (510)530-3881
Oakland, CA 94602   Fax: (510)530-1623

Subjects: Native Americans - literature, culture, history. **Holdings:** 1500 books.

★909★
Oklahoma Historical Society
Archives and Manuscript Division
Historical Bldg.   Ph: (405)521-2491
Oklahoma City, OK 73105   Fax: (405)525-3272
William D. Welge, Dir.

Subjects: Oklahoma and Indian territories, Indian tribes of Oklahoma, pioneer life, missionaries, territorial court records, explorers. **Special Collections:** Records from all state Indian agencies, except Osage Agency (3.5 million document pages; 6000 volumes); Dawes Commission Records (48 cubic feet; 242 bound volumes); Indian-Pioneer History (interviews; 112 volumes); Whipple Collection (8 cubic feet); Joseph Thoburn Collection (20 cubic feet). **Holdings:** 2900 reels of microfilm of Indian and Oklahoma affairs; 125,000 historical photographs; 28,000 reels of microfilm of newspapers; 4500 oral history tapes.

★910★
Oklahoma Historical Society
Chickasaw Council House Library
Court House Square
Box 717
Tishomingo, OK 73460   Ph: (405)371-3351
Faye Orr, Historic Property Mgr.

Subjects: Chickasaw Indian history, biographies, and statistics.
Special Collections: Oklahoma Chronicles - Chickasaw Constitution
and law books. **Holdings:** 1200 books; 150 maps; county and
Chickasaw Nation records; 70 reels of microfilm; pamphlets.

★911★
Oklahoma Historical Society
Division of Library Resources
Wiley Post Historical Bldg.   Ph: (405)521-2491
Oklahoma City, OK 73105   Fax: (405)525-3272
Edward Connie Shoemaker, Lib.Dir.

Subjects: Oklahoma and American Indian history, American west,
Oklahoma genealogy. **Holdings:** 59,500 books; 10,600 reels of
microfilm of U.S. Census, 1790-1910; 25,000 reels of microfilm of
Oklahoma newspapers, 1893 to present.

★912★
Oklahoma Historical Society
Museum of the Western Prairie
Bernice Ford Price Reference Library
1100 N. Hightower
Box 574
Altus, OK 73522   Ph: (405)482-1044
Frances Herron, Libn.

Subjects: History of southwest Oklahoma, pioneer families, Plains
Indians, cowboys, early settlers. **Special Collections:** Long
Collection (Indians of southwest); Dr. E.E. Dale History Collection;
first editions of Oklahoma University Press. **Holdings:** 1500 books;
100 bound periodical volumes; documents; oral history tapes;
archival collections; photographs.

★913★
Orange County Historical Museum
Library
812 E. Rollins Ave.
Loch Haven Park   Ph: (407)898-8320
Orlando, FL 32803   Fax: (407)896-2661
Frank Mendola, Libn.

Subjects: Local and state history, Seminole Indians. **Holdings:** 1550
volumes; 900 directories and yearbooks; 400 scrapbooks and
ledgers; 57 photograph albums; 10,000 pictures; 350 maps; 17
linear feet of vertical file materials; 19 reels of microfilm and 131
sheets of microfiche of newspapers; 1 million feet of television news
film (1950s and 1960s); 50 oral history audio tapes.

★914★
Palomar Community College
Library
Special Collections
1140 Mission Rd.   Ph: (619)744-1150
San Marcos, CA 92069   Fax: (619)744-1150
Judy J. Carter, Dir., Lib./Media Ctr.

Holdings: Fine arts (15,500 volumes); American Indian (3400
volumes); Iceland (200 volumes); World War I poster collection.

★915★
Panhandle-Plains Historical Museum
Research Center
Box 967, WT. Sta.   Ph: (806)656-2260
Canyon, TX 79016   Fax: (806)656-2250
Claire R. Kuehn, Archv./Libn.

Subjects: Texas and Southwest history; ranching; Indians of the
Great Plains; archeology of Texas Panhandle; ethnology; clothing
and textiles; fine arts; antiques; museum science. **Special
Collections:** Interviews with early settlers collected over a period of
63 years; Bob Wills Memorial Archive of Popular Music, 1915 to
present (5000 phonograph records); Southwest regional
architectural drawings, 1978 to present (microfilm). **Holdings:**

15,000 books; 12,000 cubic feet of manuscripts; 20 VF drawers of
pamphlets; 800 maps; 1600 reels of microfilm; 45 cubic feet of
manufacturers' trade literature; 250,000 historic photographs.

★916★
Parmly Billings Library
Montana Room
510 N. Broadway
Billings, MT 59101   Ph: (406)657-8290
James E. Curry, Ref.Libn.

Subjects: Western U.S. and Montana history, Battle of Little
Bighorn, Crow Indians, other Montana Indian tribes. **Special
Collections:** Local histories (100); city archives (75 archival
materials). **Holdings:** 6000 books; 100 bound periodical volumes;
120 filing drawers.

★917★
Philbrook Museum of Art
Chapman Library
Box 52510   Ph: (918)748-5306
Tulsa, OK 74152   Fax: (918)743-4230
Thomas E. Young, Libn.

Subjects: Art. **Special Collections:** Roberta Campbell Lawson
Indian Library (1105 volumes). **Holdings:** 10,000 books; 7000 bound
periodical volumes; 196 VF drawers; 450 linear ft. of archival
materials. **Remarks:** Located at 2727 South Rockford Road, Tulsa,
OK 74114.

★918★
Phoenix Indian Medical Center
Library
4212 N. 16th St.   Ph: (602)263-1200
Phoenix, AZ 85016   Fax: (602)263-1669
Jean Crosier, Adm.Libn.

Subjects: Medicine, nursing, dentistry. **Special Collections:** Indian
history; Indian health. **Holdings:** 1800 books; 2000 bound periodical
volumes; 524 medical tapes; 3000 unbound journals; 5 VF drawers
of pamphlets and reprints.

★919★
Phoenix Public Library
Arizona Room
12 E. McDowell Rd.
Phoenix, AZ 85004   Ph: (602)262-4636

Subjects: Phoenix and Arizona history, Southwestern Indians,
Southwestern water and land use, Mexican Americans,
Southwestern art. **Special Collections:** James Harvey McClintock
papers, 1864-1934. **Holdings:** 17,500 books; 225 bound periodical
volumes; Phoenix municipal records; Arizona Republic clipping file,
1977-1990.

★920★
Ponca City Cultural Center & Museums
Library
1000 E. Grand Ave.
Ponca City, OK 74601   Ph: (405)765-5268
LaWanda French, Supv.

Subjects: American Indian, anthropology, archeology, American
cowboy, museology. **Special Collections:** Personal letters and
photographs of Bryant Baker, sculptor of the Pioneer Woman;
Ponca Indian music (tape recordings). **Holdings:** 200 books; 15
bound periodical volumes; VF drawers of unbound reports, clippings,
pamphlets, dissertations, documents.

★921★
Portland Art Museum
Library
1219 S.W. Park   Ph: (503)226-2811
Portland, OR 97205   Fax: (503)226-4842
Daniel G. Lucas, Act.Libn.

Subjects: Art. **Special Collections:** Art of Indian tribes of the Pacific
Northwest; Oriental art, especially Japanese prints; English silver
books. **Holdings:** 22,442 books; 1100 bound periodical volumes;
365 pamphlet cases of catalogs relating to artists, movements, and

exhibitions; 175 pamphlet cases of museum reports and bulletins; 71,500 slides. **Remarks:** Maintained by the Oregon Art Institute.

★922★
Queens Borough Public Library
History, Travel & Biography Division
89-11 Merrick Blvd.   Ph: (718)990-0762
Jamaica, NY 11432   Fax: (718)658-8312
Deborah Hammer, Hd.

Subjects: History, Indians of North America, biography, geography, travel, exploration. **Special Collections:** Carter G. Woodson Collection of Afro-American Culture and Life; Schomburg microfilm collection; U.S. Geographic Survey topographic maps (10,300); physical/thematic maps of countries of the world (126); nautical charts (8 kits); jet/ocean/world navigation charts (520); national forest maps (75); Latin American topographic maps (97); New York State planimetric maps (968); New York state, county, road maps (78); railroad transportation zone maps (82); historic/city maps (442). **Holdings:** 143,000 books; 3550 bound periodical volumes; 6800 microforms; 1 drawer of microfiche; 36 VF drawers of pamphlets; New York Daily News, 1950 to present; newspapers on microfilm.

★923★
Rochester Museum and Science Center
Library
657 East Ave.
Box 1480
Rochester, NY 14603   Ph: (716)271-4320
Leatrice M. Kemp, Libn.

Subjects: Natural sciences, anthropology, local history, American Indians, antiques, archeology, costume, technology, museology. **Special Collections:** Albert Stone Collection of local photographs, 1904-1934 (15,000); slide library. **Holdings:** 26,000 volumes; museum bulletins; archival material and ephemera.

★924★
Roswell Museum and Art Center
Research Library
100 W. 11th St.
Roswell, NM 88201   Ph: (505)624-6744
William Ebie, Dir.

Subjects: Art - contemporary, Native American, Spanish Colonial, Western United States; rocketry; archeology. **Holdings:** 2500 books; 3600 bound periodical volumes; 3500 color slides.

★925★
St. Joseph Museum
Library
11th at Charles   Ph: (816)232-8471
Saint Joseph, MO 64501   Fax: (816)232-8482
Richard A. Nolf, Dir.

Subjects: Local and area history, Western movement, ethnology, natural history. **Special Collections:** American Indian Collection; Civil War period local history collection; Pony Express; bird, mammal, and fish exhibits. **Holdings:** 6500 volumes.

★926★
Samford University
Harwell Goodwin Davis Library
Special Collections
800 Lakeshore Dr.
Birmingham, AL 35229   Ph: (205)870-2749
Elizabeth C. Wells, Spec.Coll.Libn.

Subjects: Alabama history, literature, and imprints; Early Southeast - Indians, travel, law; genealogical source records; Southern Reconstruction; Irish history and genealogy. **Special Collections:** William H. Brantley Collection (books; 19th and 20th century manuscripts; 18th and 19th century maps); Albert E. Casey Collection (books; manuscripts; periodicals; maps of Ireland); Douglas C. McMurtrie Collection; John Ruskin Collection; John Masefield Collection; Alfred Tennyson Collection; Lafcadio Hearn Collection. **Holdings:** 25,653 books; 2562 bound periodical volumes; 806 microcards; 349 phonograph records; 2725 maps; 1477 linear feet of manuscripts; 7739 reels of microfilm; 7828 prints and photographs; 3113 microfiche; 150 oral histories; 37 atlases; 1 globe; 60 relief models.

★927★
San Antonio Museum Association
Ellen Schultz Quillin Memorial Library
Box 2601   Ph: (512)820-2131
San Antonio, TX 78299-2601   Fax: (512)820-2109
George Anne Cormier, Libn.

Subjects: Texana; art - American, Indian, folk, decorative; natural history; history; antiquities; oriental anthropology. **Holdings:** 14,000 books; 4000 bound periodical volumes; 20 drawers of documents, maps, pictures; 12 VF drawers; 25 boxes of archival materials; 17,000 slides. **Remarks:** The association maintains libraries for the Witte Memorial Museum and the San Antonio Museum of Art, located at 3801 Broadway, San Antonio, TX 78209.

★928★
San Diego Museum of Man
Scientific Library
Balboa Park
1350 El Prado   Ph: (619)239-2001
San Diego, CA 92101   Fax: (619)239-2749
Jane Bentley, Libn.

Subjects: Anthropology, pre-Columbian art, Indians of the Americas, archeology, ethnology, physical anthropology. **Special Collections:** North American Indians. **Holdings:** 6500 books; 5500 bound periodical volumes; 51 archival manuscripts.

★929★
San Diego Public Library
Special Collections
Wangenheim Room
820 E St.
San Diego, CA 92101   Ph: (619)236-5807
Eileen Boyle, Libn.

Subjects: History of printing and the development of the book with specimens ranging from cuneiform tablets to cassettes; famous presses and modern private presses; incunabula; fine book bindings. **Special Collections:** Dime novels (769 items); bookplates (6000); fore-edge paintings (185 volumes); works of Kate Greenaway (65 volumes); works of John Ruskin (250 volumes); Curtis' North American Indians (20 volumes and 20 portfolios of photographs); Monumenta Scenica (12 portfolios); Grayson's Birds of the Pacific Slope (158 plates). **Holdings:** 9550 books; selected antiquarian book dealers' catalogs; periodicals; manuscripts; autographs; artifacts.

★930★
San Juan County Archaeological Research Center & Library
P.O. Box 125   Ph: (505)632-2013
Bloomfield, NM 87413   Fax: (505)632-1707
Penny Whitten, Libn.

Subjects: Southwest archeology, history, anthropology, natural science. **Special Collections:** Slide/tape programs; historical records of San Juan Basin (3 VF drawers); Four Corners area rock art (1700 slides and photographs); archival records of excavation of Salmon Ruin Site (60 feet); Navaho Mythology Collection. **Holdings:** 2600 books and monographs; 6630 reports and pamphlets; 2250 journals and periodicals; 1 VF drawer of clippings; 1 VF drawer of photographs; 36 oral history tapes and transcriptions; 10 videotapes; 3 VF drawers of botany specimens; 5 drawers of historic maps; children's section (30 books, 4 slide shows). **Formerly:** Located in Farmington, NM. **Remarks:** Library located at the upper level of the Research Center. Maintained by the San Juan County Museum Association.

★931★
Santa Barbara Museum of Natural History
Library
2559 Puesta del Sol Rd.   Ph: (805)682-4711
Santa Barbara, CA 93105   Fax: (805)569-3170
Susan G. Dixon, Libn.

Subjects: Natural history - anthropology, botany, geology, zoology, astronomy. **Special Collections:** Chumash Indians; Harrington California Indian Archives; Stillman Berry Malacology Collection; Channel Islands Archive; Dick Smith Archives; Pacific Voyages Collection; antique nature illustrations. **Holdings:** 30,000 volumes; 200 feet of reprints.

★932★
Sara Hightower Regional Library
Special Collections
205 Riverside Pkwy.
Rome, GA 30161
Jacqueline D. Kinzer, Cur.

Ph: (404)236-4607
Fax: (404)236-4605

Subjects: Cherokee Indians, Georgia and local history, genealogy, Southern history, Civil War. **Special Collections:** J.F. Brooks Cherokeeana Collection (401 books); Ellen Louise Axson Wilson Collection; John L. Harris Papers (3 VF drawers); George M. Battey, III, Papers (5 VF drawers); Civil War collection; Yancey Lipscomb Collection (4 VF Drawers). **Holdings:** 12,000 books; 30 VF drawers; 350 maps; 7000 microforms; 450 unbound periodicals.

★933★
School of American Research
Library
Box 2188
Santa Fe, NM 87504-2188
Jane P. Gillentine, Libn.

Ph: (505)982-3583

Subjects: Anthropology, archeology, ethnology, Southwest Indian arts. **Holdings:** 6000 books; 300 bound periodical volumes.

★934★
Seton Memorial Library
Philmont Scout Ranch
Cimarron, NM 87714
Stephen Zimmer

Ph: (505)376-2281

Subjects: Books written by Ernest T. Seton, Boy Scouts, Southwest, natural history, Indian Art, Bureau of American Ethnology. **Special Collections:** Ernest T. Seton Collection (200 volumes; 7 VF drawers of manuscripts and correspondence). **Holdings:** 6000 books; 250 bound periodical volumes; 2000 photographs; local archeology reports (2 VF drawers). **Remarks:** Maintained by Boy Scouts of America-Philmont Scout Ranch.

★935★
Sharlot Hall/Prescott Historical Societies
Library/Archives
415 W. Gurley St.
Prescott, AZ 86301
Sue Abbey, Archv.

Ph: (602)445-3122

Subjects: Anglo and Indian history of the Southwest, especially Arizona; Arizona history and mining. **Special Collections:** Sharlot Hall Collection (7 cubic feet); cowboy folklore and music collection (100 cassette tapes). **Holdings:** 9000 volumes; 200 linear feet of uncataloged items; 200 oral history/folklore tapes; photographs; manuscripts; diaries; artifacts; letters.

★936★
Siouxland Heritage Museums
Library
200 W. 6th St.
Sioux Falls, SD 57102
William J. Hoskins, Cur. of Coll.

Ph: (605)339-7097

Subjects: South Dakota history; U.S. history - silver question; 19th century works on ethnology and natural science; Indians. **Special Collections:** Arthur C. Phillips Collection; Northern League Baseball records (4 linear feet); library and private papers of U.S. Senator R.F. Pettigrew (1000 volumes); South Dakota history (1500 items). **Holdings:** 9000 books; 200 bound periodical volumes; 100 maps; 150 linear feet of manuscripts; 10,000 photographs.

★937★
Skagit County Historical Museum
Historical Reference Library
Box 818
La Conner, WA 98257
Nancy Van Dyke Dickison, Archv.Mgr.

Ph: (206)466-3365

Subjects: Skagit County history, pioneer family genealogies, local Indian histories, late 19th century novels. **Special Collections:** Diaries of Grant Sisson, W.J. Cornelius, Arthur Champenois, and others, 1844-1964; Darius Kinsey Photographs; personal and legal papers of Key Pittman, U.S. Senator from Nevada, 1913-1940. **Holdings:** 1500 books; 308 bound periodical volumes; 6000

photographs; 599 newspapers; 658 business documents; 109 old letters; 106 old district school accounts/records; 81 maps; 626 clippings and clipping scrapbooks; 183 old programs/announcements; 64 pioneer diaries; 220 oral history tapes with transcripts; old American popular music, 1866-1954; local newspapers, 1900 to present.

★938★
Southern Utah State College
Library
Special Collections Department
351 W. Center St.
Cedar City, UT 84720
Blanche C. Clegg, Spec.Coll.Coord.

Ph: (801)586-7945

Subjects: Southern Paiute Indians history, local history, college history, Shakespeare. **Special Collections:** William Rees Palmer Western History Collection; Document Collection (various donors); John Laurence Seymour Collection (music, theater, humanities). **Holdings:** 7000 volumes; 925 oral history tapes; 457 phonograph records; 1445 linear feet of manuscript collections; 36,500 photographs and negatives; 804 linear feet of archives; 7530 microforms; 570 maps.

★939★
Southwest Arkansas Regional Archives (SARA)
Box 134
Washington, AR 71862
Mary Medearis, Dir.

Ph: (501)983-2633

Subjects: History of Southwest Arkansas, Caddo Indians. **Special Collections:** Rare books collection on Southwest Arkansas and Texas; census and court records for twelve southwest Arkansas counties; newspapers of southwest Arkansas; index and service records for Civil War soldiers who served in Arkansas units. **Holdings:** 1500 books; 3000 reels of microfilm; original court records of Hempstead County, 1819-1910; pictures; manuscripts; family histories; theses; sheet music; newspapers; maps; pamphlets; journals; genealogical records.

★940★
Southwest Museum
Braun Research Library
PO Box 41558
Los Angeles, CA 90041-0558
Kim Walters, Library Director

Ph: (213)221-2164
Fax: (213)224-8223

Subjects: Anthropology, Native American studies, western history. **Special Collections:** Munk Library of Arizoniana; Hector Alliott Memorial Library of Archaeology; Charles F. Lummis Collection; George Wharton James Collection; papers of Frank Hamilton Cushing, John Charles Fremont, George Bird Grinnell, Frederick Webb Hodge, Charles F. Lummis; rare Western American imprints; children's books. **Holdings:** 50,000 volumes; 100,000 pamphlets and ephemera; 120,000 photographs; 700 linear feet of manuscripts; 1300 sound recordings; government publications; VF drawers. **Remarks:** Library located at 234 Museum Dr., Los Angeles, CA 90065.

★941★
State Capital Historical Association
Library and Photo Archives
211 W. 21st Ave.
Olympia, WA 98501
Derek R. Valley, Dir.

Ph: (206)753-2580

Subjects: Washington history, Victoriana, museology, art. **Special Collections:** Collection of Washington photographs, including early photos of pioneers, towns, industries, Indians, and state governments; archives of Northwest Indian art. **Holdings:** 3000 historical photographs.

★942★
State Historical Society of Iowa
Library/Archives Bureau
600 E. Locust
Des Moines, IA 50319
Nancy Kraft, Bureau Chf.

Ph: (515)281-5111
Fax: (515)282-0502

Subjects: History - Iowa, agriculture, railroad, regional Indians; historic preservation; genealogy. **Special Collections:** State

Archives (17,000 cubic feet); historical Iowa photographs (100,000 images); Aldrich Autograph Collection (4000 items); Iowa historical maps (3000); Manuscript collections - Grenville Dodge, Charles Mason, Albert Cummins, William Boyd Allison, John A. Kasson. **Holdings:** 60,000 books; 5000 bound periodical volumes; 2500 linear feet of manuscripts; 25,000 reels of microfilm; 5000 bound newspapers; 42 VF drawers of pamphlets and clippings.

★943★
State Historical Society of Iowa
Library/Archives Bureau
402 Iowa Ave.
Iowa City, IA 52240   Ph: (319)335-3916
Nancy Kraft, Bureau Chf.

Subjects: History - Iowa, the frontier, agriculture, railroad, women, education in Iowa, Indians of the region; genealogy. **Special Collections:** Robert Lucas papers; Jonathan P. Dolliver papers; Gilbert Haugen papers; Cyrus Carpenter papers; Iowa industry house organs; historical Iowa photographs (265,000); historical Iowa maps (3000). **Holdings:** 130,000 books; 10,000 bound periodical volumes; 15,000 pamphlets; 17,000 reels of microfilm; 10,000 bound newspapers; 25 VF drawers of newspaper clippings; 1800 oral history interviews; 4000 linear feet of manuscripts.

★944★
Sunset Trading Post-Old West Museum
Library
Rte. 1
Sunset, TX 76270   Ph: (817)872-2027
Jack Glover, Owner

Subjects: Barbed wire, frontier, American Indian, cowboys and cattlemen, Civil War, Western painting, county history, guns and knives. **Special Collections:** Barbed Wire. **Holdings:** 2500 books; 200 pamphlets; clippings; drawings; Indian artifacts; Bronzes of the West by Jack Glover; unpublished stories; pictures; negatives.

★945★
Texas State Library
Local Records
Box 12927
Austin, TX 78711   Ph: (512)463-5478
Marilyn von Kohl, Dir.

Subjects: Texas - vital statistics, judicial proceedings, education, economic development, politics, family history/biography. **Special Collections:** Tidelands Case Papers of Justice Price Daniel (130 cubic feet); congressional and other papers of Representative Martin Dies; early manuscripts and photographs of Sam Houston, David G. Burnet, and others (400 cubic feet); early Texas furniture; American Indian artifacts. **Holdings:** 5200 books; 13,000 cubic feet of local government records; vital statistics records of county and district clerks on microfilm.

★946★
Thomas Gilcrease Institute of American History and Art
Library
1400 Gilcrease Museum Rd.
Tulsa, OK 74127   Ph: (918)582-3122
Sarah Erwin, Cur., Archv.Coll.

Subjects: History - Colonial, Western, Spanish Southwest, Indian. **Special Collections:** Hispanic documents, 1500-1800; John Ross papers (Chief of Cherokees, 1814-1870); Peter P. Pitchlynn papers (Chief of Choctaws); Grant Foreman Collection. **Holdings:** 50,000 books; 50 VF drawers of historic photographs and manuscripts; broadsides; maps; photostats.

★947★
Traphagen School of Fashion
Ethel Traphagen Leigh Memorial Library
686 Broadway
New York, NY 10012   Ph: (212)673-0300
Janet Harris, Dir. of Oper.

Subjects: Fashion design and illustration, history of costume, visual arts, art history, customs of mankind, American Indian arts and customs, interior decorating, architecture, fashion merchandising, fashion marketing, business management and marketing, textile arts

and industry. **Special Collections:** Rare late 18th and 19th century fashion periodicals of France, England, Germany, and America; Harper's Bazaar and Vogue, from their inception to the present; Ethnic Costume publications of many nations and religions (lithographs, original drawings). **Holdings:** 5000 books; 600 bound periodical volumes; 4 VF drawers of clippings; 550 unbound periodicals; slides. **Remarks:** Affiliated with Tobe Coburn School for Fashion Careers - Library.

★948★
Trinity College
Watkinson Library
300 Summit St.   Ph: (203)297-2268
Hartford, CT 06106   Fax: (203)297-2251
Dr. Jeffrey H. Kaimowitz, Cur.

Subjects: Americana (especially 19th century), American Indians, black history, U.S. Civil War, British history and topography, folklore, witchcraft, graphic arts, history of printing, natural history, horology, philology (especially American Indian languages), early voyages and travels, maritime history. **Holdings:** 165,000 books and bound periodical volumes; atlases; 500 maps; printed ephemera including 100 indexed scrapbooks, advertisements, fashion plates, music and theater programs, and valentines.

★949★
U.S. Department of the Interior
Bureau of Indian Affairs
Southwestern Indian Polytechnic Institute
Library
9169 Coors Blvd., N.W.
Box 10146
Albuquerque, NM 87184   Ph: (505)897-5340
Paula M. Smith, Libn.

Subjects: Vocational-technical curriculum, American Indians, recreational reading. **Special Collections:** American Indian Collection (2240 volumes; 25-35 newspapers and newsletters). **Holdings:** 26,000 books; 100 bound periodical volumes; 100 audio cassettes; 300 video cassettes; 16mm films. **Remarks:** The Bureau of Indian Affairs is part of the U.S. Department of the Interior.

★950★
U.S. Department of the Interior
Indian Arts and Crafts Board
Library
18th & C Sts., N.W., Rm. 4004-MIB
Washington, DC 20240   Ph: (202)208-3773
Robert G. Hart, Gen.Mgr.

Subjects: Contemporary Native American arts and crafts. **Remarks:** The Indian Arts and Crafts Board serves Indians, Eskimos, Aleuts, and the general public as an information, promotional, and advisory clearinghouse for all matters pertaining to the development of authentic Native American arts and crafts.

★951★
U.S. Department of the Interior
Law Branch Library
1849 C St., N.W., Rm. 7100W   Ph: (202)208-4571
Washington, DC 20240   Fax: (202)268-4714
Bernard Sussman, Act.Lib.

Subjects: Law - public land, Indian, natural resources, administrative, environmental. **Special Collections:** Pre-Federal Register regulations of the Department of the Interior (1000 pieces); Native American Legal Materials (500 microfiche). **Holdings:** 30,000 books; 2000 bound periodical volumes; 10,000 microfiche; 1000 reels of microfilm; 3000 microfiche of Indian Claims Commission materials; 10 reels of microfilm of executive orders; 1000 microfiche of Council of State Governments publications; 700 legislative histories.

★952★
U.S. Department of the Interior
Natural Resources Library
18th & C Sts., N.W.
Washington, DC 20240   Ph: (202)208-5815

Subjects: Conservation, energy and power, land use, parks, American Indians, fish and wildlife, mining, law, management.

Special Collections: Archival collection of materials published by Department of Interior (150,000 items). **Holdings:** 600,000 books; 90,000 bound periodical volumes; 7000 reels of microfilm; 40,000 unbound periodical volumes; 300,000 microfiche. **Remarks:** Library operated by Aspen System Corporation under contract to the Department of the Interior. Government manager, tel. (202)208-5435.

★953★
U.S. Department of Justice
Environment and Natural Resources Branch Library
10th & Pennsylvania Ave., N.W., Rm.
  2333
Washington, DC 20530   Ph: (202)514-2768
Leola Decker, Libn.

Subjects: Civil cases regarding lands, titles, water rights, Indian claims, hazardous waste, public works, pollution control, marine resources, fish and wildlife, environment. **Special Collections:** Legislative histories. **Holdings:** 18,000 volumes. **Formerly:** Its Land and Natural Resources - Branch Library. **Remarks:** A branch library is maintained 601 Pennsylvania Ave., N.W., Rm. 6308, Washington, DC 20530.

★954★
U.S. Library of Congress
American Folklife Center
Thomas Jefferson Bldg. - G152
Washington, DC 20540   Ph: (202)707-6590
Alan Jabbour, Dir.

Special Collections: Includes the Smithsonian Institution/Frances Densmore American Indian Collection (3700 cylinders) and the Helen Heffron Roberts' Collection of California and Northwest Indian recordings. The American Folklife Center holds the largest collection of early Indian recordings.

★955★
U.S. Library of Congress
General Reading Rooms Division
Microform Reading Room Section
Thomas Jefferson Bldg. - LJ-140B
Washington, DC 20540   Ph: (202)707-5471
Betty Culpepper, Hd.

Subjects: Includes photographs from the Smithsonian's National Anthropological Archives; annual reports from the Bureau of Indian Affairs; reports from the Indian Claims Commission; and other holdings relating to American Indian culture and history. Most sections of the Library of Congress have some information on Native Americans, although they may be included within another collection.

★956★
U.S. National Park Service
Big Hole National Battlefield
Library
Box 237   Ph: (406)689-3155
Wisdom, MT 59761   Fax: (406)689-3151
Jock F. Whitworth, Chf., I & RM
Subjects: Nez Perce War of 1877. **Holdings:** 280 books.

★957★
U.S. National Park Service
Bighorn Canyon National Recreation Area
Library
Box 458
Fort Smith, MT 59035   Ph: (406)666-2412
James E. Staebler, Pk. Ranger
Subjects: Local history, Crow Indian history, ethnology, wildlife, geology, botany, archeology. **Special Collections:** National Park Service reports and management plans for Bighorn Canyon National Recreation Area; government reports on Crow Indians of Montana. **Holdings:** 1370 books.

★958★
U.S. National Park Service
Custer Battlefield National Monument
Library
Box 39   Ph: (406)638-2622
Crow Agency, MT 59022-0039   Fax: (406)638-2623
Douglas C. McChristian, Chf.Hist.
Subjects: Battle of Little Big Horn, George Custer, Western history, Indian wars. **Special Collections:** Elizabeth B. Custer Correspondence Collection; Walter M. Camp papers. **Holdings:** 3000 books; 500 bound periodical volumes; 15,000 artifacts, relics, and correspondences; 19 reels of microfilm; rare book and manuscript collection. **Remarks:** FAX: (406)638-2623.

★959★
U.S. National Park Service
Fort Laramie National Historic Site
Library
Box 86
Fort Laramie, WY 82212   Ph: (307)837-2221
Steven R. Fullmer, Pk. Ranger
Subjects: Frontier military history, Western history, Oregon-California-Mormon trails, Plains Indians. **Holdings:** 3500 books; 200 reels of microfilm.

★960★
U.S. National Park Service
Fort Larned National Historic Site
Library
Rte. 3   Ph: (316)285-6911
Larned, KS 67550-9733   Fax: (316)285-3571
Steven R. Linderer, Supt.
Subjects: Fort Larned, 1859-1878; Plains Indians; Santa Fe Trail; military history; Indian Wars, 1848-1890; museum conservation and preservation. **Holdings:** 775 books; 110 reels of microfilm; 10 binders of national archives.

★961★
U.S. National Park Service
Gila Cliff Dwellings National Monument
Visitor Center Library
Rte. 11, Box 100
Silver City, NM 88061   Ph: (505)536-9461
Eric Finkelstein
Subjects: Archeology, natural history, Mogollon Indians. **Special Collections:** Mogollon Indian artifacts. **Holdings:** 300 books. **Remarks:** Consolidated with U.S. Forest Service to serve Gila National Forest.

★962★
U.S. National Park Service
Glacier National Park
George C. Ruhle Library
West Glacier, MT 59936   Ph: (406)888-5441
     Fax: (406)888-5581
Beth Dunagan, Pk.Libn.
Subjects: Glacier Park history, environment, geology, glaciology, mammals, Plains Indians. **Special Collections:** Schultz books on the Plains Indians. **Holdings:** 13,000 books; 3000 reprints; 10,000 museum specimens.

★963★
U.S. National Park Service
Grand Portage National Monument
Library
Box 666
Grand Marais, MN 55604   Ph: (218)387-2788
Subjects: American-Canadian fur trade, Chippewa Indian culture, Canadian-Minnesota exploration and history. **Special Collections:** Wisconsin Historical Collection (21 volumes); journals of the Hudson's Bay Company (24 volumes); works of Samuel De Champlain (6 volumes). **Holdings:** 900 books; 100 bound periodical volumes.

★964★
U.S. National Park Service
Lava Beds National Monument
Library
Box 867   Ph: (916)667-2282
Tulelake, CA 96134   Fax: (916)667-2284
Gary Hathaway, Chf., Div. of Interp.

Subjects: History of Modoc War, 1872-1873; geology and volcanology; natural history; Indian ethnography; archeology. **Holdings:** 2100 books.

★965★
U.S. National Park Service
Mound City Group National Monument
Library
16062 State Rte. 104
Chillicothe, OH 45601   Ph: (614)774-1125
William Gibson, Supt.

Subjects: Archeology, Hopewell and other prehistoric Indian cultures of Ohio, environment and environmental education, Ohio history. **Special Collections:** Reports of archeological research on Hopewell and Adena cultures conducted at monument; Hopewell Archeological Conference papers, 1978. **Holdings:** 1800 books; 650 magazines, reports, unbound articles.

★966★
U.S. National Park Service
Natchez Trace Parkway
Library & Visitor Center
R.R. 1, NT-143
Tupelo, MS 38801   Ph: (601)842-1572

Subjects: History, natural history, national parks. **Special Collections:** Papers and letters related to Choctaw and Chickasaw Indians (200 items). **Holdings:** 2300 books; 200 bound periodical volumes; 1000 color slides; 10,000 negatives.

★967★
U.S. National Park Service
Nez Perce National Historical Park
Library
Box 93   Ph: (208)843-2261
Spalding, ID 83551   Fax: (208)843-2001
Frank Walker, Supt.

Subjects: Nez Perce Indians, Nez Perce War, Indian ethnology, history of the Northwest and Idaho, Western history. **Holdings:** 1200 books; 4000 historical photographs.

★968★
U.S. National Park Service
Olympic National Park
Pioneer Memorial Museum
Library
3002 Mount Angeles Rd.
Port Angeles, WA 98362   Ph: (206)452-4501
Henry C. Warren, Chf.Pk. Naturalist

Subjects: Natural history, Northwest Coast Indians, Olympic National Park. **Special Collections:** Manuscript material and reports relating to exploration and settlement of the Olympic Peninsula; correspondence, memoranda, reports, and photographs relating to the establishment and administration of Olympic National Park. **Holdings:** 2000 books; 6 VF drawers of clippings and articles relating to natural and human history of Olympic National Park.

★969★
U.S. National Park Service
Pipestone National Monument
Library & Archives
Box 727
Pipestone, MN 56164   Ph: (507)825-5464
Vincent J. Halvorson, Supt.

Subjects: Archeology, history, ethnology of the early Indian occupation of the Northern Plains; white exploration and settlement of the region. **Special Collections:** Publications relating to ceremonial pipes and Indian smoking customs. **Holdings:** 430

volumes; manuscripts; reports; clippings; microfilm; photographs; slides.

★970★
U.S. National Park Service
Point Reyes National Seashore
Library
Point Reyes, CA 94956   Ph: (415)663-1092
                                 Fax: (415)663-8132
Carlin Finke, PK. Ranger

Subjects: Natural history, Indians, environmental education, geology, California history, sea life, mammals, botany, National Park Service. **Holdings:** 2500 books; 2075 bound periodical volumes; 425 other cataloged items; reports.

★971★
U.S. National Park Service
Southwest Regional Office
Library
P.O. Box 728   Ph: (505)988-6840
Santa Fe, NM 87504-0728   Fax: (505)988-6876
Amalin Ferguson, Libn.

Subjects: Southwestern archeology, Indians of the Southwest, Western U.S. history, natural history, history of the National Park Service. **Special Collections:** National Park Service publications and reports (3000). **Holdings:** 30,000 books; 500 unbound periodical volumes; 300 videotapes; 3000 manuscripts; 800 prints and negatives; 6000 slides; 150 maps. **Remarks:** Library holds many unpublished manuscripts and institutional reports not available elsewhere. These are primarily concerned with park units comprising the Southwest Region of the National Park Service.

★972★
U.S. Smithsonian Institute
National Anthropological Archives
National Museum of Natural History, MRC 152
10th & Constitution Ave., N.W.
Washington, DC 20560   Ph: (202)357-1976

Subjects: Anthropology, linguistics, archeology, history of anthropology, history of American Indians, history of geography. **Special Collections:** Bureau of American Ethnology manuscript collection (5000); photographs of American Indians (60,000); Center for the Study of Man; Department of Anthropology records; Institute for Social Anthropology records; River Basin Surveys; professional papers of anthropologists; records of anthropological organizations. **Holdings:** 4000 cubic feet of archives and private papers; 350,000 photographs; 500 recordings; 100 reels of microfilm.

★973★
U.S. Smithsonian Institute
National Museum of Natural History
Branch Library
Natural History Bldg., Rm. 51
10th & Constitution Ave.   Ph: (202)357-1496
Washington, DC 20560   Fax: (202)357-1896
Ann Juneau, Natural Hist.Libn.

Subjects: Paleobiology, systematic botany, geology, oceanography, ecology, entomology, vertebrate and invertebrate zoology and paleontology, mineralogy, limnology, anthropology, North and South American Indians. **Special Collections:** J.D. Smith Collection (botany); Cushman Collection (Foraminifera); Springer Collection (crinoids); Wilson Collection (copepoda); Remington-Kellogg Collection of Marine Mammalogy. **Holdings:** 329,000 books and bound periodical volumes.

★974★
University of Alberta
Humanities and Social Sciences Library
Bruce Peel Special Collections Library
Rutherford South   Ph: (403)492-5998
Edmonton, AB, Canada T6G 2J4   Fax: (403)492-4327
John Charles, Spec.Coll.Libn./Hd.

Subjects: Western Canadiana; prairie provinces; English literature, 1600-1940; Canadian drama; European drama, 17th-18th centuries;

California history; European history, 1500-1900; book arts. **Special Collections:** Includes Gregory Javitch Collection on North and South American Indians (emphasis on treaties, warfare, language, and ceremonial dances); 900 volumes. **Holdings:** 85,000 volumes; 14,250 volumes of University of Alberta dissertations and theses; 48 volumes of diaries and typescripts on Alberta early settlers and local history.

★975★
University of Arizona
College of Law Library
Tucson, AZ 85721   Ph: (602)621-1413
Ronald L. Cherry, Dir.

Subjects: Law. **Special Collections:** Natural resources; law relating to American Indians; Latin American law. **Holdings:** 169,845 volumes; 55,149 volumes in microform.

★976★
University of California, Berkeley
Native American Studies Library
3415 Dwinelle Hall
Berkeley, CA 94720   Ph: (510)642-2793
Rosalie McKay, Libn.

Subjects: Native Americans. **Special Collections:** Annual Reports of the Commissioner of Indian Affairs, 1849-1949; Survey of the Conditions of the Indians of the U.S., 1929-1944; Records of the Bureau of Indian Affairs, Record Group 75: Indian Census, 1885-1941; Harvard University Peabody Museum papers and memoirs, 1896-1957; Indian Rights Association papers, 1864-1973; Bureau of American Ethnology annual reports and bulletins; Indian Claims Commission reports; water rights; special collection on California Indians. **Holdings:** 30,000 cataloged items; 7800 monographs; dissertations on microfilm; 150 phonograph records; 200 cassettes; 67 reel-to-reel tapes; 90 videotapes; newsclipping files. **Remarks:** Library located at 103 Wheeler, Berkeley, CA.

★977★
University of California, Davis
Michael and Margaret B. Harrison Western Research Center
Department of Special Collections
Shields Library
Davis, CA 95616   Ph: (916)752-1621
Michael Harrison, Dir.

Subjects: History and development of the trans-Mississippi West, mid-19th century to present; American Indians; ethnic studies; military, local, and economic history; sociology; folklore; exploration and travel; geography; religious studies, especially the Catholic and Mormon churches; literature; art and architecture; history of printing. **Special Collections:** Books from Western fine presses; correspondence with 20th century artists, writers, and enthusiasts of the American West; original works of art. **Holdings:** 18,615 volumes.

★978★
University of California, Los Angeles
American Indian Studies Center
Library
3220 Campbell Hall   Ph: (213)825-7315
Los Angeles, CA 90024-1548   Fax: (213)206-7060
Velma S. Salabiye, Libn.

Subjects: American Indians - government relations, history, literature, art, language; Indians in California; works of Indian authorship. **Special Collections:** Dissertations and theses by and about American Indians; Indian newspapers and journals. **Holdings:** 6500 volumes; 381 reels of microfilm; 4805 pamphlets.

★979★
University of California, Los Angeles
Department of Art History
Visual Resource Collection & Services
3239 Dickson Art Center
405 Hilgard Ave.
Los Angeles, CA 90024   Ph: (213)825-3725
David K. Ziegler, Sr.Musm.Sci.

Subjects: Painting, sculpture, applied art, and architecture - European, Islamic, Japanese, Indian, American, Chinese, African;

Pre-Columbian, Oceanic, and American Indian art; contemporary art forms. **Special Collections:** The Burton Holmes Collection (hand-tinted lantern slides, 1886-1937; 19,000) **Holdings:** 260,000 slides.

★980★
University of Cincinnati
Archives and Rare Books Department
Carl Blegen Library, 8th Fl.   Ph: (513)556-1959
Cincinnati, OH 45221-0113   Fax: (513)556-2113
Alice M. Cornell, Hd. & Univ.Archv.

Subjects: University of Cincinnati, Southwestern Ohio, 18th century English literature, travel and exploration, North American Indians, baseball history, history of the book. **Holdings:** Rare Book Collection (16,000); University Archives (6000 linear feet); Urban Studies Collection (2700 linear feet); Ohio Network Collection (3000 linear feet); Baseball Research Collection (15 linear feet); History of Design Collection; University Biographical File (42 linear feet); university theses and dissertations; Southwest Ohio Public Records (177 reels of microfilm).

★981★
University of Minnesota
Law Library
120 The Law Center
Minneapolis, MN 55455   Fax: (612)625-3478
Fred Morrison, Act.Dir.

Subjects: Law - Anglo-American, foreign. **Special Collections:** Scandinavian law; American Indians; British Commonwealth legal materials, including Indian and Pakistani legal materials. **Holdings:** 510,072 volumes; 1 million microforms.

★982★
University of Missouri-Kansas City
Snyder Collection of Americana
Miller Nichols Library
5100 Rockhill Rd.   Ph: (816)235-1534
Kansas City, MO 64110   Fax: (816)333-5584
Marilyn Carbonell, Asst.Dir., Coll.Dev.

Subjects: Political campaign literature; Civil War; Indians of North America; Kansas and Missouri - history, travel, biography, fiction, poetry; 19th century Americana; early Missouri and Kansas imprints. **Holdings:** 24,837 volumes.

★983★
University of Montana
School of Law
Law Library
Missoula, MT 59812   Ph: (406)243-6171
    Fax: (406)243-2576
Maurice M. Michel, Dir.

Subjects: Law. **Special Collections:** Indian law. **Holdings:** 120,307 books.

★984★
University of Nebraska, Lincoln
Center for Great Plains Studies
205 Love Library
Lincoln, NE 68588-0475   Ph: (402)472-6220
Jon Nelson, Cur.

Subjects: Western Americana. **Special Collections:** William Henry Jackson Photographs; Patricia J. and Stanley H. Broder Collection of Indian Painting; Richard Lane Collection of Western Fiction. **Holdings:** 6500 books; 500 photographs; 300 paintings; 200 sculptures; 100 drawings and graphics.

★985★
University of New Mexico
Bainbridge Bunting Memorial Slide Library
College of Fine Arts
Albuquerque, NM 87131   Ph: (505)277-6415
Sheila Hannah, Dir.

Subjects: History of art, architecture, photography, Native American arts, Spanish Colonial arts, Pre-Columbian arts. **Holdings:** 300,000 slides.

★986★

University of New Mexico
School of Law Library
1117 Stanford, NE   Ph: (505)277-6236
Albuquerque, NM 87131-1441   Fax: (505)277-0068
Anita Morse, Dir.

Subjects: Law. **Special Collections:** American Indian law; Community Land Grant Law; Mexican and Latin American legal materials. **Holdings:** 193,819 volumes; 636,661 microforms (106,110 volume equivalents); 12,000 New Mexico Supreme Court records and briefs.

★987★

University of New Mexico
Special Collections Department
Center for Southwest Research
General Library   Ph: (505)277-6898
Albuquerque, NM 87131   Fax: (505)277-6019
Michael Miller, Hd.

Subjects: History of the American West, New Mexico history, history of Mexico and Latin America, Indians of the Southwest, southwestern architectural history. **Special Collections:** Doris Duke Collection (982 oral history tapes); Pioneer Foundation (527 tapes). **Holdings:** 36,700 volumes; 2100 tape recordings; 3150 linear feet of manuscript material; 17,000 photographs; 250 videocassettes. **Remarks:** The Special Collections Department consists of six divisions: the Anderson Room, containing Western Americana; the Coronado Room collection on the history and culture of New Mexico; the Bell Room, housing the rare book collection; the manuscript collections and architectural records, which are also housed separately; the University Archives; and the Oral History Program.

★988★

University of North Carolina at Chapel Hill
Law Library
CB 3385 Van Hecke-Wettach Bldg.   Ph: (919)962-1321
Chapel Hill, NC 27599   Fax: (919)962-1193
Laura N. Gasaway, Dir.

Subjects: Law. **Special Collections:** Native American law. **Holdings:** 265,911 volumes; 477,200 microforms.

★989★

University of North Dakota
Elwyn B. Robinson Department of Special Collections
Chester Fritz Library   Ph: (701)777-4625
Grand Forks, ND 58202   Fax: (701)777-3319
Sandra Beidler, Hd., Archv. & Spec.Coll.

Subjects: History - North and South Dakota, Northern Great Plains, Plains Indian, women, environmental; agrarian radicalism; Nonpartisan League (North Dakota); genealogy; oral history. **Special Collections:** North Dakota Book Collection (13,250 volumes); Fred G. Aandahl Book Collection (1350 volumes); Family History/Genealogy Collection (2300 volumes); North Dakota State Documents (40,000); university archives (1200 linear feet); Orin G. Libby Manuscript Collection (6000 linear feet). **Holdings:** 16,900 books; 7200 linear feet of manuscript material; 3725 reels of microfilm; 44,000 photographs; 2000 AV items.

★990★

University of Oklahoma
Law Library
300 Timberdell Rd.   Ph: (405)325-4311
Norman, OK 73019   Fax: (405)325-6282
Scott B. Pagel, Dir.

Subjects: Law. **Special Collections:** Law - Indian, water, agriculture, natural resources; Indian land titles. **Holdings:** 173,859 volumes; 75,760 volumes in microform.

★991★

University of Oklahoma
Western History Collections
630 Parrington Oval, Rm. 452
Norman, OK 73019   Ph: (405)325-3641
Donald L. DeWitt, Cur.

Subjects: American Indians, Oklahoma, American Southwest, American Trans-Mississippi West, recent U.S. history. **Special Collections:** Cherokee Nation Papers; Patrick J. Hurley papers; E.E. Dale papers; Frank E. Phillips Collection; Alan Farley Collection; Henry B. Bass Collection; Norman Brillhart Collection. **Holdings:** 55,000 books; 9000 linear feet of manuscripts; 250,000 items in photographic archives; 20,000 microforms; 3600 maps; 1400 transcripts, tapes, and discs of oral history; 5000 pamphlets and documents; 1500 linear feet of University of Oklahoma archives; newspapers, posters, broadsides.

★992★

University of the Pacific
Holt-Atherton Department of Special Collections
Stockton, CA 95211   Ph: (209)946-2404
Thomas W. Leonhardt, Dean   Fax: (209)946-2810

Subjects: Californiana, Western Americana, Pacific Northwest, Northern San Joaquin Valley, gold mining, Western authors, Native Americans, economic development of the West, ethnic history in California. **Special Collections:** Early California exploration; fur trade; John Muir papers (900 volumes, 16,500 items); Jack London family collection; Shutes Collection on Lincoln and the Civil War; Perrin Collection on William Morris and Victoriana. **Holdings:** 30,000 books; 2928 bound periodical volumes; 75 linear feet of VF pamphlets; 30,000 photographs; 700 maps; 2000 linear feet of manuscripts. **Also Known As:** Stuart Library of Western Americana. **Formerly:** Its Holt-Atherton Center for Western Studies.

★993★

University of Pennsylvania
The University Museum of Archaeology/Anthropology
Museum Library
33rd & Spruce Sts.   Ph: (215)898-7840
Philadelphia, PA 19104-6324   Fax: (215)573-2008
Jean S. Adelman, Libn.

Subjects: Archeology, anthropology, ethnology. **Special Collections:** Brinton Collection of 19th century American Indian linguistics and ethnology (2000 titles). **Holdings:** 100,000 volumes; 5000 pamphlets; 80 reels of microfilm.

★994★

University of Rochester
Government Documents and Microtext Center
Rush Rhees Library   Ph: (716)275-4484
Rochester, NY 14627   Fax: (716)473-1906
Kathleen E. Wilkinson, Govt.Docs.Libn.

Subjects: Documents - U.S. Congress, U.S. Bureau of the Census, New York State, women's studies, black studies, North American Indians, American and British literature. **Special Collections:** Goldsmiths'-Kress Collection (economic literature); slavery; papers of William Henry Seward and of the National Association for the Advancement of Colored People (NAACP); Early English Books; American Fiction; History of Women; Early British Periodicals. **Holdings:** 380 books; 391,000 uncataloged government documents in paper; 914,200 uncataloged government documents in microform; 2.4 million other microforms.

★995★

University of South Dakota
Governmental Research Library
Vermillion, SD 57069   Ph: (605)677-5702
Steven H. Feimer, Dir.

Subjects: State and local government, public administration, South Dakota government, political behavior, public finance, American Indians, public law, legislative apportionment. **Holdings:** 6000 books; 400 bound periodical volumes.

★996★
University of South Dakota
I.D. Weeks Library
Richardson Archives
Vermillion, SD 57069   Ph: (605)677-5450
Karen Zimmerman, Archv.   Fax: (605)677-5488

Subjects: History - Western U.S., frontier, South Dakota; American Indians. **Special Collections:** University Archives. **Holdings:** 10,500 books; 3528 linear feet of manuscripts.

★997★
University of South Dakota
McKusick Law Library
414 E. Clark   Ph: (605)677-5259
Vermillion, SD 57069   Fax: (605)677-5413
John F. Hagemann, Law Libn.
Subjects: Law - U.S., English, Canadian. **Special Collections:** Law - agricultural, Indian, family, water, tax, professional responsibility; arts and the law; South Dakota Supreme Court briefs (65 VF drawers); U.S. Circuit Court, 8th Circuit slip opinions. **Holdings:** 122,625 bound volumes; 6 VF drawers of pamphlets; 97,116 microfiche; 4 VF drawers of archives.

★998★
University of Tennessee at Knoxville
Special Collections
Knoxville, TN 37996-4006   Ph: (615)974-4480
     Fax: (615)974-2708
Dr. James Lloyd, Spec.Coll.Libn.
Subjects: Tennesseana, 19th century American fiction, Southern Indians, early imprints. **Special Collections:** Estes Kefauver Collection (political papers and memorabilia; 1204 feet); Radiation Research Archives (435 feet); William Congreve Collection. **Holdings:** 40,000 books; 4550 feet of processed manuscripts.

★999★
University of Tulsa
College of Law Library
3120 E. 4th Pl.   Ph: (918)631-2459
Tulsa, OK 74104   Fax: (918)631-3556
Richard E. Ducey, Dir./Assoc.Prof.
Subjects: Law. **Special Collections:** American Indian law; Energy Law and Policy Collection. **Holdings:** 245,911 volumes, including microfiche.

★1000★
University of Tulsa
McFarlin Library
Special Collections
600 S. College Ave.   Ph: (918)631-2496
Tulsa, OK 74104   Fax: (918)631-3791
Sidney F. Huttner, Cur.
Subjects: 20th century British and American literature; Indian history, law, and policy; World War I; Proletarian literature; American fiction regarding Vietnam; performing arts. **Special Collections:** Cyril Connolly Library and papers; Andre Deutsch Archive (London publisher, 1950-1988); Edmund Wilson Library; Richard Ellmann papers; Richard Murphy papers; Jean Rhys papers; Paul Scott papers; Muriel Spork papers; Rebecca West papers; Stevie Smith papers; Shleppey Indian Collection; J.B. Milam Library (Cherokee materials); Indian Claims Commission Archives; University Archives. **Holdings:** 100,000 books; 1000 bound periodical volumes; 55 boxes of Alice Robertson papers; 200,000 British and American 20th century literary manuscripts; 300 pieces of 20th century American Indian art; 150 territorial maps.

★1001★
University of Utah
Special Collections Department
Marriott Library   Ph: (801)581-8863
Salt Lake City, UT 84112   Fax: (801)581-3464
Gregory C. Thompson, Asst.Dir., Spec.Coll.
Subjects: Utah, Mountain West, Mormons, Indians. **Special Collections:** Annie Clark Tanner Memorial Trust Fund; Utah, the Mormons and the West; university contracts. **Holdings:** 93,750 books; 5525 periodical titles; 30,000 theses and dissertations; 1771 federal documents; 15,161 folders of clippings; 10,100 folders of pamphlets; 12,000 linear feet of manuscripts; 600,000 photographs; 15,000 AV items; 2257 linear feet of archives.

★1002★
Utah State Historical Society
Library
300 Rio Grande
Salt Lake City, UT 84101   Ph: (801)533-5808
Subjects: History - Utah, Mormon, Western, Indian. **Special Collections:** Utah water records (200 linear feet); Works Progress Administration records (124 linear feet). **Holdings:** 23,000 books; 50,000 bound periodical volumes; 300,000 photographs; 22,000 pamphlets; 30,000 maps; 1500 oral history tapes; 3500 linear feet of manuscripts; 5000 reels of microfilm; 160 feet of clippings files; 5500 museum objects.

★1003★
Washoe County Law Library
Court House
Box 11130   Ph: (702)328-3250
Reno, NV 89520   Fax: (702)323-0601
Sandra Marz, Law Lib.Dir.
Subjects: Law. **Special Collections:** Nevada gambling, water rights, and Indian law. **Holdings:** 38,698 books; 3540 bound periodical volumes; 4924 volumes in microform; 85 cassettes.

★1004★
Wellesley College
Margaret Clapp Library
Special Collections
Wellesley, MA 02181   Ph: (617)235-0320
Ruth Rogers, Spec.Coll.Libn.   Fax: (617)239-1139

Special Collections: Includes Alcove of North American Languages (Indian languages; 280 volumes). **Holdings:** 41,000 books; 20 linear feet of manuscripts and autographs.

★1005★
Westchester County Department of Parks, Recreation
    and Conservation
Delaware Indian Resource Center
Ward Pound Ridge Reservation
Cross River, NY 10518   Ph: (914)763-3993
Beth Herr, Cur.
Subjects: Delaware culture, Native American herbalism, Algonkian tribes of the Eastern United States, Algonkian linguistics, Northeastern United States archeology, tribes of the greater New York area. **Special Collections:** Rare books on native cultures of Southern New York; taped oral history interviews with Delaware elders (50). **Holdings:** 1000 books; 500 bound periodical volumes; 10 file boxes of unbound material.

★1006★
Western Carolina University
Hunter Library
Special Collections
Cullowhee, NC 28723   Ph: (704)227-7474
George Frizzell, Unit Hd.
Subjects: Western North Carolina, Cherokee Indians. **Special Collections:** Appalachia (1200 volumes; 220 manuscript collections); spider behavior (200 volumes); Cherokee Documents in Foreign Archives Collection, 1632-1909 (manuscript sources from foreign archives relating specifically to the Cherokee and to southern Indians in general; 821 reels of microfilm).

★1007★
Wheelwright Museum of the American Indian
Mary Cabot Wheelwright Research Library
704 Camino Lejo
Box 5153
Santa Fe, NM 87502   Ph: (505)982-4636
Steve Rogers, Cur.

Subjects: Navajo and American Indian - religion, culture, arts; comparative religions; the Southwest. **Special Collections:** Archival material on Navajo religion, sand paintings, chants, and Southwest Indian art. **Holdings:** 2000 books; 2300 periodical volumes; 100 Navajo religion manuscripts; 300 sound recordings; 1000 slides of sandpaintings and reproductions; 100 Navajo music and prayer tapes.

★1008★
Whitman College
Myron Eells Library of Northwest History
Penrose Memorial Library
345 Boyer St.   Ph: (509)527-5191
Walla Walla, WA 99362   Fax: (509)527-5900
Henry Yaple

Subjects: Pacific Northwest - geography, education, politics, government, anthropology, Indians and native peoples, archeology, religion, missions, art, architecture; regional Indian art; historical fiction about the Northwest and Northwesterners; Lewis and Clark; the Oregon Trail. **Holdings:** 6390 books; 174 periodical titles.

★1009★
Will Rogers Library
121 N. Weenonah
Claremore, OK 74017   Ph: (918)341-1564
Margaret L. Guffey, Libn.

Subjects: Will Rogers, American Indians, Oklahoma and regional history. **Holdings:** 50,000 books; 265 bound periodical volumes; 1 VF drawer of clippings and pamphlets. **Remarks:** Maintained by the City of Claremore.

★1010★
Wyandotte County Historical Society and Museum
Harry M. Trowbridge Research Library
631 N. 126th St.
Bonner Springs, KS 66012   Ph: (913)721-1078
Lisa Schwarzenholz, Archv.

Subjects: Wyandotte County and Kansas City history; Wyandot, Shawnee, and Delaware Indians. **Special Collections:** J.R. Kelley Cooperage Company business papers and ledgers, 1903-1916 (36 cubic feet); proceedings of Congresses of mid-19th century; bound magazines and school texts of the late 19th century; Early, Conley, and Farrow Family Collections, 1763-1960 (30 cubic feet of papers, books, photographs). **Holdings:** 4000 books; 1000 bound periodical volumes; clippings; 150 reels of microfilm; 5000 photographs; maps.

★1011★
Wyoming State Library
Supreme Court & State Library Bldg.   Ph: (307)777-7281
Cheyenne, WY 82002-0650   Fax: (307)777-6289
Suzanne LeBarron, State Libn.

Subjects: Wyoming, Western Americana, North American Indians, library science. **Holdings:** 113,000 books; 664 bound periodical volumes; selective depository for U.S. Government publications (1.5 million); depository for Wyoming publications (5000).

★1012★
Yakima Valley Museum and Historical Association
Archives
2105 Tieton Dr.
Yakima, WA 98902   Ph: (509)248-0747
Martin M. Humphrey, Archv.

Subjects: Area history and development, Yakima Indians, pioneers, irrigation history. **Special Collections:** Apple and pear box labels; William O. Douglas Collection (1500 books; 11,000 slides; films; photographs); local newspaper, 1889-1952 (bound volumes); records of former Yakima Mayor Betty Edmonson; papers of state legislator and HEW chairwoman Marjorie Lynch; records of Yakima

Valley Transportation Co. (railroad). **Holdings:** 5728 books; 6373 photographs; 9 file cabinets of clippings; documents; manuscripts. **Remarks:** Includes the holdings of the Gannon Museum of Wagons.

★1013★
Yakima Valley Regional Library
Reference Department
Click Relander Collection
102 N. 3rd St.   Ph: (509)452-8541
Yakima, WA 98901   Fax: (509)575-2093
Cynthia Garrick, Ref.Coord.

Subjects: Click Relander, Yakima newspaper publisher; Pacific Northwest history; Yakima and Wanapum Indians and their relationship with the U.S. government; Yakima Valley history and agriculture. **Holdings:** 169 boxes of letters, manuscripts, federal documents, photographs.

Museum Collections

Alabama

★1014★
Alabama State Archives and History Museum
c/o Alabama Department of Archives and
   History
624 Washington Ave.
Montgomery, AL 36130   Ph: (205)242-4363

Description: Collections include artifacts that trace the culture of five American Indian tribes that lived in Alabama.

★1015★
Indian Mound and Museum
S. Court St.
Florence, AL 35630   Ph: (205)760-6427

Description: The pre-Columbian Indian mound is one of the largest domiciliary Indian mounds in the Tennessee Valley. The museum contains Indian artifacts.

Arizona

★1016★
Amerind Foundation, Inc.
Museum
PO Box 248
Dragoon, AZ 85609   Ph: (602)586-3666

Description: More than 25,000 items span 10,000 years of cultural history in the Americas, focusing primarily on the native cultures of the Southwest, the Pacific Northwest, and the Arctic. An art gallery contains the works of Native Americans and includes Hopi ceremonial kachina art.

★1017★
Canyon de Chelly National Monument
Box 588   Ph: (602)674-5436
Chinle, AZ 86503   Fax: (602)674-3439
Herbert Yazhe, Superintendent

Description: Maintains collections and conducts research on the archaeology and ethnology of the Anasazi Navajo.

★1018★
Casa Grande Ruins National Monument
Box 518   Ph: (602)723-3172
Coolidge, AZ 85228   Fax: (602)723-7209
Bettie B. Gill, Contact

Description: Collections include items relating to Hohokam archaeology, local ethnology, and pre-Columbian artifacts.

★1019★
Cochise Visitor Center and Museum
c/o Willcox Chamber of Commerce
1500 N. Circle I Rd.
Willcox, AZ 85643   Ph: (602)384-2272

Description: Collections include Apache Indian artifacts.

★1020★
Colorado River Indian Tribes
Museum
Rte. 1, Box 23B   Ph: (602)669-9211
Parker, AZ 85344   Fax: (602)669-5675
Weldon B. Johnson Sr., Asst.Dir.

Description: Collections include anthropological and archaeological items pertaining to the Mojave, Chemehuevi, Navajo, Hopi, Anasazi, Hohokan, and Patayan tribes.

★1021★
Eastern Arizona College
Museum of Anthropology
Thatcher, AZ 85552-0769   Ph: (602)428-8310
Everet J. Murphy, Pres.

Description: Collections include artifacts from Mogollon, Anasazi, and Hohokam material cultures; ethnographics on the Apache, Navajo, and Hopi; botanical display utilized by prehistoric people; Southwestern weaponry; technology exhibits on axe, jewelry, pigment and pottery manufacture.

★1022★
Gila Indian Center
PO Box 457
Sacaton, AZ 85247   Ph: (602)963-3981

Description: Contains a park with reconstructed Indian villages that depict more than 2,000 years of Native American life in the Gila River Basin. The Hohokum, Papago, Maricopa, and Apache cultures are represented. A museum and craft center adjoin the park.

★1023★
Heard Museum
22 E. Monte Vista Rd.
Phoenix, AZ   Ph: (602)252-8848

Description: A museum of Native American cultures and art.

★1024★
Mohave Museum of History and Arts
400 W. Beale St.
Kingman, AZ 86401   Ph: (602)753-3195

Description: Depicts the history of northwestern Arizona with collections of turquoise, recreated Mohave and Hualapai Indian dwellings, and local artifacts and artwork.

★1025★
Navajo National Monument
HC 71, Box 3   Ph: (602)672-2366
Tonalea, AZ 86044-9704   Fax: (602)672-2345
Clarence Gorman, Superintendent

Description: Collections include archeaological materials of the Kayenti Anasazi and Navajo cultures.

★1026★
Navajo Tribal Museum
Hwy. 264
PO Box 308
Window Rock, AZ 86515   Ph: (602)871-6673
Anselm Harvey, Acting Curator

Description: Collections include Navajo history, ethnology, fine arts, Southwest archaeology, geology and paleontology, and a photo archive.

★1027★
Smoki Museum
PO Box 10224
Prescott, AZ 86304   Ph: (602)445-1230

Description: Patterned after early Pueblo structures both in architecture and interior design, it contains ceramics and other artifacts from the Tuzigoot, King, and Fitzmaurice ruins of Yavapai County. Paintings portray legends and ceremonials.

★1028★
Tonto National Monument
Hwy. 88
PO Box 707   Ph: (602)467-2241
Roosevelt, AZ 85545   Fax: (602)467-2225
Carol Kruse, Superintendent

Description: Collections include the clothing, tools, weapons, and pottery of the Salado Indians.

★1029★
Tusayan Ruin and Museum
c/o Grand Canyon National Park
PO Box 129
Grand Canyon, AZ 86023   Ph: (602)638-2305

Description: Tusayan Ruin is a small prehistoric pueblo. The museum traces the development of the Anasazi Indian culture at the canyon.

★1030★
Tuzigoot National Monument
Cottonwood and Clarkdale Rd.
PO Box 68
Clarkdale, AZ 86324   Ph: (602)634-5564
Glen E. Henderson, Superintendent

Description: Collections include artifacts found during excavation of Tuzigoot and nearby ruins.

★1031★
Walnut Canyon National Monument
Walnut Canyon Rd.
Flagstaff, AZ 86004   Ph: (602)526-3367
Sam R. Henderson, Superintendent

Description: A park museum located on the site of prehistoric ruins of the Sinagua Indian culture.

★1032★
Wupatki National Monument
HC 33, Box 444A   Ph: (602)556-7040
Flagstaff, AZ 86001   Fax: (602)556-7154
Anna Fender, Chief Ranger

Description: Exhibits include a series of displays with artifacts from the sites of the Sinagua/Anasazi cultural pattern.

★1033★
Yavapai-Apache Visitor Activity Center
PO Box 219
Camp Verde, AZ 86322   Ph: (602)567-5276

Description: Exhibits depict historic and contemporary Indian lifestyles. A slide presentation on the area's prehistoric Indian cultures and a film on the Yavapai-Apache tribe are shown.

Arkansas

★1034★
Ka-Do-Ha Discovery Museum
PO Box 669
Murfreesboro, AR 71958   Ph: (501)285-3736
Sam Johnson, Owner and Dir.

Description: The museum is housed at a Moundbuilder village and ceremonial center dating from 1000 A.D. The collection is comprised of Indian artifacts from the site as well as other areas.

California

★1035★
Cabots Old Indian Pueblo Museum
67-616 E. Desert View Ave.
PO Box 1267   Ph: (619)329-7610
Desert Hot Springs, CA 92240   Fax: (619)329-1956
Colbert H. Eyraud, CEO and Pres.

Description: Collections include Indian and Eskimo artifacts, comtemporary Native American art and jewelry, and a 35-room Hopi style structure.

★1036★
California State Indian Museum
2618 K St.
Sacramento, CA 95816   Ph: (916)324-0971
Jackie Jaquez, Pres.

Description: The museum houses a California Indian artifacts collection with a limited collection of North American Indian artifacts from other areas. It also maintains an Indian demonstration village.

★1037★
Malki Museum
Morongo Indian Reservation
11-796 Fields Rd.
Banning, CA 92220   Ph: (714)849-7289
Katherine Siva Saubel, Pres.

Description: The museum's collection includes Cahuilla and other Southern California Indian tribe artifacts, anthropology, archaeology, history, archives, ethnology, music, and natural history.

★1038★
Marin Museum of the American Indian
2200 Novato Blvd.
PO Box 864
Novato, CA 94948   Ph: (415)897-4064
Dawn Carlson, Chair.

Description: Collections include archaeological, ethnographic, and archival materials from Alaska to Peru, pertaining to Native Americans.

★1039★
Santa Rosa Junior College
Jesse Peter Native American Art Museum
1501 Mendocino Ave.
Santa Rosa, CA 95401   Ph: (707)527-4479
Foley C. Benson, Dir. and Curator

Description: Collections include Native American artifacts. Conducts research pertaining to material culture of Northwest Indians with emphasis on California and the Southwest.

Colorado

★1040★
Adams State College Museums
Richardson Hall   Ph: (719)589-7121
Alamosa, CO 81102   Fax: (719)589-7522
Dr. Joseph Hesbrook, Curator

Description: Collections include Paleo-Indian folsom points, Pueblo Indian cultural artifacts, and Navajo weaving.

★1041★
Anasazi Heritage Center
27501 Hwy. 184
Dolores, CO 81323   Ph: (303)882-4811

Description: Anasazi farming, food preparation, crafts, and trade are among the topics covered by videos, case exhibits, hands-on activities, and traveling exhibits. Preserved sites of two late Anasazi communities are nearby.

★1042★
Colorado Springs Fine Arts Center
30 W. Dale St.   Ph: (719)634-5581
Colorado Springs, CO 80903   Fax: (719)634-0570
David J. Wagner, Exec.Dir.

Description: Collections include historical and contemporary Native American art.

★1043★
Koshare Indian Museum, Inc.
115 W. 18th
PO Box 580
La Junta, CO 81050   Ph: (719)384-4411
David Bailey, CEO

Description: Collections include paintings, archaeology, anthropology, and Indian artifacts.

★1044★
Manitou Cliff Dwellings Museum
US Hwy. 24
PO Box 272
Manitou, CO 80829   Ph: (719)685-5242

Description: Depicts the lives and architectural achievements of the Indians of the Southwest during the Great Pueblo Period (A.D. 1100-1300).

★1045★
Mesa Verde National Park Museum
Mesa Verde National Park, CO 81330   Ph: (303)529-4475
Donald C. Fiero, Contact   Fax: (303)529-4465

Description: Preserves Anasazi archaeological remains dating from 550-1300 A.D.

★1046★
Southern Ute Indian Cultural Center
Hwy. 172
Box 737   Ph: (303)563-4531
Ignacio, CO 81137   Fax: (303)563-4033
Lillian Selbel, Chair.

Description: The center is located on the Southern Ute Indian reservation and maintains photo and artifact collections pertaining to Ute Indians and other Native American tribes. It sponsors art festivals, Native American dance recitals, hobby workshops, and lectures.

★1047★
Ute Indian Museum
17253 Chipeta Dr.
PO Box 1736
Montrose, CO 81402   Ph: (302)249-3098
Glen Gross, Curator

Description: The museum is located on the site of Chief Ouray's 400-acre farm. Collections include the ethnology of the Ute Indians, Indian artifacts, history, archaeology, paintings, anthropology, costumes, and Ute Indian pottery.

Connecticut

★1048★
American Indian Archaeological Institute (AIAI)
Curtis Rd.
PO Box 1260   Ph: (203)868-0518
Washington Green, CT 06793-0260   Fax: (203)868-1649
Phillip Jones, Chair.

Description: Collections contain prehistoric and historic artifacts primarily from Connecticut and the Northwestern U.S.; ethnographic items from most North American culture areas; and contemporary native art. Facilities include the Indian Habitats Trail, a reconstructed Indian village, and an arboretum of plants the Indians used in the region over the last 10,000 years.

★1049★
Tantaquidgeon Indian Museum
1819 Norwick
Uncasville, CT 06382　　　　Ph: (203)848-9145
Gladys Tantaquidgeon, Owner and Curator
Description: Collections include crafts made by Mohegan craftsmen, and artifacts from Southwestern and Northern Plains Tribes.

──────── **District of Columbia** ────────

★1050★
Indian Arts and Crafts Board
18th and C Sts., NW, Rm. 4004-M1B
U.S. Dept. of the Interior
Washington, DC 20240　　　　Ph: (202)208-3773
Robert G. Hart, Gen.Manager
Description: Maintains collections of contemporary Native American arts.

★1051★
U.S. Department of the Interior Museum
1849 C St., NW
Mail Stop 5412　　　　Ph: (202)208-4743
Washington, DC 20240　　　Fax: (202)208-6950
Charles Carter, Contact
Description: Collections include Native American Indian and Eskimo handicraft and artifacts. Conducts research on North American Indian material culture.

──────── **Florida** ────────

★1052★
Indian Temple Mound Museum
139 Miraclestrip Pkwy. SE
PO Box 4009
Fort Walton Beach, FL 32549　　　　Ph: (904)243-6521
Billy Mikel, Manager
Description: Collections include lithic and ceramic artifacts of local aboriginal origin, historic contact artifacts, ethnological and replica items, and Indian artifacts.

★1053★
San Luis Archaeological and Historic Site
c/o Museum of Florida History
500 S. Bronough St.
Tallahassee, FL 32399-0250　　　　Ph: (904)487-3711
Description: An active dig that was the site of a 17th-century Apalachee Indian village and a Spanish mission. Maintains trails with interpretive displays describing the excavations and history of the site.

──────── **Georgia** ────────

★1054★
Chief John Ross House
PO Box 863
Rossville, GA 30741　　　　Ph: (706)861-3954
W. Larry Rose, CEO
Description: Maintains collections of arrowheads and of the Cherokee alphabet.

★1055★
Chieftains Museum
501 Riverside Pkwy.
PO Box 373
Rome, GA 30162　　　　Ph: (706)291-9494
Josephine Ransom, CEO and Dir.
Description: Collections include items from archaic Indian occupation to present time.

★1056★
Etowah Indian Mounds Historical Site
813 Indian Mounds Rd. SW
Cartersville, GA 30120　　　　Ph: (706)387-3747
Elizabeth Forehand, Superintendent
Description: Collections including archaeological excavations of a prehistoric Indian center.

★1057★
Kolomoki Mounds State Park Museum
Rte. 1
Blakely, GA 31723　　　　Ph: (912)723-3398
Bill Thomas, Superintendent
Description: Collections include Indian artifacts, Mississippian mound complex, and archaeological items.

★1058★
Ocmulgee National Monument
1207 Emery Hwy.
Macon, GA 31201　　　　Ph: (912)752-8257
Mark Corey, Superintendent
Description: Collectons include Indian artifacts, and items related to Indian archaeology, anthropology, history, and ethnology.

──────── **Idaho** ────────

★1059★
College of Southern Idaho
Herett Museum
315 Falls Ave.
PO Box 1238　　　　Ph: (208)733-9554
Twin Falls, ID 83303　　　Fax: (208)734-2362
Jim Woods, Dir.
Description: Maintains collections on American Indians, archaeology, and ethnology.

★1060★
Idaho Heritage Museum
2390 Hwy. 93, S.
Twin Falls, ID 83301　　　　Ph: (208)655-4444
Description: Maintains collections of Indian artifacts, including arrowheads.

★1061★
Nez Perce National Historic Park
Hwy. 95
PO Box 93
Spalding, ID 83551　　　　Ph: (208)843-2261
Franklin C. Walker, Superintendent
Description: Collections include items relating to Nez Perce ethnology, prehistoric lithics, and 3,000 photos of the Nez Perce Indians and the local region.

Illinois

★1062★
Aurora University
Schingoethe Center for Native American Cultures
Dunham Hall
347 S. Gladstone   Ph: (708)844-5402
Aurora, IL 60506   Fax: (708)892-9286
Thomas Zarle, Univ.Pres.
Description: Collections include Native American art, and cultural materials of North American peoples from pre-historic times to the present.

★1063★
Cahokia Mounds State Historic Site
Box 681
Collinsville, IL 62234   Ph: (618)346-5160
Margaret Brown, Site Manager
Description: Maintains collections of prehistoric Indian artifacts.

★1064★
Dickson Mounds Museum
Lewiston, IL 61542   Ph: (309)547-3721
Dr. R.B. McMillan, Dir./Illinois State Museum Fax: (309)547-3189

Description: Anthropology museum and site with collections including archaeological materials from West Central Illinois, Mississippi, and Middle Woodland sites. Maintains exhibits on American prehistory, osteology, and Paleo-Indian to historic cultures.

★1065★
Hauberg Indian Museum
1510 46th Ave.
Rock Island, IL 61201   Ph: (309)788-9536
Neil Rangen, Superintendent
Description: A State Historic Site Museum located on the site of the main villages of the Sauk and Fox Indian Nations. Collections include dioramas containing life-size figures of Sauk and Fox Indians, depicting daily life in an Indian village.

★1066★
The Mitchell Indian Museum at Kendall College
2408 Orrington Ave.   Ph: (708)866-1395
Evanston, IL 60201   Fax: (708)866-1320
Dr. Thomas Kerr, CEO
Description: Contains North American Indian art and artifacts, Eskimo art, and objects from cultures of the Plains, Woodlands, Southwest, and Northwest coast. Maintains library with collections including history, anthropology, art, crafts, archaeology, religion, law, education, literature, and social problems of the American Indian.

★1067★
Starved Rock State Park
Box 116   Ph: (815)667-4906
Utica, IL 61373   Fax: (815)667-5353
Jon Blume, Superintendent
Description: A historic park and museum located on the site of a former village of the Illinois Indians, which was later conquered by Ottawa and Potawatomi Indians.

Indiana

★1068★
Angel Mounds State Historic Site
Museum
8215 Pollack Ave.
Evansville, IN 47715   Ph: (812)853-3956
Rebecca Means Harris, Historic Site Curator
Description: An Indian site museum with collections including artifacts of Middle Mississippi Indians, photos of excavations made at Angel Mounds, and a restored Indian village.

★1069★
Eiteljorg Museum of American Indian and Western Art
500 W. Washington   Ph: (317)636-9378
Indianapolis, IN 46204   Fax: (317)264-1724
Harrison Eiteljorg, Chair.
Description: Maintains collection of Native American art and artifacts, and conducts research on Native American culture.

Iowa

★1070★
Effigy Mounds National Monument
RR 1, Box 25A   Ph: (319)873-3491
Harper's Ferry, IA 52146   Fax: (319)873-3743
Thomas A. Munson, Superintendent
Description: Collections include Indian artifacts, ethnology, archaeological collections of mound excavations, and manuscript collections.

Kansas

★1071★
Coronado-Quivira Museum
105 W. Lyon
Lyons, KS 67554   Ph: (316)257-3941
Betty Romero, CEO/Dir.
Description: Collections include Coronado and Quiviran Indian artifacts.

★1072★
Indian Center Museum
650 N. Seneca
Wichita, KS 67203   Ph: (316)262-5221
Richard Mitchell, Exec.Dir.
Description: Collections include Native American art and artifacts. Conducts research on Native American life, art, and religion.

★1073★
Iowa, Sac and Fox Presbyterian Mission Museum
E. Mission Rd.
Rte. 1, Box 152C
Highland, KS 66035   Ph: (913)442-3304
Andrew L. Clements, Curator
Description: Collections include Indian archaeological artifacts. Conducts research on Iowa, Sac, and Fox tribes' migrations.

★1074★
Pawnee Indian Village Museum
Rte. 1, Box 475
Republic, KS 66964   Ph: (913)361-2255
Richard Gould, Contact
Description: An archaeology museum located on the preserved Pawnee Site. Maintains original lodge floor, hearth, collections of stone, metal and bone, tools and implements, and other artifacts illustrating Pawnee Indian life and customs.

Maine

★1075★
Abbe Museum
Sieur de Monts Spring
Acadia National Park
Box 286
Bar Harbor, ME 04609   Ph: (207)288-3519
Diane Kopec, Dir.
Description: An archaeology, anthropology, and ethnology museum, located on site at Sieur de Monts Spring, within Acadia National

Park. Collections include archaic to modern Indian artifacts and handicrafts.

★1076★
Maine Tribal Unity Museum
Quaker Hill Rd.
Unity, ME 04988   Ph: (207)948-3131
Dr. Christopher Marshall, Dir.

Description: An Indian museum with collections including Native American basketry and artifacts.

──────────── **Maryland** ────────────

★1077★
National Colonial Farm of the Accokeek Foundation, Inc.
3400 Bryan Point Rd.   Ph: (301)283-2113
Accokeek, MD 20607   Fax: (301)283-2049
Robert Ware Staus, Pres.

Description: Collections include Indian artifacts.

──────────── **Massachusetts** ────────────

★1078★
Indian House Memorial, Inc.
Main St.
PO Box 121
Deerfield, MA 01342   Ph: (413)772-0845
John Abercrombie, Pres.

Description: Collections include Native American artifacts, decorative arts, pottery, weaving, and looms.

★1079★
Trustees of Reservations
572 Essex St.   Ph: (508)921-1944
Beverly, MA 01915   Fax: (508)921-1948
Herbert W. Vaughan, Chair.

Description: An open space and historic preservation project, maintaining and protecting 71 properties in Massachusetts.

──────────── **Michigan** ────────────

★1080★
Chief Blackbird Museum
PO Box 192
Harbor Springs, MI 49740   Ph: (616)576-7731

Description: Contains Indian relics and handwork.

★1081★
Crooked Tree Arts Council
461 E. Mitchell St.   Ph: (616)347-4337
Petoskey, MI 49770   Fax: (616)347-3429
Sean Ley, CEO and Dir.

Description: Maintains a fine arts collection with emphasis on Indians of the Great Lakes area. Areas of research include the art of Ojibway, Odawa, and Nishnawbe Indians.

★1082★
Father Marquette National Memorial and Museum
Father Marquette State Park
720 Church St.
Saint Ignace, MI 49781   Ph: (906)643-8620

Description: Displays artifacts, including an Indian longhouse and canoe, and maintains exhibits which interpret early French and Indian cultures.

★1083★
Marquette Mission Park and Museum of Ojibwa Culture
500 N. State St.
Saint Ignace, MI 49781   Ph: (906)643-9161

Description: Displays include artifacts, some dating to 6,000 B.C., and reproductions relating to the Ojibwa culture.

★1084★
Sabewaing Indian Museum
612 E. Bay St.
Sebewaing, MI 48759   Ph: (517)883-3730
Jim Bunke, CEO

Description: An 1849 mission home, with collections including Native American birch bark canoes, arrowheads, and headress.

★1085★
Teysen's Woodland Indian Museum
415 W. Huron Ave.
PO Box 399
Mackinaw City, MI 49701   Ph: (616)436-7011
Kenneth Teysen, CEO

Description: Collections include Indian artifacts from the Great Lakes area, including tools, weapons, clothing, food, and trade items.

──────────── **Minnesota** ────────────

★1086★
Lac Qui Parle Indian Mission Church
RR 1, Box 125
Morton, MN 56270   Ph: (507)697-6321
Tom Ellig, Southern Dist. Man.

Description: Maintains collections and conducts research in the fields of history and archaeology.

★1087★
Lower Sioux Agency History Center
RR 1, Box 125
Morton, MN 56270   Ph: (507)697-6321

Description: Exhibits and audiovisual programs portray the history of the eastern Dakota Indians since the 18th century.

★1088★
Mille Lacs Indian Museum
SR, Box 195
Onamia, MN 56359   Ph: (612)532-3632

Description: Exhibits include life-size dioramas showing typical scenes of Ojibwa life for each season.

★1089★
Minnesota Historical Society's Grand Mound History Center
Rte. 7, Box 453
International Falls, MN 56649   Ph: (218)279-3332
Nina Archabal, CEO

Description: A prehistoric Native American burial mounds and habitation area. Research conducted on middle and late Woodland, Laurel, and Blackduck Indian cultures.

★1090★
Walker Wildlife and Indian Artifacts Museum
St. Hwy. 200
PO Box 336
Walker, MN 56484   Ph: (218)547-1257
Renee Geving, Manager

Description: Collections include Ojibway and Chippewa Indian handicraft and artifacts from 1892-1962.

Mississippi

★1091★
Grand Village of the Natchez Indians
400 Jefferson Davis Blvd.   Ph: (601)446-6502
Natchez, MS 39120   Fax: (601)359-6905
Elbert R. Hilliard, CEO

Description: Collection includes Indian ceramics, artifacts, and stone implements. Research fields include the culture of the Natchez Indians.

Missouri

★1092★
Osage Village Historic Site
PO Box 176   Ph: (314)751-8363
Jefferson City, MO 65102   Fax: (314)751-8656
Larry Grantham, Contact

Description: Houses collections of excavated materials and conducts research on Osage Indians.

Montana

★1093★
Central Montana Museum
408 NE Main St.
PO Box 818
Lewiston, MT 59457   Ph: (406)538-5436
Frank Machler, Curator

Description: The museum includes a collection of Native American artifacts.

★1094★
Chief Plenty Coups State Park
PO Box 100
Pryor, MT 59066   Ph: (406)252-1289
Annie Olson, CEO

Description: Collections include ethnographic materials of the Crow people, paintings, drawings, and pre-historic artifacts.

★1095★
Flathead Indian Museum
1 Museum Ln.
PO Box 460   Ph: (406)745-2951
Saint Ignatius, MT 59865   Fax: (406)745-2951
L. Doug Allard, Contact

Description: Maintains collections of American Indian arts and crafts from major tribes throughout the United States, and traditional dress and tools of the Flathead Indians.

★1096★
H. Earl Clack Museum
Box 1675
Havre, MT 59501   Ph: (406)265-9641
Duane Nabor, Dir.

Description: The museum maintains collections of Indian artifacts and items relating to the history of the Chippewa-Cree Indians.

★1097★
Museum of the Plains Indian and Crafts Center
U.S. Hwy. 89 and 2
PO Box 400
Browning, MT 59417   Ph: (406)338-2230
Loretta Pepion, Curator

Description: Collections include: historic, contemporary, social, and ceremonial arts of the Northern Plains Indians; traditional costumes; painted tepees; and murals.

★1098★
Pipestone County Historical Museum
113 S. Hiawatha
Pipestone, MT 56164   Ph: (507)825-2563
David Rambow, Dir.

Description: Collections include pipes, quilted and beaded clothing from the Dakota and Ojibwa tribes, Plains Indian saddles, feathered headdresses, and prehistoric items.

★1099★
Pipestone National Monument
PO Box 727
Pipestone, MT 56164   Ph: (507)825-5464
Betty McSwain, Park Ranger

Description: Maintains a collection of Indian ceremonial pipes and pipestone objects.

Nebraska

★1100★
Heritage House Museum
107 Clinton
Weeping Water, NE 68463   Ph: (402)267-4765
Deborah Freeman, Pres.

Description: The museum maintains a prehistoric Indian artifact collection with itmes that date back 20,000 years.

Nevada

★1101★
Lost City Museum
721 S. Hwy. 169
PO Box 807
Overton, NV 89040   Ph: (702)397-2193
Scott Miller, Dir.

Description: Collections include Puebloan artifacts excavated from Pueblo Grande de Nevada, Lost City, Paiute Indian artifacts, historic baskets, and southwestern Indian crafts.

New Mexico

★1102★
Acoma Tourist and Visitation Center
PO Box 309
Pueblo of Acoma, NM 87034   Ph: (505)552-6606
Violet Tenorio, Dir.

Description: Collections include photograph archives and documents relating to the history of Acoma Indians, and historic to modern pottery.

★1103★
Aztec Museum
125 N. Main St.
Aztec, NM 87410   Ph: (505)334-9829

Description: Collections include Indian artifacts.

★1104★
Aztec Ruins National Monument
Ruins Rd.
PO Box 640   Ph: (505)334-6174
Aztec, NM 87410   Fax: (505)334-6372
Charles Cooper, Superintendent

Description: Collections include archaeological materials of Chaco and Mesa Verde Anasazi Indians.

★1105★
Bandelier National Monument
State Rte. 4
HCR 1, Box 1, Ste. 15
Los Alamos, NM 87544-9701   Ph: (505)672-3861
Roy W. Weaver, Superintendent

Description: Collections include archaeological and ethnological items of Pueblo Indians of the Pajarito Plateau.

★1106★
Chaco Culture National Historic Park
Star Rte. 4, Box 6500   Ph: (505)988-6716
Bloomfield, NM 87413   Fax: (505)988-6727
Lawrence A. Belli, Superintendent

Description: Collections include items relating to the archaeology and ethnology of the Chaco Anasazi Indians and the San Juan Basin.

★1107★
Coronado State Monument
St. Hwy. 44
PO Box 95
Bernalillo, NM 87004   Ph: (505)867-5351
Nathan Stone, Manager

Description: Site of Tiwa Pueblo named Kuanua dating from 1300 A.D.

★1108★
Eastern New Mexico University
Blackwater Draw Museum
Station 9   Ph: (505)562-2202
Portales, NM 88130   Fax: (505)562-2578
Dr. John Montogomery, Dir.

Description: Maintains collections of Paleo-Indian archaeology and anthropology.

★1109★
Gadsen Museum
Barker Rd. and Hwy. 28
Box 147
Mesilla, NM 88046   Ph: (505)526-6293
Mary Veitch Alexander, Curator and Owner

Description: Collections include Indian artifacts from the Southwest.

★1110★
Indian Pueblo Cultural Center
2401 12th St., NW   Ph: (505)843-7270
Albuquerque, NM 87102   Fax: (505)842-6959
John Mihelcic, Gen.Manager

Description: Collections include contemprorary arts and crafts, architecture, daily and social dance costumes, and items relating to government, anthropology, and ethnology of the Pueblo Indians.

★1111★
Institute of American Indian Arts
Museum
1369 Cerillos Rd.
PO Box 20007
Santa Fe, NM 87504   Ph: (505)988-6281
Rick Hill, Dir.

Description: Collections include Indian artifacts, contemporary Indian arts and crafts, and an 800-tape Native American videotape archive.

★1112★
M. Tularosa Basin Historical Society
1301 White Sands Blvd.
PO Box 518
Alamogordo, NM 88310   Ph: (505)437-4760
Terry Benson, Dir.

Description: The society maintains a collection of Indian artifacts.

★1113★
Museum of Indian Arts and Culture
710 Camino Lejo
Santa Fe, NM 87501   Ph: (505)827-6344

Description: Displays Southwest Indian art, culture, and artifacts, including live exhibitions by Pueblo, Navajo, and Apache artists.

★1114★
Museum of Indian Arts and Culture
Laboratory of Anthropology
710 Camino Lejo
PO Box 2087   Ph: (505)827-6344
Santa Fe, NM 87504-2087   Fax: (505)827-6349
Stephen A. Becker, Dir.

Description: The museum maintains exhibits relating to the material culture and ethnology of the native peoples of the Southwest, including pre-historic and historic jewelry, pottery, baskets, textiles, accessories, kachinas, sculpture, and paintings.

★1115★
Red Rock Museum
Red Rock State Park
PO Box 328   Ph: (505)722-6196
Church Rock, NM 87311   Fax: (505)863-9352
John Vidal, Park Manager

Description: Collections include crafts and artifacts of the prehistoric Anasazi and historic Navajo, Hopi, Zuni, Rio Grande Pueblo, and Apache.

★1116★
School of American Research
660 Garcia St.
PO Box 2188   Ph: (505)982-3583
Santa Fe, NM 87504   Fax: (505)989-9809
Dr. Douglas W. Schwartz, Pres.

Description: The school maintains collections of representative historic Southwestern Pueblo Indian pottery, Navajo and Pueblo Indian textiles, Native American easel paintings, Navajo and Pueblo Indian jewelry, Southwest Indian basketry, and Kachinas and miscellaneous ethnographic objects pertaining to historic Southwest American Indian arts.

★1117★
Wheelwright Museum of the American Indian
701 Camino Lejo
PO Box 5153
Santa Fe, NM 87502   Ph: (805)982-4636
Susan Brown McGreevy, Pres. Bd. of Trustees

Description: Collections include Native American artifacts and art works, musical recordings of Navajo ceremonies, Navajo sandpainting reproductions, archives, and manuscripts.

──────────── **New York** ────────────

★1118★
Akwesasne Museum
Rte. 37
Hogansburg, NY 13655   Ph: (518)358-2461
Margaret Jacobs, CEO

Description: Collections include Mohawk traditional artifacts and basketry, contemporary Iroquoian artifacts and ethnological exhibitions.

★1119★
Ganondagan State Historic Site
1488 Victor Holcomb Rd.
PO Box 239
Victor, NY 14564   Ph: (716)924-5848
Edgar Brown, Pres.

Description: The site is located at a late seventeenth-century Seneca Indian settlement. It maintains collections of Seneca artifacts and trade items of European manufacture.

★1120★
Iroquois Indian Museum
Howes Cave, NY 12049   Ph: (518)234-8319
Christina B. Johannsen, Dir.

Description: Collections include contemporary art and craft work of the Iroquois Indians, pre-historic materials of the Iroquois and their immediate antecedents realting to Schoharie County, color slides, black and white prints, and a photographic collection of Iroquois arts.

★1121★
Museums at Hartwick
Hartwick College
Oneonta, NY 13820   Ph: (607)431-4480

Description: Maintains extensive collections of Upper Susquehanna Native American, Southwestern, pre-Columbian, and Mesoamerican artifacts.

★1122★
National Shrine of the Blessed Kateri Tekakwitha and Native American Exhibit
PO Box 627
Fonda, NY 12068   Ph: (518)853-3646

Description: Collections include artifacts of North American Indians. Maintains the Caughnawaga Indian village, the only completely excavated and staked-out Iroquois village in the country.

★1123★
Native American Center for the Living Arts
25 Rainbow Blvd.
Niagara Falls, NY 14303   Ph: (716)284-2427
Huron Miller, Pres.

Description: Collections include Native American archaeological, ethnographic, and contemporary art from the U.S. and Canada. Conducts research on Native American history, art, linguistics, oral history, and culture.

★1124★
Rochester Museum and Science Center
657 East Ave.
Rochester, NY   Ph: (716)271-1880

Description: A regional museum of natural science, history, and anthropology with permanent and changing exhibits. Features the permanent exhibit "At the Western Door," which interprets Native American-colonial European relations via more than 2,000 Seneca Indian artifacts, a 1790's furnished Seneca cabin, six life-size figure tableaus and a film.

★1125★
Seneca-Iroquois National Museum
Broadstreet Ext.
PO Box 442
Salamanca, NY 14779   Ph: (716)945-1738

Description: Located on the Alleghany Indian Reservation. Maintains collections of more than 300,000 articles which portray the life and culture of the Seneca and Iroquois Indians, including treaties, wampum belts, costumes, games, and modern art.

★1126★
Six Nations Indian Museum
Roakdale Rd.
HCR 1, Box 10
Onchiota, NY 12968   Ph: (518)891-0769
John Fadden, Dir.

Description: Collections include Six Nations Indians artifacts, items relating to Iroquois culture and history, and a miniature Indian village composed of the Iroquois, Delaware, Sioux, and Abenaki tribes.

★1127★
Southold Indian Museum
Bayview Rd.
PO Box 268
Southold, NY 11971   Ph: (516)765-5577
Walter L. Smith, Pres.

Description: Collections include Native American articles and artifacts, and handiworks of Eskimos.

★1128★
U.S. Smithsonian Institute
Museum of the American Indian
3753 Broadway at 155th St.
New York, NY 10032-1596   Ph: (212)283-2420
Dr. Duane King, Dir.

Description: Collections include items relating to American Indian archaeology and ethnology from North America, artifacts, textiles, agriculture, anthropology, paintings, sculpture, decorative arts, costumes, numismatic, music, medical, photo archives, manuscript collections, and Eskimo culture.

—————————— **North Carolina** ——————————

★1129★
Cherokee Indian Cyclorama Wax Museum
PO Box 485
Cherokee, NC 28719   Ph: (704)497-4521

Description: Uses dioramas, an electronic map, and narration to present 300 years of Cherokee history, from the nation's days as an empire to its virtual disappearance.

★1130★
Indian Museum of the Carolinas, Inc.
607 Turnpike Rd.
PO Box 666
Laurinburg, NC 28352   Ph: (919)276-5880
Dr. Margaret Houston, Dir.

Description: Collections include Indian artifacts, interpretive exhibits, and manuscript collections.

★1131★
Museum of the Cherokee Indian
U.S. 441
PO Box 1599
Cherokee, NC 28719   Ph: (704)497-3481
Ken Blankenship, Dir.

Description: Collections of Cherokee Indian artifacts, relics, and archives are maintained.

★1132★
Pembroke State University Center
Native American Resource Center
College Rd.
Pembroke, NC 28372   Ph: (919)521-4214
Dr. Stanley Knick, Dir.

Description: Maintains collections of Indian artifacts, art, books, cassettes, record albums, and films pertaining to Native Americans and Lumbee Indians.

★1133★
Town Creek Indian Mound State Historic Site
Montgomery County Rd. 1542
Rte. 3, Box 50
Mt. Gilead, NC 27306   Ph: (919)439-6802
Archie C. Smith Jr., Site Manager

Description: Maintains collection of Indian artifacts. Also maintains an ancient Indian mound, and reconstructed Indian structures.

——————— **North Dakota** ———————

★1134★
Knife River Indian Villages National Historic Site
RR 1, Box 168   Ph: (701)745-3300
Stanton, ND 58571   Fax: (701)745-3708
Michael Holm, Area Manager
Description: Maintains collections of Hidatsa/Mandan cultural artifacts.

★1135★
Museum of the Badlands
PO Box 198
Medora, ND 58645   Ph: (701)623-4444
Description: Collections include exhibits on the attire and crafts of North American Indian tribes.

★1136★
Turtle Mountain Chippewa Heritage Center
Hwy. 5
PO Box 257
Belcourt, ND 58316   Ph: (701)477-6140
Denise Lajimodierre, CEO and Chair.
Description: Maintains collections of Chippewa Indian artifacts and contemporary art.

——————— **Ohio** ———————

★1137★
Indian Museum of Lake County, Ohio
c/o Lake Erie College
391 W. Washington
Painesville, OH 44077   Ph: (216)352-3361
Gwen G. King, Dir.
Description: Houses a pre-contact artifacts of Ohio collection, 10,000 B.C.-1650 A.D., and a crafts and art of Native North Americans collection, 1800 to present.

★1138★
Mound City Group National Monument
16062 St. Rte. 104
Chillicothe, OH 45601   Ph: (614)774-1125
William Gibson, Superintendent
Description: Collections include archaeological artifacts from the Hopewell period.

★1139★
Moundbuilders State Memorial and Museum
7091 Brownsville Rd. SE
Glenford, OH 43739   Ph: (614)344-1920
Richard Livingston, Manager
Description: Collections include art objects and other media representing achievements of the Adeba and Hopewell cultures 1000 B.C. to 700 A.D.

★1140★
Piqua Historical Area
9845 N. Hardin Rd.
Piqua, OH 45356   Ph: (513)773-2522
Victoria Tabor Branson, Site Manager
Description: Collections include historic Indian tools, weapons, costumes, art, canoes, and trade items.

★1141★
Serpent Mound Museum
3850 State Rte. 73
Peebles, OH 45660   Ph: (513)587-2796
William E. Gustin, Area Manager
Description: The museum's collection focuses on the Adena Indian culture.

——————— **Oklahoma** ———————

★1142★
Bacone College
Aaloa Lodge Museum
99 Bacone Rd.
Muskogee, OK 74403-1597   Ph: (918)683-4581
Frances Donelson, Dir.
Description: The museum's collections include Native American stone artifacts, rugs, blankets, basketry, pottery, beadwork, and quillwork.

★1143★
Cherokee Courthouse
Rte. 2, Box 37-1
Gore, OK 74435   Ph: (918)489-5663
John Pruitt, Curator
Description: Maintains displays and exhibits on the history of the Cherokee Indians.

★1144★
Cherokee National Museum
TSA-LA-GI-Cherokee Heritage Center
Willis Rd.
PO Box 515
Tahlequah, OK 74465   Ph: (918)456-6007
Myra Moss, Exec.Dir.
Description: Collections include artifacts, paintings, a 42-structure ancient village, and a 9-structure rural village.

★1145★
Chickasaw Council House Museum
Court House Sq.
PO Box 717
Tishomingo, OK 73460   Ph: (405)371-3351
Beverly J. Wyatt, Curator
Description: Collections include articles relating to the Chickasaws' life in Oklahoma Indian territory.

★1146★
Creek Council House Museum
Town Sq.
Okmulgee, OK 74447   Ph: (918)756-2324
Janeth Slamans, Dir./Curator
Description: Collections include items relating to Indian history, archives, archaeology, and history of the Muscogee Creek Nation.

★1147★
Fort Ancient Museum
6123 St., Rte. 350
Oregonia, OK 45054   Ph: (513)932-4421
Jack K. Blosser, Area Manager
Description: Maintains collection of artifacts relating to pre-historic Indian life and culture.

★1148★
Indian City U.S.A.
PO Box 695
Anadarko, OK 73005   Ph: (405)247-5661
George F. Moran, Manager
Description: Collections include Indian artifacts and articles.

★1149★
Memorial Indian Museum
2nd and Allen Sts.
PO Box 483
Broken Bow, OK 74728   Ph: (405)584-6531
LaMarr Smith, Dir.
Description: Collections include pre-historic Indian artifacts, modern textiles, basketry, early bead work, pre-historic Indian skeletal remains, original paintings and prints, early American glass, and fossils.

★1150★
Museum of the Great Plains
601 Ferris Ave.
PO Box 68
Lawton, OK 73502   Ph: (405)581-3460
Steve Wilson, Dir.

Description: The museum maintains a photograph collection of Plains Indians.

★1151★
Museum of the Red River
812 SE Lincoln
Idabel, OK 74745   Ph: (405)286-3616
Mary Herron, Dir.

Description: The museum maintains prehistoric to contemporary American Indian collections with emphasis on local Indian history, the Caddo, and the Choctaw. It also presents interpretive exhibits of Indian cultures.

★1152★
National Hall of Fame for Famous American Indians
Hwy. 62
PO Box 548
Anadarko, OK 73005   Ph: (405)247-5555
Allie Reynolds, Pres.

Description: Collections include sculptured bronze busts of famous American Indians in an outdoor landscaped area.

★1153★
Ponca City Cultural Center & Museums
1000 E. Grand
Ponca City, OK 74601   Ph: (405)767-0427
LaWanda French, Dir.

Description: Collections include items relating to Ponca City's neighboring tribes: Ponca, Kaw, Otoe, Osage, and Tonkawa.

★1154★
Seminole Nation Museum
524 S. Wewoka Ave.
Box 1532
Wewoka, OK 74884   Ph: (405)257-5580
Garvin Peck, Pres.

Description: Maintains collections of Native American art.

★1155★
Sequoyah Home Site
Rte. 1, Box 141
Sallisaw, OK 74955   Ph: (918)775-2413
Dillard Jordan, Curator

Description: Collections include artifacts and exhibits relating to Native Americans (primarily Cherokee).

★1156★
Southern Plains Indian Museum and Crafts Center
Hwy. 62 E.
PO Box 749
Anadarko, OK 73005   Ph: (405)247-6221
Rosemary Ellison, Curator

Description: Collections include historic and contemporary Native American art.

─────────── **Oregon** ───────────

★1157★
Favell Museum of Western Art and Indian Artifacts
125 W. Main St.
PO Box 165
Klamath Falls, OR 97601   Ph: (503)882-9996
Gene H. Favell, Dir.

Description: Maintains colletion of Indian artifacts, including 60,000 arrowheads, stonework, pottery, bonework, beadwork, and quillwork.

─────────── **South Dakota** ───────────

★1158★
Akta Lakota Museum
c/o St. Joseph Indian School
PO Box 89
Chamberlain, SD 57325   Ph: (605)734-3455

Description: Displays historic artifacts and artwork of Native Americans.

★1159★
American Indian Culture Research Center Museum
Blue Cloud Abbey
PO Box 98   Ph: (605)432-5528
Marvin, SD 57251   Fax: (605)432-4754
Rev. Stanislaus Maudlin O.S.B., Dir.

Description: Collections include Maria pottery, Native American artifacts, and 30,000 photographs of Dakota Indians.

★1160★
Bear Butte State Park Visitors Center
Hwy. 79
PO Box 688
Sturgis, SD 57785   Ph: (605)347-5240
William A. Gullett, Park Manager

Description: The center is located on a Native American traditional religious site and maintains a collection of Native American clothing and religious artifacts.

★1161★
Buechel Memorial Lakota Museum
St. Francis Indian Mission
350 S. Oak St.
PO Box 499
Saint Francis, SD 57572   Ph: (605)747-2361
Lloyd One Star, Chair.

Description: The museum's collection is comprised of ethnographic materials of the reservation period of the Rosebud and Pine Ridge Sioux.

★1162★
The Heritage Center, Inc.
Red Cloud Indian School
Box 100   Ph: (605)867-5491
Pine Ridge, SD 57770   Fax: (605)867-1104
Bro. C.M. Simon S.J., Dir. and CEO

Description: Maintains the following collections: paintings by Native American artists; star quilt collection; beadwork; quill and pottery collection; Native American prints; and Northwest Coast Prints. Research fields include Native American art, Sioux artifacts, and Siouxan culture.

★1163★
Indian Museum of North America
Avenue of the Chiefs, Black Hills   Ph: (605)673-4681
Crazy Horse, SD 57730   Fax: (605)673-2185
Mrs. Anne Ziolkowski, Dir.

Description: Collections include Indian art and artifacts.

★1164★
Sioux Indian Museum and Crafts Center
515 West Blvd.
PO Box 1504
Rapid City, SD 57709   Ph: (605)348-0557
Paulette Montileaux, Curator

Description: The museum's collections include historic and contemporary Sioux art and architectural models of Native American arts and crafts.

★1165★
Tekakwitha Fine Arts Center
PO Box 208
Sisseton, SD 57262-0208   Ph: (608)698-7058
Fr. Norman Volk, Dir.

Description: The center sponsors art festivals, concerts, hobby workshops, and the annual Coteau Heritage Festival. It maintains a collection of two-dimensional art of the Lake Traverse Dakotah Sioux Reservation.

★1166★
White River Visitor Center
Rocky Fort RR
Porcupine, SD 57772   Ph: (605)455-2878

Description: Maintains Indian cultural exhibits and an audiovisual program.

——————— **Tennessee** ———————

★1167★
Red Clay State Historical Park
1140 Red Clay Park Rd. SW
Cleveland, TN 37311   Ph: (615)478-0339
Lois I. Osborne, Park Manager

Description: The park's collection includes Paleo, Archaic, Mississippian, Woodland, and historic period artifacts. The park is located on the former seat of the Cherokee government and site of eleven general councils.

——————— **Texas** ———————

★1168★
Alabama-Coushatta Tribe of Texas
Indian Museum
US Hwy. 190
Rte. 3, Box 640   Ph: (409)563-4391
Livingston, TX 77351   Free: 800-444-3507
Jo Ann Battise, Tribal Admin.

Description: Located on the Alabama-Coushatta Indian reservation, the museum's collections include a dioramic display of tribes and a living Indian village. Research is conducted in the areas of tribal history and culture.

★1169★
Caddo Indian Museum
701 Hardy St.
Longview, TX 75604   Ph: (903)759-5739
Mrs. James L. Jones, Dir.

Description: Collections include Paleo, Archaic, and Caddoan Indian cultural remains, including artifacts, tools, and weapons of stone, clay, and bone.

——————— **Utah** ———————

★1170★
Anasazi State Park
Canyon Rd.
PO Box 1329
Boulder, UT 84716   Ph: (801)335-7308
Larry Davis, Superintendent

Description: Maintains collection of artifacts representative of the Keyenta Anasazi culture during the period 1050-1200 A.D., and a diorama of Coombs Village.

★1171★
College of Eastern Utah
Prehistoric Museum
451 East 400 North
Price, UT 84501   Ph: (801)637-5060

Description: Contains exhibits of Fremont and Anasazi Indian artifacts.

★1172★
Edge of the Cedars State Park
660 West 400 North
Box 788
Blanding, UT 84511   Ph: (801)678-2238
Stephen Olsen, Superintendent

Description: Exhibits include artifacts belonging to the prehistoric Anasazi Indian Tribe, Anasazi pottery collection, and artifacts of the Navajo, Ute, and Piute Indians.

★1173★
Ute Tribal Museum
Bottle Hollow Resort
Hwy. 40
Fort Duchesne, UT 84026   Ph: (801)722-4992
Betsy Chapoose, Dir.

Description: Exhibits include Indian art work in various media, and Indian artifacts. Research includes Ute history, archaeology, and documentation of verbal Indian history through personal interviews with elderly tribe members.

——————— **Washington** ———————

★1174★
Chelan County Historical Museum and Pioneer Village
600 Cottage Ave.
PO Box 22
Cashmere, WA 98815   Ph: (509)782-3230

Description: Recreates the history of the Columbia River Indians before the arrival of the first pioneers and maintains an extensive collection of Indian artifacts.

★1175★
Makah Cultural and Research Center
PO Box 160
Neah Bay, WA 98357   Ph: (206)645-2711

Description: Contains exhibits pertaining to the Makah Indian history and culture.

★1176★
Museum of Native American Cultures
2316 W. 1st Ave.
Spokane, WA 99204   Ph: (509)456-3931

Description: Displays include paintings, artifacts, ceramics, and an extensive trade bead collection from native cultures spanning the Western Hemisphere.

★1177★
Yakima Nation Cultural Center
Fort Rd.
PO Box 151
Toppenish, WA 98948   Ph: (509)865-2800

Description: Maintains dioramas and exhibits that chronicle the history of the Yakima Indians.

Wisconsin

★1178★
Lac du Flambeau Chippewa Museum and Cultural Center
PO Box 804
Lac Du Flambeau, WI 54538   Ph: (715)588-3333
Description: Houses a collection of Indian artifacts dating back to the mid-18th century, including a 24-foot dugout canoe discovered in a local lake and thought to be about 250 years old. A four seasons display demonstrates Indian activities, clothing, and living arrangements throughout the year.

Wyoming

★1179★
Cheyenne Frontier Days and Old West Museum
PO Box 2824
Cheyenne, WY 82003   Ph: (307)778-7291
Description: Displays include Oglala Sioux Indian artifacts.

★1180★
Plains Indian Museum
Buffalo Bill Historical Center
720 Sheridan Ave.
PO Box 1000
Cody, WY 82414   Ph: (307)587-4771
Description: Maintains an extensive collection of artifacts, ceremonial items and beadwork, dress, and weaponry of the Sioux, Blackfeet, Cheyenne, Shoshone, Crow, and Arapaho tribes.

★1181★
Riverton Museum
700 E. Park Ave.
Riverton, WY 82501   Ph: (307)856-2665
Description: Collections include Shoshone and Arapaho costumes and artifacts.

★1182★
University of Wyoming
Anthropology Museum
University of Wyoming
Box 3431
Laramie, WY 82071   Ph: (307)766-5136
Description: Chronicals Wyoming's cultural history, Northwest Plains, and other North American Indians.

Research Centers

★1183★
American Indian Archaeological Institute
38 Curtis Rd.
PO Box 1260   Ph: (203)868-0518
Washington Green, CT 06793-0260   Fax: (203)868-1649
Alberto C. Meloni, Dir.
Research Activities and Fields: Discovery, preservation, and interpretation of native American cultures of the northeastern woodlands region of the U.S. Conducts surveys for prehistoric and historic evidence of human occupation. Locates, tests, and excavates prehistoric and historic sites.

★1184★
Arizona State University
Center for Indian Education
College of Education
Farmer Education Bldg., Rm. 415
Tempe, AZ 85287-1311   Ph: (602)965-6292
Karen Swisher, Dir.
Research Activities and Fields: All phases of American Indian education and related interdisciplinary issues. **Publications:** *Journal of American Indian Education* (JAIE, three times annually).

★1185★
Brown University
Center for the Study of Race and Ethnicity in America
Box 1886
Providence, RI 02912   Ph: (401)863-3080
Rhett S. Jones, Dir.
Research Activities and Fields: Racial and ethnic minorities in America, focusing on African Americans, Asian Americans, Latinos, and Native Americans. Emphasis is on interdisciplinary, comparative, and analytical studies of race, gender, and class.

★1186★
Crow Canyon Center for Southwestern Archaeology
23390 County Rd. K
Cortez, CO 81321   Ph: (303)565-8975
Ian Thompson, Dir.
Research Activities and Fields: Archeological investigation, including excavation and cataloging of artifacts. Specializes in Anasazi Indian culture, excavates sites in the Four Corners area of the southwest United States, and uses discoveries to describe ancient Anasazi social structure, behaviors, and skill levels within the society. Center offers the public the opportunity to join research expeditions.

★1187★
ERIC Clearinghouse on Rural Education and Small Schools
Appalachia Educational Laboratory
PO Box 1348
Charleston, WV 25325   Ph: (304)347-0400
Craig Howley, Codirector
Research Activities and Fields: American Indian, native Alaskan, Mexican American, migrant, outdoor, and rural education and small schools.

★1188★
Harold McCracken Research Library
PO Box 1000
Cody, WY 82414   Ph: (307)587-4771
Christina Stopka, Lib./Archivist
Research Activities and Fields: Maintains a collection of manuscripts and archival materials on western history and art, Plains Indians, and firearms technology. Major collections include the works of western artists Frank Tenney Johnson, Frederic Remington, W.H.D. Koerner, and Joseph Henry Sharp; Yellowstone National Park Special Collection; photograph collections, including Charles J. Belden, the Mercaldo Archives, and the Buffalo Bill Museum Collection.

★1189★
Humboldt State University
Center for Indian Community Development
Arcata, CA 95521   Ph: (707)826-3711
Lois J. Risling, Dir.
Research Activities and Fields: Community economic and organizational development, assesment of local needs for archeological research, regeneration of American Indian languages and literatures and the application of computer systems to publication of Indian languages. Projects include publication of textbooks and instructional material in and about Hupa, Karuk, Tolowa, Yurok, and other Indian languages. **Publications:** *The Messenger* (quarterly newsletter). **Formerly:** Center for Community Development.

★1190★
Indian Arts Research Center
School of American Research
PO Box 2188
Sante Fe, NM 87501   Ph: (505)982-3584
Michael J. Hering, Dir.

Research Activities and Fields: Maintains a collection of Southwest cultural materials, concentrating on Native American arts of the Southwest, such as ceramics, basketry, textiles, jewelry, paintings, and kachinas dating from the time of Spanish contact. Scholars, researchers, and Southwest American Indian artists are encouraged to utilize the facilities for research and aesthetic experience. **Publications:** *Annual Report and Exploration Magazine* (annually).

★1191★
Makah Cultural and Research Center
PO Box 160
Neah Bay, WA 98357   Ph: (206)645-2711
Maria Pascua, Interim Dir.

Research Activities and Fields: Language, culture, and ethnohistory of the Makah people, including comparative Wakashan linguistics, archeology, anthropology, comparative Nootkan studies, and photohistory of the reservation and people, especially in the period of change on the reservation (1880-1920). **Publications:** *Portraits in Time.*

★1192★
Montana State University
Center for Native American Studies
Bozeman, MT 59717-0234   Ph: (406)994-3881
Dr. Wayne J. Stein, Dir.

Research Activities and Fields: American Indian studies, including research on Montana tribal histories and culture and Indian-White relations. **Formerly:** American Indian Program (1975).

★1193★
Museum of the Great Plains
Elmer Thomas Park
601 Ferris Ave.
PO Box 68
Lawton, OK 73502   Ph: (405)581-3460
Steve Wilson, Dir.

Research Activities and Fields: Human ecology and prehistory in the Great Plains of North America and human adaptation to a plains environment, including studies in social psychology and on Pleistocene ecology of Domebo Mammoth Kill site, rise and decline of Wichita Indians, salvage excavations in Mangum Reservoir area, paleoIndian and plains archaic cultures, ethnology of Kiowa, Kiowa-Apache, and Comanche cultures, and archeological survey of Wichita Mountains. Conducts field excavations and provides information and technical consultation services for approved scholars and studies. **Publications:** *Great Plains Journal* (annually); *Contributions of Museum of the Great Plains* (irregularly); *Museum Newsletter.*

★1194★
Museum of New Mexico
PO Box 2087
Santa Fe, NM 87504   Ph: (505)827-6450
Thomas A. Livesay, Dir.

Research Activities and Fields: Archeology, ethnology, fine art, folk art, and history, including archeological and ethnological artifacts of Indians of southwestern U.S. and Mexico, Spanish colonial materials from Spain, Mexico, and New Mexico, historical and art collections from the Southwest, and folk art of the world. Conducts archeological excavations to document and catalog the prehistory and history of New Mexico. Also conducts anthropological investigations. **Publications:** *El Palacio* (four times per year); *Preview* six times per year.

★1195★
Navaho Initiative Project
PO Box 920
Fort Defiance, AZ 86504   Ph: (602)724-3351
James Muneta, Contact

Research Activities and Fields: Research on and development of services for handicapped Native Americans. **Publications:** *Satellite* (quarterly newsletter). **Formerly:** Dine Center for Human Development.

★1196★
New England Antiquities Research Association
305 Academy Rd.
Pembroke, NH 03275   Ph: (603)485-5655
Daniel Leary, Pres.

Research Activities and Fields: Anthropology, archeology, archeoastronomy, epigraphy, and geology. Native American studies concern the nature, origin, history, and purpose of stoneworks and related structures in the northeastern U.S. Current research includes archeology in Maine and New Hampshire. **Publications:** *NEARA Journal* (quarterly).

★1197★
Newberry Library
D'Arcy McNickle Center for the History of the
    American Indian
60 W. Walton St.
Chicago, IL 60610   Ph: (312)943-9090
Dr. Frederick E. Hoxie, Dir.

Research Activities and Fields: American Indian history, anthropology, literature, and ethnology. Programs support research in Indian-White relations, and tribal history. **Publications:** Monographs; Occasional Papers Series; Bibliographical Series; *Meeting Ground* (semiannual newsletter).

★1198★
Pembroke State University
Native American Resource Center
Pembroke, NC 28372   Ph: (919)521-4214
Stanley G. Knick Ph.D., Dir.

Research Activities and Fields: The Lumbee Indians who live in the University area and American Indian tribal histories and culture, particularly the Southeastern Indian tribes. Research interests include archaeology, ethnography, ethnohistory, and general American Indian studies. Research is conducted in conjuction with tribal organizations and with other University departments. **Publications:** *SPIRIT!* (quarterly newsletter); *Robeson Trails Archaeological Survey* (1988).

★1199★
Pennsylvania State University
American Indian Education Policy Center
320 Rackley Bldg.
University Park, PA 16802   Ph: (814)865-1489
Dr. L.A. Napier, Dir.

Research Activities and Fields: Policy issues concerning American Indian education, including training needs, leadership development, and other issues related directly or indirectly to schooling for the American Indian.

★1200★
Rochester Museum and Science Center
Research Division
657 East Ave.
PO Box 1480
Rochester, NY 14603-1480   Ph: (716)271-4320
Charles F. Hayes III, Res. Dir.

Research Activities and Fields: Anthropology, history, and natural sciences, including field studies in natural sciences, field and laboratory work in anthropology (especially American Indian and Genesee Valley region during 16th through 20th centuries), studies in historical archaeology and paleoethnobotany. **Publications:** Research Records.

★1201★
Santa Barbara Museum of Natural History
2559 Puesta del Sol Rd.
Santa Barbara, CA 93105   Ph: (805)682-4711
Dr. Dennis M. Power, Dir.

Research Activities and Fields: Anthropology, including ethnobotany, genealogy, and culture of the Chumash Indians. **Publications:** Occasional Papers Series; *Museum Bulletin* (monthly), *Annual Report*.

★1202★
Southern Methodist University
Fort Burgwin Research Center
PO Box 300
Ranchos de Taos, NM 87557   Ph: (505)758-8322
Dr. William B. Stallcup, Jr., Res. Dir.

Research Activities and Fields: Environmental sciences, archaeology, biology, and geology, including field studies in community ecology, prehistoric pithouse and pueblo settlements, osteology, demography, and ethnology. Performs archeological site preservation technology and local geology and geomorphology research.

★1203★
Southwest Museum
PO Box 41558
Los Angeles, CA 90041-0558   Ph: (213)221-2164
Jerome R. Selmer, Exec. Dir.

Research Activities and Fields: Archeology and ethnology of the Americas, especially history of the American Indian and Meso-America, both pre-Columbian and contemporary, illustrating human and cultural development. **Publications:** *Hodge Fund Publications; Southwest Museum Papers; Southwest Museum Leaflets; MASTERKEY*.

★1204★
State University of New York at Albany
Institute for Archaeological Studies
Social Science Rm.263
1400 Washington Ave.
Albany, NY 12222   Ph: (518)442-4700
Prof. Dean R. Snow,, Dir.

Research Activities and Fields: Archaeology, including northeastern archaeology, ethnology, and linguistics. Supports research conducted by faculty and graduate students on native northeastern peoples, primarily Algonquian and Iroquois tribes. **Publications:** *Man in the Northeast* (journal). **Formerly:** Absorbed the Institute for Northeast Anthropology (1988).

★1205★
University of Arizona
Arizona State Museum
Tucson, AZ 85721   Ph: (602)621-6281
Dr. Raymond H. Thompson, Dir.

Research Activities and Fields: Archaeology, ethnology, and ethnohistory, general ethnological studies among Indians, and special archeological research projects. Collaborates with state and local archeological and historical societies and clubs. **Publications:** Museum Archaeological Series; Anthropological Papers of the University of Arizona; Monograph Series; Occasional Exhibit Brochures; Informational Pamphlets; Popular Booklets.

★1206★
University of Arizona
Native American Research and Training Center
1642 E. Helen
Tucson, AZ 85719   Ph: (602)621-5075
Jennie R. Joe Ph.D., Dir.

Research Activities and Fields: Health and rehabilitation of disabled and chronically ill Native Americans. Core areas include the following: traditional Indian perceptions of disabling conditions and chronic diseases and how these perceptions affect patient responses to these conditions; development, field testing, and implementation of culturally sensitive research and rehabilitation training programs; and needs assessment and rehabilitation service delivery systems at the tribal and regional levels. Also studies the impact of government policy on the delivery of health care. Promotes self determination and parity among Native Americans in health and rehabilitation. Serves as a national resource for all North American tribes and Alaska natives.

★1207★
University of Arizona
Office of Interdisciplinary Graduate Programs
1010 N. Martin
Tucson, AZ 85719   Ph: (602)621-8368
Dr. Raphael Gruener, Dir.

Research Activities and Fields: Supports and monitors interdisciplinary research conducted by faculty committees. Projects include American Indian studies.

★1208★
University of California, Los Angeles
American Indian Studies Center
3220 Campbell Hall
Los Angeles, CA 90024   Ph: (310)825-7315
Dr. Duane Champagne, Dir.

Research Activities and Fields: American Indians, including history, culture, arts, humanities, social sciences, conditions, problems, and potentialities of that ethnic group. Seeks to benefit Los Angeles Indian community and Indian community at large. Coordinates educational, research, and action-oriented programs designed to meet needs of American Indian students at the University and of American Indian communities in general. **Publications:** *American Indian Culture and Research Journal*; American Indian Treaties Publications; Native American Pamphlet Series; American Indian Bibliographic Series; American Indian Monograph Series; Native American Politics Series; American Indian Language Series; American Indian Manuals & Handbook Series; Contemporary American Indian Issues Series. **Formerly:** Outgrowth of the American Indian Culture Program initiated at the University in 1968.

★1209★
University of Colorado—Boulder
Center for Studies of Ethnicity and Race in America
Ketchum 30
CB 339
Boulder, CO 80309-0339   Ph: (303)492-8852
Dr. Evelyn Hu-DeHart, Dir.

Research Activities and Fields: Comparative race and ethnicity and specific ethnic groups, including Afro-American, American Indian, Asian-American, and Chicano studies; African and Asian diasporal studies.

★1210★
University of Colorado—Boulder
Center for the Study of Native Languages of the
  Plains and Southwest
Dept. of Linguistics
Campus Box 295
Boulder, CO 80309-0295   Ph: (303)492-2748
Dr. Allan R. Taylor, Dir.

Research Activities and Fields: Collects data and conducts research on Native American languages of the Great Plains and Southwest, including the Siouan languages, Gros Ventre (a nearly extinct Algonquian language related to Arapaho), Kiowa, and Wichita (a nearly extinct Caddoan language). Also includes the Lakhota Project, which offers instructional materials to aid in learning Dakota Sioux language.

★1211★
University of Nebraska, Lincoln
State Museum
Nebraska Hall
Lincoln, NE 68588   Ph: (402)472-6365
Hugh H. Genoways, Dir.

Research Activities and Fields: Studies include the culture and history of the Plains Apache. **Publications:** *Bulletin of University of Nebraska State Museum; Museum Notes; Annual Report*.

★1212★
University of North Dakota
Center for Rural Health
501 Columbia Rd.
Grand Forks, ND 58203   Ph: (701)777-3848
Jack M. Geller Ph.D., Dir.

Research Activities and Fields: Rural health care delivery, especially in the areas of health manpower, the viability of rural health facilities, gerontology, Native American health care, and uncompensated care. Collaborates with other research organizations throughout the nation. **Publications:** *Focus on Rural Health* (semiannually) **Formerly:** Office of Rural Health (1986), Center for Rural Health Services, Policy and Research (1990).

★1213★
University of South Dakota
Institute of American Indian Studies
Dakota Hall, Rm. 12
414 E. Clark St.
Vermillion, SD 57069   Ph: (605)677-5209
Leonard Bruguier, Dir.

Research Activities and Fields: Indians and Indian affairs, including study of Dakota language. **Publications:** *The Bulletin* (quarterly); Reports; Papers; Conference Proceedings.

★1214★
University of South Dakota
Social Science Research Institute
Vermillion, SD 57069   Ph: (605)677-5401
Prof. Harlowe Hatle Jr., Dir.

Research Activities and Fields: Research includes studies on organizations, economic and social development, criminology, juvenile delinquency, child abuse, aged population, communications, social work and welfare, court administration, prison education, alcoholism, medical and educational problems on American Indian reservations, and follow-up on juvenile offenders. Conducts anthropological studies, including site preservation. **Formerly:** Social Research Center; Social Behavior Research Institute (1991).

★1215★
University of Utah
American West Center
1023 Annex
Salt Lake City, UT 84112   Ph: (801)581-7611
Dr. Floyd A. O'Neil, Dir.

Research Activities and Fields: Political, social, economic, and cultural studies of the North American West, American Indian history and traditions, other ethnic groups, oral history, applied historical studies, and various related research projects under government and foundation grants. **Publications:** Occasional Paper Series. **Formerly:** Western History Center (1972).

Education Programs & Services

Head Start Programs

★1216★
Cocopah Tribe
Head Start Program
PO Bin G
Somerton, AZ 85350   Ph: (602)627-2811

★1217★
Colorado River Indian Tribes
Head Start Program
Rte. 1, Box 39X
Parker, AZ 85344   Ph: (602)662-4311
Carol Daniel, Dir.

★1218★
Gila River Indian Community Council
Head Start Program
PO Box A
Sacaton, AZ 85247   Ph: (602)562-3423
Imogene Osife, Dir.

★1219★
Havasupai Tribal Council
Head Start Program
PO Box 40
Supai, AZ 86435   Ph: (602)448-2901
Jule Sinyella, Dir.

★1220★
Hopi Tribe
Head Start Program
PO Box 123
Kykotsmovi, AZ 86039   Ph: (602)734-2441
Lorraine Phee, Dir.

★1221★
Hualapai Tribe
Head Start Program
PO Box 66
Peach Springs, AZ 86434   Ph: (602)769-2399
Josephine Imus, Dir.

★1222★
Navajo Tribe
Division of Child Development
Head Start Program
PO Box 308
Window Rock, AZ 86515   Ph: (602)871-4941

★1223★
Pascua Yaqui Tribal Council
Head Start Program
7474 S. Camino De Oeste
Tucson, AZ 85746   Ph: (602)883-2838
Irene Sanchez, Dir.

★1224★
Quechan Tribal Council
Head Start Program
PO Box 890
Yuma, AZ 85364   Ph: (619)572-0264

★1225★
Salt River Pima-Maricopa Indian Community Council
Head Start Program
Rte. 1, Box 216
Scottsdale, AZ 85256   Ph: (602)941-7254
Alma Pierson, Dir.

★1226★
San Carlos Apache Tribe
Head Start Program
Box 278
San Carlos, AZ 85550   Ph: (602)475-2361
Harrison Tagle, Dir.

★1227★
Tohono O'Odham Nation
Head Start Program
PO Box 837
Sells, AZ 85634   Ph: (602)383-2221
Phyllis Anpone, Dir.

★1228★
White Mountain Apache Tribe
Head Start Program
PO Box 738   Ph: (602)338-4938
Whiteriver, AZ 85941   Fax: (602)338-4778
Norma Albert, Acting Dir.

★1229★
Hoopa Valley Business Council
Head Start Program
PO Box 1348
Hoopa, CA 95546   Ph: (619)625-4522

★1230★
Inter-Tribal Council of California
Head Start Program
2021 P St.   Ph: (916)448-8687
Sacramento, CA 95814   Fax: (916)447-6949
Toni Thompson, Dir.

★1231★
Inyo Child Care Services
Head Start Program
2742 N. Sierra Hwy.
Bishop, CA 93514   Ph: (619)872-3911

★1232★
Southern Ute Tribal Council
Head Start Program
PO Box 800   Ph: (303)563-4566
Ignacio, CO 81137   Fax: (303)563-4504
Jim Gage, Dir.

★1233★
Ute Mountain Ute Tribe
Head Start Program
General Delivery
Towaoc, CO 81334   Ph: (303)565-3751
Glenda Lopez, Dir.

★1234★
Miccosukee Tribe
Head Start Program
PO Box 44021, Tamiami Sta.
Miami, FL 33144   Ph: (305)223-8380
Griselle Alejandre, Dir.

★1235★
Seminole Tribe
Head Start Program
3006 Josie Billie Ave.
Hollywood, FL 33024

★1236★
Coeur D'Alene Tribal Council
Head Start Program
PO Box 214
Desmet, ID 83824   Ph: (208)274-6921

★1237★
Nez Perce Tribal Executive Committee
Head Start Program
PO Box 365
Lapwai, ID 83540   Ph: (208)843-2253

★1238★
Shoshone-Bannock Tribes
Head Start Program
PO Box 306
Fort Hall, ID 83203   Ph: (208)238-3700
Angela Toledo, Dir.

★1239★
Kickapoo Tribe of Kansas
Head Start Program
RR 1, Box 157A   Ph: (913)486-2131
Horton, KS 66439   Fax: (913)486-2801
Rose Finch, Dir.

★1240★
Grand Traverse Band of Ottawa and Chippewa Tribes
Head Start Program
Rte. 1, Box 135
Suttons Bay, MI 49682   Ph: (616)271-3538
Maxine Charter, Dir.

★1241★
Inter-Tribal Council of Michigan
Head Start Program
405 E. Easterday Ave.
Sault Ste. Marie, MI 49783   Ph: (906)632-6896
Irma Parish, Dir.

★1242★
Bois Forte Reservation Business Committee
Head Start Program
PO Box 16
Nett Lake, MN 55772

★1243★
Fond du Lac Reservation Business Committee
Head Start Program
105 University Rd.
Cloquet, MN 55720   Ph: (218)879-4593
Mary Ann Blacketter, Dir.

★1244★
Grand Portage Reservation Business Committee
Head Start Program
PO Box 368
Grand Portage, MN 55605   Ph: (218)475-2234
Julie Lessard, Dir.

★1245★
Leech Lake Band of Chippewa
Head Start Program
Rte. 3, Box 100
Cass Lake, MN 56633

★1246★
Mille Lacs Reservation
Head Start Program
Star Route
Onamia, MN 56359   Ph: (612)532-4181
Norma Thompson, Dir.

★1247★
Red Lake Reservation
Head Start Program
PO Box 53
Red Lake, MN 56671   Ph: (218)679-3396
Lea Defue, Dir.

★1248★
White Earth Band of Chippewa
Head Start Program
PO Box 418
White Earth, MN 56591   Ph: (218)983-3285
Blanche Niemi, Dir.

★1249★
Mississippi Band of Choctaw Indians
Head Start Program
Rte. 7, Box 21
Philadelphia, MS 39350   Ph: (601)656-5251
Dolores Saunders, Dir.

★1250★
Blackfeet Tribal Business Council
Head Start Program
PO Box 537
Browning, MT 59417   Ph: (406)338-7411

★1251★
Confederated Salish and Kootenai Tribes
Head Start Program
PO Box 266
Saint Ignatius, MT 59865   Ph: (406)745-4509
Jeanne Christopher, Dir.

★1252★
Crow Tribal Council
Head Start Program
PO Box 159
Crow Agency, MT 59022   Ph: (406)638-2697
Nora Bird, Dir.

★1253★
Fort Belknap Indian Community Council
Head Start Program
PO Box 579
Harlem, MT 59526   Ph: (406)353-2205
Carolyn Yellowroot, Dir.

★1254★
Fort Peck Tribes
Head Start Program
1027 Poplar
Poplar, MT 59255   Ph: (406)768-5155
Viola Wood, Dir.

★1255★
Northern Cheyenne Tribal Council
Head Start Program
PO Box 128
Lame Deer, MT 59043   Ph: (406)477-6347
Treva Butter, Dir.

★1256★
Rocky Boy Chippewa Cree Tribe
Head Start Program
PO Box 620
Box Elder, MT 59521   Ph: (406)395-4666
Melissa Windy Boy, Dir.

★1257★
Omaha Tribal Council
Head Start Program
PO Box 357
Macy, NE 68039   Ph: (402)837-5336
Lena Webster, Dir.

★1258★
Santee Sioux Tribal Council
Head Start Program
RR #2
Niobrara, NE 68760   Ph: (402)857-3738
Joyce Thomas, Dir.

★1259★
Winnebago Tribe of Nebraska
Head Start Program
PO Box 787
Winnebago, NE 68071   Ph: (402)878-2200
Marian Holstein, Dir.

★1260★
Inter-Tribal Council of Nevada
Head Start Program
806 Holman Way
PO Box 7440
Reno, NV 89510   Ph: (702)329-3955

★1261★
Eight Northern Pueblos, Inc.
Head Start Program
PO Box 969
San Juan Pueblo, NM 87566   Ph: (505)852-4265
Judy Cooper, Dir.

★1262★
Five Sandoval Indian Pueblos, Inc.
Head Start Program
PO Box 580
Bernalillo, NM 87004   Ph: (505)867-3351
Lucy Gutierrez, Dir.

★1263★
Jicarilla Apache Tribal Council
Head Start Program
PO Box 506
Dulce, NM 87528   Ph: (505)759-3343
Elizabeth Muniz, Dir.

★1264★
Mescalero Apache Tribal Council
Head Start Program
PO Box 176
Mescalero, NM 88340   Ph: (505)671-4494

★1265★
Pueblo of Acoma
Head Start Program
PO Box 307
Acoma, NM 87034   Ph: (505)552-6621
Cindy Sanchez, Dir.

★1266★
Pueblo of Isleta
Head Start Program
PO Box 385
Isleta Pueblo, NM 87022   Ph: (505)869-3700
Jennifer Tollesson-y-Chavez, Dir.

★1267★
Pueblo of Jemez
Head Start Program
PO Box 78
Jemez Pueblo, NM 87024   Ph: (505)834-7678
Nilla Vallo, Dir.

★1268★
Pueblo of Laguna
Head Start Program
PO Box 194
Laguna, NM 87026   Ph: (505)552-6649
Ann Ray, Dir.

★1269★
Pueblo of San Felipe
Head Start Program
PO Box H
San Felipo Pueblo, NM 87001   Ph: (505)867-2816
Santana Townsend, Dir.

★1270★
Pueblo of Taos
Head Start Program
PO Box 1846
Taos, NM 87571   Ph: (505)758-8626
Carmen Luierance, Dir.

★1271★
Santo Domingo Tribe
Head Start Program
PO Box 40
Santo Domingo, NM 87052   Ph: (505)465-2214
Barbara A. Lovelace, Prog. Dir.

★1272★
Zuni Pueblos
Head Start Program
PO Box 339
Zuni, NM 87327   Ph: (505)782-4481
Kathy Romancito, Dir.

★1273★
St. Regis Mohawk Tribe
Head Start Program
Rte. 37
Hogansburg, NY 13655   Ph: (518)358-2272
Melanie Connors, Dir.

★1274★
Seneca Nation of Indians
Head Start Program
1530 Rte. 438
Irving, NY 14081   Ph: (716)532-5577
Sheila Cooper, Dir.

★1275★
Qualla Indian Boundary
Head Start Program
PO Box 1310
Cherokee, NC 28719   Ph: (704)497-9416
Robin Schaeffer, Dir.

★1276★
Little Hoop Community College
Head Start Program
PO Box 269
Fort Totten, ND 58335   Ph: (701)766-4205
Evangelina White, Dir.

★1277★
Standing Rock Sioux Tribal Council
Head Start Program
PO Box 473   Ph: (701)854-3458
Fort Yates, ND 58538   Fax: (701)854-7299
Marcella Yellon Hammer, Acting Dir.

★1278★
Three Affiliated Tribes
Head Start Program
PO Box 687
New Town, ND 58763   Ph: (701)627-4820

★1279★
Turtle Mountain Band of Chippewa
Head Start Program
PO Box 900
Belcourt, ND 58316   Ph: (701)477-6451
Jennifer Ramey, Dir.

★1280★
Caddo Tribe
Head Start Program
PO Box 487
Binger, OK 73009   Ph: (405)656-2223

★1281★
Central Tribes of the Shawnee Area, Inc.
Head Start Program
Rte. 5, Box 148B
Shawnee, OK 74801   Ph: (405)275-0663
Denise Bettis, Dir.

★1282★
Cherokee Nation of Oklahoma
Head Start Program
PO Box 948   Ph: (918)458-5795
Tahlequah, OK 74465   Fax: (918)458-4787
Verna Thompson, Dir.

★1283★
Cheyenne-Arapaho Tribes of Oklahoma
Head Start Program
PO Box 38   Ph: (405)262-0092
Concho, OK 73022   Fax: (405)262-0745
Christine Black Owl, Dir.

★1284★
Chickasaw Nation of Oklahoma
Head Start Program
PO Box 1548   Ph: (405)436-2603
Ada, OK 74820   Fax: (405)436-4287
Belle Harjo, Dir.

★1285★
Choctaw Nation of Oklahoma
Head Start Program
PO Drawer 1210   Ph: (405)924-8280
Durant, OK 74702   Free: 800-522-6170
Linda Higginbotham, Dir.   Fax: (405)924-1150

★1286★
Creek Nation of Oklahoma
Head Start Program
PO Box 580
Okmulgee, OK 74447   Ph: (918)756-8700

★1287★
Kickapoo Tribe of Oklahoma
Kickapoo Head Start, Inc.
PO Box 399   Ph: (405)964-3676
McLoud, OK 74851   Fax: (405)964-3417
Katherine Wahpepah, Dir.

★1288★
Kiowa Tribe of Oklahoma
Head Start Program
PO Box 369
Carnegie, OK 73015   Ph: (405)654-2300
Jeannie Toppah, Dir.

★1289★
Osage Tribal Council
Head Start Program
Osage Agency Council
Pawhuska, OK 74056   Ph: (918)287-1246
Linda Kills Crow, Dir.

★1290★
Seminole Nation of Oklahoma
Head Start Program
PO Box 1498
Wewoka, OK 74884   Ph: (405)257-6663
Nolan Tiger, Dir.

★1291★
TOE Missouri Tribe
Head Start Program
Rte. 1, Box 62
Red Rock, OK 74651   Ph: (405)723-4434

★1292★
Confederated Tribes of Siletz Indians
Head Start Program
PO Box 549   Ph: (503)444-2532
Siletz, OR 97380   Fax: (503)444-2307
Denise Williams, Dir.

★1293★
Confederated Tribes of Warm Springs
Head Start Program
PO Box C
Warm Springs, OR 97761   Ph: (503)553-1161
Julie Quaid, Dir.

★1294★
Cheyenne River Sioux Tribal Council
Head Start Program
PO Box 180
Eagle Butte, SD 57625   Ph: (605)964-6835
Moses Traversi, Dir.

★1295★
Crow Creek Sioux Tribe
Head Start Program
PO Box 78   Ph: (605)245-2337
Fort Thompson, SD 57339   Fax: (605)245-2366
Susan Smith, Dir.

★1296★
Lower Brule Sioux Tribe
Head Start Program
PO Box 804   Ph: (605)473-5520
Lower Brule, SD 57548   Fax: (605)473-5606
Pat Madsen, Dir.

★1297★
Oglala Sioux Tribal Council
Head Start Program
1 Preschool Rd.
PO Box 279   Ph: (605)867-5170
Porcupine, SD 57772   Fax: (605)867-5659
Michael Her Many Horses, Exec.Dir.

★1298★
Rosebud Sioux Tribal Council
Head Start Program
PO Box 430   Ph: (605)856-2391
Rosebud, SD 57570   Fax: (605)856-2039
Lois Antoine, Dir.

★1299★
Rural America Initatives, Inc.
Head Start Program
Rte. 1, Box 1845
Rapid City, SD 57702   Ph: (605)341-3163
Allison Bates, Dir.

★1300★
Ute Indian Tribe
Head Start Program
PO Box 265
Fort Duchesne, UT 84026   Ph: (801)722-4506

★1301★
Chehalis Tribal Business Council
Head Start Program
420 Howanut Rd.
PO Box 536
Oakville, WA 98568   Ph: (206)273-5514
Robert Secena, Dir.

★1302★
Colville Confederated Tribes
Head Start Program
PO Box 150   Ph: (509)634-4711
Nespelem, WA 99155   Fax: (509)634-8799
Vicky DeSautel, Dir.

★1303★
Lower Elwha-Klallam Tribe
Head Start Program
1660 Lower Elwha Rd.
Port Angeles, WA 98362   Ph: (206)452-8471
Verna Henderson, Dir.

★1304★
Lummi Indian Business Council
Head Start Program
2616 Kwina Rd.   Ph: (206)647-6260
Bellingham, WA 98226   Fax: (206)384-5521
Ramona Menish, Dir.

★1305★
Makah Tribal Council
Head Start Program
PO Box 115
Neah Bay, WA 98357   Ph: (206)645-2201
Ann Renker, Acting Dir.

★1306★
Muckleshoot Tribal Council
Head Start Program
39015 172nd Ave. SE   Ph: (206)939-3311
Auburn, WA 98002   Fax: (206)939-5311
Dennis Goss, Gen. Manager

★1307★
Nisqually Indian Community Council
Head Start Program
4820 She-Nah-Num Dr. SE
Olympia, WA 98503   Ph: (206)456-5221
Vicky Janoe, Dir.

★1308★
Nooksack Indian Tribal Council
Head Start Program
PO Box 157   Ph: (206)592-5176
Deming, WA 98244   Fax: (206)592-5721
Lane Warbus, Dir.

★1309★
Port Gamble Klallam Tribe
Head Start Program
PO Box 280   Ph: (206)297-3138
Kingston, WA 98346   Fax: (206)297-7097
Jaclyn Haight, Dir.

★1310★
Quileute Tribal Council
Head Start Program
PO Box 279   Ph: (206)374-6163
La Push, WA 98350   Fax: (206)374-6311
Doreen Malmsten, Dir.

★1311★
Quinault Indian Nation
Head Start Program
PO Box 189   Ph: (206)962-2071
Taholah, WA 98587   Fax: (206)962-2460
Betty Boone, Dir.

★1312★
Skokomish Tribal Council
Head Start Program
N. 80 Tribal Center Rd.
Shelton, WA 98584   Ph: (206)426-4232

★1313★
Yakima Tribe
Head Start Program
PO Box 151   Ph: (509)865-5121
Toppenish, WA 98948   Fax: (509)865-6092
Philomeana Saluskin, Preschool Principal

★1314★
Bad River Tribal Council
Head Start Program
PO Box 39
Odanah, WI 54861   Ph: (715)682-4674

★1315★
Lac Courte Oreilles Governing Board
Head Start Program
Rte. 2, Box 2700   Ph: (715)634-8934
Hayward, WI 54843   Fax: (715)634-4797
Cathy Barber, Dir.

★1316★
Lac du Flambeau Tribal Council
Head Start Program
PO Box 67   Ph: (715)588-3303
Lac Du Flambeau, WI 54538   Fax: (715)588-7930
Joyce Maki, Dir.

★1317★
Oneida Tribal Business Committee
Head Start Program
3000 Seminary Rd.
PO Box 365   Ph: (414)869-1260
Oneida, WI 54155   Fax: (414)869-2194
Mary Ellen Hayes, Dir.

★1318★
Stockbridge-Munsee Tribal Council
Head Start Program
Rte. 1   Ph: (715)793-4100
Bowler, WI 54416   Fax: (715)793-4299
Theresa Martin, Dir.

★1319★
Wisconsin Winnebago Business Committee
Head Start Program
127 Main St.
PO Box 667   Ph: (715)284-4915
Black River Falls, WI 54615   Fax: (715)284-1760
Pat Marquart, Dir.

★1320★
Shoshone and Arapahoe Tribes
Head Start Program
PO Box 308
Fort Washakie, WY 82514   Ph: (307)332-7163

─────────── **Schools** ───────────

★1321★
Black Mesa Community School
RRDS, Box 215   Ph: (602)674-3632
Chinle, AZ 86503   Fax: (602)674-5201
Dorothy R. Yazzie, Dir.
School Type: Contract day school; grades K-8.

★1322★
Blackwater Community School
Rte. 1, Box 95
Coolidge, AZ 85228   Ph: (602)723-5859
S. Jo Lewis, Principal
School Type: Contract day school; grades K-2.

★1323★
Casa Blanca Day School
PO Box 940
Bapchule, AZ 85221   Ph: (602)562-3489
Geraldine Youngman, Acting Principal
School Type: BIA day school; grades K-4.

★1324★
Chilchinbeto Day School
PO Box 547
Kayenta, AZ 86033   Ph: (602)697-3448
Carl Granfors, Acting Principal
School Type: BIA day school; grades K-8.

★1325★
Chinle Boarding School
PO Box 70   Ph: (602)781-6221
Many Farms, AZ 86538   Fax: (602)674-5201
Lorraine Boyiddle, Principal
School Type: BIA on-reservation boarding school; grades K-8.

★1326★
Cibecue Community School
General Delivery   Ph: (602)332-2444
Cibecue, AZ 85911   Fax: (602)332-2586
Raymond Bierner, Principal
School Type: Grant day school; grades K-9.

★1327★
Cottonwood Day School
Chinle, AZ 86503   Ph: (602)725-3256
                                    Fax: (602)674-5201
Dr. Aty Bakker, Principal
School Type: BIA day school; grades K-8.

★1328★
Dennehotso Boarding School
PO Box LL
Dennehotso, AZ 86535   Ph: (602)658-3201
Velma Eisenberger, Principal
School Type: BIA on-reservation boarding school; grades K-8.

★1329★
Dilcon Boarding School
Star Rte.   Ph: (602)657-3211
Winslow, AZ 86047   Fax: (602)657-3370
Lula Mae Stago, Principal
School Type: BIA on-reservation boarding school; grades K-8.

★1330★
Flagstaff Dormitory
PO Box 609
Flagstaff, AZ 86002   Ph: (602)774-5270
James Kimery, Dir./Counselor
School Type: Grant peripheral dormitory; grades 9-12.

★1331★
Gila Crossing Day School
PO Box 10
Laveen, AZ 85339   Ph: (602)550-4834
Carol Howard, Acting Principal
School Type: BIA day school; grades K-6.

★1332★
Greasewood Boarding School
Ganado, AZ 86505   Ph: (602)654-3331
Beverly J. Crawford, Principal
School Type: BIA on-reservation boarding school; grades K-8.

★1333★
Greyhills High School
PO Box 160   Ph: (602)283-6271
Tuba City, AZ 86045   Fax: (602)283-6271
Andrew M. Tah, Superintendent
School Type: Grant boarding school; grades 9-12.

★1334★
Havasupai School
PO Box 40
Supai, AZ 86435   Ph: (602)448-2901
James N. Eaton, Principal
School Type: Contract day school; grades K-8.

★1335★
Holbrook Dormitory
PO Box 758
Holbrook, AZ 86025   Ph: (602)524-6223
Gary Joka, President
School Type: BIA peripheral dormitory; grades 9-12.

★1336★
Hopi Day School
PO Box 42   Ph: (602)734-2468
Kyakotsmovi, AZ 86039   Fax: (602)738-5139
Edward Vermillion, Principal
School Type: BIA day school; grades K-6.

★1337★
Hopi High School
PO Box 337   Ph: (602)738-5111
Keams Canyon, AZ 86034   Fax: (602)738-5139
Alan C. Ledford Jr., Principal
School Type: BIA day school; grades 7-12.

★1338★
Hotevilla Bacavi Community School
PO Box 48
Hotevilla, AZ 86030   Ph: (602)734-2462
Leroy Shingoitewa, Administrator
School Type: Contract day school; grades K-6.

★1339★
Hunters Point Boarding School
PO Box 99
Saint Michaels, AZ 86511   Ph: (602)871-4439
Roy H. Chase, Principal
School Type: BIA on-reservation boarding school; grades K-5.

★1340★
John F. Kennedy Day School
PO Box 130
White River, AZ 85941   Ph: (602)338-4593
Patricia L. Banashley, Principal
School Type: BIA day school; grades K-8.

★1341★
Kaibeto Boarding School
Kaibeto, AZ 86053   Ph: (602)673-3480
Oscar Tso, Principal
School Type: BIA on-reservation boarding school; grades K-8.

★1342★
Kayenta Boarding School
PO Box 188
Kayenta, AZ 86033   Ph: (602)697-3439
Loren Joseph, Principal
School Type: BIA on-reservation boarding school; grades K-8.

★1343★
Keams Canyon Boarding School
PO Box 397   Ph: (602)738-2385
Keams Canyon, AZ 86034   Fax: (602)738-5139
Dr. Theresa Delorme, Principal
School Type: Cooperative boarding school; grades K-6.

★1344★
Kinlichee Boarding School
Ganado, AZ 86505   Ph: (602)755-3439
Elsie Belone, Prinicpal
School Type: BIA on-reservation boarding school; grades K-6.

★1345★
Leupp Schools, Inc.
PO Box HC-61   Ph: (602)686-6211
Winslow, AZ 86047   Fax: (602)686-6216
Tommy C. Yazzie, Superintendent
School Type: Grant boarding school; grades K-12.

★1346★
Little Singer Community School
Star Rte. Box 239
Winslow, AZ 86047   Ph: (602)779-3788
James Shereck, Dir.
School Type: Grant day school; grades K-6.

★1347★
Low Mountain Boarding School
Chinle, AZ 86503   Ph: (602)725-3308
John C. Leffue, Principal Fax: (602)674-5201

School Type: BIA on-reservation boarding school; grades K-4.

★1348★
Lukachukai Boarding School
Lukachukai, AZ 86507   Ph: (602)787-2301
                           Fax: (602)674-5201
Larry Tsosie, Principal
School Type: BIA on-reservation boarding school; grades K-8.

★1349★
Many Farms High School
PO Box 307   Ph: (602)781-6226
Many Farms, AZ 86538   Fax: (602)674-5201
Harold King, Principal
School Type: BIA on-reservation boarding school; grades 9-12.

★1350★
Moencopi Day School
PO Box 185   Ph: (602)283-5361
Tuba City, AZ 86045   Fax: (602)738-5139
Dr. John L. Thomas, Principal
School Type: BIA day school; grades K-6.

★1351★
Navajo Mountain Boarding School
PO Box 10010
Tonalea, AZ 86044   Ph: (602)672-2851
H. C. Black, Principal
School Type: BIA on-reservation boarding school; grades K-8.

★1352★
Nazlini Boarding School
Ganado, AZ 86505   Ph: (602)755-6125
William H. Draper, Principal Fax: (602)674-5201

School Type: BIA on-reservation boarding school; grades K-6.

★1353★
Pine Springs Boarding School
PO Box 198
Houck, AZ 86506-0198   Ph: (602)871-4311
Charles W. Riley II, Principal
School Type: BIA on-reservation boarding schools; grades K-3.

★1354★
Pinon Dormitory
PO Box 159   Ph: (602)725-3250
Pinon, AZ 86510   Fax: (602)725-3232
Phyllis Badonie, Dir.
School Type: Contract peripheral dormitory; grades 1-5.

★1355★
Polacca Day School
PO Box 750   Ph: (602)737-2581
Polacca, AZ 86042   Fax: (602)738-5139
Glenn C. WhiteEagle, Principal
School Type: BIA day school; grades K-6.

★1356★
Red Lake Day School
PO Box 39
Tonalea, AZ 86044   Ph: (602)283-6325
Ray L. Interpreter, Principal
School Type: BIA day school; grades K-8.

★1357★
Rock Point Community School
Rock Point, AZ 86545   Ph: (602)659-4224
                                     Fax: (602)659-4235
Jimmy C. Begay, Dir.
School Type: Contract day school; grades K-12.

★1358★
Rocky Ridge Boarding School
PO Box 299
Kykotsmovi, AZ 86039   Ph: (602)674-3686
Fredrick M. Johnson, Principal
School Type: BIA on-reservation boarding school; grades K-8.

★1359★
Rough Rock Demonstration School
RRDS, Box 217   Ph: (602)728-3311
Chinle, AZ 86503   Fax: (602)728-3215
Carl Levi, Superintendent
School Type: Grant boarding school; grades K-12.

★1360★
Salt River Day School
Rte. 1, Box 117
Scottsdale, AZ 85256   Ph: (602)241-2810
Austin Duckles, Principal
School Type: BIA day school; grades K-6.

★1361★
San Simon School
Star Rte. 1, Box 92   Ph: (602)362-2231
Sells, AZ 85634   Fax: (602)362-2405
Della R. Williams, Principal
School Type: BIA day school; grades K-8.

★1362★
Santa Rosa Boarding School
Sells, AZ 85634   Ph: (602)361-2331
Junia Jones, Principal
School Type: BIA on-reservation boarding school; grades K-8.

★1363★
Santa Rosa Ranch School
HCO4 7570
Tucson, AZ 85735   Ph: (602)383-2359
Jean Tyson, Principal
School Type: BIA day school; grades K-8.

★1364★
Seba Dalkai Boarding School
Star Rte. 1
Winslow, AZ 86047   Ph: (602)657-3209
Holly Butler, Principal
School Type: BIA on-reservation boarding school; grades K-6.

★1365★
Second Mesa Day School
PO Box 98   Ph: (602)737-2571
Second Mesa, AZ 86043   Fax: (602)738-5139
Betty Paymella, Principal
School Type: BIA day school; grades K-6.

★1366★
Shonto Boarding School
Shonto, AZ 86054   Ph: (602)672-2340
Roland E. Smith, Principal
School Type: BIA On-Reservation Boarding School; grades K-8.

★1367★
Teecnospos Boarding School
Teecnospos, AZ 86514   Ph: (602)656-3451
Thomas Sloan, Principal
School Type: BIA on-reservation boarding school; grades K-8.

★1368★
Theodore Roosevelt School
PO Box 567
Fort Apache, AZ 85926   Ph: (602)338-4464
Linda Sue Warner, Principal
School Type: BIA on-reservation boarding school; grades 4-12.

★1369★
Tohono O'Odham High School
PO Box 513
Sells, AZ 85634   Ph: (602)362-2400
Mil Sanderson, Principal
School Type: BIA day school; grades 9-12.

★1370★
Tuba City Boarding School
PO Box 187
Tuba City, AZ 86045   Ph: (602)283-4531
Jerry E. Diebel, Principal
School Type: BIA on-reservation boarding school; grades K-8.

★1371★
Wide Ruins Boarding School
PO Box 309
Chambers, AZ 86502   Ph: (602)652-3251
Leo T. Gishie, Principal
School Type: BIA on-reservation boarding school, grades K-5.

★1372★
Winslow Dormitory
822 W. Aspinwall
Winslow, AZ 86047   Ph: (602)289-3242
Helen Higdon, Principal
School Type: BIA peripheral dormitory; grades 7-12.

★1373★
Sherman Indian High School
9010 Magnolia Ave.   Ph: (714)276-6334
Riverside, CA 92503   Fax: (714)276-6336
Joe E. Frazier, Principal
School Type: BIA off-reservation boarding school; grades 9-12.

★1374★
Ahfachkee Day School
Star Rte., Box 40   Ph: (813)983-6348
Clewiston, FL 33440   Fax: (305)581-8917
Amy Jagoda, Principal
School Type: Contract day school; grades K-6.

★1375★
Miccosukee Indian School
PO Box 440021   Ph: (305)223-8380
Tamiami Station, FL 33144   Fax: (305)223-1011
Bruce Hoffman, Principal
School Type: Contract day school; grades K-12.

★1376★
Coeur D'Alene Tribal School
PO Box 338   Ph: (208)274-6921
DeSmet, ID 83824   Fax: (208)274-3101
Don Beach, Superintendent
School Type: Grant day school; grades K-8.

★1377★
Sho'Ban School District No. 512
PO Box 306   Ph: (208)238-3975
Fort Hall, ID 83203   Fax: (208)238-3700
Gary Stears, Superintendent
School Type: Grant day school; grades 6-12.

★1378★
Sac and Fox Settlement School
Rte. 2   Ph: (515)484-4990
Tama, IA 52339   Fax: (515)484-3264
Lon Burr, Administrator
School Type: Contract day school; pre-K to grades 6.

★1379★
Kickapoo Nation School
PO Box 106
Powhattan, KS 66527   Ph: (913)474-3550
Bernard Daschell, Superintendent
School Type: Contract day school; grades K-12.

★1380★
Chitimacha Day School
Rte. 2, Box 222   Ph: (318)923-4921
Jeanerette, LA 70544   Fax: (318)923-7791
Leonard Sudduth, Principal
School Type: BIA day school; grades K-8.

★1381★
Beatrice Rafferty School
Pleasant Point Reservation   Ph: (207)853-6085
Perry, ME 04667   Fax: (207)853-6210
Sr. Maureen Wallace, Principal
School Type: Contract day school; grades K-8.

★1382★
Indian Island School
1 River Rd.
PO Box 566
Indian Island, ME 04468   Ph: (207)827-4285
Sr. Helen McKeough, Principal
School Type: Contract day school; grades K-8.

★1383★
Indian Township School
Peter Dana Point   Ph: (207)796-2362
Princeton, ME 04668   Fax: (207)796-2726
Sr. Ellen Turner, Principal
School Type: Contract day school; grades Pre-K to 8.

★1384★
Hannahville Indian School
N14911 Hannahville B1 Rd.   Ph: (906)466-2556
Wilson, MI 49896   Fax: (906)466-2418
Thomas G. Miller, Administrator
School Type: Grant day school; grades K-12.

★1385★
Chief Bug-O-Nay-Ge-Shig School
Rte. 3, Box 100   Ph: (218)665-2282
Cass Lake, MN 56633   Fax: (218)335-8309
Ted Bogda, Superintendent
School Type: Grant day school; grades K-12.

★1386★
Circle of Life Survival School
PO Box 447   Ph: (218)983-3285
White Earth, MN 56591   Fax: (218)983-3641
Dr. Jim Noonan, Principal/Admin.
School Type: Grant day school; grades K-12.

★1387★
Fond du Lac Ojibway School
105 University Rd.
Cloquet, MN 55720   Ph: (218)879-0241
Dr. Thomas Peacock, Superintendent
School Type: Grant day school; grades K-12.

★1388★
Nay-Ah-Shing School
HC 67 Box 242   Ph: (612)532-4181
Onamia, MN 56359   Fax: (612)532-4209
Leroy Machulda, Educ. Commissioner
School Type: Grant day school; grades 7-12.

★1389★
Bogue Chitto Elementary School
Rte. 2, Box 274
Philadelphia, MS 39350   Ph: (601)656-8611
James R. Burton Jr., Principal
School Type: Grant day school; grades K-8.

★1390★
Choctaw Central High School
Rte. 7, Box 72
Philadelphia, MS 39350   Ph: (601)656-8870
James Pair, Principal
School Type: Grant boarding School; grades 7-12.

★1391★
Conehatta Elementary School
Rte. 1, Box 343
Conehatta, MS 39057-9717   Ph: (601)775-8254
William P. Williamson, Principal
School Type: Grant day school; grades K-8.

★1392★
Red Water Elementary School
Rte. 4, Box 30
Carthage, MS 39051   Ph: (601)267-8500
Dr. Sharon Pyrd, Principal
School Type: Grant day school; grades K-8.

★1393★
Standing Pine Elementary School
Rte. 2, Box 236
Walnut Grove, MS 39189   Ph: (601)267-9225
Jackie Harpole, Principal
School Type: Grant day school; grades K-6.

★1394★
Tucker Elementary School
Rte. 4, Box 351
Philadelphia, MS 39350   Ph: (601)656-8775
Roseanna Thompson, Principal
School Type: Grant day school; grades K-8.

★1395★
Blackfeet Dormitory
Blackfeet Agency
Browning, MT 59417   Ph: (406)338-7441
Leonard L. Guardipee, Supervisory Guidance Counselor
School Type: BIA peripheral dormitory; grades 1-12.

★1396★
Busby School
PO Box 38   Ph: (406)592-3646
Busby, MT 59016   Fax: (406)657-6559
Robert Bailey, Superintendent
School Type: Grant day school; grades K-12.

★1397★
Two Eagle River School
PO Box 362   Ph: (406)675-0292
Pablo, MT 59855   Fax: (406)675-0292
Clarice King, Principal
School Type: Grant day school; grades 9-12.

★1398★
Duckwater Shoshone Elementary School
PO Box 38   Ph: (702)863-0242
Duckwater, NV 89314   Fax: (702)863-0301
Sheila Lupe, Administrator
School Type: Grant day school; grades K-8.

★1399★
Pyramid Lake High School
PO Box 256
Nixon, NV 89424   Ph: (702)574-0142
Harold Saylor, Principal
School Type: Contract day school; grades 9-12.

★1400★
Alamo Navajo School
PO Box 907   Ph: (505)854-2635
Magdalena, NM 87825   Fax: (505)854-2545
Eddie Mike, Dir.
School Type: Grant day school; grades K-12.

★1401★
Aztec Dormitory
1600 Lydia Pippey Rd.
Aztec, NM 87410   Ph: (505)334-6565
Jack Nolan, Contact
School Type: BIA peripheral dormitory; grades 9-12.

★1402★
Baca Community School
PO Box 509
Prewitt, NM 87045   Ph: (505)876-2769
Beatrice L. Woodward, Principal
School Type: BIA day school; grades K-3.

★1403★
Beclabito Day School
PO Box 1146   Ph: (602)656-3555
Shiprock, NM 87420   Fax: (602)656-3557
Daniel Sosnowski, Principal
School Type: Bureau of Indian Affairs day school; grades K-4.

★1404★
Borrego Pass School
Dibe Yazhi Habitiin Olta, Inc.
PO Box Drawer A
Crownpoint, NM 87313   Ph: (505)786-5237
William Poe, Principal
School Type: Grant day school; grades K-8.

★1405★
Bread Springs Day School
PO Box 1117
Gallup, NM 87305   Ph: (505)778-5665
Richard Toledo, Principal
School Type: BIA Day school; grades K-3.

★1406★
Chi-Ch'il-Tah/Jones Ranch Community School
PO Box 278
Vanderwagon, NM 87326   Ph: (505)778-5573
John L. Taylor, Principal
School Type: BIA on-reservation boarding school; grades K-8.

★1407★
Chuska Boarding School
PO Box 321   Ph: (505)733-2280
Tohatchi, NM 87325   Fax: (505)733-2222
Dr. Helen Zongolowicz, Principal
School Type: BIA on-reservation boarding school; grades K-8.

★1408★
Cove Day School
PO Box 190
Shiprock, NM 87420   Ph: (602)653-4457
Paul J. Yazzie, Principal
School Type: BIA day school; grades K-6.

★1409★
Crownpoint Community School
Drawer H
Crownpoint, NM 87313   Ph: (505)786-6160
Laura V. Garcia, Principal
School Type: BIA on-reservation boarding school; grades K-8.

★1410★
Crystal Boarding School
Navajo, NM 87328   Ph: (505)777-2385
Lena R. Wilson, Principal
School Type: BIA on-reservation boarding school; grades K-6.

★1411★
Dlo'Ay Azhi Community School
PO Box 789
Thoreau, NM 87323   Ph: (505)862-7525
Amy W. Mathis, Principal
School Type: BIA day school; grades K-6.

★1412★
Dzilth-na-o-dith-hle Community School
Star Rte. 4, Box 5003
Bloomfield, NM 87413   Ph: (505)632-1697
D. Duane Robinson, Principal
School Type: BIA day school; grades K-8, grades 9-12 (Boarding).

★1413★
Huerfano Dormitory
PO Box 639
Bloomfield, NM 87413   Ph: (505)325-3411
D. Dwane Robinson, Principal
School Type: BIA peripheral dormitory; grades 1-12; also offers a Kindergarten day school.

★1414★
Isleta Elementary School
PO Box 312
Isleta, NM 87022   Ph: (505)869-2321
Joseph V. Green, Principal
School Type: BIA day school; grades K-6.

★1415★
Jemez Day School
PO Box 238
Jemez Pueblos, NM 87024   Ph: (505)834-7304
Dr. Jannita Complo, Principal
School Type: BIA day school; grades K-6.

★1416★
Jicarilla Dormitory
PO Box 167
Dulce, NM 87528   Ph: (505)759-3910
Emilio Cordova, Contact
School Type: BIA peripheral dormitory; grades 1-12.

★1417★
Laguna Elementary School
PO Box 191   Ph: (505)552-9200
Laguna, NM 87026   Fax: (505)552-7497
Gilbert A. Sanchez, Principal
School Type: BIA day school; grades K-6.

★1418★
Lake Valley Navajo School
PO Box Drawer E
Crownpoint, NM 87313   Ph: (505)786-5392
David J. Atanasoff, Principal
School Type: BIA on-reservation boarding school; grades K-8.

★1419★
Mariano Lake Community School
PO Box 498
Crownpoint, NM 87313   Ph: (505)786-5265
Stanton D. Curtis, Principal
School Type: BIA on-reservation boarding school; grades K-5.

★1420★
Na'Neelzhiin Ji'Olta
Star Rte.
Cuba, NM 87013   Ph: (505)731-2272
Harvey Dale Allison, Principal
School Type: BIA day school; grades K-8.

★1421★
Navajo Mission Academy
1200 W. Apache
Farmington, NM 87401   Ph: (505)326-6571
Dr. Samuel Billison, Headmaster
School Type: Grant boarding school; grades 9-12.

★1422★
Nenahnezad Boarding School
PO Box 337
Fruitland, NM 87416   Ph: (505)598-6922
Rena L. Teller, Principal
School Type: BIA on-reservation boarding school; grades K-6.

★1423★
Ojo Encino Day School
Star Rte. 2
Cuba, NM 87013   Ph: (505)731-2333
Cyrus J. Chino, Principal
School Type: BIA day school; grades K-8.

★1424★
Pine Hill Schools
CPO Drawer H   Ph: (505)775-3256
Pine Hill, NM 87321   Fax: (505)775-3240
Anna Mae Pino, Dir. of Educ.
School Type: Contract boarding school; grades K-12.

★1425★
Pueblo Pintado Community School
Star Rte. 2
Cuba, NM 87013   Ph: (505)655-3341
Clyde David Kannon, Principal
School Type: BIA on-reservation boarding school; grades K-8.

★1426★
Pueblo of San Felipe
San Felipe School
PO Box E
San Felipe Pueblo, NM 87001   Ph: (505)867-3364
Edward Doler, Principal
School Type: BIA day school; grades K-6.

★1427★
San Ildefonso Day School
Rte. 5, Box 308
Santa Fe, NM 87501   Ph: (505)455-2366
Mary L. Naranjo, Principal
School Type: BIA day school; grades K-6.

★1428★
San Juan Day School
PO Box 1077
San Juan Pueblos, NM 87566   Ph: (505)852-2151
Linda P. Martinez, Principal
School Type: BIA day school; grades K-6.

★1429★
Sanostee Day School
PO Box 159
Sanostee, NM 87461   Ph: (505)723-2476
Jeanne Haskie, Principal
School Type: BIA day school; grades K-1.

★1430★
Santa Clara Day School
PO Box HHH
Espanola, NM 87532   Ph: (505)753-4406
Solomon Padilla Jr., Principal
School Type: BIA day school; grades K-6.

★1431★
Santa Fe Indian School
1501 Cerrillos Rd.
Santa Fe, NM 87501   Ph: (505)988-6291
Joseph Abeyta Jr., Superintendent
School Type: Grant boarding school; grades 7-12.

★1432★
Shiprock Alternative High School
PO Box 1799
Shiprock, NM 87420   Ph: (505)368-5144
Karen Dixon Bates, Dir.
School Type: Grant day school; Kindergarten and grades 9-12.

Grant day school; offers Kindergarten program.

★1433★
Shiprock Alternative Kindergarten
c/o Shiprock Alternative Schools, Inc.
PO Box 1799
Shiprock, NM 87420   Ph: (505)368-5170
Karen Dixon Bates, Dir.
Objectives: Grant day school; offers Kindergarten program.

★1434★
Shiprock Reservation Dormitory
PO Box 1180
Shiprock, NM 87420　　　　Ph: (505)368-5113
John Wilson, Dir.
School Type: Contract peripheral dormitory; grades 7-12.

★1435★
Sky City Community School
PO Box 349
Acoma, NM 87034　　　　Ph: (505)552-6671
Lesardo Garcia, Principal
School Type: BIA day school; grades K-8.

★1436★
Taos Day School
PO Drawer X
Taos, NM 87571　　　　Ph: (505)758-3652
Robert C. Martinez, Principal
School Type: BIA day school; grades K-6.

★1437★
Tesuque Day School
Rte. 11, Box 2
Santa Fe, NM 87501　　　　Ph: (505)982-1516
Dolly N. Smith, Principal
School Type: BIA day school; grades K-6.

★1438★
Toadlena Boarding School
PO Box 857
Toadlena, NM 87324　　　　Ph: (505)789-3201
Lena Jim, Acting Principal
School Type: BIA on-reservation boarding school; grades K-8.

★1439★
To'Hajiilee-He
PO Box 438
Laguna, NM 87026　　　　Ph: (505)831-6426
Jim Byrnes, Principal
School Type: BIA day school; grades K-12.

★1440★
Tse'ii'ahi' Community School
Drawer J
Crownpoint, NM 87313　　　　Ph: (505)786-5389
Sherry Woodfide, Principal
School Type: BIA day school; grades K-3. **Formerly:** Standing Rock Community School.

★1441★
Wingate Elementary School
PO Box 1
Fort Wingate, NM 87316　　　　Ph: (505)488-5466
David L. Braswell, Principal
School Type: BIA on-reservation boarding school; grades 1-8.

BIA on-reservation boarding school; grades 9-12.

★1442★
Wingate High School
PO Box 2
Fort Wingate, NM 87316　　　　Ph: (505)488-5402
Jay Bruce Hoover, Principal
Objectives: BIA on-reservation boarding school; grades 9-12.

★1443★
Zia Day School
San Ysidro, NM 87053　　　　Ph: (505)867-3553
Charlotte Garcia, Principal
School Type: BIA day school; grades K-6.

★1444★
Cherokee Central School
PO Box 134　　　　Ph: (704)497-6370
Cherokee, NC 28719　　　　Fax: (704)497-4373
Joyce Dugan, Acting Superintendent
School Type: Grant day school; grades K-12.

★1445★
Dunseith Day School
PO Box 759
Dunseith, ND 58329　　　　Ph: (701)263-4636
Karen Gillis, Principal
School Type: BIA day school; grades K-6.

★1446★
Four Winds Community School
PO Box 199　　　　Ph: (701)766-4161
Fort Totten, ND 58335　　　　Fax: (701)766-4766
Judy Ami, Principal
School Type: Grant day school; grades K-8.

★1447★
Mandaree Day School
PO Box 488
Mandaree, ND 58757　　　　Ph: (701)759-3311
Edward Lone Fight, Superintendent
School Type: Grant day school; grades K-12.

★1448★
Ojibwa Indian School
Box 600
Belcourt, ND 58316　　　　Ph: (701)477-3108
Cathie LaFontaine, Principal
School Type: Contract day school; grades K-8.

★1449★
Standing Rock Community School
PO Box 377
Fort Yates, ND 58538　　　　Ph: (701)854-3865
Linda Lawrence, Elem.Principle
School Type: BIA day school; grades K-12.

★1450★
Theodore Jamerson Elementary School
3315 University Dr.
Bismarck, ND 58504　　　　Ph: (701)255-3285
Anna Rubia, Principal
School Type: Grant day school; grades K-8.

★1451★
Turtle Mountain Elementary and Middle School
PO Box 440
Belcourt, ND 58316　　　　Ph: (701)477-6471
Dr. Teresa G. Delorme, Principal
School Type: Cooperative day school; grades K-8.

★1452★
Turtle Mountain High School
PO Box 440　　　　Ph: (701)477-6471
Belcourt, ND 58316　　　　Fax: (701)477-6470
Dr. Duane E. Schindler, Principal
School Type: Contract day school; grades 9-12.

★1453★
Twin Buttes Day School
Rte. 1, Box 65
Halliday, ND 58636　　　　Ph: (701)938-4396
Clifford Fox, Administrator
School Type: Grant day school; grades K-8.

★1454★
Wahpeton Indian Boarding School
Wahpeton, ND 58075   Ph: (701)642-3796
    Fax: (701)642-5880
Leroy W. Chief, Superintendent
School Type: BIA off-reservation boarding school; grades 4-8.

★1455★
White Shield School
HC1, Box 45   Ph: (701)743-4350
Roseglen, ND 58775   Fax: (701)743-4501
Ron Hauf, Principal
School Type: Grant day school; grades K-12.

★1456★
Carter Seminary
2400 Chickasaw Blvd.
Ardmore, OK 73401   Ph: (405)223-8547
Jeff Frazier, Dir.
School Type: Grant peripheral dormitory; grades 1-12.

★1457★
Eufaula Dormitory
Swadley Dr.
Eufaula, OK 74432   Ph: (918)689-2522
Greg Anderson, Administrator
School Type: Grant peripheral dormitory; grades 1-12.

★1458★
Jones Academy
Rte. 1
Hartshorne, OK 74547   Ph: (918)297-2518
Mike Bailey, Administrator
School Type: Grant peripheral school; grades 1-12.

★1459★
Riverside Indian School
Rte. 1
Anadarko, OK 37005   Ph: (405)247-6673
Cletis Satepauhoodle, Principal
School Type: BIA off-reservation boarding school; grades 2-12.

★1460★
Sequoyah High School
PO Box 948
Tahlequah, OK 74465   Ph: (918)456-0631
Jim Quetone, Superintendent
School Type: Grant off-reservation boarding school; grades 9-12.

★1461★
Chemawa Indian School
3700 Chemawa Rd. NE   Ph: (503)399-5721
Salem, OR 97305-1199   Fax: (503)399-5870
Gerald J. Gray, Principal
School Type: BIA off-reservation boarding school; grades 9-12.

★1462★
American Horse School
PO Box 660   Ph: (605)455-2480
Allen, SD 57714   Fax: (605)867-1141
Edward E. Uhrig, Principal
School Type: BIA day school; grades K-8.

★1463★
Cheyenne-Eagle Butte School
Eagle Butte, SD 57625   Ph: (605)964-8744
Dr. Cherie Farlee, Superintendent
School Type: Cooperative boarding school; grades K-12.

★1464★
Crazy Horse School
PO Box 260
Wanblee, SD 57577   Ph: (605)462-6511
Dick Vosberg, Superintendent
School Type: Grant day school; grades K-12.

★1465★
Crow Creek Reservation High School
Box 12
Stephan, SD 57346   Ph: (605)852-2455
Don Lungrenn, Superintendent
School Type: Grant boarding school; grades 7-12.

★1466★
Enemy Swim Day School
RR 1, Box 87
Waubay, SD 57273   Ph: (605)947-4605
Edna Greenhagen, Principal
School Type: Contract day school; grades K-3.

★1467★
Flandreau Indian School
Flandreau, SD 57028   Ph: (605)997-2724
    Fax: (605)997-2601
Jack Belkham, Principal
School Type: BIA off-reservation boarding school; grades 9-12.

★1468★
Fort Thompson Elementary School
PO Box 139   Ph: (605)245-2372
Fort Thompson, SD 57339   Fax: (605)245-2399
Douglas L. Daughters, Principal
School Type: Cooperative day school; grades K-6.

★1469★
Little Eagle Day School
PO Box 26
Little Eagle, SD 57639   Ph: (605)823-4235
Adele F. Little Dog, Principal
School Type: BIA day school; grades K-8.

★1470★
Little Wound Day School
PO Box 500
Kyle, SD 57752   Ph: (605)455-2461
Dr. Allen Ross, Superintendent
School Type: Grant day school; grades K-12.

★1471★
Loneman Day School
PO Box 50   Ph: (605)867-5633
Oglala, SD 57764   Fax: (605)867-5109
Dr. Ray Phipps, Principal
School Type: Grant day school; grades K-8.

★1472★
Lower Brule Day School
PO Box 245
Lower Brule, SD 57548   Ph: (605)473-5510
Bud Keller, Principal
School Type: Cooperative day school; grades K-12.

★1473★
Marty Indian School
PO Box 187
Marty, SD 57361   Ph: (605)384-5431
Everdell Wright, Superintendent
School Type: Grant boarding school; grades K-12.

★1474★
Pierre Indian Learning Center
HC 31, Box 148   Ph: (605)224-8661
Pierre, SD 57501   Fax: (605)224-4865
Darrell Jeanotte, Administrator
School Type: Contract boarding school; grades 1-8.

★1475★
Pine Ridge School
PO Box 1202   Ph: (605)867-5198
Pine Ridge, SD 57770   Fax: (605)867-1141
Imogene Horse, Principal
School Type: BIA on-reservation boarding school; grades K-12.

★1476★
Porcupine Day School
PO Box 180
Porcupine, SD 57772   Ph: (605)867-5336
Benjamin Kasyoki, Principal
School Type: Grant day school; grades K-8.

★1477★
Promise Day School
Mobridge, SD 37601   Ph: (605)733-2148
Janice Wordeman, Principal
School Type: BIA day school; grades K-8.

★1478★
Rock Creek Day School
Bullhead, SD 57621   Ph: (605)823-4971
Emmett White Temple, Principal
School Type: BIA day school; grades K-8.

★1479★
Rosebud Dormitories
PO Box 669   Ph: (605)856-4486
Mission, SD 57555   Fax: (605)747-2805
Eustance Night Shield, Contact
School Type: BIA peripheral dormitory; grades 1-12.

★1480★
St. Francis Indian School
PO Box 379   Ph: (605)747-2299
Saint Francis, SD 57572   Fax: (605)747-2379
Dr. Harlan Krein, Superintendent
School Type: Grant day school; grades K-12.

★1481★
Swift Bird Day School
CHR 3
Gettysburg, SD 67442   Ph: (605)733-2143
Merlyn Schutterle, Principal
School Type: BIA day school; grades K-8.

★1482★
Takini School
PO Box 168
Howes, SD 57748   Ph: (605)538-4399
Dr. Ken Englehardt, Superintendent
School Type: Grant day school; grades K-12.

★1483★
Tiospa Zina Tribal School
PO Box 719   Ph: (605)698-3953
Agency Village, SD 57262   Fax: (605)698-7873
Roger Bordeaux, Superintendent
School Type: Grant day school; grades K-12.

★1484★
White Horse Day School
White Horse, SD 57661   Ph: (605)733-2183
Gary Nelson, Principal
School Type: BIA day school; grades K-8.

★1485★
Wounded Knee School District
PO Box 350
Manderson, SD 57756   Ph: (605)867-5433
Robert Hacker, Principal
School Type: Grant day school; grades K-8.

★1486★
Aneth Community School
PO Drawer 600
Montezuma Creek, UT 84534   Ph: (801)651-3271
J.C. Begay, Principal
School Type: BIA on-reservation boarding school; grades K-6.

★1487★
Richfield Dormitory
PO Box 638
Richfield, UT 84701   Ph: (801)896-5101
Kevin Skenandore, Contact
School Type: BIA peripheral dormitory; grades 9-12.

★1488★
Lummi Tribal School System
2530 Kwina Rd.   Ph: (206)647-6251
Bellingham, WA 98225   Fax: (206)384-4737
Bill Hayne, Dir.
School Type: Grant day school; K-8.

★1489★
Muckleshoot Tribal School
39015 172nd Ave., SE   Ph: (206)939-3311
Auburn, WA 98002   Fax: (206)939-5311
Jim Kolessar, Superintendent
School Type: Grant day school; grades K-3.

★1490★
Wa He Lut Indian School
11110 Conine Ave., SE   Ph: (206)456-1311
Olympia, WA 98503   Fax: (206)456-1319
Barbara Przasnyski, Principal
School Type: Grant day school; pre-K to grade 8.

★1491★
Lac Courte Oreilles Ojibwa School
Rte. 2, Box 2800   Ph: (715)634-8924
Hayward, WI 54843   Fax: (715)634-4797
Eddie Benton, Administrator
School Type: Grant day school; grades K-12.

★1492★
Menominee Tribal School
Menominee Indian Tribe
PO Box 397   Ph: (715)756-2354
Keshena, WI 54135   Fax: (715)799-4525
Dr. Kenneth Lehman, Administrator
School Type: Grant day school; grades K-8.

★1493★
Oneida Tribal School
c/o Oneida Tribe
Box 365   Ph: (414)869-2795
Onieda, WI 54155-0365   Fax: (414)869-2194
Sharon A. Mousseau, Administrator
School Type: Grant day school; grades K-12.

★1494★
St. Stevens Indian School
PO Box 345
Saint Stevens, WY 82524   Ph: (307)856-4147
Margaret J. Puebla, Superintendent
School Type: Grant day school; grades pre-K to 12.

─────────── **Community Colleges** ───────────

★1495★
Navajo Community College
PO Box 126   Ph: (602)724-3311
Tsaile, AZ 86556   Fax: (602)724-3327
Al Garcia, Acting Pres.

★1496★
D-Q University
PO Box 409   Ph: (916)758-0470
Davis, CA 95617   Fax: (916)758-4891
Carlos Cordero, Pres.

★1497★
Haskell Indian Junior College
PO Box H1305   Ph: (913)749-8450
Lawrence, KS 66046   Fax: (913)749-8406
Bob Martin, Pres.

★1498★
Bay Mills Community College
Rte. 1, Box 315A   Ph: (906)248-3354
Brimley, MI 49715   Fax: (906)248-3351
Martha McCleod, Pres.

★1499★
Fond du Lac Community College
302 14th St.   Ph: (218)879-0800
Cloquet, MN 55720   Fax: (218)879-0814
Lester "Jack" Briggs, Pres.

★1500★
Blackfeet Community College
PO Box 819   Ph: (406)338-7751
Browning, MT 59417   Fax: (406)338-7808
Carol Murray, Acting Pres.

★1501★
Dull Knife Memorial College
PO Box 98   Ph: (406)477-6215
Lame Deer, MT 59043   Fax: (406)477-6219
Dr. Arthur McDonald, Pres.

★1502★
Fort Belknap Community College
PO Box 159   Ph: (406)353-2607
Harlem, MT 59526   Fax: (406)353-2841
Margaret C. Perez, Pres.

★1503★
Fort Peck Community College
PO Box 575   Ph: (406)768-5551
Poplar, MT 59255   Fax: (406)768-5552
Dr. James Shanley, Pres.

★1504★
Little Big Horn Community College
PO Box 370   Ph: (406)638-2228
Crow Agency, MT 59022   Fax: (406)638-7215
Janine Pease-Windy Boy, Pres.

★1505★
Salish Kootenai College
PO Box 117   Ph: (406)675-4800
Pablo, MT 59855   Fax: (406)675-4801
Dr. Joseph McDonald, Pres.

★1506★
Stone Child Community College
Rocky Boy Rte., Box 1082   Ph: (406)395-4313
Box Elder, MT 59521   Fax: (406)395-4836
Bert Corcoran, Acting Pres.

★1507★
Nebraska Indian Community College
PO Box 752   Ph: (402)878-2414
Winnebago, NE 68071   Fax: (402)878-2522
Thelma Thomas, Pres.

★1508★
Crownpoint Institute of Technology
PO Box 849   Ph: (505)786-5851
Crownpoint, NM 87313   Fax: (505)786-5644
James Tutt, Chancellor

★1509★
Southwest Indian Polytechnic Institute
Box 10146-9169   Ph: (505)897-5340
Albuquerque, NM 87184   Fax: (505)897-5343
Carolyn Elgin, Pres.

★1510★
Fort Berthold Community College
PO Box 490   Ph: (701)627-3665
New Town, ND 58763   Fax: (701)627-3609
Lyn Pinnick, Acting Pres.

★1511★
Little Hoop Community College
PO Box 269   Ph: (701)766-4415
Fort Totten, ND 58335   Fax: (701)766-4077
Dr. Merril Berg, Pres.

★1512★
Standing Rock College
HC1, Box 4   Ph: (701)854-3861
Fort Yates, ND 58538   Fax: (701)854-3403
Ron McNeil, Pres.

★1513★
Turtle Mountain Community College
PO Box 340   Ph: (701)477-5605
Belcourt, ND 58316   Fax: (701)477-5028
Carol Ann Davis, Pres.

★1514★
United Tribes Technical College
3315 University Dr.   Ph: (701)255-3285
Bismarck, ND 58501   Fax: (701)255-1844
Dr. David Gipp, Pres.

★1515★
Cheyenne River Community College
PO Box 220   Ph: (605)964-8635
Eagle Butte, SD 57625   Fax: (605)964-1144
Joe Lends His Horse, Pres.

★1516★
Oglala Lakota College
PO Box 490   Ph: (605)455-2321
Kyle, SD 57752   Fax: (605)455-2787
Dr. Elgin Bad Wound, Pres.

★1517★
Sinte Gleska College
PO Box 490   Ph: (605)747-2263
Rosebud, SD 57570   Fax: (605)747-2098
Dr. Lionel Bordeaux, Pres.

★1518★
Sisseton Wahpeton Community College
PO Box 689   Ph: (605)698-3966
Sisseton, SD 57262   Fax: (605)698-3132
Gwen Hill, Pres.

★1519★
Northwest Indian College
2522 Kwina Rd.   Ph: (206)676-2772
Bellingham, WA 98226   Fax: (206)738-0136
Dr. Robert Lorence, Pres.

★1520★
Lac Courte Oreilles Ojibwa Community College
RR 2, Box 2357   Ph: (715)634-4790
Hayward, WI 54843   Fax: (715)634-5049
Dr. Jasjit Minhas, Pres.

Studies Programs

Two-Year Programs

★1521★
Bacone College
Native American Studies Program
Muskogee, OK 74403   Ph: (918)683-4581
Louie Jackson, Counselor/Recruiter

★1522★
Blackfeet Community College
Native American Studies Program
Browning, MT 59417   Ph: (406)338-5421
Carol Murray, Registrar/Adm. Officer

★1523★
College of the Redwoods
Native American Studies Program
Eureka, CA 95501   Ph: (707)445-6761
                           Free: 800-458-5300
Jim Harrington, Dean of Student Serv.

★1524★
D-Q University
Native American Studies Program
Davis, CA 95617   Ph: (916)758-0470
Annzell Loufas, V. Pres.

★1525★
Dull Knife Memorial College
Native American Studies Program
Lame Deer, MT 59043   Ph: (406)477-6215
William L. Wertman, Registrar/Dir. of Adm.

★1526★
Fort Peck Community College
Native American Studies Program
Poplar, MT 59255   Ph: (406)768-5553
Patricia Stump, Dean of Student Serv.

★1527★
Lac Courte Oreilles Ojibwa Community College
Native American Studies Program
Hayward, WI 54843   Ph: (715)634-4719
Anne Penzkover, Registrar/Dir. of Adm.

★1528★
Navajo Community College
Native American Studies Program
Tsaile, AZ 86556   Ph: (602)724-3311
Louise Litzin, Registrar

★1529★
Nebraska Indian Community College
Native American Studies Program
Winnebago, NE 68071   Ph: (402)878-2414
Jeanie Eagle, Dir. of Adm./Registrar

★1530★
Palomar Community College
Native American Studies Program
San Marcos, CA 92069   Ph: (619)744-1150
Herman C. Lee, Dir. of Adm.

★1531★
Rogers State College
Native American Studies Program
Claremore, OK 74017   Ph: (918)341-7510
Betty F. Scott, Dir. of Guidance

★1532★
Rose State College
Native American Studies Program
Midwest City, OK 73110 Ph: (405)733-7308
Joe Johnson, Registrar

★1533★
Salish Kootenai College
Native American Studies Program
Pueblo, MT 59855   Ph: (406)675-4800
Cleo Kenmille, Registrar

★1534★
Santa Barbara City College
Native American Studies Program
Santa Barbara, CA 93109 Ph: (805)965-0581
Jane G. Craven, Asst. Dean of Adm. & Records

★1535★
Scottsdale Community College
Native American Studies Program
9000 E. Chaparral Rd.
Scottsdale, AZ 85256   Ph: (602)423-6139
John Silvester, Assoc. Dean of Student Serv.

★1536★
Standing Rock College
Native American Studies Program
Fort Yates, ND 58538   Ph: (701)854-3862
Linda Tudoroff, Dir. of Adm.

Four-Year Programs

★1537★
Bemidji State University
Native American Studies Program
Bemidji, MN 56601   Ph: (218)755-2027
Dr. John Quistgaard, Dir. of Adm.

★1538★
Black Hills State University
Native American Studies Program
Spearfish, SD 57783   Ph: (605)642-6343
Steve Meeker, Dir. of Adm. & Records   Free: 800-255-2487

★1539★
California State University, Sacramento
Native American Studies Program
Sacramento, CA 95819   Ph: (916)278-3901
Larry Glasmire, Dir. of Adm.

★1540★
Colgate University
Native American Studies Program
Hamilton, NY 13346   Ph: (315)824-1000
Thomas S. Anthony, Dean of Adm.

★1541★
College of St. Scholastica
Native American Studies Program
Duluth, MN 55811   Ph: (218)723-6046
Nancy J. Ferreira, Dean of Adm.

★1542★
Cornell University
American Indian Studies Program
Mt. Vernon, IA 52314   Ph: (319)895-4477
Peter S. Bryant, V.Pres. of Enrollment Serv.   Free: 800-747-1112

Remarks: Program includes Akew:kon, a residential center, library, and computer center devoted to American Indian studies.

★1543★
Dakota Wesleyan University
Native American Studies Program
Mitchell, SD 57301   Ph: (605)995-2650
Melinda Larson, Dir. of Adm.

★1544★
Dartmouth College
Native American Studies Program
Hanover, NH 03755   Ph: (603)646-2875
Karl M. Furstenberg, Dir. of Adm.

★1545★
Evergreen State College
Native American Studies Program
Olympia, WA 98505   Ph: (206)866-6000
Arnaldo Rodriguez, Dean of Enrollment Serv.

★1546★
Friends World College
Native American Studies Program
Huntington, NY 11743   Ph: (516)549-1102
Arthur Meyer, Dir. of Adm.

★1547★
Goddard College
Native American Studies Program
Plainfield, VT 05667   Ph: (802)454-8311
Gregory Dunkling, Dir. of Adm.

★1548★
Hampshire College
Native American Studies Program
Amherst, MA 01002   Ph: (413)549-4600
Olga Euben, Dir. of Adm.

★1549★
Morningside College
Native American Studies Program
Sioux City, IA 51106   Ph: (712)274-5111
David B. Reese, Dir. of Adm.   Free: 800-831-0806

★1550★
Mount Senario College
Native American Studies
Ladysmith, WI 54848   Ph: (715)532-5511
Max M. Waits, Adm. Consultant

★1551★
Northeastern State University
Native American Studies Program
Telequah, OK 74464   Ph: (918)456-5511
    Free: 800-722-9614
Noel T. Smith, Dir. of Adm./Registrar

★1552★
Northland College
Native American Studies Program
Ashland, WI 54806   Ph: (715)682-1224
James L. Miller, Dean of Student Dev. & Enrollment

★1553★
Oglala Lakota College
Native American Studies
Kyle, SD 57752   Ph: (605)455-2321
Karlene Hunter, Registrar

★1554★
Pembroke State University
Native American Studies Program
Pembroke, NC 28372   Ph: (919)521-4214
Anthony Locklear, Dir. of Adm.

★1555★
San Diego State University
Native American Studies Program
San Diego, CA 92182   Ph: (619)594-5384
Nancy C. Sprotte, Dir. of Adm.

★1556★
Sinte Gleska College
Native American Studies
Rosebud, SD 57570   Ph: (605)747-2263
Michael Benge, Dir. of Student Serv.

★1557★
Sonoma State University
Native American Studies Program
Rohnert Park, CA 94928   Ph: (707)664-2458
Dr. Frank Tansey, Dean of Adm.

★1558★
State University of New York at Buffalo
Native American Studies Program
Hayes Annex A; Main Street Campus
Buffalo, NY 14214   Ph: (716)831-2111
Kevin Durkin, Dir. of Adm.

★1559★
Union Institute
Native American Studies Program
Cincinnati, OH 45202   Ph: (513)621-6400
Dr. Charles Cunning, Dean

★1560★
University of California, Berkley
Native American Studies Program
Berkley, CA 94720   Ph: (510)642-2261
Dr. Robert L. Bailey, Dir. of Adm.

★1561★
University of California, Davis
Native American Studies Program
Tecumseh Center   Ph: (916)752-3237
Davis, CA 95616   Free: 800-523-2847
      Fax: (916)752-7097

Jack Forbes, Coordinator

★1562★
University of Minnesota, Twin Cities Campus
Native American Studies Program
Minneapolis, MN 55455   Ph: (612)625-2006
      Free: 800-826-0750

Leo D. Abbott, Dir. of Adm.

★1563★
University of Nebraska, Lincoln
Native American Studies Program
Lincoln, NE 68588   Ph: (402)472-2023
      Free: 800-742-8800

Lisa Schmidt, Dir. of High School & College Relations

★1564★
University of North Dakota
Native American Studies Program
Grand Forks, ND 58202   Ph: (701)777-3821
      Free: 800-437-5379

Donna M. Bruce, Admissions Officer

★1565★
University of Science and Arts of Oklahoma
Native American Studies Program
Chickasha, OK 73018   Ph: (405)224-3140
Jack Hudson, Registrar/Dir. of Adm.

★1566★
University of Washington
Native American Studies Program
Seattle, WA 98195   Ph: (206)543-9686
Stephanie Preston, Asst. Dir. of Adm.

★1567★
Utah State University
Native American Studies Program
Logan, UT 84322   Ph: (801)750-1106
J. Rodney Clark, Dir. of Adm.

★1568★
Washington State University
Native American Studies Program
Pullman, WA 99164   Ph: (509)335-5586
Terry Flynn, Dir. of Adm.

―――――― **Graduate Programs** ――――――

★1569★
Goddard College
Native American Studies Graduate Program
Plainfield, VT 05667   Ph: (802)454-8311
Gregory Dunkling, Dir. of Adm.

★1570★
Oglala Lakota College
Native American Studies Graduate Program
Kyle, SD 57752   Ph: (605)455-2321
Karlene Hunter, Registrar

★1571★
Rutgers University
Minority Advancement Program
North American Indian Studies Program
25 Bishop Pl.
New Brunswick, NJ 08903   Ph: (908)932-7908
Rita Broder, Asst. Dir.

★1572★
San Francisco State University
School of Ethnic Studies
American Indian Studies Program
San Francisco, CA 94132   Ph: (415)338-1693
Dr. Jim Okutsu, Grad. Coord.

★1573★
State University of New York at Buffalo
Native American Graduate Studies Program
Hayes Annex A; Main Street Campus
Buffalo, NY 14214   Ph: (716)831-2111
Kevin Durkin, Dir. of Adm.

★1574★
Union Institute
Native American Studies Doctorate Program
Cincinnati, OH 45202   Ph: (513)621-6400
Dr. Charles Cunning, Dean

★1575★
University of Arizona
College of Arts and Sciences
American Indian Studies Program
Tucson, AZ 85721   Ph: (602)621-7108
Ofelia Zepeda, Dir.

★1576★
University of California, Berkeley
Ethnic Studies Graduate Program
Berkeley, CA 94720   Ph: (510)642-2261
Dr. Robert L. Bailey, Dir. of Adm.
Remarks: Ethnic Studies program includes Native American studies.

★1577★
University of California, Los Angeles
College of Letters and Science
American Indian Studies Program
Los Angeles, CA 90024   Ph: (213)825-7420
Paul Kroskrity, Chair

★1578★
University of Hawaii at Honolulu
School of Public Health
American Indian and Alaska Native Support Program
Educational Opportunities Program
Honolulu, HI 96822   Ph: 800-927-3927
John Casken, Dir.

★1579★
University of North Dakota
School of Medicine
Indians into Medicine Program (INMED)
501 N. Columbia Rd.
Grand Forks, ND 58203   Ph: (701)777-3037
Remarks: Offers assistance to students who are preparing to study or currently studying to become physicians, nurses and other health professionals.

Scholarships, Fellowships, & Loans

★1580★
AIGC Fellowship
American Indian Graduate Center
4520 Montgomery Blvd., NE, Ste. 1-B
Albuquerque, NM 87109   Ph: (505)881-4584

Study Level: Doctorate; Graduate. **Award Type:** Fellowship.
Purpose: To help those with unmet needs as supplemental support.
Applicant Eligibility: Candidates must be enrolled members of a federally-recognized tribe or Alaska Native group or possess at least one-quarter degree of Indian blood. They must also be enrolled at an accredited college or university in the U.S. as full-time graduate students in an M.A. or Ph.D. program. Awards are need-based.
Selection Criteria: Preference is given to those applications received on or before the application deadline, former AIGC students, and those specializing in education, engineering, health, law, business and natural resources, or related fields. **Funds Available:** Approximately $1.8 million was awarded during the 1990-91 year. **Applicant Details:** Eligible applicants should call AIGC for an application. **Application Deadline:** June 3. Applicants will be notified in July.

★1581★
Ardell Bjugstad Memorial Scholarship
South Dakota Board of Regents
207 E. Capitol Ave.   Ph: (605)773-3455
Pierre, SD 57501-2408   Fax: (605)773-5320

Study Level: Undergraduate. **Award Type:** Scholarship. **Applicant Eligibility:** Applicants must be entering freshman students who are majoring in agricultural production, agribusiness, agricultural sciences, or a natural resources degree. Eligible participants are South Dakota or North Dakota residents who are enrolled members of a federally recognized tribe whose reservations are located either in South or North Dakota. Students may attend any post secondary institution which offers programs in the majors specified. **Funds Available:** One $500 scholarship is awarded annually.

★1582★
Cheyenne-Arapaho Higher Education Assistance Program Grant
Cheyenne-Arapaho Tribal Offices
PO Box 38   Ph: (405)262-0345
Concho, OK 73022   Fax: (405)262-0745

Study Level: Undergraduate. **Award Type:** Grant. **Applicant Eligibility:** Candidates must be at least one-fourth Indian, enrolled at the Concho Agency, high school or GED graduates, and approved for admission by a college. The applicant must need financial aid and show reasonable assurance of completing a four year college degree program. Graduate and/or married students are also eligible. **Funds Available:** The amount of assistance is individually determined. A new application with a current financial need evaluation must be submitted each year for renewal. **Contact:** Higher Education Assistance Program. **Applicant Details:** A completed application requires: an estimate of college expenses; a personal letter in ink that indicates academic goals and financial needs; a high school or college transcript; and indication of having filed the ACT or FAF packet, which are obtainable from the high school or college financial aid office. Recipients must maintain academic standing and social conduct acceptable to the education institution attended. They may also expect personal on-campus contact by their Native American Counselor for the purpose of providing supportive services. Grade reports or transcripts must be submitted after each term. Application and all supporting materials must be filed by June 1st for the first semester and November 1st for the second semester. Renewal application must be filed by June 1st.

★1583★
Emergency Aid and Health Profession Scholarship
Association on American Indian Affairs,
  Inc.
245 5th Ave.
New York, NY 10016-7877

Study Level: Undergraduate. **Award Type:** Scholarship. **Applicant Eligibility:** College-level American Indian and Alaskan Native students may apply after they have registered for college, and if they are in need of emergency aid. **Funds Available:** When funds are available, individual grants average between $50 and $300. **Applicant Details:** There are no application forms. A student desiring aid must write a letter and include the following information: tribal affiliation; subject of study; year in school; amount needed; brief budget of expenditures; and the name and telephone number of the college financial aid officer, and social security number. **Application Deadline:** Applications may be filed at any time after college classes are begun.

★1584★
IHS Health Professions Pre-Graduate Scholarships
Indian Health Services
5600 Fishers Ln., Rm. 6A30
Rockville, MD 20857   Ph: (301)443-1180

Study Level: Undergraduate. **Award Type:** Scholarship. **Applicant Eligibility:** Applicants must be American Indians or Alaska Natives. Candidates must be high school graduates or the equivalent, and must have the capacity to complete a health professions course of study. Applicants must be enrolled, or accepted for enrollment, in a baccalaureate degree program in specific preprofessional areas (pre-medicine and pre-dentistry). Applicants may be seniors, juniors, sophomores, or freshmen (priority given to applicants in this order). Applicants must be in good standing at the educational institution they are attending. Candidates must intend to serve Indian People upon completion of professional health care education as health care providers in the disciplines for which they are enrolled at the pregraduate level. **Funds Available:** Funding is available for a maximum of four academic years. The level of scholarship benefits is contingent upon the availability of funds appropriated each fiscal year by the Congress of the United States and, therefore, is subject to yearly changes. The Scholarship Program will provide a monthly stipend to cover living expenses including room and board. Recipients will receive the stipend only during the academic period covered by their awards, August 1 to May 31. **Contact:** IHS Area Scholarship Coordinator.

★1585★
IHS Health Professions Preparatory Scholarships
Indian Health Services
5600 Fishers Ln., Rm. 6A30
Rockville, MD 20857   Ph: (301)443-1180

Study Level: Undergraduate. **Award Type:** Scholarship. **Applicant Eligibility:** Applicants must be American Indians or Alaska Natives. Candidates must be high school graduates or the equivalent, and must have the capacity to complete a health professions course of study. Applicants must be enrolled, or be accepted for enrollment, in courses that will prepare them for acceptance into health professions schools. Courses may be either compensatory (required to improve science, mathematics, or other basic skills and knowledge) or pre-professional (required in order to qualify for admission into a health professions program). Applicants may be sophomore or freshman students (priority given to applicants in this order). Priority categories of study for 1991 enrollment are: pre-engineering; pre-medical technology; pre-nursing; pre-pharmacy; pre-physical therapy; and pre-sanitation. Applicants must be in good standing at the educational institution they are attending. Candidates must intend to serve Indian People upon completion of professional health care education as health care providers in the disciplines for which the students are taking preparatory courses. **Funds Available:** Funding is available for a maximum of two years. The level of scholarship benefits is contingent upon the availability of funds appropriated each fiscal year by the Congress of the United States and, therefore, is subject to yearly changes. The Scholarship Program will provide a monthly stipend to cover living expenses including room and board. Recipients will receive the stipend only during the academic period covered by their awards, August 1 to May 31. **Contact:** IHS Area Scholarship Coordinator.

★1586★
Indians Higher Education Grants
U.S. Bureau of Indian Affairs
Office of Indian Education Programs
1849 C St., NW
Washington, DC 20240
Study Level: Graduate; Undergraduate. **Award Type:** Grant. **Applicant Eligibility:** Applicant must be an undergraduate or graduate student who is a member of a tribal group currently served by the Bureau. Must also be able to demonstrate financial need.

★1587★
Katrin H. Lamon Fellowship
School of American Research
PO Box 2188
Santa Fe, NM 87504   Ph: (505)982-2919
Study Level: Doctorate; Postdoctorate. **Award Type:** Fellowship. **Purpose:** To support scholars pursuing significant research and writing in anthropology and related disciplines. **Applicant Eligibility:** This position is open to a Native American scholar, either pre- or post-doctoraral. Proposed project must have a humanistic focus. The school is looking for scholars whose work is of the broadest, most synthetic, and most interdisciplinary nature. It seeks applicants whose research promises to yield some significant advance in understanding human culture, behavior, history, or evolution. Projects that are narrowly focused both geographically and theoretically, or that are primarily methodological, seldom receive strong consideration. **Selection Criteria:** Applications will be evaluated primarily on the basis of overall excellence and significance of the project, in addition to such factors as clarity of presentation and the applicant's record of academic accomplishments. Preference will also be given to applicants whose fieldwork or basic research and analysis are complete and who need time to write up their results. Fellowships are awarded competitively on the basis of evaluations by a specially convened panel of scholars who represent a broad spectrum of intellectual expertise. **Funds Available:** Each resident scholar receives an apartment, an office on the School's campus, and a maximum stipend of $29,000. **Applicant Details:** The following must accompany the application form: five copies of a proposal no more than four pages in length, double-spaced (the proposal should summarize what is to be accomplished under the fellowship, describe the status of the applicant's research on the topic, and demonstrate the significance of the work); five copies of the applicant's curriculum vitae; and three letters of recommendation. **Application Deadline:** December 1.

★1588★
Michigan Indian Tuition Waiver
Michigan Commission on Indian Affairs
611 W. Ottawa St.
PO Box 30026
Lansing, MI 48909   Ph: (517)373-0654
Study Level: Undergraduate. **Award Type:** Other. **Purpose:** To provide free tuition for North American Indians to attend public state community, public junior colleges, public colleges, or public universities. **Applicant Eligibility:** Applicants must be Michigan residents for 12 consecutive months and must have not less than one-quarter blood quantum as certified by the applicant's tribal association and verified by the Michigan Commission on Indian Affairs. Must attend a Michigan public community college or university. **Funds Available:** Cost of tuition.

★1589★
Minnesota Chippewa Tribe Grant
Minnesota Chippewa Tribe
PO Box 217
Cass Lake, MN 56633   Ph: (218)335-8584
Study Level: Undergraduate. **Award Type:** Grant. **Applicant Eligibility:** Must be a member of the Minnesota Chippewa Tribe and enrolled in an institution of postsecondary education. **Selection Criteria:** First come basis. **Funds Available:** $3,000 maximum. **Contact:** Education Division. **Applicant Details:** Write for application. **Application Deadline:** January.

★1590★
Minnesota Indian Scholarship
Minnesota Higher Education Coordinating
  Board
Capitol Square Bldg., Ste. 400
550 Cedar St.
Saint Paul, MN 55101   Ph: (612)296-3974
Study Level: Undergraduate. **Award Type:** Scholarship. **Applicant Eligibility:** Must be a resident of Minnesota and a member of a recognized Indian tribe. Must be one-fourth or more of Indian ancestry. Must be a high school graduate or have GED, show ability to benefit from advanced education, and be accepted by an approved Minnesota institution. **Selection Criteria:** Must be approved by the Minnesota Indian Scholarship Committee. Award based on need. **Funds Available:** $1,450 average. **Applicant Details:** Apply to: Joe Aitken, Scholarship Officer, Indian Education, 1819 Bemidji Ave., Bemidji, MN 56601.

★1591★
National Miss Indian U.S. Scholarship
American Indian Heritage Foundation
6051 Arlington Blvd.
Falls Church, VA 22044   Ph: (703)237-7500
Study Level: Graduate; Undergraduate. **Award Type:** Award; Scholarship. **Purpose:** To promote young Indian women who continue with their Indian culture and heritage along with making a place for themselves in the white man's world. **Applicant Eligibility:** Women must be 18-26 years old, never married, pregnant, or cohabitated, and must be high school graduates. Applicant must have an Indian sponsor such as: tribe, business, or organization with a valid governing board. The women must also have a belief of and practice tribal culture and heritage. They must exhibit such positive characteristics as: listening to their elders, joining in pow-wows, and promoting Indian language if possible. **Funds Available:** First place winner receives a $10,000 cash award, $7,000 to the school of choice, $5,000 for wardrobe ($2,500 for traditional clothing and $2,500 for cultural/heritage clothing). Four runners-up receive the same kinds of prizes in descending amounts. **Contact:** Barbara Butler, Pageant Director. **Applicant Details:** Send a request for an application. **Application Deadline:** September 15.

★1592★
NNAC Gifted/Talented Artist Sponsorship
National Native American Cooperative
PO Box 1000
San Carlos, AZ 85550-1000   Ph: (602)230-3399
Study Level: Professional Development. **Purpose:** To assist in the continuation of traditional or contemporary American Indian culture. **Applicant Eligibility:** Applicant must be a Native American artist. **Selection Criteria:** Selection is based upon the applicant's ability to utilize materials provided and create art which reflects a Native American cultural experience. **Funds Available:** Beads, buckskin, silver, turquoise, gold, and other raw craft materials are presented to the artist. **Contact:** Fred Synder. **Application Deadline:** None.

★1593★
North Dakota Indian Scholarship
North Dakota Indian Affairs Commission
600 East Blvd., 1st Fl. Judicial Wing
State Capitol Bldg.   Ph: (701)224-2428
Bismarck, ND 58505-0300   Fax: (701)224-3000
Study Level: Undergraduate. **Award Type:** Scholarship. **Applicant Eligibility:** Applicant must provide certification of Indian blood or tribal enrollment, must be accepted in a North Dakota institution of higher education, and must have a 2.0 GPA. **Selection Criteria:** Students with a 3.0 average will be given priority in funding. **Funds Available:** Awards range from $200 to $2,000 depending upon scholastic ability, funds available, financial need, and total number of applicants in any one year. **Applicant Details:** Application must be accompanied by a letter of recommendation from a member of the clergy, an instructor or an employer (members of applicant's family may not provide letters of recommendation); a budget form completed by a financial aid officer at the institution attended by the applicant; and most recent official transcript. Awards are made for one academic year. A student may reapply in following years for further assistance. **Application Deadline:** June 30.

★1594★

Polingaysi Qoyawayma Scholarship

American Indian Science and Engineering
  Society
1630 30th St., Ste. 301
Boulder, CO 80301-1014   Ph: (303)492-8658

Study Level: Graduate. **Award Type:** Scholarship. **Purpose:** Promotes excellence in teaching, in memory of Polingaysi Qoyawayma (Elizabeth White), who taught for 30 years on the Hopi and Navajo reservations, and in 1954 was awarded the U.S. Department of the Interior Distinguished Service Award for teaching excellence. **Applicant Eligibility:** Applicants must be American Indian students or teachers pursuing continued teacher education in science or math. **Applicant Details:** Information can be obtained by writing to the AISES. **Application Deadline:** June.

★1595★

Presbyterian Church Native American Education
  Grants

Presbyterian Church (U.S.A.)
Office of Financial Aid for Studies
100 Witherspoon St.
Louisville, KY 40202-1396   Ph: (502)569-5745

Study Level: Graduate; Undergraduate. **Award Type:** Grant. **Applicant Eligibility:** Candidates must be American Indians, Aleuts, or Eskimos who are U.S. citizens. They must have completed at least one semester at an accredited institution of higher learning. Preference is given to Presbyterian students at the undergraduate level. **Funds Available:** Grants range from $200 to $1,500 annually depending on financial need and availability of funds. Renewal is possible with continued financial need and satisfactory academic progress. **Applicant Details:** Candidates must apply to their colleges for financial aid as well as filing an application with the Presbyterian Church (U.S.A.). **Application Deadline:** June 1.

★1596★

Presbyterian Church Native American Seminary
  Scholarships

Presbyterian Church (U.S.A.)
Office of Financial Aid for Studies
100 Witherspoon St.
Louisville, KY 40202-1396   Ph: (502)569-5745

Study Level: Graduate. **Award Type:** Scholarship. **Applicant Eligibility:** Candidates are American Indians, Aleuts, and Eskimos who are certified by the candidate's presbytery or the Presbyterian Native American Consulting Committee. Applicant must be: a seminary student preparing for a church occupation and enrolled in a seminary fully accredited by the Association of Theological Schools in the United States and Canada; a student registered with, or under the care of a presbytery and enrolled in a college program on Track 1 of the Native American Theological Association Program; a member of the Presbyterian Church (U.S.A.) from a former UPCUSA congregation, who is enrolled in a program of Theological Education by extension, such as the NATA Track III which is approved by a seminary fully accredited by the Association of Theological Schools in the United States and Canada; and a candidate, minister or member (former UPCUSA) in other church occupations pursuing an approved program of continuing education. **Funds Available:** The amount of the scholarship is determined by the Office of Financial Aid for Studies based upon recommendation by the student's Financial Officer, analysis of the applicant's financial needs, and other resources and available funds. **Contact:** Office of Financial Aid for Studies. **Applicant Details:** Candidates first contact the Financial Aid Officer of the school or seminary they attend. The officer makes a recommendation to the Office of Financial Aid for Studies.

★1597★

Seminole-Miccosukee Indian Scholarships

Florida Department of Education
Office of Student Financial Assistance
1344 Florida Education Center
Tallahassee, FL 32399-0400   Ph: (904)487-0049

Study Level: Graduate; Undergraduate. **Award Type:** Scholarship. **Purpose:** Provides financial assistance to Florida Seminole or Miccosukee Indian students who are enrolled as undergraduate or graduate students and demonstrate financial need. **Applicant Eligibility:** Applicants must be members or eligible for membership in either the Seminole Indian Tribe of Florida or the Miccosukee Indian Tribe of Florida. Candidates must meet Florida's general eligibility requirements for receipt of state aid, including: residency in Florida for purposes other than education for no less than one year prior to the first day of class of the fall term of the academic year for which the funds are received; compliance with registration requirements of the Selective Service System; and participation in the college-level communication and computation skills testing (CLAST) program. Applicants must enroll as either undergraduate or graduate students at an eligible Florida public or private college or university for a minimum of one credit hour per term. Applicants must not owe a repayment of a grant under any state or federal grant or scholarship program, and must not be in default on any state or federal student loan program unless satisfactory arrangements to repay have been made. A renewal applicant must have earned a minimum cumulative grade point average of 2.0 on a 4.0 scale. Full-time students must have earned the equivalent of 12 credit hours for each term an award was received during the academic year. Students enrolled less than full-time must earn the equivalent number of hours required for enrollment as three-quarter-time, half-time, or less than half-time students. Eligibility for renewal is determined at the end of the second semester of third quarter of each academic year. Credits earned the previous summer can be counted toward the total number of credits required. **Selection Criteria:** Renewal awards take precedence over new awards in any year in which funds are insufficient to award all eligible, timely applicants. **Funds Available:** The amount of the award is recommended by the respective tribe but may not exceed the student's annual cost of education for a maximum of eight semesters or 12 quarters of undergraduate study, or the equivalent for less than full-time enrollment. **Contact:** Applications may be obtained from the Office of Student Financial Assistance or from one of the following tribal offices: Miccosukee Tribe of Florida, c/o Higher Education Committee, PO Box 440021, Tamiami Station, Miami, FL 33144; Seminole Tribe of Florida, c/o Higher Education Committee, 6703 Sterling Rd., Hollywood, FL 33024. **Applicant Details:** Applicants must demonstrate financial need as determined by the standards established by the respective tribes. An application must be submitted to the appropriate tribal higher education committee. A renewal application must be submitted annually.

★1598★

Seneca Nation of Indians
Higher Education Scholarship

Seneca Nation of Indians
Higher Education Program
PO Box 231   Ph: (716)945-1790
Salamanca, NY 14779   Fax: (716)945-3917

Study Level: Doctorate; Graduate; Undergraduate. **Award Type:** Scholarship. **Purpose:** To assist Seneca Indians in furthering their education. **Applicant Eligibility:** Applicant must be an enrolled tribal member of the Seneca Nation of Indians. **Selection Criteria:** Based on financial need and availability of funds. **Funds Available:** $5,000 limit per student (subject to change). **Application Deadline:** Fall - July 15; Spring - December 31; Summer - May 20.

★1599★

U.S. Department of the Interior
Bureau of Indian Affairs
Job Placement and Training Scholarship

U.S. Bureau of Indian Affairs
Office of Indian Education Programs
1849 C St., NW
Washington, DC 20240

Study Level: Undergraduate. **Award Type:** Scholarship. **Purpose:** To support Native Americans' vocational training and job placement pursuits. **Applicant Eligibility:** Minimum of one-quarter of Indian blood. Applicants must also be members of a recognized tribe, band, or group of Indians and must reside on or in the proximity of an Indian reservation under the jurisdiction of the Bureau of Indian Affairs. **Funds Available:** Amount of average award is $4,500, although awards range from $800 to $6,500. **Application Deadline:** Acceptance of applications is ongoing.

★1600★
U.S. Department of the Interior
Bureau of Indian Affairs
Scholarship Grant
U.S. Bureau of Indian Affairs
Office of Indian Education Programs
1849 C St., NW
Washington, DC 20240

Study Level: Undergraduate. **Award Type:** Grant. **Applicant Eligibility:** Candidates must be Native Americans, Eskimos, Alaska natives and be members of federally recognized tribes. They must also have been accepted at an accredited college or university. **Funds Available:** Appropriated yearly by Congress with each tribe specifying the amount they wish to receive. **Contact:** Set by each Tribal Contractor. Branch of Post Secondary Education, (202)208-4871. **Applicant Details:** All application information is available from the Tribal Contractor or the Bureau Agency serving that tribe. There are no funds or applications available from the above address or the Central Office of the Bureau of Indian Affairs.

★1601★
Wisconsin Native American Student Grant
Wisconsin Higher Education Aids Board
131 W. Wilson St.
PO Box 7885
Madison, WI 53707   Ph: (608)266-0888

Study Level: Graduate; Undergraduate. **Award Type:** Grant. **Applicant Eligibility:** Must be Wisconsin residents who are at least 25 percent Native American heritage. Applicants must attend a Wisconsin institution, either public, independent, or proprietary. Awards are made to graduate as well as undergraduate students. **Funds Available:** Maximum award is $1,800 a year with a limit of five years eligibility. The Board has an informal matching arrangement with grant funds awarded by the Federal Bureau of Indian Affairs and Wisconsin tribal governments. **Applicant Details:** Application is made by the student through the use of a joint Board/BIA/Tribal form in addition to needs analysis forms.

Print & Broadcast Media

Directories

★1602★
American Indian and Alaska Native Traders Directory
Arrowstar Publishing
10134 University Park Sta.
Denver, CO 80210-1034   Ph: (303)762-6579

Covers: 3,500 American Indian-owned and Eskimo-owned arts and crafts businesses, craft persons, and artists. **Entries Include:** Company name, address. **Pages (approx.):** 140. **Frequency:** Published June 1990. **Price:** $19.95, plus $1.50 shipping.

★1603★
American Indian Archival Material: A Guide to Holdings in the Southeast
Greenwood Publishing Group, Inc.
88 Post Rd., W.
PO Box 5007
Westport, CT 06881   Ph: (203)226-3571

Covers: Manuscript repositories with significant collections on Native Americans; coverage limited to Alabama, Florida, Georgia, Kentucky, Louisiana, Mississippi, North and South Carolina, Tennessee, Virginia, and West Virginia. **Entries Include:** Repository name, location, and description of holdings. **Pages (approx.):** 325. **Frequency:** Published 1982. **Price:** $49.95.

★1604★
American Indian Education: A Directory of Organizations and Activities in American Indian Education
ERIC Clearinghouse on Rural Education
   and Small Schools (ERIC/CRESS)
Appalachia Educational Laboratory, Inc.
   (AEL)
1031 Quarrier St.
PO Box 1348
Charleston, WV 25325   Ph: (304)347-0400

Covers: Nearly 120 national, state, and local organizations, resource and evaluation centers, agencies, and other groups working in American Indian education. **Entries Include:** Name, address, phone, name and title of contact, description of programs and services. **Pages (approx.):** 35. **Frequency:** Biennial, November of even years. **Price:** $4.50.

★1605★
American Indian Index
Arrowstar Publishing
10134 University Park Sta.
Denver, CO 80210-1034   Ph: (303)762-6579

Covers: Over 6,000 Native American Indian and Native Alaskan tribes, social service organizations and agencies, newspapers, and museums. **Entries Include:** Organization name, address, subsidiary and branch names and locations (if applicable), product or service. **Pages (approx.):** 325. **Frequency:** Irregular; latest edition 1987. **Price:** $19.95, plus $1.50 shipping.

★1606★
American Indian Painters
National Museum of the American Indian
3753 Broadway
New York, NY 10032-1596   Ph: (212)283-2420

Covers: 1,190 persons, most of them living at the time of publication. **Entries Include:** Name, vital statistics, tribal affiliations, career notes, exhibitions, collections in which the artist is represented. **Pages (approx.):** 270. **Frequency:** Published in 1968; no new editions planned. **Price:** $7.50, plus $2.25 shipping.

★1607★
Education Assistance for American Indians and Alaska Natives
Master of Public Health Program for
   American Indians
School of Public Health
University of California
Warren Hall, Rm. 140
Berkeley, CA 94720   Ph: (415)642-3228

Entries Include: Name of organization or publisher, address, name of contact, phone, service programs offered. **Frequency:** Biennial, June of even years. **Price:** Free.

★1608★
Federal Programs of Assistance to Native Americans
Senate Select Committee on Indian Affairs
United States Senate
Washington, DC 20510   Ph: (202)224-2251

Covers: Programs "specifically designed to benefit Indian tribes and individuals, ...Indians or Indian tribes as eligible beneficiaries, and...(programs) deemed to be of special interest to Indians." **Entries Include:** Name, description of program, eligibility requirements, application procedures, name and address of local and Washington contacts, appropriations, other information. **Pages (approx.):** 300. **Frequency:** Irregular; previous edition 1988; latest edition 1991. **Price:** Free. **Former Title(s):** *Federal Programs of Assistance to American Indians.*

★1609★
How to Research American Indian Blood Lines
Heritage Quest
Box 40
Orting, WA 98360-0040   Ph: (206)893-5029
Entries Include: Organization name, address. **Pages (approx.):** 110. **Frequency:** Irregular; latest edition February 1987. **Price:** $9.00, plus $2.50 shipping.

★1610★
Indian America: A Traveler's Guide
John Muir Publications
PO Box 613
Santa Fe, NM 87504   Ph: (505)982-4078
Covers: Over 300 Indian tribes in the U.S. **Entries Include:** Tribe, name, council address, phone; description of activites, including public ceremonies and powwows; tribe histories. **Pages (approx.):** 448. **Frequency:** Irregular; latest edition July 1991; new edition expected July 1993 **Price:** $18.95.

★1611★
Indian Goods Retail Directory
American Business Directories, Inc.
American Business Information, Inc.
5711 S. 86th Circle
Omaha, NE 68127   Ph: (402)593-4600
Entries Include: Name, address, phone, size of advertisement, name of owner or manager, number of employees, year first in "Yellow Pages." **Frequency:** Updated continuously; printed on request. **Price:** Please inquire. Significant discounts offered for standing orders.

★1612★
Indian Reservations: A State and Federal Handbook
McFarland & Co., Inc.
Box 611
Jefferson, NC 28640   Ph: (919)246-4460
Covers: Indian reservations. **Entries Include:** Name of reservation, address, status (whether state or federal), tribal headquarters, type of land (tribal, alloted, government, etc.), description of history and culture, climate, utilities, and community facilities. **Pages (approx.):** 345. **Frequency:** Published 1986. **Price:** $45.00, plus $2.00 shipping.

★1613★
Native American Directory: Alaska, Canada, United States
National Native American Cooperative
Box 1000
San Carlos, AZ 85550-1000   Ph: (602)622-4900
Covers: Native American performing arts groups, craft materials suppliers, stores and galleries, Indian-owned motels and resorts; tribal offices, museums, and cultural centers; associations, schools; newspapers, radio and television programs and stations operated, owned, or specifically for Native Americans; calendar of events, including officially sanctioned powwows, conventions, arts and crafts shows, all-Indian rodeos, and Navajo rug auctions. **Entries Include:** Generally, organization or company name, address, descriptive comments, dates (for shows or events). **Pages (approx.):** 335. **Frequency:** Irregular; previous edition 1982; latest edition March 1992. **Price:** $44.95, plus $3.00 shipping.

★1614★
Native American Policy Network Directory
Native American Policy Network
Barry University
11300 NE 2nd Ave.
Miami, FL 33161   Ph: (305)899-3473
Covers: About 425 professors, political leaders, and others interested in Native American politics. **Entries Include:** Name, address, phone. **Pages (approx.):** 15. **Frequency:** Quarterly. **Price:** $5.00.

★1615★
Red Pages: Businesses across Indian America
LaCourse Communications Corporation
PO Box 431
Toppenish, WA 98948-0431
Covers: Native American-owned businesses. **Entries Include:** Company name, address, phone, contact name. **Frequency:** Published 1985.

★1616★
Reference Encyclopedia of the American Indian
Todd Publications
Box 301
West Nyack, NY 10994   Ph: (914)358-6213
Covers: Agencies and associations of interest to Native Americans, including reservations, tribal councils, Bureau of Indian Affairs, schools and health services, museums, cultural centers, audiovisual aids, and periodicals, approximately 1,500 Native Americans prominent in tribal affairs, business, industry, art, science, and other professions, and non-Indians active in Indian affairs and related fields. **Entries Include:** Directories include agencies' and associations', name, address, phone, titles of key personnel, and a description of activities. Biographies include name, address, and phone and biographical data. **Pages (approx.):** 1,200. **Frequency:** Biennial, even years. **Price:** $125, postpaid.

★1617★
Smoke Signals: Business Directory of Indian Country U.S.A.
Arrowstar Publishing
10134 University Park Sta.
Denver, CO 80210-1034   Ph: (303)762-6579
Covers: Approximately 3,500 American Indian and Alaska native owned and operated businesses. **Entries Include:** Company name, address. **Pages (approx.):** 220. **Frequency:** Published 1990. **Price:** $59.95, plus $1.95 shipping. **Former Title(s):** *Smoke Signals: Directory of Native Indian/Alaskan Businesses* (1990).

★1618★
Source Directory of Indian, Eskimo, and Aleut Owned-and-Operated Arts and Crafts Businesses
U.S. Indian Arts and Crafts Board
Rm. 4004-MIB
Washington, DC 20240   Ph: (202)208-3773
Covers: Over 250 Native American-owned businesses specializing in arts and crafts products. **Entries Include:** Company name, address, phone, name and title of contact, description of products and services. **Pages (approx.):** 50. **Frequency:** Irregular; latest edition 1987; updated with supplements as needed. **Price:** Free. **Former Title(s):** *Native American Owned and Operated Crafts Businesses* (1987).

★1619★
Sources of Financial Aid Available to American Indian Students
Indian Resource Development (IRD)
Box 30003, Dept. 3IRD
Las Cruces, NM 88003   Ph: (505)646-1347
Covers: About 40 government agencies, private organizations, colleges and universities, and other groups offering financial aid or work experience opportunities for North American Indian college students. **Entries Include:** Organization or institute name, address, phone, contact name, type of aid available, duration and amount, deadline, requirements, field of study, college or university selection. **Pages (approx.):** 50. **Frequency:** Annual. **Price:** $3.00.

★1620★
Who's Who in Indian Relics
Parks-Thompson Co.
1757 W. Adams
Kirkwood, MO 63122   Ph: (314)822-2409
Covers: 130 to 140 persons per volume who have outstanding collections of American Indian relics. Volume 7, published 1987, also includes roster of 1,900 other collectors. **Entries Include:** Biography and portrait of collector, description of collection, photographs of

selected items. **Pages (approx.):** 400. **Frequency:** Quadrennial; previous edition 1987; latest edition fall 1992. **Price:** $35.00 per volume, plus $2.50 shipping; payment must accompany order.

───── **Journals & Magazines** ─────

★1621★
Akwekon Literary Journal
Mohawk Nation
RR 1, Box 116
Bombay, NY 12914-9718   Ph: (518)358-9531
Description: Magazine featuring Native North American art, literature, media, and culture. **First Published:** 1984. **Frequency:** Quarterly. **Subscription:** $20. $7 single issue.

★1622★
Akwesasne Notes
Mohawk Nation
PO Box 196
Rooseveltown, NY 13683-0196   Ph: (518)358-9531
Subtitle: A Journal for Native and Natural People. **Description:** Tabloid concerning American Indians and indigenous persons worldwide. **First Published:** 1969. **Frequency:** 6x/yr. **Subscription:** $15; $35 other countries. **ISSN:** 0002-3949.

★1623★
American Indian Art Magazine
American Indian Art, Inc.
7314 E. Osborn Dr.
Scottsdale, AZ 85251   Ph: (602)994-5445
Description: Journal covering all areas of Native American art. **First Published:** November 1975. **Frequency:** Quarterly. **Subscription:** $20; $24 other countries.

★1624★
American Indian Basketry Magazine
Institute for the Study of Traditional
   American Indian Arts
PO Box 66124
Portland, OR 97266   Ph: (503)233-8131
Description: American Indian magazine featuring basketry and other native arts. **First Published:** 1979. **Frequency:** 4x/yr. **Subscription:** $30.

★1625★
American Indian Culture and Research Journal
University of California at Los Angeles
American Indian Studies Center
3220 Campbell Hale   Ph: (213)825-7315
Los Angeles, CA 90024-1548   Fax: (213)206-7060
Description: Journal focusing on American Indian life and culture. **Subscription:** $20 individuals; $30 institutions. **Former Title(s):** *American Indian Culture Center Journal.*

★1626★
American Indian Law Review
University of Oklahhoma
College of Law
300 Timberdell Rd.
Norman, OK 73019   Ph: (405)325-2840
First Published: 1973. **Frequency:** Semiannual. **Subscription:** $10.

★1627★
American Indian Quarterly
Native America Studies Program
University of California at Berkeley
NAS/3415 Dwinelle Hall
Berkeley, CA 94720-9989   Ph: (510)642-6607
Subtitle: Journal of American Indian Studies. **Description:** An interdisciplinary journal featuring anthropology, history, literature, and the arts. **First Published:** 1982. **Frequency:** Quarterly.

Subscription: $25; $45 institutions; $32 other countries; $47 institutions, other countries. **ISSN:** 0095-182X.

★1628★
Cherokee Advocate
Cherokee Nation of Oklahoma
PO Box 948
Tahlequah, OK 74465   Ph: (918)456-0671
Description: Tribal newspaper (newsletter). **First Published:** 1977. **Frequency:** Monthly. **Subscription:** $12.50.

★1629★
Daybreak
PO Box 315
Highland, MD 20777-0098
Description: National magazine of American Indian news. **Frequency:** Quarterly. **Subscription:** $12.

★1630★
Eagle's Voice
Sinte Gleska College
Box 8
Mission, SD 57555   Ph: (605)856-2321
Description: Contains literature on Native American experiences on the high plains. Text also in Lakota. **First Published:** 1975. **Also Known As:** *Wanbli Ho.*

★1631★
Hispanic Times Magazine
Hispanic Times Enterprises
Box 579
Winchester, CA 92396   Ph: (818)579-3572
Description: Business magazine aimed at Hispanics and Native Americans. **Frequency:** 5/yr. **Subscription:** $30.

★1632★
Indian Artifact Magazine
Indian Artifact Magazine, Inc.
RD 1, Box 240
Turbotville, PA 17772-9599   Ph: (717)437-3698
Description: Magazine of American Indian prehistory, including artifacts, lifestyles, customs, and archaeology. **First Published:** June 1982. **Frequency:** Quarterly. **Subscription:** $17; $21 other countries. $5 single issue. **ISSN:** 0736-265X.

★1633★
Indian Historian
Indian Historian Press
1493 Masonic Ave.
San Francisco, CA 94117   Ph: (415)626-5235
Description: Magazine covering American Indian culture and history. **First Published:** 1964. **Frequency:** Quarterly. **Subscription:** $10.

★1634★
Indian Life
Intertribal Christian Communications
PO Box 3765, Sta. B
Winnipeg, MB, Canada R2W 3R6   Ph: (204)661-9333
Description: A non-denominational Christian magazine addressing the social, cultural, and spiritual needs of North American Indians. **First Published:** November 1979. **Frequency:** 6x/yr. **Subscription:** $7. **ISSN:** 0226-9317.

★1635★
Indigenous Woman
Indigenous Women's Network
PO Box 174
Lake Elmo, MN 55042   Ph: (612)770-3861
Description: The official journal of the Indigenous Women's Association. **First Published:** 1991. **Frequency:** 2/yr. **Subscription:** $25.

★1636★
Jicarilla Chieftain
PO Box 507
Dulce, NM 87528-0507   Ph: (505)759-3242
Description: Native American news tabloid. **First Published:** January 8, 1962. **Frequency:** Every other week (Fri.). **Subscription:** $12; $18 out of state; $24 other countries.

★1637★
Journal of American Indian Education
Arizona State University
College of Education
Center for Indian Education
Farmer 415
Tempe, AZ 85287   Ph: (602)965-6292
First Published: 1961. **Frequency:** 3x/yr.

★1638★
Journal of American Indian Family Research
Histree
23011 Multon Pkwy., No. C-8
Laguna Hills, CA 92653   Ph: (714)859-1659
First Published: 1980. **Frequency:** Quarterly.

★1639★
Mountain Light News and Views from the Southwest
Southwest Learning Centers of Santa Fe
PO Box 8627
Santa Fe, NM 87504
Frequency: 2/yr.

★1640★
The Native Nevadan
Reno-Sparks Indian Colony
98 Colony Rd.
Reno, NV 89502   Ph: (702)359-9449
Description: Native American news magazine. **First Published:** 1964. **Frequency:** Monthly. **Subscription:** $15. $1.50 single issue.

★1641★
Native Peoples Magazine
5333 N. 7th St., Ste. 224C
Phoenix, AZ 85014-2803   Ph: (602)252-2236
Subtitle: The Arts and Lifeways. **Description:** Ethnic magazine portraying the culture of native peoples; targets the museum-going public expressing an interest in Native Americans. **First Published:** September 1987. **Frequency:** Quarterly. **Subscription:** $18; $29 two years; $25 other countries. **ISSN:** 0895-7606.

★1642★
News From Native California
Heyday Books
PO Box 9145
Berkeley, CA 94709   Ph: (510)549-3564
Subtitle: An Insideview of the California Indian World. **Description:** Magazine featuring material relating to California Indians, past and present. **First Published:** 1987. **Frequency:** Quarterly. **Subscription:** $15.95. $3.95 single issue.

★1643★
Northeast Indian Quarterly
American Indian Program
Cornell University
400 Caldwell Hall
Ithaca, NY 14853   Ph: (602)255-6587
First Published: 1986. **Frequency:** Quarterly. **Former Title(s):** *Indian Times.*

★1644★
Tribal College
American Indian Higher Education
  Consortium
PO Box 898   Ph: (301)778-0171
Chestertown, MD 21620   Fax: (301)778-0151
Description: The official journal of the American Indian Higher Education Consortium, focusing on post-secondary education for Native Americans. **Frequency:** 4/yr. **Subscription:** $14.00/yr.

★1645★
Whispering Wind
Written Heritage
8009 Wales St.
New Orleans, LA 70126-1952   Ph: (504)241-5866
Subtitle: American Indian: Past and Present. **Description:** Magazine covering current and historical events, crafts, and material culture of the American Indian. **First Published:** Oct. 1967. **Frequency:** 6x/yr. **Subscription:** $16; $28 two years. $4 single issue. **ISSN:** 0300-6565.

★1646★
Winds of Change
AISES Publishing, Inc.
1630 30th St., Ste. 301
Boulder, CO 80301   Ph: (303)444-9099
     Fax: (303)444-6607
Subtitle: American Indian Education and Opportunity. **Frequency:** 4/yr. **Subscription:** $24.00; $34.00 in Canada.

─────────── **Newsletters** ───────────

★1647★
AICH Newsletter
American Indian Community House, Inc.
404 Lafayette St., 2nd Fl.
New York, NY 10003   Ph: (212)598-0100
Description: Reports on activities of the organization, which serves the social, educational, and cultural needs of native Americans residing in the New York metropolitan area. Reviews news and issues of interest to American Indians. **First Published:** 1969. **Frequency:** 5/yr. **Price:** Donation requested.

★1648★
American Indian Law Center—Newsletter
American Indian Law Center, Inc.
1117 Stanford NE
PO Box 4456, Sta. A
Albuquerque, NM 87196   Ph: (505)277-5462
Description: Covers the latest developments in federal Indian law, legislation being considered for enactment, administration of Indian programs, and policy analysis. Reports congressional activity on issues affecting American Indians, administrative rulings, and judicial decisions. **First Published:** 1968. **Frequency:** Bimonthly. **Price:** $20/yr.; $15 for American Indians. **Remarks:** Publication temporarily suspended.

★1649★
American Indian Libraries Newsletter
American Indian Library Association
c/o Charles Townley
Heindel Library
Penn State Harrisburg
Middletown, PA 17057   Ph: (717)948-6070
Subscription: $10 individuals; $25 institutions. **ISSN:** 0193-8207.

★1650★
American Indian Report
Falmouth Institute
3918 Prosperity Ave., Ste. 302   Ph: (703)641-9100
Fairfax, VA 22031-3333   Fax: (703)641-1558
Frequency: Monthly. **Subscription:** $79.00.

★1651★
Arrow
St. Labre Indian School
Ashland, MT 59003   Ph: (406)784-2746

★1652★
Bureau of Catholic Indian Missions—Newsletter
Bureau of Catholic Indian Missions
2021 H St. NW   Ph: (202)331-8542
Washington, DC 20006   Fax: (202)331-8544
Description: Publishes news and concerns of the Bureau, especially those issues pertaining to the Catholic Church and the Indian community: evangelism, justice, treaties, and advocacy. Promotes healthy family living in the face of the problems affecting Indian families: divorce, drugs, suicide, and alcohol. Updates information on legislation affecting the Indian community. **First Published:** December 1977. **Frequency:** 10/yr. **Price:** Free.

★1653★
Calumet
United South and Eastern Tribes, Inc.
1101 Kermit Dr., Ste. 800
Nashville, TN 37217   Ph: (615)361-8700
Frequency: Bimonthly.

★1654★
Cherokee Boys Club—Newsletter
Cherokee Boys Club
PO Box 507
Cherokee, NC 28719   Ph: (704)497-9101
Description: Published as a service of the boys club, covering activities of the Cherokee Children's Home and the American Indian people indigenous to Tennessee and North Carolina. **First Published:** July 1965. **Frequency:** Quarterly. **Price:** Free. **ISSN:** 0890-5193.

★1655★
Cherokee Voice
Cherokee Children's Home
Box 507
Cherokee, NC 28719
First Published: 1981. **Frequency:** Quarterly.

★1656★
Commission for the Catholic Missions Among the Colored People and the Indians—Quarterly
Commission for the Catholic Missions
  Among the Colored People and the
  Indians
2021 H St. NW   Ph: (202)331-8542
Washington, DC 20006   Fax: (202)331-8544
Description: Concerned with evangelism in church programs for the Black and Indian communities in the U.S. Publishes news and updates the financial status of the Commission. Reports the ordination of priests and the activities of individuals from Black and Indian communities. **First Published:** 1977. **Frequency:** Annual. **Price:** Free.

★1657★
Cross & Feather News
Tekakwitha Conference National Center
1800 9th Ave., S., No. 20
PO Box 6768
Great Falls, MT 59406   Ph: (406)727-0147
Description: Carries articles addressing religious, social, and legislative issues concerning Native American Catholics. Reports on workshops, conferences, and meetings dealing with such topics as lay ministry, catechesis, youth and family concerns, chemical dependency, community life, social justice, and tribal concerns. **First Published:** 1979. **Frequency:** Quarterly. **Price:** Included in membership.

★1658★
Eagle's Eye
Student Leadership Development
Brigham Young University
128 ELWC   Ph: (801)378-7084
Provo, UT 84602   Fax: (801)378-6864
Description: Items of interest to Native Americans. **ISSN:** 0046-0915.

★1659★
Elder Voices
National Indian Council on Aging
6400 Uptown Blvd. NE, Ste. 510-W   Ph: (505)888-3302
Albuquerque, NM 87110   Fax: (505)888-3276
Description: Concentrates on issues affecting lives of Native American elders, such as services and related legislative issues. **First Published:** April 1977. **Frequency:** Periodic. **Price:** Free. **Former Title(s):** *NICOA News*, November 1980; *National Indian Council on Aging–Quarterly*, February 1984.

★1660★
Family Services Newsletter
Family Services Program
Toiyabe Indian Health Project, Inc.
PO Box 1296   Ph: (619)873-6394
Bishop, CA 93515   Fax: (619)873-3935
Description: Focuses on concerns of Indian families, discussing issues such as drugs and alcohol, parenting, child abuse and neglect, and women's concerns. Provides information on the Program's counseling, educational, legal, and advocacy services. **First Published:** October 1980. **Frequency:** Quarterly. **Price:** Free.

★1661★
Futures
Futures for Children   Ph: (505)247-4700
805 Tijeras, NW   Free: 800-545-6843
Albuquerque, NM 87102   Fax: (505)247-2831
Description: Supports the Futures for Children program, which seeks to find sponsors for American Indian children to contribute toward the child's education and clothing. Provides sponsors, donors, and "Friends of Futures" with news concerning the Sponsorship Program, the Self-Help Program, and the International Program. **First Published:** Summer 1961. **Frequency:** 2/yr. **Price:** Free.

★1662★
Ichana
National Committee on Indian Work of the
  Episcopal Church
815 2nd Ave.
New York, NY 10017   Ph: (212)867-8400
Description: Focuses on American Indian affairs. Informs readers of programs and projects of the Committee and other groups affiliated with the Episcopal Church. **First Published:** 1979. **Frequency:** Quarterly. **Price:** Free. **Former Title(s):** *NCIW Newsletter*.

★1663★
Indian Affairs
Association on American Indian Affairs,
  Inc.
95 Madison Ave.
New York, NY 10016   Ph: (212)689-8720
Description: Explores issues concerning American Indian affairs: reports on economic, political, and social conditions on reservations, inter-tribal relations, resource utilization, self-determination, legal defense, foster care programs, education, and health issues. **First Published:** 1949. **Frequency:** 3/yr. **Price:** $10/yr.

★1664★
Indian Arts and Crafts Association Newsletter
Indian Arts and Crafts Association
122 La Veta Dr., NE
Alburquerque, NM 87108   Ph: (505)265-9149
First Published: 1974. **Frequency:** Monthly.

★1665★
Indian Awareness Center Newsletter
Fulton County Historical Society, Inc.
Rte. 3, Box 89
Rochester, IN 46975   Ph: (219)223-4436
Description: Covers projects and activities of the Center, which encourages the awareness, appreciation, and preservation of Native American culture and traditions, especially that of the Potawatomi and Miami Indians of northern Indiana. **First Published:** 1984. **Frequency:** Quarterly. **Price:** $5/yr. for individuals; $7.50 for families and institutions.

★1666★
Indian Crusader
American Indian Liberation Crusade, Inc.
4009 Halldale Ave.
Los Angeles, CA 90062   Ph: (213)299-1810
Description: Reports on programs to aid reservation Indians. **Frequency:** Quarterly, 1954.

★1667★
Indian Law Reporter
American Indian Lawyer Training Program,
   Inc.
319 MacArthur Blvd.   Ph: (510)834-9333
Oakland, CA 94610   Fax: (510)834-3836
Description: Reports current federal, state, and tribal laws affecting Native Americans. **First Published:** 1974. **Frequency:** Monthly.

★1668★
Indian Progress
Associated Committee of Friends on
   Indian Affairs
PO Box 1661
Richmond, IN 47375   Ph: (317)962-9169
Description: Contains news of centers administered by the Committee. **Frequency:** 3/yr. **Price:** Free to individuals; $3/yr. for institutions.

★1669★
Indian Report
Friends Committee on National Legislation
245 Second St. NE
Washington, DC 20002   Ph: (202)547-6000
Description: Serves as an educational tool of the Indian program of the Committee, reporting on legislative issues affecting Native Americans. **First Published:** June 22, 1977. **Frequency:** Quarterly. **Price:** Donation requested. **Remarks:** Also available in microform.

★1670★
Indian Time
Mohawk Nation
PO Box 196
Rooseveltown, NY 13683-0196   Ph: (518)358-9531
Description: Provides news concerning the Akwesasne Mohawk reservation. **First Published:** 1983. **Frequency:** Weekly. **Price:** $40/yr., U.S.; $45 elsewhere. **ISSN:** 0893-3820.

★1671★
Inter-Tribal Association—Newsletter
Inter-Tribal Association
Vietnam Era Veterans Center
1223 Sherry Ln.
Cherokee, OK 74801   Ph: (405)273-6790
Description: Provides news of interest on American Indians who served in the Vietnam War. **Frequency:** Quarterly.

★1672★
Intercom
American Indian Community
   Communication, Information, and
   Assisstance Center
2838 W. Peterson Ave.
Chicago, IL 60659   Ph: (312)761-5000
First Published: 1987. **Frequency:** Monthly.

★1673★
Ka Ri Wen Ha Wi
Akwesasne Library
R.R. 1, Box 14 C
Hogansburg, NY 13655   Ph: (518)358-2240
Description: Publishes news of the Reservation community and the Akwesasne Library/Cultural Center. **First Published:** 1972. **Frequency:** Monthly. **Price:** Free.

★1674★
Linkages
TCI, Inc.
3410 Garfield St. NW   Ph: (202)333-6350
Washington, DC 20007-1439   Fax: (202)965-0246
Description: Covers Bureau of Indian Affairs (BIA) social service programs, especially those concerned with child abuse prevention, adoption and custody, education, and behavior. Contains notices of grants, news of legislation, and announcements of conferences and workshops.

★1675★
Meeting Ground
D'Arcy McNickle Center for the History of
   the American Indian
Newberry Library
60 W. Walton St.
Chicago, IL 60610   Ph: (312)943-9090
Description: Reports past, present, and future activities of the Center which is committed to "improving the quality of teaching and research in the field of Native American history." Recurring features include news of research, news of members, book reviews, reports on Chicago Indian community projects, and columns titled Director's Notes, Center Fellows, Alumni Notes, and New Books. **First Published:** 1974. **Frequency:** Biennially. **Price:** Free.

★1676★
NARF Legal Review
Native American Rights Fund
1506 Broadway
Boulder, CO 80302   Ph: (303)447-8760
Description: Focuses on the concerns of the Native American Rights Fund, "a nonprofit organization specializing in the protection of Indian rights." Discusses current Indian law issues. Carries staff news, news of NARF activities, and announcements of NARF services and publications. **First Published:** Summer 1973. **Frequency:** Quarterly. **Price:** Free. **ISSN:** 0739-862X. **Former Title(s):** Native American Legal Rights Fund–Announcements.

★1677★
Native American Studies
Edwin Mellen Press
240 Portage Rd.
Box 450   Ph: (716)754-8566
Lewiston, NY 14092   Fax: (716)754-4335
Frequency: Irregular.

★1678★
Native Arts Update
ATLATL
402 W. Roosevelt
Phoenix, AZ 85003   Ph: (602)253-2731
Description: Promotes the vitality of contemporary Native American artists and cultural organizations. Lists grants, fellowships, competitions, scholarships, and exhibits. **Frequency:** Quarterly. **Price:** Included in membership; $25/yr. for nonmembers, U.S.; $30, Canada; $35 elsewhere.

★1679★
Native Nations
Solidarity Foundation
404 Lafayette St.
New York, NY 10003
First Published: 1985. **Frequency:** Monthly.

★1680★
Native Sun
Detroit American Indian Center
North American Indian Association of
Detroit, Inc.
2272 Plymouth Rd.
Detroit, MI 48239   Ph: (313)963-1710
Description: Carries local and national news pertaining to Native Americans, including news of the Association, with emphasis on events of interest to American Indians in Wayne County. Covers pertinent legislation. **First Published:** March 1975. **Frequency:** Monthly. **Price:** Free.

★1681★
Native Vision
American Indian Contemporary Arts
The Monadnnock Bldg.
685 Market St., Ste. 250
San Francisco, CA 94105-4212   Ph: (415)495-7600
First Published: 1984. **Frequency:** Irregular.

★1682★
Pan-American Indian Association News
Pan-American Indian Association and
Adopted Tribal Peoples
c/o Chief Piercing Eyes
Box 244
Nocatee, FL 33864-0244   Ph: (813)494-6930
Description: Provides geneaology aid for people with Native American heritage. **First Published:** 1984. **Frequency:** Irregular. **Former Title(s):** *Tribal Advisor.*

★1683★
Pathfinder Newsletter
American Indian Heritage Foundation
6051 Arlington Blvd.   Ph: (703)237-7500
Falls Church, VA 22044   Fax: (703)532-1921
Description: Informs Indians and non-Indians about the culture and heritage of the American Indian. Addresses the spiritual and physical needs of American Indians and aims to encourage Indian youth. **First Published:** 1982. **Frequency:** Quarterly. **Price:** Included in membership; $20/yr for nonmembers.

★1684★
Pocahontas Trails—Quarterly
Pocahontas Trails Genealogical Society
6015 Robin Hill Dr.
Lakeport, CA 95453
Description: Focuses on the pursuit and study of the genealogy of Pocahontas and Powhatan. **First Published:** October 1983. **Frequency:** Quarterly. **Price:** Included in membership.

★1685★
Pottery Southwest
Albuquerque Archaeological Society
6207 Mossman Pl. NE
Albuquerque, NM 87110   Ph: (505)881-1675
Description: Carries news and queries on prehistoric pottery of the Indians in New Mexico, Arizona, Utah, Colorado, and parts of Texas and Mexico. **First Published:** January 1974. **Frequency:** Quarterly. **Price:** $3/yr. **ISSN:** 0738-8020.

★1686★
Report of the Nebraska Indian Commission
Box 19153
Denver, CO 80219-0153   Ph: (402)471-2757

★1687★
Sentinel
National Congress of American Indians
900 Pennsylvania Ave. SE
Washington, DC 20003   Ph: (202)546-9404
Description: Focuses on national issues affecting American Indians. Monitors government legislation, federal agency activities, and innovative tribal programs. **First Published:** 1944. **Frequency:** Quarterly. **Price:** Included in membership.

★1688★
Shenandoah Newsletter
Paul A. Skenandore
736 W. Oklahoma St.
Appleton, WI 54914
Description: Discusses the history and legal rights of the native peoples of Great Turtle Island. Reports news of treaty and discrimination disputes, and of the international position of American Indians in a third world setting. **First Published:** April 1973. **Frequency:** Monthly. **Price:** $13.50/yr. for individuals, $18.50 for organizations, U.S. and Canada; $20 for individuals, $30 for organizations elsewhere.

★1689★
The Source
New Mexico Office of Indian Affairs
OIA, Villa Rivera Bldg.
224 E. Palace Ave.   Ph: (505)827-6440
Santa Fe, NM 87501   Fax: (505)827-7308
Description: Provides information on intergovernmental relations, commissioner activities, culture, arts, and educational issues of the American Indians. **First Published:** 1985. **Frequency:** 3/yr.

★1690★
Spirit!
Native American Resource Center
Pembroke State University
Pembroke, NC 28372   Ph: (919)521-4214
Description: Gives news of projects and events. **First Published:** 1987. **Frequency:** Quarterly. **Price:** Free.

★1691★
University of South Dakota—Bulletin
Institute of American Indian Studies
University of South Dakota
Dakota Hall, Rm. 12
414 E. Clark St.   Ph: (605)677-5209
Vermillion, SD 57069   Fax: (605)677-5073
Description: Disseminates information on education, current affairs, and regional and national issues and activities concerning Native Americans. Offers editorials and feature articles. **First Published:** 1955. **Frequency:** Quarterly. **Price:** Donation requested. **ISSN:** 0042-0069.

★1692★
Uts'itishtaan'i
American Indian Rehabilitation Research
and Training Center
Institute for Human Development
Northern Arizona University
PO Box 5630
Flagstaff, AZ 86011   Ph: (602)523-4791
Description: Covers activities of the Center, which aims to improve the lives of American Indians with disablities. Contains articles on rehabilitation. **First Published:** 1983. **Frequency:** 2/yr. **Price:** Free.

★1693★
The WEB
American Indian Program
Cornell University
400 Caldwell Hall   Ph: (607)255-4308
Ithaca, NY 14853   Fax: (607)255-0788
Description: Focuses on Native American students at Cornell University. Reports on activities, awards, projects, scholarships,

graduations, and alumni. **First Published:** 1986. **Frequency:** 2/yr. **Price:** Free. **Former Title(s):** Update, 1988.

---------- **Newspapers** ----------

★1694★
American Indian News
PO Box 217
Fort Washakie, WY 82514

★1695★
American Indian News
Thunderbird American Indian Dancers
215 W. 23rd St.
New York, NY 10011   Ph: (212)741-9221

★1696★
Americans Before Columbus
National Indian Youth Council
318 Elm St. SE
Albuquerque, NM 87102   Ph: (505)247-2251
Frequency: Bimonthly.

★1697★
The Cherokee One Feather
Eastern Band of Cherokee Indians
PO Box 501
Cherokee, NC 28719   Ph: (704)497-5513
Description: Newspaper featuring news of interest to the local Cherokee tribe and to American Indians in general. **First Published:** 1967. **Frequency:** Weekly. **Subscription:** $20. **ISSN:** 0890-4448.

★1698★
Choctaw Community News
Mississippi Band of Choctaw Indians
Box 6010   Ph: (601)656-1521
Philadelphia, MS 39350   Fax: (601)656-1992
First Published: 1970. **Frequency:** Monthly. **Subscription:** Free.

★1699★
Circle
Boston Indian Council
105 S. Huntington Ave.
Jamaica Plain, MA 02130   Ph: (617)232-0343
Subtitle: A Paper for Native American People. **Description:** Covers information of interest to Native Americans in the Boston area as well as others. In English and Micmac. **Frequency:** Monthly. **Subscription:** $10.00.

★1700★
Daybreak Star Indian Reader
United Indians of All Tribes Foundation
1945 Yale Pl., E.
Seattle, WA 98102   Ph: (206)325-0070
Description: Geared towards children in grades 4 to 6. **Frequency:** 8/yr. **Former Title(s):** Daybreak Star.

★1701★
Eagle
Eagle Wing Press Inc.
Box 579-MO
Naugatuck, CT 06770
Description: Reports on events concerning Native Americans of New England states. **First Published:** 1981. **Frequency:** Bimonthly.

★1702★
The Indian Trader
The Indian Trader, Inc.
311 E. Aztec
PO Box 1421
Gallup, NM 87301   Ph: (505)722-6694
Description: Newspaper (tabloid) covering American Indian culture, arts, and crafts. **First Published:** September 1970. **Frequency:** Monthly. **Subscription:** $18. **ISSN:** 0046-9076.

★1703★
The Lakota Times
Native American Publishing, Inc.
1920 Lombardy Dr.   Ph: (605)341-0011
Rapid City, SD 57701-4132   Fax: (605)341-6940
Description: Newspaper of national and international readership serving Native American communities. **First Published:** July 1981. **Frequency:** Weekly. **Subscription:** $30; $38 out of state. **ISSN:** 0744-2238.

★1704★
Navaho
Maazo Publishing
Box 1245
Window Rock, AZ 86515   Ph: (602)729-2233
Description: Covers Navaho Indian culture. **Frequency:** Quarterly.

★1705★
The Navajo Times
The Navajo Nation
PO Box 310
Window Rock, AZ 86515-0310   Ph: (602)871-6641
Subtitle: The Newspaper of the Navajo People. **First Published:** 1957. **Frequency:** Thur. (morn.). **Subscription:** $25. **Formerly:** The Navajo Times Today and Navajo Nation Times.

★1706★
News from Indian Country
Indian Country Communications, Inc.
Rte. 2, Box 2900 A
Hayward, WI 54843   Ph: (715)634-5226
Subtitle: The Journal. **Description:** Newspaper covering national, state, and local Native American news and features. **First Published:** 1977. **Frequency:** Monthly. **Subscription:** $15; $24 libraries; $25 other countries.

★1707★
Rawhide Press
Spokane Tribe of Indians
Spokane Tribal Business Council
Box 373
Wellprint, WA 99040   Ph: (509)258-4581
Description: Concerned with Indian culture and history. **Frequency:** Monthly. **Former Title(s):** Smoke Signals.

★1708★
Wotani-Wowapi
Fort Peck Assiniboine and Sioux Tribes
Box 1027
Poplar, MT 59225   Ph: (406)768-5155
First Published: 1969. **Frequency:** Weekly. **Former Title(s):** Wotanin.

★1709★
Yakima Nation Review
Yakima Indian Nation
PO Box 151
Toppenish, WA 98948   Ph: (509)865-5121
Description: Newspaper serving the Yakima Indian Nation. Covers tribal, state, federal government, and general news. **First Published:** May 1970. **Frequency:** 2x/mo. (Fri.). **Subscription:** $15.

Radio Stations

★1710★
KABR-AM
PO Box 907
Alamo, NM 87825   Ph: (505)854-2543
Frequency: 1500. **Network Affiliation:** Independent. **Format:** News;
Eclectic; Top 40; Country; Ethnic (Navajo language). **Owner:** Trowen
(T.C.) Hulett.

★1711★
KCIE-FM
PO Box 603
Dulce, NM 87528   Ph: (505)759-3681
Warren Cassador, Station Mgr.
Frequency: 90.5. **Format:** Eclectic. **Owner:** Jicarilla Apache Tribe.

★1712★
KEYA-FM
PO Box 190
Belcourt, ND 58316   Ph: (701)477-5686
Michael V. Vann, Pres.
Founded: 1975. **Frequency:** 88.5. **Format:** Country. **Owner:**
Belcourt School District No. 7.

★1713★
KHNE-FM
PO Box 83111
Lincoln, NE 68503   Ph: (402)472-3611
Frequency: 89.1. **Network Affiliation:** National Public Radio (NPR);
American Public Radio (APR). **Format:** Public Radio; Classical;
News; Jazz; Ethnic (American Indian); Folk. **Owner:** Nebraska
Educational Telecommunications Commission.

★1714★
KIDE-FM
PO Box 1220
Hoopa, CA 95546   Ph: (916)625-4245
Joe Orozco, Station Mgr.
Founded: 1980. **Frequency:** 91.3. **Format:** Eclectic. **Owner:** Hoopa
Valley Communication Corporation.

★1715★
KILI-FM
Lakota Communications
PO Box 150
Porcupine, SD 57772   Ph: (605)867-5002
Larry Swalley, Dir.
Frequency: 90.1. **Format:** Eclectic.

★1716★
KINI-FM
PO Box 419
Saint Francis, SD 57572
Mark Iyotte, Gen. Mgr.
Founded: 1976. **Frequency:** 96.1. **Format:** Eclectic; News. **Owner:**
Rosebud Educational Society, Inc.

★1717★
KMHA-FM
PO Box 699
New Town, ND 58763   Ph: (701)627-3333
Doreen Yellowbird, Gen. Mgr.
Founded: 1983. **Frequency:** 91.3. **Format:** Eclectic. **Owner:** Fort
Berthold Communications Enterprise.

★1718★
KNNB-FM
Hwy. 73, Skill Center Rd.
Box 310   Ph: (602)338-5229
Whiteriver, AZ 85941   Fax: (602)338-4778
Phoebe L. Nez, Gen. Mgr.
Frequency: 88.1. **Format:** Eclectic. **Owner:** Apache Radio
Broadcasting Corp.

★1719★
KSUT-FM
PO Box 737   Ph: (303)247-4900
Ignacio, CO 81173   Fax: (303)563-4033
Carlos Sena, Gen. Mgr.
Frequency: 89.1 and 91.3. **Network Affiliation:** National Public
Radio (NPR), American Public Radio (APR). **Format:** Eclectic.
Owner: KUTE, Inc.

★1720★
KTDB-FM
PO Box 40, Drawer B
Pine Hills, NM 87357-089B   Ph: (505)775-3215
Bernard J. Bustos, Station Mgr.
Founded: 1972. **Frequency:** 89.7. **Format:** Public Radio; Talk;
Ethnic (Indian Cultural Affairs); News; Country. **Owner:** Ramah
Navajo School Board, Inc.

★1721★
KTNN-AM
PO Box 2569   Ph: (602)871-2666
Window Rock, AZ 86515   Fax: (602)871-3479
Freddie Howard, Gen. Mgr.
Frequency: 660. **Network Affiliation:** NBC. **Format:** Contemporary
Country. **Owner:** KTNN-AM.

★1722★
KWSI-FM
20450 Empire Blvd.   Ph: (503)553-1965
Bend, OR 97701   Free: 800-422-0117
                                    Fax: (503)553-3348
Nat Shaw, Prog. Dir.
Frequency: 96.5. **Network Affiliation:** CNN. **Format:** Adult
Contemporary. **Owner:** Confederated Tribes of Warm Springs.

★1723★
KWSO-FM
PO Box 489   Ph: (503)553-1968
Warm Springs, OR 97761   Fax: (503)553-3348
Gerald L. Smith, Station Mgr.
Founded: 1986. **Frequency:** 91.9. **Format:** Public Radio; Eclectic;
Ethnic. **Owner:** Confederated Tribes of Warm Springs.

★1724★
WASG-AM
1210 S. Main St.   Ph: (205)368-5500
Altmore, AL 36052   Fax: (205)368-4227
R. Dale Gehman, Gen. Mgr.
Founded: 1981. **Frequency:** 550. **Network Affiliation:** NBC Talknet,
ABC. **Format:** Contemporary Country; Agricultural News; Talk.
Owner: Alabama Native American Broadcasting Co.

★1725★
WOJB-FM
Rte. 2
Hayward, WI 54843   Ph: (715)634-2100
Camille Lacapa-Morrison, Gen. Mgr.
Frequency: 88.9. **Format:** Eclectic; Native American Music. **Owner:**
Lac Courte Oreilles Ojibwa Broadcasting Corporation.

★1726★
WYRU-AM
PO Box 711
Red Springs, NC 28377
Michael Flanagan, Gen. and Station Mgr.

Ph: (919)843-5946
Fax: (919)521-8625

Founded: 1970. **Frequency:** 1160. **Network Affiliation:** Southern Farm. **Format:** Religious. **Owner:** Carolina Sunbelt Radio Media.

Publishers

★1727★
Acoma Books
PO Box 4
Ramona, CA 92065

Ph: (619)789-1288

Subjects: Native Americans, southwestern U.S. **Principal Officials and Managers:** Robert E. Neutrelle.

★1728★
Akwesasne Notes
Mohawk Nation
PO Box 196
Rooseveltown, NY 13683

Ph: (518)358-9531

Description: Publishes on the history, philosophy, religion, and ecology of the native people of the Americas. Reaches market through direct mail. **Total Titles in Print:** 8. **Selected Titles:** *Basic Call to Consciousness, Tales of the Iroquois, Vols. I-II* by Tehanetorens. **Principal Officials and Managers:** Douglas George, Editor; Susan Rourke, Manager.

★1729★
American Indian Archaeological Institute
38 Curtis Rd.
PO Box 1260
Washington Green, CT 06793-0260

Ph: (203)868-0518
Fax: (203)868-1649

Description: Publishes on New England archaeology and American Indian prehistory and history. Distributes books from other publishers. Offers a quarterly *Artifacts*. Reaches market through direct mail. **Total Titles in Print:** 5. **Selected Titles:** *Native Harvests: Botanicals and Recipes of the American Indian* by Barrie Kavasch; *Memories of Sweet Grass* by Adelphena Logan; *6LF21: A Paleo-Indian Site in Western Connecticut, A Guide to New England Artifacts*, both by Roger Moeller; *A Key into the Language of Woodsplint Baskets* edited by Ann McMullen and Russell G. Handsman. **Principal Officials and Managers:** Susan F. Payne, Director; Russell Handsman, Director of Research; Trudi Lamb Richmond, Director of Education.

★1730★
American Indian Basketry and Other Native Arts
PO Box 66124
Portland, OR 97266

Ph: (503)233-8131

Description: Publishes mostly monographs devoted to traditional native American arts. **Total Titles in Print:** 20. **Selected Titles:** *Miwok Indian Basketry* by Craig Bates; *Washoe Indian Basketry* by Marvin Cohodas; *Columbia River/Plateau Indian Beadwork, American Indian Art: Values and Aesthetics, Traditional Arts of the Indians of Western Oregon*, all by John M. Gogol. **Principal Officials and Managers:** John M. Gogol, Editor and Publisher.

★1731★
Amerind Foundation, Inc.
PO Box 248
Dragoon, AZ 85609

Ph: (602)586-3666

Description: Nonprofit archaeological research institution and museum specializing in the Native American cultures of the Americas. Publications result from archaeological field work. Also offers archaeological site maps, files, and photographic collections. Reaches market through direct mail. **Selected Titles:** *Casas Grandes: A Fallen Trading Center of the Gran Chichimeca, Vols. 1-8* by Charles Di Peso, John Rinaldo, and Gloria Fenner; *An Archaeological Site Near Gleeson, Arizona; Archaeological Notes on Texas Canyon, Arizona*, both by William Shirley Fulton; *Amerind*

New World Studies Series, Vol. 1: Exploring the Hohokam: Prehistoric Desert Peoples of the American Southwest edited by George J. Gumerman. **Principal Officials and Managers:** Dr. Anne I. Woosley, Director; William Duncan Fulton, President; Peter Formo, Vice-President; Michael W. Hard, Treasurer; Elizabeth F. Husband, Secretary.

★1732★
Angel Mounds State Historic Site
8215 Pollack Ave.
Evansville, IN 47715

Ph: (812)853-3956

Description: Publications deal with Angel Mounds, the Indians who lived there, and special exhibits. Offers a newsletter. **Subjects:** Native Americans. **Total Titles in Print:** 1. **Selected Titles:** *Ancient Treasures of the Americas*. **Principal Officials and Managers:** Rebecca Harris, Curator; Peggy Brooks, Assistant Curator.

★1733★
Anthropology Film Center Foundation
1626 Canyon Rd.
Santa Fe, NM 87501

Ph: (505)983-4127

Description: Provides consultation and research services, seminars, publications, teaching, research films, and reports on visual anthropology/documentary filmmaking. Distributed by Zia Cine, Inc. **Selected Titles:** *A Filmography for American Indian Education.* **Principal Officials and Managers:** Joan S. Williams, Executive Director.

★1734★
Arizona Desert Bighorn Sheep Society, Inc.
PO Box 7545
Phoenix, AZ 85011

Ph: (602)957-0773

Subjects: History, Seri Indians. **Total Titles in Print:** 2. **Selected Titles:** *The Wilderness of Big Horn Sheep and Seri Indians* by Charles Sheldon; *Borrego: The Fall and Rise of Desert Bighorn Sheep in Arizona* by Hook-Lee. **Principal Officials and Managers:** Dean Bowdoin, President; Bill Hook, Treasurer; Tom Martin, Secretary.

★1735★
Arrowstar Publishing
10134 University Park Sta.
Denver, CO 80210-0134

Ph: (303)692-6579

Description: American Indian-owned and operated publishing company with preference for American Indian works. Accepts unsolicited manuscripts. Reaches market through direct mail. **Number of New Titles:** 1989 - 3, 1990 - 3; Total Titles in Print - 15. **Selected Titles:** *While We're At It, Let's Find You a Job* by Frazier and Guthrie; *American Indian Index, Snake Signals, American Indian Funding Guide*, all by Frazier; *Job Development Services for American Indians* by Jones; *Traders Directory*. **Principal Officials and Managers:** John Bell, Vice-President, Marketing.

★1736★
Artlist
PO Box 35552
Albuquerque, NM 87175

Ph: (505)881-3248

Description: Publishes a reference source of auction prices of American Indian art. Offers appraisals. **Number of New Titles:** 1989 - 2, 1990 - 1; Total Titles in Print - 3. **Selected Titles:** *North American Indian Arts: An Index of Prices and Auctions* Laurence C. and Maurine M. Smith. **Principal Officials and Managers:** Laurence C. Smith, Owner.

★1737★
Association on American Indian Affairs
245 5th Ave., Ste. 1801
New York, NY 10016

Ph: (212)689-8720

Description: A private, nonprofit, national citizens organization providing technical and legal assistance to American Indian tribes and communities at their request. Also publishes the newsletter *Indian Affairs*. **Selected Titles:** *Indian Affairs; The Destruction of American Indian Families; Tribal Bond Handbook; Arts and Crafts Resource Guide; Economic and Community Development Resource Guide for Native Americans*. **Principal Officials and Managers:** Joy Hanley, President; Gary N. Kimble, Executive Director; David Risling,

Vice-President; Jo Motanic Lewis, Secretary; Owanah Anderson, Treasurer.

★1738★
Augustana College
Center for Western Studies
Box 727
Sioux Falls, SD 57197   Ph: (605)336-4007

Description: Publishes historical and cultural nonfiction dealing with the Midwest. Offers a biannual publication, *CWS Newsletter.* Accepts unsolicited manuscripts. Distributes for Nordland Heritage Foundation and University of Nebraska Press. Reaches market through direct mail and trade sales. **Subjects:** Immigration, settlement of the West, Sioux (Dakota) Indian culture. Cheyenne Indian history, Crow Indian history, Blackfoot Indian history. **Number of New Titles:** 1989 - 3, 1990 - 3, 1991 (est.) - 3; Total Titles in Print - 24. **Selected Titles:** *An Illustrated History of the Arts of South Dakota* by Arthur R. Huseboe; *Tomahawk and Cross: Lutheran Missionaries among the Northern Plains Tribes, 1858-1866* by Gerhard M. Schmutterer; *The Last Contrary: The Story of Wesley Whiteman (Black Bear)* by Warren G. Schwartz; *Natural History of the Black Hills and Badlands* by Sven G. Froiland; *Poems and Essays of Herbert Krause* edited by Arthur R. Huesboe; *The Quartzite Border* by Gordon Iseminger. **Principal Officials and Managers:** Arthur R. Huseboe, Executive Director; Barbara J. Ries, Office Manager; Harry Thompson, Curator and Managing Editor; Dean Schuler, Development Director.

★1739★
Avanyu Publishing, Inc.
PO Box 27134
Albuquerque, NM 87125   Ph: (505)266-6128

Description: Publishes on the ethnography of American Indians. Accepts unsolicited manuscripts. Distributed by University of New Mexico Press. Reaches market through direct mail, commission representatives, and wholesales. Alternate telephone number: (505)243-8485. **Number of New Titles:** 1989 - 3, 1990 - 2, 1991 (est.) - 6; Total Titles in Print - 14. **Selected Titles:** *Zuni Katcinas* by Ruth Bunzel; *Zuni Indians* by Matilda Coxe Stevenson; *Hopi Snake Ceremonies* by Jesse Walter Fewkes; *The Navajo* by J. B. Moore; *Historic Navajo Weaving* by Tyrone Campbell; *Petroglyphs and Pueblo Myths of the Rio Grande* by C. Rudolph. **Principal Officials and Managers:** J. Brent Ricks, President; Alexander E. Anthony, Jr., Secretary.

★1740★
Bear Claw Press
1407 W. Paterson St.
Flint, MI 48504   Ph: (313)238-2569

Description: Publishes materials for and about Native American cultures and ecology-wilderness literature. Presently inactive. **Subjects:** Native American narratives, poetry. **Total Titles in Print:** 4. **Selected Titles:** *The Seven Visions of Bull Lodge* edited by George Horst Capture; *Adirondacks: A Poetic Narrative* by Greg Kuzma; *Who Met the Ice Lynx, Born Tying Knots: Swampy Cree Naming Poems,* both by Howard Norman. **Principal Officials and Managers:** David Robbins, Publisher and Editor; Richard A. Pohrt, Manager.

★1741★
Bear Tribe Medicine Society
PO Box 9167
Spokane, WA 99209   Ph: (509)258-7755

Description: Publishes books, a magazine, *Wildfire Networking,* and cassette tapes. Offers lectures and chants. Reaches market through direct mail and trade sales. **Subjects:** Native American people, earth awareness, personal and spiritual growth. **Number of New Titles:** 1989 - 1, 1990 - 1, 1991 (est.) - 1; Total Titles in Print - 8. **Selected Titles:** *Buffalo Hearts* by Sun Bear; *The Bear Tribe's Self Reliance Books* by Sun Bear, Wabun, Nimimosha and the Tribe; *Sun Bear: The Path of Power* as told to Wabun and Barry Weinstock; *The Book of the Vision Quest* by Steven Foster and Meredith Little. **Principal Officials and Managers:** Sun Bear, Medicine Chief; Wabun Bear, Medicine Helper.

★1742★
Beechwood Books
720 Wehapa Circle
Leeds, AL 35094   Ph: (205)699-6935

Description: Publishes on Indians and history of the southeastern United States. Reaches market through direct mail and Baker & Taylor. **Number of New Titles:** 1992 (est.) - 2; Total Titles in Print - 4. **Selected Titles:** *World of the Southern Indians, Southern Indian Myths and Legends, Grand Old Days of Birmingham Golf,* all by Brown; *The Story of Coal and Iron in Alabama* by Armes. **Principal Officials and Managers:** Virginia Pounds-Brown, Owner; Laurella Owens, Editor.

★1743★
Bell Books Ltd.
528 Varsity Estates Bay NW
Calgary, AB, Canada T3B 2W8   Ph: (403)288-5021

Description: Publishes on native Indian topics. Reaches market through direct mail. Mail returned from address above; no forwarding address available. **Selected Titles:** *Ruffled Feathers; Religion for People.* **Principal Officials and Managers:** William I. C. Wuttunee, President.

★1744★
Blanche P. Browder
5133 Jeffries Rd.
Raleigh, NC 27606   Ph: (919)851-0679

Description: Publishes on the Cherokee Indian history of North Carolina, and on local history and genealogy. **Selected Titles:** *De Soto and Other Spanish Explorers and Their Historians, Cherokee Indians and Those Who Came After,* both by Nathaniel C. Browder.

★1745★
Bowman Books
2 Middle Grove Rd.
Greenfield Center, NY 12833   Ph: (518)584-1728

Selected Titles: *The Faithful Hunter: Abenaki Stories* by Joseph Bruchac.

★1746★
Central States Archaeological Societies, Inc.
646 Knierim Pl.
Kirkwood, MO 63122   Ph: (314)821-7675

Description: Publishes books and a journal on the archaeology and history of both prehistoric and historic American Indians. Accepts unsolicited manuscripts. **Selected Titles:** *The Cherry Valley Report* by Gregory Perino; *The Guebert Site-Kaskaskia Report* by Mary E. Good; *Memoir.* **Principal Officials and Managers:** Richard A. Watts, Business Manager; Alan L. Banks, Editor; Pat Fleming, Secretary-Treasurer.

★1747★
Ciga Press
PO Box 654
Fallbrook, CA 92028   Ph: (619)728-9308

Description: Publishes some genealogical materials, but mostly publishes Osage Indian materials. Reaches market through direct mail, museums, and historical societies. **Subjects:** Indian culture, history, genealogy, anthropology. **Number of New Titles:** 1989 - 1; Total Titles in Print - 7. **Selected Titles:** *A History of the Osage People; Turn of the Wheel: A Burns-Tinker Genealogy, A System for Keeping Genealogical Research Records, Osage Indian Bands and Clans, Osage Indian Customs and Myths, Osage Mission Baptisms, Marriages and Interments 1820-1886,* all by Louis F. Burns. **Principal Officials and Managers:** Ruth Blake, Managing Editor; Louis F. Burns, Editor.

★1748★
Council for Indian Education
517 Rimrock Rd.
Billings, MT 59102   Ph: (406)252-1800

Description: Publishes fiction and nonfiction related to American Indian life and culture, suitable for use in the education of Native American children. Accepts unsolicited manuscripts. Reaches market through direct mail. **Number of New Titles:** 1990 - 5, 1991 -

8, 1992 (est.) - 5; Total Titles in Print - 85. **Selected Titles:** *Quest for Courage* by Stormy Rodolph; *Keeper of Fire* by James Magorian; *Chant of the Red Man* by Hap Gilliland; *Cheyenne Fire Fighters* by Henry Tall Bull and Tom Weist; *Geronimo Chino* by Paula Paul; *Sacajawea: A Native American Heroine* by Martha F. Bryant. **Principal Officials and Managers:** Hap Gilliland, Executive Editor; Ellen Williams, Business Manager.

★1749★
Creative Products of America, Inc.
4201 N. Marshall Way
Scottsdale, AZ 85251   Ph: (602)941-9348
Description: Publishes archival quality reproductions of unusual fine arts (paintings, graphics). **Selected Titles:** *Kiowa Indian Art* by Oscar Jacobson and Jamake Highwater; *Pueblo Indian Painting* by Hartley Burr Alexander and Jamake Highwater. **Principal Officials and Managers:** Arnold Horwitch, Managing Director. **Formerly:** Bell Editions, Inc.

★1750★
Cree Productions Inc.
12555 127th St.
Edmonton, AB, Canada T5L 1A4   Ph: (403)455-9317
Description: Dedicated to the preservation of Cree language and culture. Mail returned from address above; no forwarding address available. **Selected Titles:** *Let's Learn Cree; Cree Picture Dictionary; Great Outdoor Kitchen; Cree Reader; Conversational Cree Advanced; Legends of Wesakecha.* **Principal Officials and Managers:** Anne Anderson-Irvine, President; Connie Bennett, Secretary.

★1751★
Dancing Feather
4434 Wilmette St.
Fort Wayne, IN 46806   Ph: (219)456-4390
Description: Publishes American Indian philosophy and spirituality in poetic form. All profits are donated to Indian schools. Also offers lectures. Reaches market through reviews. Dancing Feather, a Mohawk Indian, is also known as Thomas Leonard Ebbing. **Total Titles in Print:** 3. **Selected Titles:** *Rhythm of the Drum, Melody of the Forest, Song Eternal,* all by Dancing Feather. **Principal Officials and Managers:** Thomas Leonard Ebbing, Author and Publisher.

★1752★
DCA Publishers
6709 Esther Ave., NE
Albuquerque, NM 87109   Ph: (505)823-2914
Description: Publishes materials on management and fundraising for American Indian tribes and organizations. Presently inactive. **Total Titles in Print:** 5. **Selected Titles:** *Funding Guide for Native Americans; Grants to Indians; How to Write Winning Proposals; Tribal Economic Development Directory; Management for the 1980's.* **Principal Officials and Managers:** Dean Chavers, Owner and President; Antonia Chavers, Owner.

★1753★
Diablo Books
1317 Canyonwood, No. 1
Walnut Creek, CA 94595   Ph: (415)939-8644
Description: Publishes local and California Indian history. Reaches market through direct mail, wholesalers, schools, and libraries. **Number of New Titles:** 1990 - 1; Total Titles in Print - 2. **Selected Titles:** *Contra Costa County: An Illustrated History,* by Emanuels; *Indians of the Yosemite* by Galen Clark; *California Indians: An Illustrated Guide; California's Contra Costa County: An Illustrated History.* **Principal Officials and Managers:** George Emanuels, Proprietor.

★1754★
Eagle's View Publishing
6756 North Fork Rd.
Liberty, UT 84310   Ph: (801)393-3991
Description: Specializes in Native American and frontier craft books. Reaches market through commission representatives, direct mail, telephone sales, and wholesalers. **Number of New Titles:** 1989 - 5, 1990 - 4, 1991 (est.) - 4; Total Titles in Print - 20. **Selected Titles:**

Techniques of Beading Earrings, More Techniques of Beading Earrings, both by Deon DeLange; *The Technique of Porcupine Quill Decoration among the Indians of North America, Beads and Beadwork of the American Indians,* both by William C. Orchard; *Crow Indian Beadwork: A Descriptive and Historical Study* by William Wildschut and John C. Ewers; *The Technique of North American Indian Beadwork.* **Principal Officials and Managers:** Monte Smith, Publisher; Sue K. Smith, Sales Manager; Denise Knight, Editor-in-Chief.

★1755★
Earth Art Inc.
Box 166
Fulton, MI 49052   Ph: (616)646-9545
Description: Offers mailing labels of American Indian reservations, organizations, and individuals. Reaches market through direct mail and advertising. **Subjects:** American Indians, ecology, modeling, nature, education, hobbies. **Number of New Titles:** 1989 - 1; Total Titles in Print - 22. **Selected Titles:** *More about...* by Cal Noell; *Resources for Parents of Gifted Children; American Indian Reference Book; American Indian Recipes; American Indian Cookbook; Recipes for the Birds.* **Principal Officials and Managers:** Cal Noell, Glenda Beach, Owners.

★1756★
East Plateau Indian Cooperative
905 E. 3rd Ave.
Spokane, WA 99202-2246   Ph: (509)535-1158
Description: Publishes Native American calendars. Offers audio cassettes of Indian tales and provides market access for Indian artists who produce art and craftwork. Reaches market through direct mail and trade sales. **Number of New Titles:** 1989 - 1, 1990 - 1; Total Titles in Print - 3. **Principal Officials and Managers:** Kathy Hutson, Chairor; John LeBret, Secretary-Treasurer; Leonard Hendrickx, Manager.

★1757★
Ervin Stuntz
20451 Tyler Rd.
Walkerton, IN 46574   Ph: (219)586-3766
Description: Self-publisher of books on American Indians. Operates an American Indian artifacts museum. Reaches market through direct mail and telephone sales. **Selected Titles:** *The Indians of Today, The Incredible Wheel of Time, Vols. 1-2, Who Were the Savages, The Story of My Life, The Life of the Indian, Our First Americans,* all by Ervin Stuntz. **Principal Officials and Managers:** Ervin Stuntz.

★1758★
Fantail Native Design
c/o Pacific Science Center
200 2nd Ave., N.
Seattle, WA 98109   Ph: (204)489-4604
Description: Publishes books related to Native American history and the natural sciences. Also produces Native American prints and notecards. Reaches market through direct mail, telephone sales, and trade sales. **Selected Titles:** *Return of the Comet: An Activity Book* by Dennis Schatz; *Stone Trap Fishing/Cod Lure Fishing* by Patricia Cosgrove. **Principal Officials and Managers:** George Moynihan, Director; Jan Clow, Publications Manager.

★1759★
Five Civilized Tribes Foundation Museum
Agency Hill at Honor Heights Dr.
Muskogee, OK 74401   Ph: (918)683-1701
Description: Publishes on the history and heritage of Five Tribes and area of Muskogee, Oklahoma. **Total Titles in Print:** 3. **Selected Titles:** *The Cherokees: An Illustrated History* by Billy M. Jones and Odie B. Faulk; *Muskogee: City and County* by Odie B. Faulk; *Pow Wow Chow Cookbook: A Collection of Recipes from Five Tribe Families.* **Principal Officials and Managers:** Debra G. Synar, Director.

★1760★
Fogelman Publishing Co.
RD 1, Box 240
Turbotville, PA 17772-9599   Ph: (717)437-3698
Description: Publishes to educate collectors and laymen on American Indian artifacts. Offers a chronological type chart for projectiles and knives of the Northeast. Reaches market through direct mail and wholesalers. **Subjects:** Indian artifacts. **Number of New Titles:** 1989 - 8; Total Titles in Print - 72. **Selected Titles:** *Projectile Point Typology for Pennsylvania and the Northeast, Shoop: Pennsylvania's Famous Paleo Site* both by Gary L. Fogelman; *Fluted Points in Lycoming County* by Gary Fogelman and Richard P. Johnston; *Pennsylvania Lithics Book, No. 34, Pennsylvania Artifacts Series.* **Principal Officials and Managers:** Gary L. Fogelman, Editor and Publisher.

★1761★
Frank Kenan Barnard
8240 Lindley Mill Rd.
Graham, NC 27253   Ph: (919)376-3242
Description: Publishes a book on identifying Indian artifacts. Reaches market through telephone sales. **Total Titles in Print:** 1. **Selected Titles:** *How to Find and Identify Arrowheads and Other Indian Artifacts* by Frank Kenan Barnard.

★1762★
Fulcrum Publishing
350 Indiana St., Ste. 350   Ph: (303)277-1623
Golden, CO 80401   Free: 800-992-2908
          Fax: (303)277-1623
Description: Publishes in many areas including Native American books. **Selected Titles:** *Keepers of the Animals–Native American Stories and Wildlife Activities for Children; Keepers of the Earth–Native American Stories and Environmental Activities for Children; Native American Stories.*

★1763★
Fun Publishing Co.
PO Box 2049
Scottsdale, AZ 85252   Ph: (602)946-2093
Description: Publishes the Children's American Indian Book Series. **Selected Titles:** *The Navajo Indian Book; The Navajo Design Book; The Plains Indian Book; The Kachina Doll Book 1; The Kachina Doll Book 2.* **Principal Officials and Managers:** Howard Greenlee, President.

★1764★
Gallup Distributing Co.
205 Sunde Ave.
Gallup, NM 87301   Ph: (505)863-4304
Description: Distributor of mass market paperbacks and magazines. **Subjects:** Indian titles. **Principal Officials and Managers:** Walter W. Tyler, Owner and Manager.

★1765★
George M. White Books
PO Box 365
Ronan, MT 59864   Ph: (406)676-3766
Description: Publishes paperback books on Native American handicrafts. Also sells bronze figurines. **Selected Titles:** *Craft Manual of North American Footwear, Craft Manual of Northwest Beading, Craft Manual of Yukon Tlingit, Craft Manual of Alaskan Eskimo, Windshield Geology of the Flathead, Living in Montana,* all by G. M. White.

★1766★
Havasupai Tribal Council
PO Box 10
Supai, AZ 86435   Ph: (602)448-2731
Description: Publishes on the history of the Havasupai Indian tribe. Reaches market through direct mail. **Total Titles in Print:** 1. **Selected Titles:** *Havsuw 'Baaja: People of the Blue Green Water* by Stephen Hirst. **Principal Officials and Managers:** Clark Jack, Jr., Tribal Chairor; Rex Tilousi, Vice-Chairor; James Uquqlla, Jr., Lucinda Watahomigie, Roland Mana Kaja, Council Members.

★1767★
Heyday Books
PO Box 9145
Berkeley, CA 94709   Ph: (415)549-3564
Description: Publishes books on natural history of California and on American Indians. Also publishes maps and nature trail guides. Offers a quarterly publication, *News from Native California.* **Number of New Titles:** 1989 - 7, 1990 - 6; Total Titles in Print - 28. **Selected Titles:** *Towards History of Needs* by Ivan Illich; *Disorderly House* by James Mills; *The Ohlone Way* by Malcolm Margolin; *Harvest Gypsies* by John Steinbeck; *Humphrey the Wayward Whale* by Ernest Callenbach. **Principal Officials and Managers:** Malcolm Margolin, Director.

★1768★
Hothem House
PO Box 458
Lancaster, OH 43130   Ph: (614)653-9030
Description: Publishes books on American Indian artifacts. Reaches market through direct mail and trade sales. **Number of New Titles:** 1989 - 1, 1990 - 2, 1991 (est.) - 2; Total Titles in Print - 7. **Selected Titles:** *Treasures of the Mound Builders, Indian Flints of Ohio, Ornamental and Ceremonial Artifacts, North American Indian Axes, Collecting Indian Knives, Arrowheads and Projectile Points,* all by Lar Hothem. **Principal Officials and Managers:** Lar Hothem, Owner.

★1769★
Indian Country Press
292 Walnut
Irvine Park Offices
Saint Paul, MN 55102   Ph: (612)292-1861
Description: "As an Indian-initiated, Indian-oriented, and Indian-controlled alternative school, the Red School House has recognized from the onset the need for Indian-developed and produced curricular materials reflecting in a positive, undistorted way Indian philosophy, viewpoints, and historical facts." Mail returned from address above; no forwarding address available. **Selected Titles:** *The Mishomis Book, A Mishomis Book: Coloring Book Series, A Culture Based Assessment,* all by Edward Benton Banai; *The Sounding Voice* by Benton Banai and Sherry Blakey; *Un Gi Dah So Win: Counting* by Cherie Neima; *The Red Writer* by Edward Benton Banai and Cherie Neima. **Principal Officials and Managers:** Edward Benton Banai, Executive Director.

★1770★
Indian Historian Press
1493 Masonic Ave.
San Francisco, CA 94117   Ph: (415)626-5235
Description: Principal interest is the American Indians of North America; also covers indigenous peoples of the western hemisphere. **Total Titles in Print:** 34. **Selected Titles:** *Legends of the Lakota* by James LaPointe; *Tsali* by Denton R. Bedford; *The Missions of California: A Legacy of Genocide* edited by R. Custo; *Pima and Papage Ritual Oratory* by Don Bahr; *Give or Take a Century, An Eskimo Chronicle* by J. Senungetek; *A Thousand Years of American Indian Storytelling* by J. Costo. **Principal Officials and Managers:** Jeannette Henry, Editor; Rupert Costo, President.

★1771★
Indian Press/Publications
1869 2nd Ave.
New York, NY 10467   Ph: (212)882-3207
Description: Publishes the history and advancement of the American Indian. Mail returned from address above; no forwarding address available. **Selected Titles:** *The Saga of Chief Crazy Horse* by Garrett Springer. **Principal Officials and Managers:** M. Comachu, Paul Weldon, Editors.

★1772★
Indian Resource Development (IRD)
Box 30003/Dept. 3IRD
New Mexico State University
Las Cruces, NM 88003-0003   Ph: (505)646-1347
Description: Publishes materials to help American Indians develop managerial, scientific, and technical skills. Offers a semiannual newsletter aimed at recruiting high school students into college and

engineering, business, and science related careers. Also offers video cassettes. Accepts unsolicited manuscripts. Reaches market through direct mail. **Selected Titles:** *Sources of Financial Aid Available to American Indian Students, Annual Report of Indian Resource Development, Indian Math Camp of New Mexico,* all by Lance Lujan; *A Sacred Trust* (video cassette). **Principal Officials and Managers:** Lance Lujan, Director; Jimmy Shendo, Program Coordinator; Lena Seoutewa, Secretary.

★1773★
Indian University Press
Bacone College
Muskogee, OK 74401   Ph: (918)683-4581

Description: Publishes materials for the teaching and preservation of Indian languages, including bilingual materials. Also publishes important writing by Indians and historical materials relating to the history of Indian territory, including family histories. Accepts one unsolicited manuscript per year. Reaches market through direct mail. **Total Titles in Print:** 10. **Selected Titles:** *A Cherokee Prayer Book,* by Howard Meredith; *Cherokee-English Interlinear First Epistle of John* by Ralph E. Dawson, III; *Christmas in Those Days* by Mary Lou Ziegenfuss; *China Illustrata* translated by Charles B. Van Tuyl; *On the Landing* by Michael W. Simpson; *Estyut Omagat–Creek Writings* by Lewis Oliver. **Principal Officials and Managers:** Lisa E. Johnson, Publications Director; Charles Van Tuyl, Director.

★1774★
Institute for the Development of Indian Law
1104 Glyndon St., SE
Vienna, VA 22180   Ph: (703)938-7822

Description: Founded by three Indian attorneys for the purpose of strengthening the Indian people through legal and historical research, publication, and advocacy. **Selected Titles:** *Indian Sovereignty, Federal Trust Relationship, Indian Jurisdiction, Indians and U.S. Government, Indian Treaties,* all by Kirke Kickingbird et al. **Principal Officials and Managers:** Kirke Kickingbird, Executive Director.

★1775★
Institute for the Study of Traditional American Indian Arts
PO Box 66124
Portland, OR 97266   Ph: (503)233-8131

Subjects: Traditional American Indian arts. **Total Titles in Print:** 20. **Selected Titles:** *Yakima Indian Beadwork; Columbia River/Plateau Indian Beadwork, Traditional Arts of the Indians of Western Oregon,* both by John M. Gogol; *Traditional Miwok Basketry* by Craig D. Bates; *Washoe Indian Basketry* by Marvin Cohodas; *Utility Basketry of the Northwest Indians* by K. Johanneson. **Principal Officials and Managers:** John M. Gogol, Director.

★1776★
Inter-Tribal Indian Ceremonial Association
PO Box 1
Church Rock, NM 87311   Ph: (505)863-3896

Description: Publishes a book on Navajo rugs; plans to produce other pamphlets on Indian crafts, as well as a quarterly magazine. Offers a newsletter, cards, maps, lapel pins, T-shirts, fine art posters, Indian information service, slides, and video cassettes of Indian dances and Indian art. Reaches market through direct mail. **Total Titles in Print:** 1. **Selected Titles:** *So You Want to Buy a Navajo Rug* **Principal Officials and Managers:** Laurance Linford, Executive Director; Flo Barton, President; Horace Manzanares, Chairor.

★1777★
Janet Herren, Publisher
4750 Crystal Springs Dr.
Bainbridge Island, WA 98110   Ph: (206)842-3484

Description: Publishes a book on a Northwest Indian legend. **Total Titles in Print:** 1. **Selected Titles:** *Stolen Princess: A Northwest Indian Legend* by Willard Morss and Janet Morss Herren. **Principal Officials and Managers:** Janet Herren, Publisher.

★1778★
Lion's Head Publishing Co.
2436 S. U.S. 33
Albion, IN 46701   Ph: (219)635-2165

Subjects: American Indians, fiction. **Selected Titles:** *Five Forts: Story of Indian Wars of the Old Northwest, Voice of the Turtle: Biography of Miami Warchief Little Turtle,* both by John Ankenbruck. **Principal Officials and Managers:** John Ankenbruck, President.

★1779★
MacRae Publications
PO Box 652
1605 Cole St.
Enumclaw, WA 98022   Ph: (206)825-3737

Subjects: American Indians. **Selected Titles:** *Spider Woman, Navaho Shepherd and Weaver,* both by Gladys Reichard; *Pomo Indian Basketry* by S. A. Barrett; *The Cheyenne Indians: The Sun Dance* by George Dorsey; *Indian Stories from the Pueblos* by Frank Applegate; *The Vanishing Race* by Joseph Dixon. **Principal Officials and Managers:** Ken MacRae, Owner.

★1780★
MacRae's Indian Book Distributors
1605 Cole St.
PO Box 652
Enumclaw, WA 98002   Ph: (206)825-3737

Description: Distributor. Reaches market through direct mail. **Subjects:** American Indians. **Principal Officials and Managers:** Ken MacRae, Owner.

★1781★
Malki Museum
Malki Museum Press
Morongo Indian Reservation
11-795 Fields Rd.
Banning, CA 92220   Ph: (714)849-7289

Description: Publishes books and pamphlets about the Indian peoples of California and Baja California. Also publishes the *Journal of California and Great Basin Anthropology* in cooperation with the Department of Anthropology, University of California, Riverside. **Selected Titles:** *Lost Copper: Collected Poems* by Wendy Rose; *Encounter with an Angry God, Mirror and Pattern,* both by Carobeth Laird; *The Calhuilla Indians* by Harry James; *Eye of the Flute* by Fernando Librado; *Willie Boy* by Harry Lawton; *When Animals Were People* by Kay Sanger. **Principal Officials and Managers:** Harry W. Lawton, Managing Director; Tom Blackburn, Editorial Director; Katherine Siva Saubel, Chairor of Editorial Board; Roderick Linton, Publications Manager.

★1782★
Maverick Distributors
PO Drawer 7289
Bend, OR 97708   Ph: (503)382-2728

Description: Wholesale distributor of Native American books.

★1783★
Memento Publications, Inc.
PO Box 58646
Dallas, TX 75258   Ph: (808)734-8611

Subjects: American Indians. **Selected Titles:** *The Way of an Indian* by Frederic Remington. **Principal Officials and Managers:** Travis Johnson, Publisher.

★1784★
Michigan Indian Press
45 Lexington NW
Grand Rapids, MI 49504   Ph: (616)774-8331

Description: Publishes books that dispel negative stereotypes about Native Americans and instead educate the general public about Native American culture, history, heritage, and beliefs. Offers the *Turtle Talk* newsletter. Distributes for Red School House and Lotus Light. Accepts unsolicited manuscripts. Reaches market through direct mail, telephone sales, and trade sales. **Number of New Titles:** 1991 (est.) - 4; Total Titles in Print - 3. **Selected Titles:** *People of Three Fires: The Ottawa, Potawatami, and Ojibway of Michigan* by

James A. Clifton et al; *Walk in Peace: Legends and Stories of the Michigan Indians* by Simon Otto; *Aube Na Bing: A Pictorial History of Michigan Indians*. **Principal Officials and Managers:** J. Wagner Wheeler, Executive Director.

★1785★
Museum of Ojibwa Culture
500 N. State St.
Saint Ignace, MI 49781   Ph: (906)643-9161

Description: Publishes books on the museum's exhibits and on 17th-century upper Michigan history. Also publishes a newsletter to friends of the museum. **Total Titles in Print:** 2. **Selected Titles:** *The Story of Wafted Across, Southern Feather's Story,* both by Margaret Peacock. **Principal Officials and Managers:** Carol Hosler, Museum Director.

★1786★
National Indian Law Library
1522 Broadway
Boulder, CO 80302-6296   Ph: (303)447-8760

Description: A clearinghouse for federal Indian legal materials, primarily for attorneys. Reaches market through direct mail. **Subjects:** Indian law, American Indian history. **Number of New Titles:** 1990 - 3; Total Titles in Print - 4. **Selected Titles:** *National Indian Law Library Catalogue; Top 50: A List of Significant Cases Affecting Native Americans Law; Issues Affecting Native Americans in the United States Supreme Court.* **Principal Officials and Managers:** John E. Echohawk, Executive Director; Ethel Abeita, Deputy Director; Marylin Pourier, Development Officer; Susan R. Hart, Controller; Deana Harragarra Waters, Lawyer Librarian.

★1787★
National Museum of the American Indian
3753 Broadway
New York, NY 10032-1596   Ph: (212)283-2420

Description: Formerly known as Museum of the American Indian. **Subjects:** Native peoples of North, Middle, and South America, new world archaeology. **Number of New Titles:** 1990 - 1; Total Titles in Print - 35. **Selected Titles:** *Beads and Beadwork of the American Indians* by William C. Orchard; *Native American Painting* by David M. Fawcett and Lee A. Callander; *Shawnee Home Life: The Paintings of Earnest Spybuck* by L. A. Callander and R. Slivka; *Native Americans on Film and Video, Vol. 2,* by Elizabeth Weatherford and Emelia Seubert; *The Native Peoples of the Northeast Woodlands* by Judith A. Brundin with Mary C. Bradford; *New York City in Indian Possession* by R. P. Bolton. **Principal Officials and Managers:** Duane King, Assistant Director; Ellen Jamieson, Publications Manger.

★1788★
National Native American Co-op
PO Box 5000
San Carlos, AZ 85550-0301   Ph: (602)230-3399

Description: Publishes a directory listing Native American tribal offices, organizations, corporations, museums, libraries, and cultural events. Publications available in microform. Offers American Indian information packets, crafts, and flags. Mailing List services also available. Reaches market through direct mail and telephone and trade sales. **Number of New Titles:** 1991 (est.) - 1; Total Titles in Print - 1. **Selected Titles:** *Native American Directory.* **Principal Officials and Managers:** Fred Synder, Director and Consultant.

★1789★
Native American Images
2104 Nueces
PO Box 746
Austin, TX 78767   Ph: (512)472-3049

Description: Features exhibit posters, limited edition prints, original stone lithographs, and paintings by American Indians and Southwestern artists. Color brochures of current works available. **Selected Titles:** *Crow Parade* by Steve Forbis; *Council of the Medicine Men* by Paladine Roye; *Polik-Mana* by David Dawangyumptewa; *Broken Promises* by Donald Vann. **Principal Officials and Managers:** Christopher Pearsall, Staff Member.

★1790★
Navajo Community College
Navajo Community College Press
Tsaile, AZ 86556   Ph: (602)724-3311

Description: Publishes books on the American Indian with emphasis on the Navajo in historical and contemporary contexts. Reaches market through direct mail, trade sales, and wholesalers. **Subjects:** History, life, culture, mythology, traditions, education, political aspirations, progress of the tribe, nonfiction, fiction, poetry. **Total Titles in Print:** 27. **Selected Titles:** *The Tribally Controlled Indian Colleges* by Norman T. Oppelt; *A Political History of the Navajo Tribe* by Dr. Robert W. Young; *Navajo Stories of Long Walk Period* edited by B. Johnson; *Earth Power Coming: Short Fiction in Native American Literature* edited by S. Ortiz; *The Sacred: Ways of Knowledge, Sources of Life* by Beck and Walters; *The Myth and Prayers of the Great Star Chant and the Myth of the Coyote Chant* by Mary C. Wheelwright. **Principal Officials and Managers:** Anna L. Walters, Director.

★1791★
Navajo Curriculum Center
Star Rte. 1
RRDS., Box 217
Chinle, AZ 86503   Ph: (602)728-3311

Description: Publishes bilingual curriculum materials and other major publications dealing with Navajo life, history, and culture. Offers maps, cards, and calendars. Reaches market through direct mail, trade sales, and wholesalers. **Total Titles in Print:** 20. **Selected Titles:** *Coyote Stories of the Navajo People* by Robert A. Roessel; *Navajo Biographies, Vol. 1* by Virginia Hoffman and Broderick Johnson; *Navajo History, Vol. I* by Ethelon Yazzie; *Contemporary Navajo Affairs* by Norman K. Eck; *Women in Navajo Society* by Ruth Roessel; *Kinaalada: The Navajo Puberty Ceremony* by Shirley M. Begay. **Principal Officials and Managers:** Carl Levi, Executive Director; Regina Lynch, Coordinator.

★1792★
Origins Program
4632 Vincent Ave., S.
Minneapolis, MN 55410   Ph: (612)922-8175

Description: Publishes catalogs and books to accompany exhibitions of tribal art and books on multicultural understanding. Also offers audio and video cassettes on Indian and Eskimo topics, and on museum collections of tribal art. Reaches market through commission representatives and distributors, including BookPeople and Quality Books, Inc. **Subjects:** Indian and Eskimo art and culture, multiculturalism. **Number of New Titles:** 1990 - 1, 1991 - 2; Total Titles in Print - 2. **Selected Titles:** *Tsonakwa and Yolaikia: Legends in Stone, Bone and Wood* edited by Crawford and West; *Dark Lady Dreaming: Quilts and Drawings* by Amy Cordova and Pam Eyden; *To Hold Us Together* by Linda Crawford; *Beyond the Suitcase* edited by Helen E. Stub; *The Elders: Passing It On* edited by Linda Crawford. **Principal Officials and Managers:** Linda Crawford, Director; Jo Devlin, Curator; Helen Stub, Registrar. **Formerly:** Arts and Learning Services Foundation.

★1793★
Parks-Thompson Company
1757 W. Adams
Saint Louis, MO 63122   Ph: (314)822-2409

Description: Publishes books pertaining to Indians and archaeology. **Total Titles in Print:** 7. **Selected Titles:** *Who's Who in Indian Relics, Nos. 1-2,* both by Wachtel; *Who's Who in Indian Relics, Nos. 3-4,* both by Parks-Thompson; *Who's Who in Indian Relics, Nos. 5-7,* both by Thompson. **Principal Officials and Managers:** Ben W. Thompson, Editor and Publisher.

★1794★
P.B. Graphics
5300 Desoto Dr., Ste. 119
Houston, TX 77091   Ph: (713)956-4062

Description: Publishes and distributes American Indian art posters. Featured artists include R. C. Gorman and Amado Pena. Mail returned from address above; no forwarding address available.

★1795★
Persimmon Press
118 Tillinghast Pl.
Buffalo, NY 14216   Ph: (716)838-3633
Description: Publishes monographs on prehistoric archaeology and how the New World became peopled. Accepts unsolicited manuscripts. Distributes for Buffalo Museum of Science, Atlantic Archaeology, Ltd., and St. Johns, Newfoundland. Reaches market through direct mail and Center for the Study of the First Americans. **Number of New Titles:** 1990 - 2, 1991 (est.) - 1; Total Titles in Print - 5. **Selected Titles:** *Adams: The Manufacturing of Flaked Stone Tools at a Palaeo Indian Site in Kentucky* by Thomas N. Sanders; *Guide to the Palaeo-Indian Artifacts of North America* by Richard M. Gramly; *Debert: A Palaeo-Indian Site in Nova Scotia* by George MacDonald; *Adkins: A Palaeo-Indian Encampment and Associated Stone Structure* by R. M. Gramly; *A Palaeo-Indian Site in Eastern Pennsylvania: An Early Hunting Culture*, by J. Witthoft. **Principal Officials and Managers:** R. M. Gramley, Owner.

★1796★
Peter Lang Publishing, Inc.
62 W. 45th St., 4th Fl.
New York, NY 10036-4202   Ph: (212)302-6740
Description: Scholarly publisher in the humanities and social sciences specializing in book-length scholarly monographs. Titles include a series of academic books on American Indians.

★1797★
R. Schneider Publishers
312 Linwood Ave.
Stevens Point, WI 54481   Ph: (715)341-0020
Description: Publishes on the crafts and technology of the American Indian. Reaches market through direct mail, trade sales, and wholesalers. **Subjects:** Crafts and technology, primarily American Indian. **Number of New Titles:** 1989 - 1; Total Titles in Print - 13. **Selected Titles:** *Crafts of the North American Indians, Natural History of the Minocki of the Lakeland Region of Wisconsin*, both by R. Schneider; *A Small Upright Spinning Wheel, A Table Swift, A No-Lathe Saxony-Style Spinning Wheel*, all by R. and M. Schneider; *Ojibwa Crafts* by Carrie Lyford. **Principal Officials and Managers:** Richard C. Schneider, Owner.

★1798★
Raven Hail Books
PO Box C-900, No. 230
Scottsdale, AZ 85252   Ph: (602)945-2790
Description: Self-publishes books on Cherokee Indians. Reaches market through direct mail. **Number of New Titles:** 1989 - 1; Total Titles in Print - 5. **Selected Titles:** *Native American Foods (Foods the Indians Gave Us) Coloring Book, Windsong: Texas Cherokee Princess, The Raven Speaks, The Pleiades Stones, The Raven's Tales (Cherokee Indian Legends)*, all by Raven Hail. **Principal Officials and Managers:** Raven Hail, Owner.

★1799★
Ray Manley Publishing
238 S. Tucson Blvd.
Tucson, AZ 85716   Ph: (602)623-0307
Subjects: Indian jewelry and crafts of southwestern tribes, Indian lands. **Selected Titles:** *Collecting Southwestern Indian Arts and Crafts, Indian Lands, Hopi Kachinas*, all by Clara Lee Tanner; *The Fine Art of Navajo Weaving* by Steve Getzwiller. **Principal Officials and Managers:** Naurice Koonce, Mickey Prim, Alan Manley, Carolyn Robinson.

★1800★
Robert F. Brand
1029 Lake Ln.
Pennsburg, PA 18073   Ph: (215)679-8134
Description: Publishes books, articles, and audio-visual materials on the North American Indian. Reaches market through direct mail. Annual Sales: $6000. **Total Titles in Print:** 1. **Selected Titles:** *How to Collect North American Indian Artifacts* by Robert F. Brand.

★1801★
Sequoyah Books
PO Box 5474
New York, NY 10163   Ph: (604)374-0616
Description: Publishes limited editions of reference works on American Indians; also packages and/or co-publishes with others more general books on American Indians. Sequoyah Books handles all book publication work of the Confederation of American Indians, Council of American Indian Artists, Gay American Indians, and American Indian Economic Development Fund. Reaches market through direct mail, trade sales, and reviews. **Subjects:** American Indian history, art, culture, languages. **Total Titles in Print:** 5. **Selected Titles:** *Economics of the Iroquois* by Adam Starchild; *History of the Seminole and Miccosukee Tribes* by Harry A. Kersey, Jr.; *Handbook of Federal and State Indian Reservations; The U.S. Army, Public Opinion, and President Grant's Indian Peace Policy* by Robert C. Key; *The Federal Government and the Creek Indians, 1775-1813* by Frank H. Akers, Jr. **Principal Officials and Managers:** David McCord, Executive Director.

★1802★
Sierra Oaks Publishing Co.
1370 Sierra Oaks Ln.
New Castle, CA 95658-9791   Ph: (916)663-1474
Description: Produces books on the history and culture of American Indians. Also publishes a line of children's titles on American Indian topics and legends. Reaches market through direct mail, trade sales, Pacific Pipeline, and Quality Books, Inc., and Treasure Chest Publications. **Number of New Titles:** 1989 - 2; Total Titles in Print - 15. **Selected Titles:** *American Indian Identity* by Clifford Trafzer; *Strangers in a Stolen Land* by Richard Carrico; *Grandmother Stories of the Northwest* by Nashone; *A Trip to a Pow Wow, ABC's the American Indian Way*, both Richard Redhawk; *Indian Wars of the Red River Valley* by William Leckie. **Principal Officials and Managers:** Richard W. Smith, Publisher; Stephanie Morris, Managing Editor; Louise N. Smith, Art Director.

★1803★
Southwest Museum
PO Box 41558
Los Angeles, CA 90041-0558   Ph: (213)221-2164
Description: Publishes on native American history, anthropology, and archaeology. Offers photo cards of Indian images. Reaches market through direct mail. **Total Titles in Print:** 68. **Selected Titles:** *Five Prehistoric Archaeology Sites in Los Angeles* by E. F. Walker; *Native Faces: Indian Cultures in American Art* by Patricia Trenton and Patrick Houlihan; *Visit to the Missions of Southern California in February and March 1874* by Henry Oak; *Two Maya Monuments in Yucatan* by Hasso von Winning. **Principal Officials and Managers:** Jerome Selmer, Executive Director; Jeanette Leeper O'Malley, Assistant Director; Dr. Kathleen Whitaker, Chief Curator.

★1804★
Starwood Publishers
PO Box 40503
Washington, DC 20016   Ph: (202)362-7404
Description: Publisher of the new "Library of Congress Classics" series. The first to be published was *The First Americans: Photographs from the Library of Congress*, a collection of photographs from the turn of the century, many of which were taken by Edward S. Curtis.

★1805★
Strawberry Press
PO Box 451, Bowling Green Sta.
New York, NY 10004   Ph: (212)522-3227
Description: Formed to publish young and established Native American (American Indian) authors in chapbook, broadside, and postcard formats. **Subjects:** Native American poetry, fiction, and art. **Total Titles in Print:** 7. **Selected Titles:** *Visions in Ink: Drawings of Native Nations* by Kahionhes; *Sketches in Winter, with Crows* by Peter Blue Cloud; *Without Warning* by Charlotte DeClue; *Where You First Saw the Eyes of Coyote* by Linda Noel; *Covers: Poems and Drawings* by Rakwaho. **Principal Officials and Managers:** Maurice Kenny, Editor and Publisher; A. M. Warr, Daniel Thompson (Rokwaho), Charlotte Finkenberg, Board of Directors.

★1806★
Tejas Art Press
207 Terrell Rd.
San Antonio, TX 78209   Ph: (512)826-7803

Description: A nonprofit publisher; encourages poets, dramatists, and artists from U.S. Indian tribes. Reaches market through direct mail. Presently inactive. **Total Titles in Print:** 4. **Selected Titles:** *The Ancient Song of Quetzalcoatl* by John H. Cornyn; *All the Wondrousness* by Catherine E. Whitmar; *Art in Clay* by Robert Willson; *One More Shiprock Night* by Luci Tapahonso; *A Story in Glass.* **Principal Officials and Managers:** Robert Willson, Editor and Publisher.

★1807★
Treasure Chest Publications
1802 W. Grant
Tucson, AZ 85745   Ph: (602)623-9558

Description: Focuses on Indian arts and crafts books. **Number of New Titles:** 1990 - 4; Total Titles in Print - 32. **Selected Titles:** *Turquoise Gem of the Centuries; Fetishes and Carvings of the Southwest; Indian Jewelry Making, Vols. I-II; What You Need to Know about Your Gold and Silver,* all by Oscar Branson; *Navajo Sand Painting Art* by Mark Bahti. **Principal Officials and Managers:** Oscar Branson, President; Sterling Mahan, General Manager.

★1808★
Tribal Press
Rte. 2, Box 599
Cable, WI 54821   Ph: (715)794-2247

Description: Publishes a book on the life and work of sculptor Peter Toth, ''who is dedicating his life to honor the American Indians.'' Also produces postcards. **Total Titles in Print:** 1. **Selected Titles:** *Indian Giver* by Peter Wolf Toth. **Principal Officials and Managers:** Peter Toth, Author and Publisher.

★1809★
Trust for Native American Cultures and Crafts
PO Box 142
Greenville, NH 03048   Ph: (603)878-2944

Description: Disseminates information on traditional native technologies. Offers videotapes, field research, and posters. Reaches market through direct mail. **Total Titles in Print:** 1. **Selected Titles:** *Making the Attikamek Snowshoe* by Henri Vaillancourt; *Beavertail Snowshoes* (videotape); *Building an Algonquin Birchbark Canoe* (videotape); *Indian Hide Tanning* (videotape). **Principal Officials and Managers:** Henri Vaillancourt, John Todd Crocker, Trustees.

★1810★
University of California, Los Angeles
American Indian Studies Center
3220 Campbell Hall
Los Angeles, CA 90024-1548   Ph: (213)825-7315

Description: Publishes books, documents, and video cassettes on Native American subjects for researchers, scholars, and professionals. Offers the *American Indian Culture and Research Journal.* Accepts unsolicited manuscripts. Some publications available on microfiche. Reaches market through direct mail, trade sales, Baker & Taylor, Blackwell North America, Midwest Library Service, and other distributors. **Number of New Titles:** 1990 - 1, 1991 (est.) - 1; Total Titles in Print - 30. **Selected Titles:** *American Indian Policy and Cultural Values: Conflict and Accommodation* by Jennie Joe; *Preserving Traditional Arts* by Susan Dyal; *Migration Tears* by Michael Kabotie; *Issues for the Future of American Indian Studies* by Susan Guyette and Charlotte Heth; *Shadow Country* by Paula Gunn Allen; *The Light on the Tent Wall* by Mary TallMountain. **Principal Officials and Managers:** Duane Champagne, Acting Director and Publications Editor; Judith St. George, Managing Editor; Troy Johnson, Book Review Editor; Laura Cannis, Velma S. Salabiye, Assistant Editors.

★1811★
University of New Mexico
Institute for Native American Development
1812 Las Lomas NE
Albuquerque, NM 87131   Ph: (505)277-3917

Description: Provides outreach services for Native American communities in the areas of specialized seminars, research, and publications. Also offers posters. Reaches market through direct mail. **Number of New Titles:** 1989 - 1; Total Titles in Print - 5. **Selected Titles:** *American Indian Energy Resources and Development* edited by Roxanne Dunbar Ortiz; *Irredeemable America: The Indians' Estate and Land Claims* by Imre Sutton; *Economic Development in American Indian Reservations* by Roxanne Dunbar Ortiz; *Public Policy Impacts on American Indian Economic Development* by C. Matthew Snipp. **Principal Officials and Managers:** Ted Jojola, Director; Edwina Abeita, Staff Assistant.

★1812★
University of Oklahoma
University of Oklahoma Press
1005 Aspen Ave.
Norman, OK 73019   Ph: (405)325-5111

Description: Publishes scholarly books on many topics, including a new series devoted to American Indian literature and criticism.

★1813★
University of South Dakota
University of South Dakota Press
c/o Dept. of Social Behavior
414 E. Clark St.
Vermillion, SD 57069-2390   Ph: (605)677-5401

Description: Founded to further the publishing interests of the University of South Dakota. Has mainly published Native American literature, as well as some books about South Dakota and other books pertinent to education and the university. **Number of New Titles:** 1990 - 3, 1991 - 5, 1992 (est.) - 5; Total Titles in Print - 34. **Selected Titles:** *To have this Land* by Hall; *Whatever it Takes* by Moses; *Cante ohitika Win* by Reyer; *Ptebloka* by Two Bulls; *Fort Pierre Chouteau* by Schuler. **Principal Officials and Managers:** Gil French, Managing Editor.

Videos

★1814★
Abnaki: The Native People of Maine
Centre Productions, Inc.
1800 30th St., Ste. 207
Boulder, CO 80301   Ph: (303)444-1166
    Free: 800-824-1166

Description: This film follows the Abnaki Indians in their efforts to accomplish their legal victory. Furthermore, we explore the historical, cultural and spiritual factors that have contributed to the survival of their Native American heritage. **Release Date:** 1984. **Length:** 29 mins. **Format:** Beta, VHS, 3/4″ U-matic Cassette.

★1815★
Aboriginal Rights: I Can Get It For You Wholesale
Native American Public Broadcasting
  Consortium
PO Box 86111
1800 N. 33rd St.
Lincoln, NE 68501   Ph: (402)472-3522

Description: This tape debates the pro side of Native American aboriginal rights, claiming precedence and respect for nature as its major arguments. **Release Date:** 1976. **Length:** 60 mins. **Format:** VHS, 3/4″ U-matic Cassette, 1″ Broadcast Type ″C″, 2″ Quadruplex Open Reel.

★1816★
Acorns: Staple Food of California Indians
University of California at Berkeley
  Extension Media Center
2176 Shattuck Ave.
Berkeley, CA 94704   Ph: (510)642-0460
Description: Pomo tribe members demonstrate traditional acorn harvesting, storing, and processing methods that have evolved over generations. **Release Date:** 1962. **Length:** 28 mins. **Format:** 3/4″ U-matic Cassette, Other than listed.

★1817★
Akwesasne: Another Point of View
Icarus Films
200 Park Ave., S., Ste. 1319
New York, NY 10003   Ph: (212)674-3375
Description: This program explores some of the social, political, and legal obstacles faced by traditional Mowhawks in recent years in their struggle to retain traditional rights. **Release Date:** 1981. **Length:** 28 mins. **Format:** 3/4″ U-matic Cassette.

★1818★
The American as Artist: A Portrait of Bob Penn
Native American Public Broadcasting
  Consortium
PO Box 86111
1800 N. 33rd St.
Lincoln, NE 68501   Ph: (402)472-3522
Description: An essay on American Indian artist Penn and his experimental work, examining both the art and his position as a Native American artist. **Release Date:** 1976. **Length:** 29 mins. **Format:** VHS, 3/4″ U-matic Cassette, 1″ Broadcast Type ″C″, 2″ Quadraplex Open Reel.

★1819★
The American Indian
Dallas County Community College District
Center for Educational Telecommunications
Dallas Telecourses
9596 Walnut St.   Ph: (214)952-0303
Mesquite, TX 75243   Fax: (214)952-0329
Description: This program examines the history of the American Indian from the turn of the century to the present day. **Release Date:** 1980. **Length:** 28 mins. **Format:** 3/4″ U-matic Cassette.

★1820★
American Indian After the White Man Came
Handel Film Corporation
8730 Sunset Blvd.
West Hollywood, CA 90069   Ph: (213)657-8990
Description: An examination of the profound impact white expansion had upon the many existing native tribes and the formation of government policies. **Release Date:** 1972. **Length:** 27 mins. **Format:** Beta, VHS, 3/4″ U-matic Cassette. **Credits:** Narrated by: Iron Eyes Cody.

★1821★
American Indian Artists: Part I
Native American Public Broadcasting
  Consortium
PO Box 86111
1800 N. 33rd St.
Lincoln, NE 68501   Ph: (402)472-3522
Description: A series looking at the work and lifestyle of six American Indian artists. **Release Date:** 1976. **Length:** 29 mins. **Format:** VHS, 3/4″ U-matic Cassette, 1″ Broadcast Type ″C″, 2″ Quadraplex Open Reel.

★1822★
American Indian Artists: Part II
Native American Public Broadcasting
  Consortium
PO Box 86111
1800 N. 33rd St.
Lincoln, NE 68501   Ph: (402)472-3522
Description: Three more American Indian artists display and discuss their work. **Release Date:** 1982. **Length:** 29 mins. **Format:** VHS, 3/4″ U-matic Cassette, 1″ Broadcast Type ″C″, 2″ Quadraplex Open Reel.

★1823★
American Indian Before the White Man
Handel Film Corporation
8730 Sunset Blvd.
West Hollywood, CA 90069   Ph: (213)657-8990
Description: A comprehensive study of the Indian, tracing the early Asiatic descendants who fanned out into Mexico and the Americas. The Apache and Navajo tribes are explored in detail. **Release Date:** 1972. **Length:** 19 mins. **Format:** Beta, VHS, 3/4″ U-matic Cassette. **Credits:** Narrated by: Iron Eyes Cody.

★1824★
American Indian Collection: Geronimo and the Apache Resistance
PBS Video
1320 Braddock Pl.
Alexandria, VA 22314-1698   Ph: (703)739-5380
Description: This presentation chronicles the years of unfair treatment handed out to the Apache tribe and the efforts of American soldiers to apprehend Geronimo and his warriors after their revolt against this tyranny. Part of the ″Odyssey″ series. **Release Date:** 1991. **Length:** 60 mins. **Format:** VHS.

★1825★
American Indian Collection: Myths and Moundbuilders
PBS Video
1320 Braddock Pl.
Alexandria, VA 22314-1698   Ph: (703)739-5380
Description: Recently, archaeologists discovered that huge earthen mounds scattered throughout the central U.S. were built by Indians. Part of the ″Odyssey″ series. **Release Date:** 1991. **Length:** 60 mins. **Format:** Beta, VHS.

★1826★
American Indian Collection: Seasons of the Navajo
PBS Video
1320 Braddock Pl.
Alexandria, VA 22314-1698   Ph: (703)739-5380
Description: An extended Navajo family deals with modern life through tribal communion in this documentary. Part of the ″Odyssey″ series. **Release Date:** 1991. **Length:** 60 mins. **Format:** VHS.

★1827★
American Indian Collection: Spirit of Crazy Horse
PBS Video
1320 Braddock Pl.
Alexandria, VA 22314-1698   Ph: (703)739-5380
Description: This documentary explores the culture, customs, and legacy of the great Sioux tribe and their efforts to retain their traditions and honor in a modern world. Part of the ″Odyssey″ series. **Release Date:** 1991. **Length:** 54 mins. **Format:** VHS.

★1828★
American Indian Collection: Winds of Change—A Matter of Promises
PBS Video
1320 Braddock Pl.
Alexandria, VA 22314-1698   Ph: (703)739-5380
Description: This documentary examines the problems facing Native Americans as they try to hold onto ancient customs and values in a modern society. The ways of the Navajo nation in Arizona and New Mexico, the Lummi tribe in Washington State, and the Onondaga in

New York are detailed. Part of the "Odyssey" series. **Release Date:** 1991. **Length:** 60 mins. **Format:** VHS. **Credits:** Hosted by: N. Scott Momaday.

★1829★
American Indian Influence on the United States
Dana Productions
6249 Babcock Ave.
North Hollywood, CA 91606   Ph: (213)877-9246
Description: A look at how life in the U.S. has been influenced by the Indian–economically, sociologically, philosophically, and culturally. **Release Date:** 1972. **Length:** 20 mins. **Format:** Beta, VHS, 1/2″ Reel-EIAJ, 3/4″ U-matic Cassette, Other than listed. **Credits:** Narrated by: Barry Sullivan.

★1830★
The American Indian Series
University of California at Berkeley
   Extension Media Center
2176 Shattuck Ave.
Berkeley, CA 94704   Ph: (510)642-0460
Description: Members of several northern California Indian tribes depict unique elements of a way of life as it flourished before the imposition of European culture. **Release Date:** 196?. **Length:** 30 mins. **Format:** 3/4″ U-matic Cassette, Other than listed.

★1831★
The American Indian Speaks
Britannica Films
310 S. Michigan Ave.   Ph: (312)347-7958
Chicago, IL 60604   Fax: (312)347-7966
Description: This powerful documentary lets the Indian speak about his people and heritage, about the white man and the future. **Release Date:** 1973. **Length:** 23 mins. **Format:** Beta, VHS, 3/4″ U-matic Cassette.

★1832★
American Indian Sweat Lodge Ceremony
Artistic Video
87 Tyler Ave.
Sound Beach, NY 11789   Ph: (516)744-0449
Description: The entire ceremony, which is one of North America's oldest, is shown. **Release Date:** 1987. **Length:** 90 mins. **Format:** Beta, VHS.

★1833★
The American Indian Today
NETCHE (Nebraska ETV Council for
   Higher Education)
Box 83111
Lincoln, NE 68501   Ph: (402)472-3611
Description: This is a lesson which contains material on American Indians circa 1969. **Release Date:** 1969. **Length:** 30 mins. **Format:** 1/2″ Reel-EIAJ.

★1834★
American Indians Before European Settlement
Coronet/MTI Film & Video   Ph: (708)940-1260
108 Wilmot Rd.   Free: 800-621-2131
Deerfield, IL 60015   Fax: (708)940-3640
Description: This account of American Indian life relates their culture to their environment in five different geographic regions, prior to the coming of the European settlers. **Release Date:** 1959. **Length:** 11 mins. **Format:** Beta, VHS, 3/4″ U-matic Cassette, Other than listed.

★1835★
The American Indian's Sacred Ground
Wood Knapp & Company, Inc.
Knapp Press
5900 Wilshire Blvd.   Ph: (213)937-5486
Los Angeles, CA 90036   Free: 800-521-2666
Description: The mythical and geological aspects of the Native American sacred grounds are examined here, with discussions on architecture, communication, and the natural and spiritual world;

filmed at sites throughout the United States. **Release Date:** 1991. **Length:** 60 mins. **Format:** VHS.

★1836★
American Indians: Yesterday and Today
FilmFair Communications   Ph: (818)985-0244
10621 Magnolia Blvd.   Free: 800-423-2461
North Hollywood, CA 91601   Fax: (818)980-8492
Description: In this program, Native Americans from three different tribes tell the stories of their people–how they survived the earliest days and what their lives are like today. **Release Date:** 1982. **Length:** 19 mins. **Format:** Beta, VHS, 3/4″ U-matic Cassette.

★1837★
Amiotte
Native American Public Broadcasting
   Consortium
PO Box 86111
1800 N. 33rd St.
Lincoln, NE 68501   Ph: (402)472-3522
Description: A film outlining the career and life of Native American artist Arthur Amiotte. **Release Date:** 1976. **Length:** 29 mins. **Format:** VHS, 3/4″ U-matic Cassette, 1″ Broadcast Type "C", 2″ Quadraplex Open Reel.

★1838★
An Ancient Gift
University of California at Berkeley
   Extension Media Center
2176 Shattuck Ave.
Berkeley, CA 94704   Ph: (510)642-0460
Description: The important role that sheep play in the lives of the Navajo is explored. **Release Date:** 1986. **Length:** 16 mins. **Format:** VHS, 3/4″ U-matic Cassette.

★1839★
Ancient Indian Cultures of Northern Arizona
Victorian Video Productions
PO Box 1540   Ph: (916)346-6184
Colfax, CA 95713-1540   Free: 800-848-0284
Description: Concentrates on the Sinagua and Anasazi people and how they survived under harsh conditions. Also looks at five national monuments: Montezuma Castle, Wupatki, Tuzigoot, Walnut Canyon, and Sunset Crater. **Release Date:** 1985. **Length:** 30 mins. **Format:** Beta, VHS.

★1840★
Ancient Spirit, Living Word: The Oral Tradition
Native American Public Broadcasting
   Consortium
PO Box 86111
1800 N. 33rd St.
Lincoln, NE 68501   Ph: (402)472-3522
Description: An exploration of the Native American oral story-telling tradition. **Release Date:** 1983. **Length:** 58 mins. **Format:** VHS, 3/4″ U-matic Cassette, 1″ Broadcast Type "C", 2″ Quadraplex Open Reel.

★1841★
Annie and the Old One
Phoenix/BFA Films
468 Park Ave., S.   Ph: (212)684-5910
New York, NY 10016   Free: 800-221-1274
Description: The Old One is the beloved grandmother of a little Navajo girl named Annie. Annie questions the Old One about the cycle of life. Adapted from a book by Miska Miles. **Release Date:** 1976. **Length:** 15 mins. **Format:** Beta, VHS.

★1842★
Another Wind Is Moving
University of California at Berkeley
  Extension Media Center
2176 Shattuck Ave.
Berkeley, CA 94704   Ph: (510)642-0460
Description: Since Indian schools have begun to shut down in larger and larger numbers, it is increasingly more difficult for Native Americans to learn about their culture. **Release Date:** 1986. **Length:** 59 mins. **Format:** VHS, 3/4″ U-matic Cassette.

★1843★
The Apache Indian
Coronet/MTI Film & Video   Ph: (708)940-1260
108 Wilmot Rd.   Free: 800-621-2131
Deerfield, IL 60015   Fax: (708)940-3640
Description: An examination of Apache life and culture, from ancient times to the present, from tribal ceremonies to advanced education. **Release Date:** 1975. **Length:** 10 mins. **Format:** Beta, VHS, 3/4″ U-matic Cassette, Other than listed.

★1844★
Apache Mountain Spirit
Native American Public Broadcasting
  Consortium
1800 N. 33rd St.
PO Box 86111
Lincoln, NE 68501   Ph: (402)472-3522
Description: When Robert takes up with a bad crowd, the Gaan, Apache Mountain spirits, touch and test him. He allows the spirits to direct his life and use his powers within for good purposes. **Release Date:** 1985. **Length:** 59 mins. **Format:** VHS, 1″ Broadcast Type ″C″, 3/4″ U-matic Cassette.

★1845★
The Art of Being Indian: Filmed Aspects of the
  Culture of the Sioux
Native American Public Broadcasting
  Consortium
PO Box 86111
1800 N. 33rd St.
Lincoln, NE 68501   Ph: (402)472-3522
Description: The refined art of being truly Sioux is thoroughly surveyed, past, present and future. Features art by Bob Penn, Seth Eastman, Stanley Morrow and George Catlin. **Release Date:** 1976. **Length:** 29 mins. **Format:** VHS, 3/4″ U-matic Cassette, 1″ Broadcast Type ″C″, 2″ Quadraplex Open Reel.

★1846★
The Art of Navajo Weaving
Arts America, Inc.
12 Havermeyer Pl.
Greenwich, CT 06830   Ph: (203)637-1454
Description: Watch as skilled veterans perform the art of Navajo weaving. This video also shows the Durango Collection, the world's largest private collection of Navajo weaving. **Release Date:** 1988. **Length:** 56 mins. **Format:** Beta, VHS.

★1847★
As Long As the Grass Is Green
Atlantis Productions
1252 La Granada Dr.
Thousand Oaks, CA 91360   Ph: (805)495-2790
Description: A summer experience with the children of the Woodland Indians of North America. Nonnarrative. **Release Date:** 1973. **Length:** 11 mins. **Format:** Beta, VHS, 3/4″ U-matic Cassette.

★1848★
Basketry of the Pomo: Forms and Ornamentation
University of California at Berkeley
  Extension Media Center
2176 Shattuck Ave.
Berkeley, CA 94704   Ph: (510)642-0460
Description: This look at the basketry of the Pomo Indians of northern California illustrates the great variety of shapes and designs

descriptive of animals. **Release Date:** 1962. **Length:** 21 mins. **Format:** 3/4″ U-matic Cassette, Other than listed.

★1849★
Basketry of the Pomo: Introductory Film
University of California at Berkeley
  Extension Media Center
2176 Shattuck Ave.
Berkeley, CA 94704   Ph: (510)642-0460
Description: The Pomo Indians of northern California were the world's most expert basketmakers. This program shows Indians gathering raw materials for baskets, and creating baskets with graceful geometric forms. **Release Date:** 1962. **Length:** 30 mins. **Format:** 3/4″ U-matic Cassette, Other than listed.

★1850★
Basketry of the Pomo: Techniques
University of California at Berkeley
  Extension Media Center
2176 Shattuck Ave.
Berkeley, CA 94704   Ph: (510)642-0460
Description: A detailed look at the basketry techniques of the Pomo Indians of northern California, showing precisely how the various weaves were executed. **Release Date:** 1962. **Length:** 33 mins. **Format:** 3/4″ U-matic Cassette, Other than listed.

★1851★
Beautiful Tree: Chishkale
University of California at Berkeley
  Extension Media Center
2176 Shattuck Ave.
Berkeley, CA 94704   Ph: (510)642-0460
Description: A look at how the Pomo Indians of northern California removed poisonous tannic acid from the acorns of the tan oak chishkale (the beautiful tree) to feed the tribe. **Release Date:** 1965. **Length:** 20 mins. **Format:** 3/4″ U-matic Cassette, Other than listed.

★1852★
Beyond Tradition
Home Vision Cinema   Ph: (312)878-2600
5547 N. Ravenswood Ave.   Free: 800-826-3456
Chicago, IL 60640-1199   Fax: (312)878-8648
Description: Indian art, from prehistoric to modern, is set to haunting accompaniment of guitar and flute. **Release Date:** 1982. **Length:** 45 mins. **Format:** Beta, VHS.

★1853★
Black Coal, Red Power
Indiana University Center for Media &
  Teaching Resources   Ph: (812)855-8087
Bloomington, IN 47405-5901   Fax: (812)855-8404
Description: The strip mining of coal on Navajo and Hopi reservations in Arizona is examined for its effects on the ecology and the economy of the Indian population. **Release Date:** 1972. **Length:** 41 mins. **Format:** 3/4″ U-matic Cassette, Other than listed.

★1854★
The Black Hills: Who Owns the Land
NETCHE (Nebraska ETV Council for
  Higher Education)
Box 83111
Lincoln, NE 68501   Ph: (402)472-3611
Description: Examines the historical record of lands in South Dakota and the question of who owns them–the Indians? **Release Date:** 1989. **Length:** 60 mins. **Format:** Beta, VHS, 3/4″ U-matic Cassette.

★1855★
Boldt Decision: Impacts and Implementation
University of Washington Instructional
  Media Services
Kane Hall, DG-10
Seattle, WA 98195   Ph: (206)543-9909
Description: A discussion of the court ruling by U.S. Judge George Boldt who ruled that treaty Indians in Washington are entitled to half

the harvestable catch of salmon and steelhead. **Release Date:** 1976. **Length:** 60 mins. **Format:** 3/4″ U-matic Cassette.

★1856★
Boldt Decision: Update
University of Washington Instructional
 Media Services
Kane Hall, DG-10
Seattle, WA 98195　　　　　　　Ph: (206)543-9909

Description: A look at the impact of the court ruling by U.S. Judge George Boldt that treaty Indians in Washington are entitled to half the harvestable catch of salmon and steelhead. **Release Date:** 1976. **Length:** 60 mins. **Format:** 3/4″ U-matic Cassette.

★1857★
Box of Treasures
Documentary Educational Resources
101 Morse St.　　　　　　Ph: (617)926-0491
Watertown, MA 02172　　　Fax: (617)926-9519

Description: This film is a focus on Kwakiutl society, a native American Indian community, and their struggle to redefine cultural identity. **Release Date:** 1986. **Length:** 28 mins. **Format:** 3/4″ U-matic Cassette.

★1858★
Boy of the Navajos
Coronet/MTI Film & Video　　　Ph: (708)940-1260
108 Wilmot Rd.　　　　　　　Free: 800-621-2131
Deerfield, IL 60015　　　　　Fax: (708)940-3640

Description: The story of Tony, a present-day Navajo boy as he herds sheep in the Arizona desert, and spends evenings with his family in the hogan. **Release Date:** 1975. **Length:** 11 mins. **Format:** Beta, VHS, 3/4″ U-matic Cassette, Other than listed.

★1859★
Boy of the Seminoles (Indians of the Everglades)
Coronet/MTI Film & Video　　　Ph: (708)940-1260
108 Wilmot Rd.　　　　　　　Free: 800-621-2131
Deerfield, IL 60015　　　　　Fax: (708)940-3640

Description: The story of Naha, a Seminole boy, as he travels into the swamp to return the baby alligator captured by his dog. Life among the Seminole people is illustrated. **Release Date:** 1956. **Length:** 11 mins. **Format:** Beta, VHS, 3/4″ U-matic Cassette, Other than listed.

★1860★
Broken Journey
Native American Public Broadcasting
 Consortium
1800 N. 33rd St.
PO Box 86111
Lincoln, NE 68501　　　　　　Ph: (402)472-3522

Description: Focuses on the problem of alcohol for Native Americans by listening to stories told by men and women incarcerated for alcohol related problems. Aimed at Native American youth. **Length:** 27 mins. **Format:** VHS, 1″ Broadcast Type ″C″, 3/4″ U-matic Cassette.

★1861★
Broken Rainbow
Direct Cinema Limited　　　　Ph: (213)652-8000
PO Box 69799　　　　　　　　Free: 800-345-6748
Los Angeles, CA 90069-9976　Fax: (213)652-2346

Description: An acclaimed documentary about the U.S. Government's relocation of 12,000 Navajo Indians. They described it as a Hopi-Navajo land settlement, but actually did it to facilitate energy development. **Release Date:** 1985. **Length:** 70 mins. **Format:** Beta, VHS, 3/4″ U-matic Cassette, Other than listed. **Credits:** Narrated by: Martin Sheen; Burgess Meredith; Buffy Sainte-Marie.

★1862★
Buckeyes: Food of California Indians
University of California at Berkeley
 Extension Media Center
2176 Shattuck Ave.
Berkeley, CA 94704　　　　　Ph: (510)642-0460

Description: This program shows how the Nisenan Indians of California harvested buckeyes and processed them by stone boiling and leaching. Buckeyes were an important staple of their diet. **Release Date:** 1961. **Length:** 13 mins. **Format:** 3/4″ U-matic Cassette, Other than listed.

★1863★
By This Song I Walk: Navajo Song
Norman Ross Publishing Inc.　　Ph: (212)765-8200
330 W. 58th St.　　　　　　　Free: 800-648-8850
New York, NY 10019　　　　　Fax: (212)765-2393

Description: When the harmony of life is disrupted, the Navajo sings to restore balance and symmetry, as shown in this program (Navajo with English subtitles). **Release Date:** 1981. **Length:** 25 mins. **Format:** Beta, VHS, 3/4″ U-matic Cassette.

★1864★
California Riviera
New & Unique Videos
2336 Sumac Dr.　　　　　　　Ph: (619)282-6126
San Diego, CA 92105　　　　　Fax: (619)283-8264

Description: A look at the history, culture, archaeology, and oceanography of southern California. Included is an interview with the present members of the ancient Juaneno Indian tribe who have extensive ancestral knowledge of the area. **Release Date:** 1989. **Length:** 50 mins. **Format:** Beta, VHS.

★1865★
Calumet, Pipe of Peace
University of California at Berkeley
 Extension Media Center
2176 Shattuck Ave.
Berkeley, CA 94704　　　　　Ph: (510)642-0460

Description: This program discusses rituals surrounding the calumet, or peace pipe, which was smoked to insure safe conduct, to placate hostile nations, to control the weather, and to conclude peace treaties. **Release Date:** 1964. **Length:** 23 mins. **Format:** 3/4″ U-matic Cassette, Other than listed.

★1866★
Canyon de Chelly & Hubbell Trading Post
Victorian Video Productions
PO Box 1540　　　　　　　　Ph: (916)346-6184
Colfax, CA 95713-1540　　　　Free: 800-848-0284

Description: Visit these national parks of New Mexico and Arizona that contain Anasazi cliff dwellings and Navajo craftsmen. **Release Date:** 1979. **Length:** 30 mins. **Format:** Beta, VHS.

★1867★
Celebration/The Pipe is the Altar
Intermedia Arts of Minnesota, Inc.
425 Ontario St. SE
Minneapolis, MN 55414　　　　Ph: (612)627-4444

Description: Two programs looking at various traditional Indian rituals. **Release Date:** 1980. **Length:** 26 mins. **Format:** Beta, VHS, 3/4″ U-matic Cassette.

★1868★
A Century of Silence...Problems of the American Indian
Atlantis Productions
1252 La Granada Dr.
Thousand Oaks, CA 91360　　　Ph: (805)495-2790

Description: This film correlates the current problems of the American Indian to the past 100 years of contact with the white culture. Also addressed, are the issues of cultural conflict, assimilation, and activism within the Indian community. **Release Date:** 197?. **Length:** 28 mins. **Format:** Beta, VHS, 3/4″ U-matic Cassette.

★1869★
Cesar's Bark Canoe
Education Development Center, Inc.
55 Chapel St., Ste. 901   Ph: (617)969-7100
Newton, MA 02160   Free: 800-225-4276
Description: Cree Indian Cesar Newashish uses a knife and axe to construct a canoe from a birch tree. With no spoken commentary, this program highlights each stage of construction with on-screen text in three languages–Cree, French, and English. **Release Date:** 1978. **Length:** 58 mins. **Format:** 3/4″ U-matic Cassette, Other than listed.

★1870★
Cherokee
Cinema Guild
1697 Broadway   Ph: (212)246-5522
New York, NY 10019   Fax: (212)246-5525
Description: This program explores the dilemma the Cherokee face in preserving their traditions and captures the beauty of the pageants and ceremonies still performed today. **Release Date:** 1976. **Length:** 26 mins. **Format:** 3/4″ U-matic Cassette, Other than listed.

★1871★
Children of the Long-Beaked Bird
Bullfrog Films, Inc.
PO Box 149   Ph: (215)779-8226
Oley, PA 19547   Free: 800-543-3764
    Fax: (215)370-1978
Description: This is an intimate look at a modern Native American Family that disproves the stereotype commonly placed on American Indians. **Release Date:** 1976. **Length:** 29 mins. **Format:** Beta, VHS, 3/4″ U-matic Cassette.

★1872★
Children of the Plains Indians
CRM/McGraw-Hill Films
674 Via de la Valle
PO Box 641
Del Mar, CA 92014
Description: A view of Indian life on the Great Plains before the arrival of white settlers, featuring intimate scenes of many tribal activities. **Release Date:** 1962. **Length:** 20 mins. **Format:** Beta, VHS, 3/4″ U-matic Cassette.

★1873★
A Circle of Women
Island Visual Arts
8920 Sunset Blvd., 2nd Fl.   Ph: (213)288-5382
Los Angeles, CA 90069   Fax: (213)276-5476
Description: Modern women meet women elders of Native American Tribes in an effort to link their cultures, and create an awareness of wisdom long discarded by the modern world. **Release Date:** 1991. **Length:** 60 mins. **Format:** VHS.

★1874★
Civilized Tribes
Cinema Guild
1697 Broadway   Ph: (212)246-5522
New York, NY 10019   Fax: (212)246-5525
Description: In the Southeast part of the country, the five civilized tribes–the Seminoles, the Creek, the Choctaw, the Chickasaw, and the Cherokee–make their home. This program explores the Hollywood reservation in Florida where a village has been reconstructed to document the Seminole's earlier life. Also in Philadelphia, Miss., the Choctaw tribal people discuss their struggle to become a successful independent business community. **Release Date:** 1976. **Length:** 26 mins. **Format:** 3/4″ U-matic Cassette, Other than listed.

★1875★
Clouded Land
Intermedia Arts of Minnesota, Inc.
425 Ontario St. SE
Minneapolis, MN 55414   Ph: (612)627-4444
Description: The land claim dispute on the White Earth Reservation in Minnesota is explored by highlighting its' effect on two Indian and two non-Indian families directly involved in the conflict. **Release Date:** 1987. **Length:** 58 mins. **Format:** 3/4″ U-matic Cassette.

★1876★
Clues to Ancient Indian Life
AIMS Media
9710 De Soto Ave.
Chatsworth, CA 91311-9734   Free: 800-367-2467
    Fax: (818)341-6700
Description: The kinds of clues ancient Indians left behind, and the importance of preserving these artifacts for study are explored on this video. **Release Date:** 1962. **Length:** 10 mins. **Format:** Beta, VHS, 3/4″ U-matic Cassette.

★1877★
The Colors of Pride
National Film Board of Canada
1251 Avenue of the Americas, 16th Fl.
New York, NY 10020-1173   Ph: (212)586-5131
Description: A visit with four Indian painters whose work in recent years has stirred international interest. **Release Date:** 1973. **Length:** 28 mins. **Format:** Beta, VHS, 3/4″ U-matic Cassette.

★1878★
A Common Destiny
Mystic Fire Video
PO Box 1092
Cooper Sta.   Ph: (212)941-0999
New York, NY 10276   Fax: (212)941-1443
Description: Comprises two films: ''Walking in Both Worlds'' concerns Jewell Praying Wolf James, a Lummi tribesman of the Pacific Northwest who seeks Native American participation in United States land management while noting native people must walk with one foot in the Indian world and the other in the non-Indian world. ''The Hopi Prophecy'' tells of Thomas Banyacya, spokesman for Hopi high religious leaders, as he interprets prophetic sacred tribal symbols and calls for universal peace and spiritual connectedness with the earth. **Release Date:** 1990. **Length:** 52 mins. **Format:** VHS.

★1879★
Completing Our Circle
CRM/McGraw-Hill Films
674 Via de la Valle
PO Box 641
Del Mar, CA 92014
Description: The traditions of the Plains and West Coast Indians, the Inuit, and the first Europeans and settlers in Western Canada are shown in this program. Their art and craftsmanship are presented as a way to express both individual identity and oneness with other men. **Release Date:** 1978. **Length:** 27 mins. **Format:** Beta, VHS, 3/4″ U-matic Cassette.

★1880★
Conquista
Center for Humanities, Inc.
Communications Park
Box 1000   Ph: (914)666-4100
Mount Kisco, NY 10549   Free: 800-431-1242
Description: A look at how the history of the Old West was affected by the fateful meeting of the plains Indian and the horse. **Release Date:** 1974. **Length:** 20 mins. **Format:** Beta, VHS, 3/4″ U-matic Cassette. **Credits:** Narrated by: Richard Boone.

★1881★
Contemporary and Native American Readings
Videotakes
187 Parker Ave.
Rte. 71
Manasquan, NJ 08736

Ph: (908)528-5000
Free: 800-526-7002

Description: Chamberlain reads and interprets work from Joseph Campbell about Native Americans. He also interprets an address from Native Americans to the President regarding the obligation of Americans to protect the Earth. **Release Date:** 19??. **Length:** ? mins. **Format:** VHS. **Credits:** Narrated by: Richard Chamberlain.

★1882★
Contrary Warriors: A Film of the Crow Tribe
Direct Cinema Limited
PO Box 69799
Los Angeles, CA 90069-9976

Ph: (213)652-8000
Free: 800-345-6748
Fax: (213)652-2346

Description: The century-long struggle for survival of Native Americans is explored in this film. **Release Date:** 1986. **Length:** 60 mins. **Format:** Beta, VHS, 3/4″ U-matic Cassette.

★1883★
A Conversation with Vine Deloria, Jr.
Norman Ross Publishing Inc.
330 W. 58th St.
New York, NY 10019

Ph: (212)765-8200
Free: 800-648-8850
Fax: (212)765-2393

Description: The writer discusses the gulf between Indian and non-Indian culture and the ''schizophrenia'' of white expectations for the Indian. **Release Date:** 1981. **Length:** 29 mins. **Format:** Beta, VHS, 3/4″ U-matic Cassette.

★1884★
Crow Dog
Cinema Guild
1697 Broadway
New York, NY 10019

Ph: (212)246-5522
Fax: (212)246-5525

Description: A video portrait of medicine man Leonard Crow Dog, the Sioux Nation's spiritual leader and spokesperson for the traditionalist (those Sioux who wish to retain the beliefs and customs of their forefathers). **Release Date:** 1979. **Length:** 57 mins. **Format:** Beta, VHS, 3/4″ U-matic Cassette.

★1885★
Crow Dog's Paradise
Centre Productions, Inc.
1800 30th St., Ste. 207
Boulder, CO 80301

Ph: (303)444-1166
Free: 800-824-1166

Description: A look at a Sioux Indian enclave where the Crow Dog family preserves the spiritual and intellectual heritage of their traditional American Indian culture. **Release Date:** 1979. **Length:** 28 mins. **Format:** Beta, VHS, 3/4″ U-matic Cassette.

★1886★
Dance to Give Thanks
Native American Public Broadcasting
  Consortium
1800 N. 33rd St.
PO Box 86111
Lincoln, NE 68501

Ph: (402)472-3522

Description: Looks at the 184th annual He-De-Wa-Chi (Festival of Joy) of the Omaha Indian Tribe. Learn about the history of the festival as well as see traditional and fancy dancing by tribe members. **Length:** 30 mins. **Format:** VHS, 1″ Broadcast Type ″C″, 3/4 U-matic Cassette.

★1887★
Daughters of the Anasazi
Facets Multimedia, Inc.
1517 W. Fullerton Ave.
Chicago, IL 60614

Ph: (312)281-9075

Description: An examination of the ancient techniques used in producing traditional pottery in the Southwest. Filmed in New Mexico. **Release Date:** 1990. **Length:** 28 mins. **Format:** VHS.

★1888★
Desert Regions: Nomads and Traders
Phoenix/BFA Films
468 Park Ave., S.
New York, NY 10016

Ph: (212)684-5910
Free: 800-221-1274

Description: A look at the Navajo Indians of Monument Valley and the Bedouins of Jordan. **Release Date:** 1980. **Length:** 15 mins. **Format:** Beta, VHS, 3/4″ U-matic Cassette.

★1889★
Dineh: The People
Native American Public Broadcasting
  Consortium
PO Box 86111
1800 N. 33rd St.
Lincoln, NE 68501

Ph: (402)472-3522

Description: This documentary covers the impending relocation of several thousand Navajo from a joint-use land area in the Navajo Reservation. **Release Date:** 1976. **Length:** 77 mins. **Format:** VHS, 3/4″ U-matic Cassette, 1″ Broadcast Type ″C″, 2″ Quadraplex Open Reel.

★1890★
Dinshyin
University of California at Berkeley
  Extension Media Center
2176 Shattuck Ave.
Berkeley, CA 94704

Ph: (510)642-0460

Description: Ethnographical chronicle of the many peoples who have lived in and around the Canyon de Chelley in northeastern Arizona, focusing on the Navajo, who came to the area 700 years ago. **Release Date:** 1974. **Length:** 22 mins. **Format:** 3/4″ U-matic Cassette, Other than listed.

★1891★
Distant Voice...Thunder Words
Native American Public Broadcasting
  Consortium
1800 N. 33rd St.
PO Box 86111
Lincoln, NE 68501

Ph: (402)472-3522

Description: Discusses the role of the oral tradition in modern Native American literature. Includes interviews with storytellers and other experts. **Release Date:** 1990. **Length:** 59 mins. **Format:** VHS, 1″ Broadcast Type ″C″, 3/4 U-matic Cassette.

★1892★
The Divided Trail: A Native American Odyssey
Phoenix/BFA Films
468 Park Ave., S.
New York, NY 10016

Ph: (212)684-5910
Free: 800-221-1274

Description: The program follows the lives of three members of the Chicago Indian Village. One is a recovered alcoholic; another is a reformed militant; the final member has gone through a severe emotional crisis due to a conflict between her political actions and sense of personal identity. **Release Date:** 1978. **Length:** 33 mins. **Format:** Beta, VHS, 3/4″ U-matic Cassette.

★1893★
Do We Want Us To?
National AudioVisual Center
National Archives & Records
  Administration
Customer Services Section PZ
8700 Edgeworth Dr.
Capitol Heights, MD 20743-3701

Ph: (301)763-1896

Description: The story about the heritage of the Tlingket Indians helps students recognize and understand the consequences of one culture arriving in the land of another. **Release Date:** 1979. **Length:** 20 mins. **Format:** Beta, VHS, 3/4″ U-matic Cassette, Other than listed.

★1894★
Dream Dances of the Kashia Pomo
University of California at Berkeley
  Extension Media Center
2176 Shattuck Ave.
Berkeley, CA 94704   Ph: (510)642-0460
Description: A look at the five dances of the Kashia Pomo Indians, the Bole Maru, nearly a century after it first evolved. The five dances reflect recent influences including Christianity and World War II. **Release Date:** 1964. **Length:** 30 mins. **Format:** 3/4" U-matic Cassette, Other than listed.

★1895★
Dreamspeaker
Filmakers Library, Inc.
124 E. 40th
New York, NY 10016   Ph: (212)808-4980
Description: A powerful drama depicting an encounter between a disturbed youth and an Indian shaman. Presents the Indian views on death and the life cycle. **Release Date:** 1977. **Length:** 75 mins. **Format:** Beta, VHS, 3/4" U-matic Cassette.

★1896★
The Drum
New Dimension Media, Inc.   Ph: (503)484-7125
85895 Lorane Hwy.   Free: 800-288-4456
Eugene, OR 97405   Fax: (503)484-5267
Description: A Native American ritual shows the importance of people keeping their heritage alive. **Release Date:** 1987. **Length:** 15 mins. **Format:** Beta, VHS.

★1897★
The Drum Is the Heart
Intermedia Arts of Minnesota, Inc.
425 Ontario St. SE
Minneapolis, MN 55414   Ph: (612)627-4444
Description: A program that studies the modernized rituals of the Blackfoot Indians. **Release Date:** 1982. **Length:** 29 mins. **Format:** Beta, VHS, 3/4" U-matic Cassette.

★1898★
The Eagle and the Condor
Native American Public Broadcasting
  Consortium
PO Box 86111
1800 N. 33rd St.
Lincoln, NE 68501   Ph: (402)472-3522
Description: This tape follows the South American tour of Native American entertainers from Brigham Young University's Lamanite Generation. **Release Date:** 1976. **Length:** 29 mins. **Format:** VHS, 3/4" U-matic Cassette, 1" Broadcast Type "C", 2" Quadraplex Open Reel.

★1899★
Early Man in North America
Films, Inc.
5547 N. Ravenswood Ave.   Ph: (312)878-2600
Chicago, IL 60640-1199   Free: 800-323-4222
Description: Early man in North America was by no means a nomadic hunter. Evidence which exists throughout the U.S. today tells of large Indian cities, advanced building structures, and other works requiring thousands of laborers. **Release Date:** 1972. **Length:** 12 mins. **Format:** Beta, VHS, 3/4" U-matic Cassette.

★1900★
The Earth Is Our Home
Media Project, Inc.
PO Box 4093
Portland, OR 97208   Ph: (503)223-5335
Description: The film depicts the vestiges of prehistoric life ways among the Northern Paiute Indians. **Release Date:** 1979. **Length:** 30 mins. **Format:** Beta, VHS, 1/2" Reel-EIAJ, 3/4" U-matic Cassette.

★1901★
Earthshapers
Native American Public Broadcasting
  Consortium
1800 N. 33rd St.
PO Box 86111
Lincoln, NE 68501   Ph: (402)472-3522
Description: A look at the sacred mounds created by the Woodland Native people. **Length:** 14 mins. **Format:** VHS, 1" Broadcast Type "C", 3/4" U-matic Cassette.

★1902★
Emergence
Pictures of Record
119 Kettle Creek Rd.
Weston, CT 06883   Ph: (203)227-3387
Description: This tape is an animated reconstruction of an ancient Navajo myth about a mystic underworld. **Release Date:** 1982. **Length:** 14 mins. **Format:** VHS, 3/4" U-matic Cassette.

★1903★
An End to Isolation
National Municipal League, Inc.
55 W. 44th St.
New York, NY 10036   Ph: (212)730-7930
Description: Explains how American Indians living in the city can assure themselves a fair share of jobs, social services, and political power. **Release Date:** 1976. **Length:** 30 mins. **Format:** 1/2" Reel-EIAJ, 3/4" U-matic Cassette.

★1904★
End of the Trail: The American Plains Indian
CRM/McGraw-Hill Films
674 Via de la Valle
PO Box 641
Del Mar, CA 92014
Description: This program covers the history of the American Plains Indian in the post-Civil War era. It shows the impact that the westward movement had on them and explores their folklore, pointing out the contributions they have made to generations of Americans. Available as a whole or in two parts. **Release Date:** 1967. **Length:** 16 mins. **Format:** Beta, VHS, 3/4" U-matic Cassette.

★1905★
Excavation of Mound 7
National AudioVisual Center
National Archives & Records
  Administration
Customer Services Section PZ
8700 Edgeworth Dr.
Capitol Heights, MD 20743-3701   Ph: (301)763-1896
Description: Archaeology work in the field and in the lab to piece together the mysteries of the Pueblo Indians of New Mexico. **Release Date:** 1973. **Length:** 44 mins. **Format:** Beta, VHS, 3/4" U-matic Cassette, Other than listed.

★1906★
The Exiles
University of California at Berkeley
  Extension Media Center
2176 Shattuck Ave.
Berkeley, CA 94704   Ph: (510)642-0460
Description: A depiction of three young American Indians who come to Los Angeles and get involved in drinking, gambling, and fighting, in anguish and frustration. **Release Date:** 1961. **Length:** 72 mins. **Format:** 3/4" U-matic Cassette, Other than listed.

★1907★
Eyanopopi: The Heart of the Sioux
Centre Productions, Inc.
1800 30th St., Ste. 207   Ph: (303)444-1166
Boulder, CO 80301   Free: 800-824-1166
Description: An explanation as to why the Black Hills of South Dakota are so important to the Sioux. **Release Date:** 1990. **Length:** 30 mins. **Format:** Beta, VHS, 3/4" U-matic Cassette.

★1908★
Faithkeeper
Mystic Fire Video
PO Box 1092
Cooper Sta.   Ph: (212)941-0999
New York, NY 10276   Fax: (212)941-1443
Description: Oren Lyons, an Onondaga chief and leader in the
international environmental movement discusses with Bill Moyers
the history and philosophy of Native Americans, including their
respect for nature and their responsibility for future generations.
Release Date: 1991. **Length:** 58 mins. **Format:** VHS. **Credits:**
Hosted by: Bill Moyers.

★1909★
The First Americans
Troll Associates
320 Rte. 17
Mahwah, NJ 07430   Ph: (201)529-4000
Description: A tape which explains the different Indian tribes of
North America, and tells about their customs. **Release Date:** 1988.
Length: 60 mins. **Format:** VHS. **Credits:** Hosted by: Hugh Downs.

★1910★
The First Americans
New York State Education Department
Center for Learning Technologies
Media Distribution Network, Rm. C-7,
  Concourse Level
Albany, NY 12230   Ph: (518)474-1265
Description: Topics and issues related to the American Indian are
discussed in a talk show format in this series of twenty programs.
Release Date: 197?. **Length:** 30 mins. **Format:** Beta, VHS, 1/2"
Reel-EIAJ, 3/4" U-matic Cassette, 2" Quadraplex Open Reel.

★1911★
The First Americans
Dallas County Community College District
Center for Educational Telecommunications
Dallas Telecourses
9596 Walnut St.   Ph: (214)952-0303
Mesquite, TX 75243   Fax: (214)952-0329
Description: The 30,000 years of cultural development of the
American Indian provide a background for the story of America.
Release Date: 1979. **Length:** 29 mins. **Format:** 3/4" U-matic
Cassette.

★1912★
First Frontier
Wombat Film and Video   Ph: (708)328-6700
930 Pitner   Free: 800-323-5448
Evanston, IL 60202   Fax: (708)328-6706
Description: A history of Native Americans from 1540 to 1814
including dramatizations of key events. **Release Date:** 1989.
Length: 57 mins. **Format:** Beta, VHS, 3/4" U-matic Cassette.

★1913★
Folklore of the Muscogee (Creek) People
Native American Public Broadcasting
  Consortium
PO Box 86111
1800 N. 33rd St.
Lincoln, NE 68501   Ph: (402)472-3522
Description: Dr. Ruth Arrington narrates an analysis of the
significance of Creek folklore. **Release Date:** 1983. **Length:** 29
mins. **Format:** VHS, 3/4" U-matic Cassette, 1" Broadcast Type "C",
2" Quadraplex Open Reel.

★1914★
Forest Spirits
Great Plains National (GPN)
PO Box 80669   Ph: (402)472-2007
Lincoln, NE 68501-0669   Free: 800-228-4630
Description: The plight of the Oneida and Menominee Indians comes
under scrutiny in this series, in an effort to reaffirm the heritage and
traditions of these North American Indians. Programs are available

individually. **Release Date:** 1977. **Length:** 30 mins. **Format:** Beta,
VHS, 3/4" U-matic Cassette.

★1915★
Forever in Time: The Art of Edward S. Curtis
Cinema Guild
1697 Broadway   Ph: (212)246-5522
New York, NY 10019   Fax: (212)246-5525
Description: A biography of the man who devoted much of his life to
photographing the American Indian in the early part of the twentieth
century. Curtis was unable to fulfill his dream of photographing every
North American tribe before his death in 1952, but he uncovered
previously unknown aspects of the Battle of Little Big Horn. **Release
Date:** 1990. **Length:** 50 mins. **Format:** VHS.

★1916★
The Forgotten American
Carousel Film & Video
260 5th Ave., Rm. 705
New York, NY 10001   Ph: (212)683-1660
Description: Shows how the white man exploits the American
Indian. Documents hopelessness and despair, minimal food and
housing, inadequate educational facilities, and limited employment
opportunity. **Release Date:** 1972. **Length:** 25 mins. **Format:** Beta,
VHS, 3/4" U-matic Cassette.

★1917★
Forgotten Frontier
Native American Public Broadcasting
  Consortium
PO Box 86111
1800 N. 33rd St.
Lincoln, NE 68501   Ph: (402)472-3522
Description: A document of the Spanish missionary settlements in
southern Arizona and the agricultural, political and religious
influences they had on the Native Americans of the area. **Release
Date:** 1976. **Length:** 29 mins. **Format:** VHS, 3/4" U-matic Cassette,
1" Broadcast Type "C", 2" Quadraplex Open Reel.

★1918★
Forty-Seven Cents
University of California at Berkeley
  Extension Media Center
2176 Shattuck Ave.
Berkeley, CA 94704   Ph: (510)642-0460
Description: This program documents how officials of the Bureau of
Indian Affairs, the Indian Claims Commission, and a lawyer
representing the Pit River Indian Nation of Northern California
obtained from the tribe a land settlement many of its members did
not want. **Release Date:** 1973. **Length:** 45 mins. **Format:** VHS, 3/4"
U-matic Cassette.

★1919★
Four Corners of Earth
Native American Public Broadcasting
  Consortium
PO Box 86111
1800 N. 33rd St.
Lincoln, NE 68501   Ph: (402)472-3522
Description: A film documenting the cultural evolution of Seminole
women. Changing traditional values in the modern world are viewed
from the perspective of women living on South Florida Seminole
reservations. **Release Date:** 1984. **Length:** 30 mins. **Format:** VHS,
3/4" U-matic Cassette, 1" Broadcast Type "C", 2" Quadraplex
Open Reel.

★1920★
Game of Staves
University of California at Berkeley
  Extension Media Center
2176 Shattuck Ave.
Berkeley, CA 94704   Ph: (510)642-0460
Description: Pomo Indians demonstrate the game of staves, a
variation of dice, played by most of the Indian tribes of North

America. **Release Date:** 1962. **Length:** 10 mins. **Format:** 3/4" U-matic Cassette, Other than listed.

★1921★
Gannagaro
Native American Public Braodcasting
  Consortium
1800 N. 33rd St.
PO Box 86111
Lincoln, NE 68501   Ph: (402)472-3522
Description: Explores the Seneca, one of the five Iroquois nations of New York state, and the events that occured in 1687 when the French invaded their village and destroyed it. Combines footage from the archaelogical dig, interviews, and museum artifacts. **Release Date:** 1986. **Length:** 28 mins. **Format:** VHS, 1" Broadcast Type "C", 3/4" U-matic Cassette.

★1922★
Geronimo: The Final Campaign
Centre Productions, Inc.
1800 30th St., Ste. 207   Ph: (303)444-1166
Boulder, CO 80301   Free: 800-824-1166
Description: This video takes a look at one of the most respected and well-known Indian warriors. **Release Date:** 1988. **Length:** 30 mins. **Format:** Beta, VHS, 3/4" U-matic Cassette.

★1923★
Geronimo Jones
Learning Corporation of America
108 Wilmot Rd.   Ph: (708)940-1260
Deerfield, IL 60015-9990   Free: 800-621-2131
Description: Perceptive study of the conflict which faces an Indian boy, torn between pride in his heritage and his future in modern American society. **Release Date:** 1970. **Length:** 21 mins. **Format:** Beta, VHS, 3/4" U-matic Cassette. **Credits:** Directed by: Bert Salzman.

★1924★
The Gift of Santa Fe
Native American Public Broadcasting
  Consortium
1800 N. 33rd St.
PO Box 86111
Lincoln, NE 68501   Ph: (402)472-3522
Description: A visit to the internationally reknowned Santa Fe Indian Market, a weekend-long display of Native American art, including pottery, jewelry, carvings, weavings, and paintings. Features the work of Lucy M. Lewis, a 90-year-old master potter. **Length:** 22 mins. **Format:** VHS, 1" Broadcast Type "C", 3/4" U-matic Cassette.

★1925★
Girl of the Navajos
Coronet/MTI Film & Video   Ph: (708)940-1260
108 Wilmot Rd.   Free: 800-621-2131
Deerfield, IL 60015   Fax: (708)940-3640
Description: The story of Nanabah, a Navajo girl, as she recalls her feelings of loneliness and fear the first time she had to herd her family's sheep into the canyon. **Release Date:** 1977. **Length:** 15 mins. **Format:** Beta, VHS, 3/4" U-matic Cassette, Other than listed.

★1926★
The Girl Who Loved Wild Horses
Random House Media
Department 467
400 Hahn Rd.
Westminster, MD 21157   Free: 800-492-0782
Description: A Plains Indian girl loves the horses that live near her tribe. A Paul Globe story. **Release Date:** 1985. **Length:** 9 mins. **Format:** VHS.

★1927★
The Good Mind
Native American Public Broadcasting
  Consortium
PO Box 86111
1800 N. 33rd St.
Lincoln, NE 68501   Ph: (402)472-3522
Description: A comparative essay on Christian and American Indian beliefs, and how the two have merged. **Release Date:** 1983. **Length:** 30 mins. **Format:** VHS, 3/4" U-matic Cassette, 1" Broadcast Type "C", 2" Quadraplex Open Reel.

★1928★
Great American Indian Heroes
Troll Associates
320 Rte. 17
Mahwah, NJ 07430   Ph: (201)529-4000
Description: A selection of brief profiles of eight different noted Indians. **Release Date:** 1988. **Length:** 82 mins. **Format:** VHS.

★1929★
The Great Movie Massacre
Video Tech
19346 3rd Ave. NW
Seattle, WA 98177   Ph: (206)546-5401
Description: The motion picture image of the Indian warrior is seen in clips from Robert Altman's "Buffalo Bill and the Indians," starring Paul Newman. From the "Images of Indians" series. **Release Date:** 1982. **Length:** 30 mins. **Format:** Beta, VHS, 3/4" U-matic Cassette, Other than listed. **Credits:** Narrated by: Will Sampson.

★1930★
Great Spirit Within the Hole
Intermedia Arts of Minnesota, Inc.
425 Ontario St. SE
Minneapolis, MN 55414   Ph: (612)627-4444
Description: This film looks at the occasional restriction of Indian religious leaders from giving spiritual aid to Indians in prison. **Release Date:** 1983. **Length:** 60 mins. **Format:** Beta, VHS, 3/4" U-matic Cassette.

★1931★
Had You Lived Then: Life in the Woodlands Before
  the White Man Came
AIMS Media
9710 De Soto Ave.
Chatsworth, CA 91311-9734   Free: 800-367-2467
     Fax: (818)341-6700
Description: Indians show how their ancestors lived before the white man came and how deer were important in the survival of the Indians. **Release Date:** 1976. **Length:** 12 mins. **Format:** Beta, VHS, 3/4" U-matic Cassette.

★1932★
Haudensaunee: Way of the Longhouse
New York State Education Department
Center for Learning Technologies
Media Distribution Network, Rm. C-7,
  Concourse Level
Albany, NY 12230   Ph: (518)474-1265
Description: A historical overview of the lifestyles and attitudes of the Haudenosaunee Iroquois tribe. **Release Date:** 1984. **Length:** 13 mins. **Format:** Beta, VHS, 1/2" Reel-EIAJ, 3/4" U-matic Cassette, 2" Quadraplex Open Reel.

★1933★
Health Care Crisis at Rosebud
Native American Public Broadcasting
  Consortium
PO Box 86111
1800 N. 33rd St.
Lincoln, NE 68501   Ph: (402)472-3522
Description: An exploration of the reasons behind the Rosebud Reservation's lack of physicians. **Release Date:** 1973. **Length:** 21

mins. **Format:** VHS, 3/4″ U-matic Cassette, 1″ Broadcast Type ″C″, 2″ Quadraplex Open Reel.

★1934★
Heart of the Earth Survival School/Circle of the Winds
Intermedia Arts of Minnesota, Inc.
425 Ontario St. SE
Minneapolis, MN 55414   Ph: (612)627-4444
Description: Two programs about the alternative schooling available to American Indians. **Release Date:** 1980. **Length:** 32 mins. **Format:** Beta, VHS, 3/4″ U-matic Cassette.

★1935★
Heathen Injuns and the Hollywood Gospel
Video Tech
19346 3rd Ave. NW
Seattle, WA 98177   Ph: (206)546-5401
Description: This program from the ″Images of Indians″ series looks at Hollywood's portrayal of Native American religion and values and the stereotyping of Indian women. **Release Date:** 1982. **Length:** 30 mins. **Format:** Beta, VHS, 3/4″ U-matic Cassette, Other than listed. **Credits:** Narrated by: Will Sampson.

★1936★
Heritage of Craftsmanship
Michigan Media
University of Michigan
400 4th St.
Ann Arbor, MI 48109   Ph: (313)764-8228
Description: A look at the role of Indian craftsmanship in Indian life, past and present. Part of the ″Silent Heritage″ series. **Release Date:** 1966. **Length:** 29 mins. **Format:** 3/4″ U-matic Cassette, Other than listed.

★1937★
Herman Red Elk: A Sioux Indian Artist
Native American Public Broadcasting
   Consortium
PO Box 86111
1800 N. 33rd St.
Lincoln, NE 68501   Ph: (402)472-3522
Description: A look at the work of this renowned traditional skin painter. **Release Date:** 1975. **Length:** 29 mins. **Format:** VHS, 3/4″ U-matic Cassette, 1″ Broadcast Type ″C″, 2″ Quadraplex Open Reel.

★1938★
Hisatsinom: The Ancient Ones
Native American Public Broadcasting
   Consortium
1800 N. 33rd St.
PO Box 86111
Lincoln, NE 68501   Ph: (402)472-3522
Description: Explores the culture of the Anasazi people of the Colorado and San Juan River valleys through story, song, dance, and ceremony. **Length:** 24 mins. **Format:** VHS, 1″ Broadcast Type ″C″, 3/4″ U-matic Cassette.

★1939★
The History and Problems of Winnebago Indians
NETCHE (Nebraska ETV Council for
   Higher Education)
Box 83111
Lincoln, NE 68501   Ph: (402)472-3611
Description: A native Winnebago describes the history and migration of the tribe and conditions on the Northeast Nebraska reservation in 1970. **Release Date:** 1970. **Length:** 30 mins. **Format:** 1/2″ Reel-EIAJ.

★1940★
Home of the Brave
Cinema Guild
1697 Broadway   Ph: (212)246-5522
New York, NY 10019   Fax: (212)246-5525
Description: An examination into the problems being faced by the native populations of North and South America. Of primary concern to the Indians is the increasing industrial development and pollution on their land. **Release Date:** 1984. **Length:** 53 mins. **Format:** Beta, VHS, 3/4″ U-matic Cassette.

★1941★
Honored by the Moon
Women Make Movies
225 Lafayette St., Ste. 206   Ph: (212)925-0606
New York, NY 10012   Fax: (212)925-2052
Description: An exploration of the special cultural prejudices faced by Native American lesbians and gays. **Release Date:** 1990. **Length:** 15 mins. **Format:** Beta, VHS, 3/4″ U-matic Cassette.

★1942★
The Honour of All
Native American Public Broadcasting
   Consortium
1800 N. 33rd St.
PO Box 86111
Lincoln, NE 68501   Ph: (402)472-3522
Description: Looks at the Alkali Lake Indian Band's struggle to overcome its problem with alcoholism and gives guidelines on how other communities can pull together to overcome alcoholism and drug abuse. Individual program titles: The Honour of All, Part I; The Honour of All, Part II; Sharing Innovations that Work. Tapes are available individually or as a series. **Release Date:** 1987. **Length:** 41 mins. **Format:** VHS, 1″ Broadcast Type ″C″, 3/4″ U-matic Cassette.

★1943★
Hopewell Heritage
Michigan Media
University of Michigan
400 4th St.
Ann Arbor, MI 48109   Ph: (313)764-8228
Description: This is a study of the excavation and recreation of the Hopewell Indian culture. **Release Date:** 1964. **Length:** 30 mins. **Format:** 3/4″ U-matic Cassette, Other than listed.

★1944★
The Hopi
Victorian Video Productions
PO Box 1540   Ph: (916)346-6184
Colfax, CA 95713-1540   Free: 800-848-0284
Description: A look at the everyday life of the members of this particular Indian tribe. **Release Date:** 1989. **Length:** 30 mins. **Format:** Beta, VHS.

★1945★
The Hopi Indian
Coronet/MTI Film & Video   Ph: (708)940-1260
108 Wilmot Rd.   Free: 800-621-2131
Deerfield, IL 60015   Fax: (708)940-3640
Description: The Hopi Indians hold most firmly to their traditional ways. This program shows them in daily routines and special celebrations. **Release Date:** 1975. **Length:** 11 mins. **Format:** Beta, VHS, 3/4″ U-matic Cassette, Other than listed.

★1946★
Hopi Indian Arts and Crafts
Coronet/MTI Film & Video   Ph: (708)940-1260
108 Wilmot Rd.   Free: 800-621-2131
Deerfield, IL 60015   Fax: (708)940-3640
Description: This program emphasizes Hopi skills and observes them weaving, making baskets, silversmithing, and making ceramics to sell in their cooperative store. **Release Date:** 1975. **Length:** 10 mins. **Format:** Beta, VHS, 3/4″ U-matic Cassette, Other than listed.

★1947★
Hopi Pottery
Norman Beerger Productions
3217 S. Arville St.
Las Vegas, NV 89102-7612   Ph: (702)876-2328
Description: How Hopi pottery relates to that Indian tribe's way of life is explained. **Release Date:** 1988. **Length:** 65 mins. **Format:** Beta, VHS.

★1948★
Hopi Prayer for Peace
Wishing Well Distributing   Ph: (414)864-2395
PO Box 2   Free: 800-888-9355
Wilmot, WI 53192   Fax: (414)862-2398
Description: Elders of the Hopi Nation repeat their appeal to the world for peace. **Release Date:** 1990. **Length:** 27 mins. **Format:** VHS.

★1949★
Hopi: Songs of the Fourth World
New Day Films
121 W. 27th St., Ste. 902   Ph: (212)645-8210
New York, NY 10001   Fax: (212)645-8652
Description: The life of the Hopi Indians as it remains today is implicit in their relationship with the environment. **Release Date:** 1985. **Length:** 58 mins. **Format:** Beta, VHS, 3/4″ U-matic Cassette, Other than listed.

★1950★
Hopiit
Intermedia Arts of Minnesota, Inc.
425 Ontario St. SE
Minneapolis, MN 55414   Ph: (612)627-4444
Description: A visually exciting look at the life of the Hopi Indian, which dispels many cliches about Native Americans. **Release Date:** 1982. **Length:** 15 mins. **Format:** Beta, VHS, 3/4″ U-matic Cassette.

★1951★
Hopis: Guardians of the Land
FilmFair Communications   Ph: (818)985-0244
10621 Magnolia Blvd.   Free: 800-423-2461
North Hollywood, CA 91601   Fax: (818)980-8492
Description: This program shows how the land of the Hopi Indians has been desecrated by men seeking coal and water from the soil. **Release Date:** 1971. **Length:** 10 mins. **Format:** Beta, VHS, 3/4″ U-matic Cassette.

★1952★
How Hollywood Wins the West
Video Tech
19346 3rd Ave. NW
Seattle, WA 98177   Ph: (206)546-5401
Description: Scenes from "Soldier Blue" and D.W. Griffith's "America" show how the film industry has only portrayed the colonization of the West from the white man's viewpoint. From the "Images of Indians" series. **Release Date:** 1982. **Length:** 30 mins. **Format:** Beta, VHS, 3/4″ U-matic Cassette, Other than listed. **Credits:** Narrated by: Will Sampson.

★1953★
How the West Was Lost
Cinema Guild
1697 Broadway   Ph: (212)246-5522
New York, NY 10019   Fax: (212)246-5525
Description: The way of life of the Plains Indians changed dramatically with the westward movement of the white man. This program highlights the prime of Plains Indian civilization and focuses upon the contemporary Indian effort to maintain a sense of their own identity. **Release Date:** 1976. **Length:** 26 mins. **Format:** 3/4″ U-matic Cassette, Other than listed.

★1954★
How the West Was Won...and Honor Lost
CRM/McGraw-Hill Films
674 Via de la Valle
PO Box 641
Del Mar, CA 92014
Description: The gradual defeat of the Indians by American settlers in the 1800s is charted in this program from the "North American Indian" series. **Release Date:** 1971. **Length:** 25 mins. **Format:** Beta, VHS, 3/4″ U-matic Cassette.

★1955★
Hupa Indian White Deerskin Dance
Barr Films
12801 Schabarum Ave.   Ph: (818)338-7878
PO Box 7878   Free: 800-234-7878
Irwindale, CA 91706-7878   Fax: (818)814-2672
Description: Records a dance of the Hupa Indians of Northwestern California, describing the artifacts used and the traditional dance pattern and song. **Release Date:** 1958. **Length:** 11 mins. **Format:** Beta, VHS, 3/4″ U-matic Cassette.

★1956★
I Am Different From My Brother: Dakota Name-Giving
Native American Public Broadcasting
   Consortium
PO Box 86111
1800 N. 33rd St.
Lincoln, NE 68501   Ph: (402)472-3522
Description: A documentary about the Name-Giving ceremony for three young Flandreau Dakota Sioux Indian children. **Release Date:** 1981. **Length:** 20 mins. **Format:** VHS, 3/4″ U-matic Cassette, 1″ Broadcast Type "C", 2″ Quadraplex Open Reel.

★1957★
I Will Fight No More Forever
New York State Education Department
Center for Learning Technologies
Media Distribution Network, Rm. C-7,
   Concourse Level
Albany, NY 12230   Ph: (518)474-1265
Description: The tragic saga of the Nez Perce Indians, who were forced from their reservations in the Pacific Northwest by white settlers, which led to war and ultimate decimation. **Release Date:** 1982. **Length:** 10 mins. **Format:** Beta, VHS, 3/4″ U-matic Cassette.

★1958★
Iisaw: Hopi Coyote Stories
Norman Ross Publishing Inc.   Ph: (212)765-8200
330 W. 58th St.   Free: 800-648-8850
New York, NY 10019   Fax: (212)765-2393
Description: These singing tales reinforce the Hopi ethic by describing what happens to those who shirk hard work (Hopi with English subtitles). **Release Date:** 1981. **Length:** 18 mins. **Format:** Beta, VHS, 3/4″ U-matic Cassette.

★1959★
Images of Indians
Video Tech
19346 3rd Ave. NW
Seattle, WA 98177   Ph: (206)546-5401
Description: A five-part series that traces the stereotypical Hollywood treatment of Indians through the years. Programs are available separately. **Release Date:** 1982. **Length:** 30 mins. **Format:** Beta, VHS, 3/4″ U-matic Cassette, Other than listed. **Credits:** Narrated by: Will Sampson.

★1960★
In Quest of a Vision
American Educational Films
3807 Dickerson Rd.
Nashville, TN 37207   Free: 800-822-5678
Description: The culture of the Great Basin Indians is shown within the framing story of a young tribesman's journey toward spiritual

fulfillment. **Release Date:** 1976. **Length:** 30 mins. **Format:** Beta, VHS, 3/4″ U-matic Cassette.

★1961★
In Search of the First Americans
Carolina Biological Supply Company
2700 York Rd.   Ph: (919)584-0381
Burlington, NC 27215   Free: 800-334-5551
Description: This program examines the early history of prehistoric man in North America. **Release Date:** 1988. **Length:** 28 mins. **Format:** Beta, VHS.

★1962★
In the White Man's Image
Native American Public Broadcasting
   Consortium
1800 N. 33rd St.
PO Box 86111
Lincoln, NE 68501   Ph: (402)472-3522
Description: Explores the cultural genocide that occured in the Carlisle School for Indian Students which impacted on generations of Native Americans. At the school, students were taught to read and write English, and were placed in uniforms and drilled like soldiers in order to "civilize" them. Includes interviews with former students. **Release Date:** 1991. **Length:** 51 mins. **Format:** VHS, 1″ Broadcast Type "C", 3/4 U-matic Cassette.

★1963★
Indian Artists of the Southwest
Britannica Films
310 S. Michigan Ave.   Ph: (312)347-7958
Chicago, IL 60604   Fax: (312)347-7966
Description: Three Pueblo Indian tribes (Zuni, Hopi, and Navajo) introduce four of their major art forms: stone and silverwork, pottery making, weaving, and kachina carving. **Release Date:** 1972. **Length:** 15 mins. **Format:** Beta, VHS, 3/4″ U-matic Cassette.

★1964★
Indian Arts at the Phoenix Heard Museum
Native American Public Broadcasting
   Consortium
PO Box 86111
1800 N. 33rd St.
Lincoln, NE 68501   Ph: (402)472-3522
Description: This is a survey of the Heard Museum's collection of southwestern Indian art. **Release Date:** 1975. **Length:** 28 mins. **Format:** VHS, 3/4″ U-matic Cassette, 1″ Broadcast Type "C", 2″ Quadraplex Open Reel.

★1965★
Indian Boy of the Southwest
Phoenix/BFA Films
468 Park Ave., S.   Ph: (212)684-5910
New York, NY 10016   Free: 800-221-1274
Description: Toboya, a Hopi Indian boy, tells us about his life and his home. **Release Date:** 1963. **Length:** 15 mins. **Format:** Beta, VHS, 3/4″ U-matic Cassette.

★1966★
Indian Country
Cinema Guild
1697 Broadway   Ph: (212)246-5522
New York, NY 10019   Fax: (212)246-5525
Description: This program offers a thorough survey of contemporary Indian life extending to the social, religious, and political aspects. **Release Date:** 1976. **Length:** 26 mins. **Format:** 3/4″ U-matic Cassette, Other than listed.

★1967★
Indian Country
PBS Video
1320 Braddock Pl.
Alexandria, VA 22314-1698   Ph: (703)739-5380
Description: An examination of life on the Quinault Indian Reservation in Washington which assesses the effectiveness of its

leader Joe De LaCruz. **Release Date:** 1988. **Length:** 60 mins. **Format:** Beta, VHS, 3/4″ U-matic Cassette.

★1968★
Indian Crafts: Hopi, Navajo, and Iroquois
Phoenix/BFA Films
468 Park Ave., S.   Ph: (212)684-5910
New York, NY 10016   Free: 800-221-1274
Description: The many diversified arts and crafts of these Indian cultures are demonstrated by their basket making, pottery making, kachina carving, weaving, jewelry making, and mask carving. **Release Date:** 1980. **Length:** 12 mins. **Format:** Beta, VHS, 3/4″ U-matic Cassette.

★1969★
Indian Family of Long Ago (Buffalo Hunters of the Plains)
Britannica Films
310 S. Michigan Ave.   Ph: (312)347-7958
Chicago, IL 60604   Fax: (312)347-7966
Description: This video presentation recreates the life of Plains Indians in the Dakotas and adjoining territories two hundred years ago. **Release Date:** 1957. **Length:** 14 mins. **Format:** Beta, VHS, 3/4″ U-matic Cassette.

★1970★
Indian Heroes of America
Atlantis Productions
1252 La Granada Dr.
Thousand Oaks, CA 91360   Ph: (805)495-2790
Description: This video presents biographical sketches of seven American Indian personalities whose lives paralleled 300 years of historic events from the coming of the white man to the final capitulation. **Release Date:** 197?. **Length:** 17 mins. **Format:** Beta, VHS, 3/4″ U-matic Cassette.

★1971★
Indian and His Homeland: American Images, 1590-1876
Finley-Holiday Film Corporation
PO Box 619
Dept. CS
Whittier, CA 90608   Free: 800-345-6707
                                 Fax: (213)693-4756
Description: Enhance your knowledge of the American Indian way of life, the way it was before the arrival of European civilization. Video is presented in a fascinating collage of paintings done by such artists as Catlin, Bodmer, Audubon, and Moran. **Release Date:** 1991. **Length:** 30 mins. **Format:** VHS.

★1972★
Indian Legacy
January Productions
210 6th Ave., Dept. VSF   Ph: (201)423-4666
PO Box 66   Free: 800-451-7450
Hawthorne, NJ 07507   Fax: (201)423-5569
Description: A series of five programs that will teach children about American Indians and their customs. **Release Date:** 1988. **Length:** 52 mins. **Format:** VHS.

★1973★
Indian Self-Rule
Documentary Educational Resources
101 Morse St.   Ph: (617)926-0491
Watertown, MA 02172   Fax: (617)926-9519
Description: This documentary traces the history of white-Indian relations from nineteenth century treaties through the present, as tribal leaders, historians, teachers, and other Indians gather at a 1983 conference organized to reevaluate the significance of the Indian/Reorganization Act of 1934. **Release Date:** 1986. **Length:** 58 mins. **Format:** 3/4″ U-matic Cassette.

★1974★
An Indian Summer
Atlantis Productions
1252 La Granada Dr.
Thousand Oaks, CA 91360 Ph: (805)495-2790
Description: A summer experience with Chippewa Indian children on a woodland reservation and their relationship to animals and to the environment are shown. **Release Date:** 1975. **Length:** 11 mins. **Format:** Beta, VHS, 3/4″ U-matic Cassette.

★1975★
The Indian Way
New York State Education Department
Center for Learning Technologies
Media Distribution Network, Rm. C-7,
   Concourse Level
Albany, NY 12230 Ph: (518)474-1265
Description: This program looks at how traditional Indian values clash with modern times. **Release Date:** 196?. **Length:** 30 mins. **Format:** Beta, VHS, 1/2″ Reel-EIAJ, 3/4″ U-matic Cassette, 2″ Quadraplex Open Reel.

★1976★
The Indians
Center for Humanities, Inc.
Communications Park
Box 1000 Ph: (914)666-4100
Mount Kisco, NY 10549 Free: 800-431-1242
Description: This film is a portrait of Indian life and culture in Colorado before, during, and after the white settlers came. **Release Date:** 1970. **Length:** 31 mins. **Format:** Beta, VHS, 3/4″ U-matic Cassette.

★1977★
Indians Americans
Michigan Media
University of Michigan
400 4th St.
Ann Arbor, MI 48109 Ph: (313)764-8228
Description: This video examines two extremes of American Indian life–racial and cultural extinction in the East and cultural preservation on reservations in the West. Part of the "Silent Heritage" series. **Release Date:** 1966. **Length:** 29 mins. **Format:** 3/4″ U-matic Cassette, Other than listed.

★1978★
Indians in the Americas (Revised)
Phoenix/BFA Films
468 Park Ave., S. Ph: (212)684-5910
New York, NY 10016 Free: 800-221-1274
Description: This updated program follows America's valuable Indian heritage, from early Indian cultures to modern ones in both North and South America. **Release Date:** 1985. **Length:** 22 mins. **Format:** Beta, VHS, 3/4″ U-matic Cassette.

★1979★
Indians of California: Part 1, Village Life
Barr Films
12801 Schabarum Ave. Ph: (818)338-7878
PO Box 7878 Free: 800-234-7878
Irwindale, CA 91706-7878 Fax: (818)814-2672
Description: This program describes life in a primitive Indian village, including trading, house building, basket making, and songs and dances. **Release Date:** 1964. **Length:** 15 mins. **Format:** Beta, VHS, 3/4″ U-matic Cassette.

★1980★
Indians of California: Part 2, Food
Barr Films
12801 Schabarum Ave. Ph: (818)338-7878
PO Box 7878 Free: 800-234-7878
Irwindale, CA 91706-7878 Fax: (818)814-2672
Description: This program describes how primitive Indians obtained their food. Includes bow and arrow making, deer hunting, and

gathering and preparing acorns. **Release Date:** 1964. **Length:** 14 mins. **Format:** Beta, VHS, 3/4″ U-matic Cassette.

★1981★
Indians of Early America
Britannica Films
310 S. Michigan Ave. Ph: (312)347-7958
Chicago, IL 60604 Fax: (312)347-7966
Description: This film recreates activities of representative early North American Indian Tribes, including Iroquois, Sioux, and Pueblo. **Release Date:** 1957. **Length:** 22 mins. **Format:** Beta, VHS, 3/4″ U-matic Cassette.

★1982★
Iowa's Ancient Hunters
University of Iowa
Audiovisual Center
C-215 Seashore Hall
Iowa City, IA 52242 Ph: (319)335-2539
Description: This documentary shows the location and excavation of the Cherokee Dig, where remnants of three prehistoric societies have been found in northwest Iowa. **Release Date:** 1978. **Length:** 28 mins. **Format:** 3/4″ U-matic Cassette.

★1983★
The Iroquois
Michigan Media
University of Michigan
400 4th St.
Ann Arbor, MI 48109 Ph: (313)764-8228
Description: The story of the Iroquois Indian. With great pride in their unique heritage, the Iroquois Indians of New York State plan for their future despite loss of lands promised to them. Part of the "Silent Heritage" series. **Release Date:** 1966. **Length:** 29 mins. **Format:** 3/4″ U-matic Cassette, Other than listed.

★1984★
Iroquois Social Dance I & II
Green Mountain Cine Works, Inc.
53 Hamilton Ave.
Staten Island, NY 10301 Ph: (718)981-0120
Description: Two programs, available individually, presenting social dances of the Mohawk Indians. Part I is about the dances in general; Part II illustrates the techniques. **Release Date:** 1980. **Length:** 18 mins. **Format:** Beta, 3/4″ U-matic Cassette.

★1985★
Ishi, The Ending People
Centre Productions, Inc.
1800 30th St., Ste. 207 Ph: (303)444-1166
Boulder, CO 80301 Free: 800-824-1166
Description: This film is based on the true story of the Yahi people of Northern California. It centers around a young Yahi named Ishi who came out of hiding in 1911 to tell the story of his ancient tribe. **Release Date:** 1983. **Length:** 15 mins. **Format:** Beta, VHS, 3/4″ U-matic Cassette.

★1986★
Itam Hakim Hopiit (We Someone, The Hopi)
American Federation of Arts
41 E. 65th St. Ph: (212)988-7700
New York, NY 10021 Fax: (212)861-2487
Description: A realistic/surrealistic visualization of Hopi philosophy and prophesy. **Release Date:** 1984. **Length:** 60 mins. **Format:** Beta, VHS, 3/4″ U-matic Cassette.

★1987★
Joe KillsRight: Oglala Sioux
Downtown Community TV Center
87 Lafayette St.
New York, NY 10013 Ph: (212)966-4510
Description: A profile of Joe KillsRight, an Oglala Sioux who came to New York City to find work and found a hostile urban environment much different from the reservation. **Release Date:** 1980. **Length:**

25 mins. **Format:** 1/2″ Reel-EIAJ, 3/4″ U-matic Cassette, Other than listed.

★1988★
Journey to the Sky: A History of the Alabama Coushatta Indians

Native American Public Broadcasting
Consortium
PO Box 86111
1800 N. 33rd St.
Lincoln, NE 68501   Ph: (402)472-3522

Description: Chief Fulton Battise tells a campfire tale of his tribe, metaphorically recounting the history of his tribe and its first meeting with white men. **Release Date:** 1980. **Length:** 53 mins. **Format:** VHS, 3/4″ U-matic Cassette, 1″ Broadcast Type ″C″, 2″ Quadraplex Open Reel.

★1989★
Kashia Men's Dances: Southwestern Pomo Indians

University of California at Berkeley
Extension Media Center
2176 Shattuck Ave.
Berkeley, CA 94704   Ph: (510)642-0460

Description: This program preserves four authentic Pomo dances as performed, in elaborate costumes and headdresses, on the Kashia Reservation on the northern California coast. **Release Date:** 1963. **Length:** 40 mins. **Format:** 3/4″ U-matic Cassette, Other than listed.

★1990★
Keep Your Heart Strong

Native American Public Broadcasting
Consortium
1800 N. 33rd St.
PO Box 86111
Lincoln, NE 68501   Ph: (402)472-3522

Description: Explores contemporary Native American culture through the Pow Wow. Explains why traditional values are important to today's culture. **Release Date:** 1986. **Length:** 58 mins. **Format:** VHS, 1″ Broadcast Type ″C″, 3/4 U-matic Cassette.

★1991★
Keeper of the Western Door

New York State Education Department
Center for Learning Technologies
Media Distribution Network, Rm. C-7,
Concourse Level
Albany, NY 12230   Ph: (518)474-1265

Description: Various aspects of the tradition and culture of the Seneca Nations of Indians are examined in this series. **Release Date:** 198?. **Length:** 15 mins. **Format:** Beta, VHS, 1/2″ Reel-EIAJ, 3/4″ U-matic Cassette, 2″ Quadraplex Open Reel.

★1992★
Kevin Alec

The Media Guild
11722 Sorrento Valley Rd., Ste. E   Ph: (619)755-9191
San Diego, CA 92121   Fax: (619)755-4931

Description: Examines the life of an eleven-year-old boy who lives on the Fountain Indian Reserve with his grandmother. From the ″Who Are You″ series. **Release Date:** 1978. **Length:** 17 mins. **Format:** Beta, VHS, 3/4″ U-matic Cassette.

★1993★
Kiliwa: Hunters and Gatherers of Baja California

University of California at Berkeley
Extension Media Center
2176 Shattuck Ave.
Berkeley, CA 94704   Ph: (510)642-0460

Description: This program documents aspects of hunting and gathering, food preparation, and shelter construction by a group of Baja California Indians. **Release Date:** 1975. **Length:** 14 mins. **Format:** 3/4″ U-matic Cassette, Other than listed.

★1994★
Lakota Quillwork: Art & Legend

One West Media
PO Box 5766
559 Onate Pl.
Sante Fe, NM 87501   Ph: (505)983-8685

Description: Lakota Indian women demonstrate their intricate craft with porcupine quills. **Release Date:** 1986. **Length:** 28 mins. **Format:** VHS, 3/4″ U-matic Cassette.

★1995★
Lament of the Reservation

CRM/McGraw-Hill Films
674 Via de la Valle
PO Box 641
Del Mar, CA 92014

Description: A record of life on an open Indian reservation, showing the sacrifices that must be made by the natives in order to remain a true Indian. Part of the ″North American Indian″ series. **Release Date:** 1971. **Length:** 24 mins. **Format:** Beta, VHS, 3/4″ U-matic Cassette.

★1996★
The Last of the Caddoes

Phoenix/BFA Films
468 Park Ave., S.   Ph: (212)684-5910
New York, NY 10016   Free: 800-221-1274

Description: Set in rural Texas in the 1930s, this program follows a young boy through a summer of self-discovery as he learns about his part-Indian heritage. **Release Date:** 1982. **Length:** 29 mins. **Format:** Beta, VHS, 3/4″ U-matic Cassette.

★1997★
Last Chance for the Navajo

CRM/McGraw-Hill Films
674 Via de la Valle
PO Box 641
Del Mar, CA 92014

Description: The problems faced by Navajo Indians today are spelled out, including economic, employment and cultural difficulties. **Release Date:** 1978. **Length:** 27 mins. **Format:** Beta, VHS, 3/4″ U-matic Cassette.

★1998★
Legacy in Limbo

Native American Public Broadcasting
Consortium
1800 N. 33rd St.
PO Box 86111
Lincoln, NE 68501   Ph: (402)472-3522

Description: Discusses the plight of the Museum of the American Indian in New York City. Because of it's small size, only a fraction of the artifacts can be displayed in the museum. The remainder sit in a Bronx warehouse. Although the museum is willing to move, politicians are blocking this step. **Release Date:** 1990. **Length:** 60 mins. **Format:** VHS, 1″ Broadcast Type ″C″, 3/4″ U-matic cassette.

★1999★
The Legend of the Boy and the Eagle

Coronet/MTI Film & Video   Ph: (708)940-1260
108 Wilmot Rd.   Free: 800-621-2131
Deerfield, IL 60015   Fax: (708)940-3640

Description: A Hopi Indian boy is caught between his love for the sacred eagle of the tribe and the conflicting values of group and individual. **Release Date:** 1990. **Length:** 21 mins. **Format:** Beta, VHS, 1/2″ Reel-EIAJ, 3/4″ U-matic Cassette, Other than listed.

★2000★
Legend Days Are Over
Pyramid Film & Video
Box 1048
2801 Colorado Ave.
Santa Monica, CA 90406

Ph: (310)828-7577
Free: 800-421-2304
Fax: (310)453-9083

Description: An elegy evoking the American Indian experience. **Release Date:** 1973. **Length:** 5 mins. **Format:** Beta, VHS, 3/4″ U-matic Cassette.

★2001★
Letter from an Apache
Pictures of Record
119 Kettle Creek Rd.
Weston, CT 06883

Ph: (203)227-3387

Description: The life of Dr. Carlos Montezuma, an Apache, and people as he remembers them, rendered in the style of 19th century Indian paintings. **Release Date:** 1983. **Length:** 12 mins. **Format:** VHS, 3/4″ U-matic Cassette. **Credits:** Narrated by: Fred Hellerman.

★2002★
Live and Remember
Centre Productions, Inc.
1800 30th St., Ste. 207
Boulder, CO 80301

Ph: (303)444-1166
Free: 800-824-1166

Description: This documentary captures the hardships and contradictions that modern Indians live with. **Release Date:** 1987. **Length:** 29 mins. **Format:** Beta, VHS, 3/4″ U-matic Cassette.

★2003★
Long Lance
National Film Board of Canada
1251 Avenue of the Americas, 16th Fl.
New York, NY 10020-1173

Ph: (212)586-5131

Description: Based on a true story, this film explores the mysterious origins of Chief Buffalo Child Long Lance. **Release Date:** 1987. **Length:** 55 mins. **Format:** Beta, VHS, 3/4″ U-matic Cassette.

★2004★
The Longest Trail
University of California at Berkeley
  Extension Media Center
2176 Shattuck Ave.
Berkeley, CA 94704

Ph: (510)642-0460

Description: View a Native American celebration in which a dance commemorates the crossing of the Bering Straits. **Release Date:** 1986. **Length:** 58 mins. **Format:** VHS, 3/4″ U-matic Cassette.

★2005★
The Longhouse People
National Film Board of Canada
1251 Avenue of the Americas, 16th Fl.
New York, NY 10020-1173

Ph: (212)586-5131

Description: Deals with the life and religion of the Iroquois Indians, showing a rain dance, a healing ceremony, and the celebration in honor of a newly chosen chief. **Release Date:** 1951. **Length:** 24 mins. **Format:** Beta, VHS, 3/4″ U-matic Cassette.

★2006★
Look What We've Done to This Land
Blue Sky Productions
PO Box 548
Santa Fe, NM 87501

Ph: (505)988-2995

Description: Questions pertinent issues of energy consumption and strip-mining in the West. Covers the effects of mining operations on Navajo and Hopi Indians. **Release Date:** 1973. **Length:** 22 mins. **Format:** 3/4″ U-matic Cassette, Other than listed.

★2007★
Loving Rebel
Centre Productions, Inc.
1800 30th St., Ste. 207
Boulder, CO 80301

Ph: (303)444-1166
Free: 800-824-1166

Description: This documentary profiles Helen Hunt Jackson, one of the nineteenth century's foremost advocates of Native American rights. This video features readings from Jackson's poems, novels, essays and other writings as well as rare photographs and drawings of the writer's world. **Release Date:** 1987. **Length:** 25 mins. **Format:** Beta, VHS, 3/4″ U-matic Cassette.

★2008★
Lucy Covington: Native American Indian
Britannica Films
310 S. Michigan Ave.
Chicago, IL 60604

Ph: (312)347-7958
Fax: (312)347-7966

Description: Lucy Covington, an active leader and spokesperson for the Colville Indians, retells the history of her people as it has been handed down through oral tradition. **Release Date:** 1979. **Length:** 16 mins. **Format:** Beta, VHS, 3/4″ U-matic Cassette.

★2009★
Man Belongs to the Earth
National AudioVisual Center
National Archives & Records
  Administration
Customer Services Section PZ
8700 Edgeworth Dr.
Capitol Heights, MD 20743-3701

Ph: (301)763-1896

Description: This program features Chief Dan George who offers profound insight into the native American view of nature. **Release Date:** 1974. **Length:** 22 mins. **Format:** Beta, VHS, 3/4″ U-matic Cassette, Other than listed. **Credits:** Narrated by: James Whitmore.

★2010★
Man of Lightning
Native American Public Broadcasting
  Consortium
PO Box 86111
1800 N. 33rd St.
Lincoln, NE 68501

Ph: (402)472-3522

Description: Two Cherokee folktales that delineate the nature of Indian culture before European influence are enacted. **Release Date:** 1982. **Length:** 29 mins. **Format:** VHS, 3/4″ U-matic Cassette, 1″ Broadcast Type ″C″, 2″ Quadraplex Open Reel.

★2011★
Maria! Indian Pottery of San Ildefonso
Arts America, Inc.
12 Havermeyer Pl.
Greenwich, CT 06830

Ph: (203)637-1454

Description: Noted Indian pottery maker Maria Martinez demonstrates traditional Indian ways, beginning with the spreading of sacred corn before the clay is gathered. Clay mixing, pottery construction, hand decorating, and building of the firing mound are also viewed. **Release Date:** 1972. **Length:** 27 mins. **Format:** Beta, VHS, 3/4″ U-matic Cassette, Other than listed.

★2012★
Maria of the Pueblos
Centron Films
108 Wilmot Rd.
Deerfield, IL 60015-9990

Ph: (312)940-1260
Free: 800-621-2131

Description: This video traces the life of Maria Martinez, the world's most famous and successful Indian potter, while giving an understanding of the culture, philosophy, art, and economic conditions of the Pueblo Indians. **Release Date:** 1971. **Length:** 15 mins. **Format:** Beta, VHS, 3/4″ U-matic Cassette.

★2013★

Meet the Sioux Indian
International Film Bureau, Inc. (IFB)
332 S. Michigan Ave.
Chicago, IL 60604-4382   Ph: (312)427-4545

Description: This video shows how the Sioux Indians adapted to their environment and found food, shelter, and clothing on the Western plains. Worldwide distribution rights. **Release Date:** 1956. **Length:** 11 mins. **Format:** Beta, VHS, 3/4″ U-matic Cassette, Other than listed.

★2014★

Menominee
Native American Public Broadcasting
  Consortium
PO Box 86111
1800 N. 33rd St.
Lincoln, NE 68501   Ph: (402)472-3522

Description: The trials and current plight of the Menominee Indians of northwestern Wisconsin are related in this study. **Release Date:** 1974. **Length:** 59 mins. **Format:** VHS, 3/4″ U-matic Cassette, 1″ Broadcast Type ″C″, 2″ Quadraplex Open Reel.

★2015★

A Message from Native America
Lionel Television Productions
66 1/2 Windward
Venice, CA 90291

Description: This is a recitation of Hopi and other prophecies which declare that we can have peace and joy if we return to the way of the creator, but if we continue on our present course, disaster will be the inevitable outcome. **Release Date:** 1982. **Length:** 14 mins. **Format:** Beta, VHS, 3/4″ U-matic Cassette.

★2016★

The Metis
CRM/McGraw-Hill Films
674 Via de la Valle
PO Box 641
Del Mar, CA 92014

Description: This is the story of the Metis people of North America, who trace their ancestry to both Indian and European roots in the seventeenth century. **Release Date:** 1978. **Length:** 27 mins. **Format:** Beta, VHS, 3/4″ U-matic Cassette.

★2017★

Minorities in Agriculture: The Winnebago
Native American Public Broadcasting
  Consortium
PO Box 86111
1800 N. 33rd St.
Lincoln, NE 68501   Ph: (402)472-3522

Description: A retrospective look at the Winnebago Indians of Nebraska, their heritage and modern troubles. **Release Date:** 1984. **Length:** 29 mins. **Format:** VHS, 3/4″ U-matic Cassette, 1″ Broadcast Type ″C″, 2″ Quadraplex Open Reel.

★2018★

Minority Youth: Adam
Phoenix/BFA Films
468 Park Ave., S.   Ph: (212)684-5910
New York, NY 10016   Free: 800-221-1274

Description: Adam is an American Indian. In the show, he speaks candidly about his cultural heritage and his place in today's society. **Release Date:** 1971. **Length:** 10 mins. **Format:** Beta, VHS, 3/4″ U-matic Cassette.

★2019★

Miss Indian America
Native American Public Broadcasting
  Consortium
PO Box 86111
1800 N. 33rd St.
Lincoln, NE 68501   Ph: (402)472-3522

Description: This is a filmed record of the 1973 Miss Indian America pageant held in Sheridan, Wyoming. **Release Date:** 1973. **Length:** 59 mins. **Format:** VHS, 3/4″ U-matic Cassette, 1″ Broadcast Type ″C″, 2″ Quadraplex Open Reel.

★2020★

Mistress Madeleine
National Film Board of Canada
1251 Avenue of the Americas, 16th Fl.
New York, NY 10020-1173   Ph: (212)586-5131

Description: This drama focuses on a half-Native American woman during the mid-nineteenth century, whose life is nearly ruined by prejudice. **Release Date:** 1987. **Length:** 57 mins. **Format:** Beta, VHS, 3/4″ U-matic Cassette.

★2021★

Monument Valley: Navajo Homeland
Finley-Holiday Film Corporation
PO Box 619
Dept. CS
Whittier, CA 90608   Free: 800-345-6707
                           Fax: (213)693-4756

Description: Witness the majestic, beautiful lands of Monument Valley and learn the reasons for the Navajo bond with this, their homeland. Rare footage of Navajo customs and spiritual practices make this video a unique reference to the true identity of the Navajo Indian. **Release Date:** 1991. **Length:** 30 mins. **Format:** VHS.

★2022★

Moon Drum
Island Visual Arts
8920 Sunset Blvd., 2nd Fl.   Ph: (213)288-5382
Los Angeles, CA 90069   Fax: (213)276-5476

Description: John Whitney uses computer graphics to present Native American art and music, including the Pueblo, Hopi, Oglala Sioux, Plains, and Pacific Northwest tribes. **Release Date:** 19??. **Length:** 60 mins. **Format:** VHS.

★2023★

More Than Bows and Arrows
Video Tech
19346 3rd Ave. NW
Seattle, WA 98177   Ph: (206)546-5401

Description: A coast-to-coast look at the technology being used by Indians, Eskimos, and Aleuts. **Release Date:** 1978. **Length:** 56 mins. **Format:** Beta, VHS, 3/4″ U-matic Cassette, Other than listed.

★2024★

Mother Corn
Native American Public Broadcasting
  Consortium
PO Box 86111
1800 N. 33rd St.
Lincoln, NE 68501   Ph: (402)472-3522

Description: The historical and religious role that corn plays in Hopi and Pueblo life is portrayed. **Release Date:** 1977. **Length:** 29 mins. **Format:** VHS, 3/4″ U-matic Cassette, 1″ Broadcast Type ″C″, 2″ Quadraplex Open Reel.

★2025★

Mother of Many Children
National Film Board of Canada
1251 Avenue of the Americas, 16th Fl.
New York, NY 10020-1173   Ph: (212)586-5131

Description: A collection and story of womanhood as expressed through the lives of Agatha Marie Goudine, a 108-year-old woman of the Hobbema Indian tribe, and young Elizabeth and Sarah. **Release**

Date: 1980. **Length:** 58 mins. **Format:** Beta, VHS, 3/4″ U-matic Cassette.

★2026★
Mountain Wolf Woman
Her Own Words Productions
PO Box 5264
Madison, WI 53705   Ph: (608)271-7083

Description: Narrated by her granddaughter, Mountain Wolf Woman's story is presented in her own words. Technically excellent, with some beautiful photographs, this film presents bits and pieces of a fascinating life. **Release Date:** 1990. **Length:** 17 mins. **Format:** VHS.

★2027★
The Movie Reel Indians
Video Tech
19346 3rd Ave. NW
Seattle, WA 98177   Ph: (206)546-5401

Description: Several examples of stereotypical portrayals of American Indians in Hollywood films are shown in this final program from the ''Images of Indians'' series. **Release Date:** 1982. **Length:** 30 mins. **Format:** Beta, VHS, 3/4″ U-matic Cassette, Other than listed. **Credits:** Narrated by: Will Sampson.

★2028★
The Music of the Devil, the Bear and the Condor
Cinema Guild
1697 Broadway   Ph: (212)246-5522
New York, NY 10019   Fax: (212)246-5525

Description: The sacred and magical ceremonies of the Aymara Indians are the focus of this documentary. **Release Date:** 1989. **Length:** 52 mins. **Format:** Beta, VHS, 3/4″ U-matic Cassette.

★2029★
The Mystery of the Anasazi
Time-Life Video and Television
1450 E. Parham Rd.   Ph: (804)266-6330
Richmond, VA 23280   Free: 800-621-7026

Description: This film documents the attempts of archeologists in the southwestern United States to determine who the Anasazi were and where they came from. **Release Date:** 1976. **Length:** 59 mins. **Format:** Beta, VHS, 3/4″ U-matic Cassette, Other than listed.

★2030★
The Mystery of the Lost Red Paint People: The Discovery of a Prehistoric North American Sea Culture
Bullfrog Films, Inc.   Ph: (215)779-8226
PO Box 149   Free: 800-543-3764
Oley, PA 19547   Fax: (215)370-1978

Description: An expedition revealing archaeological discoveries around the periphery of the North Atlantic. **Release Date:** 1987. **Length:** 57 mins. **Format:** Beta, VHS, 3/4″ U-matic Cassette.

★2031★
Nations Within a Nation
Native American Public Broadcasting
   Consortium
1800 N. 33rd St.
PO Box 86111
Lincoln, NE 68501   Ph: (402)472-3522

Description: Examines the historical, legal, and social issues of sovereignty for tribal governments. **Length:** 59 mins. **Format:** VHS, 1″ Broadcast Type ''C'', 3/4″ U-matic Cassette.

★2032★
Native America Speaks
Lionel Television Productions
66 1/2 Windward
Venice, CA 90291

Description: Peace pipe symbolism, the religious ceremony of the sweat lodge, and the spiritual significance of group dancing are featured in segments taken from the 1979 World Symposium on Humanity, illustrating Native American culture. **Release Date:** 1980. **Length:** 25 mins. **Format:** Beta, VHS, 3/4″ U-matic Cassette.

★2033★
Native American Art—Lost and Found
American Federation of Arts
41 E. 65th St.   Ph: (212)988-7700
New York, NY 10021   Fax: (212)861-2487

Description: Fourteen American Indian artists, working in various mediums including wood carving and pottery, display their work and talk about the personal and historical meanings of such handicrafts. **Release Date:** 1986. **Length:** 22 mins. **Format:** Beta, VHS, 3/4″ U-matic Cassette.

★2034★
Native American Catholics: People of the Spirit
Franciscan Communications
1229 S. Santee St.   Ph: (213)746-2916
Los Angeles, CA 90015   Free: 800-421-8510

Description: A look at the ways that converted Indians show their faith in God. **Release Date:** 1987. **Length:** 28 mins. **Format:** Beta, VHS, 3/4″ U-matic Cassette.

★2035★
Native American Images
Native American Public Broadcasting
   Consortium
PO Box 86111
1800 N. 33rd St.
Lincoln, NE 68501   Ph: (402)472-3522

Description: This is a profile of three Austin-based Native American artists: Paladine H. Roye, Donald Vann, and Steve Forbes. **Release Date:** 1984. **Length:** 29 mins. **Format:** VHS, 3/4″ U-matic Cassette, 1″ Broadcast Type ''C'', 2″ Quadraplex Open Reel.

★2036★
Native American Indian Artist Series
Arts America, Inc.
12 Havermeyer Pl.
Greenwich, CT 06830   Ph: (203)637-1454

Description: A series on Native American Artists and their art including jewelry, prints, paintings and pottery. **Release Date:** 1990. **Length:** 29 mins. **Format:** VHS.

★2037★
Native American Prophecy & Ceremony
Wishing Well Distributing   Ph: (414)864-2395
PO Box 2   Free: 800-888-9355
Wilmot, WI 53192   Fax: (414)862-2398

Description: A look at the customs of the peace pipe, ritual dancing, and the sweat lodge, combined with Native American warnings concerning the future. **Release Date:** 1990. **Length:** 25 mins. **Format:** VHS.

★2038★
Native American Series
Journal Films, Inc.   Ph: (708)328-6700
930 Pitner Ave.   Free: 800-323-5448
Evanston, IL 60202   Fax: (708)328-6706

Description: This program series is based on geological, archeological, and historical evidence and will help young people understand the origin, diversity, and life-style of the American Indian. Programs are available individually. **Release Date:** 1976. **Length:** 18 mins. **Format:** Beta, VHS, 3/4″ U-matic Cassette.

★2039★
Native American Sweat Lodge Ceremony
Wishing Well Distributing   Ph: (414)864-2395
PO Box 2   Free: 800-888-9355
Wilmot, WI 53192   Fax: (414)862-2398

Description: An introduction to the physical and spiritual benefits of this centuries-old Native American custom. **Release Date:** 1990. **Length:** 90 mins. **Format:** VHS.

★2040★
The Native Americans
Cinema Guild
1697 Broadway
Ph: (212)246-5522
New York, NY 10019
Fax: (212)246-5525
Description: This series explores the reasons behind the white man's seizure of Indian land from colonial times to the present, shows why the Indian is our country's most underprivileged ethnic group, and highlights the Indians' current attempts to take their rightful place in our democracy. Programs are available individually. **Release Date:** 1981. **Length:** 26 mins. **Format:** 3/4″ U-matic Cassette, Other than listed.

★2041★
The Native Land
Atlantis Productions
1252 La Granada Dr.
Thousand Oaks, CA 91360
Ph: (805)495-2790
Description: This is an insight into Indian life and thoughts about land and heritage, told from the Indian's point of view. **Release Date:** 1976. **Length:** 17 mins. **Format:** Beta, VHS, 3/4″ U-matic Cassette.

★2042★
Native Land
Cinema Guild
1697 Broadway
Ph: (212)246-5522
New York, NY 10019
Fax: (212)246-5525
Description: The history of the native North and South Americans is traced with emphasis on the role mythology has played within their cultures. **Release Date:** 1986. **Length:** 58 mins. **Format:** Beta, VHS, 3/4″ U-matic Cassette. **Credits:** Hosted by: Jamake Highwater.

★2043★
Native Self Reliance
Bullfrog Films, Inc.
Ph: (215)779-8226
PO Box 149
Free: 800-543-3764
Oley, PA 19547
Fax: (215)370-1978
Description: A study of solar technology projects developed by six American Indians. **Release Date:** 1980. **Length:** 20 mins. **Format:** Beta, VHS, 3/4″ U-matic Cassette.

★2044★
Natwaniwa: A Hopi Philosophical Statement
Norman Ross Publishing Inc.
Ph: (212)765-8200
330 W. 58th St.
Free: 800-648-8850
New York, NY 10019
Fax: (212)765-2393
Description: What the Hopi does in his field is a rehearsal for his future life, as shown in this program (Hopi with English subtitles). **Release Date:** 1981. **Length:** 27 mins. **Format:** Beta, VHS, 3/4″ U-matic Cassette.

★2045★
The Navajo
Victorian Video Productions
PO Box 1540
Ph: (916)346-6184
Colfax, CA 95713-1540
Free: 800-848-0284
Description: Spokesmen for the largest and one of the wealthiest tribes in the United States discuss the problems of preserving their culture in the advancing modern world. Part of the "Silent Heritage" series. **Release Date:** 1966. **Length:** 29 mins. **Format:** VHS, 3/4″ U-matic Cassette, Other than listed.

★2046★
The Navajo
Centre Productions, Inc.
1800 30th St., Ste. 207
Ph: (303)444-1166
Boulder, CO 80301
Free: 800-824-1166
Description: This program brings to light the fascinating blend of ancient Navajo culture with modern ideas about education and medicine that exists today within the tribe. **Release Date:** 1983. **Length:** 11 mins. **Format:** Beta, VHS, 3/4″ U-matic Cassette.

★2047★
Navajo
Native American Public Broadcasting
  Consortium
1800 N. 33rd St.
PO Box 86111
Lincoln, NE 68501
Ph: (402)472-3522
Description: Two children leave their modern lifestyle to spend time with their grandparents on a Navajo Reservation. There they learn about Navajo traditions, including the matriarchal society and the desire to live in peace with the earth. **Release Date:** 1979. **Length:** 29 mins. **Format:** VHS, 1″ Broadcast Type "C", 3/4″ U-amtic Cassette.

★2048★
Navajo: A Study in Cultural Contrast
Journal Films, Inc.
Ph: (708)328-6700
930 Pitner Ave.
Free: 800-323-5448
Evanston, IL 60202
Fax: (708)328-6706
Description: This program journeys to the southwestern desert region, the home of the Navajo. It views the environment, family structure, traditions, ceremonies, and art forms of people untouched by modern civilization. **Release Date:** 1968. **Length:** 15 mins. **Format:** Beta, VHS, 3/4″ U-matic Cassette.

★2049★
Navajo Code Talkers
One West Media
PO Box 5766
559 Onate Pl.
Sante Fe, NM 87501
Ph: (505)983-8685
Description: This video examines the contributions of Navajo cryptographers in World War II. **Release Date:** 1986. **Length:** 27 mins. **Format:** VHS, 3/4″ U-matic Cassette.

★2050★
Navajo Country
International Film Bureau, Inc. (IFB)
332 S. Michigan Ave.
Chicago, IL 60604-4382
Ph: (312)427-4545
Description: The creativity of the nomadic Navajos is presented. **Release Date:** 1983. **Length:** 10 mins. **Format:** Beta, VHS, 3/4″ U-matic Cassette, Other than listed.

★2051★
The Navajo Film Themselves
Museum of Modern Art, Circulating Film
  Library
11 W. 53rd St.
New York, NY 10019
Ph: (212)708-9530
Description: Navajo weaving and silversmithing are featured in this silent film. **Release Date:** 1966. **Length:** 18 mins. **Format:** VHS, Other than listed.

★2052★
Navajo Girl
Center for Humanities, Inc.
Communications Park
Box 1000
Ph: (914)666-4100
Mount Kisco, NY 10549
Free: 800-431-1242
Description: Daily life on an Indian reservation is depicted in this story about 10-year-old Kathy Begay and her Navajo family. **Release Date:** 1973. **Length:** 21 mins. **Format:** Beta, VHS, 3/4″ U-matic Cassette.

★2053★
Navajo Health Care Practices
University of Arizona
Biomedical Communications
Tucson, AZ 85724
Ph: (602)626-7343
Description: This program explores the traditions and healing practices of a Navajo family. **Release Date:** 1977. **Length:** 40 mins. **Format:** 3/4″ U-matic Cassette, Other than listed.

★2054★
The Navajo Indian
Coronet/MTI Film & Video
108 Wilmot Rd.
Deerfield, IL 60015

Ph: (708)940-1260
Free: 800-621-2131
Fax: (708)940-3640

Description: This is an examination of modern Navajo life, and how they adjust to contemporary changes while they continue their life as herdsman, weavers, and silversmiths. **Release Date:** 1975. **Length:** 10 mins. **Format:** Beta, VHS, 3/4″ U-matic Cassette, Other than listed.

★2055★
Navajo Land Issue
Journal Films, Inc.
930 Pitner Ave.
Evanston, IL 60202

Ph: (708)328-6700
Free: 800-323-5448
Fax: (708)328-6706

Description: This program examines a unique land issue that exists between two separate Indian tribes, the Navajo and the Hopi. **Release Date:** 197?. **Length:** 12 mins. **Format:** Beta, VHS, 3/4″ U-matic Cassette.

★2056★
Navajo: Legend of the Glittering World
Finley-Holiday Film Corporation
PO Box 619
Dept. CS
Whittier, CA 90608

Free: 800-345-6707
Fax: (213)693-4756

Description: This is a look at what's left of the Navajo legacy in the Southwestern desert. **Release Date:** 1986. **Length:** 25 mins. **Format:** Beta, VHS.

★2057★
Navajo, Race for Prosperity
Cinema Guild
1697 Broadway
New York, NY 10019

Ph: (212)246-5522
Fax: (212)246-5525

Description: This program offers a contemporary view of life on the Navajo reservation and focuses upon the development of industries on the reservation. An arts and crafts cooperative provides a source of income and at the same time keeps alive the beautiful art of the Navajo. **Release Date:** 1976. **Length:** 26 mins. **Format:** 3/4″ U-matic Cassette, Other than listed.

★2058★
Navajos: The Last Red Indians
Time-Life Video and Television
1450 E. Parham Rd.
Richmond, VA 23280

Ph: (804)266-6330
Free: 800-621-7026

Description: This video documents the Navajo's fight to preserve their way of life against the inroads of the white man's culture. It contains uncensored scenes of tribal rituals and ceremonies. **Release Date:** 1972. **Length:** 35 mins. **Format:** Beta, VHS, 3/4″ U-matic Cassette, Other than listed.

★2059★
Neshnabek: The People
University of California at Berkeley
   Extension Media Center
2176 Shattuck Ave.
Berkeley, CA 94704

Ph: (510)642-0460

Description: A look at the Potowatomi Indians of Kansas is provided. **Release Date:** 1979. **Length:** 45 mins. **Format:** VHS, 3/4″ U-matic Cassette.

★2060★
The New Indians
National Geographic Society
PO Box 2118
Washington, DC 20013-2118

Ph: (202)857-7378
Free: 800-447-0647

Description: This video offers a look at contemporary tribes and the problems they face. **Release Date:** 1977. **Length:** 59 mins. **Format:** 3/4″ U-matic Cassette, Other than listed.

★2061★
The New Pequot: A Tribal Portrait
Native American Public Broadcasting
   Consortium
1800 N. 33rd St.
PO Box 86111
Lincoln, NE 68501

Ph: (402)472-3522

Description: Focuses on Connecticut's Mashantucket Pequot Indians, a tribe which was close to extinction in the 1970s, and the roadblocks they overcame to survive. **Length:** 60 mins. **Format:** VHS, 1″ Broadcast Type ″C″, 3/4″ U-matic Cassette.

★2062★
Nez Perce: Portrait of a People
Native American Public Broadcasting
   Consortium
1800 N. 33rd St.
PO Box 86111
Lincoln, NE 68501

Ph: (402)472-3522

Description: Historic photos, stories, and scenery combine to give a history of the Nez Perce tribe. **Length:** 23 mins. **Format:** VHS, 1″ Broadcast Type ″C″, 3/4″ U-matic Cassette.

★2063★
Ni'bthaska of the Umunhon
Native American Public Broadcasting
   Consortium
1800 N. 33rd St.
PO Box 86111
Lincoln, NE 68501

Ph: (402)472-3522

Description: Follows the life of a 13-year old boy from the Omaha tribe during his first summer of manhood. Condensed from the "We Are One" series. Individual program titles: Turning of the Child; Becoming a Warrior; The Buffalo Hunt. Tapes are available individually or as a series. **Release Date:** 1987. **Length:** 30 mins. **Format:** VHS, 1″ Broadcast Type ″C″, 3/4″ U-matic Cassette.

★2064★
No Address
National Film Board of Canada
1251 Avenue of the Americas, 16th Fl.
New York, NY 10020-1173

Ph: (212)586-5131

Description: This is an examination of the plight of Native Americans, lured off their reservations by the promise of jobs and a better life, only to end up homeless in large cities. **Release Date:** 1988. **Length:** 56 mins. **Format:** Beta, VHS, 3/4″ U-matic Cassette.

★2065★
No Turning Back
One West Media
PO Box 5766
559 Onate Pl.
Sante Fe, NM 87501

Ph: (505)983-8685

Description: A lengthy portrait of Boots Wagner, a Navajo Indian turned preacher, whose mission is to save the souls of the "pagan" American Indian race. **Release Date:** 1987. **Length:** 58 mins. **Format:** VHS, 3/4″ U-matic Cassette.

★2066★
North American Indian Legends
Phoenix/BFA Films
468 Park Ave., S.
New York, NY 10016

Ph: (212)684-5910
Free: 800-221-1274

Description: Legends of American Indians describe tribal traditions, explain natural events, and express values of the people. The legends in this film represent the original stories of three tribes. **Release Date:** 1973. **Length:** 21 mins. **Format:** Beta, VHS, 3/4″ U-matic Cassette.

★2067★
The North American Indian Series
CRM/McGraw-Hill Films
674 Via de la Valle
PO Box 641
Del Mar, CA 92014
Description: These three programs offer a vital new perspective on the plight of one of our most misunderstood minority groups–the American Indian. **Release Date:** 1971. **Length:** 20 mins. **Format:** Beta, VHS, 3/4" U-matic Cassette.

★2068★
North American Indians and Edward S. Curtis
Phoenix/BFA Films
468 Park Ave., S.   Ph: (212)684-5910
New York, NY 10016   Free: 800-221-1274
Description: Vintage footage taken by Edward Curtis around the turn of the century helps viewers understand about different Indian tribes. **Release Date:** 1985. **Length:** 30 mins. **Format:** Beta, VHS, 3/4" U-matic Cassette.

★2069★
North American Indians Today
National Geographic Society
PO Box 2118   Ph: (202)857-7378
Washington, DC 20013-2118   Free: 800-447-0647
Description: A look at Indian life today, and the problems they face. **Release Date:** 1977. **Length:** 25 mins. **Format:** 3/4" U-matic Cassette, Other than listed.

★2070★
The Northern Plains
Michigan Media
University of Michigan
400 4th St.
Ann Arbor, MI 48109   Ph: (313)764-8228
Description: An examination of the history of the legendary Plains warriors–the Sioux and Crow tribes–who fought tenaciously against the United States for their land and means of survival. **Release Date:** 1966. **Length:** 29 mins. **Format:** 3/4" U-matic Cassette, Other than listed.

★2071★
Now That the Buffalo's Gone
The Media Guild
11722 Sorrento Valley Rd., Ste. E   Ph: (619)755-9191
San Diego, CA 92121   Fax: (619)755-4931
Description: This program reviews the history and present-day situation of the American Indians. **Release Date:** 1969. **Length:** 75 mins. **Format:** Beta, VHS, 3/4" U-matic Cassette.

★2072★
Obsidian Point-Making
University of California at Berkeley
   Extension Media Center
2176 Shattuck Ave.
Berkeley, CA 94704   Ph: (510)642-0460
Description: A Tolowa Indian demonstrates an ancient method of fashioning an arrow point from obsidian, using direct percussion and pressure-flaking techniques. **Release Date:** 1964. **Length:** 13 mins. **Format:** 3/4" U-matic Cassette, Other than listed.

★2073★
Omaha Tribe: The Land, The People, The Family
NETCHE (Nebraska ETV Council for
   Higher Education)
Box 83111
Lincoln, NE 68501   Ph: (402)472-3611
Description: This series on the Omaha Tribe provides historical perspective, a view of the present population, and a close look at the life-style of a three-generation Omaha family. **Release Date:** 1979. **Length:** 30 mins. **Format:** 1/2" Reel-EIAJ, 3/4" U-matic Cassette.

★2074★
On the Path to Self-Reliance
Native American Public Broadcasting
   Consortium
PO Box 86111
1800 N. 33rd St.
Lincoln, NE 68501   Ph: (402)472-3522
Description: The Seminole tribe of Florida is examined amidst its current success and financial self-sufficiency. Narrated by Chairman James Billie. **Release Date:** 1982. **Length:** 45 mins. **Format:** VHS, 3/4" U-matic Cassette, 1" Broadcast Type "C", 2" Quadraplex Open Reel.

★2075★
On the Totem Trail
Journal Films, Inc.   Ph: (708)328-6700
930 Pitner Ave.   Free: 800-323-5448
Evanston, IL 60202   Fax: (708)328-6706
Description: A school assignment about Indians helps two students discover the rich heritage of the Pacific Northwest Tribes. **Release Date:** 197?. **Length:** 30 mins. **Format:** Beta, VHS, 3/4" U-matic Cassette.

★2076★
1,000 Years of Muscogee (Creek) Art
Native American Public Broadcasting
   Consortium
PO Box 86111
1800 N. 33rd St.
Lincoln, NE 68501   Ph: (402)472-3522
Description: Experts and anthropologists survey the history of Creek art. **Release Date:** 1982. **Length:** 28 mins. **Format:** VHS, 3/4" U-matic Cassette, 1" Broadcast Type "C", 2" Quadraplex Open Reel.

★2077★
The Origin of the Crown Dance and Ba'ts'oosee
Norman Ross Publishing Inc.   Ph: (212)765-8200
330 W. 58th St.   Free: 800-648-8850
New York, NY 10019   Fax: (212)765-2393
Description: An Apache elder tells the story of a boy who became a gaan, a supernatural being with curative powers (Apache with English subtitles). **Release Date:** 1981. **Length:** 40 mins. **Format:** Beta, VHS, 3/4" U-matic Cassette.

★2078★
Oscar Howe: The Sioux Painter
Centron Films
108 Wilmot Rd.   Ph: (312)940-1260
Deerfield, IL 60015-9990   Free: 800-621-2131
Description: Oscar Howe, a native Sioux Indian, has won fifteen grand or first awards in national art competitions through his paintings. **Release Date:** 1973. **Length:** 27 mins. **Format:** Beta, VHS, 3/4" U-matic Cassette. **Credits:** Narrated by: Vincent Price.

★2079★
Our Native American Friends
Britannica Films
310 S. Michigan Ave.   Ph: (312)347-7958
Chicago, IL 60604   Fax: (312)347-7966
Description: From the "Friends" units these three programs: Apache Indian Friends, Miccosukee Indian Friends, and Eskimo Friends, are combined to tell of different ethnic groups in the United States. **Release Date:** 1979. **Length:** 10 mins. **Format:** Beta, VHS, 3/4" U-matic Cassette.

★2080★
Our Sacred Land
Intermedia Arts of Minnesota, Inc.
425 Ontario St. SE
Minneapolis, MN 55414   Ph: (612)627-4444
Description: A look at the tumultuous history of the restriction of Sioux's rights to visit and worship on their sacred, unreserved land. **Release Date:** 1984. **Length:** 28 mins. **Format:** Beta, VHS, 3/4" U-matic Cassette.

★2081★
Our Totem is the Raven
Phoenix/BFA Films
468 Park Ave., S.   Ph: (212)684-5910
New York, NY 10016   Free: 800-221-1274
Description: Fifteen-year-old David, an urban Indian boy, has little interest in his cultural heritage. His grandfather takes him into the forest to give him an understanding of his forefathers. **Release Date:** 1972. **Length:** 21 mins. **Format:** Beta, VHS, 3/4″ U-matic Cassette.

★2082★
The People Are Dancing Again
Media Project, Inc.
PO Box 4093
Portland, OR 97208   Ph: (503)223-5335
Description: This program documents the plight of Oregon's Siletz tribe and their struggle to regain federal recognition of their tribe. **Release Date:** 1976. **Length:** 28 mins. **Format:** Beta, VHS, 1/2″ Reel-EIAJ, 3/4″ U-matic Cassette.

★2083★
People of the Buffalo
Britannica Films
310 S. Michigan Ave.   Ph: (312)347-7958
Chicago, IL 60604   Fax: (312)347-7966
Description: This program demonstrates the relationship between the buffalo and the Plains Indians, showing the Indians' dependence on the creature, and explaining how the westward advance of settlers disrupted this natural relationship. **Release Date:** 1980. **Length:** 15 mins. **Format:** Beta, VHS, 3/4″ U-matic Cassette.

★2084★
People of the Dawn
CC Films
National Council of Churches
475 Riverside Dr.
Rm. 860
New York, NY 10115-0050   Ph: (212)870-2575
Description: A look at Indian tribes native to Maine, their history of broken treaties with the U.S., and their current grants of land and funds. **Release Date:** 1984. **Length:** 30 mins. **Format:** 3/4″ U-matic Cassette.

★2085★
People of the First Light
Great Plains National (GPN)
PO Box 80669   Ph: (402)472-2007
Lincoln, NE 68501-0669   Free: 800-228-4630
Description: This series tells the story of descendant tribes of the Eastern Woodland Algonquin Indians and shows how these tribes have maintained their cultural identity. Programs are available individually. **Release Date:** 1979. **Length:** 30 mins. **Format:** Beta, VHS, 3/4″ U-matic Cassette.

★2086★
People of the Macon Plateau
Native American Public Broadcasting
  Consortium
1800 N. 33rd St.
PO Box 86111
Lincoln, NE 68501   Ph: (402)472-3522
Description: Provides a picture of the tribes from the Eastern United States. **Length:** 10 mins. **Format:** VHS, 1″ Broadcast Type "C", 3/4″ U-matic Cassette.

★2087★
Picking Tribes
Women Make Movies
225 Lafayette St., Ste. 206   Ph: (212)925-0606
New York, NY 10012   Fax: (212)925-2052
Description: A young woman's struggle to find an identity between her Black American and Native American heritages is examined through vintage photographs and watercolor animation. **Release**

Date: 1988. **Length:** 7 mins. **Format:** Beta, VHS, 3/4″ U-matic Cassette.

★2088★
Picuris Indians
Arts America, Inc.
12 Havermeyer Pl.
Greenwich, CT 06830   Ph: (203)637-1454
Description: A documentary of the lifestyle of the Picuris Indians at their ancient pueblo in the mountains of north central New Mexico. Includes ancient sacred dances performed on film for the first time. **Release Date:** 1988. **Length:** 60 mins. **Format:** VHS.

★2089★
Pine Nuts
University of California at Berkeley
  Extension Media Center
2176 Shattuck Ave.
Berkeley, CA 94704   Ph: (510)642-0460
Description: Members of the Paviotso and Paiute tribes demonstrate how the pine nuts were harvested and prepared as food, since the Indians long ago came to depend upon the pinon tree as a source of food. **Release Date:** 1961. **Length:** 13 mins. **Format:** 3/4″ U-matic Cassette, Other than listed.

★2090★
Places Not Our Own
National Film Board of Canada
1251 Avenue of the Americas, 16th Fl.
New York, NY 10020-1173   Ph: (212)586-5131
Description: A native American family is forced to live as squatters on the outskirts of town, during a drought in 1929. **Release Date:** 1987. **Length:** 56 mins. **Format:** Beta, VHS, 3/4″ U-matic Cassette.

★2091★
Politics, Peyote, and Passamaquoddy
Michigan Media
University of Michigan
400 4th St.
Ann Arbor, MI 48109   Ph: (313)764-8228
Description: A look at the Indian role in politics, their religious customs, and their languages, all of which have served to perpetuate the American Indian's independence. Part of the "Silent Heritage" series. **Release Date:** 1966. **Length:** 29 mins. **Format:** 3/4″ U-matic Cassette, Other than listed.

★2092★
Pomo Shaman
University of California at Berkeley
  Extension Media Center
2176 Shattuck Ave.
Berkeley, CA 94704   Ph: (510)642-0460
Description: The final night of an Indian healing ceremony is shown in this shortened version of "Sucking Doctor." **Release Date:** 1964. **Length:** 20 mins. **Format:** VHS, 3/4″ U-matic Cassette.

★2093★
Pow-Wow!
Centron Films
108 Wilmot Rd.   Ph: (312)940-1260
Deerfield, IL 60015-9990   Free: 800-621-2131
Description: A display of North American Indian dances at a gathering of more than twenty tribes. **Release Date:** 1980. **Length:** 16 mins. **Format:** Beta, VHS, 3/4″ U-matic Cassette.

★2094★
Powerless Politics
Anti-Defamation League of B'nai B'rith
Audio-Visual Department
823 United Nations Plaza
New York, NY 10017   Ph: (212)490-2525
Description: The impact of the Bureau of Indian Affairs on the simplest details of life on the reservation today is examined. **Release Date:** 1986. **Length:** 30 mins. **Format:** Beta, VHS, 3/4″ U-matic Cassette.

★2095★
Prehistoric Man
Center for Humanities, Inc.
Communications Park
Box 1000   Ph: (914)666-4100
Mount Kisco, NY 10549   Free: 800-431-1242
Description: A look at the developement of the Indians of the American West, from prehistoric times until the Spanish explorers. **Release Date:** 1970. **Length:** 17 mins. **Format:** Beta, VHS, 3/4" U-matic Cassette.

★2096★
Pride, Purpose and Promise: Paiutes of the Southwest
Native American Public Broadcasting
  Consortium
PO Box 86111
1800 N. 33rd St.
Lincoln, NE 68501   Ph: (402)472-3522
Description: A profile of the Arizona and Nevada-based Paiute tribe–past, present and future. **Release Date:** 1982. **Length:** 28 mins. **Format:** VHS, 3/4" U-matic Cassette, 1" Broadcast Type "C", 2" Quadraplex Open Reel.

★2097★
The Primal Land
Cinema Guild
1697 Broadway   Ph: (212)246-5522
New York, NY 10019   Fax: (212)246-5525
Description: A documentary contrasting Native American and Western culture. Emphasis is placed on the different perceptions of the natural environment, science, the arts, and language. **Release Date:** 1984. **Length:** 58 mins. **Format:** Beta, VHS, 3/4" U-matic Cassette. **Credits:** Hosted by: Jamake Highwater.

★2098★
The Primal Mind
Cinema Guild
1697 Broadway   Ph: (212)246-5522
New York, NY 10019   Fax: (212)246-5525
Description: The differences between Native American and Western cultures are explored in this documentary, written and hosted by renowned author Jamake Highwater. **Release Date:** 1984. **Length:** 58 mins. **Format:** Beta, VHS, 3/4" U-matic Cassette.

★2099★
The Probable Passing of Elk Creek
Cinema Guild
1697 Broadway   Ph: (212)246-5522
New York, NY 10019   Fax: (212)246-5525
Description: This video explores the conflict between a proposed dam, the white community it may flood, and the Indian tribal homeland it will destroy. **Release Date:** 1983. **Length:** 60 mins. **Format:** Beta, VHS, 3/4" U-matic Cassette. **Credits:** Directed by: Robert Wilson.

★2100★
Proud Moments
Treehaus Communications
Box 249
Loveland, OH 45140   Free: 800-638-4287
Description: A look at the efforts of a nurse from Boston who works among the Navajos. **Release Date:** 1989. **Length:** 57 mins. **Format:** Beta, VHS, 3/4" U-matic Cassette.

★2101★
Pueblo Arts
International Film Bureau, Inc. (IFB)
332 S. Michigan Ave.
Chicago, IL 60604-4382   Ph: (312)427-4545
Description: A pot is built using the coil technique of the Pueblos. **Release Date:** 198?. **Length:** 11 mins. **Format:** Beta, VHS, 3/4" U-matic Cassette, Other than listed.

★2102★
Pueblo Peoples: First Encounters
Native American Public Broadcasting
  Consortium
1800 N. 33rd St.
PO Box 86111
Lincoln, NE 68501   Ph: (402)472-3522
Description: Using historic accounts and contemporary interpretations of events, this program discusses the Pueblos reaction to the Spanish invaders in 1539 and 1540. **Release Date:** 1991. **Length:** 30 mins. **Format:** VHS, 1" Broadcast Type "C", 3/4" U-matic Cassette.

★2103★
Pueblo Renaissance
Cinema Guild
1697 Broadway   Ph: (212)246-5522
New York, NY 10019   Fax: (212)246-5525
Description: This program provides an authentic view of the sacred traditions and the ancient religious and agricultural ceremonies of the Pueblo people. **Release Date:** 1976. **Length:** 26 mins. **Format:** 3/4" U-matic Cassette, Other than listed.

★2104★
The Real People
Great Plains National (GPN)
PO Box 80669   Ph: (402)472-2007
Lincoln, NE 68501-0669   Free: 800-228-4630
Description: The thoughts and values of the American Indian life are examined in this series about seven tribes of the Northwest Plateau: the Spokane, Colville, Kalispel, Kooteni, Nez Perce, Coeur d'Alene and Flathead. Programs available individually. **Release Date:** 1976. **Length:** 28 mins. **Format:** Beta, VHS, 3/4" U-matic Cassette, Other than listed.

★2105★
Red Road: Towards the Techno-Tribal
Native American Public Broadcasting
  Consortium
PO Box 86111
1800 N. 33rd St.
Lincoln, NE 68501   Ph: (402)472-3522
Description: This program views the contemporary philosophy of Native Americans in relation to the technological influences on tribal life. **Release Date:** 1984. **Length:** 27 mins. **Format:** VHS, 3/4" U-matic Cassette, 1" Broadcast Type "C", 2" Quadraplex Open Reel.

★2106★
Red Sunday
Pyramid Film & Video
Box 1048   Ph: (310)828-7577
2801 Colorado Ave.   Free: 800-421-2304
Santa Monica, CA 90406   Fax: (310)453-9083
Description: This program examines the Battle of Little Big Horn, using a wealth of original drawings, photographs and paintings. **Release Date:** 1975. **Length:** 28 mins. **Format:** Beta, VHS, 3/4" U-matic Cassette.

★2107★
Return of the Raven—The Edison Chiloquin Story
Televideos
PO Box 22   Ph: 800-284-3367
Lorane, OR 97451   Free: 800-2VI-DEOS
Description: This film documents the life of Chiloquin, a Native American who struggled with the U.S. Congress in an effort to preserve traditional values, and won. **Release Date:** 1985. **Length:** 47 mins. **Format:** Beta, VHS, 3/4" U-matic Cassette.

★2108★
Return of the Sacred Pole
Native American Public Broadcasting
  Consortium
1800 N. 33rd St.
PO Box 86000
Lincoln, NE 68501   Ph: (402)472-3522
Description: Recounts the events of returning a sacred pole, a spirit endowed artifact, to the Omaha tribe after a 100-year stay at the Peabody Museum at Harvard University. **Release Date:** 1989. **Length:** 30 mins. **Format:** VHS, 1″ Broadcast Type ″C″, 3/4″ U-matic Cassette.

★2109★
Return to Sovereignty
University of California at Berkeley
  Extension Media Center
2176 Shattuck Ave.
Berkeley, CA 94704   Ph: (510)642-0460
Description: This is a documentary about how government policy has changed concerning the American Indians. The Kickapoo tribe from Kansas are used as examples. **Release Date:** 1987. **Length:** 46 mins. **Format:** VHS, 3/4″ U-matic Cassette.

★2110★
Rolling Thunder: The Unity of Man and Nature
Facets Multimedia, Inc.
1517 W. Fullerton Ave.
Chicago, IL 60614   Ph: (312)281-9075
Description: Rolling Thunder, a medicine man of intertribal status, examines man as a dominator of nature verses man living in harmony with nature. He also talks of his visits to the spirit world and his shamanistic healing methods. **Release Date:** 19??. **Length:** 90 mins. **Format:** VHS.

★2111★
Run, Appaloosa, Run
Coronet/MTI Film & Video   Ph: (708)940-1260
108 Wilmot Rd.   Free: 800-621-2131
Deerfield, IL 60015   Fax: (708)940-3640
Description: An Indian girl and Holy Smoke, her stallion, share happiness and tragedy in this adventure. **Release Date:** 1966. **Length:** 48 mins. **Format:** Beta, VHS, 1/2″ Reel-EIAJ, 3/4″ U-matic Cassette, Other than listed.

★2112★
The Runaway
Native American Public Broadcasting
  Consortium
1800 N. 133rd St.
PO Box 86111
Lincoln, NE 68501   Ph: (402)472-3522
Description: Discusses the situation of 14-year old Darlene Horse, a Native American girl who ran away from a difficult home situation, including her family's problems with alcohol. **Length:** 29 mins. **Format:** VHS, 1″ Broadcast Type ″C″, 3/4 U-matic Cassette.

★2113★
Running on the Edge of the Rainbow: Laguna Stories and Poems
Norman Ross Publishing Inc.   Ph: (212)765-8200
330 W. 58th St.   Free: 800-648-8850
New York, NY 10019   Fax: (212)765-2393
Description: A reflection on the nature of Laguna storytelling, its functions, and the problems of being an Indian poet. **Release Date:** 1981. **Length:** 28 mins. **Format:** Beta, VHS, 3/4″ U-matic Cassette.

★2114★
Sacajawea
FilmFair Communications   Ph: (818)985-0244
10621 Magnolia Blvd.   Free: 800-423-2461
North Hollywood, CA 91601   Fax: (818)980-8492
Description: Still photos and animation bring to life the Indian woman who helped Lewis and Clark on their trip through the

American West. **Release Date:** 1989. **Length:** 25 mins. **Format:** Beta, VHS, 3/4″ U-matic Cassette.

★2115★
Sacred Ground: The North American Indian's Relationship to the Land
Wood Knapp & Company, Inc.
Knapp Press
5900 Wilshire Blvd.   Ph: (213)937-5486
Los Angeles, CA 90036   Free: 800-521-2666
Description: A look at a variety of Native American societies, focusing on mythology, anthropology, and social structure. **Release Date:** 1991. **Length:** 60 mins. **Format:** VHS. **Credits:** Hosted by: Cliff Robertson.

★2116★
Science or Sacrilege: The Study of American Indian Remains
University of California at Santa Barbara
Instructional Development
Santa Barbara, CA 93106   Ph: (805)961-3518
Description: This program deals with the issue of whether or not American Indian Skeletal remains and artifacts should be preserved in museums for study by anthropologists and other scientists. **Release Date:** 1983. **Length:** 41 mins. **Format:** Beta, VHS, 3/4″ U-matic Cassette.

★2117★
Seasons of a Navajo
PBS Video
1320 Braddock Pl.
Alexandria, VA 22314-1698   Ph: (703)739-5380
Description: A look at the traditional Navajo way of life, including their music, folklore and ceremonies. Features scenes of Arizona's Monument Valley and the Anasazi ruins. **Release Date:** 1985. **Length:** 60 mins. **Format:** VHS, 3/4″ U-matic Cassette.

★2118★
Seminole Indians
International Film Bureau, Inc. (IFB)
332 S. Michigan Ave.
Chicago, IL 60604-4382   Ph: (312)427-4545
Description: The lives of Seminole Indians are presented in this program. **Release Date:** 1982. **Length:** 11 mins. **Format:** Beta, VHS, 3/4″ U-matic Cassette, Other than listed.

★2119★
Shadow Catcher
Phoenix/BFA Films
468 Park Ave., S.   Ph: (212)684-5910
New York, NY 10016   Free: 800-221-1274
Description: This is a program about photographer-anthropologist Edward Curtis and the Indian people he worked with from 1895 to 1930. Includes all of Curtis' recoverable film footage of life among the Kwakiutl, Hopi, and Navaho Indians. **Release Date:** 1975. **Length:** 88 mins. **Format:** Beta, VHS, 3/4″ U-matic Cassette.

★2120★
The Shadow Walkers
Agency for Instructional Technology (AIT)
1111 W. 17th St.
Box A   Ph: (812)339-2203
Bloomington, IN 47402-0120   Free: 800-457-4509
Description: A set of programs designed to bring out the pride associated with being a Native American. **Release Date:** 1989. **Length:** 30 mins. **Format:** Beta, VHS, 3/4″ U-matic Cassette.

★2121★
Shadow of the Warrior
National AudioVisual Center
National Archives & Records
   Administration
Customer Services Section PZ
8700 Edgeworth Dr.
Capitol Heights, MD 20743-3701   Ph: (301)763-1896

Description: This video for Veterans Administration center psychology professionals deals with the lives and problems of American Indian Vietnam veterans. **Release Date:** 1985. **Length:** 42 mins. **Format:** Beta, VHS, 3/4″ U-matic Cassette.

★2122★
The Shaman's Journey
Wishing Well Distributing   Ph: (414)864-2395
PO Box 2   Free: 800-888-9355
Wilmot, WI 53192   Fax: (414)862-2398

Description: A look at Native American healing practices, coupled with a tour of Central and South American historic sites. **Release Date:** 1990. **Length:** 90 mins. **Format:** VHS.

★2123★
Shinnecock: A Story of a People
Phoenix/BFA Films
468 Park Ave., S.   Ph: (212)684-5910
New York, NY 10016   Free: 800-221-1274

Description: This video features a look at the history, heritage, and present-day status of the Shinnecock Indians. **Release Date:** 1976. **Length:** 20 mins. **Format:** Beta, VHS, 3/4″ U-matic Cassette.

★2124★
The Silent Enemy
Video Yesteryear
Box C   Ph: (203)426-2574
Sandy Hook, CT 06482   Free: 800-243-0987

Description: An interesting documentary which tells the Ojibway Indian's way of life before the arrival of the white man. The title is a reference to hunger. **Release Date:** 1930. **Length:** 110 mins. **Format:** Beta, VHS, 8mm.

★2125★
Silent Heritage: The American Indian
Michigan Media
University of Michigan
400 4th St.
Ann Arbor, MI 48109   Ph: (313)764-8228

Description: To seek the truth about the American Indian and give him an opportunity to express his views, a film crew from the University of Michigan Media Resources Center traveled to six states, interviewing representatives from major tribes. All programs available individually. **Release Date:** 1966. **Length:** 29 mins. **Format:** 3/4″ U-matic Cassette, Other than listed.

★2126★
Sinew-Backed Bow and its Arrows
University of California at Berkeley
   Extension Media Center
2176 Shattuck Ave.
Berkeley, CA 94704   Ph: (510)642-0460

Description: This program follows the construction of a sinew-backed bow–the finest of the bows used by American Indians–by a Yurok craftsman. Demonstrations of the making of arrows are also included. **Release Date:** 1961. **Length:** 24 mins. **Format:** 3/4″ U-matic Cassette, Other than listed.

★2127★
Sioux Legends
AIMS Media
9710 De Soto Ave.
Chatsworth, CA 91311-9734   Free: 800-367-2467
                                Fax: (818)341-6700

Description: Recreates philosophies and religion of the Sioux culture and its identification with the forces of nature. **Release Date:** 1974. **Length:** 20 mins. **Format:** Beta, VHS, 3/4″ U-matic Cassette.

★2128★
The Six Nations
Cinema Guild
1697 Broadway   Ph: (212)246-5522
New York, NY 10019   Fax: (212)246-5525

Description: In upstate New York stands the Iroquois League, a federation older than the U.S. itself, consisting of the Mohawk, Oneida, Onondaga, Seneca, Cayuga, and Tuscarora tribes. This program tells how these tribes consider themselves to be a sovereign independent nation and reject the American way of life in favor of a self-sufficient existence on their own land. **Release Date:** 1976. **Length:** 26 mins. **Format:** 3/4″ U-matic Cassette, Other than listed.

★2129★
Smithsonian: Catlin and the Indians
CRM/McGraw-Hill Films
674 Via de la Valle
PO Box 641
Del Mar, CA 92014

Description: An examination of the paintings of George Catlin, who recorded the now-extinct way of life of the Plains Indians–the forms and rituals of a vanished society. From the "Smithsonian" series. **Release Date:** 1967. **Length:** 24 mins. **Format:** Beta, VHS, 3/4″ U-matic Cassette. **Credits:** Hosted by: Bill Ryan.

★2130★
Snaketown
University of California at Berkeley
   Extension Media Center
2176 Shattuck Ave.
Berkeley, CA 94704   Ph: (510)642-0460

Description: An ancient Indian site in Arizona is excavated. **Release Date:** 1969. **Length:** 45 mins. **Format:** VHS, 3/4″ U-matic Cassette.

★2131★
Something Seneca
New York State Education Department
Center for Learning Technologies
Media Distribution Network, Rm. C-7,
   Concourse Level
Albany, NY 12230   Ph: (518)474-1265

Description: A series of programs looking at modern Native American culture, for the high school student. Electronically enhanced for video. **Release Date:** 1978. **Length:** 14 mins. **Format:** Beta, VHS, 1/2″ Reel-EIAJ, 3/4″ U-matic Cassette.

★2132★
Sometimes We Feel
Barr Films
12801 Schabarum Ave.   Ph: (818)338-7878
PO Box 7878   Free: 800-234-7878
Irwindale, CA 91706-7878   Fax: (818)814-2672

Description: A young Indian tells of the proud history of his people, and explains how they are now reduced to a life of sorrow, poverty, and neglect on their desert reservation. **Release Date:** 1974. **Length:** 10 mins. **Format:** Beta, VHS, 3/4″ U-matic Cassette.

★2133★
Songs of My Hunter Heart: Laguna Songs and Poems
Norman Ross Publishing Inc.   Ph: (212)765-8200
330 W. 58th St.   Free: 800-648-8850
New York, NY 10019   Fax: (212)765-2393

Description: A look at the inroads made upon traditional Laguna Pueblo life by the discovery of uranium deposits and extensive mining. **Release Date:** 1981. **Length:** 34 mins. **Format:** Beta, VHS, 3/4″ U-matic Cassette.

★2134★
Southwest Indian Arts and Crafts
Coronet/MTI Film & Video   Ph: (708)940-1260
108 Wilmot Rd.   Free: 800-621-2131
Deerfield, IL 60015   Fax: (708)940-3640

Description: The fine workmanship of the Southwest Indians is seen in Navajo rugs, San Ildefanso and Acoma pottery, and much more.

Release Date: 1973. Length: 14 mins. Format: Beta, VHS, 3/4″ U-matic Cassette, Other than listed.

★2135★
Southwest Indians of Early America
Coronet/MTI Film & Video   Ph: (708)940-1260
108 Wilmot Rd.   Free: 800-621-2131
Deerfield, IL 60015   Fax: (708)940-3640
Description: An examination of the prosperous ancestors of the Hopi, Pima, and Papaga Indians in the Southwestern United States. **Release Date:** 1973. **Length:** 14 mins. **Format:** Beta, VHS, 3/4″ U-matic Cassette, Other than listed.

★2136★
Spirit of the Hunt
Centre Productions, Inc.
1800 30th St., Ste. 207   Ph: (303)444-1166
Boulder, CO 80301   Free: 800-824-1166
Description: This film is a fascinating account of the spiritual elements of what the buffalo means to the Indians of the Plains of North America. **Release Date:** 1982. **Length:** 29 mins. **Format:** Beta, VHS, 3/4″ U-matic Cassette.

★2137★
Stone Age Americans
International Film Bureau, Inc. (IFB)
332 S. Michigan Ave.
Chicago, IL 60604-4382   Ph: (312)427-4545
Description: This is a study of the Indians of the Mesa Verde in Colorado, who disappeared after thirteen centuries of development. **Release Date:** 1970. **Length:** 21 mins. **Format:** Beta, VHS, 3/4″ U-matic Cassette, Other than listed.

★2138★
Stories of American Indian Culture: Hawk, I'm Your Brother
Best Film & Video Corporation   Ph: (516)487-4515
98 Cutter Mill Rd.   Free: 800-527-2189
Great Neck, NY 11021   Fax: (516)487-4834
Description: A young boy develops a special relationship with a majestic hawk and learns what it means to fly. Based on Byrd Baylor's award winning children's books, this video offers the Native American's unique perspective on life. **Release Date:** 1991. **Length:** 25 mins. **Format:** VHS. **Credits:** Narrated by: Will Rogers, Jr.

★2139★
Stories of American Indian Culture: The Other Way to Listen
Best Film & Video Corporation   Ph: (516)487-4515
98 Cutter Mill Rd.   Free: 800-527-2189
Great Neck, NY 11021   Fax: (516)487-4834
Description: Children are shown the unique Native American perspective on desert life and what one can "hear" in the desert. Based on Byrd Baylor's award winning children's books. **Release Date:** 1991. **Length:** 20 mins. **Format:** VHS. **Credits:** Narrated by: Will Rogers, Jr.

★2140★
Stories of American Indian Culture: The Way to Start a Day
Best Film & Video Corporation   Ph: (516)487-4515
98 Cutter Mill Rd.   Free: 800-527-2189
Great Neck, NY 11021   Fax: (516)487-4834
Description: Video version of Byrd Baylor's children's books which introduce young people to Native American culture, emphasizing the unique perspective on nature. This edition offers computer animated versions of illustrator Peter Parnall's work. **Release Date:** 1990. **Length:** 12 mins. **Format:** VHS. **Credits:** Narrated by: Will Rogers, Jr.

★2141★
Strength of Life—Knokavtee Scott
Native American Public Broadcasting
  Consortium
PO Box 86111
1800 N. 33rd St.
Lincoln, NE 68501   Ph: (402)472-3522
Description: The life and work of Cherokee/Creek jewelry craftsman Scott is explored, as is his inspirational devotion to the Spiro Mounds in Oklahoma. **Release Date:** 1984. **Length:** 27 mins. **Format:** VHS, 3/4″ U-matic Cassette, 1″ Broadcast Type "C", 2″ Quadraplex Open Reel.

★2142★
Sucking Doctor
University of California at Berkeley
  Extension Media Center
2176 Shattuck Ave.
Berkeley, CA 94704   Ph: (510)642-0460
Description: A group of Indians from the Southwest perform a ritual healing. **Release Date:** 1964. **Length:** 45 mins. **Format:** VHS, 3/4″ U-matic Cassette.

★2143★
Summer Legend
Churchill Films
12210 Nebraska Ave.   Ph: (213)207-6600
Los Angeles, CA 90025   Fax: (213)207-1330
Description: This is an animated version of the Micmac Indian legend that explains the changing of the seasons. **Release Date:** 1988. **Length:** 8 mins. **Format:** Beta, VHS, 3/4″ U-matic Cassette.

★2144★
Sun Bear on Earth Changes
Wishing Well Distributing   Ph: (414)864-2395
PO Box 2   Free: 800-888-9355
Wilmot, WI 53192   Fax: (414)862-2398
Description: A presentation of Native American prophecies concerning the state of the world. **Release Date:** 1990. **Length:** 60 mins. **Format:** VHS.

★2145★
The Sun Dagger
Bullfrog Films, Inc.   Ph: (215)779-8226
PO Box 149   Free: 800-543-3764
Oley, PA 19547   Fax: (215)370-1978
Description: Robert Redford narrates the extraordinary culture of the Anasazi Indians who built the calendar and thrived in the harsh environment of Chaco Canyon, New Mexico, one thousand years ago. A 29 minute version is available. **Release Date:** 1983. **Length:** 58 mins. **Format:** Beta, VHS, 3/4″ U-matic Cassette.

★2146★
Surviving Columbus
PBS Video
1320 Braddock Pl.
Alexandria, VA 22314-1698   Ph: (703)739-5380
Description: A look at the first encounters between New Mexico's Pueblo Indians and the first European explorers, led by Coronado. The focus is on the explorers' search for non-existent gold, and the havoc they wrought. **Release Date:** 1990. **Length:** 30 mins. **Format:** VHS, 3/4″ U-matic Cassette.

★2147★
Tahtonka
AIMS Media
9710 De Soto Ave.
Chatsworth, CA 91311-9734   Free: 800-367-2467
                                 Fax: (818)341-6700
Description: Historic look at the Plains Indians from the pre-horse era to the Wounded Knee massacre, showing their dependence on the buffalo. **Release Date:** 1968. **Length:** 30 mins. **Format:** Beta, VHS, 3/4″ U-matic Cassette.

★2148★
Tales of the Muscogee
Centre Productions, Inc.
1800 30th St., Ste. 207   Ph: (303)444-1166
Boulder, CO 80301   Free: 800-824-1166
Description: This program is narrated, scored and illustrated by members of the Indian tribe. It examines the folklore of the tribe and demonstrates how this ancient folklore can teach today's children about morality. **Release Date:** 1983. **Length:** 15 mins. **Format:** Beta, VHS, 3/4″ U-matic Cassette.

★2149★
The Taos Pueblo
Bullfrog Films, Inc.   Ph: (215)779-8226
PO Box 149   Free: 800-543-3764
Oley, PA 19547   Fax: (215)370-1978
Description: A look at the dramatically beautiful, 1000 year-old pueblo in Taos, New Mexico to discover more about the traditions that the resident Indians are trying to preserve. **Release Date:** 1987. **Length:** 9 mins. **Format:** Beta, VHS, 3/4″ U-matic Cassette.

★2150★
That One Good Spirit—An Indian Christmas Story
Native American Public Broadcasting
  Consortium
PO Box 86111
1800 N. 33rd St.
Lincoln, NE 68501   Ph: (402)472-3522
Description: Clay animation is used to enact an Ute Christmas myth. **Release Date:** 1981. **Length:** 16 mins. **Format:** VHS, 3/4″ U-matic Cassette, 1″ Broadcast Type ″C″, 2″ Quadraplex Open Reel.

★2151★
They Promised to Take Our Land
Cinema Guild
1697 Broadway   Ph: (212)246-5522
New York, NY 10019   Fax: (212)246-5525
Description: When Europeans began to colonize the New World there were hundreds of Indian tribes spread across the continent. By 1900 the Indians had been greatly reduced in number and forced to live on tracts of land alloted by the white man. In this program, Navajo tribal chairman Peter Macdonald discusses the ″rip-off″ of Indian resources dating back 100 years. **Release Date:** 1976. **Length:** 26 mins. **Format:** 3/4″ U-matic Cassette, Other than listed.

★2152★
Those Who Sing Together
CRM/McGraw-Hill Films
674 Via de la Valle
PO Box 641
Del Mar, CA 92014
Description: The folklore and music of the Plains Indians and the tribes of the Pacific Northwest are chronicled in this program. **Release Date:** 1978. **Length:** 28 mins. **Format:** Beta, VHS, 3/4″ U-matic Cassette.

★2153★
A Time to Be Brave
Beacon Films
930 Pinter Ave.   Ph: (312)328-6700
Evanston, IL 60202   Free: 800-323-5448
Description: In the northern wilderness, a young Ojibway girl must overcome her fears in order to save her father's life. **Release Date:** 1982. **Length:** 28 mins. **Format:** Beta, VHS, 3/4″ U-matic Cassette.

★2154★
Tomorrow's Yesterday
Brigham Young University
101 Fletcher Building
Provo, UT 84602   Ph: (801)378-3456
Description: Shows American Indians as they were, as they are, and as they hope to be. Stresses the positive things they are doing to meet the challenge of modern civilization without losing their cultural heritage. **Release Date:** 1971. **Length:** 29 mins. **Format:** 3/4″ U-matic Cassette.

★2155★
Totem Pole
University of California at Berkeley
  Extension Media Center
2176 Shattuck Ave.
Berkeley, CA 94704   Ph: (510)642-0460
Description: The development of the seven types of totem poles is lyrically presented, and each is discussed in terms of a social system and mythology. The carving of a pole by a tribal chief is also shown. **Release Date:** 1963. **Length:** 27 mins. **Format:** 3/4″ U-matic Cassette, Other than listed.

★2156★
Track of the Moonbeast
Prism Entertainment
1888 Century Park, E., Ste. 1000   Ph: (213)277-3270
Los Angeles, CA 90067   Fax: (213)203-8036
Description: An American Indian uses mythology to capture the Moonbeast, a lizard-like creature that is roaming the deserts of New Mexico. **Release Date:** 1976. **Length:** 90 mins. **Format:** Beta, VHS. **Credits:** Cast Member: Chase Cordell; Donna Leigh Drake. Directed by: Richard Ashe.

★2157★
Trail of Broken Treaties
Cinema Guild
1697 Broadway   Ph: (212)246-5522
New York, NY 10019   Fax: (212)246-5525
Description: An examination of the past and present injustices suffered by the Indian and a look at the attempts of Indian leaders to improve the situation. **Release Date:** 1976. **Length:** 26 mins. **Format:** 3/4″ U-matic Cassette, Other than listed.

★2158★
The Treasure: Indian Heritage
Phoenix/BFA Films
468 Park Ave., S.   Ph: (212)684-5910
New York, NY 10016   Free: 800-221-1274
Description: A contemporary study of cultural values in conflict-two teenage Indian brothers impatient with their father's traditional ways. **Release Date:** 1970. **Length:** 13 mins. **Format:** Beta, VHS, 3/4″ U-matic Cassette.

★2159★
Treaties Made, Treaties Broken
CRM/McGraw-Hill Films
674 Via de la Valle
PO Box 641
Del Mar, CA 92014
Description: The Treaty of Medicine Creek grants the Indians of Washington State fishing and hunting rights in perpetuity. Today, the treaty is in dispute. From the ″North American Indian″ series. **Release Date:** 1971. **Length:** 18 mins. **Format:** Beta, VHS, 3/4″ U-matic Cassette.

★2160★
The Treaty of 1868 Series
Native American Public Broadcasting
  Consortium
1800 N. 33rd St.
PO Box 86111
Lincoln, NE 68501   Ph: (402)472-3522
Description: Explores whether the Lakota Sioux Indians or the United States government own the Black Hills of South Dakota, which the Lakota regard as sacred ground. Individual program titles: The Treaty of 1868; The Black Hills Claim. Tapes are available individually or as a series. **Release Date:** 1987. **Length:** 28 mins. **Format:** VHS, 1″ Broadcast Type ″C″, 3/4″ U-matic Cassette.

★2161★
Treaty Rights or Civil Rights
Michigan Media
University of Michigan
400 4th St.
Ann Arbor, MI 48109   Ph: (313)764-8228

Description: An explanation of the importance of treaty rights and constitutional civil rights in protecting Indian reservations and preserving the Indian way of life. Part of the "Silent Heritage" series. **Release Date:** 1966. **Length:** 29 mins. **Format:** 3/4″ U-matic Cassette, Other than listed.

★2162★
The Trial of Leonard Peltier
Intermedia Arts of Minnesota, Inc.
425 Ontario St. SE
Minneapolis, MN 55414   Ph: (612)627-4444

Description: This documentary tells the unusual story of the United States Government's murder case against American Indian Movement leader Leonard Peltier. **Release Date:** 1977. **Length:** 16 mins. **Format:** 3/4″ U-matic Cassette, Other than listed.

★2163★
Turtle Shells
Native American Public Broadcasting
  Consortium
1800 N. 33rd St.
PO Box 86111
Lincoln, NE 68501   Ph: (402)472-3522

Description: Explores the crafting of Native American women's leg rattles, from choosing the turtle shell to the final fitting. Demonstrated by Christine Hannena, a Muscogee Creek Indian of Oklahoma. **Length:** 26 mins. **Format:** VHS, 1″ Broadcast Type "C", 3/4″ U-matic cassette.

★2164★
Two Worlds
Anti-Defamation League of B'nai B'rith
Audio-Visual Department
823 United Nations Plaza
New York, NY 10017   Ph: (212)490-2525

Description: An examination of the condition of the American Indian today and the problems rising from the effort to integrate them into the mainstream of American life. **Release Date:** 1986. **Length:** 30 mins. **Format:** Beta, VHS, 3/4″ U-matic Cassette.

★2165★
The Uncertain Future
Michigan Media
University of Michigan
400 4th St.
Ann Arbor, MI 48109   Ph: (313)764-8228

Description: A discussion of the major problems of the American Indian of today and tomorrow, such as low income, poor education, and termination of helpful government programs. Part of "Silent Heritage" series. **Release Date:** 1966. **Length:** 29 mins. **Format:** 3/4″ U-matic Cassette, Other than listed.

★2166★
Urban Indians
Downtown Community TV Center
87 Lafayette St.
New York, NY 10013   Ph: (212)966-4510

Description: This is the true story of an Oglala Sioux who came to New York City looking for a job, but wound up a drug addict. **Release Date:** 1984. **Length:** 20 mins. **Format:** 1/2″ Reel-EIAJ, 3/4″ U-matic Cassette, Other than listed.

★2167★
The Wake
National Film Board of Canada
1251 Avenue of the Americas, 16th Fl.
New York, NY 10020-1173   Ph: (212)586-5131

Description: A contemporary, single, Native American mother must face the difficulties of prejudice. **Release Date:** 1987. **Length:** 58 mins. **Format:** Beta, VHS, 3/4″ U-matic Cassette.

★2168★
Walking with Grandfather
Native American Public Broadcasting
  Consortium
1800 N. 33rd St.
PO Box 86111
Lincoln, NE 68501   Ph: (402)472-3522

Description: Stories drawn from the oral tradition of many North American Indian tribes that present basic human values. Individual program titles: The Arrival; The Woods; The Mountain; The Valley; The Stream; The Gift. Tapes are available individually or as a series. **Release Date:** 1988. **Length:** 14 mins. **Format:** VHS, 1″ Broadcast Type "C", 3/4″ U-matic Cassette.

★2169★
Walking in a Sacred Manner
International Film Bureau, Inc. (IFB)
332 S. Michigan Ave.
Chicago, IL 60604-4382   Ph: (312)427-4545

Description: The appreciation that Indians have for the physical, spiritual and psychological well being of man is documented. **Release Date:** 1983. **Length:** 23 mins. **Format:** Beta, VHS, 3/4″ U-matic Cassette, Other than listed.

★2170★
Warpaint and Wigs
Video Tech
19346 3rd Ave. NW
Seattle, WA 98177   Ph: (206)546-5401

Description: This program from the "Images of Indians" series shows how the movie image of the Indian has affected the self-image of Native Americans. **Release Date:** 1982. **Length:** 30 mins. **Format:** Beta, VHS, 3/4″ U-matic Cassette, Other than listed. **Credits:** Narrated by: Will Sampson.

★2171★
Warriors
Intermedia Arts of Minnesota, Inc.
425 Ontario St. SE
Minneapolis, MN 55414   Ph: (612)627-4444

Description: This film focuses on American Indians who fought in the Vietnam War. **Release Date:** 1987. **Length:** 58 mins. **Format:** 3/4″ U-matic Cassette.

★2172★
Water Is So Clear That a Blind Man Could See
Indiana University Center for Media &
  Teaching Resources   Ph: (812)855-8087
Bloomington, IN 47405-5901   Fax: (812)855-8404

Description: A look at New Mexico's Taos Indians, who believe that all life is sacred, and have lived in harmony with nature for over a century. Their land is now threatened by lumber companies. **Release Date:** 1970. **Length:** 30 mins. **Format:** 3/4″ U-matic Cassette, Other than listed.

★2173★
Way of Our Fathers
University of California at Berkeley
  Extension Media Center
2176 Shattuck Ave.
Berkeley, CA 94704   Ph: (510)642-0460

Description: Members of several northern California Indian tribes depict unique elements of a way of life as it flourished before the coming of the white man. **Release Date:** 1972. **Length:** 33 mins. **Format:** 3/4″ U-matic Cassette, Other than listed.

★2174★
We Are One: A Series
Native American Public Broadcasting
  Consortium
1800 N. 33rd St.
PO Box 86111
Lincoln, NE 68501   Ph: (402)472-3522
Description: Focuses on 13-year old Ni'bathaska and his sister Mi'onbathin and the daily activities of their lives as Omaha Indians in early 19th century Nebraska. A teacher's guide is included with each tape. Individual program titles: Morning Comes; Learning from Others; Turning of the Child; Storytelling; Becoming a Warrior; Preparing for the Summer Hunt; The Dare; The Buffalo Hunt. Tapes are available individually or as a series. **Release Date:** 1986. **Length:** 20 mins. **Format:** VHS, 1″ Broadcast Type ″C″, 3/4″ U-matic Cassette.

★2175★
We Are a River Flowing
Intermedia Arts of Minnesota, Inc.
425 Ontario St. SE
Minneapolis, MN 55414   Ph: (612)627-4444
Description: Ten-year old Fiona travels from her home in Belfast, Ireland to the Pine Ridge Indian reservation as a part of a program for children of political turmoil. This film makes a striking between the Irish and Indian societies. **Release Date:** 1985. **Length:** 40 mins. **Format:** Beta, VHS, 3/4″ U-matic Cassette.

★2176★
A Weave of Time
Direct Cinema Limited   Ph: (213)652-8000
PO Box 69799   Free: 800-345-6748
Los Angeles, CA 90069-9976   Fax: (213)652-2346
Description: A look at Navajo life in the 1930s. **Release Date:** 1987. **Length:** 60 mins. **Format:** Beta, VHS, 3/4″ U-matic Cassette.

★2177★
What Is an American Part 2
Pyramid Film & Video
Box 1048   Ph: (310)828-7577
2801 Colorado Ave.   Free: 800-421-2304
Santa Monica, CA 90406   Fax: (310)453-9083
Description: The program explains to children how Puerto Rican and American Indian cultures have enriched our American experience. **Release Date:** 1979. **Length:** 12 mins. **Format:** Beta, VHS, 3/4″ U-matic Cassette.

★2178★
Where the Buffaloes Begin
Random House Media
Department 467
400 Hahn Rd.
Westminster, MD 21157   Free: 800-492-0782
Description: Olaf Baker's story about the lives of Native Americans is brought to life. **Release Date:** 1985. **Length:** 14 mins. **Format:** VHS. **Credits:** Narrated by: Jamake Highwater.

★2179★
White Apache
Imperial Entertainment Corporation
4640 Lankershim Blvd., 4th Fl.
North Hollywood, CA 91602
Description: Emotionally charged saga of a man barred from both Indian and White societies. The film focuses on the impact of prejudice toward a white man raised by Apaches. **Release Date:** 1988. **Length:** 90 mins. **Format:** Beta, VHS.

★2180★
White Man's Way
Native American Public Broadcasting
  Consortium
1800 N. 33rd St.
PO Box 86111
Lincoln, NE 68501   Ph: (402)472-3522
Description: Looks at the U.S. Indian School in Nebraska where, beginning in the late 1800's, Indian children from numerous tribes were sent to learn the ways of the white man and were forbidden to practice their own lifestyles. **Release Date:** 1986. **Length:** 30 mins. **Format:** VHS, 1″ Broadcast Type ″C″, 3/4″ U-matic Cassette.

★2181★
Who Discovered America
Films, Inc.
5547 N. Ravenswood Ave.   Ph: (312)878-2600
Chicago, IL 60640-1199   Free: 800-323-4222
Description: Different theories about who the Indians were and where they came from are discussed, as well as their discovery of corn, which made their world possible and still flourishes throughout today's world. **Release Date:** 1972. **Length:** 14 mins. **Format:** Beta, VHS, 3/4″ U-matic Cassette.

★2182★
Winter on an Indian Reservation
Atlantis Productions
1252 La Granada Dr.
Thousand Oaks, CA 91360   Ph: (805)495-2790
Description: A look at the lives of children on a forest reservation in the Great Lakes area. Also available in a non-narrative version. **Release Date:** 1973. **Length:** 11 mins. **Format:** Beta, VHS, 3/4″ U-matic Cassette.

★2183★
Wooden Box: Made by Steaming and Bending
University of California at Berkeley
  Extension Media Center
2176 Shattuck Ave.
Berkeley, CA 94704   Ph: (510)642-0460
Description: This program follows every stage of making the Kwakiutl box, elaborately carved and painted boxes made by steaming and bending a single wooden slab using no nails, screws, or glue. **Release Date:** 1962. **Length:** 33 mins. **Format:** 3/4″ U-matic Cassette, Other than listed.

★2184★
Woodland Indians of Early America
Coronet/MTI Film & Video   Ph: (708)940-1260
108 Wilmot Rd.   Free: 800-621-2131
Deerfield, IL 60015   Fax: (708)940-3640
Description: Authentic reconstructions and scenes in the eastern and Great Lakes regions provide settings for this study of woodland Indian life prior to European influence. **Release Date:** 1980. **Length:** 10 mins. **Format:** Beta, VHS, 3/4″ U-matic Cassette, Other than listed.

★2185★
Woonspe (Education and the Sioux)
Native American Public Broadcasting
  Consortium
PO Box 86111
1800 N. 33rd St.
Lincoln, NE 68501   Ph: (402)472-3522
Description: A program that indicts the current state of Native American education. **Release Date:** 1974. **Length:** 28 mins. **Format:** VHS, 3/4″ U-matic Cassette, 1″ Broadcast Type ″C″, 2″ Quadraplex Open Reel.

★2186★
The Wounded Knee Affair
Journal Films, Inc.   Ph: (708)328-6700
930 Pitner Ave.   Free: 800-323-5448
Evanston, IL 60202   Fax: (708)328-6706
Description: The siege of Wounded Knee, South Dakota in 1973 by a group of American Indians to draw international attention to their problems is examined. **Release Date:** 197?. **Length:** 17 mins. **Format:** Beta, VHS, 3/4″ U-matic Cassette.

★2187★
You Are on Indian Land
National Film Board of Canada
1251 Avenue of the Americas, 16th Fl.
New York, NY 10020-1173   Ph: (212)586-5131
Description: This film documents the 1969 demonstration by Mohawk Indians of the St. Regis Reserve on the international bridge between Canada and the United States near Cornwall, Ontario. **Release Date:** 1987. **Length:** 37 mins. **Format:** Beta, VHS, 3/4″ U-matic Cassette.

Alaska Natives

<hr>

Tribal Communities

<hr>

──────── Alaska ────────

★2188★
Native Village of Akhiok
Box 5072
Akhiok, AK 99615   Ph: (907)836-2229
Nick Peterson Sr., Pres.
BIA Area Office: Juneau. **BIA Agency:** Anchorage.

★2189★
Akiachak Native Community
PO Box 70
Akiachak, AK 99552   Ph: (907)825-4626
Willie Kasayulie, Pres.
BIA Area Office: Juneau. **BIA Agency:** Bethel.

★2190★
Akiak Native Community
PO Box 52165
Akiak, AK 99552   Ph: (907)765-7112
Michael Williams, Pres.
BIA Area Office: Juneau. **BIA Agency:** Bethel.

★2191★
Native Village of Akutan
General Delivery
Akutan, AK 99553   Ph: (907)698-2232
Leon Prokopioff, Pres.
BIA Area Office: Juneau. **BIA Agency:** Anchorage.

★2192★
Village of Alakanuk
PO Box 167
Alakanuk, AK 99554   Ph: (907)238-9515
Dennis Sheldon, Pres.
BIA Area Office: Juneau. **BIA Agency:** Bethel.

★2193★
Alatna Traditional Council
General Delivery
Alatna, AK 99720   Ph: (907)968-2241
Harding Sam, Chief
BIA Area Office: Juneau. **BIA Agency:** Fairbanks.

★2194★
Native Village of Aleknagik
PO Box 115
Aleknagik, AK 99555   Ph: (907)842-2229
Patrick Kohler Sr., Pres.
BIA Area Office: Juneau. **BIA Agency:** Anchorage.

★2195★
Allakaket Traditional Council
General Delivery
Allakaket, AK 99720   Ph: (907)968-2241
Bergman Moses, Chief
BIA Area Office: Juneau. **BIA Agency:** Fairbanks.

★2196★
Ambler Traditional Council
General Delivery
Ambler, AK 99796   Ph: (907)445-2181
Louie Commack, Pres.
BIA Area Office: Juneau. **BIA Agency:** Nome.

★2197★
Anaktuvuk Pass Village Council
General Delivery
Anaktuvuk Pass, AK 99721   Ph: (907)661-3113
Raymond Paneak, Pres.
BIA Area Office: Juneau. **BIA Agency:** Fairbanks.

★2198★
Native Village of Kanatak
c/o BIA Anchorage Agency
1675 C St.
Anchorage, AK 99501   Ph: (907)271-4111
, Pres.
BIA Area Office: Juneau. **BIA Agency:** Anchorage.

★2199★
Angoon Community Association
PO Box 188
Angoon, AK 99820   Ph: (907)788-3994
Wally Frank, Pres.
BIA Area Office: Juneau. **BIA Agency:** Southeast.

★2200★
Native Village of Napamute
General Delivery
Aniak, AK 99557
BIA Area Office: Juneau.

★2201★
Village of Aniak
PO Box 176
Aniak, AK 99557   Ph: (907)675-4349
William A. Morgan Sr., Pres.
BIA Area Office: Juneau. **BIA Agency:** Bethel.

★2202★
Anvik Village
General Delivery
Anvik, AK 99558   Ph: (907)663-6346
Ken Chase, Chief
BIA Area Office: Juneau. **BIA Agency:** Fairbanks.

★2203★
Arctic Village Traditional Council
PO Box 22050
Arctic Village, AK 99722   Ph: (907)587-5320
Trible Gilbert, First Chief
BIA Area Office: Juneau. **BIA Agency:** Fairbanks.

★2204★
Venetie Village Council
General Delivery
Arctic Village, AK 99781
Gidgeon Jones, First Chief
BIA Area Office: Juneau. **BIA Agency:** Fairbanks.

★2205★
Native Village of Atka
Atka Rural Village
Atka, AK 99502   Ph: (907)767-8001
George Kudrin, Pres.
BIA Area Office: Juneau. **BIA Agency:** Anchorage.

★2206★
Village of Atmautluak
General Delivery
Atmautluak, AK 99559   Ph: (907)553-5610
Oscar Nick, Pres.
BIA Area Office: Juneau. **BIA Agency:** Bethel.

★2207★
Atqasuk Village Council
General Delivery
Atqasuk, AK 99791
Jimmy Nayukok, Pres.
BIA Area Office: Juneau. **BIA Agency:** Fairbanks.

★2208★
Inupiat Community of Arctic Slope
PO Box 934
Barrow, AK 99723   Ph: (907)825-6907
George Edwardsen, Pres.
BIA Area Office: Juneau. **BIA Agency:** Fairbanks.

★2209★
Native Village of Barrow
Box 1139
Barrow, AK 99723   Ph: (907)852-4411
Rex A. Okakok, Pres.
BIA Area Office: Juneau. **BIA Agency:** Fairbanks.

★2210★
Beaver Village Council
General Delivery
Beaver, AK 99724   Ph: (907)628-6126
Paul Williams Sr., First Chief
BIA Area Office: Juneau. **BIA Agency:** Fairbanks.

★2211★
Native Village of Belkofski
General Delivery
Belkofski, AK 99695   Ph: (907)497-2260
Maggie Kenezuroff, Pres.
BIA Area Office: Juneau. **BIA Agency:** Anchorage.

★2212★
Orutsararmuit Native Council
PO Box 927
Bethel, AK 99559   Ph: (907)543-2608
Thaddeus Tikiun Jr., Pres.
BIA Area Office: Juneau. **BIA Agency:** Bethel.

★2213★
Native Village of Evansville
General Delivery
Bettles Field, AK 99726   Ph: (907)692-5035
Naomi Costello, Clerk
BIA Area Office: Juneau. **BIA Agency:** Fairbanks.

★2214★
Brevig Mission Traditional Council
General Delivery
Brevig Mission, AK 99785   Ph: (907)642-3851
Robert Rock, Pres.
BIA Area Office: Juneau. **BIA Agency:** Nome.

★2215★
Native Village of Buckland
General Delivery
Buckland, AK 99727   Ph: (907)494-2121
Jimmie Geary Sr., Pres.
BIA Area Office: Juneau. **BIA Agency:** Nome.

★2216★
Native Village of Cantwell
PO Box 94
Cantwell, AK 99729   Ph: (907)768-2151
David Nicklie, Pres.
BIA Area Office: Juneau. **BIA Agency:** Anchorage.

★2217★
Chalkyitsik Village Council
General Delivery
Chalkyitsik, AK 99788   Ph: (907)773-1232
John Druck, Chief
BIA Area Office: Juneau. **BIA Agency:** Fairbanks.

★2218★
Chefornak Traditional Council
PO Box 29
Chefornak, AK 99561   Ph: (907)867-8850
Peter Tom, Pres.
BIA Area Office: Juneau. **BIA Agency:** Bethel.

★2219★
Native Village of Chanega
General Delivery
Chenega, AK 99562
John Totemoff, Pres.
Ph: (907)573-5111
BIA Area Office: Juneau. **BIA Agency:** Anchorage.

★2220★
Chevak Traditional Council
PO Box 5514
Chevak, AK 99563
Joseph V. Paniyak, Pres.
Ph: (907)858-7428
BIA Area Office: Juneau. **BIA Agency:** Bethel.

★2221★
Native Village of Chickaloon
PO Box 1105
Chickaloon, AK 99674
Alan Larson, Pres.
Ph: (907)746-0505
BIA Area Office: Juneau. **BIA Agency:** Anchorage.

★2222★
Native Village of Chignik Lagoon
General Delivery
Chignik Lagoon, AK 99565
Clemens Grunert, Pres.
Ph: (907)840-2206
BIA Area Office: Juneau. **BIA Agency:** Anchorage.

★2223★
Native Village of Chignik
General Delivery
Chignik Lake, AK 99563
Johnny Lind, Pres.
Ph: (907)749-8001
BIA Area Office: Juneau. **BIA Agency:** Anchorage.

★2224★
Native Village of Chignik Lake
PO Box 33
Chignik Lake, AK 99548
Willard Lind Jr., Pres.
Ph: (907)845-2122
BIA Area Office: Juneau. **BIA Agency:** Anchorage.

★2225★
Native Village of Chitina
PO Box 31
Chitina, AK 99566
Roy Eskilida, Pres.
Ph: (907)823-2215
BIA Area Office: Juneau. **BIA Agency:** Anchorage.

★2226★
Village of Chuathbaluk
General Delivery
Chuathbaluk, AK 99557
George Yaska, Chief
Ph: (907)467-4313
BIA Area Office: Juneau. **BIA Agency:** Bethel.

★2227★
Native Village of Eklutna
Star Rte. 2, Box 7450
Chugiak, AK 99567
Peter Ezi, Pres.
Ph: (907)688-3962
BIA Area Office: Juneau. **BIA Agency:** Anchorage.

★2228★
Native Village of Chuloonawick
General Delivery
Chuloonawick, AK 99581
Russ Akers, Pres.
Ph: (907)949-1147
BIA Area Office: Juneau. **BIA Agency:** Bethel.

★2229★
Circle Village Council
PO Box 8
Circle, AK 99733
Larry Nathaniel, First Chief
Ph: (907)733-1232
BIA Area Office: Juneau. **BIA Agency:** Fairbanks.

★2230★
Native Village of Clark's Point
PO Box 16
Clark's Point, AK 99569
Joseph Clark, Pres.
Ph: (907)236-1221
BIA Area Office: Juneau. **BIA Agency:** Anchorage.

★2231★
Village of Nelson Lagoon
General Delivery
Cold Bay, AK 99571
Paul Gunderson, Pres.
Ph: (907)989-2205
BIA Area Office: Juneau. **BIA Agency:** Anchorage.

★2232★
Native Village of Kluti-kaah
PO Box 68
Copper Center, AK 99573
Carl Pete, Pres.
Ph: (907)822-5241
BIA Area Office: Juneau. **BIA Agency:** Anchorage.

★2233★
Native Village of Eyak
PO Box 693
Cordova, AK 99574
Agnes Nichols, Chm.
Ph: (907)464-3622
BIA Area Office: Juneau. **BIA Agency:** Anchorage.

★2234★
Craig Community Association
PO Box 244
Craig, AK 99821
Jeff Sheakley, Vice Pres.
Ph: (907)826-3247
BIA Area Office: Juneau. **BIA Agency:** Southeast.

★2235★
Village of Crooked Creek
General Delivery
Crooked Creek, AK 99575
Marie Irman, Pres.
Ph: (907)432-2227
BIA Area Office: Juneau. **BIA Agency:** Bethel.

★2236★
Native Village of Deering
PO Box 36043
Deering, AK 99736
James Moto Jr., Pres.
Ph: (907)363-2136
BIA Area Office: Juneau. **BIA Agency:** Nome.

★2237★
Healy Lake Village Council
PO Box 667
Delta Junction, AK 99737
Linda Erickson, Pres.
Ph: (907)452-7915
BIA Area Office: Juneau. **BIA Agency:** Fairbanks.

★2238★
Dillingham Village Council
PO Box 216
Dillingham, AK 99576
Sally H. Smith, Pres.
Ph: (907)842-2384
BIA Area Office: Juneau. **BIA Agency:** Anchorage.

★2239★
Native Village of Diomede
General Delivery
Diomede, AK 99762   Ph: (907)686-8001
David Soolook, Pres.
BIA Area Office: Juneau.

★2240★
Dot Lake Village Council
PO Box 272
Dot Lake, AK 99737   Ph: (907)882-2693
William Miller, Pres.
BIA Area Office: Juneau. **BIA Agency:** Fairbanks.

★2241★
Douglas Indian Association
PO Box 434
Douglas, AK 99824   Ph: (907)463-5219
George Goenett, Pres.
BIA Area Office: Juneau. **BIA Agency:** Southeast.

★2242★
Eagle Village Council
PO Box 19
Eagle, AK 99738   Ph: (907)547-2238
Ruth Ridley, Contact
BIA Area Office: Juneau. **BIA Agency:** Fairbanks.

★2243★
Native Village of Eek
General Delivery
Eek, AK 99578   Ph: (907)536-5129
Steven White, Pres.
BIA Area Office: Juneau. **BIA Agency:** Bethel.

★2244★
Egegik Village Council
PO Box 189
Egegik, AK 99579   Ph: (907)233-2231
Richard Alto, Pres.
BIA Area Office: Juneau. **BIA Agency:** Anchorage.

★2245★
Native Village of Ekuk
General Delivery
Ekuk, AK 99576   Ph: (907)842-5937
Peter Heyano, Pres.
BIA Area Office: Juneau. **BIA Agency:** Anchorage.

★2246★
Ekwok Village Council
PO Box 49
Ekwok, AK 99580   Ph: (907)464-3311
Luki Akelkok Sr., Pres.
BIA Area Office: Juneau. **BIA Agency:** Anchorage.

★2247★
Native Village of Elim
PO Box 39070
Elim, AK 99739   Ph: (907)890-3441
John Jemewouk, Pres.
BIA Area Office: Juneau. **BIA Agency:** Nome.

★2248★
Emmonak Village Council
General Delivery
Emmonak, AK 99581   Ph: (907)949-1335
Billy Charles, Pres.
BIA Area Office: Juneau. **BIA Agency:** Bethel.

★2249★
False Pass Village Council
180 Umiak Dr.
False Pass, AK 99583   Ph: (907)548-2227
Gilda Shellikoff, Vice President
BIA Area Office: Juneau. **BIA Agency:** Anchorage.

★2250★
Birch Creek Village Council
General Delivery
Fort Yukon, AK 99740   Ph: (907)628-6126
Randall Baalam, Chief
BIA Area Office: Juneau. **BIA Agency:** Fairbanks.

★2251★
Native Village of Ft. Yukon
Box 126
Fort Yukon, AK 99740   Ph: (907)662-2581
Clarence Alexander, First Chief
BIA Area Office: Juneau. **BIA Agency:** Fairbanks.

★2252★
Native Village of Marshall
PO Box 110
Fortuna Ledge, AK 99585   Ph: (907)679-6632
Alex Evan, Pres.
BIA Area Office: Juneau. **BIA Agency:** Bethel.

★2253★
Native Village of Ohogamiut
General Delivery
Fortuna Ledge, AK 99585   Ph: (907)679-6740
Ludwig Papp, Pres.
BIA Area Office: Juneau. **BIA Agency:** Bethel.

★2254★
Gulkana Village Council
PO Box 254
Gakona, AK 99586   Ph: (907)822-5213
Gronia Ewan, Pres.
BIA Area Office: Juneau. **BIA Agency:** Anchorage.

★2255★
Native Village of Chistochina
PO Box 241
Gakona, AK 99586   Ph: (907)822-3503
Evelyn Beeter, Pres.
BIA Area Office: Juneau. **BIA Agency:** Anchorage.

★2256★
Native Village of Gakona
PO Box 124
Gakona, AK 99586   Ph: (907)822-3497
David Gene, Pres.
BIA Area Office: Juneau. **BIA Agency:** Anchorage.

★2257★
Galena Village Council
Box 182
Galena, AK 99741   Ph: (907)656-1366
Paddy Nollner, Chief
BIA Area Office: Juneau. **BIA Agency:** Fairbanks.

★2258★
Native Village of Gambell
PO Box 133
Gambell, AK 99742   Ph: (907)985-5014
Herbert Apassingok, Pres.
BIA Area Office: Juneau. **BIA Agency:** Nome.

★2259★
Native Village of Tazlina
PO Box 188
Glennallen, AK 99588   Ph: (907)822-5965
Robert Marshall, Pres.
BIA Area Office: Juneau. **BIA Agency:** Anchorage.

★2260★
Chinik Eskimo Community
PO Box 62020
Golovin, AK 99762   Ph: (907)779-3671
Tonsashay Esparza, Pres.
BIA Area Office: Juneau. **BIA Agency:** Nome.

★2261★
Native Village of Goodnews Bay
General Delivery
Goodnews Bay, AK 99589   Ph: (907)697-8614
James M. Smith, Pres.
BIA Area Office: Juneau. **BIA Agency:** Bethel.

★2262★
Organized Village of Grayling
General Delivery
Grayling, AK 99590   Ph: (907)453-5128
Marvin Deacon, Pres.
BIA Area Office: Juneau. **BIA Agency:** Fairbanks.

★2263★
Chilkoot Indian Association
PO Box 490
Haines, AK 99827   Ph: (907)766-2310
Roy Clayton, Pres.
BIA Area Office: Juneau. **BIA Agency:** Southeast.

★2264★
Holy Cross Village Council
PO Box 203
Holy Cross, AK 99602   Ph: (907)476-7196
Richard Peters, First Chief
BIA Area Office: Juneau. **BIA Agency:** Fairbanks.

★2265★
Port Graham Village Council
Port Graham via
Homer, AK 99603   Ph: (907)284-2227
Eleanor McMullen, Pres.
BIA Area Office: Juneau. **BIA Agency:** Anchorage.

★2266★
Hoonah Indian Association
PO Box 144
Hoonah, AK 99829   Ph: (907)945-3600
Jim Austin, Pres.
BIA Area Office: Juneau. **BIA Agency:** Southeast.

★2267★
Native Village of Hooper Bay
PO Box 37
Hooper Bay, AK 99604   Ph: (907)758-4915
Louis Bunyan, Pres.
BIA Area Office: Juneau. **BIA Agency:** Bethel.

★2268★
Native Village of Piamuit
General Delivery
Hooper Bay, AK 99604   Ph: (907)758-4420
Janet Napoleon, Pres.
BIA Area Office: Juneau. **BIA Agency:** Bethel.

★2269★
Hughes Village Council
General Delivery
Hughes, AK 99745   Ph: (907)889-2206
Carlson Koyukuk, First Chief
BIA Area Office: Juneau. **BIA Agency:** Fairbanks.

★2270★
Huslia Village Council
General Delivery
Huslia, AK 99746   Ph: (907)829-2256
Tony Sam Sr., Chief
BIA Area Office: Juneau. **BIA Agency:** Fairbanks.

★2271★
Hydaburg Cooperative Association
Box 305
Hydaburg, AK 99922   Ph: (907)285-3761
Robert Sanderson, Pres.
BIA Area Office: Juneau. **BIA Agency:** Southeast.

★2272★
Igiugig Village Center
PO Box 4008
Igiugig, AK 99613   Ph: (907)533-3211
Trefim Andrew, Pres.
BIA Area Office: Juneau. **BIA Agency:** Anchorage.

★2273★
Kokhanok Village Council
PO Box 1007
Iliamna, AK 99606   Ph: (907)282-2202
John Nelson, Pres.
BIA Area Office: Juneau. **BIA Agency:** Anchorage.

★2274★
Native Village of Iliamna
PO Box 286
Iliamna, AK 99606   Ph: (907)571-1246
Lorene Arce, Pres.
BIA Area Office: Juneau. **BIA Agency:** Anchorage.

★2275★
Newhalen Village Council
PO Box 165
Iliamna, AK 99606   Ph: (907)571-1226
Raymond Wassillie, Pres.
BIA Area Office: Juneau. **BIA Agency:** Anchorage.

★2276★
Ivanoff Bay Village Council
General Delivery
Ivanoff Bay, AK 99502   Ph: (907)699-2204
Archie Kalmakoff, Pres.
BIA Area Office: Juneau. **BIA Agency:** Anchorage.

★2277★
Central Council of the Tlingit and Haida Indian Tribes
  of Alaska
320 W. Willoughby Ave., Ste. 300
Juneau, AK 99801   Ph: (907)586-1432
Edward K. Thomas, Pres.
BIA Area Office: Juneau. **BIA Agency:** Fairbanks.

★2278★
Organized Village of Kake
PO Box 316
Kake, AK 99830-0316   Ph: (907)785-6471
Roselyn Fay, Pres.
BIA Area Office: Juneau. **BIA Agency:** Southeast.

★2279★
Kaktovik Village of Barter Island
PO Box 8
Kaktovik, AK 99747   Ph: (907)640-6120
Archie Brower, Pres.
BIA Area Office: Juneau. **BIA Agency:** Fairbanks.

★2280★
Village of Lower Kalskag
PO Box 27
Kalskag, AK 99626   Ph: (907)471-2228
Polassa Evan, Pres.
BIA Area Office: Juneau. **BIA Agency:** Bethel.

★2281★
Village of (Upper) Kalskag
General Delivery
Kalskag, AK 99607   Ph: (907)471-2218
Annie Lou Williams, Pres.
BIA Area Office: Juneau. **BIA Agency:** Bethel.

★2282★
Native Village of Kaltag
General Delivery
Kaltag, AK 99748   Ph: (907)534-2230
Franklin Madros, Chief
BIA Area Office: Juneau. **BIA Agency:** Nome.

★2283★
Native Village of Karluk
PO Box 22
Karluk, AK 99608   Ph: (907)241-2224
Ronny Lind, Pres.
BIA Area Office: Juneau. **BIA Agency:** Anchorage.

★2284★
Native Village of Kasaan
General Delivery
Kasaan, AK 99924   Ph: (907)542-2214
Louis Thompson, Pres.
BIA Area Office: Juneau. **BIA Agency:** Southeast.

★2285★
Native Village of Kasaan
PO Box 19
Kasigluk, AK 99609   Ph: (907)477-6927
Howard R. Tinker, Pres.
BIA Area Office: Juneau. **BIA Agency:** Bethel.

★2286★
Kenaitze Indian Tribe
PO Box 988
Kenai, AK 99611   Ph: (907)283-3633
Clara Swan, Chairperson
BIA Area Office: Juneau. **BIA Agency:** Anchorage.

★2287★
Native Village of Salamatof
PO Box 2682
Kenai, AK 99611   Ph: (907)283-7864
James Segura, Pres.
BIA Area Office: Juneau. **BIA Agency:** Anchorage.

★2288★
Ketchikan Indian Corporation
429 Deermount Ave.
Ketchikan, AK 99901   Ph: (907)225-5158
Ronald W. Leighton, Pres.
BIA Area Office: Juneau. **BIA Agency:** Southeast.

★2289★
Organized Village of Saxman
Rte. 2, Box 2
Ketchikan, AK 99901   Ph: (907)225-4166
Christine Collison, Pres.
BIA Area Office: Juneau. **BIA Agency:** Southeast.

★2290★
Kiana Traditional Council
PO Box 69
Kiana, AK 99749   Ph: (907)475-2109
Ben Atoruk, Pres.
BIA Area Office: Juneau. **BIA Agency:** Nome.

★2291★
King Cove Traditional Council
PO Box 13
King Cove, AK 99612   Ph: (907)497-2340
Simeon Kuzchikin, Pres.
BIA Area Office: Juneau. **BIA Agency:** Anchorage.

★2292★
Ugashik Village Council
General Delivery via
King Salmon, AK 99613
Roy Matsuno, Pres.
BIA Area Office: Juneau. **BIA Agency:** Anchorage.

★2293★
Native Village of Kipnuk
PO Box 57
Kipnuk, AK 99614   Ph: (907)896-5427
Luke Amik, Pres.
BIA Area Office: Juneau. **BIA Agency:** Bethel.

★2294★
Native Village of Kivalina
Box 32
Kivalina, AK 99750   Ph: (907)645-2137
David Swan, Pres.
BIA Area Office: Juneau. **BIA Agency:** Nome.

★2295★
Klawock Cooperative Extension
PO Box 112
Klawock, AK 99925   Ph: (907)755-2265
James Martinez, Pres.
BIA Area Office: Juneau. **BIA Agency:** Southeast.

★2296★
Chilkat Indian Village of Klukwan
PO Box 210   Ph: (907)767-5505
Klukwan, AK 99827-0210   Fax: (907)767-5515
Joe Hotch, Pres.
BIA Area Office: Juneau. **BIA Agency:** Southeast.

★2297★
Native Village of Hamilton
General Delivery
Koatlik, AK 99620   Ph: (907)899-4027
Willie Kamkoff, Pres.
BIA Area Office: Juneau. **BIA Agency:** Bethel.

★2298★
Kobuk Traditional Council
General Delivery
Kobuk, AK 99751   Ph: (907)948-2217
Elmer Ward, Pres.
BIA Area Office: Juneau. **BIA Agency:** Nome.

★2299★
Shoonaq Tribe of Kodiak
PO Box 1974
Kodiak, AK 99615   Ph: (907)486-4449
Margaret Roberts, Pres.
BIA Area Office: Juneau.

★2300★
Koliganek Village Council
General Delivery
Koliganek, AK 99576   Ph: (907)282-2202
Gus H. Johnson Jr., Pres.
BIA Area Office: Juneau. **BIA Agency:** Anchorage.

★2301★
Kongiganak Traditional Council
General Delivery
Kongiganak, AK 99559   Ph: (907)557-5638
Tommy Andrew, Pres.
BIA Area Office: Juneau. **BIA Agency:** Bethel.

★2302★
Bill Moore's Slough Native Village
Genera Delivery
Kotlik, AK 99620   Ph: (907)899-4712
Mark Okitkun, Tribal Admin.
BIA Area Office: Juneau. **BIA Agency:** Bethel.

★2303★
Village of Kotlik
PO Box 20096
Kotlik, AK 99620   Ph: (907)899-4326
Pius Akaran, Pres.
BIA Area Office: Juneau. **BIA Agency:** Bethel.

★2304★
Native Village of Kotzebue
PO Box 296
Kotzebue, AK 99752   Ph: (907)442-3467
Pete Schaeffer, Chm.
BIA Area Office: Juneau. **BIA Agency:** Nome.

★2305★
Native Village of Koyuk
PO Box 81
Koyuk, AK 99753   Ph: (907)963-3651
Raymond Douglas, Pres.
BIA Area Office: Juneau. **BIA Agency:** Nome.

★2306★
Koyukuk Village Council
General Delivery
Koyukuk, AK 99754   Ph: (907)927-2214
Leo Lolnitz, Chief
BIA Area Office: Juneau. **BIA Agency:** Fairbanks.

★2307★
Organized Village of Kwethluk
General Delivery
Kwethluk, AK 99621   Ph: (907)757-6814
Joseph Guy, Pres.
BIA Area Office: Juneau. **BIA Agency:** Bethel.

★2308★
Native Village of Kwigillingok
PO Box 49
Kwigillingok, AK 99622   Ph: (907)588-8114
Owen Lewis, Pres.
BIA Area Office: Juneau. **BIA Agency:** Bethel.

★2309★
Native Village of Larsen Bay
PO Box 35
Larsen Bay, AK 99624   Ph: (907)847-2207
Valen Reft, Pres.
BIA Area Office: Juneau. **BIA Agency:** Anchorage.

★2310★
Levelock IRA Council
General Delivery
Levelock, AK 99625   Ph: (907)287-3030
Edwin Peterson, Pres.
BIA Area Office: Juneau. **BIA Agency:** Anchorage.

★2311★
Lime Village Council
General Delivery
Lime Village, AK 99627   Ph: (907)526-5126
Phillip Bobby, Pres.
BIA Area Office: Juneau. **BIA Agency:** Bethel.

★2312★
Manley Village Council
General Delivery
Manley Hot Springs, AK 99756   Ph: (907)672-3271
Dorothy Shockley, Pres.
BIA Area Office: Juneau. **BIA Agency:** Fairbanks.

★2313★
Manokotak Village Council
PO Box 169
Manokotak, AK 99628   Ph: (907)289-1027
Schwalbe Nukwak, Pres.
BIA Area Office: Juneau. **BIA Agency:** Anchorage.

★2314★
McGrath Native Village
PO Box 134
McGrath, AK 99627   Ph: (907)524-3024
Ann Egrass, Chief
BIA Area Office: Juneau. **BIA Agency:** Bethel.

★2315★
Telida Village Council
Box 217
McGrath, AK 99627   Ph: (907)843-8115
Steve Eluska, First Chief
BIA Area Office: Juneau. **BIA Agency:** Bethel.

★2316★
Native Village of Mekoryuk
PO Box 66
Mekoryuk, AK 99630   Ph: (907)827-8828
Solomon Williams, Pres.
BIA Area Office: Juneau. **BIA Agency:** Bethel.

★2317★
Metlakatla Indian Community Council
PO Box 8   Ph: (907)886-4441
Metaklatla, AK 99926   Fax: (907)886-7997
Ted A. Littlefield, Mayor
BIA Area Office: Portland. **BIA Agency:** Metlakatla.

★2318★
Minto Village Council
PO Box 26
Minto, AK 99758   Ph: (907)798-7112
Berkman Silas, Chief
BIA Area Office: Juneau. **BIA Agency:** Fairbanks.

★2319★
Native Village of Mountain Village
PO Box 32007
Mountain Village, AK 99632   Ph: (907)591-2048
Robert Beans, Pres.
BIA Area Office: Juneau. **BIA Agency:** Bethel.

★2320★
Naknek Native Village Council
PO Box 106
Naknek, AK 99633   Ph: (907)246-4210
Dolly Hermann, Pres.
BIA Area Office: Juneau. **BIA Agency:** Anchorage.

★2321★
Nanwalek Village Council
General Delivery
Napakiak, AK 99634   Ph: (907)281-9219
Vincent Kvasnikoff, Pres.
BIA Area Office: Juneau. **BIA Agency:** Anchorage.

★2322★
Native Village of Napakiak
General Delivery
Napakiak, AK 99634   Ph: (907)589-2227
Daniel Nelson, Pres.
BIA Area Office: Juneau. **BIA Agency:** Bethel.

★2323★
Napaskiak Village Council
General Delivery
Napaskiak, AK 99559   Ph: (907)737-7626
Paul Guy, Pres.
BIA Area Office: Juneau. **BIA Agency:** Bethel.

★2324★
Nenana Native Association
PO Box 356
Nenana, AK 99760   Ph: (907)479-6211
Dennis Argall, Chief
BIA Area Office: Juneau. **BIA Agency:** Fairbanks.

★2325★
New Stuyahok Village Council
General Delivery
New Stuyahok, AK 99636   Ph: (907)693-8002
Peter Gumlikpuk, Pres.
BIA Area Office: Juneau. **BIA Agency:** Anchorage.

★2326★
Newtok Village Council
General Delivery
Newtok, AK 99681   Ph: (907)237-2314
Larry Charles, Pres.
BIA Area Office: Juneau. **BIA Agency:** Bethel.

★2327★
Nickolai Village Council
General Delivery
Nickolai, AK 99691   Ph: (907)524-3741
Paul Petruska, Pres.
BIA Area Office: Juneau. **BIA Agency:** Bethel.

★2328★
Native Village of Nightmute
General Delivery
Nightmute, AK 99690   Ph: (907)647-6427
Dick Anthony, Pres.
BIA Area Office: Juneau. **BIA Agency:** Bethel.

★2329★
Umkumiut Village Council
General Delivery
Nightmute, AK 99690   Ph: (907)647-6312
Simon Angus, Pres.
BIA Area Office: Juneau. **BIA Agency:** Bethel.

★2330★
Native Village of Nikolski
General Delivery
Nikolski, AK 99638   Ph: (907)576-2208
Mr. Val Dushkin, Pres.
BIA Area Office: Juneau. **BIA Agency:** Anchorage.

★2331★
Ninilckik Traditional Council
PO Box 282
Ninilchik, AK 99639   Ph: (907)567-3313
Grassim Oskolkoff, Pres.
BIA Area Office: Juneau. **BIA Agency:** Anchorage.

★2332★
Native Village of Noatak
PO Box 89
Noatak, AK 99761   Ph: (907)485-2173
Benjamin Sherman, Pres.
BIA Area Office: Juneau. **BIA Agency:** Nome.

★2333★
King Island Native Community
PO Box 992
Nome, AK 99762   Ph: (907)443-5494
Gabriel Payenna, Chief
BIA Area Office: Juneau. **BIA Agency:** Nome.

★2334★
Native Village of Council
PO Box 1707
Nome, AK 99762
Barbara Gray, Pres.

★2335★
Nome Eskimo Community
PO Box 401
Nome, AK 99762   Ph: (907)443-2246
Danny Karmun, Pres.
BIA Area Office: Juneau. **BIA Agency:** Nome.

★2336★
Nondalton Village Council
General Delivery
Nondalton, AK 99640   Ph: (907)294-2254
Melvin Trefon, Pres.
BIA Area Office: Juneau. **BIA Agency:** Anchorage.

★2337★
Noorvik Native Community
PO Box 71
Noorvik, AK 99763   Ph: (907)636-2144
William Zibell, Pres.
BIA Area Office: Juneau. **BIA Agency:** Nome.

★2338★
Northway Village Council
PO Box 455
Northway, AK 99764   Ph: (907)778-2250
Robert Silas, Pres.
BIA Area Office: Juneau. **BIA Agency:** Fairbanks.

★2339★
Native Village of Nuigsut
General Delivery
Nuigsut, AK 99723   Ph: (907)480-6714
Maggie Kavalsky, Mayor
BIA Area Office: Juneau. **BIA Agency:** Fairbanks.

★2340★
Nulato Village Council
General Delivery
Nulato, AK 99765   Ph: (907)898-0255
Ivan Sipary, Pres.
BIA Area Office: Juneau. **BIA Agency:** Fairbanks.

★2341★
Native Village of Nunapitchuk
PO Box 190
Nunapitchuk, AK 99641   Ph: (907)527-5705
Chuck Chaliak, Pres.
BIA Area Office: Juneau. **BIA Agency:** Bethel.

★2342★
Village of Old Harbor
PO Box 109
Old Harbor, AK 99643   Ph: (907)286-2204
Ron Bertsen, Pres.
BIA Area Office: Juneau. **BIA Agency:** Anchorage.

★2343★
Oscarville Traditional Council
PO Box 1554
Oscarville, AK 99559   Ph: (907)737-7321
Ignati Jacob, Pres.
BIA Area Office: Juneau. **BIA Agency:** Bethel.

★2344★
Village of Ouzinkie
PO Box 13
Ouzinkie, AK 99644   Ph: (907)680-2259
Alex Ambrosia, Pres.
BIA Area Office: Juneau. **BIA Agency:** Anchorage.

★2345★
Pedro Bay Village Council
PO Box 47020
Pedro Bay, AK 99647   Ph: (907)850-2225
Johnny Jacko, Pres.
BIA Area Office: Juneau. **BIA Agency:** Anchorage.

★2346★
Village of Perryville
PO Box 110
Perryville, AK 99648   Ph: (907)852-2203
Elia J. Phillips, Pres.
BIA Area Office: Juneau. **BIA Agency:** Anchorage.

★2347★
Petersburg Indian Association
PO Box 588
Petersburg, AK 99833   Ph: (907)772-3636
Gertrude Lyons, Pres.
BIA Area Office: Juneau. **BIA Agency:** Southeast.

★2348★
Village of Pilot Point
PO Box 449
Pilot Point, AK 99649   Ph: (907)797-2208
Mark Reamey, Pres.
BIA Area Office: Juneau. **BIA Agency:** Anchorage.

★2349★
Pilot Station Traditional Council
PO Box 5040
Pilot Station, AK 99650   Ph: (907)549-3512
Nicky Myer, Acting Pres.
BIA Area Office: Juneau. **BIA Agency:** Bethel.

★2350★
Native Village of Pitka's Point
PO Box 127
Pitka's Point, AK 99658   Ph: (907)438-2833
Ruth Riley, Pres.
BIA Area Office: Juneau. **BIA Agency:** Bethel.

★2351★
Platinum Village Council
General Delivery
Platinum, AK 99651   Ph: (907)979-8126
James T. Kasayulie, Pres.
BIA Area Office: Juneau. **BIA Agency:** Bethel.

★2352★
Point Hope Village Council
PO Box 91
Point Hope, AK 99766   Ph: (907)368-2453
Ernie Frankson, Pres.
BIA Area Office: Juneau. **BIA Agency:** Nome.

★2353★
Native Village of Point Lay
PO Box 101
Point Lay, AK 99759   Ph: (907)833-2428
Annie Martin, Pres.
BIA Area Office: Juneau. **BIA Agency:** Fairbanks.

★2354★
Village Council of Port Heiden
PO Box 49007
Port Heiden, AK 99459   Ph: (907)284-2218
Orville Linde, Pres.
BIA Area Office: Juneau. **BIA Agency:** Anchorage.

★2355★
Native Village of Port Lions
PO Box 253
Port Lions, AK 99550   Ph: (907)454-2234
Mara Lukin, Pres.
BIA Area Office: Juneau. **BIA Agency:** Anchorage.

★2356★
Portage Creek Village Council
General Delivery
Portage Creek, AK 99576   Ph: (907)842-5218
Dan Pauk, Pres.
BIA Area Office: Juneau. **BIA Agency:** Anchorage.

★2357★
Native Village of Kwinhagak
PO Box 58
Quinhagak, AK 99655   Ph: (907)556-8449
John O. Mark, Pres.
BIA Area Office: Juneau. **BIA Agency:** Bethel.

★2358★
Rampart Village Council
General Delivery
Rampart, AK 99767   Ph: (907)358-3115
Linda Evans, Chief
BIA Area Office: Juneau. **BIA Agency:** Fairbanks.

★2359★
Village of Red Devil
General Delivery
Red Devil, AK 99656   Ph: (907)447-9901
Nick Willis, Pres.
BIA Area Office: Juneau. **BIA Agency:** Bethel.

★2360★
Ruby Native Council
Box 21
Ruby, AK 99768   Ph: (907)468-4406
Donald Honea Sr., Pres.
BIA Area Office: Juneau. **BIA Agency:** Fairbanks.

★2361★
Native Village of Russian Mission
General Delivery
Russian Mission, AK 99657   Ph: (907)584-5111
Nick Pitka, Acting Pres.
BIA Area Office: Juneau. **BIA Agency:** Bethel.

★2362★
St. George Island Village Council
PO Box 940
Saint George, AK 99660   Ph: (907)859-2205
Gilbert G. Kashevarof, Pres.
BIA Area Office: Juneau. **BIA Agency:** Anchorage.

★2363★
Native Village of Algaaciq
General Delivery
Saint Mary's, AK 99658   Ph: (907)438-2932
Francis Thompson, Pres.
BIA Area Office: Juneau. **BIA Agency:** Bethel.

★2364★
Native Village of Andreafski
General Delivery
Saint Mary's, AK 99658   Ph: (907)438-2317
Daniel Stevens Sr., Pres.
BIA Area Office: Juneau. **BIA Agency:** Bethel.

★2365★
Native Village of St. Michael
PO Box 59090
Saint Michael, AK 99659   Ph: (907)923-3831
Susanna Horn, Pres.
BIA Area Office: Juneau. **BIA Agency:** Nome.

★2366★
Aleut Community of St. Paul Island
General Delivery
Saint Paul Island, AK 99660   Ph: (907)546-2211
Simeon Swetsof, Pres.
BIA Area Office: Juneau. **BIA Agency:** Anchorage.

★2367★
Village of Sand Point
PO Box 189
Sand Point, AK 99661   Ph: (907)383-3525
Dick Jacobson, Pres.
BIA Area Office: Juneau. **BIA Agency:** Anchorage.

★2368★
Native Village of Savoonga
PO Box 129
Savoonga, AK 99769   Ph: (907)984-6414
Truman Kava, Pres.
BIA Area Office: Juneau. **BIA Agency:** Nome.

★2369★
Native Village of Scammon Bay
General Delivery
Scammon Bay, AK 99662   Ph: (907)558-5529
Aloysius Aguchak Sr., Pres.
BIA Area Office: Juneau. **BIA Agency:** Bethel.

★2370★
Native Village of Selawik
PO Box 59
Selawik, AK 99770   Ph: (907)484-2225
Louis M. Skin, Pres.
BIA Area Office: Juneau. **BIA Agency:** Nome.

★2371★
Native Village of Seldovia
Drawer L
Seldovia, AK 99663   Ph: (907)234-7625
Fred H. Elvsaas, Pres.
BIA Area Office: Juneau. **BIA Agency:** Bethel.

★2372★
Shageluk IRA Council
General Delivery
Shageluk, AK 99665   Ph: (907)473-8221
Hamilton Hamilton Sr., Chief
BIA Area Office: Juneau. **BIA Agency:** Bethel.

★2373★
Native Village of Shaktoolik
PO Box 75
Shaktoolik, AK 99771   Ph: (907)955-3701
Edgar Jackson, Pres.
BIA Area Office: Juneau. **BIA Agency:** Nome.

★2374★
Native Village of Sheldon's Point
General Delivery
Sheldon's Point, AK 99666   Ph: (907)498-4226
Paul J. Manumik, Pres.
BIA Area Office: Juneau. **BIA Agency:** Bethel.

★2375★
Native Village of Shishmaref
General Delivery
Shishmaref, AK 99772   Ph: (907)649-3821
William Barr, Pres.
BIA Area Office: Juneau. **BIA Agency:** Nome.

★2376★
Native Village of Shungnak
General Delivery
Shungnak, AK 99773   Ph: (907)437-2170
Levi Cleveland, Pres.
BIA Area Office: Juneau. **BIA Agency:** Nome.

★2377★
Sitka Community Association
PO Box 1450
Sitka, AK 99835   Ph: (907)747-3207
Pete Esquiro, Pres.
BIA Area Office: Juneau. **BIA Agency:** Southeast.

★2378★
Village of Sleetmute
PO Box 21
Sleetmute, AK 99668   Ph: (907)449-9901
Jane Zaukar, Pres.
BIA Area Office: Juneau. **BIA Agency:** Bethel.

★2379★
Village of Solomon
General Delivery
Solomon, AK 99762
BIA Area Office: Juneau.

★2380★
South Naknek Village Council
PO Box 70106
South Naknek, AK 99670   Ph: (907)246-3324
Carvil Zimin, Pres.
BIA Area Office: Juneau. **BIA Agency:** Anchorage.

★2381★
Stebbins Community Association
PO Box 2
Stebbins Village, AK 99761   Ph: (907)934-3561
Fred Pete Sr., Pres.
BIA Area Office: Juneau. **BIA Agency:** Nome.

★2382★
Stevens Village Council
General Delivery
Stevens Village, AK 99774   Ph: (907)478-9226
Harold Simons, First Chief
BIA Area Office: Juneau. **BIA Agency:** Fairbanks.

★2383★
Village of Stoney River
General Delivery
Stoney River, AK 99557   Ph: (907)537-3220
Nattie Donhauser, Pres.
BIA Area Office: Juneau.

★2384★
Takotna Village Council
General Delivery
Takotna, AK 99675   Ph: (907)298-2212
Dorothy Anderson, Pres.
BIA Area Office: Juneau. **BIA Agency:** Bethel.

★2385★
Tanacross Village Council
General Delivery
Tanacross, AK 99776   Ph: (907)883-4131
Jerry Isaac, Pres.
BIA Area Office: Juneau. **BIA Agency:** Bethel.

★2386★
Tanana IRA Native Council
PO Box 93
Tanana, AK 99777   Ph: (907)366-7160
Dennis Charley, Pres.
BIA Area Office: Juneau. **BIA Agency:** Fairbanks.

★2387★
Native Village of Tatitlek
PO Box 171
Tatitlek, AK 99677   Ph: (907)325-2311
Gary Kompkoff, Pres.
BIA Area Office: Juneau. **BIA Agency:** Anchorage.

★2388★
Teller Village Council
PO Box 548
Teller, AK 99778   Ph: (907)642-3401
Dale Okpealuk, Pres.
BIA Area Office: Juneau. **BIA Agency:** Nome.

★2389★
Village of Mary's Igloo
PO Box 571
Teller, AK 99778   Ph: (907)642-3731
Becky Pushruk, Pres.
BIA Area Office: Juneau.

★2390★
Tetlin Village Council
PO Box 520
Tetlin, AK 99780   Ph: (907)883-2202
Donald Joe, Pres.
BIA Area Office: Juneau. **BIA Agency:** Fairbanks.

★2391★
Traditional Council of Togiak
PO Box 209
Togiak, AK 99678   Ph: (907)493-5029
Andrew Franklin, Pres.
BIA Area Office: Juneau. **BIA Agency:** Anchorage.

★2392★
Mentasta Village
General Delivery
Tok, AK 99780   Ph: (907)291-2319
Eva Johns, Pres.
BIA Area Office: Juneau. **BIA Agency:** Anchorage.

★2393★
Native Village of Toksook Bay
General Delivery
Toksook Bay, AK 99637   Ph: (907)427-7114
Joseph Asuluk, Pres.
BIA Area Office: Juneau. **BIA Agency:** Bethel.

★2394★
Tuluksak Native Community
General Delivery
Tuluksak, AK 99679   Ph: (907)695-6828
Nick Alexie Sr., Pres.
BIA Area Office: Juneau. **BIA Agency:** Bethel.

★2395★
Native Village of Tuntutuliak
PO Box 77
Tuntutuliak, AK 99680   Ph: (907)256-2315
Peter Pavilla, Pres.
BIA Area Office: Juneau. **BIA Agency:** Bethel.

★2396★
Native Village of Tununak
PO Box 77
Tununak, AK 99681   Ph: (907)652-6527
Joe Post, Pres.
BIA Area Office: Juneau. **BIA Agency:** Bethel.

★2397★
Twin Hills Tribal Council
General Delivery
Twin Hills, AK 99576   Ph: (907)525-4820
Arthur Sharp, Pres.
BIA Area Office: Juneau. **BIA Agency:** Anchorage.

★2398★
Native Village of Tyonek
PO Box 82009
Tyonek, AK 99682-0009   Ph: (907)279-1941
Emil McCord Sr., Pres.
BIA Area Office: Juneau. **BIA Agency:** Anchorage.

★2399★
Qualingin Tribal Council
PO Box 339
Uhalaska, AK 99685
Okalena Gregory, Pres.
BIA Area Office: Juneau. **BIA Agency:** Anchorage.

★2400★
Unalakleet Village Council
PO Box 70
Unalakleet, AK 99684   Ph: (907)624-3622
Stanton Katchatag, Pres.
BIA Area Office: Juneau. **BIA Agency:** Nome.

★2401★
Wainwright Traditional Council
PO Box 184
Wainwright, AK 99782   Ph: (907)763-2726
George Agnassaga, Pres.
BIA Area Office: Juneau. **BIA Agency:** Fairbanks.

★2402★
Native Village of Wales
General Delivery
Wales, AK 99783   Ph: (907)664-3351
Victor Ongtowasruk, Pres.
BIA Area Office: Juneau. **BIA Agency:** Nome.

★2403★
Knik Village Council
PO Box 2130
Wasilla, AK 99687   Ph: (907)373-2161
Paul Theodore, Pres.
BIA Area Office: Juneau. **BIA Agency:** Anchorage.

★2404★
Native Village of White Mountain
PO Box 82
White Mountain, AK 99784   Ph: (907)638-3651
Dorothy Barr, Pres.
BIA Area Office: Juneau. **BIA Agency:** Nome.

★2405★
Wrangell Cooperative Association
PO Box 868
Wrangell, AK 99929   Ph: (907)874-5854
Marleita Wallace, Pres.
BIA Area Office: Juneau. **BIA Agency:** Southeast.

★2406★
Yakutat Native Association
PO Box 418
Yakutat, AK 99689   Ph: (907)784-3238
Nettie Vale, Exec.Dir.
BIA Area Office: Juneau. **BIA Agency:** Southeast.

National Organizations

★2407★
Alaska Federation of Natives (AFN)
411 W. Fourth Ave., Ste. 301
Anchorage, AK 99501   Ph: (907)274-3611
Julie Kitka, Pres.
Description: Serves as an advocate for Alaskan Eskimos, Indians, and Aleuts before Congress, the Alaska state legislature, and other federal and state agencies. Bestows awards, including Parents of the Year and AFN Citizen of the Year. **Founded:** 1966. **Members:** 80,000. **State Groups:** 6. **Publications:** *AFN Newsletter*, quarterly.

Includes president's report, information on winners of awards, and convention schedule. • *Annual Report*.

★2408★
American Indian Library Association (AILA)
c/o Amer. Library Assn.
50 E. Huron St.
Chicago, IL 60611
Naomi Caldwell Wood, Pres.
Description: Individuals and institutions interested in promoting the development, maintenance, and improvement of libraries, library systems, and cultural information services on reservations and in communities of Native Americans and Native Alaskans. Develops and encourages adoption of standards for Indian libraries; provides technical assistance to Indian tribes on establishing and maintaining archives systems. Works to enhance the capabilities of libraries to assist Indians who are writing tribal histories and to perpetuate knowledge of Indian language, history, legal rights, and culture. Seeks support for the establishment of networks for exchange of information among Indian tribes. Communicates the needs of Indian libraries to legislators and the library community. Coordinates development of courses, workshops, institutes, and internships on Indian library services. **Founded:** 1979. **Publications:** *American Indian Libraries Newsletter*, periodic.

★2409★
American Native Press Research Association (ANPRA)
University of Arkansas at Little Rock
Dept. of English
2801 S. University Ave.
Little Rock, AR 72204   Ph: (501)569-3160
Johnye E. Strickland, Corr.Sec.-Treas.
Description: Membership includes contributors to the American Indian and Alaska Native Periodicals Project, nonprofit educational and cultural institutions, and individuals interested in the study of the American native press. Purposes are to: promote and foster academic research concerning the American native press, those involved in it, and American native periodical literature as a whole; disseminate research results; refine methodologies for discussing the American native press. **Founded:** 1984. **Members:** 70.

★2410★
Americans for Indian Opportunity (AIO)
3508 Garfield St. NW
Washington, DC 20007   Ph: (202)338-8809
LaDonna Harris, Exec.Dir.
Description: Promotes economic self-sufficiency for American Indian tribes and individuals, and political self-government for members of American Indian tribes. Seeks to: help American Indians, Eskimos, and Aleuts establish self-help programs at the local level; improve communications among Native Americans and with non-Indians; educate the public on the achievements and current needs of Native Americans. Supports projects in education, health, housing, job development, and training opportunities for Indian young people. Assists in establishing local centers with similar goals. Monitors federal agencies to ensure the fair and proper administration of Indian programs and to obtain federal programs and grants of benefit to Indians on a local or national scale. Conducts research; bestows awards; compiles statistics. Maintains speakers' bureau. Holds seminars. **Founded:** 1970. **State Groups:** 7. **Publications:** *Red Alert*, periodic. • Also publishes *You Don't Have to Be Poor to Be Indian* and other resource information.

★2411★
Bureau of Catholic Indian Missions (BCIM)
2021 H St. NW   Ph: (202)331-8542
Washington, DC 20006   Fax: (202)331-8544
Rev.Msgr. Paul A. Lenz, Exec.Dir.
Description: Purpose is to conduct religious, charitable, and educational activities at American Indian and Eskimo missions. Maintains speakers' bureau; conducts research programs. **Founded:** 1874. **Publications:** *Bureau of Catholic Indian Missions-Newsletter*, monthly. • *Bureau of Catholic Indian Missions-Quarterly*.

★2412★
Cook Inlet Native Association (CINA)
1569 S. Bragaw, Ste. 200
Anchorage, AK 99508   Ph: (907)337-1800
Jane Goldbeck, Exec.Dir.

Description: Alaskan natives and American Indians dedicated to nurturing pride in the heritage and traditions of the Alaska native and preserving the customs, folklore, and art of the people. Promotes the potentials, opportunities, and physical, economic, and social well-being of Alaskan natives and American Indians. Offers training programs for word processors, clerical workers, bank tellers, and job-seeking techniques. Sponsors competitions; bestows awards; contributes to charitable programs. Maintains museum; compiles statistics. **Founded:** 1964. **Members:** 1472. **State Groups:** 140. **Publications:** *Trail Blazer*, quarterly. Newsletter.

★2413★
Institute of American Indian Arts (IAIA)
PO Box 20007
Santa Fe, NM 87504   Ph: (505)988-6463
Kathryn Harris Tijerina, Pres.

Description: Federally chartered private institution. Offers learning opportunities in the arts and crafts to Native American youth (Indian, Eskimo, or Aleut). Emphasis is placed upon Indian traditions as the basis for creative expression in fine arts including painting, sculpture, museum studies, creative writing, printmaking, photography, communications, design, and dance, as well as training in metal crafts, jewelry, ceramics, textiles, and various traditional crafts. Students are encouraged to identify with their heritage and to be aware of themselves as members of a race rich in architecture, the fine arts, music, pageantry, and the humanities. All programs are based on elements of the Native American cultural heritage that emphasize differences between Native American and non-Native American cultures. Sponsors Indian arts-oriented junior college offering Associate of Fine Arts degrees in various fields as well as seminars, an exhibition program, and traveling exhibits. Maintains extensive library, museum, and biographical archives. Provides placement service. **Founded:** 1962. **State Groups:** 10. **Publications:** *Faculty Handbook*, annual. • *School Catalog*, annual. • *Student Handbook*, annual. **Formerly:** (1962) Sante Fe Indian School.

★2414★
Maniilaq Association (MA)
PO Box 256
Kotzebue, AK 99752   Ph: (907)442-3311
Marie N. Greene, Pres.

Description: Tribal organization serving 11 Alaskan Eskimo villages ranging from 60 to 3000 in population. Works to: promote health and social welfare in the Northwest Arctic Borough region of Alaska; preserve and promote the Eskimo customs, arts, and language; advance education in all forms; stimulate economic activity and social understanding between natives and non-natives. Maintains group home, senior citizen center, nursing wing, social rehabilitation center, and youth camp; manages Maniilaq Medical Center. Provides women's crisis program, prematernal home, and placement and children's services. Bestows awards. Programs include: Adult Education; Agriculture; Counseling Services; Dental and Eye Care; Emergency Medical Services; Environmental Health Services; Health Aide Training; Health Education; Housing Improvement; Maternal-Child Health; Public Assistance; Public Health Nursing; Realty; Safety Education; Substance Abuse Treatment; Tribal Doctors; WIC. **Founded:** 1966. **Members:** 6500. **Regional Groups:** 4. **Local Groups:** 13. **Publications:** *Annual Report*. • *Maniilaq Directory*, annual. • *Northwest Arctic NUNA*, 10/year. Newsletter; includes local news and program information. • Also publishes books. • Also publishes books. **Formerly:** (1972) Northwest Alaska Native Association; (1981) Mauneluk Association.

★2415★
National Congress of American Indians (NCAI)
900 Pennsylvania Ave. SE
Washington, DC 20003   Ph: (202)546-9404

Description: Tribes representing 600,000 Indians (155) and individuals (2000). Seeks to: protect, conserve, and develop Indian natural and human resources; serve legislative interests of Indian tribes; improve health, education, and economic conditions. Administers NCAI Fund for educational and charitable purposes.

Conducts research on Indian problems as a service to Indian tribes. Offers training seminars. Bestows congressional awards; compiles statistics. NCAI claims to be the oldest and largest national membership organization of American Indians and Alaskan natives. **Founded:** 1944. **Members:** 2155. **State Groups:** 15. **Publications:** *Annual Conference Report*. • *Sentinel*, periodic. Bulletin providing information on political and legislative news. Includes survey results, calendar of events, and federal register notices.

★2416★
National Indian Council on Aging (NICOA)
6400 Uptown Blvd. NE
City Centre, Ste. 510-W
Albuquerque, NM 87110   Ph: (505)888-3302
Dave Baldridge, Exec.Dir.

Description: Native Americans. Seeks to bring about improved, comprehensive services to the Indian and Alaskan native elderly. Objectives are: to act as a focal point for the articulation of the needs of the Indian elderly; to disseminate information on Indian aging programs; to provide technical assistance and training opportunities to tribal organizations in the development of their programs. Conducts research on the needs of Indian elderly. **Founded:** 1976. **Members:** 300. **State Groups:** 8. **Publications:** *Elder Voices*, quarterly. • Also publishes proceedings, reports, and monographs. Write to request publication list.

★2417★
National Indian Education Association (NIEA)
1819 H St. NW, Ste. 800
Washington, DC 20006   Ph: (202)835-3001
Donna Rhodes, Pres.

Description: American Indians; associate members are non-Indians. Advocates educational programs to improve the social and economic well-being of American Indians and Alaskan natives. Represents diversity of geographic and tribal backgrounds. Focuses on exchange of ideas, techniques, and research methods among the participants in Indian/native education. **Founded:** 1970. **Members:** 2000. **State Groups:** 1. **Publications:** quarterly. *Indian Education Newsletter*, 4/year.

★2418★
National Indian Health Board (NIHB)
1385 S. Colorado Blvd. Ste. A-708
Denver, CO 80222   Ph: (303)759-3075
Levi Mestegh, Exec.Dir.

Description: Indians of all tribes and natives of Alaskan villages. Advocates the improvement of health conditions which directly or indirectly affect American Indians and Alaskan Natives. Seeks to inform the public of the health condition of Native Americans; represents Indians and their interests. Conducts seminars and workshops on health subjects. Provides technical assistance to members and Indian organizations. Bestows awards to nominated individuals who have made significant contributions in the Indian health field. **Founded:** 1969. **Members:** 12. **Regional Groups:** 12. **State Groups:** 6. **Publications:** *Conference Report*, annual. • *NIHB Health Reporter*, bimonthly. • Also publishes special reports on health issues and produces audiotapes.

★2419★
National Indian Social Workers Association (NISWA)
PO Box 27463
Albuquerque, NM 87125
Mary Kihega, Sec.-Treas.

Description: Advocates for the rights of American Indians and Alaska Natives in social services areas. Provides training and technical assistance to tribal and nontribal organizations in subjects including counseling, program development, and planning and administration. Encourages publication of articles and books which clearly depict characteristics of American Indian and Alaska Native life; encourages American Indian and Alaska Native students to enter the field of social work. Holds seminars on Indian child welfare. Conducts survey research on major advocacy issues; sponsors competitions; bestows Indian Social Worker of the Year Award. Maintains speakers' bureau; compiles statistics. **Founded:** 1970. **Members:** 200. **Regional Groups:** 7. **Publications:** *National Indian Social Workers Association–The Association*, periodic. Newsletter; includes calendar of events and news of members, research, and awards. **Formerly:** (1981) Association of American Indian Social Workers; (1984) Association of American Indian and Alaskan Native Social Workers. Presently inactive.

★2420★
National Indian Traders Association
3575 S. Fox
Englewood, CO 80110   Ph: (303)762-6579
Dr. Moto, Pres.

Description: Promotes Native American and Native Alaskan-produced arts and crafts. Provides a clearinghouse and consultation. **Founded:** 1981. **Publications:** *National Indian Arts and Crafts Directory*, biannual.

★2421★
National Urban Indian Council (NUIC)
10068 University Station
Denver, CO 80210   Ph: (303)750-2695
Gregory W. Frazier, Chief Exec.

Description: According to the council, more than 50% of the American Indians and Alaska Natives in the U.S. now reside off their reservations. Because of this transition and the resulting problems that have arisen, the council was formed to serve as a coalition through which urban-based American Indian and Alaskan Native groups could communicate among themselves and with the public for mutual support and sharing of information. Compiles statistics; bestows awards; operates speakers' bureau and private personnel placement service. Conducts research; maintains 200 volume library. **Founded:** 1977. **Members:** 500. **Regional Groups:** 10. **Local Groups:** 150. **Publications:** *American Indian Review*, quarterly. • *Bulletin*, 9-10/year. • Also publishes *Source Document*, *American Indians*, and *Alaska Natives*.

★2422★
Native American Program, Commission for Multicultural Ministries of ELCA (NAPCMM-ECL)
8765 W. Higgens Rd.
Chicago, IL 60631   Ph: (312)380-2838

Description: A program of the Evangelical Lutheran Church in America. Maintains a nine member board of American Indians and Alaskan natives. Acts as advocate and consultant to Lutheran churches on behalf of the needs of Indian communities. Supports American Indian and Alaskan native rights in ways consistent with Christian faith and life. **Founded:** 1987.

★2423★
Tekakwitha Conference National Center (TCNC)
PO Box 6759
Great Falls, MT 59406   Ph: (406)727-0147
Fred A. Buckles Jr., Exec.Dir.

Description: Catholic missionaries among American Indians; Eskimo and American Indian deacons and laypersons involved in ministry. Develops Catholic evangelization in the areas of Native American ministry, catechesis, liturgy, family life, evangelical liberation, ecumenical cooperation, and urban ministry, spirituality, and theology. Provides a forum for the exchange of ideas among Catholic Native Americans, Eskimos, and missionaries. Encourages development of Native American ministry by Indian people and attempts to assure Native American representation in the decision-making bodies of the church. Maintains 2000 volume library on scripture, theology, liturgy, religion, and Native Americans. **Founded:** 1939. **Members:** 12,000. **Regional Groups:** 3. **State Groups:** 6. **Publications:** *Cross and Feather News*, quarterly. Provides cultural, governmental, and spiritual information for Native Americans and Eskimos. Also includes book reviews, employment opportunities, and obituaries.

Regional, State/Provincial, & Local Organizations

★2424★
Aleutian Pribiloff Island Association
401 E. Fireweed, Ste. 201   Ph: (907)276-2700
Anchorage, AK 99503   Fax: (907)276-4894
Dimitri Philimonof, Exec.Dir.

★2425★
Association of Alaska Native Contractors
700 W. 58th, Unit F   Ph: (907)562-1866
Anchorage, AK 99518   Fax: (907)561-3006
Linda J. E. Henerikson, Pres.

★2426★
Yukon-Kuskokwim Health Corporation
PO Box 528
Bethel, AK 99559   Ph: (907)543-3321
Gene Pelpola, Pres.

★2427★
Copper River Health Director
PO Drawer H   Ph: (907)822-3333
Copper Center, AK 99573   Fax: (907)822-5247
Evelyn Beeter, Exec.Dir.

★2428★
Bristol Bay Area Health Corporation
PO Box 130
Dillingham, AK 99576   Ph: (907)842-5266
Robert Clark, Exec.Dir.

Description: Offers an alcohol recovery program.

★2429★
Fairbanks Native Association
201 1st Ave., 2nd Fl.   Ph: (907)452-1648
Fairbanks, AK 99701   Fax: (907)456-4148
Sam Demientiff, Exec.Dir.

★2430★
Institute of Alaska Native Arts
524 3rd Ave.
PO Box 80583   Ph: (907)456-7491
Fairbanks, AK 99708   Fax: (907)451-7268
Caroline A. Derrick, Exec. Officer

★2431★
Tanana Chiefs Health Authority
122 1st Ave.
Fairbanks, AK 99701   Ph: (907)452-8251

★2432★
Sealaska Heritage Foundation
1 Sealaska Plaza, Ste. 201
Juneau, AK 99801   Ph: (907)463-4844
David G. Katzeek, Exec.Dir.

★2433★
Southeast Alaska Regional Health Corporation
3245 Hospital Dr.   Ph: (907)463-4040
Juneau, AK 99801   Fax: (907)463-4012

★2434★
Kodiak Area Native Association
402 Center Ave.
Kodiak, AK 99615   Ph: (907)486-5725
Kelly Simeoneff, Pres.

★2435★
Mauneluk Association
PO Box 256
Kotzebue, AK 99752
Marie Green, Pres.

Ph: (907)442-3311
Fax: (907)442-2381

★2436★
Norton Sound Health Corporation
PO Box 966
Nome, AK 99762
Carolyn Michael, Pres.

Ph: (907)443-3311
Fax: (907)443-3139

Federal Government Agencies

★2437★
U.S. Department of Health and Human Services
Office of State and Community Programs
Office for American Indian, Alaskan Native and Native Hawaiian Programs
330 Independence Ave. SW
Washington, DC 20201

Ph: (202)619-2957

★2438★
U.S. Department of Housing and Urban Development
Office of Indian and Alaska Native Programs
451 7th St. SW
Washington, DC 20410

Ph: (202)708-0420

★2439★
U.S. Department of the Interior
Bureau of Indian Affairs
Juneau Area Office
9109 Mendenhall Mall Rd., Ste. 5
PO Box 3-8000
Juneau, AK 99802-1219
Niles Cesar, Dir.

Ph: (907)586-7177
Fax: (907)586-7169

Territory Includes: Alaska.

Federal Domestic Assistance Programs

★2440★
U.S. Department of Health and Human Services
Public Health Service
Indian Health Service
2101 E. Jefferson Blvd., Ste. 603
Rockville, MD 20852
Kay Carpentier, Grants Management Contact

Ph: (301)443-5204

Catalog Number: 93.905. **Objectives:** To conduct research and developmental activities in areas of Indian health care which further the performance of health responsibilities of the Indian Health Service. **Applicant Eligibility:** There are two groups of eligible applicants: (1) Federally recognized Indian tribes and tribal organizations which are contracting with the Indian Health Service under the authority of the Indian Self-Determination and Education Assistance Act; and (2) Indian Health Service components, including Service units and area offices. **Beneficiary Eligibility:** American Indian Tribes and Alaska Natives.

★2441★
U.S. Department of Health and Human Services
Public Health Service
Indian Health Service
Health Management Development Program
2101 E. Jefferson Blvd., Ste. 603
Rockville, MD 20857
B. Bowman, Contact

Ph: (301)443-5204

Catalog Number: 93.228. **Objectives:** To improve the quality of the health of American Indians and Native Alaskans by providing a full range of curative, preventive and rehabilitative health services; and to increase the capability of American Indians and Native Alaskans to manage their own health programs. **Applicant Eligibility:** Federally-recognized tribes and tribal organizations. **Types of Assistance:** Project Grants. **Beneficiary Eligibility:** Individuals who are members of an eligible applicant tribe, band, group, or village and who may be regarded as within the scope of the Indian health and medical service program and who are regarded as an Indian by the community in which he lives as evidenced by such factors as tribal membership, enrollment, residence on tax exempt land, ownership of restricted property, active participation in tribal affairs or other relevant factors in keeping with general Bureau of Indian Affairs practices in the jurisdiction.

★2442★
U.S. Department of Health and Human Services
Public Health Service
Indian Health Service
Health Professions Preparatory Scholarship Program for Indians
12300 Twinbrook Pkwy., Ste. 100
Rockville, MD 20852
Wes Picciotti, Contact

Ph: (301)443-6197

Catalog Number: 93.971. **Objectives:** To make scholarships to Indians for the purpose of completing compensatory pre-professional education to enable the recipient to qualify for enrollment or re-enrollment in a health professions school. **Applicant Eligibility:** Scholarship awards are made to individuals of American Indian or Native Alaskan descent, who have successfully completed high school education or high school equivalency and who have been accepted for enrollment in a compensatory, pre-professional general education course or curriculum. **Types of Assistance:** Project Grants. **Beneficiary Eligibility:** Individuals of American Indian or Native Alaskan descent.

★2443★
U.S. Department of Health and Human Services
Public Health Service
Indian Health Service
Health Professions Scholarship Program
200 Independence Ave. SW
Washington, DC 20201
Barbara N. Rosenberg, Grants Management Officer

Ph: (202)245-0146

Catalog Number: 93.972. **Objectives:** To promote service delivery improvement through research studies, and application of knowledge. **Applicant Eligibility:** Individuals of American Indian or Native Alaskan descent are given priority. Applicants for new awards: (1) must be accepted by an accredited U.S. educational institution for a full-time course of study leading to a degree in medicine, osteopathy, dentistry, or other participating health profession which is deemed necessary by the Indian Health Service; (2) be eligible for or hold an appointment as a Commissioned Officer in the Regular or Reserve Corps of the Public Health Service; or (3) be eligible for civilian service in the Indian Health Service. **Types of Assistance:** Project Grants.

★2444★
U.S. Department of Health and Human Services
Public Health Service
Indian Health Service
Research and Demonstration Projects for Indian Health
5600 Fishers Ln.
Rockville, MD 20852
Douglas Black, Contact

Ph: (301)443-5204

Catalog Number: 93.933. **Objectives:** To promote improved health care among American Indians and Alaska Natives through research studies, and demonstration projects. **Applicant Eligibility:** Federally recognized Indian tribes; tribal organizations; nonprofit intertribal organizations; nonprofit urban Indian organizations contracting with the Indian Health Service under Title V of the Indian Health Care Improvement Act; public or private nonprofit health and education entities; and State and local government health agencies. **Types of Assistance:** Project Grants. **Beneficiary Eligibility:** American Indians/Alaska Natives will be the ultimate beneficiaries of the funded projects either directly or indirectly depending upon the nature of the project. For example, those individuals who participate in research studies and receive services will be direct beneficiaries while those impacted by policy changes resulting from analyses of Indian health care issues will be indirect beneficiaries.

★2445★
U.S. Department of Housing and Urban Development
Community Planning and Development
Indian Community Development Block Program
451 7th St. SW
Washington, DC 20410   Ph: (202)708-1322

Catalog Number: 14.223. **Objectives:** To provide assistance to Indian Tribes and Alaskan Native Villages in the development of viable Indian communities. **Applicant Eligibility:** Any Indian tribe, band, group, or nation, including Alaskan Indians, Aleuts, and Eskimos, and any Alaskan Native Village which is eligible for assistance under the Indian Self-Determination and Education Assistance Act. **Types of Assistance:** Project Grants. **Beneficiary Eligibility:** Indian tribes and Alaskan Native Villages as defined above.

★2446★
U.S. Department of Housing and Urban Development
Public and Indian Housing
Washington, DC 20410   Ph: (202)755-0950

Catalog Number: 14.850. **Objectives:** To provide and operate cost-effective, decent, safe and sanitary dwellings for lower income families through an authorized local Public Housing Agency (PHA) or Indian Housing Authority (IHA). **Applicant Eligibility:** Public Housing Agencies and Indian Housing Authorities established in accordance with State or Tribal law are eligible. Other lower income individuals may be served under certain limited cirumstances. **Types of Assistance:** Direct Payments for Specified Use. **Beneficiary Eligibility:** Lower inocme families. "Families" include individuals who are 62 years old or older, disabled , or handicapped, or the remaining member of a tenant family.

★2447★
U.S. Department of the Interior
Bureau of Indian Affairs
Office of Indian Education Programs
Higher Education Grant Program
18th & C Sts. NW
Washington, DC 20245   Ph: (202)208-4871
Dr. Reginald Rodriguez, Contact

Catalog Number: 15.114. **Objectives:** To provide finanical aid to eligible Indian students to enable them to attended accredited institutions of higher education. **Applicant Eligibility:** Must be a member of an Indian tribe or Alaska Native Village being served by the Bureau, be enrolled or accepted for enrollment in an accredited college, and have financial need as determined by the institution's financial aid office. **Types of Assistance:** Project Grants. **Beneficiary Eligibility:** Same as applicant eligibility.

★2448★
U.S. Department of the Interior
Bureau of Indian Affairs
Trust and Economic Development
Indian Loans—Economic Development
18th & C Sts. NW
Washington, DC 20240   Ph: (202)208-5324
R.K. Nephew, Contact

Catalog Number: 15.124. **Objectives:** To provide assistance to Indians, Alaska Natives, tribes, and Indian organizations to obtain financing from private and governmental sources which serve other citizens. When otherwise unavailable, financial assistance through the Bureau is provided eligible applicants for any purpose that will promote the economic development of a Federal Indian reservation. **Applicant Eligibility:** Indians, Alaska Natives, tribes, and Indian organizations. Individual applicants must be a member of a federally recognized tribe. Organizational applicants must have a form of organization satisfactory to the Assistant Secretary for Indian Affairs. **Types of Assistance:** Direct Loans; Guaranteed/Insured Loans; Provisions of Specialized Services. **Beneficiary Eligibility:** Same as applicant eligibility.

★2449★
U.S. Department of the Interior
Indian Arts and Crafts Board
Indian Arts and Crafts Development
1849 C St. NW
Washington, DC 20240   Ph: (202)208-3773

Catalog Number: 15.850. **Objectives:** To encourage and promote the development of American Indian arts and crafts. **Applicant Eligibility:** Native Americans, Indian, Eskimo, and Aleut individuals and organizations, federally recognized Indian tribal governments, State and local governments, and nonprofit organizations. **Types of Assistance:** Use of Property, Facilities, and Equipment; Advisory Services and Counseling; Investigation of Complaints. **Beneficiary Eligibility:** Same as applicant eligibility.

★2450★
U.S. Department of Labor
Employment and Training Administration
Division of Indian and Native American Programs
Native American Employment and Training Programs
200 Constitution Ave. NW
Washington, DC 20210   Ph: (202)535-0500
Paul Mayrand, Contact

Catalog Number: 17.251. **Objectives:** To afford job training to Native Americans facing serious barriers to employment, who are in special need of such training to obtain productive employment. To reduce the economic disadvantages among Indians and others of Native American descent and to advance the economic and social development of such people. **Applicant Eligibility:** Indian tribes, bands or groups, Alaska Native villages or groups, and Hawaiian Native communities meeting the eligibility criteria, public bodies or private nonprofit agencies selected by the Secretary. Tribes, bands and groups may also form consortia in order to qualify for designation as a grantee. An independently eligible grantee shall be an Indian or Native American entity which has: (1) An identifiable Native American resident population of at least 1,000 individuals (for new grantees) within its designated service area, and (2) the capability to administer Indian and Native American employment and training programs. **Types of Assistance:** Formula Grants. **Beneficiary Eligibility:** Members of State or federally recognized Indian tribes, bands and other individuals of Native American descent, such as, but not limited to, the Kalamaths in Oregon, Micmac and Miliseet in Maine, the Lumbees in North Carolina and South Carolina, Indians variously descibed as terminated or landless, Eskimos and Aleuts in Alaska, and Hawaiian Natives. ("Hawaiian Native" means an individual any of whose ancestors were natives prior to 1778 of the area which now comprises the State of Hawaii.) Applicants must also be economically disadvantaged, unemployed, or underemployed. A Native American grantee may apply in some cases enroll participants who are not economically disadvantaged, unemployed, or underemployed in upgrading and retraining programs.

State/Provincial & Local Government Agencies

★2451★
Alaska Education Department
Rural and Native Education
PO Box F
Juneau, AK 99811-0500   Ph: (907)465-2800
Edna MacLean, Contact

★2452★
Alaska Governor's Office
Assistant for Alaska Native Affairs
Pouch A
Juneau, AK 99811

★2453★
Alaska State Council on the Arts
411 W. 4th Ave., Ste. 1E   Ph: (907)297-1558
Anchorage, AK 99501   Fax: (907)279-4330
Christine D'Arcy, Contact
Description: Provides grants to support Native Alaskan arts and crafts.

★2454★
U.S. Department of the Interior
Bureau of Indian Affairs
Anchorage Agency
PO Box 100120   Ph: (907)271-4088
Anchorage, AK 99510   Fax: (907)868-4083

★2455★
U.S. Department of the Interior
Bureau of Indian Affairs
Bethel Agency
PO Box 347   Ph: (907)543-2726
Bethel, AK 99559   Fax: (907)543-3574

★2456★
U.S. Department of the Interior
Bureau of Indian Affairs
Fairbanks Agency
101 12th Ave.
Box 16   Ph: (907)456-0222
Fairbanks, AK 99707   Fax: (907)870-0225

★2457★
U.S. Department of the Interior
Bureau of Indian Affairs
Metlakatla Field Station
PO Box 560   Ph: (907)886-2791
Metlakatla, AK 99926   Fax: (907)886-7738

★2458★
U.S. Department of the Interior
Bureau of Indian Affairs
Nome Agency
PO Box 1108   Ph: (907)443-2284
Nome, AK 99762   Fax: (907)443-2317

★2459★
U.S. Department of the Interior
Bureau of Indian Affairs
Southeast Agency
PO Box 3-8000   Ph: (907)586-7304
Juneau, AK 99802   Fax: (907)871-7169

Library Collections

★2460★
Chilkat Valley Historical Society
Sheldon Museum & Cultural Center
Box 269
Haines, AK 99827   Ph: (907)766-2366
Rebecca Nelson, Asst.Cur.
Subjects: Tlingit art and culture; Alaskan history. **Special Collections:** Porcupine Mining Company account books, 1897-1916; logbooks from two harbor boats, 1910-1930. **Holdings:** 1150 books; 5600 feet of home movies; Haines and Skagway newspapers on microfilm; AV programs on historical and resource subjects; photographs, 1897 to present; autographed correspondence;

journals, manuscripts, deeds from circa 1900; maps; charts; 27 linear feet of blueprints.

★2461★
ERIC Clearinghouse on Rural Education and Small Schools
Library
1031 Quarrier St.
Box 1348
Charleston, WV 25325   Free: 800-624-9120
                                           Fax: (304)347-0487
Subjects: Education - rural, small schools, Mexican American, American Indian, Alaska Native, migrant, outdoor. **Holdings:** 300,000 documents on ERIC microfiche. **Also Known As:** CRESS. **Remarks:** Electronic mail address(es): CRESS.ERIC (GTE).

★2462★
Institute of American Indian and Alaska Native Culture and Arts Development
Library
College of Santa Fe Campus
St. Michael's Dr.
Box 20007   Ph: (505)988-6670
Santa Fe, NM 87504   Fax: (505)988-6446
Mary Young, Dir. of Libs.
Subjects: American Indian culture, history and technique of American Indian fine arts. **Special Collections:** Exhibition catalogs. **Holdings:** 18,000 books; 8 file drawers of archival materials; 9000 art slides; 4000 Indian slides; 24 file drawers of art catalogs; 27,826 Smithsonian Indian photographs; 8 file drawers of Indian newspapers; 60 tapes, 88 cassettes and 585 phonograph records of Indian music recordings; Indian newspapers. **Remarks:** Institute is not affiliated with the College of Santa Fe.

★2463★
Nome Library/Kegoayah Kozga Public Library
Front St.
Box 1168
Nome, AK 99762   Ph: (907)443-5133
Dee J. McKenna, Libn.
Subjects: Alaska, Eskimo and Gold Rush artifacts. **Special Collections:** Alaskana (75 rare volumes). **Holdings:** 14,000 books; 3000 cassette tapes; 1200 AV programs; old photographs; bilingual and oral history materials.

★2464★
Society of Jesus, Oregon Province
Archives
Crosby Library, Gonzaga University
E. 502 Boone Ave.   Ph: (509)328-4220
Spokane, WA 99258   Fax: (509)484-2804
Rev. Neill R. Meany, S.J., Archv.
Subjects: History - Northwest Church, Alaska Church and missions, Doukhobor, local; Alaskan and Indian languages. **Special Collections:** Joset Papers; Cataldo Papers; Crimont Papers; Neil Byrne Papers; Monaghan Papers; Cowley Papers; Prando Papers; Jesuit Mission Papers. **Holdings:** 3600 books; 800 bound periodical volumes; 123,000 manuscripts; 25,000 photographs.

★2465★
Tongass Historical Museum
Library
629 Dock St.   Ph: (907)225-5600
Ketchikan, AK 99901   Fax: (907)225-5075
Roxana Adams, Musm.Dir.
Subjects: Alaska - forestry, mining, fishing, Indians. **Special Collections:** Ketchikan Spruce Mills manuscript collection (500 cubic feet); regional photographs of Alaskan industries and Indians (20,000). **Holdings:** 500 books; 500 cubic feet of regional archives. **Formerly:** Tongass Historical Society, Inc. **Remarks:** Library cooperates with Alaska State Historical Library, Pouch G, Juneau, AK 99801.

★2466★
Totem Heritage Center
Library
c/o 629 Dock St.   Ph: (907)225-5900
Ketchikan, AK 99901   Fax: (907)225-5075
Roxana Adams, Musm.Dir.

Subjects: Northwest Coast Indian art, culture, and history. **Special Collections:** Northwest Coast totem poles (31). **Holdings:** 500 books; 150 bound periodical volumes; 2500 photographs; 50 manuscripts. **Remarks:** Maintained by the City of Ketchikan Museum Department.

★2467★
U.S. Department of the Interior
Indian Arts and Crafts Board
Library
18th & C Sts., N.W., Rm. 4004-MIB
Washington, DC 20240   Ph: (202)208-3773
Robert G. Hart, Gen.Mgr.

Subjects: Contemporary Native American arts and crafts. **Remarks:** The Indian Arts and Crafts Board serves Indians, Eskimos, Aleuts, and the general public as an information, promotional, and advisory clearinghouse for all matters pertaining to the development of authentic Native American arts and crafts.

★2468★
U.S. National Park Service
Sitka National Historical Park
Library
Box 738   Ph: (907)747-6281
Sitka, AK 99835   Fax: (907)747-5938
Tim Stone, Chf.Pk. Ranger

Subjects: Pacific Northwest Coast Indians, arts and crafts, ethnology, archeology, Southeast Alaska history, natural history, Russian American history. **Special Collections:** Park archives; Old Kasaan National Monument. **Holdings:** 1500 books; 200 clippings and special papers; 55 tapes; 14 films.

★2469★
University of Alaska, Fairbanks
Alaska Native Language Center
Research Library
Box 900111   Ph: (907)474-7874
Fairbanks, AK 99775-0120   Fax: (907)474-7720
Michael Krauss, Dir.

Subjects: Alaskan native, Athabaskan, Eyak, Tlingit, Haida, Tsimshian, and Eskimo-Aleut languages; Amerindian linguistics. **Holdings:** 8000 books, journals, unpublished papers, field notes, and archival materials. **Remarks:** Said to contain practically everything written in or on any Alaska native language, including languages shared in Canada and the Soviet Union.

Museum Collections

★2470★
Alaska Indian Arts, Inc.
23 Ft. Seward Dr.
PO Box 271
Haines, AK 99827   Ph: (907)766-2160
Carl W. Heinmiller, CEO

Description: Collections include Tlingit Indian costumes, Indian art, and ethnology. It maintains a totem village with tribal house and totem poles.

★2471★
Alaska State Museum
395 Whittier St.
Juneau, AK 99801   Ph: (907)465-2901

Description: Preserves and exhibits the culture and art of Alaska's native peoples.

★2472★
Anchorage Museum of History and Art
121 W. 7th Ave.   Ph: (907)343-4326
Anchorage, AK 99501   Fax: (907)343-6149
Patricia B. Wolf, Dir.

Description: The museum contains collections of Alaskan art and artifacts of all periods.

★2473★
Baranov Museum
Erskine House
101 Marine Way
Kodiak, AK 99615   Ph: (907)486-5920
Peggy Dyson, Pres.

Description: Collections include items from the Kodiak and Aleutian Islands and Eskimo artifacts.

★2474★
Clausen Memorial Museum
203 Fram St.
PO Box 708
Petersburg, AK 99833   Ph: (907)772-3598
Michale Edgington, Exec.Dir.

Description: The museum's collections reflect the diversity of the peoples who have lived in the area, including Tlingit, European, and Asian. Collections include a Tlingit canoe and tools.

★2475★
Cook Inlet Historical Society
121 W. 7th Ave.
Anchorage, AK 99501   Ph: (907)343-4326
William E. Davis, Pres.

Description: The society maintains a collection of native artifacts.

★2476★
Fort William H. Seward
PO Box 518   Ph: (907)766-2702
Haines, AK 99827   Free: 800-458-3579

Description: Accommodates carvers who use traditional Indian methods for creating totems, dance masks, and other items. Maintains a replica of a tribal house, and several totem poles.

★2477★
Kotzebue Museum, Inc.
PO Box 46   Ph: (907)442-3401
Kotzebue, AK 99752   Fax: (907)442-3742
Caleb Pungowiyi, City Manager and CEO

Description: Collections contain Eskimo artifacts, arts and crafts, costumes, and Indian artifacts.

★2478★
Samuel K. Fox Museum
Seward and D Sts.
PO Box 273   Ph: (907)842-2322
Dillingham, AK 99576   Fax: (907)842-5691
Mark Weber, Dir.

Description: The museum maintains collections of Southwestern Yup'ik Eskimo arts and crafts; basket weaving; skin sewing; wood, ivory, and bone carving; Alaskan culture memorabilia; Southwestern Yup'ik, Siberian Yup'ik, and Inupiat Eskimo artifacts; and historical photographs and prints.

★2479★
Sheldon Jackson Museum
104 College Dr.   Ph: (907)747-8981
Sitka, AK 99835   Fax: (907)747-3004
Irene Schuler, Pres.

Description: Collections include: Haida argillite carvings; Eskimo implements, ivory carvings, masks, skin clothing, baskets, kayaks, umiak; Athapaskan birchbark canoes, skin clothing, implements; Tlingit totem poles, Shaman charms, baskets, ceremonial equipment and garments.

★2480★
Sheldon Museum and Cultural Center
25 Main St.
PO Box 269
Haines, AK 99827
Ph: (907)766-2366
Cynthia L. Jones, Curator
Description: The center maintains a collection of Tlingit and other Northwest Coast Indian artifacts, including some Eskimo/Athapascan.

★2481★
Simon Paneak Memorial Museum
PO Box 21085
Ph: (907)661-3413
Anaktuvuk Pass, AK 99721
Fax: (907)661-3429
Jeslie Kaleak, CEO
Description: The museum maintains a collection on Nunamuit Eskimo history and traditions.

★2482★
Tongass Historical Museum
629 Dock St.
Ph: (907)225-5600
Ketchikan, AK 99901
Fax: (907)225-5075
Roxana Adams, Dir.
Description: Collections contain Indian artifacts, as well as objects and photos relating to the Tlingit, Haida, and Tsimshian cultures.

★2483★
Totem Heritage Center
629 Dock St.
Ph: (907)225-5900
Ketchikan, AK 99901
Fax: (907)225-5075
Roxana Adams, Dir.
Description: The center maintains an Alaska Totem collection and a collection of Northwest Coast Indian art. It sponsors a Native Arts Studies program and awards a certificate of merit in carving/design or textile arts.

★2484★
Wrangell Museum
PO Box 1050
Wrangell, AK 98929
Ph: (907)874-3770
Description: Contains collection of Tlingit Indian hand tools, spruce root and cedar baskets, ceremonial headdresses and blankets.

★2485★
Yugtarvik Regional Museum and Bethel Visitor Center
Box 388
Bethel, AK 99559
Ph: (907)543-2098
Gordon H. Hills, Curator
Description: Collections include Yup'ik Eskimo artifacts of southwestern Alaska, the Kuskokwim delta, and the Yukon delta.

California

★2486★
Cabots Old Indian Pueblo Museum
67-616 E. Desert View Ave.
PO Box 1267
Ph: (619)329-7610
Desert Hot Springs, CA 92240
Fax: (619)329-1956
Colbert H. Eyraud, CEO and Pres.
Description: Collections include Indian and Eskimo artifacts, comtemporary Native American art and jewelry, and a 35-room Hopi style structure.

★2487★
Marin Museum of the American Indian
2200 Novato Blvd.
PO Box 864
Novato, CA 94948
Ph: (415)897-4064
Dawn Carlson, Chair.
Description: Collections include archaeological, ethnographic, and archival materials from Alaska to Peru, pertaining to Native Americans.

District of Columbia

★2488★
U.S. Department of the Interior Museum
1849 C St., NW
Mail Stop 5412
Ph: (202)208-4743
Washington, DC 20240
Fax: (202)208-6950
Charles Carter, Contact
Description: Collections include Native American Indian and Eskimo handicraft and artifacts. Conducts research on North American Indian material culture.

Illinois

★2489★
The Mitchell Indian Museum at Kendall College
2408 Orrington Ave.
Ph: (708)866-1395
Evanston, IL 60201
Fax: (708)866-1320
Dr. Thomas Kerr, CEO
Description: Contains North American Indian art and artifacts, Eskimo art, and objects from cultures of the Plains, Woodlands, Southwest, and Northwest coast. Maintains library with collections including history, anthropology, art, crafts, archaeology, religion, law, education, literature, and social problems of the American Indian.

New York

★2490★
Southold Indian Museum
Bayview Rd.
PO Box 268
Southold, NY 11971
Ph: (516)765-5577
Walter L. Smith, Pres.
Description: Collections include Native American articles and artifacts, and handiworks of Eskimos.

★2491★
U.S. Smithsonian Institute Museum of the American Indian
3753 Broadway at 155th St.
New York, NY 10032-1596
Ph: (212)283-2420
Dr. Duane King, Dir.
Description: Collections include items relating to American Indian archaeology and ethnology from North America, artifacts, textiles, agriculture, anthropology, paintings, sculpture, decorative arts, costumes, numismatic, music, medical, photo archives, manuscript collections, and Eskimo culture.

Research Centers

★2492★
ERIC Clearinghouse on Rural Education and Small Schools
Appalachia Educational Laboratory
PO Box 1348
Charleston, WV 25325
Ph: (304)347-0400
Craig Howley, Codirector
Research Activities and Fields: American Indian, native Alaskan, Mexican American, migrant, outdoor, and rural education and small schools.

★2493★
University of Alaska, Anchorage
Arctic Environmental Information and Data Center
707 A St.
Anchorage, AK 99501   Ph: (907)257-2733
Sal Cuccarese, Acting Dir.

Research Activities and Fields: Investigation, analysis, and synthesis of environmental problems related to Alaska. Provides assistance on resource management issues in Alaska, including Native land selection under the Alaska Native Claims Settlement Act and environmental effects of development projects. Conducts field studies, sociocultural impact studies, and background analyses on policy and development questions debated by the International Whaling Commission, the U.S. Congress, and the Alaska legislature. Serves as one of twelve Computer Mapping and Analysis System Stations (CMAS) in the U.S. for NOAA. The Alaska Climate Center conducts climate-related research, including studies on the superstructure of icing, solar-radiation measurements, and wind measurements. It also maintains historical records for the state. **Publications:** *Alaska Climate Center Technical Notes* (occasionally); *Alaska Climate Summaries.* Also produces books, environmental atlases, bibliographies with indexes, pamphlets, maps, posters, and radio and video features.

★2494★
University of Alaska, Anchorage
Center for Alcohol and Addiction Studies
3211 Providence Dr.
Anchorage, AK 99508   Ph: (907)786-1805
Dennis Fisher Ph.D., Dir.

Research Activities and Fields: Basic, applied, and evaluative research in alcohol and substance abuse and intervention strategies in Alaska. Conducts epidemiological studies of drug use in the state, social impact and public policy research pertaining to drug use/abuse, and survey and cross-cultural research to define personality and social antecedents and correlates of drug use/abuse. Also conducts a statewide survey of substance use/abuse in Alaska.

★2495★
University of Alaska, Anchorage
Institute of Social and Economic Research
3211 Providence Dr.
Anchorage, AK 99508   Ph: (907)786-7710
Prof. Edward L. Gorsuch, Dir.

Research Activities and Fields: Regional economics, Alaska Native studies, federal-state relations, regional and rural economic development, natural resources management, policy studies, transportation system development, workforce development, rural and vocational education, energy development, social and economic impacts, and northern and Pacific Rim development. Also studies issue confronting the State's economy, population, and social and political institutions. **Publications:** *Alaska Review of Social and Economic Conditions* (irregularly). **Formerly:** Institute of Social, Economic and Government Research.

★2496★
University of Alaska, Fairbanks
Alaska Native Language Center
Box 900111
Fairbanks, AK 99775-0120   Ph: (907)474-7874
Dr. Michael E. Krauss, Dir.

Research Activities and Fields: Linguistic research and documentation of the twenty Native Indian, Aleut, and Eskimo languages of Alaska, including preparation of comprehensive native language dictionaries, which currently cover 11 Alaskan languages.

★2497★
University of Alaska, Fairbanks
Alaska Quaternary Center
Univ. of Alaska Museum
907 Yukon Dr.
Fairbanks, AK 99775-1200   Ph: (907)474-7817
Dr. Craig Gerlach, Dir.

Research Activities and Fields: Quaternary studies in northern regions including studies in Quaternary volcanism, and the ethnohistory of Alaskan Natives. **Publications:** *AQC Newsletter* (six times per year). **Formerly:** Office of Quaternary Studies (1983).

★2498★
University of Alaska, Fairbanks
Center for Cross-Cultural Studies
Fairbanks, AK 99775-0900   Ph: (907)474-7143
Dr. Gerald V. Mohatt, Dir.

Research Activities and Fields: Cross-cultural education, human services and behavioral sciences, and rural development in Alaska. Current projects include studies on using research knowledge to improve teacher education for rural Alaska, patterns of alcohol use in Alaska, sociolinguistic investigation of patterns affecting literacy performance, and improving science education of Alaska Native teachers. Funds many small research grants for the faculty of the college. **Formerly:** Center for Northern Education Research.

Education Programs & Services

———— Head Start Programs ————

★2499★
Association of Village Council Presidents
Head Start Program
PO Box 219
Bethel, AK 99559   Ph: (907)543-3521
Helen Morris, Dir.

★2500★
Bristol Bay Native Association
Head Start Program
PO Box 310
Dillingham, AK 99576   Ph: (907)842-4059

★2501★
Cook Inlet Tribal Council
Head Start Program
670 W. Firewood Ln.
Anchorage, AK 99503   Ph: (907)276-3343
Lisa Dolchok, Dir.

★2502★
Fairbanks Native Association
Head Start Program
201 1st Ave.
Fairbanks, AK 99701   Ph: (907)452-1648
Jean Demmert, Dir.

★2503★
Kawerak, Inc.
Head Start Program
Pouch 948
Nome, AK 99762   Ph: (907)443-5231
Joe Putnam, Dir.

★2504★
Metlakatla Indian Community Council
Head Start Program
PO Box 8
Metlakatla, AK 99926   Ph: (907)886-5151

★2505★
Tanana Chiefs Conference
Head Start Program
122 1st Ave.
Fairbanks, AK 99701   Ph: (907)452-8251
Sarah Kuenzli, Dir.

★2506★
Tlingit and Haida Central Council
Head Start Program
320 W. Willoughby, Ste. 300
Juneau, AK 99801   Ph: (907)586-1432
Rina Hart, Dir.

Studies Programs

Four-Year Programs

★2507★
University of Alaska, Fairbanks
Alaska Native Studies, Inupiaq Eskimo Studies, and
  Yupik Eskimo Studies Programs
Fairbanks, AK 99775-0885   Ph: (907)474-6243
James T. Mansfield, Assoc.Dir. of Admissions

★2508★
University of Alaska, Fairbanks
Alaskan Native Studies Program
Fairbanks, AK 99775   Ph: (907)474-6243
James T. Mansfield Nageak, Assoc. Dir. of Adm. & Records

Graduate Programs

★2509★
University of Hawaii at Honolulu
School of Public Health
American Indian and Alaska Native Support Program
Educational Opportunities Program
Honolulu, HI 96822   Ph: 800-927-3927
John Casken, Dir.

Scholarships, Fellowships, & Loans

★2510★
AIGC Fellowship
American Indian Graduate Center
4520 Montgomery Blvd., NE, Ste. 1-B
Albuquerque, NM 87109   Ph: (505)881-4584
Study Level: Doctorate; Graduate. **Award Type:** Fellowship.
Purpose: To help those with unmet needs as supplemental support.
Applicant Eligibility: Candidates must be enrolled members of a
federally-recognized tribe or Alaska Native group or possess at least
one-quarter degree of Indian blood. They must also be enrolled at an
accredited college or university in the U.S. as full-time graduate
students in an M.A. or Ph.D. program. Awards are need-based.
Selection Criteria: Preference is given to those applications
received on or before the application deadline, former AIGC
students, and those specializing in education, engineering, health,
law, business and natural resources, or related fields. **Funds
Available:** Approximately $1.8 million was awarded during the 1990-
91 year. **Applicant Details:** Eligible applicants should call AIGC for
an application. **Application Deadline:** June 3. Applicants will be
notified in July.

★2511★
Emergency Aid and Health Profession Scholarship
Association on American Indian Affairs,
  Inc.
245 5th Ave.
New York, NY 10016-7877
Study Level: Undergraduate. **Award Type:** Scholarship. **Applicant
Eligibility:** College-level American Indian and Alaskan Native
students may apply after they have registered for college, and if they
are in need of emergency aid. **Funds Available:** When funds are
available, individual grants average between $50 and $300.
Applicant Details: There are no application forms. A student
desiring aid must write a letter and include the following information:
tribal affiliation; subject of study; year in school; amount needed;
brief budget of expenditures; and the name and telephone number of
the college financial aid officer, and social security number.
Application Deadline: Applications may be filed at any time after
college classes are begun.

★2512★
IHS Health Professions Pre-Graduate Scholarships
Indian Health Services
5600 Fishers Ln., Rm. 6A30
Rockville, MD 20857   Ph: (301)443-1180
Study Level: Undergraduate. **Award Type:** Scholarship. **Applicant
Eligibility:** Applicants must be American Indians or Alaska Natives.
Candidates must be high school graduates or the equivalent, and
must have the capacity to complete a health professions course of
study. Applicants must be enrolled, or accepted for enrollment, in a
baccalaureate degree program in specific preprofessional areas (pre-
medicine and pre-dentistry). Applicants may be seniors, juniors,
sophomores, or freshmen (priority given to applicants in this order).
Applicants must be in good standing at the educational institution
they are attending. Candidates must intend to serve Indian People
upon completion of professional health care education as health care
providers in the disciplines for which the students are enrolled at the
pregraduate level. **Funds Available:** Funding is available for a
maximum of four academic years. The level of scholarship benefits is
contingent upon the availability of funds appropriated each fiscal
year by the Congress of the United States and, therefore, is subject
to yearly changes. The Scholarship Program will provide a monthly
stipend to cover living expenses including room and board.
Recipients will receive the stipend only during the academic period
covered by their awards, August 1 to May 31. **Contact:** IHS Area
Scholarship Coordinator.

★2513★
IHS Health Professions Preparatory Scholarships
Indian Health Services
5600 Fishers Ln., Rm. 6A30
Rockville, MD 20857   Ph: (301)443-1180
Study Level: Undergraduate. **Award Type:** Scholarship. **Applicant
Eligibility:** Applicants must be American Indians or Alaska Natives.
Candidates must be high school graduates or the equivalent, and
must have the capacity to complete a health professions course of
study. Applicants must be enrolled, or be accepted for enrollment, in
courses that will prepare them for acceptance into health
professions schools. Courses may be either compensatory (required
to improve science, mathematics, or other basic skills and
knowledge) or pre-professional (required in order to qualify for
admission into a health professions program). Applicants may be
sophomore or freshman students (priority given to applicants in this
order). Priority categories of study for 1991 enrollment are: pre-
engineering; pre-medical technology; pre-nursing; pre-pharmacy;
pre-physical therapy; and pre-sanitation. Applicants must be in good
standing at the educational institution they are attending. Candidates
must intend to serve Indian People upon completion of professional
health care education as health care providers in the disciplines for
which the students are taking preparatory courses. **Funds
Available:** Funding is available for a maximum of two years. The
level of scholarship benefits is contingent upon the availability of
funds appropriated each fiscal year by the Congress of the United
States and, therefore, is subject to yearly changes. The Scholarship
Program will provide a monthly stipend to cover living expenses
including room and board. Recipients will receive the stipend only
during the academic period covered by their awards, August 1 to
May 31. **Contact:** IHS Area Scholarship Coordinator.

★2514★
Presbyterian Church Native American Education
  Grants
Presbyterian Church (U.S.A.)
Office of Financial Aid for Studies
100 Witherspoon St.
Louisville, KY 40202-1396   Ph: (502)569-5745
Study Level: Graduate; Undergraduate. **Award Type:** Grant.
Applicant Eligibility: Candidates must be American Indians, Aleuts,
or Eskimos who are U.S. citizens. They must have completed at
least one semester at an accredited institution of higher learning.
Preference is given to Presbyterian students at the undergraduate
level. **Funds Available:** Grants range from $200 to $1,500 annually
depending on financial need and availability of funds. Renewal is
possible with continued financial need and satisfactory academic
progress. **Applicant Details:** Candidates must apply to their colleges
for financial aid as well as filing an application with the Presbyterian
Church (U.S.A.). **Application Deadline:** June 1.

★2515★
Presbyterian Church Native American Seminary
  Scholarships
Presbyterian Church (U.S.A.)
Office of Financial Aid for Studies
100 Witherspoon St.
Louisville, KY 40202-1396   Ph: (502)569-5745
Study Level: Graduate. **Award Type:** Scholarship. **Applicant
Eligibility:** Candidates are American Indians, Aleuts, and Eskimos
who are certified by the candidate's presbytery or the Presbyterian
Native American Consulting Committee. Applicant must be: a
seminary student preparing for a church occupation and enrolled in a
seminary fully accredited by the Association of Theological Schools
in the United States and Canada; a student registered with, or under
the care of a presbytery and enrolled in a college program on Track 1
of the Native American Theological Association Program; a member
of the Presbyterian Church (U.S.A.) from a former UPCUSA
congregation, who is enrolled in a program of Theological Education
by extension, such as the NATA Track III which is approved by a
seminary fully accredited by the Association of Theological Schools
in the United States and Canada; and a candidate, minister or
member (former UPCUSA) in other church occupations pursuing an
approved program of continuing education. **Funds Available:** The
amount of the scholarship is determined by the Office of Financial
Aid for Studies based upon recommendation by the student's
Financial Officer, analysis of the applicant's financial needs, and
other resources and available funds. **Contact:** Office of Financial Aid
for Studies. **Applicant Details:** Candidates first contact the Financial
Aid Officer of the school or seminary they attend. The officer makes
a recommendation to the Office of Financial Aid for Studies.

★2516★
U.S. Department of the Interior
Bureau of Indian Affairs
Scholarship Grant
U.S. Bureau of Indian Affairs
Office of Indian Education Programs
1849 C St., NW
Washington, DC 20240
Study Level: Undergraduate. **Award Type:** Grant. **Applicant
Eligibility:** Candidates must be Native Americans, Eskimos, Alaska
natives and be members of federally recognized tribes. They must
also have been accepted at an accredited college or university.
Funds Available: Appropriated yearly by Congress with each tribe
specifying the amount they wish to receive. **Contact:** Set by each
Tribal Contractor. Branch of Post Secondary Education, (202)208-
4871. **Applicant Details:** All application information is available from
the Tribal Contractor or the Bureau Agency serving that tribe. There
are no funds or applications available from the above address or the
Central Office of the Bureau of Indian Affairs.

Print & Broadcast Media

Directories

★2517★
American Indian and Alaska Native Traders Directory
Arrowstar Publishing
10134 University Park Sta.
Denver, CO 80210-1034   Ph: (303)762-6579
Covers: 3,500 American Indian-owned and Eskimo-owned arts and
crafts businesses, craft persons, and artists. **Entries Include:**
Company name, address. **Pages (approx.):** 140. **Frequency:**
Published June 1990. **Price:** $19.95, plus $1.50 shipping.

★2518★
American Indian Index
Arrowstar Publishing
10134 University Park Sta.
Denver, CO 80210-1034   Ph: (303)762-6579
Covers: Over 6,000 Native American Indian and Native Alaskan
tribes, social service organizations and agencies, newspapers, and
museums. **Entries Include:** Organization name, address, subsidiary
and branch names and locations (if applicable), product or service.
Pages (approx.): 325. **Frequency:** Irregular; latest edition 1987.
Price: $19.95, plus $1.50 shipping.

★2519★
Education Assistance for American Indians and
  Alaska Natives
Master of Public Health Program for
  American Indians
School of Public Health
University of California
Warren Hall, Rm. 140
Berkeley, CA 94720   Ph: (415)642-3228
Entries Include: Name of organization or publisher, address, name
of contact, phone, service programs offered. **Frequency:** Biennial,
June of even years. **Price:** Free.

★2520★
Native American Directory: Alaska, Canada, United
  States
National Native American Cooperative
Box 1000
San Carlos, AZ 85550-1000   Ph: (602)622-4900
Covers: Native American performing arts groups, craft materials
suppliers, stores and galleries, Indian-owned motels and resorts;
tribal offices, museums, and cultural centers; associations, schools;
newspapers, radio and television programs and stations operated,
owned, or specifically for Native Americans; calendar of events,
including officially sanctioned powwows, conventions, arts and
crafts shows, all-Indian rodeos, and Navajo rug auctions. **Entries
Include:** Generally, organization or company name, address,
descriptive comments, dates (for shows or events). **Pages
(approx.):** 335. **Frequency:** Irregular; previous edition 1982; latest
edition March 1992. **Price:** $44.95, plus $3.00 shipping.

★2521★
Smoke Signals: Business Directory of Indian Country
  U.S.A.
Arrowstar Publishing
10134 University Park Sta.
Denver, CO 80210-1034   Ph: (303)762-6579
Covers: Approximately 3,500 American Indian and Alaska native
owned and operated businesses. **Entries Include:** Company name,
address. **Pages (approx.):** 220. **Frequency:** Published 1990. **Price:**
$59.95, plus $1.95 shipping. **Former Title(s):** *Smoke Signals:
Directory of Native Indian/Alaskan Businesses* (1990).

★2522★
Source Directory of Indian, Eskimo, and Aleut Owned-and-Operated Arts and Crafts Businesses
U.S. Indian Arts and Crafts Board
Rm. 4004-MIB
Washington, DC 20240   Ph: (202)208-3773
Covers: Over 250 Native American-owned businesses specializing in arts and crafts products. **Entries Include:** Company name, address, phone, name and title of contact, description of products and services. **Pages (approx.):** 50. **Frequency:** Irregular; latest edition 1987; updated with supplements as needed. **Price:** Free. **Former Title(s):** *Native American Owned and Operated Crafts Businesses* (1987).

Journals & Magazines

★2523★
Alaska Native Magazine
PO Box 220230
Anchorage, AK 99522   Ph: (907)277-7192
Description: Magazine focuses on social, political and economic issues involving the native community. **First Published:** November 1982. **Frequency:** Quarterly. **Subscription:** $17.50. $2.95 per single issue. **ISSN:** 0745-8851.

Newsletters

★2524★
Northwest Arctic NUNA
Maniilaq Association
PO Box 256   Ph: (907)442-3311
Kotzebue, AK 99752   Free: 800-478-3312
Description: Reflects the aims of the Association, a health corporation promoting public health and social welfare in Alaskan Eskimo villages. Reports on Inupiaq Eskimo customs, arts, and language to promote understanding between natives and non-natives. Highlights programs of the Association and profiles members. **Frequency:** 8-10/yr. **Price:** Included in membership.

Newspapers

★2525★
Tundra Times
Eskimo, Indian, Aleut Publishing Co.
PO Box 104480
Anchorage, AK 99510-4480   Ph: (907)274-2512
Description: Statewide Native American newspaper. **First Published:** 1962. **Frequency:** Weekly (Mon.). **Subscription:** $20; $35 other countries. **ISSN:** 0049-4801.

Radio Stations

★2526★
KBRW-AM
1695 Okpik St.
PO Box 109   Ph: (907)852-6811
Barrow, AK 99723   Fax: (907)852-4791
Don Rinker, Gen. Mgr.
Founded: 1975. **Frequency:** 680. **Network Affiliation:** American Public Radio (APR); AP. **Format:** Eclectic. **Owner:** Silakkuagvik Communications.

★2527★
KDLG-AM
PO Box 670
Dillingham, AK 99576   Ph: (907)842-5281
Les Robinson, Mgr.
Founded: 1975. **Frequency:** 670. **Network Affiliation:** American Public Radio (APR). **Format:** Full Service. **Owner:** Dillingham City Schools.

★2528★
KOTZ-AM
PO Box 78
Kotzebue, AK 99752   Ph: (907)442-3434
Rob Rawls, Gen. Mgr.
Frequency: 720. **Network Affiliation:** National Public Radio (NPR). **Format:** News; Eclectic. **Owner:** Kotzubue Broadcasting Inc.

★2529★
KYUK-AM
640 Radio St.
Pouch 468
Bethel, AK 99559   Ph: (907)543-3131
Jerry Bringham, Gen. Mgr.
Founded: 1971. **Frequency:** 640. **Format:** Eclectic. **Owner:** Bethel Broadcasting Inc.

Publishers

★2530★
Alaska Historical Society
PO Box 100299
Anchorage, AK 99510-0299   Ph: (907)276-1596
Description: Publishes books on Alaska history, emphasizing monographs, documents, and translations. Also publishes a quarterly newsletter and a semiannual journal *Alaska History*. Accepts unsolicited manuscripts on Alaska. Reaches market through wholesalers. **Total Titles in Print:** 11. **Selected Titles:** *Archeology of Cook Inlet* by Delaguna; *Diary of Visit of Lady Franklin* by De Armond; *Alaska Salmon Hatcheries* by Patricia Roppell; *Recollections of the Yukon: Memories.* by Francois Mercier; *Alaska's Heritage* by J. Antonson and W. Hanable; *Transportation in Alaska's Past* edited by G. Stein. **Principal Officials and Managers:** Nancy Gross, President.

★2531★
Alaska International Art Institute
20681 Leonard Rd.
Saratoga, CA 95070-4201   Ph: (408)867-4421
Total Titles in Print: 4. **Selected Titles:** *Wendy's Windows; Welcome Aboard; First Ladies of Alaska; Tongues and Totems: Comparative Arts of the Pacific Basin* by Starr and Richard Davis. **Principal Officials and Managers:** Starr Davis, Secretary.

★2532★
Alaska Pacific University
Alaska Pacific University Press
4101 University Dr.
Anchorage, AK 99508   Ph: (907)564-8304
Description: Publishes and distributes books on Alaskan themes, including Alaska native life, legends and history, contemporary issues, and fiction. Also publishes textbooks. **Number of New Titles:** 1989 - 1, 1990 - 2, 1991 (est.) - 2; Total Titles in Print - 15. **Selected Titles:** *People of Kauwerak: Legends of the Northern Eskimo* by William Oquilluk; *Minus 31 and the Wind Blowing: 9 Reflections about Living on Land* by John Haines; *The Nelson Island Eskimo* by A. Fienup-Riordan; *Wolf Smeller: A Biography of John Fredson, Native Alaskan* by Clara Childs MacKenzie; *Communicating in Japanese* by Heshiki Kazumi; *Going Up in Flames: The Promises and Pledges of Alaska Statehood under Attack* by Malcom Roberts. **Principal Officials and Managers:** Jan Ingram, Managing Editor; Jennifer Stoudenmire, Press Assistant.

★2533★
Epicenter Press
Box 60529
Fairbanks, AK 99706   Ph: (907)474-4969

Description: Publishes historical books on Alaska. Accepts unsolicited manuscripts. Reaches market through direct mail, telephone sales, and Pacific Pipeline. **Number of New Titles:** 1989 - 2, 1990 - 2, 1991 (est.) - 1; Total Titles in Print - 7. **Selected Titles:** *Reaching for a Star: The Final Campaign for Alaska Statehood* by G. Bowkett; *Four Generations on the Yukon* by Kent Sturgis; *Steamboats on the Chena: The Founding and Development of Fairbanks Alaska* by Hendrick and Savage; *Art and Eskimo Power: The Life and Times of Alaskan Howard Rock* by L. Morgan. **Principal Officials and Managers:** Lael Morgan, Kent Sturgis, Partners.

★2534★
Greatland Graphics
PO Box 100333
Anchorage, AK 99510   Ph: (907)562-5723

Description: Publishes materials related to Alaska. Offers a calendar, *Northern Light: The Alaskan Photographers' Calendar.* Also offers two posters, *Last Train to Nowhere* and *Kayak.* Accepts unsolicited manuscripts; send letter of query first. Reaches market through commission representatives and direct mail. **Number of New Titles:** 1989 - 2, 1990 - 2; Total Titles in Print - 4. **Selected Titles:** *The Native People of Alaska* by Steve J. Langdon; *Black Tides: The Alaska Oil Spill* by Brian O'Donoghue; *The Road North: A Woma n's Adventure Driving the Alaska Highway, 1946-47* by Iris Woolcock. **Principal Officials and Managers:** Edward Bovy, Owner.

★2535★
Maniilaq Association
PO Box 256
Kotzebue, AK 99752   Ph: (907)442-3311

Description: Native corporation concerned with retaining the Eskimo traditions and beliefs. Offers brochures, annual reports, newsletters, a monthly newspaper, calendars, and posters. Reaches market through direct mail. **Total Titles in Print:** 2. **Selected Titles:** *Maniilaq Annual Report and Directory; Northwest Arctic Nuna.* **Principal Officials and Managers:** Michael Lacey, Media Planner.

★2536★
Origins Program
4632 Vincent Ave., S.
Minneapolis, MN 55410   Ph: (612)922-8175

Description: Publishes catalogs and books to accompany exhibitions of tribal art and books on multicultural understanding. Also offers audio and video cassettes on Indian and Eskimo topics, and on museum collections of tribal art. Reaches market through commission representatives and distributors, including BookPeople and Quality Books, Inc. **Subjects:** Indian and Eskimo art and culture, multiculturalism. **Number of New Titles:** 1990 - 1, 1991 - 2; Total Titles in Print - 2. **Selected Titles:** *Tsonakwa and Yolaikia: Legends in Stone, Bone and Wood* edited by Crawford and West; *Dark Lady Dreaming: Quilts and Drawings* by Amy Cordova and Pam Eyden; *To Hold Us Together* by Linda Crawford; *Beyond the Suitcase* edited by Helen E. Stub; *The Elders: Passing It On* edited by Linda Crawford. **Principal Officials and Managers:** Linda Crawford, Director; Jo Devlin, Curator; Helen Stub, Registrar. **Formerly:** Arts and Learning Services Foundation.

★2537★
Spirit Mountain Press
PO Box 1214
558 Gaffney St.
Fairbanks, AK 99707   Ph: (213)221-2164

Description: Promotes Alaskan literature, especially biographies of native Alaskans and long term residents. Also offers note cards, posters, and prints. Reaches market through direct mail, trade sales, and wholesalers. Mail returned from address above; no forwarding address available. **Total Titles in Print:** 14. **Selected Titles:** *Henry Ekada, Stanley Dayo, Chuck and Gladys Dart, Altona Brown, Goodwin Semakin,* all edited by Madison and Yarber; *Sacred Fire* by Larry Laraby. **Principal Officials and Managers:** Larry M. Laraby, Owner.

★2538★
Tanadgusix Corporation
Saint Paul Island, AK 99660   Ph: (206)537-7877

Subjects: Aleut history, St. Paul guide. **Selected Titles:** *Slaves of the Harvest* by Barbara Boyle Torrey; *Pribilof Islands, A Guide to St. Paul* by Susan Hackley Johnson. **Principal Officials and Managers:** Anthony Philemonoff, C.E.O.; Victor Merculieff, Land Manager.

★2539★
University of Alaska, Anchorage
Institute of Social and Economic Research ((ISER))
3211 Providence Dr.
Anchorage, AK 99508   Ph: (907)786-7710

Description: Publishes research concerning social and economic issues in Alaska. Offers the periodical, *Alaska Review of Social and Economic Conditions.* **Selected Titles:** *Alaska State Government and Politics* edited by Gerald A. McBeath and Thomas A. Morehouse; *An Alaska Census of Transportation* by John T. Gray and J. Philip Rowe; *Subsistence and the North Slope Inupiat: Effects of Energy Development* by John A. Kruse; *Alaska's Small Rural High Schools: Are They Working* by Judith Kleinfeld; *Alaska's Elections, 1958-1984* by Thomas Morehouse; *Poverty and Public Assistance among Alaska Natives* by Matthew Berman. **Principal Officials and Managers:** Lee Gorsuch, Director and Publisher; Linda Leask, Editor.

★2540★
University of Alaska, Fairbanks
Alaska Native Language Center
Box 900111
Fairbanks, AK 99775-0120   Ph: (907)474-7874

Description: ANLC was established by act of State Legislature in 1972 to document Alaska Native languages and to provide for their future. Reaches market through direct mail. **Number of New Titles:** 1989 - 3, 1990 - 5, 1991 (est.) - 5; Total Titles in Print - 132. **Selected Titles:** *Ugiuvangmiut Quliapyuit: King Island Tales: Eskimo History and Legends* edited by Kaplan; *Bakk'aatugh Ts unhuniy: Stories We Live By: Traditional Athabaskan Stories* by Attla; *In Honor of Eyak: The Art of Anna Nelson Harry* edited by Krauss; *Shem Pete's Alaska: Annotated Placenames/Stories of Dena'ina Culture* edited by Kari and Fall; *Unangam Ungiikangin Kayux Tunusangin: Aleut Tales and Narratives Collected 1909-1910 by Waldemar Jochelson* edited by Bersland and Dirks; *K'etetaalkkaanee: The One Who Paddled Among the People and Animals: The Story of an Ancient Traveler.* **Principal Officials and Managers:** Michael E. Krauss, Professor of Linguistics and Director of Research.

★2541★
University of Alaska, Fairbanks
University of Alaska Press
1st Fl. Gruening Bldg.
Fairbanks, AK 99775-1580   Ph: (907)474-6389

Description: Publishes scholarly nonfiction on Alaska, the circumpolar north, and North Pacific rim. Offers maps and videos. Distributes for Geophysical Institute, KUAC-TV, University of Alaska Museum, and Alaska Association for the Arts. Reaches market through direct mail, trade sales, and wholesalers, including Rainforest Publishing, Pacific Pipeline, and Fairbanks News Agency. **Subjects:** Native studies, regional history, politics, natural sciences, biographies, translations. **Number of New Titles:** 1989 - 6, 1990 - 5; Total Titles in Print - 43. **Selected Titles:** *William D. Berry 1954-1956: Alaskan Field Sketches* compiled by Elizabeth Berry; *Birds of the Seward Peninsula* by Brian Kessel; *Chills and Fever: Early History of Health and Disease in Alaska* by Robert Fortuine; *The White Pass: Gateway to the Klondike* by Roy Minter; *Enjoying a Life in Science: The Autobiography of P. F. Scholander.* **Principal Officials and Managers:** Claus-M. Naske, Executive Director; Debbie Van Stone, Manager; Carla Helfferich, Managing Editor; Pam Odom, Administrative Assistant.

★2542★
User-Friendly Press
6552 Lakeway Dr.
Anchorage, AK 99502-1949   Ph: (907)243-8947

Description: Publishes on the Athabaskan Indians of Cook Inlet, Alaska. Offers editing and proofreading services. Reaches market through direct mail and trade sales. **Subjects:** Poetry, Alaskan history. **Total Titles in Print:** 2. **Selected Titles:** *Canoeing in the Rain, On the Trail of Eklutna,* both by Ann Chandonnet; *To Recognize This Dying* by Joe Napora; *Spring Comes again to Arnett* by Patrick Worth Gray; *Citizen R. K. Does Not Live* by Ryszard Krynicki, introduced by Stanislaw Baranczak; *Columbus Names the Flower: Mr. Cognito's 12 year Anthology.* **Principal Officials and Managers:** Ann Chandonnet, Publisher.

Videos

★2543★
Angoon One Hundred Years Later
Native American Public Broadcasting
  Consortium
PO Box 86111
1800 N. 33rd St.
Lincoln, NE 68501   Ph: (402)472-3522
Description: A commemoration of the destruction of the Tlingit Indian village of Angoon, Alaska in 1882 by the U.S. Naval Force. **Release Date:** 1982. **Length:** 30 mins. **Format:** VHS, 3/4″ U-matic Cassette, 1″ Broadcast Type ″C″, 2″ Quadraplex Open Reel.

★2544★
Angotee
International Film Bureau, Inc. (IFB)
332 S. Michigan Ave.
Chicago, IL 60604-4382   Ph: (312)427-4545
Description: A documentary account of an Eskimo boy's life from infancy to maturity. **Release Date:** 1953. **Length:** 31 mins. **Format:** Beta, VHS, 3/4″ U-matic Cassette, Other than listed.

★2545★
At the Autumn River Camp: Parts 1 & 2
Education Development Center, Inc.
55 Chapel St., Ste. 901   Ph: (617)969-7100
Newton, MA 02160   Free: 800-225-4276
Description: The autumn existence of the Netsilik Eskimos is related in these programs. Hunting, fishing, sewing tent roofs, and igloo building are a few of the jobs that are handled by the Native Alaskans. **Release Date:** 1967. **Length:** 30 mins. **Format:** 3/4″ U-matic Cassette, Other than listed.

★2546★
At the Caribou Crossing Place: Parts 1 & 2
Education Development Center, Inc.
55 Chapel St., Ste. 901   Ph: (617)969-7100
Newton, MA 02160   Free: 800-225-4276
Description: A documentary of the day-to-day existence of a family of Netsilik Eskimos. **Release Date:** 1967. **Length:** 30 mins. **Format:** 3/4″ U-matic Cassette, Other than listed.

★2547★
At the Spring Sea Ice Camp: Parts 1-3
Education Development Center, Inc.
55 Chapel St., Ste. 901   Ph: (617)969-7100
Newton, MA 02160   Free: 800-225-4276
Description: A record of the everyday life of a family of Netsilik Eskimos, as they hunt seals through the sea-ice in the springtime. **Release Date:** 1967. **Length:** 27 mins. **Format:** 3/4″ U-matic Cassette, Other than listed.

★2548★
At the Winter Sea Ice Camp: Parts 1-4
Education Development Center, Inc.
55 Chapel St., Ste. 901   Ph: (617)969-7100
Newton, MA 02160   Free: 800-225-4276
Description: A way of life that is no more is seen in the lifestyle of the Netsilik Eskimos. We see them at work during the frigid Canadian winter, when special care must be taken to survive. **Release Date:** 1967. **Length:** 35 mins. **Format:** 3/4″ U-matic Cassette, Other than listed.

★2549★
Building a Kayak: Parts 1 and 2
Education Development Center, Inc.
55 Chapel St., Ste. 901   Ph: (617)969-7100
Newton, MA 02160   Free: 800-225-4276
Description: Two Netsilik Eskimos show the work involved in building a kayak from seal skins, sinews, bone and scraps of wood. **Release Date:** 1967. **Length:** 32 mins. **Format:** 3/4″ U-matic Cassette, Other than listed.

★2550★
Easter in Igloolik: Peter's Story
Bullfrog Films, Inc.   Ph: (215)779-8226
PO Box 149   Free: 800-543-3764
Oley, PA 19547   Fax: (215)370-1978
Description: Viewers are provided with a look at life in a modern Arctic Eskimo community. **Release Date:** 1987. **Length:** 24 mins. **Format:** Beta, VHS, 3/4″ U-matic Cassette. **Credits:** Cast Member: Peter Arnatsiaq.

★2551★
Eskimo Artist: Kenojuak
National Film Board of Canada
1251 Avenue of the Americas, 16th Fl.
New York, NY 10020-1173   Ph: (212)586-5131
Description: Kenojuak, an eskimo artist, depicts her works and sources of inspiration. She transfers her designs into stone, which express her beliefs and understandings of the ecological unity. **Release Date:** 1964. **Length:** 20 mins. **Format:** Beta, VHS, 3/4″ U-matic Cassette.

★2552★
Eskimo Family
Britannica Films
310 S. Michigan Ave.   Ph: (312)347-7958
Chicago, IL 60604   Fax: (312)347-7966
Description: Follows Anakudluk and his family on their annual trek from winter camp to spring hunting grounds. **Release Date:** 1959. **Length:** 17 mins. **Format:** Beta, VHS, 3/4″ U-matic Cassette.

★2553★
The Eskimo: Fight for Life
Education Development Center, Inc.
55 Chapel St., Ste. 901   Ph: (617)969-7100
Newton, MA 02160   Free: 800-225-4276
Description: Six families of Netsilik heritage are seen hunting the frozen ice masses for food and animal skins, building an igloo, conversing with each other, and enacting their food sharing ritual. Aside from showing the Netsilik's daily activities, the program focuses particularly on the eskimo's patience, industry, strength, and family security. Part of the ″Eskimo Survival″ series. **Release Date:** 1971. **Length:** 51 mins. **Format:** 3/4″ U-matic Cassette, Other than listed.

★2554★
The Eskimo in Life and Legend (The Living Stone)
Britannica Films
310 S. Michigan Ave.   Ph: (312)347-7958
Chicago, IL 60604   Fax: (312)347-7966
Description: Relates the dramatic story of a great seal hunter who carved the image of his wish from a piece of stone-a wish that later came true. Shows the Eskimo way of life, his legends, and his art. **Release Date:** 1960. **Length:** 22 mins. **Format:** Beta, VHS, 3/4″ U-matic Cassette.

★2555★
Eskimo Summer
Education Development Center, Inc.
55 Chapel St., Ste. 901   Ph: (617)969-7100
Newton, MA 02160   Free: 800-225-4276
Description: This program includes all of the Netsilik activities on the land. In spring, they begin to fish, gather moss and heather, and search for bird eggs. Summer activities include building a kayak for caribou hunting. As summer progresses they move farther inland to trap salmon returning up river, hunt caribou, and prepare to return to

the sea and ice. Part of the "People of the Seal" series. **Release Date:** 19??. **Length:** 52 mins. **Format:** 3/4" U-matic Cassette, Other than listed.

★2556★
Eskimo Survival Series
Education Development Center, Inc.
55 Chapel St., Ste. 901   Ph: (617)969-7100
Newton, MA 02160   Free: 800-225-4276

Description: A series of programs on the North American Eskimo: a look at their lives, their homes, their rituals and their struggles. Highlighted are the Netsilik Eskimos. Programs are available individually. **Release Date:** 1971. **Length:** 54 mins. **Format:** 3/4" U-matic Cassette, Other than listed.

★2557★
Eskimo Winter
Education Development Center, Inc.
55 Chapel St., Ste. 901   Ph: (617)969-7100
Newton, MA 02160   Free: 800-225-4276

Description: As the sea freezes, the Netsilik move far out into the Bay, search for seal holes, and build their igloos near good seal-hunting spots. The program concentrates on seal hunting, on which the Eskimos' lives depend. We are shown how the families divide up the food and put every part of the animal to good use, after which they begin their annual inland trek. Part of the "People of the Seal" series. **Release Date:** 19??. **Length:** 52 mins. **Format:** 3/4" U-matic Cassette, Other than listed.

★2558★
Eskimos: A Changing Culture
Phoenix/BFA Films
468 Park Ave., S.   Ph: (212)684-5910
New York, NY 10016   Free: 800-221-1274

Description: Using the Eskimos of Nunivak Island in the Bering Sea, this show examines the changes as they have occurred in the lifetime of the present generation. **Release Date:** 1971. **Length:** 17 mins. **Format:** Beta, VHS, 3/4" U-matic Cassette.

★2559★
Expressions of Eskimo Culture
Michigan Media
University of Michigan
400 4th St.
Ann Arbor, MI 48109   Ph: (313)764-8228

Description: Inuit (Eskimo) culture is shown, as expressed in rich and beautiful prints and carvings. **Release Date:** 1979. **Length:** 29 mins. **Format:** 3/4" U-matic Cassette, Other than listed.

★2560★
Eyes of the Spirit
KET, The Kentucky Network Enterprise
    Division   Ph: (606)233-3000
2230 Richmond Rd., Ste. 213   Free: 800-354-9067
Lexington, KY 40502   Fax: (606)266-3562

Description: A look at Yup'ik Eskimo mask carvers in action. **Release Date:** 1983. **Length:** 30 mins. **Format:** Beta, VHS, 3/4" U-matic Cassette.

★2561★
Fishing at the Stone Weir, Parts I & II
Education Development Center, Inc.
55 Chapel St., Ste. 901   Ph: (617)969-7100
Newton, MA 02160   Free: 800-225-4276

Description: In the summertime, a group of Netsilik Eskimos fish by the side of the river using three-pronged leisters, spearing the fish and stringing them on a thong. **Release Date:** 1967. **Length:** 30 mins. **Format:** 3/4" U-matic Cassette, Other than listed.

★2562★
From the First People
Documentary Educational Resources
101 Morse St.   Ph: (617)926-0491
Watertown, MA 02172   Fax: (617)926-9519

Description: This program is about change and contemporary life in Shungnak, a village on the Kobuk River in northwestern Alaska. **Release Date:** 1977. **Length:** 45 mins. **Format:** 3/4" U-matic Cassette.

★2563★
Group Hunting on the Spring Ice, Parts I-III
Education Development Center, Inc.
55 Chapel St., Ste. 901   Ph: (617)969-7100
Newton, MA 02160   Free: 800-225-4276

Description: Late in June, the hunters of a Netsilik Eskimo tribe go out in search of seal pups for food. **Release Date:** 1967. **Length:** 30 mins. **Format:** 3/4" U-matic Cassette, Other than listed.

★2564★
Haa Shagoon
University of California at Berkeley
    Extension Media Center
2176 Shattuck Ave.
Berkeley, CA 94704   Ph: (510)642-0460

Description: One day in the life of the Tlingit Indian tribe from Alaska is documented. **Release Date:** 1983. **Length:** 29 mins. **Format:** VHS, 3/4" U-matic Cassette.

★2565★
High Arctic: Life with the Northernmost Eskimos
Cornell University
Audio Visual Resource Center
8 Business & Technology Park   Ph: (607)255-2091
Ithaca, NY 14850   Fax: (607)255-9946

Description: This tape looks at the culture and society of a tribe of Eskimos who make their home a few hundred miles from the North Pole. **Release Date:** 1963. **Length:** 65 mins. **Format:** Beta, VHS, 1/2" Reel-EIAJ, 3/4" U-matic Cassette, 2" Quadraplex Open Reel.

★2566★
Hitting Sticks—Healing Hearts
River Tracks Productions
PO Box 9
Manley Hot Springs, AK 99756

Description: This documentary, produced at the request of village elders, provides an in-depth view of an Athabaskan memorial potlatch in the village of Minto, Alaska. This video centers on death, grieving, love, community, music, and tradition. **Release Date:** 1991. **Length:** 58 mins. **Format:** VHS.

★2567★
Hunters of the Seal
Time-Life Video and Television
1450 E. Parham Rd.   Ph: (804)266-6330
Richmond, VA 23280   Free: 800-621-7026

Description: Documents the dramatic contrast between the old and the new for the Netsilik Eskimo, and their struggle to find meaning in their new lives. **Release Date:** 1976. **Length:** 30 mins. **Format:** Beta, VHS, 3/4" U-matic Cassette, Other than listed.

★2568★
Huteetl: A Koyukon Memorial Potlatch
River Tracks Productions
PO Box 9
Manley Hot Springs, AK 99756

Description: Documents the final death rites for a young couple who died in a plane crash in 1981. A memorial potlatch was given over a year later and more than 200 people joined the residents of Hughes, Alaska, for the week-long celebration releasing the deceased spirit. **Release Date:** 1983. **Length:** 55 mins. **Format:** VHS.

★2569★
Inuit Kids
Bullfrog Films, Inc.
PO Box 149
Oley, PA 19547
Ph: (215)779-8226
Free: 800-543-3764
Fax: (215)370-1978

Description: A film which helps children get the feel of Arctic life by sharing moments in the lives of two thirteen year old boys. **Release Date:** 1987. **Length:** 15 mins. **Format:** Beta, VHS.

★2570★
Inuit Legends Series
Beacon Films
930 Pinter Ave.
Evanston, IL 60202
Ph: (312)328-6700
Free: 800-323-5448

Description: These programs are three Eskimo legends of courage and sacrifice in puppet animation for young viewers. **Release Date:** 1982. **Length:** 6 mins. **Format:** Beta, VHS, 3/4″ U-matic Cassette.

★2571★
Jigging for Lake Trout
Education Development Center, Inc.
55 Chapel St., Ste. 901
Newton, MA 02160
Ph: (617)969-7100
Free: 800-225-4276

Description: In springtime, the Netsilik Eskimos go fishing through lake ice for freshwater trout. **Release Date:** 1967. **Length:** 32 mins. **Format:** 3/4″ U-matic Cassette, Other than listed.

★2572★
Lumaaq—An Eskimo Legend
National Film Board of Canada
1251 Avenue of the Americas, 16th Fl.
New York, NY 10020-1173
Ph: (212)586-5131

Description: Without commentary, this program depicts the story of a legend widely believed by the Povungnituk Eskimos. **Release Date:** 1975. **Length:** 8 mins. **Format:** Beta, VHS, 3/4″ U-matic Cassette.

★2573★
Matthew Aliuk: Eskimo in Two Worlds
Learning Corporation of America
108 Wilmot Rd.
Deerfield, IL 60015-9990
Ph: (708)940-1260
Free: 800-621-2131

Description: This is the story of a proud people's struggle for cultural survival in a changing world. **Release Date:** 1973. **Length:** 18 mins. **Format:** Beta, VHS, 3/4″ U-matic Cassette.

★2574★
More Than Bows and Arrows
Video Tech
19346 3rd Ave. NW
Seattle, WA 98177
Ph: (206)546-5401

Description: A coast-to-coast look at the technology being used by Indians, Eskimos, and Aleuts. **Release Date:** 1978. **Length:** 56 mins. **Format:** Beta, VHS, 3/4″ U-matic Cassette, Other than listed.

★2575★
Old Dances, New Dancers
KET, The Kentucky Network Enterprise
  Division
2230 Richmond Rd., Ste. 213
Lexington, KY 40502
Ph: (606)233-3000
Free: 800-354-9067
Fax: (606)266-3562

Description: A filmed record of the first annual Young People's Eskimo Dance Awareness Festival in Chevak, Alaska. **Release Date:** 1983. **Length:** 30 mins. **Format:** Beta, VHS, 3/4″ U-matic Cassette.

★2576★
On the Spring Ice
Documentary Educational Resources
101 Morse St.
Watertown, MA 02172
Ph: (617)926-0491
Fax: (617)926-9519

Description: The danger of moving ice and walrus hunting are the topics of this program. **Release Date:** 1975. **Length:** 45 mins. **Format:** 3/4″ U-matic Cassette.

★2577★
Our Native American Friends
Britannica Films
310 S. Michigan Ave.
Chicago, IL 60604
Ph: (312)347-7958
Fax: (312)347-7966

Description: From the "Friends" units these three programs: Apache Indian Friends, Miccosukee Indian Friends, and Eskimo Friends, are combined to tell of different ethnic groups in the United States. **Release Date:** 1979. **Length:** 10 mins. **Format:** Beta, VHS, 3/4″ U-matic Cassette.

★2578★
People of the Seal Series
Education Development Center, Inc.
55 Chapel St., Ste. 901
Newton, MA 02160
Ph: (617)969-7100
Free: 800-225-4276

Description: A summary of the entire migratory cycle of the Netsilik Eskimo, from summer to winter, including their seasonal activities and rituals. Programs are available individually. **Release Date:** 19??. **Length:** 52 mins. **Format:** 3/4″ U-matic Cassette, Other than listed.

★2579★
Sananguagat: Inuit Masterworks
National Film Board of Canada
1251 Avenue of the Americas, 16th Fl.
New York, NY 10020-1173
Ph: (212)586-5131

Description: This program alternates between an exhibition of Eskimo carvings and views of the daily life in the Iglootik settlement of the Northwest Territories. **Release Date:** 1974. **Length:** 25 mins. **Format:** Beta, VHS, 3/4″ U-matic Cassette.

★2580★
Songs In Minto Life
One West Media
PO Box 5766
559 Onate Pl.
Sante Fe, NM 87501
Ph: (505)983-8685

Description: The interrelationship between songs and life of the Minto Indians of Alaska is documented here. **Release Date:** 1986. **Length:** 30 mins. **Format:** VHS, 3/4″ U-matic Cassette.

★2581★
Stalking Seal on the Spring Ice, Parts I & II
Education Development Center, Inc.
55 Chapel St., Ste. 901
Newton, MA 02160
Ph: (617)969-7100
Free: 800-225-4276

Description: On the shore of Pelly Bay, a family of Netsilik Eskimos stalk a seal, kill it and then use the animal for food, sinew and clothing. **Release Date:** 1967. **Length:** 30 mins. **Format:** 3/4″ U-matic Cassette, Other than listed.

★2582★
Tanana River Rat
River Tracks Productions
PO Box 9
Manley Hot Springs, AK 99756

Description: Focusing on contemporary life in Interior Alaska, this film portrays the story of two brothers who are forced to come together after being separated by the 1991 Alaska Native land claims. **Release Date:** 1989. **Length:** 57 mins. **Format:** VHS.

★2583★
They Never Asked Our Fathers
Native American Public Broadcasting
  Consortium
1800 N. 33rd St.
PO Box 86111
Lincoln, NE 68501
Ph: (402)472-3522

Description: Focuses on the Yup'ik Eskimos of Nunivaq, who have lost their land to the U.S. government. Includes historic photographs, documents, interviews, and scenes of life in the Bering Sea area. **Release Date:** 1982. **Length:** 58 mins. **Format:** VHS, 1″ Broadcast Type "C", 3/4″ U-matic Cassette.

★2584★
Tukiki and His Search for a Merry Christmas
Coronet/MTI Film & Video Ph: (708)940-1260
108 Wilmot Rd. Free: 800-621-2131
Deerfield, IL 60015 Fax: (708)940-3640
Description: The Christmastime adventures of a small Eskimo boy named Tukiki are related. **Release Date:** 1980. **Length:** 25 mins. **Format:** Beta, VHS, 3/4″ U-matic Cassette, Other than listed.

★2585★
Tununeremiut: The People of Tununak
Documentary Educational Resources
101 Morse St. Ph: (617)926-0491
Watertown, MA 02172 Fax: (617)926-9519
Description: This program portrays aspects of the lives of the Eskimos of Tununak in Alaska. **Release Date:** 1972. **Length:** 35 mins. **Format:** 3/4″ U-matic Cassette.

★2586★
The Wedding of Palo
Video Yesteryear
Box C Ph: (203)426-2574
Sandy Hook, CT 06482 Free: 800-243-0987
Description: The classic documentary co-filmed by Danish explorer Rasmussen about Eskimo life in a northern district of Greenland. **Release Date:** 1935. **Length:** 72 mins. **Format:** Beta, VHS. **Credits:** Directed by: Knud Rasmussen; Knud Rasmussen; Friedrich Dalsheim.

★2587★
World Eskimo Art
New York State Education Department
Center for Learning Technologies
Media Distribution Network, Rm. C-7,
   Concourse Level
Albany, NY 12230 Ph: (518)474-1265
Description: How Eskimo art relates to the Eskimo lifestyle is examined. **Release Date:** 1971. **Length:** 30 mins. **Format:** Beta, VHS, 1/2″ Reel-EIAJ, 3/4″ U-matic Cassette, 2″ Quadraplex Open Reel.

★2588★
Yesterday, Today: The Netsilik Eskimo
Education Development Center, Inc.
55 Chapel St., Ste. 901 Ph: (617)969-7100
Newton, MA 02160 Free: 800-225-4276
Description: A look at one day in the life of a Netsilik Eskimo family for whom life is no longer a constant struggle. They have left their igloos for rented government housing, receive their government provided family allowance checks to use at the co-op store, and hunt from snowmobiles. We are shown how their traditional self-sufficient way of life has been replaced by the interdependency and specialization of modern life. Part of the "Eskimo Survival" series. **Release Date:** 1971. **Length:** 57 mins. **Format:** 3/4″ U-matic Cassette, Other than listed.

★2589★
You Can't Grow Potatoes Up There!
Kinetic Film Enterprises, Ltd.
255 Delaware Ave., Ste. 340
Buffalo, NY 14202 Ph: (716)856-7631
Description: This program illustrates the importance of seal hunting in the traditional life of the Arctic Inuit Eskimos. **Release Date:** 1981. **Length:** 27 mins. **Format:** 3/4″ U-matic Cassette.

Native Hawaiians

National Organizations

★2590★
ALU LIKE, Inc.
1624 Mapunapuna St.
Honolulu, HI 96819-4417   Ph: (808)836-8940
Haunani Apoliona, Pres.

Description: A community based organization seeking "to assist Hawaiian natives in their efforts to achieve social and economic excellence." ALU LIKE, Inc. has been named the sole administrator of a variety of government funded programs designed to help native Hawaiians, including: Employment and Training Program; Hawaii Computer Training Center; Offender/Ex-Offender Project; Native Hawaiian Substance Abuse Prevention Project; Native Hawaiian Vocational Education Program; Ke Ola Pono No Na Kupuna Project; Business Development Center; and the Native Hawaiian Library Project. Operates five Island Centers. **Founded:** 1974. **Publications:** *No No Lima Hano No'eau O ALU LIKE*, monthly newsletter.

★2591★
Congress of the Hawaiian People
98-1364 Akaaka St.
Aiea, HI 96701   Ph: (808)488-6905
John Agare, Pres.

Description: Coalition of Hawaiian organizations and individuals who seek to preserve the cultural heritage and improve the social, economic, and educational welfare of native Hawaiian people and their communities.

★2592★
E Ola Mau
1374 Nu'uanu Ave., Ste. 201   Ph: (808)533-1628
Honolulu, HI 96817   Fax: (808)521-2967
Nanette K. Judd MPH, Pres.

Description: Native Hawaiian health care providers, including traditional healers (Kupuna lapa'au), physicians, nurses, health aides, dentists, nutritionists, psychologists, pharmacists, and others involved in the health care profession. Works to achieve good health among native Hawaiians by developing "self-determination, self-responsibility, self-reliance, and initiative in seeking optimal health and life." **Founded:** 1986. **Also Known As:** Live On.

★2593★
Hui Na-auao
3415 Ka'ohinani Dr.   Ph: (808)595-6647
Honolulu, HI 96817   Fax: (808)595-8105
Elizabeth Pa Martin, Pres.

Description: Coalition of over fifty organizations that serve Hawaiian natives. Seeks to promote awareness of Native Hawaiian sovereignity and self-determination. Will be administering the Sovereignty and Self-Determination Community Education Project, a three year project funded by a grant from the U.S. Department of Health and Human Services Administration for Native Americans.

★2594★
Native Hawaiian Advisory Council (NHAC)
1088 Bishop St., Ste. 1204   Ph: (808)523-1445
Honolulu, HI 96813   Fax: (808)599-4380
Elizabeth Pa Martin, Exec.Dir.

Description: Strives to protect the rights and entitlements of people of native Hawaiian ancestry. Monitors governments and lawmakers to ensure that laws covering these rights and entitlements are properly enforced. Current projects include the Native Hawaiian Water Resources Control Project, a community awareness program designed to strengthen the ability of Hawaiian natives to manage and control their water resources. In conjunction with this project, NHAC conducts workshops, assists Hawaiian natives in declaring their water resources for certification, testifies on the State Water Commission and reviews its actions, and participates with the viewpoint of Hawaiian natives in the development of water laws. Established a database of water uses and claims in Hawaii. **Publications:** *KE KIA'I, The Guardian*, monthly newsletter.

★2595★
Native Hawaiian Library Project (NHLP)
2810 Pa'a St., Ste. 1-A
Honolulu, HI 96819   Ph: (808)839-7784
Mahealani Merryman, Prog. Admin.

Description: Administered by ALU LIKE, Inc. and funded by the Library Services and Construction Act Admendement of 1984 which appropriated funds to establish library programs and services for Native Americans. Seeks to increase availability of library resources for native Hawaiians, encourage parent and child reading programs, and strengthen adult literacy skills. Sponsors programs and projects designed to increase access to libraries and information services for native Hawaiians, including the Library Resource Van; Remote Regions (provides library services by mail); Parent Workshops; Homework Centers; a Fellowship Program; and Literacy and Library Promotions.

★2596★
Native Hawaiian Vocational Education Program
   (NHVEP)
2879 Pa'a St., Ste. 201
Honolulu, HI 96819-4406   Ph: (808)839-7922
Robert Allen, Admin.

Description: Administered by ALU LIKE, Inc. and funded by the U.S. Congress with the goals of improving the academic and employment skills of native Hawaiian high school students, increasing and retaining the number of native Hawaiians in community college vocational education programs, and establishing vocational educational services to assist native Hawaiian adults in becoming productive members of the labor force.

★2597★
University of Hawaii at Hilo
Center for Gifted and Talented Native Hawaiian
   Children
Hilo, HI 96720-4091   Ph: (808)933-3678

Description: Seeks "to increase opportunities for native Hawaiian children to participate in educational enrichment activities." Serves children from kindergarten through grade 12 with programs that incorporate self-esteem, talent enhancement, student and parent support services, and Hawaiian culture and values. **Also Known As:** Na Pua No'eau.

Regional, State/Provincial, & Local Organizations

Hawaii

★2598★
Hale Naua III Society of Hawaiian Art
99-919 Kalawina Pl.
Aiea, HI 96701   Ph: (808)487-6949
Rocky Kaiouliokahihikoloehu Jensen, Dir.

Description: Serves Hawaiian artists of native descent. Provides exhibits, lectures, workshops, and historical tours.

★2599★
Hui Malama Ola Na 'Oiwi
Kona Office
PO Box 447   Ph: (808)323-3618
Captain Cook, HI 96704   Fax: (808)323-3096

★2600★
Hui No Ke Ola Pono
Hana Office
4293-A Hana Hwy.
Hana, HI 96713   Ph: (808)248-7502

★2601★
Queen Liliuokalani Children's Center
Windward Oahu Office
53-516 Kamehameha Hwy.   Ph: (808)293-8577
Hauula, HI 96717   Fax: (808)293-5182

★2602★
ALU LIKE, Inc.
Hawaii Island Center
32 Kinoole St., Ste. 218
Hilo, HI 96720   Ph: (808)961-2625

★2603★
Hui Malama Ola Na 'Oiwi
305 Wailuku Dr., Ste. 3   Ph: (808)969-9220
Hilo, HI 96720   Fax: (808)961-4794
Anuhea Reimann-Gieger, Pres.

Description: Responsible for providing health care services to the native Hawaiian residents of the island of Hawai'i under the Native Hawaiian Health Care Act. Operates three local offices in Captain Cook, Waimea, and Pahoa.

★2604★
Abigail K. Kawananakoa Trust
420 Kekau Pl.
Honolulu, HI 96817   Ph: (808)533-7370
Abigail Kawananakoa, Pres.

Description: Funds a Halau and offers instruction in the Hawaiian art of Hula.

★2605★
ALU LIKE, Inc. Business Development Center
1120 Mauna Kea St., Ste. 273   Ph: (808)524-1225
Honolulu, HI 96817   Fax: (808)522-5314
James Mi'ikeha, Admin.

Description: Offers professional and technical services to small business owners through the Business Services Center. Also operates the Entrepreneurship Training Program and the Management and Technical Assistance Program for individuals of Hawaiian descent.

★2606★
ALU LIKE, Inc.
Ohau Island Center
1505 Dillingham Blvd., Ste. 218
Honolulu, HI 96817   Ph: (808)847-3868

★2607★
Daughters of Hawaii
2913 Pali Hwy.   Ph: (808)595-6291
Honolulu, HI 96817   Fax: (808)595-4395
Ellen Vasconcellos, Regent

Description: Nonprofit organization that works to perpetuate the memory and spirit of old Hawaii and preserve the nomenclature and pronunciation of the Hawaiian language. Holds meetings and conducts classes.

★2608★
Hawaii Community Foundation (HCF)
Irving A. Singer Foundation
222 Merchant St., 2nd Fl.
Honolulu, HI 96813   Ph: (808)537-6333

Description: Offers a small one-time grant to individuals of Hawaiian ancestry. Contact HCF for application details.

★2609★
Hawaii Cultural Research Foundation (HCRF)
PO Box 4590
Honolulu, HI 96813   Ph: (808)524-0884
Hanakaulani A. Ferreria, Contact

Description: Offers grants supporting research in Hawaiian arts and philosophy.

★2610★
Hawaii Stitchery and Fibre Art Guild
PO Box 61364
Honolulu, HI 96839   Ph: (808)737-0002
Rebecca Kendro, Pres.

Description: Conducts classes, lectures, and workshops that encourage the development of Hawaiian stitchery and related fiber arts as media for creative expression.

★2611★
Hawaiian Canoe Racing Association
169 S. Kukui St.
Honolulu, HI 96813
Michael Tongg, Pres.
Ph: (808)526-1969
Fax: (808)524-4028
Description: Works to promote and perpetuate the tradition of Hawaiian canoe racing and Hawaiian canoes.

★2612★
Historic Hawaii Foundations
PO Box 1658
Honolulu, HI 96806
Mrs. Phyllis G. Fox, Pres.
Ph: (808)537-9564
Fax: (808)526-3989
Description: Nonprofit organization working to preserve historic buildings, objects, and sites in Hawaii.

★2613★
Kalihi-Palama Culture and Art Society
357 N. King St.
Honolulu, HI 96817
Hazel Naone, Pres.
Ph: (808)521-6905
Description: Sponsors ongoing culture and arts workshops, hula competitions, the state prison's annual art exhibit, and an annual conference on traditional Hawaiian poetry, chants, and hula.

★2614★
Kapiolani Community College
Office of Community Services
4303 Diamond Head Rd.
Honolulu, HI 96816
Regina Edwards, Dir.
Ph: (808)734-9211
Fax: (808)734-9447
Description: Provides interpretive programs on Hawaii's cultural heritage and walking tours of Old Honolulu to the general public. Also available are a variety of non-credit workshops and seminars relating to culture and the arts.

★2615★
Ke Ola Mamo
1374 Nu'uanu Ave., Ste. 200
Honolulu, HI 96817
Claire Hughes, Pres.
Ph: (808)599-5200
Fax: (808)523-9983
Description: Responsible for providing health care services to the native Hawaiian residents of the island of O'ahu under the Native Hawaiian Health Care Act. Also operates offices in Kahuku and Kailua.

★2616★
Lawrence Newbold Brown Memorial Foundation
c/o Hawaiian Trust Co., Ltd.
PO Box 3170
Honolulu, HI 96802
Zadoc W. Brown, Pres.
Ph: (808)531-5743
Description: Offers small grants to tax-exempt charitable organizations that are involved in the preservation and promotion of native Hawaiian music.

★2617★
Naimi Noeau
1210 Laukahi St.
Honolulu, HI 96821
Bruce Ka'imiloa Chrisman, Dir.
Ph: (808)373-3730
Fax: (808)947-9324
Description: Group of artists and other individuals who strive to foster and preserve native Hawaiian arts and crafts.

★2618★
Papa Ola Lokahi
Kawaiaha'o Plaza
567 S. King St., Ste. 102
Honolulu, HI 96813
Larry Miike MD, JD, Exec.Dir.
Ph: (808)536-9453
Fax: (808)545-1783
Description: Provides statewide planning and support to the five native Hawaiian health care service providers in the state of Hawai'i under the Native Hawaiian Health Care Act.

★2619★
Queen Liliuokalani Children's Center
1300 Halona St.
Honolulu, HI 96817
Ph: (808)847-1302
Description: Offers child welfare services to orphaned native Hawaiian children, including foster care, counseling, and adoption services. Operates an auxiliary, Hui Hanai.

★2620★
Royal Hawaiian Band
2805 Monsarrat Ave.
Honolulu, HI 96815
Aaron Mahi, Dir.
Ph: (808)922-5331
Fax: (808)924-2841
Description: Has performed Hawaiian music for more than 150 years; tours worldwide.

★2621★
State Council on Hawaiian Heritage
PO Box 3022
Honolulu, HI 96807
Mrs. Keahi Allen, Dir.
Ph: (808)586-0335
Fax: (808)586-0335
Description: Conducts seminars in dance and presents the annual King Kamehameha Hula Competition. Also sponsors conferences and seminars on storytelling, legends, and related topics.

★2622★
Ke Ola Mamo
Ko'olaulao Office
601 Haole Camp Rd.
Kahuku, HI 96731
Ph: (808)293-5414

★2623★
Halau Mohala Ilima
1110 Aalapapa Dr.
Kailua, HI 96734
Ph: (808)261-0689
Description: Provides instruction in hula and Hawaiian culture. Participates in major hula events and competitions statewide.

★2624★
Ke Ola Mamo
Waimanalo Office
1051 Keolu Dr., Ste. 240
Kailua, HI 96734

★2625★
ALU LIKE, Inc.
Hawaii Island Center
Kailua-Kona Annex
74-5622 Alapa St., 2nd Fl.
Kailua-Kona, HI 96740
Ph: (808)326-1899

★2626★
ALU LIKE, Inc.
Hawaii Island Center
Kamuela Annex
Mamalahoa Hwy.
PO Box 2065
Kamuela, HI 96743
Ph: (808)885-4700

★2627★
Ho'Ola Lahui Hawai'i
Kapa'a Office
PO Box 29
Kapa'a, HI 96746
Ph: (808)822-2058
Fax: (808)822-3694

★2628★
Ka Imi Naauao O Hawaii Nei
PO Box 218
Kaumakani, HI 96747
Roselle F.K. Bailey, President
Ph: (808)335-3628
Description: Offers instruction in hula dancing and in Hawaiian culture.

★2629★
ALU LIKE, Inc.
Molokai Island Center
PO Box 392
Kaunakakai, HI 96748   Ph: (808)553-5393

★2630★
Na Pu'uwai
53 Farrington St.
PO Box 130   Ph: (808)567-6831
Kaunakakai, HI 96748   Fax: (808)567-9004
Emmett Aluli MD, Pres.
Description: Responsible for providing health care services to the native Hawaiian residents of the islands of Molokai, Kalaupapa, and Lana'i under the Native Hawaiian Health Care Act.

★2631★
Lahaina Arts Society
649 Wharf St.
Lahaina, HI 96761   Ph: (808)661-0111
Daniel Schroyer, Dir.
Description: Nonprofit organization that conducts classes, operates galleries, and awards scholarships to promote art and culture.

★2632★
ALU LIKE, Inc.
Kauai Island Center
4334 Rice St., Ste. 204-C
Lihue, HI 96766   Ph: (808)245-8545

★2633★
Hui Malama Ola Na 'Oiwi
Puna Office
PO Box 1455
Pahoa, HI 96778

★2634★
Kalani Honua
PO Box 4500   Ph: (808)965-7828
Pahoa, HI 96778   Fax: (808)965-9443
Richard Koob, Founder
Description: Intercultural conference and retreat center that includes the site of an ancient Hawaiian school and has accomodations and workshop facilities for more than 100 participants. Offers seminars and an artist-in-residence program.

★2635★
Halau Hula O Mililani
85-711 Kaupuni Pl.
Waianae, HI 96792   Ph: (808)696-2145
Mililani Allen, Dir.
Description: Hula school that also provides instruction in traditional Hawaiian crafts, language, and culture.

★2636★
Hale Ola Ho'opakolea, Inc.
89-137 Nanakuli Ave.
Waianae, HI 96792   Ph: (808)668-2361
Description: Provides outpatient alcohol and drug abuse treatment to native Hawaiians.

★2637★
Queen Liliuokalani Children's Center
Leeward Oahu Office
87-1876 Farrington Hwy.   Ph: (808)293-8577
Waianae, HI 96792   Fax: (808)668-8811

★2638★
Waianae Coast Culture and Arts Society
89-188 Farrington Hwy.
Waianae, HI 96792   Ph: (808)668-1549
Mrs. Agnes Cope, Dir.
Description: Works for community participation in traditional and artistic heritages of ethno-culture through activities in cultural workshops and presentations of dance, music, and craft.

★2639★
ALU LIKE, Inc.
Maui Island Center
400 Hookahi St., Ste. 209
Wailuku, HI 96793   Ph: (808)242-9774

★2640★
Hui No Ke Ola Pono
2307 Main St.
PO Box 894   Ph: (808)244-4647
Wailuku, HI 96793   Fax: (808)242-6676
Joseph Kamaka MD, Pres.
Description: Responsible for providing health care services to the native Hawaiian residents of the island of Maui under the Native Hawaiian Health Care Act. Also operates an office in Hana.

★2641★
Ho'Ola Lahui Hawai'i
Waimea Medical Clinic
PO Box 909   Ph: (808)338-0031
Waimea, HI 96796   Fax: (808)338-1845
Wayne Fukino MD, Pres.
Description: Responsible for providing health care services to the native Hawaiian residents of the islands of Kaua'i and Ni'ihau under the Native Hawaiian Health Care Act. Also operates an office in Kapa'a.

★2642★
Hui Malama Ola Na 'Oiwi
Waimea Office
PO Box 6288
Waimea, HI 96743   Ph: (808)885-0489

—————————— **Washington** ——————————

★2643★
Wakinikona Hawaiian Club
c/o Tukwila Senior Center
Seattle, WA 98168   Ph: (206)776-9420
Doug Kaapana, Pres.
Description: Promotes traditional Native Hawaiian culture and history. Performs ancient Hawaiian music and dance, such as the hula "kahiko" using the "melee" instrument. Sponsors the Hawaiian Summer Festival in Seattle.

Federal Government Agencies

★2644★
U.S. Department of Health and Human Services
Office of State and Community Programs
Office for American Indian, Alaskan Native and Native
  Hawaiian Programs
330 Independence Ave. SW
Washington, DC 20201   Ph: (202)619-2957

Federal Domestic Assistance Programs

★2645★
U.S. Department of Education
Office of Assistant Secretary for Educational
  Research and Improvement
**Library Services for Indian Tribes and Hawaiian
  Natives**
555 New Jersey Ave. NW
Washington, DC 20208-5517   Ph: (202)219-1323
Beth Fine, Program Officer

Catalog Number: 84.163. **Objectives:** Includes providing incentives for the establishment and expansion of tribal library programs for Hawaiian natives. **Applicant Eligibility:** Federally recognized Indian tribes and organizations that primarily serve Hawaiian Natives that are recognized by the Governor of the state of Hawaii may apply. Only Indian tribes and Hawaiian Native organizations that have received a basic grant are eligible to apply for special projects awards. **Types of Assistance:** Project grants (discretionary). **Beneficiary Eligibility:** Members of Indian tribes and Hawaiian Natives will benefit.

★2646★
U.S. Department of Education
Office of the Assistant Secretary for Elementary and
  Secondary Education
**Native Hawaiian Model Curriculum Development
Kamehameha Elementary Education Program (KEEP)**
400 Maryland Ave. SW
Washington, DC 20202   Ph: (202)401-1342
John Fiegel, Contact

Catalog Number: 84.208. **Objectives:** To implement and increase the impact of the Kamehameha Elementary Education Program Model Demonstration Curriculum. **Applicant Eligibility:** (1)State of Hawaii (University of Hawaii); (2)State of Hawaii (Department of Education); (3) Kamehameha Schools/Bernice Pauahi Bishop Estate; and (4) the State of Hawaii may apply. **Types of Assistance:** Direct Payments for Specified Use. **Beneficiary Eligibility:** Same as applicant eligibility.

★2647★
U.S. Department of Education
Office of the Assistant Secretary for Elementary and
  Secondary Education
**School Improvement Program
Native Hawaiian Gifted and Talented**
400 Maryland Ave. SW
Washington, DC 20202   Ph: (202)401-1342
John Fiegel, Contact

Catalog Number: 84.210. **Objectives:** To provide financial assistance to the University of Hawaii at Hilo to :(1) Establish a Native Hawaiian Gifted and Talented Center at the University of Hawaii at Hilo; and (2) to demonstrate programs designed to address the special needs of Native Hawaiian elementary and secondary school students who are gifted and talented. Support services are also provided to their families as needed. **Applicant Eligibility:** The University of Hawaii at Hilo may apply. **Types of Assistance:** Direct Payments for Specified Use. **Beneficiary Eligibility:** Gifted and talented native Hawaiian elementary and secondary educational students will benefit.

★2648★
U.S. Department of Education
Office of the Assistant Secretary for Elementary and
  Secondary Education
**School Improvement Programs
Native Hawaiian Family-Based Education Centers**
400 Maryland Ave. SW
Washington, DC 20202   Ph: (202)401-1342
John Fiegel, Contact

Catalog Number: 84.209. **Objectives:** To develop and operate a minimum of eleven family-based education centers throughout the Hawaiian Islands. **Applicant Eligibility:** Native Hawaiian organizations including Native Hawaiian educational organizations may apply. **Types of Assistance:** Direct Payments for Specified Use. **Beneficiary Eligibility:** Infants up to three years old and their parents, also preschoolers four and five years old and their parents will benefit.

★2649★
U.S. Department of Education
Office of the Assistant Secretary for Vocational and
  Adult Education
**Division of National Programs
Vocational Education—Indian and Hawaiian Natives**
Washington, DC 20202-7242   Ph: (202)732-2380
Kate Homberg, Hawaiian Natives Prog.

Catalog Number: 84.101. **Objectives:** To make grants and contracts with Indian tribes or tribal organizations and to organizations primarily serving and representing Hawaiian Natives to plan, conduct, and administer programs or portions of programs authorized byu and consistent with the Carl D. Perkins Vocational Education Act. **Applicant Eligibility:** (1) A tribal organization or an Indian tribe which is eligible to contract with the Secretary of the Interior for the administration of programs under the Indian Self-Determination and Education Assistance Act of 1975 or under the Act of April 16, 1934. (2) Any organization primarily serving and representing Hawaiian Natives which is recognized by the Governor of Hawaii. **Types of Assistance:** Project Grants (Cooperative Agreements); Project Grants (Contracts). **Beneficiary Eligibility:** Federally recognized Indian tribes and Hawaiian Natives will benefit.

★2650★
U.S. Department of Education
Office of Special Education and Rehabilitative
  Services
Native Hawaiian Special Education
330 C St. SW
Washington, DC 20202   Ph: (202)732-1107
Dr. Martin J. Kaufman, Contact

Catalog Number: 84.221. **Objectives:** To operate projects addressing the special education needs of Native Hawaiian students. **Applicant Eligibility:** State of Hawaii or Native Hawaiian organizations may apply. **Types of Assistance:** Project Grants. **Beneficiary Eligibility:** Native Hawaiian students with handicaps served by grantees will benefit.

★2651★
U.S. Department of Health and Human Services
Administration on Aging
**American Indian, Alaskan Native, & Native Hawaiian
  Programs
Special Programs for the Aging, Title VI—Part B
  Grants to Native Hawaiians**
330 Independence Ave. SW
Washington, DC 20201   Ph: (202)619-2957

Catalog Number: 93.655. **Objectives:** To promote the delivery of supportive services, including nutrition services to older Indians, Alaskan Natives, and Native Hawaiians. Services are comparable to services provided under Title III of the Older Americans Act of 1965, as amended. **Applicant Eligibility:** Includes public or nonprofit organizations which serve Native Hawaiian Elders, which represent at least 50 Indians or Hawaiians 60 years of age or older. Applicants must document that they have or will have the ability to deliver social and nutrition services. **Types of Assistance:** Project grants. **Beneficiary Eligibility:** Indians or Native Hawaiians who are 60 years of age and older, and in the case of nutrition, their spouses.

★2652★
U.S. Department of Health and Human Services
Public Health Service
Indian Health Service
Native Hawaiian Health Centers
5600 Fishers Ln.
Rockville, MD 20857   Ph: (301)443-8134
Elizabeth A. Hickey, Contact

Catalog Number: 93.932. **Objectives:** To elevate the health status of Native Hawaiians living in Hawaii by providing primary health care and health education to create changes within the health care system that will address the health needs of the Native Hawaiians. **Applicant Eligibility:** An entity qualifies to apply if it is a (1) a Native Hawaiian health center; (2) a Native Hawaiian organization; or (3) a public or nonprofit private health provider. Native Hawaiian Health Centers are entities which (1) are organized under the laws of the State of Hawaii; (2) provide or arrange for health care services through practitioners licensed by the State of Hawaii, where licensure requirements are applicable; (3) are public or nonprofit entities; and (4) have Native Hawaiian health practitioners significantly participating in the planning, management, monitoring, and evaluation of health services. Native Hawaiians organizations are entities which (1) serve the interests of Native Hawaiians; (2) are (a) recognized by Papa Ola Lokahi (an organization composed of E Ola Mau; the Office of Hawaiian Affairs of the State of Hawaii; ALU LIKE Inc.; the University of Hawaii; and the Office of Hawaiian Health of the Hawaii State Department of Health) for the purpose of planning, conducting or administrating programs (or portions of programs) authorized under the Native Hawaiian Health Care Act of 1988 for the benefit of Native Hawaiians, and (b) certified by Papa Ola Lokahi as having the qualification and capacity to provide the services, and meet the requirements of the contracts the organizations enter into **Types of Assistance:** Project Grants. **Beneficiary Eligibility:** Native Hawaiians.

★2653★
U.S. Department of Labor
Employment and Training Administration
Division of Indian and Native American Programs
Native American Employment and Training Programs
200 Constitution Ave. NW
Washington, DC 20210   Ph: (202)535-0500
Paul Mayrand, Contact

Catalog Number: 17.251. **Objectives:** To afford job training to Native Americans facing serious barriers to employment, who are in special need of such training to obtain productive employment. To reduce the economic disadvantages among Indians and others of Native American descent and to advance the economic and social development of such people. **Applicant Eligibility:** Indian tribes, bands or groups, Alaska Native villages or groups, and Hawaiian Native communities meeting the eligibility criteria, public bodies or private nonprofit agencies selected by the Secretary. Tribes, bands and groups may also form consortia in order to qualify for designation as a grantee. An independently eligible grantee shall be an Indian or Native American entity which has: (1) An identifiable Native American resident population of at least 1,000 individuals (for new grantees) within its designated service area, and (2) the capability to administer Indian and Native American employment and training programs. **Types of Assistance:** Formula Grants. **Beneficiary Eligibility:** Members of State or federally recognized Indian tribes, bands and other individuals of Native American descent, such as, but not limited to, the Kalamaths in Oregon, Micmac and Miliseet in Maine, the Lumbees in North Carolina and South Carolina, Indians variously descibed as terminated or landless, Eskimos and Aleuts in Alaska, and Hawaiian Natives. ("Hawaiian Native" means an individual any of whose ancestors were natives prior to 1778 of the area which now comprises the State of Hawaii.) Applicants must also be economically disadvantaged, unemployed, or underemployed. A Native American grantee may apply in some cases enroll participants who are not economically disadvantaged, unemployed, or underemployed in upgrading and retraining programs.

State/Provincial & Local Government Agencies

Hawaii

★2654★
Hawaii Accounting and General Services Department
King Kamehameha Celebration Commission
355 N. King St.
Honolulu, HI 96817   Ph: (808)548-4512
Antoinette Lee, Chairman

★2655★
Hawaii Culture and the Arts Foundation
335 Merchant St., Rm. 202
Honolulu, HI 96813   Ph: (808)548-4145
Wendell Silva, Contact

★2656★
Hawaii Health Department
Health Resources Administration
Office of Hawaiian Health
1250 Punchbowl St.   Ph: (808)548-8816
Honolulu, HI 96813   Fax: (808)548-3263
Fern Clark, Contact

★2657★
Hawaiian Home Lands Department
335 Merchant St., Rm. 307
PO Box 1879   Ph: (808)548-6450
Honolulu, HI 96805   Fax: (808)586-3835
Ilima A. Piianaia, Dir./Chairman

Publications: *Ka Nuhou*, monthly newsletter.

★2658★
State of Hawaii
Office of Hawaiian Affairs (OHA)
711 Kapiolani Blvd., 5th Fl.   Ph: (808)586-3777
Honolulu, HI 96813-5249   Fax: (808)586-4745
Clayton Hee, Bd. of Trustees Chairman

Description: An independent branch of the state government "responsible for the performance, development, and coordination of programs and activities relating to Hawaiians." **Publications:** *Ka Wai Ola O OHA*, monthly newspaper.

Library Collections

★2659★
Bernice Pauahi Bishop Museum
Library
1525 Bernice St.
Box 19000-A
Honolulu, HI 96817   Ph: (808)848-4147
Maguerite K. Ashford, Hd.Libn.

Subjects: Includes Hawaiiana. **Special Collections:** Includes Fuller Collection of Pacific Books; 19th century Hawaiian language newspapers; Carter Collection of Hawaiiana; early Pacific voyages; and Pacific island language texts.

★2660★
Lyman House Memorial Museum
Kathryn E. Lyle Memorial Library
276 Haili St.
Hilo, HI 96720   Ph: (808)935-5021
Gloria Kobayashi, Contact
Subjects: Includes Hawaiian history, mythology and legends, religions, and local family genealogies. **Holdings:** 7500 books; 11,500 photographs; 200 blueprints; 6 charts; 84 daguerreotypes; 2500 peices of ephemera; 735 glassplates; 5 journals; 2000 letters; 190 maps; 13 newsletters; 200 prints; 6000 clippings; 660 New England newspapers, 1808-1900; historical materials on early Hawaii. **Subscription:** 34 journals and other serials.

★2661★
Maui Historical Society
Library
2375-A Main St.
Wailuku, HI 96793   Ph: (808)244-3326
Gail Bartholomew, Libn.
Subjects: Hawaii, Maui. **Holdings:** 600 books; 6 VF drawers of mounted clippings; 4 VF drawers of photographs; 1 drawer of slides; and historical files, archeological files, and archives and manuscripts.

★2662★
U.S. Library of Congress
Rare Book and Special Collections Division
Thomas Jefferson Bldg., Rm. 204
Washington, DC 20540   Ph: (202)707-5434
Special Collections: Includes a Hawaiian collection.

★2663★
U.S. National Park Service
Pu'uhonau o Honaunau National Historical Park
Library
Box 129   Ph: (808)328-2288
Honaunau, HI 96726   Fax: (808)328-9485
Blossom Sapp, Park Ranger
Subjects: Includes Hawaiian culture and history. **Holdings:** 400 books; 180 manuscripts.

Museum Collections

★2664★
Bailey House Museum
2375A Main St.   Ph: (808)244-3326
Wailuku, HI 96793   Fax: (808)242-4378
John Cooper, Exec.Dir.
Description: Collections include Native Hawaiian artifacts. Conducts research on local history and archaeology of Maui County.

★2665★
Bernice Pauahi Bishop Museum
1525 Bernice St.
PO Box 19000-A   Ph: (808)847-3511
Honolulu, HI 96817-0916   Fax: (808)841-8968
Siegfried S. Kagawa, Pres.
Description: The state museum of cultural and natural history with exhibits relating to Hawaii and the Pacific, including a collection of Hawaiian royal artifacts.

★2666★
Hawaii Children's Museum
650 Iwilei Rd.   Ph: (808)522-0040
Honolulu, HI 96817   Fax: (808)545-7961
Description: Has hands-on exhibits relating to Hawaiian and other cultures.

★2667★
Hulihee Palace
75-5718 Alii Dr.
Kailua-Kona, HI 96740   Ph: (808)329-1877
Julia L. Soehren, 4th Vice-Regent and CEO
Description: Collections include ancient Hawaiian artifacts.

★2668★
Iolani Palace
King and Richards Sts.
PO Box 2259   Ph: (808)522-0822
Honolulu, HI 96804   Fax: (808)532-1051
Alice F. Guild, Managing Dir.
Description: Collections include artifacts of the Hawaiian monarchy (1882-1893), and original artifacts of Iolani Palace.

★2669★
Kamuela Museum
Kamuela, HI 96743   Ph: (808)885-4724
Description: Includes a large Hawaiian cultural collection, including royal artifacts and pieces that were originally in the Iolani palace.

★2670★
Kauai Museum
4428 Rice St.
PO Box 248
Lihue, HI 96766   Ph: (808)245-6931
Dan Dahl, Dir.
Description: Maintains Hawaiiana collection with particular emphasis on items of the island of Kauai, a Kauai photo collection, and ethnic and heritage displays.

★2671★
Lahaina Restoration Foundation
Dickenson and Front Sts.
PO Box 338
Maui, HI 96761   Ph: (808)661-3262
James C. Luckey, Exec.Dir.
Description: Collections include Hawaiian stone artifacts and tools.

★2672★
Lyman Mission House Memorial Museum
276 Haili St.   Ph: (808)935-5021
Hilo, HI 96720   Fax: (808)969-7685
Richard Henderson, Pres.
Description: Collections include 19th and early 20th century Hawaiian Artists' Gallery, Hawaiian cultural relics, and ethnic displays of seven national groups living in Hawaii.

★2673★
Mission Houses Museum
553 S. King St.
Honolulu, HI 96813   Ph: (808)531-0481
Deborah Pope, CEO
Description: Maintains collection of Polynesian artifacts, including domestic artifacts, household furnishings, and Hawaiian language materials.

★2674★
Moanalua Gardens Foundation
1352 Pineapple Pl.
Honolulu, HI 96819   Ph: (808)839-5334
Paulie K. Jennings, Exec.Dir.
Description: Collections include items relating to Hawaiian cultural history.

★2675★
Pu'uhonua O Honaunau National Historical Park
PO Box 129   Ph: (808)328-2326
Honaunau, HI 96726   Fax: (808)328-9485
Jerry Y. Shimoda, Superintendent
Description: Maintains collections of Hawaiian artifacts and burial remains.

★2676★
Queen Emma Summer Palace
2913 Pali Hwy.
Honolulu, HI 96817
Mildred Nolan, CEO and Regent

Ph: (808)595-3167
Fax: (808)595-1395

Description: Former home of Queen Emma and King Kamehameha IV. Collections include household furnishings and personal effects of Queen Emma and her family, period pieces, portraits, photographs, Hawaiian artifacts, tapa, feather work, and Hawaiian quilts.

Research Centers

★2677★
Bernice Pauahi Bishop Museum
1525 Bernice St.
PO Box 19000-A
Honolulu, HI 96817-0916
W. Donald Duckworth, Pres. & Dir.

Ph: (808)847-3511

Research Activities and Fields: Interests include Hawaiian archeology, Hawaiian language, art, culture, and Hawaii's ethnic groups. **Publications:** *Bishop Museum Bulletins* (irregularly); *Bishop Museum Occasional Papers* (annually); Special Publications (irregularly); Bishop Museum Miscellaneous Publications; Anthropology Departmental Report Series (irregularly).

★2678★
University of Hawaii at Manoa
Center for Oral History
Social Science Research Institute
Porteus Hall 724
2424 Maile Way
Honolulu, HI 96822
Warren S. Nishimoto, Dir.

Ph: (808)956-6259

Research Activities and Fields: Records and preserves through oral interviews the recollections of Hawaii's people. Transcript topics include life histories of Native Hawaiians, perspectives on Hawaii's statehood, and social and labor history. Serves as a resource center for researchers, students, and the general community. **Publications:** *Oral History Recorder* (quarterly newsletter). Develops books, articles, catalogs, photo displays, brochures, and videotapes based on oral histories.

Education Programs & Services

Schools

★2679★
Hale Kako'o Punana Leo/Hilo
1744 Kino'ole St.
Hilo, HI 96720
Namaka Rawlins, Contact

Ph: (808)959-4979

School Type: Hawaiian Immersion schools support center.

★2680★
Hale Kako'o Punana Leo/Honolulu
2002-L Hunnewell St.
Honolulu, HI 96822
Lilinoe Andrews, Contact

Ph: (808)941-0584

School Type: Hawaiian Immersion schools support and materials development center.

★2681★
Kamehameha Schools/Bernice Pauahi Bishop Estate (KS/BE)
Education Group
Program Services Division
Kapalama Heights
Honolulu, HI 96817

Ph: (808)842-8881
Fax: (808)842-8875

Description: Exists to carry out the legacy of Bernice Pauahi Bishop (Ke Ali'i Pauahi, the last direct descendent of the royal line of Kamehameha). KS/BE offers a variety of educational services, both independently and in conjunction with the Hawaii State Department of Education, and gives preference to children of Hawaiian ancestry. Programs include: Parent-Infant Program; Traveling Pre-schools; 23 Center-based Pre-Schools; KEEP—Kamehameha's Elementary Education Program (elementary language arts); Pre-service Education for Teachers of Minorities (PETOM); Kamehameha Elementary School (grades K-6); Kamehameha Secondary School (grades 7-12; college prep); Alternative and Continuing Education programs; Hawaiian Studies Institute; Summer programs; Kamehameha Schools Intermediate Reading Program (KSIRP); Post-High Scholarship and Counseling Program; Kamehameha Talent Search; Native Hawaiian Higher Education Program; Native Hawaiian Health Professions Scholarship Program; and the Native Hawaiian Drug-Free Schools and Communities Program. Operates the KS Press, which publishes a small group of educational materials with a focus on Hawaiian studies.

★2682★
Kapa'a Elementary School
4886 Kawaihau Rd.
Kapa'a, HI 96746
Puanani Wilhelm, Contact

Ph: (808)822-4141

School Type: Hawaiian Immersion school; grades 1-8.

★2683★
Keaukaha Elementary School
240 Desha Ave.
Hilo, HI 96720
Nako'olani Warrington, Contact

Ph: (808)935-1959

School Type: Hawaiian Immersion school; grades 1-8.

★2684★
Kualapu'u Elementary School
Kualapu'u, HI 96757
Manuwai Peters, Contact

Ph: (808)567-6126

School Type: Hawaiian Immersion school; grades 1-8.

★2685★
Pa'ia Elementary School
955 Baldwin Ave.
Pa'ia, HI 96779
Kaiki Kawai'ae'a, Contact

Ph: (808)579-9967

School Type: Hawaiian Immersion school; grades 1-8.

★2686★
Punana Leo O Hilo
1744 Kino'ole St.
Hilo, HI 96720
Leina'ala Poepoe, Dir.

Ph: (808)959-4700

School Type: Hawaiian Immersion preschool.

★2687★
Punana Leo O Honolulu
1313 Kamehameha IV Rd.
Honolulu, HI 96819
Wehi Na'auao, Dir.

Ph: (808)841-6655

School Type: Hawaiian Immersion preschool.

★2688★
Punana Leo O Kaua'i
PO Box 2093
Puhi, HI 96766
Kau'i Kanoho, Dir.

Ph: (808)245-1755

School Type: Hawaiian Immersion Preschool.

★2689★
Punana Leo O Kona
73-1385 Ihumoe St.
Kailua-Kona, HI 96740
Rayann Godden, Contact
School Type: Hawaiian Immersion preschool.

★2690★
Punana Leo O Maui
PO Box 337
Wailuku, HI 96793 Ph: (808)244-5676
Hokulani Holt-Padilla, Dir.
School Type: Hawaiian Immersion preschool.

★2691★
Punana Leo O Moloka'I
PO Box 102
Kualap'u, HI 96757 Ph: (808)567-9211
Leilani Camara, Contact
School Type: Hawaiian Immersion preschool.

★2692★
Punana Leo O Wai'anae
PO Box 1848
Wai'anae, HI 96792 Ph: (808)696-2565
Renee Bishaw, Contact
School Type: Hawaiian Immersion preschool.

★2693★
Pu'ohala Elementary School
45-233 Kulauli St.
Kane'ohe, HI 96744 Ph: (808)235-1361
Malia Souki, Contact
School Type: Hawaiian Immersion school; grades 1-8.

★2694★
Waiau Elementary School
98-450 Ho'okanike St.
Pearl City, HI 96782 Ph: (808)456-9222
Kalani Akana, Contact
School Type: Hawaiian Immersion School; grades 1-8.

Studies Programs

Four-Year Programs

★2695★
University of Hawaii at Hilo
Hawaiian Studies Program
523 W. Lanikaula St.
Hilo, HI 96720-4091 Ph: (808)933-3414
Winifred Tatsuta, Dir. of Admissions

★2696★
University of Hawaii at Manoa
Hawaiian Studies Program
Honolulu, HI 96822 Ph: (808)948-8975
Donald R. Fukuda, Dir. of Admissions

Print & Broadcast Media

Newsletters

★2697★
Ka Nuhou
Hawaiian Home Lands Department
Community Relations/Information Office
335 Merchant St., Rm. 342
Honolulu, HI 96813 Ph: (808)586-3822
Description: Provides information to and about the beneficiaries of the Hawaiian Homes Commission Act of 1920. **Frequency:** Monthly.

★2698★
KE KIA'I, The Guardian
Native Hawaiian Advisory Council
1088 Bishop St., Ste. 1204 Ph: (808)523-1445
Honolulu, HI 96813 Fax: (808)599-4380
Description: Funded by the NHAC's Native Hawaiian Water Resources Project. Provides information to the Native Hawaiian community to assist them in asserting and exercising control over their resources. **Frequency:** Monthly.

★2699★
No Na Lima Hana No'eau O ALU LIKE
ALU LIKE, Inc.
1024 Mapunapuna St.
Honolulu, HI 96819-4417 Ph: (808)836-8940
Description: In-house newsletter of ALU LIKE, Inc., a private, nonprofit, community based, 501(3)(c) advocate for native Hawaiian social and economic self sufficiency. **First Published:** 1989. **Frequency:** Monthly.

Newspapers

★2700★
Ka Wai Ola O OHA
Office of Hawaiian Affairs
711 Kapi'olani Blvd., Ste. 500
Honolulu, HI 96813-5249 Ph: (808)586-3777
Subtitle: The Living Water of OHA. **Description:** Articles and information for the native Hawaiian community. Distributed to 55,000 households, Hawaii state and county government offices, private and community agencies, and others. **First Published:** 1982. **Frequency:** Monthly. **Subscription:** Free.

Radio Stations

★2701★
KAHU-AM
400 Hualani
Hilo, HI 96720 Ph: (808)959-2056
Frequency: 1060. **Format:** Ethnic (Hawaiian).

★2702★
KAOI-FM
1728-C Kaahumanu Ave.
Wailuku, HI 96793 Ph: (808)244-9145
Frequency: 95.1. **Format:** Adult Contemporary; Contemporary Hit Radio (CHR); Ethnic (Hawaiian). **Owner:** KA-OI Communications, Inc., at above address.

★2703★
KCCN-AM
900 Fort St., Ste. 400
Honolulu, HI 96813   Ph: (808)536-2728
Frequency: 1420. **Format:** Traditional Hawaiian music. **Owner:** KCCN Broadcasting Co. Inc.

★2704★
KCCN-FM
900 Fort St., Ste. 400
Honolulu, HI 96813   Ph: (808)536-2728
Frequency: 100.3. **Format:** Ethnic (Contemporary Island Music). **Owner:** KCCN Broadcasting Co. Inc.

★2705★
KINE-FM
741 Bishop
Honolulu, HI 96813   Ph: (808)524-7100
Frequency: 105.1. **Format:** Ethnic (Hawaiian). **Owner:** Bob Sinclair.

★2706★
KKON-AM
Kealakekua
Kona, HI 96740   Ph: (808)323-2200
Frequency: 790. **Format:** Ethnic (Hawaiian).

★2707★
KLEI-AM
4120 Marina Dr.
Santa Barbara, CA 93110   Ph: (808)262-6988
Frequency: 1130. **Format:** Hawaiian; Easy Listening. **Owner:** Merit Media International, at above address.

★2708★
KLUA-FM
Kona, HI 96740   Ph: (808)329-8688
Frequency: 93.9. **Format:** Ethnic (Hawaiian).

★2709★
KMVI-AM
250 Waiehu Beach Rd.
Wailuku, HI 96793   Ph: (808)242-6611
    Fax: (808)244-8017
Frequency: 550. **Format:** Ethnic (Hawaiian); Adult Contemporary. **Owner:** Obie Communications Inc. of Maui, at above address.

★2710★
KPOA-FM
658 Front St.
Lahaina, HI 96761   Ph: (808)667-9110
Frequency: 93.5. **Format:** Ethnic (Hawaiian). **Owner:** Lahaina Broadcasting Co. Ltd.

★2711★
KPUA-AM
1145 Kilauea Ave.
Hilo, HI 96720   Ph: (808)935-5461
Frequency: 670. **Network Affiliation:** CNN Radio. **Format:** Adult Contemporary; News; Middle-of-the-Road (MOR); Ethnic (Hawaiian). **Owner:** Hawaii Broadcasting Co., Inc.

★2712★
KUAI-AM
4469 Waialo Rd.
PO Box 720
Eleele, HI 96705   Ph: (808)335-3171
Frequency: 720. **Network Affiliation:** Mutual Broadcasting System. **Format:** Full Service; Ethnic (Hawaiian). **Owner:** American Islands Broadcasting Corp.

Publishers

★2713★
Aloha Publishing
PO Box 7165
Honolulu, HI 96821   Ph: (808)922-0977
Description: Specializes in Hawaiian history for visitors. Accepts unsolicited manuscripts. Reaches market through commission representatives, trade sales, and Pacific Trade Group. **Total Titles in Print:** 11. **Selected Titles:** *Hawaii's Tragic Princess, Hawaiian Monarchy, Women of Old Hawaii, Hawaii's Whaling Days*, all by Maxine Mrantz; *Hawaii's Volcanoes: Legends and Facts* by Joseph Mullins; *Supernatural Hawaii* by Margaret Stone. **Principal Officials and Managers:** Mark Mrantz, Owner.

★2714★
Bamboo Ridge Press
PO Box 61781
Honolulu, HI 96839-1781   Ph: (808)599-4823
Description: Publishes books by or about Hawaii's people. Publications include collections of short stories, anthologies of contemporary Hawaiian literature, collections of legends, and collections of poetry. Reaches market through direct mail, telephone sales, and wholesalers. **Annual Sales:** $10,000. **Number of New Titles:** 1988 - 3, 1989 - 3, 1990 (est.) - 2; Total Titles in Print - 21. **Selected Titles:** *Sun, Short Stories and Drama* by Darrell H. Y. Lum; *Malama/Hawaiian Land and Water* edited by Dana Naone Hall; *Guilt Payment* by Ty Pak; *Expounding the Doubtful Points* by Wing Tek Lum; *Hilo Rains* by Juliet Kono; *Speed of Darkness* by Rodney Morales. **Principal Officials and Managers:** Eric Chock, Darrell Lum, Editors.

★2715★
Barnhart Press
PO Box 27940
Los Angeles, CA 90027   Ph: (213)462-0767
Description: Publishes on ancient Kahuna secrets from old Hawaii. Reaches market through DeVorss & Co. **Selected Titles:** *Mana Magic* by John Bainbridge. **Principal Officials and Managers:** D. Nowacki, Manager.

★2716★
Bernice Pauahi Bishop Museum
Bishop Museum Press
PO Box 19000-A
Honolulu, HI 96819   Ph: (808)847-3511
Description: Publishes popular and scientific titles on natural and cultural history of Hawaii and the Pacific. Reaches market through trade sales, wholesalers, and direct contact. **Subjects:** Natural history, cultural history, Hawaiiana, Pacifiana. **Number of New Titles:** 1989 - 12, 1991 (est.) - 16; Total Titles in Print - 1200. **Selected Titles:** *In Gardens of Hawaii* by M. C. Neal; *Arts and Crafts of Hawaii* by P. H. Buck; *A Pictorial History of the Japanese in Hawaii 1885-1924* by Franklin Odo and Kazuko Sinoto; *Olelo No'Eau: Hawaiian Proverbs and Practical Sayings* by Mary Kawena Pukui; *Pacific Island Names: A Map and Name Guide to the New Pacific* by L. S. Motteler; *Outrigger Canoes of Bali and Madura, Indonesia* by Adrian Horridge. **Principal Officials and Managers:** Frank Satlow, Director; Barbara Pope, Design and Production; Tautasi Manicas, Sales and Marketing; Randy Rego, Sales Assistant; Jessica Barmark, Editorial Assistant.

★2717★
Bess Press
PO Box 22388
Honolulu, HI 96823   Ph: (808)734-7159
Description: A regional publisher of Asian, Pacific, and Hawaiian history, language, and cultural materials. Also publishes adult and children's trade books. Offers a map of Hawaii and an eight-part filmstrip package on the Hawaiians of old. Reaches market through wholesalers. **Number of New Titles:** 1989 - 10, 1990 - 10, 1991 - 9; Total Titles in Print - 59. **Selected Titles:** *Whales of the World* by Spencer Tinker; *Pacific Nations and Territories* by Reilly Ridgell; *The Hawaiian Sentence Book* by Robert Lokomaika'iokalani

Snakenberg; *How to Hook and Cookbook* by Mike Sokamoto; *Okage Sama De: The Japanese in Hawaii, 1885-1985* by Dorothy Hazama and Jane Komeiji; *Go for Broke: A Pictorial History of the Japanese American 100th Infantry Battalion and the 442nd Regimental Combat Team* by Chester Tanaka. **Principal Officials and Managers:** Benjamin E. Bess III, Publisher; Ann L. Rayson, Editor.

★2718★
Editions Ltd.
2909 Waialae Ave., No. 43
Honolulu, HI 96826   Ph: (808)735-7644

Description: Publishes limited editions and collectors' books on Hawaiian history, sociology, religion, and art. Also produces calendars and maps. Reaches market through direct mail and wholesalers. **Number of New Titles:** 1989 - 3; Total Titles in Print - 12. **Selected Titles:** *The Early Mapping of Hawaii* by Gary L. Fitzpatrick and Riley M. Moffat; *Hawaii Goes to War* by Desoto Brown; *The Hawaiian Calabash* by Irving Jenkins; *The Russian Discovery of Hawaii* by Glynn Barrat; *The View from Diamond Head* by Don Hubbard and David Franzen; *Waikiki Beachboy* by Grady Timmons. **Principal Officials and Managers:** Gaylord Wilcox, President; Carol M. Wilcox, David A. Rick, Vice-Presidents.

★2719★
Hawaii Seahorse Press
PO Box 2791
Kamuela, HI 96743   Ph: (808)538-1981

Description: Publishes historical and contemporary novels on Hawaii. Reaches market through direct mail and Pacific Trade Group. Formerly listed as Seahorse Press. **Selected Titles:** *Mahele O Maui, The Road to Hana Maui*, both by Lynn Nakkim. **Principal Officials and Managers:** Nalani Kai, Lynn Nakkim, Editors.

★2720★
Heritage Press of the Pacific
1279-203 Ala Kapuna St.
Honolulu, HI 96819   Ph: (808)839-1238

Description: Publishes Hawaiian history and fiction. Reaches market through direct mail. **Total Titles in Print:** 3. **Selected Titles:** *Hawaiian Tales, The Niihau Incident, Crisis: The Japanese Attack on Pearl Harbor and Southeast Asia*, all by Allan Beekman. **Principal Officials and Managers:** Allan Beekman, Owner.

★2721★
Hogarth Press Hawaii, Inc.
Box 10606
Honolulu, HI 96816   Ph: (808)536-4216

Description: Promotes and publishes Hawaiian literature for children and adults. Reaches market through wholesalers. Mail returned from address above; no forwarding address available. **Selected Titles:** *Hawaii's Royal History* by R. Carey. **Principal Officials and Managers:** John Patrick O'Connell, President; Eileen Solecki, Secretary-Treasurer.

★2722★
Hui Hanai
1300 Halona St.
Honolulu, HI 96817   Ph: (202)293-2686

Description: Hui Hanai is an auxiliary of the Queen Liliuokalani Children's Center. Publishes on Hawaiian ethnohistory and sociology. All books are distributed exclusively by Trade Publishing Co. **Number of New Titles:** 1990 - 1; Total Titles in Print - 2. **Selected Titles:** *Nana I Ke Kumu, Vol. 1* by Pukui, Heartig, and Lee; *Vol. 2* by Pukui, Heartig, and McDermott; *By Royal Command* by Curtis P. Iaukea. **Principal Officials and Managers:** Agnes Conrad, President.

★2723★
Kauai Museum Association Ltd.
4428 Rice St.
Lihue, HI 96766   Ph: (808)245-6931

Description: Publishes on the history, flora, and fauna of the island of Kauai. Also produces maps, calendars, and prints. Reaches market through direct mail and commission representatives. **Total Titles in Print:** 5. **Selected Titles:** *Early Kauai Hospitality* by Dora

Jane Cole and Juliet Rice Wichman; *Amelia, Moki*, both by Juliet Rice Wichman; *Hawaiian Quilting on Kauai* by Edith Rice Plews; *Kauai: The Separate Kingdom* by Edward Joesting. **Principal Officials and Managers:** Juliet Rice Wichman, President; Beryl Moir, Vice-President; Hilda Cannon, Second Vice-President; Tom Whittemore, Treasurer; Hilda Camnon, Secretary; David P. Penhalcow, Director.

★2724★
Ku Pa'a Inc.
3180 Pacific Heights Rd.
Honolulu, HI 96813   Ph: (808)531-7985

Description: Publishes creative writing about Hawaii and the South Pacific. **Number of New Titles:** 1991 - 3, 1992 (est.) - 4. **Selected Titles:** *The Art of Featherwork in Old Hawaii, Wainea Summer*, both by John Dominis Holt; *The Last Village in Kona* by Mason Altiery; *Ka Poe Kahiko O Waianae* by Waianae Coast Culture and Arts; *Iolani Luahine* by Francis Haar; *Na Ki'i Pohaku: A Petroglyph Primer* by P. F. Kwiatkowski. **Principal Officials and Managers:** John Dominis Holt, President; Frances Damon Holt, Vice-President; Erminie MacKenzie, Secretary-Treasurer. **Formerly:** Topgallant Publishing Co., Inc.

★2725★
Lani Goose Publications, Inc.
583 Kamoku St., Ste. 3803
Honolulu, HI 96826   Ph: (808)947-7330

Description: Publishes legends of Hawaii with read-along cassettes for elementary-age children. Reaches market through Pacific Trade Group. **Number of New Titles:** 1989 - 1; Total Titles in Print - 4. **Selected Titles:** *Legends of Hawaii As Told By Lani Goose, Legends of Oahu As Told By Lani Goose, Legends of Maui As Told By Lani Goose, Lani Goose Sings...for Hawaii's Children*, all by Elithe Manu 'Aipo Kahn. **Principal Officials and Managers:** Art Freedman, President.

★2726★
Lyman Mission House Memorial Museum
276 Haili St.
Hilo, HI 96720   Ph: (808)935-5021

Description: Publishes on Hawaiian history. Also offers newsletters. Reaches market through direct mail and museum gift shop. **Selected Titles:** *Sarah Joiner Lyman of Hawaii: Her Own Story* by Sarah Joiner Lyman; *Hilo 1825-1925: A Century of Paintings and Drawings* by David W. Forbes and Thomas K. Kunichika; *Japanese Painting, Calligraphy, and Lacquer* by Howard Link and Kazuo Noda; *Kane, Kanaloa, Ku and Lona, Na Akua Nui o Hawaii; Gourds in the Garden at Work and in the Gardens (of Old); Symbols of Royalty*. **Principal Officials and Managers:** Leon H. Bruno, Museum Director.

★2727★
Makapu'u Press
PO Box 264
Bend, OR 97709   Ph: (503)388-2892

Description: Publishes illustrated books on Hawaiian and Japanese culture. Reaches market through telephone sales and personal contact. **Subjects:** Hawaiiana, natural history, folklore. **Number of New Titles:** 1989 - 2. **Selected Titles:** *Legends of the Hawaiian Forest, Legends of the Hawaiian Waters*, both by Robin Koma Lee; *Haiku of Ko-Un Shiu* by Yotaro Okuno. **Principal Officials and Managers:** Robin K. Lee, Publisher and Editor; John D. Simpson, Manager.

★2728★
Mele Loke Publishing Co.
PO Box 240142
Honolulu, HI 96824-0142   Ph: (808)734-8611

Description: Promotes Hawaiian culture through song and dance. Also offers microform publications, records, filmstrips, and cassettes of songs by Carol Roes. Reaches market through direct mail and trade sales. **Subjects:** Hawaiian culture, music, dance. **Total Titles in Print:** 42. **Selected Titles:** *Children's Songs from Hawaii, Songs of Hawaii and Spirituals, Hulas from Hawaii, Song Stories of Hawaii, It Can Happen Only in Hawaii, Eight Islands*, all by Carol Roes. **Principal Officials and Managers:** Carol Roes, Owner; Joan Lindsey, Instructor and Director, Hula Studio.

★2729★
Wonder View Press
823 Olive Ave.
Wahiawa, HI 96786   Ph: (808)621-2288
Description: Specializes in local-interest publications with emphasis on histories of Hawaiian locales, people, and traditions. Reaches market through direct mail, trade sales, and Pacific Trade Group. **Total Titles in Print:** 5. **Selected Titles:** *Waipahu: A Brief History; Wahiawa: From Dream to Community,* both by Lani Nedbalek; *Plantation Village Cookbook; Country Cookbook; The Second Plantation Village Cookbook.* **Principal Officials and Managers:** Leon Nedbalek, Lani Nedbalek, General Partners.

Aboriginal Canadians

Tribal Communities

Alberta

★2730★
Whitefish Lake Indian Band
General Delivery
Atikameg, AB, Canada T0G 0C0
Robert James Grey, Chief
Ph: (403)767-3914

★2731★
Kehewin Indian Band
PO Box 6218
Bonnyville, AB, Canada T9N 2G8
Gordon Gadwa, Chief
Ph: (403)826-3333

★2732★
Peigan Nation
PO Box 70
Brocket, AB, Canada T0K 0H0
Leonard Walter Bastien, Chief
Ph: (403)965-3940

★2733★
Duncan's Indian Band
PO Box 148
Brownvale, AB, Canada T0H 0L0
Donald Testawich, Chief
Ph: (403)597-3777

★2734★
Woodland Cree Indian Band
General Delivery
Cadotte Lake, AB, Canada T0H 0N0
John Wilbert Cardinal, Chief
Ph: (403)629-3803

★2735★
Tsuu T'Ina Nation (Sarcee)
3700 Anderson Rd., SW
Calgary, AB, Canada T2W 3C4
Roy Albert Whitney, Chief
Ph: (403)281-4455

★2736★
Dene Tha' Tribe Band
PO Box 120
Chateh, AB, Canada T0H 0S0
Harry Chonkolay, Chief
Ph: (403)321-3842

★2737★
Bigstone Cree Band
General Delivery
Desmarais, AB, Canada T0G 0T0
Eric Alook, Chief
Ph: (403)891-3836

★2738★
Driftpile Indian Band
General Delivery
Driftpile, AB, Canada T0G 0V0
Eugene Germain Laboucan, Chief
Ph: (403)355-3868

★2739★
Paul Indian Band
PO Box 89
Duffield, AB, Canada T0E 0N0
Walter Rain, Chief
Ph: (403)892-2691

★2740★
Sucker Creek Band
PO Box 65
Enilda, AB, Canada T0G 0W0
Jim Badger, Chief
Ph: (403)523-4426

★2741★
Cree Indian Band
PO Box 90
Fort Chipewyan, AB, Canada T0P 1B0
Archie Waquan, Chief
Ph: (403)697-3740

★2742★
Fort Chipewyan Indian Band
PO Box 366
Fort Chipewyan, AB, Canada T0P 1B0
Patrice Marcel, Chief
Ph: (403)697-3730

★2743★
Fort McKay Indian Band
PO Box 5360
Fort McMurray, AB, Canada T9H 3G4
Mary Dorothy McDonald, Chief
Ph: (403)828-4220

★2744★
Fort McMurray Indian Band
PO Box 8217, Clearwater Station
Fort McMurray, AB, Canada T9H 4J1
Bernice Cree, Chief
Ph: (403)334-2293

★2745★
Janvier Indian Band
9206 McCormack Dr.
Fort McMurray, AB, Canada T9H 1C7   Ph: (403)559-2272
Walter Janvier, Chief

★2746★
Tallcree Indian Band
PO Box 367
Fort Vermilion, AB, Canada T0H 1N0   Ph: (403)927-3727
Bernard John Meneen, Chief

★2747★
Frog Lake Indian Band
Frog Lake, AB, Canada T0A 1M0   Ph: (403)943-3737
Elmer Thomas Abraham, Chief

★2748★
Siksika Nation Band
PO Box 249
Gleichen, AB, Canada T0J 1N0   Ph: (403)264-7250
Strater Crow Foot, Chief

★2749★
Alexis Indian Band
PO Box 7
Glenevis, AB, Canada T0E 0X0   Ph: (403)967-2225
Howard Mustus, Chief

★2750★
Saddle Lake Band
Goodfish Lake Group
Goodfish Lake, AB, Canada T0A 1R0   Ph: (403)636-3622
Allan Percy Houle, Chief

★2751★
Cold Lake First Nations Band
PO Box 1769
Grand Centre, AB, Canada T0A 1T0   Ph: (403)594-7183
Baptiste Blackman, Chief

★2752★
Grouard Indian Band
General Delivery
Grouard, AB, Canada T0G 1C0   Ph: (403)751-3800
Frank Thomas Halcrow, Chief

★2753★
Boyer River Indian Band
PO Box 270
High Level, AB, Canada T0H 1Z0   Ph: (403)927-3697
Harvey Bulldog, Chief

★2754★
Little Red River Cree Nation Indian Band
PO Box 1165
High Level, AB, Canada T0H 1Z0   Ph: (403)759-3912
A.J. Sewepagaham, Chief

★2755★
Ermineskin Indian Band
PO Box 219
Hobbema, AB, Canada T0C 1N0   Ph: (403)420-0008
John Baptiste Ermineskin, Chief

★2756★
Louis Bull Indian Band
PO Box 130
Hobbema, AB, Canada T0C 1N0   Ph: (403)423-2064
Simon Threefingers, Chief

★2757★
Montana Indian Band
PO Box 70
Hobbema, AB, Canada T0C 1N0   Ph: (403)585-3744
Leo Cattleman, Chief

★2758★
Samson Indian Band
PO Box 159
Hobbema, AB, Canada T0C 1N0   Ph: (403)421-4926
Victor Buffalo, Chief

★2759★
Horse Lake Indian Band
PO Box 303
Hythe, AB, Canada T0H 2C0   Ph: (403)356-2248
Dale Robert Horseman, Chief

★2760★
Swan River Indian Band
PO Box 270
Kinuso, AB, Canada T0G 1K0   Ph: (403)775-3536
Charles Henry Chalifoux, Chief

★2761★
Beaver Lake Indian Band
PO Box 960
Lac La Biche, AB, Canada T0A 2C0   Ph: (403)623-4549
Alphonse Lameman, Chief

★2762★
Heart Lake Indian Band
PO Box 447
Lac La Biche, AB, Canada T0A 2C0   Ph: (403)623-2130
Eugene Monias, Chief

★2763★
Alexander Indian Band
PO Box 510
Morinville, AB, Canada T0G 1P0   Ph: (403)939-5887
Joseph Stanley Arcand, Chief

★2764★
Stoney Indian Band
Bearspaw Group
PO Box 40
Morley, AB, Canada T0L 1N0   Ph: (403)881-3770
Johnny Ear, Chief

★2765★
Stoney Indian Band
Chiniki Group
PO Box 40
Morley, AB, Canada T0L 1N0   Ph: (403)881-3770
Kenneth Soldier, Chief

★2766★
Stoney Indian Band
Wesley Group
PO Box 40
Morley, AB, Canada T0L 1N0   Ph: (403)881-3770
John Snow, Chief

★2767★
Lubicon Lake Indian Band
PO Box 6731
Peace River, AB, Canada T8S 1S5   Ph: (403)639-3945
Bernard Ominayak, Chief

★2768★
O'Chiese Indian Band
PO Box 1570
Rocky Mountain House, AB, Canada T0M
1T0   Ph: (403)989-3943
Caroline Beaver Bones, Chief

★2769★
Sunchild Cree Indian Band
PO Box 747
Rocky Mountain House, AB, Canada T0M
1T0   Ph: (403)989-3740
Harry Goodrunning, Chief

★2770★
Saddle Lake Indian Band
Saddle Lake Group
Development Projects
PO Box 100
Saddle Lake, AB, Canada T0A 3T0   Ph: (403)726-3829
Carl Quinn, Chief

★2771★
Sawridge Indian Band
PO Box 326
Slave Lake, AB, Canada T0G 2A0   Ph: (403)849-4311
Walter Patrick Twinn, Chief

★2772★
Blood Indian Band
PO Box 60
Standoff, AB, Canada T0L 1Y0   Ph: (403)737-3753
Roy Fox, Chief

★2773★
Sturgeon Lake Indian Band
PO Box 757
Valleyview, AB, Canada T0H 3N0   Ph: (403)524-3307
Ronald Sunshine, Chief

★2774★
Enoch Indian Band
Site 2, RR 1
PO Box 2
Winterburn, AB, Canada T0E 2N0   Ph: (403)470-4505
Howard Peacock, Chief

───── **British Columbia** ─────

★2775★
Canim Lake Indian Band
PO Box 1030
100 Mile House, BC, Canada V0K 2E0 Ph: (604)397-2227
Gabriel Roy Christopher, Chief

★2776★
Sumas Indian Band
3092 Sumas Mountain Rd.
RR 4
Abbotsford, BC, Canada V2S 4N4   Ph: (604)852-4040
Lester Vernon Ned, Chief

★2777★
Chehalis Indian Band
Chehalis Rd.
RR 1, Compt. 66
Agassiz, BC, Canada V0M 1A0   Ph: (604)796-2116
Rose Charlie, Chief

★2778★
Seabird Island Indian Band
PO Box 650
Agassiz, BC, Canada V0M 1A0   Ph: (604)796-2177
Archibald Charles, Chief

★2779★
Ahousaht Indian Band
General Delivery
Ahousaht, BC, Canada V0R 1A0   Ph: (604)670-9563
Louie M. Frank Sr., Chief

★2780★
Nimpkish Indian Band
PO Box 210
Alert Bay, BC, Canada V0N 1A0   Ph: (604)974-5556
Patrick Alfred, Chief

★2781★
Tanakteuk Indian Band
PO Box 327
Alert Bay, BC, Canada V0N 1A0   Ph: (604)974-5489
William McKenzie Glendale, Chief

★2782★
Tlatlasikwala Indian Band
c/o Whe-La-La-U Area Council
PO Box 150
Alert Bay, BC, Canada V0N 1A0   Ph: (604)974-5501
Thomas Wallace, Chief

★2783★
Anaham Indian Band
General Delivery
Alexis Creek, BC, Canada V0L 1A0   Ph: (604)394-4212
Andrew Harry, Chief

★2784★
Ulkatcho Indian Band
General Delivery
Anahim Lake, BC, Canada V0L 1C0   Ph: (604)742-3260
Cassidy Sill, Chief

★2785★
Ashcroft Indian Band
PO Box 440
Ashcroft, BC, Canada V0K 1A0   Ph: (604)453-9154
Mae Boomer, Chief

★2786★
Oregon Jack Creek Band
PO Box 940
Ashcroft, BC, Canada V0K 1A0   Ph: (604)453-9098
Robert S. Pasco, Chief

★2787★
Taku River Tlingit Indian Band
Box 132
Atlin, BC, Canada V0W 1A0   Ph: (403)651-7615
Sylvester Jack Sr., Chief

★2788★
North Thompson Indian Band
PO Box 220
Barriere, BC, Canada V0E 1E0   Ph: (604)672-9995
Nathan Louis Matthew, Chief

★2789★
Bella Coola Indian Band
PO Box 65
Bella Coola, BC, Canada V0T 1C0   Ph: (604)799-5613
Edward Moody, Chief

★2790★
Boothroyd Indian Band
PO Box 295
Boston Bar, BC, Canada V0K 1C0   Ph: (604)867-9211
Wilfred George Campbell, Chief

★2791★
Boston Bar Indian Band
SS 1
Boston Bar, BC, Canada V0K 1C0   Ph: (604)867-9349
Herman Phillips, Chief

★2792★
Pauquachin Indian Band
PO Box 517
Brentwood Bay, BC, Canada V0S 1K0   Ph: (604)656-0191
Edwin Mitchell, Chief

★2793★
Tsartlip Indian Band
PO Box 70
Brentwood Bay, BC, Canada V0S 1A0   Ph: (604)652-3988
Daniel Sam Sr., Chief

★2794★
Blueberry River Indian Band
PO Box 3009
Buick, BC, Canada V0C 2R0   Ph: (604)630-2584
Joe Apsassin, Chief

★2795★
Broman Lake Indian Band
PO Box 760
Burns Lake, BC, Canada V0J 1E0   Ph: (604)698-7330
Maureen Ogen, Chief

★2796★
Burns Lake indian Band
PO Bag 9000
Burns Lake, BC, Canada V0J 1E0   Ph: (604)692-7097
Robert Charlie, Chief

★2797★
Cheslatta Carrier Nation Indian Band
PO Box 909
Burns Lake, BC, Canada V0J 1E0   Ph: (604)694-3334
Marvin Charlie, Chief

★2798★
Lake Babine Indian Band
PO Box 879
Burns Lake, BC, Canada V0J 1E0   Ph: (604)692-7555
Wilf Adams, Chief

★2799★
Nee-Tahi-Buhn Indian Band
RR 2, Box 28
Burns Lake, BC, Canada V0J 1E0   Ph: (604)694-3301
Pius Jack, Chief

★2800★
Bonaparte Indian Band
PO Box 669
Cache Creek, BC, Canada V0K 1H0   Ph: (604)457-9624
Nels Terry Porter, Chief

★2801★
Pavilion Indian Band
PO Box 609
Cache Creek, BC, Canada V0K 1H0   Ph: (604)256-4204
Marvin Bob, Chief

★2802★
Campbell River Indian Band
1400 Weiwaikum Rd.
Campbell River, BC, Canada V9W 5W8   Ph: (604)286-6949
Roy Anthony Roberts, Chief

★2803★
Ehattesaht Indian Band
Box 716
Campbell River, BC, Canada V9W 6J3   Ph: (604)287-4353
Earl J. Smith, Chief

★2804★
Homalco Indian Band
PO Box 789
Campbell River, BC, Canada V9W 6Y4   Ph: (604)287-4922
Richard Harry, Chief

★2805★
Kwiakah Indian Band
1440 Island Hwy.
Campbell River, BC, Canada V9W 2E3   Ph: (604)286-1295
Stephen George Dick, Chief

★2806★
Mamaleleqala Qwe'Qwa'Sot'Enox Indian Band
1400 Weiwakum Rd.
Campbell River, BC, Canada V9W 5W8   Ph: (604)287-2955
Robert Sewid, Chief

★2807★
Dease River Indian Band
Good Hope Lake
PO Box 3500
Cassiar, BC, Canada V0C 1E0   Ph: (604)239-3000
Peter Chief, Chief

★2808★
Adams Lake Indian Band
PO Box 588
Chase, BC, Canada V0E 1M0   Ph: (604)679-8841
Harvey Jules, Chief

★2809★
Little Shuswap Band
PO Box 1100
Chase, BC, Canada V0E 1M0   Ph: (604)679-3203
Felix Arnouse, Chief

★2810★
Neskonlith Indian Band
PO Box 608
Chase, BC, Canada V0E 1M0   Ph: (604)679-3295
Madene Joyce Manuel, Chief

★2811★
Halalt Indian Band
RR 1
Chemainus, BC, Canada V0R 1K0   Ph: (604)246-4736
George Norris, Chief

★2812★
Penelakut Indian Band
PO Box 360
Chemainus, BC, Canada V0R 1K0   Ph: (604)246-2321
Earl Wilbur Jack, Chief

★2813★
Saulteaux Indian Band
PO Box 414
Chetwynd, BC, Canada V0C 1J0   Ph: (604)788-3955
Stewart Cameron, Chief

★2814★
Alexis Creek Indian Band
PO Box 69
Chilanko, BC, Canada V0L 1H0   Ph: (604)481-3335
Irvine Charleyboy, Chief

★2815★
Kwaw-Kwaw-A-Pilt Indian Band
PO Box 412
Chilliwack, BC, Canada V2P 6H7   Ph: (604)858-0662
Harold Henry, Chief

★2816★
Skwah Indian Band
PO Box 178
Chilliwack, BC, Canada V2P 6H7   Ph: (604)792-9204
Leslie Williams, Chief

★2817★
Squiala Indian Band
PO Box 392
Chilliwack, BC, Canada V2P 6J7   Ph: (604)792-8300
Robert B. Jimmie, Chief

★2818★
Quatsino Indian Band
PO Box 100
Coal Harbour, BC, Canada V0N 1K0   Ph: (604)949-6245
Stephen Clair, Chief

★2819★
Tlowitsis-Mumtagila Band
c/o Whe-La-La-U Area Council
PO Box 150
Coquitlam, BC, Canada V3J 1P5   Ph: (604)974-5501
John Smith, Chief

★2820★
Comox Indian Band
3320 Comox Rd.
Courtenay, BC, Canada V9N 3P8   Ph: (604)339-4545
Norman Frank, Chief

★2821★
St. Mary's Indian Band
Mission Rd.
Site 15, RR 1
Cranbrook, BC, Canada V1C 4H4   Ph: (604)426-5717
Agnes McCoy, Chief

★2822★
Lower Kootenay Indian Band
PO Box 1107
Creston, BC, Canada V0B 1G0   Ph: (604)428-4428
Wayne Louie, Chief

★2823★
Anderson Lake Indian Band
PO Box 88
D'arcy, BC, Canada V0N 1L0   Ph: (604)452-3221
Lawrence Patrick, Chief

★2824★
Tsawwassen Indian Band
N. Tsawwassen Dr., Bldg. 132
Delta, BC, Canada V4K 3N2   Ph: (604)943-2112
Frederick A. Jacobs, Chief

★2825★
Lakahahmen Indian Band
41290 Lougheed Hwy.
Deroche, BC, Canada V0M 1G0   Ph: (604)826-7976
George Campo, Chief

★2826★
Canoe Creek Indian Band
General Delivery
Dog Creek, BC, Canada V0L 1J0   Ph: (604)440-5645
William Harry, Chief

★2827★
Cowichan Indian Band
1802 Tzouhalem Rd.
PO Box 880
Duncan, BC, Canada V9L 3Y2   Ph: (604)748-3196
Dennis Alphonse, Chief

★2828★
Spallumcheen Indian Band
PO Box 430
Enderby, BC, Canada V0E 1V0   Ph: (604)838-6496
Cindy Williams, Chief

★2829★
Nadleh Whuten Band
PO Box 36
Fort Fraser, BC, Canada V0J 1N0   Ph: (604)690-7211
Ernie Nooski, Chief

★2830★
Langley Indian Band
PO Box 117
Fort Langley, BC, Canada V0X 1J0   Ph: (604)888-2488
Alfred J. Gabriel, Chief

★2831★
Fort Nelson Indian Band
293 Alaska Hwy.
RR 1
Fort Nelson, BC, Canada V0C 1R0   Ph: (604)774-7688
Sally Behn, Chief

★2832★
Prophet River Indian Band
PO Box 3250
Fort Nelson, BC, Canada V0C 1R0   Ph: (604)774-1025
Liza Wolf, Chief

★2833★
Nak'Azdli Indian Band
PO Box 1329
Fort Saint James, BC, Canada V0J 1P0   Ph: (604)996-7171
Leonard Thomas, Chief

★2834★
Tl'azt'en Nation
PO Box 670
Fort Saint James, BC, Canada V0J 1P0   Ph: (604)648-3212
Edward John, Chief

★2835★
Stellaquo Indian Band
PO Box 760
Fraser Lake, BC, Canada V0J 1S0   Ph: (604)699-8747
Robert Michell, Chief

★2836★
Gitwinksihlkw Indian Band
PO Box 1
Gitwinksihlkw, BC, Canada V0J 3T0   Ph: (604)633-2294
Harvey Fraser Nyce, Chief

★2837★
Mowachaht Indian Band
PO Box 459
Gold River, BC, Canada V0P 1G0   Ph: (604)283-2532

★2838★
Tobacco Plains Indian Band
PO Box 21
Grasmere, BC, Canada V08 1R0   Ph: (604)887-3461
Josephine Shottanana, Chief

★2839★
Lakalzap Indian Band
Greenville, BC, Canada V0J 1X0   Ph: (604)621-3212
Henry Moore, Chief

★2840★
Stone Indian Band
General Delivery
Hanceville, BC, Canada V0L 1K0   Ph: (604)394-4295
Anthony Myers, Chief

★2841★
Douglas Indian Band
PO Box 339
Harrison Hot Springs, BC, Canada V0M
1K0   Ph: (604)820-3082
Neil Phillips, Chief

★2842★
Hartley Bay Indian Band
Hartley Bay, BC, Canada V0V 1A0   Ph: (604)851-2500
William Clifton, Chief

★2843★
Gitanmaax Indian Band
PO Box 440
Hazelton, BC, Canada V0J 1Y0   Ph: (604)842-5297
Gary Patsey Jr., Chief

★2844★
Glen Vowell Band
PO Box 157
Hazelton, BC, Canada V0J 1Y0   Ph: (604)842-5241
Marvin Norman Sampson, Chief

★2845★
Chawathil Indian Band
PO Box 1659
Hope, BC, Canada V0X 1L0   Ph: (604)869-9994
Herman W. Dennis Peters, Chief

★2846★
Ohamil Indian Band
RR 2, Site 22, C4
Hope, BC, Canada V0X 1L0   Ph: (604)869-2627
Audrey Diana Kelly, Chief

★2847★
Peters Indian Band
16650 Peters Rd.
RR 1
Hope, BC, Canada V0X 1L0   Ph: (604)794-7059
Frank Peters, Chief

★2848★
Skawahlook Indian Band
PO Box 1668
Hope, BC, Canada V0X 1L0   Ph: (604)796-9877
Anna Delores Chapman, Chief

★2849★
Union Bar Indian Band
PO Box 788
Hope, BC, Canada V0X 1L0   Ph: (604)869-9466
Andrew Alex, Chief

★2850★
Yale Indian Band
PO Box 1869
Hope, BC, Canada V0X 1L0   Ph: (604)863-2423
Robert Hope, Chief

★2851★
Shuswap Indian Band
PO Box 790
Invermere, BC, Canada V0A 1K0   Ph: (604)342-6361
Paul Ignatius Sam, Chief

★2852★
Iskut Indian Band
Iskut, BC, Canada V0J 1K0   Ph: (604)234-3331
Louis Louie, Chief

★2853★
Kamloops Indian Band
315 Yellowhead Hwy.
Kamloops, BC, Canada V2H 1H1   Ph: (604)828-9700
Clarence Thomas Jules, Chief

★2854★
Whispering Pines Band
RR 1, Site 8, Comp. 4
Kamloops, BC, Canada V2C 1Z3   Ph: (604)579-5772

★2855★
Westbank Indian Band
515 Hwy. 97 S.
Kelowna, BC, Canada V1Z 3J2   Ph: (604)769-5666
Robert Louie, Chief

★2856★
Lower Similkameen Band
PO Box 100
Keremeos, BC, Canada V0X 1N0   Ph: (604)499-5528
Barnett Allison, Chief

★2857★
Upper Similkameen Indian Band
PO Box 100
Keremeos, BC, Canada V0X 1N0   Ph: (604)499-5528
Edward Allison, Chief

★2858★
Kincolith Indian Band
Kincolith, BC, Canada V0J 1B0   Ph: (604)326-4212
Stuart Christopher Doolan, Chief

★2859★
Tsawataineuk Indian Band
Kingcome Inlet, BC, Canada V0N 2B0
Edward Dawson, Chief

★2860★
Kispiox Indian Band
RR 1, Box 25
Kispiox, BC, Canada V0J 1Y0   Ph: (604)842-5248
Brian Williams, Chief

★2861★
Kitamaat Indian Band
Haisla
PO Box 1101
Kitamaat Village, BC, Canada V0T 2B0   Ph: (604)639-9361
Gerald Victor Amos, Chief

★2862★
Kitkatla Indian Band
Kitkatla, BC, Canada V0V 1C0   Ph: (604)628-9305
David Moody, Chief

★2863★
Gitwangak Indian Band
PO Box 400
Kitwanga, BC, Canada V0J 2A0   Ph: (604)849-5591
Glenford Williams, Chief

★2864★
Kitwancool Indian Band
PO Box 340
Kitwanga, BC, Canada V0J 2A0   Ph: (604)849-5222
Elmer Philemon Derrick, Chief

★2865★
Kitasoo Indian Band
Klemtu, BC, Canada V0T 1L0   Ph: (604)839-1255
Leslie Neasloss, Chief

★2866★
Kyuquot Indian Band
Kyuquot, BC, Canada V0P 1J0   Ph: (604)332-5259
Richard H. Leo, Chief

★2867★
Chemainus Indian Band
RR 1
Ladysmith, BC, Canada V0R 2E0   Ph: (604)245-7155
Robert Daniels, Chief

★2868★
Lyackson Indian Band
PO Box 1798
Ladysmith, BC, Canada V0R 2E0   Ph: (604)245-3829
Gordon Thomas, Chief

★2869★
Scowlitz Indian Band
PO Box 76
Lake Errock, BC, Canada V0M 1N0   Ph: (604)826-5813
Clarence Martin Pennier, Chief

★2870★
Nanoose Indian Band
RR 1, Box 124
Lantzville, BC, Canada V0R 2H0   Ph: (604)390-3661
Leonard Wayne Edwards, Chief

★2871★
Bridge River Indian Band
PO Box 190
Lillooet, BC, Canada V0K 1V0   Ph: (604)256-7423
Susan James, Chief

★2872★
Cayoose Creek Indian Band
PO Box 484
Lillooet, BC, Canada V0K 1V0   Ph: (604)256-4136
Perry Redan, Chief

★2873★
Fountain Indian Band
PO Box 1330
Lillooet, BC, Canada V0K 1V0   Ph: (604)256-4227
Roger Adolf, Chief

★2874★
Lillooet Indian Band
PO Box 615
Lillooet, BC, Canada V0K 1V0   Ph: (604)256-4118
William Machell, Chief

★2875★
High Bar Indian Band
c/o Fraser Canyon Indian Admin.
PO Box 400
Lytton, BC, Canada V0K 1Z0   Ph: (604)455-2279
Rosemarie Haller, Chief

★2876★
Kanaka Bar Indian Band
PO Box 210
Lytton, BC, Canada V0K 1Z0   Ph: (604)455-2279
James Frank, Chief

★2877★
Lytton Indian Band
PO Box 20
Lytton, BC, Canada V0K 1Z0   Ph: (604)455-2304
Byron James Spinks, Chief

★2878★
Micomen Indian Band
PO Box 328
Lytton, BC, Canada V0K 1Z0   Ph: (604)455-2279
Cyril Spence, Chief

★2879★
Siska Indian Band
PO Box 358
Lytton, BC, Canada V0K 1Z0   Ph: (604)455-2219
Guy Dunstan, Chief

★2880★
Skuppah Indian Band
PO Box 116
Lytton, BC, Canada V0K 1Z0   Ph: (604)455-2279
John McIntyre, Chief

★2881★
Masset Indian Band
PO Box 189
Masset, BC, Canada V0T 1M0   Ph: (604)626-3337
Michael Thomas Nicoll, Chief

★2882★
Matsqui Indian Band
31753 Harris Rd.
RR #1, PO Box 229
Matsqui, BC, Canada V0X 1S0   Ph: (604)826-6145
David McKay, Chief

★2883★
McLeod Lake Indian Band
General Delivery
McLeod Lake, BC, Canada V0J 2G0   Ph: (604)750-4415
Harry Chingy, Chief

★2884★
Coldwater Indian Band
PO Bag 4600
Merritt, BC, Canada V0K 2B0   Ph: (604)378-6174
F. Gordon Antoine, Chief

★2885★
Lower Nicola Indian Band
RR 1, Site 17, Comp. 18
Merritt, BC, Canada V0K 2B0   Ph: (604)378-5157
Donald Moses, Chief

★2886★
Nooaitch Indian Band
PO Bag 6000
Merritt, BC, Canada V0K 2B0   Ph: (604)378-6141
Linday May Shackelly, Chief

★2887★
Shackan Indian Band
Bag 6000
Merritt, BC, Canada V0K 2B0   Ph: (604)378-6141
Percy Anthony Joe, Chief

★2888★
Upper Nicola Indian Band
PO Bag 3700
Merritt, BC, Canada V0K 2B0   Ph: (604)350-3342
George Saddleman, Chief

★2889★
Malahat Indian Band
PO Box 111
Mill Bay, BC, Canada V0R 2P0   Ph: (604)743-3231
Randolph Daniels, Chief

★2890★
Samahquam Indian Band
PO Box 3068
Mission, BC, Canada V2V 4J3   Ph: (604)894-5262

★2891★
West Moberly Indian Band
General Delivery
Moberly Lake, BC, Canada V0C 1X0   Ph: (604)788-3663
George Desjarlais, Chief

★2892★
Mount Currie Indian Band
PO Box 165
Mount Currie, BC, Canada V0N 2K0   Ph: (604)894-6115
Katherine Wallace, Chief

★2893★
Nanaimo Indian Band
1145 Totem Rd.
Nanaimo, BC, Canada V9R 1H1   Ph: (604)753-3481
Robert E. Thomas, Chief

★2894★
Ohiaht Indian Band
PO Box 82, Sta. A
Nanaimo, BC, Canada V9R 5K4   Ph: (604)752-3994
Telford K. Dennis, Chief

★2895★
Nemaiah Valley Indian Band
Nemaiah Valley Post Office
Nemaiah Valley, BC, Canada V0L 1X0
Annie C. Williams, Chief

★2896★
Gitlakdamix Indian Band
New Aiyansh, BC, Canada V0J 1A0   Ph: (604)633-2215
Herbert Morven, Chief

★2897★
Hagwilget Indian Band
PO Box 460
New Hazelton, BC, Canada V0J 2J0   Ph: (604)842-6258
Jack Alex Sebastian, Chief

★2898★
Burrard Indian Band
3082 Ghumlye Dr.
North Vancouver, BC, Canada V7H 1B3   Ph: (604)929-3454
Leonard George, Chief

★2899★
Squamish Indian Band
PO Box 86131
North Vancouver, BC, Canada V7L 4J5   Ph: (604)985-7711
Philip L.
Norman Joe

★2900★
Osoyoos Indian Band
RR 3, Site 25, Comp. 1
Oliver, BC, Canada V0H 1T0   Ph: (604)498-4906
Clarence Joseph Louie, Chief

★2901★
Skookumchuck Indian Band
PO Box 190
Pemberton, BC, Canada V0M 2L0   Ph: (604)894-6037
Paul Williams, Chief

★2902★
Penticton Indian Band
Site 80, Comp. 19, RR 2
Penticton, BC, Canada V2A 6J7   Ph: (604)493-0048
Archie Jack, Chief

★2903★
Katzie Indian Band
10946 Katzie Rd.
Pitt Meadows, BC, Canada V3Y 1Z3   Ph: (604)465-8961
Ed Pierre, Chief

★2904★
Ditidaht Indian Band
PO Box 340
Port Alberni, BC, Canada V9Y 7M8
G. Jackie Thompson, Chief

★2905★
Opetchesaht Indian Band
PO Box 211
Port Alberni, BC, Canada V9Y 7M7   Ph: (604)724-4041
Daniel Watts, Chief

★2906★
Sheshaht Indian Band
Box 1218
Port Alberni, BC, Canada V9Y 7M1   Ph: (604)724-1225
Adam Shewish, Chief

★2907★
Uchucklesaht Indian Band
Box 157
Port Alberni, BC, Canada V9Y 7M7   Ph: (604)724-1832
Charlie Cootes, Chief

★2908★
Coquitlam Indian Band
65 Colony Farm Rd.
Port Coquitlam, BC, Canada V3C 3V4   Ph: (604)941-4995
Patsy Chaffee, Chief

★2909★
Gwa'sala-'Nakwaxda'xw Indian Band
PO Box 998
Port Hardy, BC, Canada V0N 2P0   Ph: (604)949-8343
Paddy Walkus, Chief

★2910★
Kwakiutl Indian Band
PO Box 1440
Port Hardy, BC, Canada V0N 2P0   Ph: (604)949-6012
Alfred Hunt, Chief

★2911★
Oweekeno Indian Band
PO Box 3500
Port Hardy, BC, Canada V0N 2P0
Frank Johnson, Chief

★2912★
Kwa-Wa-Aineuk Indian Band
PO Box 344
Port McNeill, BC, Canada V0N 2R0   Ph: (604)949-8732
Charlie Williams, Chief

★2913★
Pacheenaht Indian Band
General Delivery
Port Renfrew, BC, Canada V0S 1K0   Ph: (604)647-5521
Kenneth Jones, Chief

★2914★
Lax-Kw-alaams Indian Band
206 Shashaak St.
Port Simpson, BC, Canada V0V 1H0   Ph: (604)625-3474
Lawrence Helin, Chief

★2915★
Sliammon Indian Band
Sliammon Rd.
RR 2
Powell River, BC, Canada V8A 4Z3   Ph: (604)483-9646
Gene Louie, Chief

★2916★
Fort George Indian Band
RR 1, Site 27, Comp. 60
Prince George, BC, Canada V2N 2H8   Ph: (604)963-8451
Peter Quaw, Chief

★2917★
Fort Ware Band
3-1257 4th Ave.
Prince George, BC, Canada V21 3J5   Ph: (604)563-4161
Emil McCook, Chief

★2918★
Ingenika Indian Band
101-1551 Ogilvie
Prince George, BC, Canada V2N 1W7   Ph: (604)562-8882
Gordon Pierre, Chief

★2919★
Metlakatla Indian Band
PO Box 459
Prince Rupert, BC, Canada V8J 3R1   Ph: (604)628-9294
Brian James Sparrow, Chief

★2920★
Qualicum Indian Band
Site 347, C-1, RR 3
Qualicum Beach, BC, Canada V0R 2T0   Ph: (604)757-9337
Robert Mark Recalma, Chief

★2921★
Cape Mudge Indian Band
PO Box 220
Quathiaski Cove, BC, Canada V0P 1N0   Ph: (604)285-3316
Ralph Dick Sr., Chief

★2922★
Skidegate Indian Band
RR 1, PO Box 699
Queen Charlotte City, BC, Canada V0T
1S0   Ph: (604)559-4496
Paul Edward Pearson, Chief

★2923★
Alexandria Band
RR 2, PO Box 4
Quesnel, BC, Canada V2J 3H6   Ph: (604)993-4324
Thomas Billboy, Chief

★2924★
Kluskus Indian Band
395A Kinchant St.
Quesnel, BC, Canada V2J 2R5   Ph: (604)992-8186
Roger Jimmie, Chief

★2925★
Nazko Indian Band
PO Box 4534
Quesnel, BC, Canada V2J 3H8   Ph: (604)992-9810
Stanley Boyd, Chief

★2926★
Red Bluff Indian Band
1515 Arbutus Rd., Box 4693
Quesnel, BC, Canada V2J 3J9   Ph: (604)747-2900
Frank Boucher, Chief

★2927★
Toosey Indian Band
General Delivery
Riske Creek, BC, Canada V0L 1T0   Ph: (604)659-5655
Francis Laceese, Chief

★2928★
Doig River Indian Band
PO Box 55
Rose Prairie, BC, Canada V0C 2H0   Ph: (604)787-4466
Gerry Attachie, Chief

★2929★
Cheam Indian Band
10704 Hwy. 9
Rosedale, BC, Canada V0X 1X0   Ph: (604)794-7924
Theodore Douglas, Chief

★2930★
Popkum Indian Band
PO Box 68
Rosedale, BC, Canada V0X 1X0   Ph: (604)794-7924
James Murphy, Chief

★2931★
Tsawout Indian Band
Box 121
Saanichton, BC, Canada V0S 1M0   Ph: (604)652-9101
Norman Underwood, Chief

★2932★
Aitchelitz Indian Band
8150 Aitkens Rd., RR 1
Sardis, BC, Canada V2R 1A9   Ph: (604)792-2404
Johnny George, Chief

★2933★
Skowkale Indian Band
PO Box 365
Sardis, BC, Canada V2R 1A7   Ph: (604)792-0730
Steven Point, Chief

★2934★
Tzeachten Indian Band
Box 278
Sardis, BC, Canada V2R 1A6   Ph: (604)858-3888
Kenneth Malloway, Chief

★2935★
Yakweakwioose Indian Band
7176 Chilliwack River Rd.
RR 2
Sardis, BC, Canada V2R 1B1   Ph: (604)858-6726
Frank Malloway, Chief

★2936★
Skeetchestn Indian Band
PO Box 178
Savona, BC, Canada V0K 2J0   Ph: (604)373-2493
Ronald Eric Ignace, Chief

★2937★
Sechelt Indian Band
PO Box 740
Sechelt, BC, Canada V0N 3A0   Ph: (604)688-3017
Thomas Paul, Chief

★2938★
Seton Lake Indian Band
General Delivery
Shalalth, BC, Canada V0N 3C0   Ph: (604)259-8227
Rodney J. Louie, Chief

★2939★
Tseycum Indian Band
Box 2596
Sidney, BC, Canada V8L 4C1   Ph: (604)656-0858
David Bill, Chief

★2940★
Kwicksutaineuk-Ah-Kwaw-Ah-Mish Indian Band
General Delivery
Simoon Sound, BC, Canada V0P 1S0
Alice Smith, Chief

★2941★
Moricetown Indian Band
RR 1, Site 15, Box 1
Smithers, BC, Canada V0J 2N0   Ph: (604)847-2133
Stanislaus George Nikal, Chief

★2942★
Beecher Bay Indian Band
3843 E. Sooke Rd.
RR 1, PO Box 2
Sooke, BC, Canada V0S 1N0   Ph: (604)478-3535
Patricia Ann Chipps, Chief

★2943★
Sooke Indian Band
2184 Lazzar Rd.
RR 3, PO Box 5
Sooke, BC, Canada V0S 1N0   Ph: (604)642-3957
Lawrence D. Underwood, Chief

★2944★
Gitsegukla Indian Band
36 Cascade Ave.
RR 1
South Hazelton, BC, Canada V0J 2R0   Ph: (604)849-5595
Kenneth H. Russell, Chief

★2945★
Klahoose Indian Band
PO Box 9
Squirrel Cove, BC, Canada V0P 1T0   Ph: (604)935-6650
Kathy Francis, Chief

★2946★
Takla Lake Indian Band
General Delivery
Takla Landing, BC, Canada V0J 2T0
Roy French, Chief

★2947★
Tahltan Indian Band
Telegraph Creek, BC, Canada V0J 2W0   Ph: (604)235-3241
Ronnie Carlick, Chief

★2948★
Kitselas Indian Band
4562 Queensway
Terrace, BC, Canada V8G 3X6   Ph: (604)635-5084
Ralph Wright, Chief

★2949★
Kitsumkalum Indian Band
House of Sim-Oi-Ghets
PO Box 544
Terrace, BC, Canada V8G 4B5   Ph: (604)635-6177
Steve Roberts, Chief

★2950★
Hesquiaht Indian Band
PO Box 2000
Tofino, BC, Canada V0R 2Z0
Richard Lucas Sr., Chief

★2951★
Tla-o-qui-aht First Nations Band
PO Box 18
Tofino, BC, Canada V0R 2Z0   Ph: (604)725-3223
Francis F. Frank, Chief

★2952★
Toquaht Indian Band
Box 759
Ucluelet, BC, Canada V0R 3A0   Ph: (604)726-4230
Burt Mack, Chief

★2953★
Ucluelet Indian Band
Box 699
Ucluelet, BC, Canada V0R 3A0   Ph: (604)726-7342
Robert Mundy, Chief

★2954★
Musqueam Indian Band
6370 Salish Dr.
Vancouver, BC, Canada V6N 2C6   Ph: (604)263-3261
Wendy Grant, Chief

★2955★
Stony Creek Indian Band
RR 1, Site 12, Comp. 26
Vanderhoof, BC, Canada V0J 3A0   Ph: (604)567-9293
Geoffrey Thomas, Chief

★2956★
Soowahlie Indian Band
PO Box 696
Vedder Crossing, BC, Canada V0X 1Z0   Ph: (604)858-4603
William Commodore, Chief

★2957★
Okanagan Indian Band
RR 7, Site 8, Comp. 20
Vernon, BC, Canada V1T 7Z3   Ph: (604)542-4328
Albert Saddleman, Chief

★2958★
Esquimalt Indian Band
1113A Admirals Rd.
Victoria, BC, Canada V9A 6V2   Ph: (604)381-7861
Andrew Benedict Thomas, Chief

★2959★
Songhees Indian Band
1500 A-Admirals Rd.
Victoria, BC, Canada V9A 2R1   Ph: (604)386-1043
Edward Norman George, Chief

★2960★
Heiltsuk Indian Band
PO Box 880
Waglisla, BC, Canada V0T 1Z0   Ph: (604)957-2381
Arlene Wilson, Chief

★2961★
Semiahmoo Indian Band
16010 Beach Rd.
RR 7
White Rock, BC, Canada V4B 5A8 Ph: (604)536-1794
Bernard Charles, Chief

★2962★
Alkali Indian Band
PO Box 4479
Williams Lake, BC, Canada V2G 2V5 Ph: (604)440-5611
William Chelsea, Chief

★2963★
Soda Creek Indian Band
RR 4, Site 15, Comp. 2
Williams Lake, BC, Canada V2G 4M8 Ph: (604)297-6323
Beverly Ann Sellers, Chief

★2964★
Williams Lake Indian Band
Sugarcane
RR 3, Box 4
Williams Lake, BC, Canada V2G 1M3 Ph: (604)296-3507
Eric Michael Gilbert, Chief

★2965★
Columbia Lake Indian Band
PO Box 130
Windermere, BC, Canada V0B 2L0 Ph: (604)342-6301
Joseph Nicholas, Chief

★2966★
Halfway River Indian Band
PO Box 59
Wonowon, BC, Canada V0C 2N0 Ph: (604)787-4452
Gerry Hunter, Chief

★2967★
Spuzzum Indian Band
RR 1
Yale, BC, Canada V0K 2S0 Ph: (604)863-2205
James Edward Johnson, Chief

★2968★
Nuchatlaht Indian Tribe
PO Box 40
Zeballos, BC, Canada V0P 2A0 Ph: (604)761-4520
Walter Michael, Chief

─────────── **Manitoba** ───────────

★2969★
Berens River Indian Band
Berens River Post Office
Berens River, MB, Canada R0B 0A0 Ph: (204)382-2161
Lester Oliver Everett, Chief

★2970★
Birdtail Sioux Indian Band
PO Box 22
Beulah, MB, Canada R0M 0B0 Ph: (204)568-4540
Henry Skywater, Chief

★2971★
Gamblers Indian Band
PO Box 293
Binscarth, MB, Canada R0J 0G0 Ph: (204)532-2464
Louis Tanner, Chief

★2972★
Indian Birch Band
Birch River, MB, Canada R0L 0E0 Ph: (204)236-4201
Charles Audy, Chief

★2973★
Bloodvein Indian Band
General Delivery
Bloodvein, MB, Canada R0C 0J0 Ph: (204)395-2148
Helen Cook, Chief

★2974★
Barren Lands Indian Band
General Delivery
Brochet, MB, Canada R0B 0B0 Ph: (204)323-2300
John W. Bighetty, Chief

★2975★
Pine Creek Indian Band
Camperville, MB, Canada R0L 0J0 Ph: (204)524-2478
Clifford McKay, Chief

★2976★
Crane River Indian Band
Crane River, MB, Canada R0L 0M0 Ph: (204)732-2490
John H. McDonald, Chief

★2977★
Cross Lake Indian Band
Cross Lake, MB, Canada R0B 0J0 Ph: (204)676-2218
Syndey Garrioch, Chief

★2978★
Jackhead Indian Band
Dallas, MB, Canada R0C 0S0 Ph: (204)276-2366
Bert Traverse, Chief

★2979★
Chemawawin First Nation Band
Easterville, MB, Canada R0C 0V0 Ph: (204)329-2161
Alpheus Brass, Chief

★2980★
Ebb and Flow Indian Band
Ebb and Flow, MB, Canada R0L 0R0 Ph: (204)448-2134
Alfred Beaulieu, Chief

★2981★
Long Plain Indian Band
General Delivery
Edwin, MB, Canada R0H 0G0 Ph: (204)252-2731
Peter Yellowquill, Chief

★2982★
Keeseekoowenin Indian Band
PO Box 100
Elphinstone, MB, Canada R0J 0N0 Ph: (204)625-2004
Harry Bone, Chief

★2983★
Rolling River Band
PO Box 145
Erickson, MB, Canada R0J 0P0 Ph: (204)636-2211
Dennis Whitebird, Chief

★2984★
Fairford Indian Band
Fairford, MB, Canada R0C 0X0 Ph: (204)659-5705
Andrew Anderson, Chief

★2985★
Fort Alexander Indian Band
Fort Alexander, MB, Canada R0E 0P0 Ph: (204)367-2287
Jerry Fontaine, Chief

★2986★
Fox Lake Indian Band
PO Box 369
Gilliam, MB, Canada R0B 0L0
Robert Wavey, Chief
Ph: (204)652-2219

★2987★
Roseau River Indian Band
PO Box 30
Ginew, MB, Canada R0A 2R0
Lawrence Henry, Chief
Ph: (204)427-2312

★2988★
God's Lake Indian Band
God's Lake Narrows, MB, Canada R0B
0M0
Peter Watt, Chief
Ph: (204)335-2552

★2989★
God's River Indian Band
God's River, MB, Canada R0B 0N0
Marcel Okemaw, Chief
Ph: (204)335-2011

★2990★
Grand Rapids First Nation Band
PO Box 500
Grand Rapids, MB, Canada R0C 1E0
Harold Turner, Chief
Ph: (204)639-2219

★2991★
Sioux Valley Indian Band
PO Box 38
Griswold, MB, Canada R0M 0S0
Robert Bone, Chief
Ph: (204)855-2671

★2992★
Dauphin River Indian Band
General Delivery
Gypsumville, MB, Canada R0C 1J0
Emery Stagg, Chief
Ph: (204)659-6370

★2993★
Lake St. Martin Indian Band
PO Box 69
Gypsumville, MB, Canada R0C 1J0
David E. Traverse, Chief
Ph: (204)659-4539

★2994★
Little Sask Indian Band
Post Office
Gypsumville, MB, Canada R0C 1J0
Hector Shorting, Chief
Ph: (204)659-4584

★2995★
Peguis Indian Band
PO Box 219
Hodgson, MB, Canada R0C 1N0
Louis J. Stevenson, Chief
Ph: (204)645-2359

★2996★
War Lake Indian Band
General Delivery
Ilford, MB, Canada R0B 0S0
Alex Ouskan, Chief
Ph: (204)288-4315

★2997★
Garden Hill First Nation Indian Band
Island Lake, MB, Canada R0B 0T0
Jack Fiddler, Chief
Ph: (204)456-2085

★2998★
Fisher River Indian Band
Koostatak, MB, Canada R0C 1S0
Lorne Cochrane, Chief
Ph: (204)645-2171

★2999★
Northlands Indian Band
Lac Brochet, MB, Canada R0B 2E0
Simon Samuel, Chief
Ph: (204)337-2001

★3000★
Little Grand Rapids Indian Band
Little Grand Rapids, MB, Canada R0B
0V0
Oliver Owens, Chief
Ph: (204)397-2264

★3001★
Sandy Bay Indian Band
Marius, MB, Canada R0H 0T0
Angus Starr, Chief
Ph: (204)843-2462

★3002★
Buffalo Point First Nation Band
PO Box 37
Middlebro, MB, Canada R0A 1B0
James Thunder, Chief
Ph: (204)437-2133

★3003★
Moose Lake Indian Band
Moose Lake, MB, Canada R0B 0Y0
Jim Tobacco, Chief
Ph: (204)678-2113

★3004★
Poplar River First Nation Band
Negginan, MB, Canada R0B 0Z0
Verna Mitchell, Chief
Ph: (204)244-2267

★3005★
Nelson House Indian Band
General Delivery
Nelson House, MB, Canada R0B 1A0
Norman Linklater, Chief
Ph: (204)484-2332

★3006★
Norway House Indian Band
PO Box 218
Norway House, MB, Canada R0B 1B0
Alan James Ross, Chief
Ph: (204)359-6721

★3007★
Little Black River Indian Band
O'Hanley, MB, Canada R0E 1K0
Franklin Abraham, Chief
Ph: (204)367-4411

★3008★
Oxford House Indian Band
Oxford House, MB, Canada R0B 1C0
Gabriel Hart, Chief
Ph: (204)538-2156

★3009★
Shoal River Indian Band
Pelican Rapids, MB, Canada R0L 1L0
Ronald Cook, Chief
Ph: (204)587-2012

★3010★
Oak Lake Sioux Indian Band
PO Box 146
Pipestone, MB, Canada R0M 1T0
Mike Kay, Chief
Ph: (204)854-2959

★3011★
Dakota Plains Indian Band
PO Box 110
Portage La Prairie, MB, Canada R1N 3B2
Ernest Smoke, Chief
Ph: (204)252-2288

★3012★
Dakota Tipi Indian Band
PO Box 1569
Portage La Prairie, MB, Canada R1N 3P1   Ph: (204)857-4381
Dennis Pashe, Chief

★3013★
Mathias Colomb Indian Band
Pukatawagan, MB, Canada R0B 1G0   Ph: (204)553-2090
Pascal Bighetty, Chief

★3014★
Red Sucker Lake Indian Band
Red Sucker Lake, MB, Canada R0B 1H0   Ph: (204)469-9300
John H. Harper, Chief

★3015★
Waywayseecappo First Nation Treaty Four—1874
PO Box 340
Rossburn, MB, Canada R0J 1V0   Ph: (204)859-2883
Murray Clearsky, Chief

★3016★
St. Theresa Point Indian Band
Saint Theresa Point, MB, Canada R0B
1J0   Ph: (204)462-2106
Jack Flett, Chief

★3017★
Brokenhead Indian Band
Scanterbury, MB, Canada R0E 1W0   Ph: (204)766-2494
Wendell Sinclair, Chief

★3018★
Shamattawa First Nation Band
Shamattawa, MB, Canada R0B 1K0   Ph: (204)565-2340
Tommy McKay, Chief

★3019★
Valley River Indian Band
Valley River General Delivery
Shortdale, MB, Canada R0L 1W0   Ph: (204)546-3334
Mervin Lynxleg Sr., Chief

★3020★
Waterhen Indian Band
Skownan, MB, Canada R0L 1Y0   Ph: (204)628-3373
Harvey Nepinak, Chief

★3021★
Split Lake Cree First Nation Band
Split Lake, MB, Canada R0B 1P0   Ph: (204)342-2045
Norman Flett, Chief

★3022★
Swan Lake Indian Band
PO Box 368
Swan Lake, MB, Canada R0G 2S0   Ph: (204)836-2101
Roy Mckinney, Chief

★3023★
Fort Churchill Indian Band
Tadoule Lake, MB, Canada R0B 2C0   Ph: (204)684-2022
Peter Thorassie Sr., Chief

★3024★
The Pas Indian Band
PO Box 297
The Pas, MB, Canada R9A 1K4   Ph: (204)623-5483
Charles Constant, Chief

★3025★
Lake Manitoba Indian Band
Vogar, MB, Canada R0C 3C0   Ph: (204)768-3492
Raymond Swan, Chief

★3026★
Hollow Water Indian Band
Wanipigow, MB, Canada R0E 2E0   Ph: (204)363-7278
Roderick Bushie, Chief

★3027★
Wasagamack Indian Band
Wasagamack, MB, Canada R0B 1Z0   Ph: (204)457-2337
Elijah Knott, Chief

★3028★
York Factory Indian Band
York Landing, MB, Canada R0B 2B0   Ph: (204)342-2210
Eric Saunders, Chief

——————— **Northwest Territories** ———————

★3029★
Aklavik Indian Band
PO Box 118
Aklavik, NT, Canada X0E 0A0   Ph: (403)978-2340
Eugene Pascal, Chief

★3030★
Arctic Red River Indian Band
General Delivery
Arctic Red River, NT, Canada X0E 0B0   Ph: (403)953-3201
Peter Ross, Chief

★3031★
Fort Franklin Indian Band
General Delivery
Fort Franklin, NT, Canada X0E 0G0   Ph: (403)589-3151
Raymond Taniton, Chief

★3032★
Fort Good Hope Indian Band
General Delivery
Fort Good Hope, NT, Canada X0E 0H0   Ph: (403)598-2231
Everett Kakfwi, Chief

★3033★
Fort Liard Indian Band
General Delivery
Fort Liard, NT, Canada X0G 0A0   Ph: (403)770-4141
Steve Kotchea, Chief

★3034★
Tetlit Gwich'in Council
PO Box 86
Fort McPherson, NT, Canada X0E 0J0   Ph: (403)952-2330
James Ross, Chief

★3035★
Fort Norman Indian Band
General Delivery
Fort Norman, NT, Canada X0E 0K0   Ph: (403)588-3341
David Etchinelle, Chief

★3036★
Fort Providence Indian Band
General Delivery
Fort Providence, NT, Canada X0E 0L0   Ph: (403)699-3441
Joachim Bonnetrouge, Chief

★3037★
Dog Rib Rae Indian Band
PO Box 8
Fort Rae, NT, Canada X0E 0Y0   Ph: (403)392-6471
Edward Erasmus, Chief

★3038★
Fort Resolution Indian Band
General Delivery
Fort Resolution, NT, Canada X0E 0M0   Ph: (403)394-5281
Bernadette Unka, Chief

★3039★
Fort Simpson Indian Band
PO Box 469
Fort Simpson, NT, Canada X0E 0N0   Ph: (403)695-3328
Jim Antoine, Chief

★3040★
Fitz/Smith—Alta-Northwest Territories Native Band
PO Box 960
Fort Smith, NT, Canada X0E 0P0   Ph: (403)872-2986
Henry Beaver, Chief

★3041★
Fort Wrigley Indian Band
General Delivery
Fort Wrigley, NT, Canada X0E 1E0   Ph: (403)581-3321
Alma Ekenale, Chief

★3042★
Hay River Indian Band
PO Box 1638
Hay River, NT, Canada X0E 0R0   Ph: (403)874-6701
Pat Martel, Chief

★3043★
Inuvik Native Band
PO Box 2570
Inuvik, NT, Canada X0E 0T0   Ph: (403)979-3344
Cece McCauley, Chief

★3044★
Kakisa Lake
General Delivery
Kakisa Lake, NT, Canada X0E 0L0   Ph: (403)699-9949
Lloyd Chicot, Chief

★3045★
Lac La Martre
General Delivery
Lac La Martre, NT, Canada X0E 1P0   Ph: (403)573-3012
Isidore Zoe, Chief

★3046★
Nahanni Butte Indian Band
General Delivery
Nahanni Butte, NT, Canada X0E 0N0   Ph: (403)695-7223
Peter Marcellais, Chief

★3047★
Lutsel K'E Dene Indian Band
General Delivery
Snowdrift, NT, Canada X0E 1A0   Ph: (403)370-3551
Antoine Michel, Chief

★3048★
Sambaa K'e Dene Indian Band
General Delivery
Trout Lake, NT, Canada X0E 0N0   Ph: (403)695-9800
Edward Jumbo, Chief

★3049★
Yellowknives Dene Indian Band
PO Box 2514
Yellowknife, NT, Canada X1A 2P8   Ph: (403)873-4307
Jonas Sangris, Chief

─────────── **Ontario** ───────────

★3050★
Wapekeka Indian Band
Angling Lake, ON, Canada P0V 1B0   Ph: (807)537-2315
Norman Brown, Chief

★3051★
Gull Bay Indian Band
Gull Bay Post Office
Armstrong, ON, Canada P0T 1P0   Ph: (807)982-2188
John Roger King, Chief

★3052★
Whitesand Indian Band
PO Box 68
Armstrong, ON, Canada P0T 1A0   Ph: (807)583-2177
Doug Sinoway, Chief

★3053★
Attawapiskat Indian Band
PO Box 248
Attawapiskat, ON, Canada P0L 1A0   Ph: (705)997-2166
Ignace Gull, Chief

★3054★
Gibson Indian Band
PO Box 327
Bala, ON, Canada P0C 1A0   Ph: (705)762-3343
Stephen Stock, Chief

★3055★
Nipigon Indian Band
Nipigon Ojibway First Nation
Rocky Bay Reserve
PO Box 241
Beardmore, ON, Canada P0T 2G0   Ph: (807)885-5441

★3056★
Bearskin Lake Indian
Post Office
Bearskin Lake, ON, Canada P0V 1E0   Ph: (807)363-2518
Tom Kamenawatamin, Chief

★3057★
Big Trout Lake Indian Band
Big Trout Lake, ON, Canada P0V 1G0   Ph: (807)537-2263
Stanley Sainnawap, Chief

★3058★
Wawakapewin Indian Band
Big Trout Lake, ON, Canada P0V 1G0
Jermiah Nanokeesic, Chief

★3059★
Whitefish River Indian Band
Birch Island, ON, Canada P0P 1A0   Ph: (705)285-4335
Leona Nahwegahbow, Chief

★3060★
Mississauga Indian Band
PO Box 1299
Blind River, ON, Canada P0R 1B0   Ph: (705)356-1621
Douglas Daybutch, Chief

★3061★
Caldwell Indian Band
PO Box 163
215 Main St.
Bothwell, ON, Canada N0P 1C0   Ph: (519)695-3642
Larry Johnson, Chief

★3062★
Magnetawan Indian Band
RR #1
PO Box 15
Britt, ON, Canada P0G 1A0   Ph: (705)383-2477
Joan Noganosh, Chief

★3063★
Constance Lake Indian Band
Constance Lake Indian Reserve
General Delivery
Calstock, ON, Canada P0L 1B0   Ph: (705)463-4511
Mark Spence, Chief

★3064★
Cat Lake Indian Band
Cat Lake, ON, Canada P0V 1J0
Albert Wesley, Chief

★3065★
Brunswick House Indian Band
PO Box 1319
Chapleau, ON, Canada P0M 1K0   Ph: (705)864-0174
Joseph Saunders Sr., Chief

★3066★
Chapleau Cree Band
PO Box 400
Chapleau, ON, Canada P0M 1K0   Ph: (705)864-0784
Doreen Cachagee, Chief

★3067★
Chapleau Ojibway Indian Band
PO Box 279
Chapleau, ON, Canada P0M 1K0   Ph: (705)864-1090
Joanne Nakogee, Chief

★3068★
New Post Indian Band
RR #2, Box 2, Comp. 0
Cochrane, ON, Canada P0L 1C0   Ph: (705)272-5685
Peter Archibald Sr., Chief

★3069★
Mohawks of Akwesasne Indian Band
PO Box 579
Cornwall, ON, Canada K6H 5T3   Ph: (613)575-2250
Michael Mitchell, Chief

★3070★
Curve Lake Indian Band
Curve Lake Post Office
Curve Lake, ON, Canada K0L 1R0   Ph: (705)657-8045
Melville Wilson Jacob, Chief

★3071★
Serpent River Indian Band
48 Village Rd.
Cutler, ON, Canada P0P 1B0   Ph: (705)844-2418
Earl Commanda, Chief

★3072★
Deer Lake Indian Band
PO Box 335
Deer Lake, ON, Canada P0V 1N0   Ph: (807)775-0053
Fred Meekis, Chief

★3073★
Mohawks of the Bay of Quinte Indian Band
RR No. 1
Deseronto, ON, Canada K0K 1X0   Ph: (613)396-3424
Earl Hill, Chief

★3074★
Naicatchewenin Indian Band
RR 1
Devlin, ON, Canada P0W 1C0   Ph: (807)486-3407
Robert Smith, Chief

★3075★
Wabigoon Lake Ojibway Nation
General Delivery
Dinorwic, ON, Canada P0V 1P0   Ph: (807)938-6684
Christine Garneau, Chief

★3076★
Eagle Lake Indian Band
Eagle River, ON, Canada P0V 1S0   Ph: (807)755-5526
Arnold Gardner, Chief

★3077★
Rainy River Indian Band
PO Box 450
Emo, ON, Canada P0W 1E0   Ph: (807)482-2479
William Wilson, Chief

★3078★
Chippewas of Kettle & Stony Point Indian Band
RR No. 2
Forest, ON, Canada N0N 1J0   Ph: (519)786-2125
Thomas S. Bressette, Chief

★3079★
Albany Indian Band
Albany Island
General Delivery
Fort Albany, ON, Canada P0L 1HW   Ph: (705)278-1044
Edmund Metatawabin, Chief

★3080★
Couchiching Indian Band
c/o PO Box 723
Fort Frances, ON, Canada P9A 3M9   Ph: (807)274-3228
Joan Mainville, Chief

★3081★
Lac La Croix Indian Band
PO Box 640
Fort Frances, ON, Canada P9A 3M9   Ph: (705)485-2431
Stephen Jourdain, Chief

★3082★
Nicikousemencaning Band
PO Box 68
Fort Frances, ON, Canada P9A 3M5   Ph: (807)481-2536
Kelvin Morrison, Chief

★3083★
Strangecoming Indian Band
c/o PO Box 609
Fort Frances, ON, Canada P9A 3M6   Ph: (807)274-2188
Janice Henderson, Chief

★3084★
Fort Severn Indian Band
Fort Severn, ON, Canada P0V 1W0   Ph: (807)478-2572
Elias (Ennis) Crow, Chief

★3085★
Mattagami Indian Band
Gogama, ON, Canada P0M 1W0   Ph: (705)894-2072
Delores B. Legace, Chief

★3086★
Algonquins of Golden Lake Band
Golden Lake, ON, Canada K0J 1X0   Ph: (613)625-2800
Clifford Milnese, Chief

★3087★
Grassy Narrows First Nation Band
General Delivery
Grassy Narrows, ON, Canada P0X 1B0   Ph: (807)925-2201
Raphael Fobister, Chief

★3088★
Mississaugas of the Credit Band
RR No. 6
Hagersville, ON, Canada N0A 1H0   Ph: (416)768-1133
Maurice Laforme, Chief

★3089★
Ojibways of the Pic River First Nation
Heron Bay, ON, Canada P0T 1R0   Ph: (807)229-1749
Roy Michano, Chief

★3090★
Kasabonika Indian Band
Kasabonika Lake, ON, Canada P0V 1Y0   Ph: (807)535-2547
Jeremiah McKay, Chief

★3091★
Albany Indian Band
Village of Kashechewan
General Delivery
Kashechewan, ON, Canada P0L 1S0   Ph: (705)275-4440
Dan Koosees, Chief

★3092★
Hiawatha First Nation Band
RR No. 2
Keene, ON, Canada K0L 2G0   Ph: (705)295-4421
Carl Francis Cowie, Chief

★3093★
Washagamis Bay Indian Band
PO Box 625
Keewatin, ON, Canada P0X 1C0   Ph: (807)543-2532
Alfred Sinclair, Chief

★3094★
Shoal Lake No. 39 Indian Band
Kejick Post Office
Kejick, ON, Canada P0X 1E0   Ph: (807)733-2560
Eli Mandamin, Chief

★3095★
Shoal Lake No. 40 Indian Band
Kejick, ON, Canada P0X 1E0   Ph: (807)733-2315
Lloyd Redsky, Chief

★3096★
Dalles Indian Band
PO Box 1770
Kenora, ON, Canada P9N 3X7   Ph: (807)548-1929
Jerry Perrault, Chief

★3097★
Rat Portage Indian Band
PO Box 1850
Kenora, ON, Canada P9N 3X8   Ph: (807)548-5663
George Kakeway, Chief

★3098★
Wabauskang Indian Band
PO Box 1730
Kenora, ON, Canada P9N 3X7   Ph: (807)547-2555
Barney Petiquan, Chief

★3099★
Kingfisher Lake Indian Band
Kingfisher Lake, ON, Canada P0V 1Z0   Ph: (807)532-0067
James Mamakwa, Chief

★3100★
Lac Seul Indian Band
General Delivery
Lac Seul, ON, Canada P0V 2A0   Ph: (807)582-3211
Roger Southwind, Chief

★3101★
Sucker Creek Indian Band
RR 1, PO Box 21
Little Current, ON, Canada P0P 1K0   Ph: (705)368-2228
Patrick Madahbee, Chief

★3102★
Ginoogaming First Nation
PO Box 89
Longlac, ON, Canada P0T 2A0   Ph: (807)876-2241
Leslie O'Nabigon, Chief

★3103★
Long Lake No. 58 Indian Band
PO Box 609
Longlac, ON, Canada P0T 2A0   Ph: (807)876-2292
Sydney Abraham, Chief

★3104★
Rocky Bay Indian Band
Macdiarmid, ON, Canada P0T 2B0   Ph: (807)885-3401
Moses Kowtiash, Chief

★3105★
Moose Deer Point Indian Band
PO Box 119
Mactier, ON, Canada P0C 1H0   Ph: (705)375-5209
James Edward Williams, Chief

★3106★
Spanish River Band
PO Box 610
Massey, ON, Canada P0P 1P0   Ph: (705)865-5421
Nelson Toulouse, Chief

★3107★
Matachewan Indian Band
General Delivery
Matachewan, ON, Canada P0K 1M0   Ph: (705)565-2288
Robert Batisse, Chief

★3108★
Wahgoshig Band
PO Box 722
Matheson, ON, Canada P0K 1N0   Ph: (705)567-4891
Clifford Diamond, Chief

★3109★
Seine River Indian Band
General Delivery
Mine Centre, ON, Canada P0W 1H0   Ph: (807)599-2224
Andrew Johnson, Chief

★3110★
Pic Mobert Indian Band
Mobert, ON, Canada P0M 2J0   Ph: (807)822-2131
James Kwissiwa, Chief

★3111★
Dokis Indian Band
Dokis Bay
Monetville, ON, Canada P0M 2K0   Ph: (807)763-2200
Tim Restoule, Chief

★3112★
Moose Factory Indian Band
PO Box 190
Moose Factory, ON, Canada P0L 1W0   Ph: (705)658-4619
Norman F. Wesley, Chief

★3113★
Big Grassy Indian Band
General Delivery
Morson, ON, Canada P0W 1J0   Ph: (807)488-5552
Fred Copenace, Chief

★3114★
Big Island Indian Band
General Delivery
Morson, ON, Canada P0W 1J0   Ph: (807)488-5602
Pauline Big George, Chief

★3115★
Chippewas of the Thames First Nation Band
R.R. No. 1
Muncey, ON, Canada N0L 1Y0   Ph: (519)264-1528
Del Riley, Chief

★3116★
Munsee-Delaware Nation Indian Band
RR 1
Muncey, ON, Canada N0L 1Y0   Ph: (519)289-5396
Leroy Dolson, Chief

★3117★
Aroland Indian Band
PO Box 390
Nakina, ON, Canada P0T 2H0   Ph: (807)329-5970
William Magiskan, Chief

★3118★
Martin Falls Indian Band
Ogoki Post
Nakina, ON, Canada P0T 2L0   Ph: (807)349-2509
Eli Moonias, Chief

★3119★
Whitefish Lake Indian Band
PO Box 39
Naughton, ON, Canada P0M 2M0   Ph: (705)692-3651
Larry Naponse, Chief

★3120★
Ojibways of Onegaming Band
PO Box 160
Nestor Falls, ON, Canada P0X 1K0   Ph: (807)484-2162
Anthony Copenace, Chief

★3121★
Flying Post Indian Band
PO Box 937
Nipigon, ON, Canada P0T 2J0   Ph: (807)886-2443
Frances Ray, Chief

★3122★
Red Rock Indian Band
PO Box 1030
Nipigon, ON, Canada P0T 2J0   Ph: (807)887-2510
Betty Paakunainen, Chief

★3123★
Shawanaga Indian Band
RR 1
Nobel, ON, Canada P0G 1G0   Ph: (705)366-2526
Howard Pamajewon, Chief

★3124★
North Spirit Lake Indian Band
c/o Box 70
North Spirit Lake, ON, Canada P0V 2G0
Peter Campbell, Chief

★3125★
Six Nations of the Grand River Indian Band
PO Box 1
Ohsweken, ON, Canada N0A 1M0   Ph: (519)445-2201
William Montour, Chief

★3126★
Osnaburg Indian Band
Osnaburg, ON, Canada P0V 2H0   Ph: (807)928-2414
Aloysius L. Kaminaiwash, Chief

★3127★
Parry Island First Nation Band
PO Box 253
Parry Sound, ON, Canada P2A 2X4   Ph: (705)746-2531
John I. Rice, Chief

★3128★
Whitefish Bay Indian Band
Pawitik, ON, Canada P0X 1L0   Ph: (807)226-5411
George Crow, Chief

★3129★
Beausoleil Indian Band
Cedar Point Post Office
Penetanguishene, ON, Canada L0K 1C0   Ph: (705)247-2051
Jeffrey Monaque, Chief

★3130★
Henvey Inlet Indian Band
Pickerel, ON, Canada P0G 1J0   Ph: (705)857-2331
Charlotte Contin, Chief

★3131★
Eabametoong First Nation Band
Eabamet Lake
PO Box 70
Pickle Lake, ON, Canada P0T 1L0   Ph: (807)242-7361
Cornelius Missewace, Chief

★3132★
Lansdowne House Indian Band
Pickle Lake, ON, Canada P0T 1Z0   Ph: (807)479-2570
Roy Moonias Jr., Chief

★3133★
Muskrat Dam Indian Band
Muskrat Dam
Pickle Lake, ON, Canada P0V 3B0
Charlie Morris, Chief

★3134★
Summer Beaver Indian Band
Summer Beaver
Pickle Lake, ON, Canada P0T 3B0   Ph: (807)593-2131
Sandy Yellowhead, Chief

★3135★
Webequi Indian Band
Webequi
Pickle Lake, ON, Canada P0T 3A0   Ph: (807)353-6531
Roy Spence, Chief

★3136★
Pikangikum Indian Band
Pikangikum, ON, Canada P0V 2L0   Ph: (807)773-5578
Peter Quill, Chief

★3137★
Poplar Hill Indian Band
PO Box 315
Poplar Hill, ON, Canada P0V 2M0   Ph: (807)595-2577
Garry Mark Owen, Chief

★3138★
Scugog Indian Band
RR 5
Port Perry, ON, Canada L9L 1B6   Ph: (416)985-3337
MJ Yvonne Edgar, Chief

★3139★
Chippewas of Rama First Nation Indian Band
Rama Rd.
Post Office 35
Rama, ON, Canada L0K 1T0   Ph: (705)325-3611
George C. St. Germain, Chief

★3140★
McDowell Lake Indian Band
PO Box 315
Red Lake, ON, Canada P0V 2M0   Ph: (807)727-2803
Aglaba James, Chief

★3141★
Alderville Indian Band
RR No. 46
Roseneath, ON, Canada K0K 2X0   Ph: (416)352-2011
Leonard C. Gray, Chief

★3142★
Sachigo Lake Indian Band
Sachigo Lake, ON, Canada P0V 2P0   Ph: (807)595-2577
Titus Tait, Chief

★3143★
Kee-Way-Win Indian Band
Sandy Lake, ON, Canada P0V 1V0   Ph: (807)774-1215
George Kakepetum, Chief

★3144★
Sandy Lake Indian Band
Sandy Lake, ON, Canada P0V 1V0   Ph: (807)774-3421
Jonas Fiddler, Chief

★3145★
Chippewas of Sarnia Indian Band
978 Tashmoo Ave.
Sarnia, ON, Canada N7T 7H5   Ph: (519)336-8410
Phillip A. Maness, Chief

★3146★
Batchewana Indian Band
236 Frontenac St.
Sault Ste. Marie, ON, Canada P6A 5K9   Ph: (705)759-0914
Harvey Bell, Chief

★3147★
Garden River First Nation Band
Site 5, RR No. 4
PO Box 7
Sault Ste. Marie, ON, Canada P6A 5K9   Ph: (705)942-4011
Darrell E. Boissoneau, Chief

★3148★
Missanabie Cree
217 John St.
Sault Ste. Marie, ON, Canada P6A 1P4   Ph: (705)942-0123
Arthur Nolan, Spokesperson

★3149★
Saugeen Nation Indian Band
General Delivery
Savant Lake, ON, Canada P0V 2S0   Ph: (807)584-2908
Edward Machimity, Chief

★3150★
Pays Plat Indian Band
PO Box 819
Scheiber, ON, Canada P0T 2S0   Ph: (807)824-2541
Aime Bouchard, Chief

★3151★
Sheguiandah Indian Band
Sheguiandah, ON, Canada P0P 1W0   Ph: (705)368-2781
Maxie Assinewai, Chief

★3152★
Sheshegwaning Indian Band
Sheshegwanin, ON, Canada P0P 1X0   Ph: (705)283-3292
Joseph Endanawas, Chief

★3153★
New Slate Falls Indian Band
Slate Falls
Sioux Lookout, ON, Canada P0V 2T0
Gordon Carpenter, Chief

★3154★
Northwest Angle No. 37 Band
General Delivery
Sioux Narrows, ON, Canada P0X 1N0   Ph: (807)226-5353
Joseph Powassin, Chief

★3155★
Saugeen Indian Band
RR 1
Southampton, ON, Canada N0H 2L0   Ph: (519)797-2218
Vernon Roote, Chief

★3156★
Oneidas of the Thames Indian Band
RR 2
Southwold, ON, Canada N0L 2G0   Ph: (519)652-3244
Alfred L. Day, Chief

★3157★
Nipissing Indian Band
RR 1
Sturgeon Falls, ON, Canada P0H 2G0   Ph: (705)753-2050
Philip Goulais, Chief

★3158★
Cockburn Island Band
434 Brock St., Upper Unit
Sudbury, ON, Canada P3B 2G7   Ph: (705)688-1952
Irene Kells, Chief

★3159★
Chippewas of Georgina Island Indian Band
RR No. 2
Sutton West, ON, Canada L0E 1R0   Ph: (705)437-1337
James Clayton (Eric) Charles, Chief

★3160★
Temagami Indian Band
Bear Island
Temagami, ON, Canada P0H 2H0   Ph: (705)237-8943
Gary Potts, Chief

★3161★
Moravian of the Thames Indian Band
RR 3
Thamesville, ON, Canada N0P 2K0   Ph: (519)692-3936
Richard Snake, Chief

★3162★
Thessalon Indian Band
RR 3, PO Box 9
Thessalon, ON, Canada P0R 1L0   Ph: (705)842-2323
Alfred Bisaillon, Chief

★3163★
Fort William Indian Band
Station F
PO Box 786
Thunder Bay, ON, Canada P7C 4Z2   Ph: (807)623-9543
Christi Pervais, Chief

★3164★
Sandpoint Indian Band
921 Athabasca St.
Thunder Bay, ON, Canada P7C 3E5   Ph: (807)622-2081
Dan R. McGuire, Chief

★3165★
Lac des Milles Lacs Indian Band
Lac Des Milles Lac
Upsala, ON, Canada P0T 2Y0
Kelvin Chicago, Chief

★3166★
Wahnapitae Indian Band
PO Box 128
Wahnapitae, ON, Canada P0M 3C0   Ph: (705)694-5632
Norman Recollect, Chief

★3167★
Walpole Island Indian Band
RR 3
Wallaceburg, ON, Canada N8A 4K9   Ph: (519)627-1481
Robert L. Williams, Chief

★3168★
Michipicoten Indian Band
RR No. 1, Ste. 7
PO Box 26
Wawa, ON, Canada P0S 1K0   Ph: (705)856-4455
Evelyn Stone, Chief

★3169★
North Caribou Lake Indian Band
Weagamow Lake, ON, Canada P0V 2Y0   Ph: (807)469-5191
Caleb Sakchekapo, Chief

★3170★
West Bay Indian Band
Excelsior Post Office
West Bay, ON, Canada P0P 1G0   Ph: (705)377-5362
Stewart Roy, Chief

★3171★
Islington Indian Band
Whitedog Post Office
Whitedog, ON, Canada P0X 1P0   Ph: (807)927-2068
Roy McDonald, Chief

★3172★
Chippewas of Nawash Indian Band
RR No. 5
Wiarton, ON, Canada N0H 2T0   Ph: (519)534-1689
Ralph Akiwenzie, Chief

★3173★
Wikwemikong Indian Band
PO Box 112
Wikwemikong, ON, Canada P0P 2J0   Ph: (705)859-3122
Joseph Henry Peltier, Chief

★3174★
Weenusk Indian Band
General Delivery
Winisk, ON, Canada P0L 2H0   Ph: (705)473-2554
Abraham Hunter, Chief

★3175★
Wunnumin Indian Band
Wunnumin Lake, ON, Canada P0V 2Z0   Ph: (807)442-0051
Simon Winnepetonga, Chief

───────── **Quebec** ─────────

★3176★
Bande indienne d'Abitibiwinni
C.P. 36, Pikogan
Amos, PQ, Canada J9T 3A3   Ph: (819)732-6591
Harry McDougall, Chief

★3177★
Bande indienne des Abenakis de Wolinak
Reserve indienne de Wolinak
4680 boul. Danube
Becancour, PQ, Canada G0X 1B0   Ph: (819)294-9835
Raymond Bernard, Chief

★3178★
Bande indienne de Betsiamites
20, rue Messek, C.P. 40
Betsiamites, PQ, Canada G0H 1B0   Ph: (418)567-2265
Jean-Louis Bacon, Chief

★3179★
Mistissini Indian Band
Mistassini Lake, Baie-Du-Poste
Chibougamau, PQ, Canada G0W 1C0   Ph: (418)923-3253
Henry Mianscum, Chief

★3180★
Chisasibi Indian Band
PO Box 150
Chisasibi, PQ, Canada J0M 1E0   Ph: (819)855-2878
Violet Pachano, Chief

★3181★
Eastmain Indian Band
Eastmain, PQ, Canada J0M 1W0   Ph: (819)977-0211
Kenneth Gilpin, Chief

★3182★
Bande indienne de Gaspe
C.P. 69, Fontenelle
Gaspe, PQ, Canada G0E 1H0   Ph: (418)368-6005
Placide Jeannotte, Chief

★3183★
Mohawks of Kahnawake
PO Box 720
Kahnawake, PQ, Canada J0L 1B0   Ph: (514)632-7500
Joseph Norton, Chief

★3184★
Bande indienne Montagnais de la Romaine
La Romaine, PQ, Canada G0G 1M0   Ph: (418)229-2917
Georges Bacon, Chief

★3185★
Bande indienne du Lac Simon
Lac Simon
Lac Simon, PQ, Canada J0Y 3M0   Ph: (819)736-2351
Louis Jerome, Chief

★3186★
Bande indienne des Montagnais des Escoumins
27 de la Reserve, C.P. 820
Les Escoumins, PQ, Canada G0T 1K0   Ph: (418)233-2509
Denis Ross, Chief

★3187★
Bande indienne du Grand Lac Victoria
Louvicourt, PQ, Canada J0Y 1Y0   Ph: (819)736-2351
Donat Papatisse, Chief

★3188★
Kitigan Zibi Anishinabeg Indian Band
PO Box 309
Maniwaki, PQ, Canada J9E 3C9   Ph: (819)449-5170
Jean-Guy Whiteduck, Chief

★3189★
Les Atikamekw de Manawan
135, Rue Kicik
Manouane, PQ, Canada J0K 1M0   Ph: (819)971-8813
Henri Ottawa, Chief

★3190★
Micmacs of Gesgapegiag Indian Band
Maria Indian Reserve
PO Box 368
Maria, PQ, Canada G0C 1Y0   Ph: (418)759-3441
Douglas Martin, Chief

★3191★
Bande indienne de Mingan
C.P. 319
Mingan, PQ, Canada G0G 1V0   Ph: (418)949-2234
Philippe Pietacho, Chief

★3192★
Bande indienne des Montagnais de Natashquan
Natashquan, PQ, Canada G0G 2E0   Ph: (418)726-3529
Joseph Tettaut, Chief

★3193★
Nemaska Indian Band
Lac Champion
Nemiscau, PQ, Canada J0Y 3B0   Ph: (819)673-2512
Lawrence Jimiken, Chief

★3194★
Temiskaming Indian Band
PO Box 336
Notre Dame Du Nord, PQ, Canada J0Z
  3B0   Ph: (819)723-2335
Carol McBride, Chief

★3195★
Bande indienne d'Odanak
58, rue Wabanaki
Odanak, PQ, Canada J0G 1H0   Ph: (514)568-2810
Albert O'Bomsawin, Chief

★3196★
Kanesatake Indian Band
PO Box 607
Oka, PQ, Canada J0N 1E0   Ph: (514)479-8373
Jerry Peltier, Chief

★3197★
Montagnais du Lac St. Jean
151, rue Ouiatchouan
Pointe-Bleue, PQ, Canada G0W 2H0   Ph: (418)275-2473
Remi Kurtness, Chief

★3198★
Whapmagoostui Indian Band
PO Box 390
Poste de la Baleine, PQ, Canada J0M
  1G0   Ph: (819)929-3503
Robbie Dick, Chief

★3199★
Algonquins of Barriere Lake Indian Band
La Verendrye Park
Rapid Lake, PQ, Canada J0W 2G0   Ph: (819)824-1734
Jean Maurice Matchewan, Chief

★3200★
Restigouche Indian Band
17 Riverside West
Restigouche, PQ, Canada G0C 2R0   Ph: (418)788-2136
Ronald Jacques, Chief

★3201★
Bande indienne d'Obedjiwan
Reserve indienne d'Obedjiwan
Roberval, PQ, Canada G0W 3B0   Ph: (819)974-8837
Paul Mequish, Chief

★3202★
Montagnais de Pakua Shipi Indian Band
Saint Augustin, PQ, Canada G0G 2R0   Ph: (418)947-2726
Charles Mark, Chief

★3203★
Viger Indian Band
39-3400 Losch Blvd.
Saint Hubert, PQ, Canada J3Y 5T6   Ph: (514)656-9731
Gaetane Aubin, Grand Chief

★3204★
Bande indienne de Weymontachie
Reserve indienne de Weymontachie
Sanmaur, PQ, Canada G0A 4M0   Ph: (819)666-2237
Marcel Boivin, Chief

★3205★
Montagnais de Schefferville
Case postale 1390
Scheferville, PQ, Canada G0G 2T0   Ph: (418)585-2601
Alexandre McKenzie, Chief

★3206★
Naskapis of Quebec Indian Band
PO Box 970
Scheferville, PQ, Canada G0G 2T0   Ph: (418)585-2370
George Shecanapish, Chief

★3207★
**Bande indienne des Montagnais de Uashat et
  Maliotenam**
C.P. 8000
Sept-Iles, PQ, Canada G4R 4L9   Ph: (418)962-0327
Elie Jacques Jourdain, Chief

★3208★
Kipawa Indian Band
Kebaoweck Indian Reserve
PO Box 787
Temiscamingue, PQ, Canada J0Z 3R0   Ph: (819)627-3455
Jimmy Constant, Chief

★3209★
Wolf Lake Indian Band
PO Box 1060
Temiscamingue, PQ, Canada J0Z 3R0   Ph: (819)627-3628
Harold St. Denis, Chief

★3210★
Bande indienne de la Nation Huronne-Wendat
145, rue Chef Aime Romain
Village des Hurons, PQ, Canada G0A 4V0   Ph: (418)843-3767
Max (Magella) Gros-Louis, Chief

★3211★
Waskaganish Band
PO Box 60
Waskaganish, PQ, Canada J0M 1R0   Ph: (819)895-8843
Billy Diamond, Chief

★3212★
Waswanipi Indian Band
Waswanipi River, PQ, Canada J0Y 3C0   Ph: (819)753-2587
Allan Happyjack, Chief

★3213★
Wemindji Indian Band
Weminedji, PQ, Canada J0M 1L0   Ph: (819)978-0265
Walter Hughboy, Chief

★3214★
Long Point Indian Band
PO Box 1
Winneway River, PQ, Canada J0Z 2J0   Ph: (819)722-2441
Jerry Polson, Chief

───────── Saskatchewan ─────────

★3215★
Okanese Indian Band
PO Box 593
Balcarres, SK, Canada S0G 0C0   Ph: (306)334-2532
Marie Ann Daywalker, Chief

★3216★
Peepeekisis Indian Band
PO Box 492
Balcarres, SK, Canada S0G 0C0   Ph: (306)334-2573
J. Enoch Poitras, Chief

★3217★
Starblanket Indian Band
PO Box 456
Balcarres, SK, Canada S0G 0C0   Ph: (306)334-2206
Irvin G. Starblanket, Chief

★3218★
One Arrow Indian Band
PO Box 2
Batoche, SK, Canada S0K 0K0   Ph: (306)423-5900
Richard John, Chief

★3219★
John Smith Indian Band
PO Box 9
Birch Hills, SK, Canada S0J 0G0   Ph: (306)764-1282
Everette Bear, Chief

★3220★
Black Lake Indian Band
General Delivery
Black Lake, SK, Canada S0J 0H0   Ph: (306)284-2044
Daniel Robillard, Chief

★3221★
Cowessess Indian Band
PO Box 607
Broadview, SK, Canada S0G 0K0   Ph: (306)696-2520
Lionel Sparvier, Chief

★3222★
Kahkewistahaw Indian Band
PO Box 609
Broadview, SK, Canada S0G 0K0   Ph: (306)696-3291
Louis Carl Taypotat, Chief

★3223★
Mosquito Grizzly Bear's Head Band
Cando, SK, Canada S0K 0V0
Jenny Spyglas, Chief

★3224★
Red Pheasant Indian Band
PO Box 70
Cando, SK, Canada S0K 0V0   Ph: (306)937-7717
Leonard Wuttunee, Chief

★3225★
Canoe Lake Indian Band
Canoe Narrows, SK, Canada S0M 0K0   Ph: (306)829-2150
Frank Iron, Chief

★3226★
White Bear Indian Band
PO Drawer 700
Carlyle, SK, Canada S0C 0R0   Ph: (306)577-2461
Bernard Shephard, Chief

★3227★
Moosomin Indian Band
PO Box 45
Cochin, SK, Canada S0M 0L0
Gerald SwiftWolfe, Chief

★3228★
Saulteaux Indian Band
PO Box 1
Cochin, SK, Canada S0M 0L0   Ph: (306)386-2324
Gabriel Gopher, Chief

★3229★
Cumberland House Indian Band
PO Box 220
Cumberland House, SK, Canada S0E 0S0   Ph: (306)888-2152
Pierre Settee, Chief

★3230★
Piapot Indian Band
PO Box 178
Cupar, SK, Canada S0G 0Y0   Ph: (306)781-4848
Clayton Kaiswatum, Chief

★3231★
Big River Indian Band
PO Box 519
Debden, SK, Canada S0J 0S0   Ph: (306)724-4700
John Keenatch, Chief

★3232★
Buffalo River Indian Band
Dillon, SK, Canada S0M 0S0   Ph: (306)282-2033
Alex Gordon Billette, Chief

★3233★
Beardy & Okemasis Indian Band
PO Box 340
Duck Lake, SK, Canada S0K 1J0   Ph: (306)467-4523
Richard John Napoleon Gamble, Chief

★3234★
Fond du Lac Indian Band
Fond du Lac, SK, Canada S0G 0W0   Ph: (306)686-2102
August Mercredi, Chief

★3235★
Muscowpetung Indian Band
PO Box 1310
Fort Qu'Appelle, SK, Canada S0G 1S0   Ph: (306)723-4710
Paul Poitras, Chief

★3236★
Pasqua Indian Band
PO Box 968
Fort Qu'Appelle, SK, Canada S0G 1S0   Ph: (306)332-5697
Lindsay Cyr, Chief

★3237★
Standing Buffalo Indian Band
General Delivery
Fort Qu'Appelle, SK, Canada S0G 1S0   Ph: (306)332-4685
Melvin Isnana, Chief

★3238★
Sweetgrass Indian Band
PO Box 147
Gallivan, SK, Canada S0M 0X0   Ph: (306)937-2990
Edward Wayne Standinghorn, Chief

★3239★
Little Black Bear Indian Band
PO Box 102
Goodeve, SK, Canada S0A 1C0   Ph: (306)334-2269
Clarence A. Bellegarde, Chief

★3240★
Sakimay Indian Band
PO Box 339
Grenfell, SK, Canada S0G 2B0   Ph: (306)697-2831
Samuel Bunnie, Chief

★3241★
Cote Indian Band
PO Box 1659
Kamsack, SK, Canada S0A 1S0   Ph: (306)542-2694
Alfred J. Stevenson, Chief

★3242★
Keeseekoose Indian Band
PO Box 1120
Kamsack, SK, Canada S0A 1S0   Ph: (306)542-2516
Albert James Musqua, Chief

★3243★
Pheasant Rump Nakota
General Delivery
Kisby, SK, Canada S0C 1L0   Ph: (306)462-2002
Calvin J. McArthur, Chief

★3244★
Big C Indian Band
PO Box 145
La Loche, SK, Canada S0M 1G0   Ph: (306)822-2021
Frank Piche, Chief

★3245★
Lac La Ronge Indian Band
PO Box 480
La Ronge, SK, Canada S0J 1L0   Ph: (306)425-2183
Harry Cook, Chief

★3246★
Mistawasis Indian Band
PO Box 250
Leask, SK, Canada S0J 1M0   Ph: (306)466-4800
Noel Daniels, Chief

★3247★
Muskeg Lake Indian Band
PO Box 130
Leask, SK, Canada S0J 1M0   Ph: (306)466-4959
Harry Lafond, Chief

★3248★
Pelican Lake
PO Box 9
Leoville, SK, Canada S0J 1N0   Ph: (306)984-2313
Leon Thomas, Chief

★3249★
Muskowekwan Indian Band
PO Box 298
Lestock, SK, Canada S0A 2G0   Ph: (306)274-2061
Albert Pinacie, Chief

★3250★
Onion Lake Band
PO Box 900
Lloydminster, SK, Canada S9V 1C3   Ph: (306)344-2107
Donald Cardinal, Chief

★3251★
Island Lake Indian Band
PO Box 460
Loon Lake, SK, Canada S0M 1L0   Ph: (306)837-4845
Ernest Crookedneck, Chief

★3252★
Makwa Sahgaiehcan Indian Band
PO Box 340
Loon Lake, SK, Canada S0M 1L0   Ph: (306)837-2150
Gerald Kiseyinewakup, Chief

★3253★
Nikaneet Indian Band
PO Box 548
Maple Creek, SK, Canada S0N 1N0   Ph: (306)662-9196
Gordon Oakes, Chief

★3254★
Flying Dust Indian Band
PO Box 2410
Meadow Lake, SK, Canada S0M 1V0   Ph: (306)236-4437
Richard Gladue, Chief

★3255★
James Smith Indian Band
PO Box 1059
Melfort, SK, Canada S0E 1A0   Ph: (306)864-3636
Walter Constant, Chief

★3256★
Montreal Lake Indian Band
General Delivery
Montreal Lake, SK, Canada S0J 1Y0   Ph: (306)663-5349
Edward Henderson, Chief

★3257★
Key Indian Band
PO Box 70
Norquay, SK, Canada S0A 2V0   Ph: (306)594-2020
Dennis O'Soup, Chief

★3258★
Shoal Lake of the Cree Nation
Pakwaw Lake, SK, Canada S0E 1G0   Ph: (306)768-3551
Dennis Whitecap, Chief

★3259★
English River Band
Patuanak, SK, Canada S0M 2H0   Ph: (306)396-2055
Louis George, Chief

★3260★
Little Pine Indian Band
PO Box 70
Paynton, SK, Canada S0M 2J0   Ph: (306)398-4942
John Victor Semaganis, Chief

★3261★
Poundmaker Indian Band
PO Box 220
Paynton, SK, Canada S0M 2J0   Ph: (306)398-4971
Teddy Lee Antoine, Chief

★3262★
Peter Ballantyne Indian Band
Pelican Narrows, SK, Canada S0P 0E0   Ph: (306)632-2125
Ronald Michel, Chief

★3263★
Joseph Bighead Indian Band
PO Box 309
Pierceland, SK, Canada S0M 2K0   Ph: (306)839-2277
Ernest Sundown, Chief

★3264★
Wahpeton Indian Band
PO Box 128
Prince Albert, SK, Canada S6V 5R4   Ph: (306)764-6649
Lorne Waditaka, Chief

★3265★
Day Star Indian Band
PO Box 277
Punnichy, SK, Canada S0A 3C0   Ph: (306)835-2834
Cameron Kinequon, Chief

★3266★
Gordon Indian Band
Punnichy, SK, Canada S0A 3C0   Ph: (306)835-2232
Wayne Morris, Chief

★3267★
Kawacatoose Indian Band
Quinton, SK, Canada S0A 3G0   Ph: (306)835-2125
Richard Poorman, Chief

★3268★
Red Earth Indian Band
Red Earth, SK, Canada S0E 1K0   Ph: (306)768-3640
Philip Head, Chief

★3269★
Yellowquill Indian Band
PO Box 97
Rose Valley, SK, Canada S0E 1M0   Ph: (306)322-2281
Henry Neapetung, Chief

★3270★
Lucky Man Indian Band
401 Packham Pl.
Saskatoon, SK, Canada S7N 2I7   Ph: (306)384-8410
Andrew King, Chief

★3271★
Moosewoods Indian Band
RR 5, PO Box 149
Saskatoon, SK, Canada S7K 3J8   Ph: (306)477-0908
Charles R. Eagle, Chief

★3272★
Ahtahkakoop Indian Band
PO Box 220
Shell Lake, SK, Canada S0J 2G0   Ph: (306)468-2326
Clifford Sifton Ahenakew, Chief

★3273★
Sturgeon Lake Indian Band
Site 12, RR 1
PO Box 5
Shellbrook, SK, Canada S0J 2E0   Ph: (306)764-1872
Henry Daniels, Chief

★3274★
Carry the Kettle Indian Band
PO Box 57
Sintaluta, SK, Canada S0G 4N0   Ph: (306)727-2135
James L. O'Watch, Chief

★3275★
Witchekan Lake Indian Band
PO Box 879
Spiritwood, SK, Canada S0J 2M0   Ph: (306)883-2787
Mike Fineday, Chief

★3276★
Ocean Man
PO Box 157
Stoughton, SK, Canada S0G 4T0   Ph: (306)457-2697
Laura Big Eagle, Chief

★3277★
Kinistin Indian Band
PO Box 2590
Tisdale, SK, Canada S0E 1T0   Ph: (306)873-5590
Albert Scott, Chief

★3278★
Turnor Lake Indian Band
Turnor Lake, SK, Canada S0M 3E0   Ph: (306)894-2030
Jean Campbell, Chief

★3279★
Thunderchild Indian Band
PO Box 340
Turtleford, SK, Canada S0M 2Y0   Ph: (306)845-3424
Charles Paddy Sr., Chief

★3280★
Fishing Lake Indian Band
PO Box 508
Wadena, SK, Canada S0A 4J0   Ph: (306)338-3838
Allan Paquacan, Chief

★3281★
Waterhen Lake Indian Band
Waterhen Lake, SK, Canada S0M 3B0   Ph: (306)236-6717
Robert Fiddler, Chief

★3282★
Ochapowace Indian Band
PO Box 550
Whitewood, SK, Canada S0J 5C0   Ph: (306)696-2637
George Denton, Chief

★3283★
Hatchet Lake Indian Band
Wollaston Lake, SK, Canada S0J 3C0   Ph: (306)633-2003
Edward Benoanie, Chief

★3284★
Wood Mountain Indian Band
PO Box 104
Wood Mountain, SK, Canada S0H 4L0   Ph: (306)266-2027
William Goodtrack, Chief

——————————— Yukon ———————————

★3285★
White River First Nation Indian Band
General Delivery
Beaver Creek, YT, Canada Y0B 1A0   Ph: (403)862-7802
Rose Marie Blair
Joe Smith

★3286★
Kluane First Nation Band
General Delivery
Mile 1093, Alaska Hwy.
Burwash Landing, YT, Canada Y0B 1H0
George K. Johnson, Chief
Ph: (403)841-4274
Fax: (403)841-5900

★3287★
Carcross/Tagish First Nations Indian Band
PO Box 130
Carcross, YT, Canada Y0B 1B0
Doris McLean, Chief
Ph: (403)821-4251

★3288★
Little Salmon-Carmacks Indian Band
General Delivery
Carmacks, YT, Canada Y0B 1C0
Eric Fairclough, Chief
Ph: (403)863-5576

★3289★
Dawson Indian Band
PO Box 599
Dawson City, YT, Canada Y0B 1G0
Steve Taylor, Chief
Ph: (403)993-5385

★3290★
Champagne/Aishihik Indian Band
General Delivery
PO Box 5309
Haines Junction, YT, Canada Y0B 1L0
Paul Birckel, Chief
Ph: (403)634-2288

★3291★
Na-Cho Ny'A'K-Dun Indian Band
Box 220
Mayo, YT, Canada Y0B 1M0
Albert Peter, Chief
Ph: (403)996-2265

★3292★
Vuntut Gwitchin Indian Band
General Delivery
Old Crow, YT, Canada Y0B 1N0
Roger Kaye, Chief
Ph: (403)966-3261

★3293★
Selkirk Indian Band
General Delivery
Pelly Crossing, YT, Canada Y0B 1P0
Pat Vanbibber Jr., Chief
Ph: (403)537-3331

★3294★
Ross River Indian Band
General Delivery
Ross River, YT, Canada Y0B 1S0
Clifford McLeod, Chief
Ph: (403)969-2278

★3295★
Telsin Tlingit Indian Band
General Delivery
Teslin, YT, Canada Y0A 1B0
David Keenan, Chief
Ph: (403)390-2532

★3296★
Liard Indian Reserve—Number Three
PO Box 489
Watson Lake, YT, Canada Y0A 1C0
George Miller, Deputy Chief
Ph: (604)779-3161

★3297★
Liard River Band
PO Box 328
Watson Lake, YT, Canada T0A 1C0
Dixon Lutz, Chief
Ph: (403)536-2131

★3298★
Kwanlin Dun Indian Band
PO Box 1217
Whitehorse, YT, Canada Y1A 5A5
Lena Rose Johns, Chief
Ph: (403)667-6465

National Organizations

★3299★
Assembly of First Nations National Indian Brotherhood
55 Murray St., 5th Fl.
Ottawa, ON, Canada K1N 5M3
Ovide Mercurdi, National Chief
Ph: (613)236-0673
Fax: (613)238-5780

Description: Serves as a representative of Canada's First Nations to the government on issues of concern to Native Americans, including economic development, education, environment, health, and housing. **Founded:** 1969. **Publications:** *AFN Bulletin.*

★3300★
Canadian Alliance in Solidarity with the Native People (CASNP)
16 Spadina Rd., Ste. 302
Toronto, ON, Canada M5R 2S7
Brian Wright-McLeod, Coord.
Ph: (416)964-0169

Description: Native and non-native individuals. Seeks to educate the public about issues of concern to native people, such as spirituality, self-determination, child welfare, and the environment. Assists Native peoples in obtaining services and benefits to which they are entitled. Works to provide support for the indigenous peoples of the world. Conducts workshops and panel discussions. **Founded:** 1960. **Members:** 1200. **Regional Groups:** 5. **State Groups:** 1. **Local Groups:** 7. **Publications:** *The Phoenix,* quarterly. Journal covering issues from Native perspectives. Includes book and video reviews. • Also publishes *Resource/Reading List, Indian Giver: A Legacy of North American Native Peoples,* and *Native Rights in Canada* (books). **Formerly:** (1972) Indian-Eskimo Association of Canada; (1984) Canadian Association in Support of the Native Peoples.

★3301★
Canadian Native Arts Foundation
77 Mowat Ave., Ste. 321
Toronto, ON, Canada M6K 3E3
John Kim Bell, Dir.
Ph: (416)588-3328
Fax: (416)588-9198

Description: Promotes the culture of Native Canadians.

★3302★
First Peoples' Fund
134 Adelaide St., E., No. 304
Toronto, ON, Canada M5C 1K9
Shelly Brant, Assoc. Prog. Dir.
Ph: (416)360-1708
Fax: (416)360-5219

★3303★
Four Arrows (FA)
PO Box 1332
Ottawa, ON, Canada K1P 5R4
Ph: (613)234-5887

Description: Individuals seeking to protect the human and political rights of indigenous peoples of the Americas. Promotes intercultural exchange, spiritual strength, and communication among Indian people; encourages self-sufficiency projects; supports revitalization of Indian communities through culture, tradition, and spiritual strength. Sponsors programs in education and agricultural development for Mexican Indian youth. Has sponsored development projects in Guatemala. **Founded:** 1968. **Members:** 100. **Regional Groups:** 4. **Publications:** *Guatemala: The Horror and the Hope.* **Also Known As:** Las Cuatro Flechas. **Formerly:** (1977) White Roots of Peace.

★3304★
Indian and Inuit Nurses Association
55 Murray St.   Ph: (613)230-1864
Ottawa, ON, Canada K1N 5M3   Fax: (613)729-6903
Description: Organization of registered nurses and student nurses of Canadian Indian and Inuit descent.

★3305★
Indigenous Bar Association of Canada
1338 Wellington St.   Ph: (613)729-9491
Ottawa, ON, Canada K1Y 3B7   Fax: (613)729-6903
Roger Jones, Dir.
Description: Association for indigenous lawyers, judges and retired judges, and law school graduates and students who are practicing or studying in Canada. Members also include persons who have made significant contributions towards the advancement of justice for indigenous people in Canada.

★3306★
Indigenous Survival International (ISI)
47 Clarence St., Ste. 400   Ph: (613)236-0673
Ottawa, ON, Canada K1N 9K1   Fax: (613)238-5780
David Monture, Exec.Dir.

★3307★
Institute for Encyclopedia of Human Ideas on Ultimate Reality and Meaning
Regis College
15 St. Mary St.
Toronto, ON, Canada M4Y 2R5   Ph: (416)922-2476
Tibor Horvath, Dir.
Description: Researches the ideology of North American Indians.
Founded: 1970. **Publications:** *Ultimate Reality and Meaning*, newsletter.

★3308★
National Aboriginal Communications Society
PO Box 2250   Ph: (403)623-3301
Lac La Biche, AB, Canada T0A 2C0   Fax: (403)623-3302
Ray Fox, Pres./CEO

★3309★
National Aboriginal Youth Council (NAYC)
120-1 Laval St.
Ottawa, ON, Canada K1L 7Z4   Ph: (613)741-7488

★3310★
National Association of Friendship Centres (NAFC)
251 W. Laurier Ave.   Ph: (613)563-4844
Ottawa, ON, Canada K1P 5J6   Fax: (613)235-4957
Jerome Berthelette, Exec.Dir.

★3311★
National Committee of Indian Cultural Education Centres (NAITC)
RR 3
Cornwall Island, ON, Canada K6H 5R7 Ph: (613)932-9452
Harold Tarbell, Coord.

★3312★
Native Fishing Association
1755 E. Hastings St., Ste. 202   Ph: (604)255-5457
Vancouver, BC, Canada V5L 1T1   Fax: (604)255-0955
David Barrett, Exec.Dir.
Description: Works in association with the Native Brotherhood of British Columbia.

★3313★
Native Women's Association of Canada (NWAC)
9 Melrose Ave.   Ph: (613)722-3033
Ottawa, ON, Canada K1Y 1T8   Fax: (613)722-7687
Gail Stacey-Moore, National Speaker
Description: Strives to be the national voice for Native women; address issues in a manner which reflects the changing needs of Native women in Canada; assist and promote common goals towards self-determination and self-sufficiency for Native peoples; promote equal opportunities for Native women in programs and activities; serve as a resource among Native communities; cultivate and teach cultural and historical traditions; assist Native women's organizations and community projects; advance issues and concerns of Native women; and provide a network between Native women.
Founded: 1974.

★3314★
World Council of Indigenous Peoples
555 King Edward Ave.   Ph: (613)230-9030
Ottawa, ON, Canada K1N 6N5   Fax: (613)230-9340
Donald Rojas, Pres.

★3315★
World Council of Indigenous Peoples (WCIP)
555 King Edward Ave., 2nd Fl.   Ph: (613)230-9030
Ottawa, ON, Canada K1N 6N5   Fax: (613)230-9340
Donald Rojas Maroto, Pres.
Description: Organizations in 30 countries representing indigenous peoples. Objectives are to: further economic self-suffiency and attain self-determination; ensure unity and encourage the exchange of information among all indigenous peoples; abolish physical, economic, and social injustices suffered by indigenous peoples; establish and strengthen the principles of equality among indigenous people and people of surrounding nations. Conducts investigations and research on refuges for political prisoners. Maintains library.
Founded: 1975. **Members:** 36. **Regional Groups:** 5. **Publications:** *Boletin del CMPI*, periodic. *WCIP Newsletter*, periodic.

Regional, State/Provincial, & Local Organizations

Alberta

★3316★
Bonnyville Canadian Native Friendship Centre
5106 50th St.
Box 5399   Ph: (403)826-3374
Bonnyville, AB, Canada T9N 2G5   Fax: (403)826-2540
Dorothy Schnie, Exec.Dir.

★3317★
Kehewin Cultural Education Centre
Box 6218   Ph: (403)826-3333
Bonnyville, AB, Canada T9N 2G8   Fax: (403)826-2355
Dale Yutzky, Principal

★3318★
Metis Association of Alberta
PO Box 6497   Ph: (403)826-7483
Bonnyville, AB, Canada T9N 2H1   Fax: (403)826-7603

★3319★
Oldman River Cultural Centre
PO Box 70   Ph: (403)965-3939
Brocket, AB, Canada T0K 0H0   Fax: (403)965-3931
Jo Ann Yellowhorn, Coord.

★3320★
Calgary Native Friendship Society
140 2nd Ave. SW   Ph: (403)264-1155
Calgary, AB, Canada T2P 0B9   Fax: (403)265-9275
Laverna McMaster, Exec.Dir.

★3321★
Metis Association of Alberta
Bay 7 3140 14th Ave. NE   Ph: (403)569-8800
Calgary, AB, Canada T2A 6J4   Fax: (403)569-8959

★3322★
Tsut'ina K'osa
Sarcee Cultural Program
3700 Anderson Rd. SW
Box 135   Ph: (403)238-2677
Calgary, AB, Canada T2W 3C4   Fax: (403)251-6061
Jeanette Starlight, Dir.

★3323★
Ninastako Cultural Centre
Box 1299   Ph: (403)737-3774
Cardston, AB, Canada T0K 0K0   Fax: (403)737-3786
Gloria Wells, Dir.

★3324★
Aboriginal Multi-Media Society of Alberta
15001 112th Ave.   Ph: (403)455-2700
Edmonton, AB, Canada T5M 2V6   Fax: (403)455-7639
Bert Crow Foot, Gen.Manager

★3325★
Alberta Indian Investment Corporation
10621 100th Ave.   Ph: (403)428-6731
Edmonton, AB, Canada T5J 0B3   Fax: (403)425-9018
Fred Gladstone, Pres.

★3326★
Alberta Native Friendship Centres Association
10339 124th St., Ste. 503   Ph: (403)482-5196
Edmonton, AB, Canada T5N 1R1   Fax: (403)482-2032
Tony Callihoo, Coord.

★3327★
Canadian Native Friendship Centre
11016 127th St.   Ph: (403)452-7811
Edmonton, AB, Canada T5M 0T2   Fax: (403)452-8754
Lloyd Sutton, Exec.Dir.

★3328★
Metis Association of Alberta
13140 St. Albert Tr.   Ph: (403)455-2200
Edmonton, AB, Canada T5L 4R8   Fax: (403)452-8946
Larry Desmeules, Pres.

★3329★
Metis Child and Family Services Society
10950 124th St.   Ph: (403)452-6100
Edmonton, AB, Canada T5M 0H5   Fax: (403)452-8944
Connie Campbell, Exec.Dir.

★3330★
Native Council of Canada
Alberta Office
PO Box 39004   Ph: (403)429-6003
Edmonton, AB, Canada T5B 0T5   Fax: (403)428-6964
Richard Long, Exec.Dir.

★3331★
Indian Association of Alberta
RR 1, Box 516, Site 2   Ph: (403)470-5751
Enoch, AB, Canada T0E 2N0   Fax: (403)470-3077
Regena Crowchild, Pres.

★3332★
Nistawoyou Association Friendship Centre
8310 Manning Ave.   Ph: (403)743-8555
Fort McMurray, AB, Canada T9H 1W1   Fax: (403)791-4041
Noella Harpe, Exec.Dir.

★3333★
Grand Centre Friendship Centre
Box 1978   Ph: (403)594-7526
Grand Centre, AB, Canada T0A 1T0   Fax: (403)594-7360
Fernie Marty, Exec.Dir.

★3334★
Grande Prairie Friendship Centre
10507 98th Ave.   Ph: (403)532-5722
Grande Prairie, AB, Canada T8V 4L1   Fax: (403)539-5121
Brian Kelly, Exec.Dir.

★3335★
High Level Native Friendship Centre Society
PO Box 1735   Ph: (403)926-3355
High Level, AB, Canada T0H 1Z0   Fax: (403)926-2038
Elmor Cardinal, Exec.Dir.

★3336★
High Prairie Native Friendship Centre
4919 51st Ave.
Box 1448   Ph: (403)523-4512
High Prairie, AB, Canada T0G 1E0   Fax: (403)523-3055
Loraine Duguay, Exec.Dir.

★3337★
Traditional Native Healing Society
PO Box 1882
High Prarie, AB, Canada T0G 1E0   Ph: (403)523-4355
Russell and Yvonne Miller, Contacts

★3338★
Beaver Lake Cultural Centre
Beaver Lake Indian Band
Box 960   Ph: (403)623-4549
Lac La Biche, AB, Canada T0A 2C0   Fax: (403)623-4523
Al Lameman, Chief

★3339★
Lac La Biche Canadian Native Friendship Centre
10210 101st St.
Box 2338   Ph: (403)623-3249
Lac La Biche, AB, Canada T0A 2C0   Fax: (403)623-2733
William Landstrom, Pres.

★3340★
Metis Association of Alberta
PO Box 1350   Ph: (403)623-3039
Lac La Biche, AB, Canada T0A 2C0   Fax: (403)623-2733

★3341★
Sik-Ook-Kotok Centre
535 13th St., N., Ste. 10   Ph: (403)328-2414
Lethbridge, AB, Canada T1H 2S6   Fax: (403)327-0087
Mike Bruised, Exec.Dir.

★3342★
Lloydminster Native Friendship Centre
5010 41st St.   Ph: (403)875-6558
Lloydminster, AB, Canada T9V 1B7   Fax: (403)875-3812
George Hougham, Exec.Dir.

★3343★
Nakoda Institute
Stoney Tribal Organization
PO Box 40   Ph: (403)881-3770
Morley, AB, Canada T0L 1N0   Fax: (403)881-2187
Ian Getty, Dir.

★3344★
Alberta Native Women's Association
9423 84th Ave.
Peace River, AB, Canada T8S 1G0   Ph: (403)624-6190
Carrie Cotton, Pres.

★3345★
Metis Association of Alberta
9418 94th Ave.   Ph: (403)624-4219
Peace River, AB, Canada T8S 1J7   Fax: (403)524-3477

★3346★
Sagitawa Friendship Centre
10108 100th Ave.
PO Box 5083   Ph: (403)624-2443
Peace River, AB, Canada T8S 1R7   Fax: (403)624-2728
Sylvia Johnson, Exec.Dir.

★3347★
Napi Friendship Centre
PO Box 657   Ph: (403)627-4224
Pincher Creek, AB, Canada T0K 1W0   Fax: (403)256-4627
Carol Specht, Exec.Dir.

★3348★
Red Deer Native Friendship Society
5217 Gaetz Ave.
Red Deer, AB, Canada T4N 4B4   Ph: (403)340-0020
Caroline Yellowhorn, Exec.Dir.

★3349★
Rocky Native Friendship Centre Society
PO Box 1927
Rocky Mountain House, AB, Canada T0M   Ph: (403)845-2788
1T0   Fax: (403)845-3093
Carrie Mason, Exec.Dir.

★3350★
Saddle Lake Cultural Education Program
Box 102   Ph: (403)726-3829
Saddle Lake, AB, Canada T0A 3T0   Fax: (403)726-3788
Keith Lapatac, Dir.

★3351★
Manniwanis Native Friendship Centre
PO Box 2519
Saint Paul, AB, Canada T0A 3A0   Ph: (403)645-4630
Bob Harrison, Dir.

★3352★
Metis Association of Alberta
PO Box 1787   Ph: (403)849-4654
Slave Lake, AB, Canada T0G 2A0   Fax: (403)849-2890

★3353★
Slave Lake Native Friendship Centre
416 6th Ave. NE   Ph: (403)849-3039
Slave Lake, AB, Canada T0G 2A2   Fax: (403)849-2402
Peggy Roberts, Exec.Dir.

★3354★
Voice of Alberta Native Women's Society
PO Box 60   Ph: (403)737-3753
Standoff, AB, Canada T0L 1Y0   Fax: (403)737-2336
Welton Goodstriker, Exec.Coord.

─────────── **British Columbia** ───────────

★3355★
Bella Coola-Nuxalk Education Authority
PO Box 778   Ph: (604)799-5453
Bella Coola, BC, Canada V0T 1C0   Fax: (604)799-5426
Peter Siwallace, Education Admin.

★3356★
Saanich Cultural Education Centre
7449 W. Saanich Rd.
Box 368   Ph: (604)652-1811
Brentwood Bay, BC, Canada V0S 1A0   Fax: (604)652-6929
Philip Paul, Dir.

★3357★
Tansi Friendship Centre
PO Box 418   Ph: (604)788-2996
Chetwynd, BC, Canada V0C 1J0   Fax: (604)788-2353
Beverly Davis, Exec.Dir.

★3358★
Nawican Friendship Centre
1320 102nd Ave.
Dawson Creek, BC, Canada V1G 4H4   Ph: (604)782-5202
Keith Hall, Exec.Dir.

★3359★
Nawican Friendship Centre
1320 102nd Ave.
PO Box 593
Dawson Creek, BC, Canada V1G 4H4   Ph: (604)782-5202

★3360★
Alliance Tribal Council
130 N. Tsawwassen Dr.   Ph: (604)943-6712
Delta, BC, Canada V4K 3N2   Fax: (604)943-5367
Chief Frederick A. Jacobs, Chair.

★3361★
Valley Native Friendship Centre Society
PO Box 1015   Ph: (604)748-2242
Duncan, BC, Canada V9L 3Y2   Fax: (604)748-2238
Debbie Williams, Exec.Dir.

★3362★
Fort Nelson-Liard Native Friendship Society
PO Box 1266   Ph: (604)774-2993
Fort Nelson, BC, Canada V0C 1R0   Fax: (604)774-2998
Andrea Bidulka, Exec.Dir.

★3363★
Fort Nelson/Liard Native Friendship Society
PO Box 1266   Ph: (604)774-2993
Fort Nelson, BC, Canada V0C 1R0   Fax: (604)774-3730

★3364★
Fort St. John Friendship Society
10208 95th Ave.   Ph: (604)785-8566
Fort Saint John, BC, Canada V1J 2J6   Fax: (604)785-1507
Ruby Roe, Exec.Dir.

★3365★
British Columbia Native Women's Society
345 Yellowhead Hwy.   Ph: (604)828-9796
Kamloops, BC, Canada V2H 1H1   Fax: (604)828-9803
Clorinda Saskamoose, Admin.

★3366★
Interior Indian Friendship Centre
125 Palm St.   Ph: (604)376-1296
Kamloops, BC, Canada V1J 8J7   Fax: (604)376-2275

★3367★
Lillooet Friendship Centre
PO Box 1270
357 Main St.   Ph: (604)256-4146
Lillooet, BC, Canada V0K 1V0   Fax: (604)256-7928

★3368★
Mission Indian Friendship Centre
33150A 1st Ave.   Ph: (604)826-1281
Mission, BC, Canada V2V 1G4   Fax: (604)826-4056

★3369★
Tillicum Haus Society
602 Haliburton St.   Ph: (604)753-8291
Nanaimo, BC, Canada V9R 4W5   Fax: (604)753-6560

★3370★
Tillicum Haus Society
927 Haliburton
RR1, Site A, Comp. 13   Ph: (604)753-8291
Nanaimo, BC, Canada V9R 5K1   Fax: (604)753-6560
Grace Nielson, Exec.Dir.

★3371★
Native Courtworker and Counseling Association
32415 W. Esplanade   Ph: (604)687-0281
North Vancouver, BC, Canada V7L 1A6   Fax: (604)985-8933
Brian Chromko, Contact

★3372★
Okanagan Indian Educational Resources Society
257 Brunswick St.   Ph: (604)493-7181
Penicton, BC, Canada V2A 5P9   Fax: (604)493-5302
Don Fiddler, Dir.

★3373★
Port Alberni Friendship Centre
3555 4th Ave.   Ph: (604)723-8281
Port Alberni, BC, Canada V9Y 4H3   Fax: (604)723-1877
Wally Samuel, Exec.Dir.

★3374★
Sliammon Cultural Centre
RR 2, Sliammon Rd.   Ph: (604)483-9646
Powell River, BC, Canada V8A 4Z0   Fax: (604)483-9769
Elizabeth Harry, Education Coord.

★3375★
Prince George Native Friendship Centre
144 George St.   Ph: (604)564-3568
Prince George, BC, Canada V2L 1P9   Fax: (604)563-0924
Dan George, Exec.Dir.

★3376★
Friendship House Association of Prince Rupert
PO Box 512   Ph: (604)627-1717
Prince Rupert, BC, Canada V8J 3R5   Fax: (604)627-7533
Fred Anderson, Exec.Dir.

★3377★
Quesnel Tillicum Society Friendship Centre
319 N.Fraser Dr.   Ph: (604)992-8347
Quesnel, BC, Canada V2J 1Y8   Fax: (604)992-5708
Doug Sanderson, Exec.Dir.

★3378★
British Columbia Association of Indian Friendship Centres
3-2475 Mt. Newton Crossroads   Ph: (604)652-0210
Saanichton, BC, Canada V0S 1M0   Fax: (604)652-3102
Gwen Underwood, Coord.

★3379★
Coqualeetza Education Training Centre
PO Box 370   Ph: (604)858-9431
Sardis, BC, Canada V2R 1A7   Fax: (604)858-8488
Shirley D. Leon, Mngr.

★3380★
Dzel K'ant Friendship Centre
PO Box 2290   Ph: (604)847-3525
Smithers, BC, Canada V0J 2N0   Fax: (604)847-3600

★3381★
Smithers Friendship Centre
PO Box 2920   Ph: (604)847-5211
Smithers, BC, Canada V0J 2N0   Fax: (604)847-5144
Lila Wallace, Exec.Dir.

★3382★
Semiahmoo House Society
201-15585 24th Ave.   Ph: (604)536-1242
Surrey, BC, Canada V4A 2J4   Fax: (604)536-9507
Alanna Hendren, Exec.Dir.

★3383★
Kermode Friendship Society
3313 Kalum St.   Ph: (604)635-4906
Terrace, BC, Canada V8G 2N7   Fax: (604)635-3013
Dorothy Davidson, Exec.Dir.

★3384★
Native Communications Society of British Columbia
4562-B Greensway
PO Box 1090   Ph: (604)638-8137
Terrace, BC, Canada V8G 4V1   Fax: (604)638-8027
Emma Williams, Pres.
Also Known As: Northern Native Broadcasting.

★3385★
Aboriginal Council of British Columbia
990 Homer St., No. 204   Ph: (604)682-4897
Vancouver, BC, Canada V6B 2W7   Fax: (604)682-3550
Beryl Harris, Exec.Coord.

★3386★
Aboriginal People's Business Association (APBA)
c/o Centre for Native Small Business
680-1155 W. Georgia St.   Ph: (604)687-7166
Vancouver, BC, Canada V6E 3H4   Fax: (604)687-5519
David Anderson, Exec.Dir.

★3387★
Alliance of Tribal Nations
503-68 Water St.   Ph: (604)684-1066
Vancouver, BC, Canada V6B 1A4   Fax: (604)684-9498

★3388★
Allied Indian & Metis Society
2716 Clark Dr.   Ph: (604)874-9610
Vancouver, BC, Canada V5N 3H6   Fax: (604)874-3858
Marjorie White, Dir.

★3389★
British Columbia Aboriginal Peoples' Fisheries Commission
990 Homer St., Ste. 204   Ph: (604)682-4897
Vancouver, BC, Canada V6B 2W7   Fax: (604)682-3550
Simon Lucas, Chief

★3390★
Centre for Native Small Business
680-1155 W. Georgia St.   Ph: (604)687-7166
Vancouver, BC, Canada V6E 3H4   Fax: (604)687-5519

★3391★
Indian Arts and Crafts Society of British Columbia
530 Hornby St., Ste. 402   Ph: (604)682-8988
Vancouver, BC, Canada V6C 2E7   Fax: (604)682-8994
Jill Fiske, General Manager

★3392★
Lu'Ma Native Housing Society
201-4720 Main St.   Ph: (604)876-0811
Vancouver, BC, Canada V5V 3R7   Fax: (604)876-0999
Helen Lambert, Dir.

★3393★
Native Brotherhood of British Columbia
1755 E. Hastings, No. 200   Ph: (604)255-4696
Vancouver, BC, Canada V5L 1T1   Fax: (604)251-7107
Robert Clifton, Pres.

★3394★
Native Communications Society of British Columbia
540 Burrard St., No. 302   Ph: (604)684-7375
Vancouver, BC, Canada V6C 2K1   Fax: (604)684-5375
Lynn Jorgenson, Pres.

★3395★
Native Investment and Trade Association
1501111 Melville St.
PO Box 10   Ph: (604)275-0307
Vancouver, BC, Canada V6E 3V6   Fax: (604)684-0881
Vernita Helin, Dir.

★3396★
Union of British Columbia Indian Chiefs
73 Water St., 1st Fl.   Ph: (604)684-0231
Vancouver, BC, Canada V6B 1A1   Fax: (604)684-5726
Saul Terry, Pres./Chief

★3397★
United Native Nations
736 Granville St., 8th Fl.   Ph: (604)688-1821
Vancouver, BC, Canada V6O 1G3   Fax: (604)688-1823
Ernie Grey, Pres.

★3398★
Urban Images for Native Women
1-245 E. Broadway   Ph: (605)875-9211
Vancouver, BC, Canada V5G 1W4   Fax: (604)872-1845
Darlene Kelly, Prog. Coord.

★3399★
Vancouver Indian Centre Society
1607 E. Hastings St.   Ph: (604)251-4844
Vancouver, BC, Canada V5L 1S7   Fax: (604)251-1986
Art Paul, Exec.Dir.

★3400★
Victoria Native Friendship Centre
533 Yates St., Penthouse   Ph: (604)384-3211
Victoria, BC, Canada V8W 1K7   Fax: (604)384-1586
Sandra Douglas-Tubb, Exec.Dir.

★3401★
Heiltsuk Cultural Education Centre
Box 880   Ph: (604)957-2626
Waglisla, BC, Canada V0T 1Z0   Fax: (604)957-2544
Jennifer Carpenter, Program Mngr.

★3402★
Cariboo Friendship Society
99 3rd Ave.   Ph: (604)398-6831
Williams Lake, BC, Canada V2G 1J1   Fax: (604)398-6115
Gail Madrigga, Exec.Dir.

───────── **Manitoba** ─────────

★3403★
Interlake Reserves Tribal Council
PO Box 580   Ph: (204)659-4465
Ashern, MB, Canada R0C 0E0   Fax: (204)659-2147
Darlene Woodhouse, Acting Admin.

★3404★
Brandon Friendship Centre
303 9th St.   Ph: (204)727-1407
Brandon, MB, Canada R7A 4A8   Fax: (204)726-0902
Ken Norquay, Exec.Dir.

★3405★
Cross Lake Cultural/Education Centre
Cross Lake Indian Reserve   Ph: (204)676-2166
Cross Lake, MB, Canada R0B 0J0   Fax: (204)676-2117
Ernest Munoz, Coord.

★3406★
Dauphin Friendship Centre
210 1st Ave. NE
Dauphin, MB, Canada R7A 1A7   Ph: (204)638-5707
Les Campbell, Exec.Dir.

★3407★
West Region Tribal Council
Indian Cultural Education Program
21 4th Ave. NW   Ph: (204)638-8225
Dauphin, MB, Canada R7N 1H9   Fax: (204)638-8062
Wally Swain, Program Head

★3408★
Flin Flon Indian and Metis Friendship Centre
57 Church St.
Box 188
Flin Flon, MB, Canada R8A 1M7   Ph: (204)687-3900
Marcie Johnson, Exec.Dir.

★3409★
Peguis Cultural Centre
Box 219   Ph: (204)645-2359
Hodgson, MB, Canada R0C 1N0   Fax: (204)645-2360
Daphne Stevenson, Contact

★3410★
Lynn Lake Friendship Centre
625 Gordon Ave.
Box 460   Ph: (204)356-2407
Lynn Lake, MB, Canada R0B 0W0   Fax: (204)356-8223
Vicki Stowman-Sinclair, Exec.Dir.

★3411★
Norway House Cultural Education Centre
Norway House Indian Band
PO Box 218   Ph: (204)359-6313
Norway House, MB, Canada R0B 1B0
Joyce Osborne, Dir.

★3412★
Sagkeeng Cultural Centre, Inc.
Box 749   Ph: (204)367-2129
Pine Falls, MB, Canada R0E 1M0   Fax: (204)367-4249
Felix Boubard, Dir.

★3413★
Portage Friendship Centre
21 Royal Rd., S.
Box 1118
Portage La Prairie, MB, Canada R1N   Ph: (204)239-6333
   3C5   Fax: (204)239-6534
Richard Chaske, Exec.Dir.

★3414★
Ka-Wawiyak Centre
Box 235
Powerview, MB, Canada R0E 1P0   Ph: (204)367-8820
Rhonda Houston, Exec.Dir.

★3415★
Riverton & District Friendship Centre
PO Box 359
Riverton, MB, Canada R0C 2R0
Marlene Monkman, Exec.Dir.   Ph: (204)378-2927

★3416★
Brokenhead Cultural Centre
Brokenhead Indian Band   Ph: (204)766-2494
Scanterbury, MB, Canada R0E 1W0   Fax: (204)766-2306
Chief Wendell Sinclair, Pres.

★3417★
Selkirk Friendship Centre
425 Eveline St.
Selkirk, MB, Canada R1A 2J5   Ph: (204)482-7525
Jim Sinclair, Exec.Dir.

★3418★
Swan River Indian & Metis Friendship Centre
1413 Main St., E.
Box 1448   Ph: (204)734-9301
Swan River, MB, Canada R0L 1Z0   Fax: (204)734-3090
Elbert Chartrand, Exec.Dir.

★3419★
Indian Council of First Nations of Manitoba, Inc.
PO Box 3848, Otineka Mall   Ph: (204)623-7227
The Pas, MB, Canada R9A 1S4   Fax: (204)623-4041
Andrew Kirkness, Grand Chief

★3420★
The Pas Friendship Centre
81 Edwards Ave.
Box 2638   Ph: (204)623-6459
The Pas, MB, Canada R9A 1M3   Fax: (204)623-4268
Judy Elaschuk, Exec.Dir.

★3421★
Ma-Mow-We-Tak Friendship Centre, Inc.
122 Hemlock Cres.   Ph: (204)778-7337
Thompson, MB, Canada R8N 0R6   Fax: (204)677-3195
Larry Soldier, Exec.Dir.

★3422★
Manitoba Keewatinowi Okimakanak
23 Station Rd.   Ph: (204)778-4431
Thompson, MB, Canada R8N 0N6   Fax: (204)778-7655
Chief Pasquel Bighetty, Chair.

★3423★
Native Communications Inc.
76 Severn Cres.   Ph: (204)778-8343
Thompson, MB, Canada R8N 1M6   Fax: (204)778-6659
Ron Nadeau, Chief Exec. Officer

★3424★
Aboriginal Council of Winnipeg
273 Selkirk Ave.   Ph: (204)589-6343
Winnipeg, MB, Canada R2W 2L5   Fax: (204)582-0256
Eric Robinson, Dir.
Formerly: Winnipeg Council of Treaty & Status Indians.

★3425★
Aboriginal Women of Manitoba
78 Grey Friars St.
Winnipeg, MB, Canada R3T 3J5   Ph: (204)269-0033
Pauline Busch, Pres.

★3426★
Arctic Co-Operatives Ltd.
1741 Wellington Ave.   Ph: (204)786-4481
Winnipeg, MB, Canada R3H 0G1   Fax: (204)783-2851
Bill Lyall, Pres.

★3427★
Canadian Council for Native Business
240 Graham Ave, No. 300   Ph: (204)947-6436
Winnipeg, MB, Canada R3C 45   Fax: (204)956-0995
Barbara Bruce, Exec.Dir.
Also Known As: Conseil Canadien pour le Commerce Autochtone.

★3428★
First Nations Confederacy Inc.
203-286 Smith St.   Ph: (204)944-8245
Winnipeg, MB, Canada R3C 1K4   Fax: (204)943-1482
Lorie Daniels, Exec.Dir.

★3429★
Indian and Metis Friendship Centre
239 Magnus Ave.   Ph: (204)586-8441
Winnipeg, MB, Canada R2W 2B6   Fax: (204)582-8261
Stirling Ranville, Exec.Dir.

★3430★
Indigenous Women's Collective of Manitoba
388 Donald St., No. 120   Ph: (204)944-8709
Winnipeg, MB, Canada R2B 2J4   Fax: (204)949-1336
Winnie Giebrecht, Pres.

★3431★
Intertribal Christian Communications
PO Box 3765, Sta. B   Ph: (204)661-9333
Winnipeg, MB, Canada R2W 3R6   Fax: (204)661-3982
Ed Wilson, Dir.

★3432★
Manitoba Association of Friendship Centres
208-424 Logan Ave.   Ph: (204)943-8082
Winnipeg, MB, Canada R3A 0R4   Fax: (204)943-0106
Richard Chaske, Pres.

★3433★
Manitoba Indian Education Association Inc.
352 Donald St.   Ph: (204)947-0421
Winnipeg, MB, Canada R3B 2HH   Fax: (204)942-3067
George Desnomie, Exec.Dir.

★3434★
Manitoba Metis Federation
408 McGregor St.   Ph: (204)586-8474
Winnipeg, MB, Canada R2W 4X5   Fax: (204)947-1816
W. Yvon Dumont, Pres.

★3435★
Native Alcoholism Council of Manitoba
160 Salter St.   Ph: (204)586-8395
Winnipeg, MB, Canada R2W 4K1   Fax: (204)589-3921
Bertha Fontaine, Exec.Dir.

★3436★
Native Employment Services
338 Donald St., No. 210   Ph: (204)989-7110
Winnipeg, MB, Canada R3B 2J4   Fax: (204)989-9113

★3437★
Native Women's Transition Centre
105 Akins St.   Ph: (204)989-8240
Winnipeg, MB, Canada R2W 4E4   Fax: (204)586-1101
Lucille Bruce, Dir.

New Brunswick

★3438★
Fredericton Native Friendship Centre
173 King St.
PO Box 20167   Ph: (506)459-5283
Fredericton, NB, Canada E3B 7B2   Fax: (506)459-1756
Debra Alivisatos, Exec.Dir.

★3439★
New Brunswick Aboriginal Peoples Council
320 St. Mary's St.   Ph: (506)458-8422
Fredericton, NB, Canada E3A 2S4   Fax: (506)450-3749
Dennis Gideon, Acting Pres.

★3440★
New Brunswick Native Indian Women's Council
65 Brunswick St., No. 258
Fredericton, NB, Canada E3B 1G5   Ph: (506)458-1114
Christine Boone, Contact

★3441★
Union of New Brunswick Indians
35 Dedam St.   Ph: (506)458-9444
Fredericton, NB, Canada E3A 2V2   Fax: (506)458-2850
Ronald Perley, Pres.

★3442★
New Brunswick Native Employment Counsellors
65 Brunswick St.   Ph: (506)450-7984
Fredricton, NB, Canada E3B 1G5   Fax: (506)451-9386
Doreen Joe, Contact

★3443★
Oromocto Indian Nation Association
PO Box 417   Ph: (506)357-2083
Oromocto, NB, Canada E2V 2J2   Fax: (506)357-2628
Danielle Thurlow, Contact

Newfoundland

★3444★
Federation of Newfoundland Indians
General Delivery
Benoit's Cave, NF, Canada A0L 1A0   Ph: (709)789-2797
Gerrard Webb, Pres.

★3445★
Labrador Metis Association
PO Box 599, Sta. B
Happy Valley, NF, Canada A0P 1E0   Ph: (709)896-3880
Ruby Durno, Contact

★3446★
Labrador Native Women's Association
Box 1101, Sta. B
Happy Valley, NF, Canada A0P 1M0   Ph: (709)896-8420
Annette Blake, Pres.

★3447★
Labrador Friendship Centre
PO Box 767, Sta. B
Happy Valley/Goose Bay, NF, Canada
  A0P 1E0   Ph: (709)896-8302
Renne Simms, Exec.Dir.

★3448★
Council of the Conne River Micmacs
Conne River Reserve   Ph: (709)882-2470
Micmac Territory, NF, Canada A0H 1J0   Fax: (709)882-2292
Chief Shane McDonald, Contact

★3449★
Labrador Inuit Association
PO Box 70   Ph: (709)922-2942
Nain, NF, Canada A0P 1L0   Fax: (709)922-2931
Angela Dewe, Contact

★3450★
Okalakatiget Society
PO Box 160   Ph: (709)922-2896
Nain, NF, Canada A0P 1L0   Fax: (709)922-2293
Heather Levecque, Exec.Dir.

★3451★
Torngusok Cultural Institute
PO Box 40   Ph: (709)922-2158
Nain, NF, Canada A0P 1L0   Fax: (709)922-2863
Gary Baikie, Dir.

★3452★
St. John's Native Friendship Centre
61 Cashin Ave.   Ph: (709)726-5902
Saint John's, NF, Canada A1E 3B4   Fax: (709)754-2364
Myrtle Blandford, Exec.Dir.

★3453★
St. John's Native Friendship Centre
PO Box 2414, Sta. C   Ph: (709)726-5902
Saint John's, NF, Canada A1C 6E7   Fax: (709)754-2364

★3454★
Naskapi-Montagnais Innu Association
PO Box 119
Sheshatsiu, NF, Canada A0P 1M0   Ph: (709)497-8392
Greg Penashue, Pres.

Northwest Territories

★3455★
Kitkmeot Inuit Association
PO Box 18   Ph: (403)983-2458
Cambridge Bay, NT, Canada X0E 0C0   Fax: (403)983-2701
Jim Eetoorook, Pres.

★3456★
Zhahti Koe Friendship Centre
General Delivery   Ph: (403)699-3411
Fort Providence, NT, Canada X0E 0Y0   Fax: (403)699-4355
Dorothy Minozda, Exec.Dir.

★3457★
Deh Cho Society
PO Box 470
Fort Simpson, NT, Canada X0E 0N0   Ph: (403)695-2577

★3458★
Uncle Gabe's Friendship Centre
PO Box 957   Ph: (403)872-3013
Fort Smith, NT, Canada X0E 0P0   Fax: (403)872-5313

★3459★
Soaring Eagle Friendship Centre
PO Box 396
Hay River, NT, Canada X0E 0R0   Ph: (403)874-6581

★3460★
Ingamo Hall Friendship Centre
PO Box 1293   Ph: (403)979-2166
Inuvik, NT, Canada X0E 0T0   Fax: (403)979-2873
Benita Chlow, Exec.Dir.

★3461★
Inuvialuit Communications Society
PO Box 1704
Inuvik, NT, Canada X0E 0T0
Vincent Teddy, V.Pres.
Ph: (403)979-2067
Fax: (403)979-2744

★3462★
Inuvialuit Development Corporation
Bag Service No. 7
Inuvik, NT, Canada X0E 0T0
Frank Hansen, Chairperson
Ph: (403)979-2419
Fax: (403)979-3256

★3463★
Inuvialuit Regional Corporation
107 MacKenzie Rd.
PO Box 2120
Inuvik, NT, Canada X0E 0T0
Ann Matheson, Exec.Dir.
Ph: (403)979-2737
Fax: (403)979-2135

★3464★
Rae Edzo Friendship Centre
PO Box 85
Rae, NT, Canada X0E 0Y0
Bertha Rabesca, Exec.Dir.
Ph: (403)392-6000
Fax: (403)392-6093

★3465★
Sappujjijit Friendship Centre
PO Box 58
Ranklin Outlet, NT, Canada X0C 0G0
Ph: (403)645-2488

★3466★
Metis Association of the Northwest Territories
PO Box 1375
Yellowknife, NT, Canada X1A 2P1
Gary Bohnet, Pres.
Ph: (403)873-3505
Fax: (403)873-3395

★3467★
Native Communications Society of the Western Northwest Territories
PO Box 1919
Yellowknife, NT, Canada X1A 2P4
Ph: (403)873-2661
Free: 800-661-0711
Fax: (403)920-4205

Catherine MacQuarrie, Exec.Dir.

★3468★
Native Women's Association of the Northwest Territories
PO Box 2321
Yellowknife, NT, Canada X1A 2P7
Angie Lance, Exec.Dir.
Ph: (403)873-5509
Fax: (403)873-3152

★3469★
Northwest Territories Arts and Crafts Society
PO Box 2765
Yellowknife, NT, Canada X1A 2R1
Sonny McDonald, Pres.
Ph: (403)920-2854
Fax: (403)873-8753

★3470★
Northwest Territories Council of Friendship Centres
PO Box 2667
Yellowknife, NT, Canada X1A 2P9
Tom Eagle, Chair.
Ph: (403)873-2864
Fax: (403)873-5185

★3471★
Northwest Territories Council of Friendship Centres
PO Box 2667
Yellowknife, NT, Canada X1A 2P9
Tom Eagle, Pres.
Ph: (403)873-2864
Fax: (403)873-5185

★3472★
Tree of Peace Friendship Centre
PO Box 2667
Yellowknife, NT, Canada X1A 2P9
Tom Eagle, Exec.Dir.
Ph: (403)920-2288
Fax: (403)873-5185

Nova Scotia

★3473★
Baffin Region Inuit Association
PO Box 219
Frobisher Bay, NS, Canada X0A 0H0
Paul Keevookta, Exec.Dir.
Ph: (819)979-5391
Fax: (819)979-4325

★3474★
Micmac Native Friendship Centre
2158 Gottingen St.
Halifax, NS, Canada B3K 3B4
Ph: (902)420-1576
Fax: (902)423-6130

★3475★
Micmac Native Learning Centre
2158 Gottingen St.
Halifax, NS, Canada B3K 3B4
Gordon V. King, Exec.Dir.
Ph: (902)420-1576
Fax: (902)423-6130

★3476★
Native Communications Society of Nova Scotia
PO Box 344
Sydney, NS, Canada B1P 6H2
Theresa Moore, Contact
Ph: (902)539-0045
Fax: (902)564-0430

★3477★
Union of Nova Scotia Indians
PO Box 961
Sydney, NS, Canada B1P 6J4
Carl Gould, Sec./Treas.
Ph: (902)539-4107
Fax: (902)564-2137

★3478★
Native Council of Nova Scotia
PO Box 1320
Truro, NS, Canada B2N 5N2
Dwight Dorey, Pres.
Ph: (902)895-1523
Fax: (902)895-0024

★3479★
Nova Scotia Native Women's Association
PO Box 805
Truro, NS, Canada B2N 5E8
Clara Gloade, Pres.
Ph: (902)893-7402

Ontario

★3480★
Atikokan Native Friendship Centre
PO Box 1510
Atikokan, ON, Canada P0T 1C0
Roberta McMahon, Exec.Dir.
Ph: (807)597-1213
Fax: (807)597-1520

★3481★
Barrie Native Friendship Centre
21 Owen St.
Barrie, ON, Canada L4M 3G8
Merlle Assance-Beedie, Exec.Dir.
Ph: (705)721-7689
Fax: (705)725-1648

★3482★
Indian Arts and Crafts of Ontario
10 Woodwary Tr.
Brantford, ON, Canada N3B 5Z6
Wellington Staats, Pres.
Ph: (519)751-0040
Fax: (519)751-2790

★3483★
Pine Tree Native Centre of Brant
154 Dahousie St.
Brantford, ON, Canada N3T 2J4
Nancy Hill, Exec.Dir.
Ph: (519)752-5132

★3484★
Ininew Friendship Centre
190 3rd Ave.
Box 1499   Ph: (705)272-4497
Cochrane, ON, Canada P0L 1C0   Fax: (705)272-3597
Howard Restoule, Exec.Dir.

★3485★
Dryden Native Friendship Centre
53 Arthur St.   Ph: (807)223-4180
Dryden, ON, Canada P8N 1J7   Fax: (807)223-7136
Irene St. Goddard, Exec.Dir.

★3486★
Fort Erie Indian Friendship Centre
303 Nigle Rd.   Ph: (416)871-8931
Fort Erie, ON, Canada L2A 5H2 Fax: (416)871-9655
Wayne Hill, Exec.Dir.

★3487★
United Native Friendship Centre
PO Box 752   Ph: (807)274-3207
Fort Frances, ON, Canada P9A 3N1 Fax: (807)274-4110
Frank Bruyere, Exec.Dir.

★3488★
Thunderbird Friendship Centre
PO Box 430   Ph: (807)854-1060
Geraldton, ON, Canada P0T 1M0 Fax: (807)854-0861
Beverley Bottle, Exec.Dir.

★3489★
Hamilton Regional Indian Centre
712 Main St., E.   Ph: (416)548-9593
Hamilton, ON, Canada L8M 1K8   Fax: (416)545-4077
Cathy Staats, Exec.Dir.

★3490★
Grand Council Treaty No. 3
PO Box 1720   Ph: (807)548-4215
Kenora, ON, Canada P7N 3X7   Fax: (807)548-5041
Peter Kelly, Grand Chief

★3491★
Lake of the Woods Ojibway Cultural Centre
PO Box 159   Ph: (807)548-5744
Kenora, ON, Canada P9N 3X3   Fax: (807)548-1591
Joseph Red Thunderboy, Dir.

★3492★
Ne-Chee Friendship Centre
PO Box 241   Ph: (807)468-5440
Kenora, ON, Canada P9N 3X3   Fax: (807)468-5340
Joe Seymour, Exec.Dir.

★3493★
N'Amerind Friendship Centre
260 Colbourne St.   Ph: (519)672-0131
London, ON, Canada N6B 2S6   Fax: (519)672-0717
Tom Doxtator, Exec.Dir.

★3494★
Georgian Bay Native Friendship Centre
366 Midland Ave.   Ph: (705)526-5589
Midland, ON, Canada L4R 3K7   Fax: (705)526-7662
Fred Jackson, Exec.Dir.

★3495★
Moosonee Native Friendship Centre
PO Box 478   Ph: (705)472-2811
Moosonee, ON, Canada P0L 1Y0   Fax: (705)336-2929
Bill Morrison, Exec.Dir.

★3496★
Inuit Art Foundation
2081 Merivale Rd.   Ph: (613)224-8189
Nepean, ON, Canada K2G 1G9   Fax: (613)224-2907
Marybelle Mitchell, Exec.Dir.

★3497★
Niagara Regional Indian Centre
Niagara-on-the-Lake
RR 4, Queenston & Taylor Rds.   Ph: (416)688-6484
Niagara, ON, Canada L0S 1J0   Fax: (416)688-4033
Vince Hill, Dir.

★3498★
North Bay Indian Friendship Centre
980 Cassells St.   Ph: (705)472-2811
North Bay, ON, Canada P1B 4A6 Fax: (705)472-5251
Bill Butler, Exec.Dir.

★3499★
Union of Ontario Indians
PO Box 711   Ph: (705)497-9127
North Bay, ON, Canada P1B 8J8 Fax: (705)497-9135
Nora Bothwell, Prog. Manager

★3500★
Six Nations Child and Family Support Centre
Oshweken Post Office
Oshweken, ON, Canada N0A 1M0   Ph: (519)445-2211
Kalen Porter, Dir.
Formerly: Six Nations Crisis Intervention Centre.

★3501★
Cree Naskapi Commission
305-222 Queen St.   Ph: (613)234-4288
Ottawa, ON, Canada K1P 5V9   Fax: (613)234-8102
Brian Shawana, Dir.

★3502★
Indigenous Survival International (ISI Canada)
298 Elgin St., No. 105   Ph: (613)236-0673
Ottawa, ON, Canada K2P 1M3   Fax: (613)230-3595
Dan Smith, Contact

★3503★
Inuit Broadcasting Corporation
251 Laurier Ave., W., No. 703   Ph: (613)235-1892
Ottawa, ON, Canada K1P 5J6   Fax: (613)230-8824
Debbie Brisebois, Exec.Dir.

★3504★
Inuit Circumpolar Conference
170 Laurier Ave., No. 504   Ph: (613)563-2642
Ottawa, ON, Canada K1P 5V5   Fax: (613)565-3089
Corinee Gray, Dir.

★3505★
Inuit Development Corporation
280 Albert St., Ste. 902
Ottawa, ON, Canada K1P 5G8   Ph: (613)238-4981

★3506★
Inuit Tapirisat of Canada
170 Laurier Ave., W., No. 510   Ph: (613)238-8181
Ottawa, ON, Canada K1P 5V5   Fax: (613)234-1991
Rosemary Kuptana, Pres.

★3507★
Inuit Women's Association
200 Elgin St., Ste. 804   Ph: (613)238-3977
Ottawa, ON, Canada K2P 1L5   Fax: (613)238-1787
Martha Flaherty, Pres.

★3508★
Inuit Youth Council
170 Laurier Ave.   Ph: (613)238-8181
Ottawa, ON, Canada K1P 5Z5   Fax: (613)234-1991
Sheila Lumsden, Pres.

★3509★
Native Business Institute of Canada
2055 Carling Ave., No. 101   Ph: (613)761-9734
Ottawa, ON, Canada K2A 1G6   Fax: (613)725-9031
Frank Craddock, Exec.Dir.

★3510★
Native Council of Canada
384 Bank St., 2nd Fl.   Ph: (613)238-3511
Ottawa, ON, Canada K2P 1Y4   Fax: (613)230-6273
Ron George, Dir.
Also Known As: Conseil National des Autochtones du Canada.

★3511★
Nunasi Corporation
280 Albert St., Ste. 904   Ph: (613)238-4981
Ottawa, ON, Canada K1P 5G8   Fax: (613)238-5230
Pat Lyall, Pres.

★3512★
Odawa Native Friendship Centre
396 Maclaren St.   Ph: (613)238-8591
Ottawa, ON, Canada K2P 0M8   Fax: (613)238-6106
Jim Eagle, Exec.Dir.

★3513★
Tungavik Federation of Nunavut
130 Slater St., Ste. 800   Ph: (613)238-1096
Ottawa, ON, Canada K1P 6E2   Fax: (613)238-4131
James Tetoolooh, Pres.

★3514★
Parry Sound Friendship Centre
13 Bowes St.   Ph: (705)746-5970
Parry Sound, ON, Canada 92A 2K7 Fax: (705)746-2612
Vera Pawis-Tabobondung, Exec.Dir.

★3515★
Sault Ste. Marie Indian Friendship Centre
13 Bowes St.   Ph: (705)746-5970
Parry Sound, ON, Canada P2A 2K7 Fax: (705)746-2612
Vera Pawis-Tabobondung, Exec.Dir.

★3516★
Red Lake Indian Friendship Centre
PO Box 244   Ph: (807)727-2847
Red Lake, ON, Canada P0V 2M0   Fax: (807)727-3253
Kim Harder, Exec.Dir.

★3517★
Ontario Metis and Aboriginal Association (OMAA)
158 Sackville Rd.   Ph: (705)949-5161
Sault Ste. Marie, ON, Canada P6B 4T6   Free: 800-461-5112
Olaf Biolenaa, Pres.

★3518★
Nishnawbe-Gamik Friendship Centre
PO Box 1299   Ph: (807)737-1903
Sioux Lookout, ON, Canada P0V 2T0   Fax: (807)737-1805
Laura Wynn, Exec.Dir.

★3519★
Wawatay Communications Society
16 5th Ave.
Box 1180
Sioux Lookout, ON, Canada P0V 2T0

★3520★
Association of Iroquois and Allied Indians
RR 2   Ph: (519)652-3251
Southwold, ON, Canada N0L 2G0   Fax: (519)679-1653
Harry Doxtator, Grand Chief

★3521★
N'Swakamok Native Friendship Centre
110 Elm St.   Ph: (705)674-2128
Sudbury, ON, Canada P3C 1T5   Fax: (705)671-9699
Marie Meawasige, Exec.Dir.

★3522★
Ontario Native Women's Association
115 N. May St., No. 101   Ph: (807)623-3442
Thunder Bay, ON, Canada P7C 3N8 Fax: (807)623-1104
Marlene Pierre, Exec.Dir.

★3523★
Thunder Bay Indian Friendship Centre
401 N. Cumberland St.   Ph: (807)345-5840
Thunder Bay, ON, Canada P7A 4P7 Fax: (807)344-8945
Anne Cox, Exec.Dir.

★3524★
Timmins Native Friendship Centre
170 2nd Ave.   Ph: (705)268-6262
Timmins, ON, Canada P4N 1G1   Fax: (705)268-6266
Peter Sackaney, Exec.Dir.

★3525★
**Association for Native Development in the Performing
    and Visual Arts**
39 Spiadina   Ph: (416)972-0871
Toronto, ON, Canada M5R 2S9   Fax: (416)972-0892
Made Nixon, Exec.Dir.

★3526★
Canadian Council for Native Business
204 St. George St., 2nd Fl.   Ph: (416)961-8663
Toronto, ON, Canada M5R 2N5   Fax: (416)961-3995
Patrick Lavelle, Pres./CEO
Also Known As: Conseil Canadien pour le Commerce Autochtone.

★3527★
Chiefs of Ontario
22 College St., 2nd Fl.   Ph: (416)972-0212
Toronto, ON, Canada M5G 1K2   Fax: (416)972-0217

★3528★
Joint Indian Association Committee of Ontario
22 College St., 2nd Fl.   Ph: (416)972-0212
Toronto, ON, Canada M5G 1K2   Fax: (416)972-0217
Andrea Chrisjohn, Dir.
Also Known As: Chiefs of Ontario.

★3529★
Native Canadian Centre of Toronto
16 Spadina Rd.   Ph: (416)964-9087
Toronto, ON, Canada M5R 2S7   Fax: (416)964-2111
Gail Mason, Dir.

★3530★
Native Skills Centre
401 Richmond St., W.   Ph: (416)581-1392
Toronto, ON, Canada M5V 1X3   Fax: (416)581-1723
Leslie MacGregor, Dir.

★3531★
Ontario Federation of Indian Friendship Centres
234 Eglinton Ave., E., No. 207   Ph: (416)484-1411
Toronto, ON, Canada M4P 1K5   Fax: (416)484-6893
Sylvia Maracle, Exec.Dir.

★3532★
Ontario Native Council on Justice
22 College St., No. 102
Toronto, ON, Canada M5G 1K6
Carol Monthgnes, Exec.Dir.
Ph: (416)969-9119
Fax: (416)969-9120

★3533★
Inuit Non-Profit Housing Corporation
175 Montreal Rd., Ste. 3302
Vanier, ON, Canada K1L 6E4
Sam Metcalfe, Pres.
Ph: (613)744-5193
Fax: (613)744-7530

★3534★
Ojibwa Cultural Foundation
Excelsior Post Office
West Bay, ON, Canada P0P 1G0
Mary Lou Fox Radulovich, Dir.
Ph: (705)377-4902
Fax: (705)377-5460

★3535★
Can Am Indian Friendship Centre
1648 Ellrofe Ave.
Windsor, ON, Canada N8Y 3X7
Terry Doxtator, Exec.Dir.
Ph: (519)948-8365
Fax: (519)948-8419

—— **Prince Edward Island** ——

★3536★
Aboriginal Women's Association of Prince Edward Island
PO Box 213
Charlottetown, PE, Canada C1A 7K4
Mary Moore, Pres.
Ph: (902)675-3850

★3537★
Native Council of Prince Edward Island
33 Allen St.
Charlottetown, PE, Canada C1A 2V6
Graham Tuplin, Pres.
Ph: (902)892-5314
Fax: (902)368-7464

★3538★
Lennox Island Cultural Educational Centre
PO Box 134
Lennox Island, PE, Canada G0B 1P0
Irene Labobe, Dir.
Ph: (902)831-2779

—— **Quebec** ——

★3539★
Grand Council of the Crees
2 Lakeshore, Nemaska
Baie James, PQ, Canada J0Y 3B0
Also Known As: Grand Conseil des Crees.
Ph: (819)673-2600
Fax: (819)673-2606

★3540★
Cree Indian Centre
95 rue Jaculet
Chibougamau, PQ, Canada G8P 2G1
Jacqueline Patti, Contact
Ph: (418)748-7667
Fax: (418)748-6954

★3541★
Kativik School Board
305 Mimosa Ave.
Dorval, PQ, Canada H9S 3K5
Annie Poppert, Head
Ph: (514)636-8120
Fax: (819)361-2157

★3542★
Taqramiut Nipingat Inc.
185 Dorval Ave., Ste. 501
Dorval, PQ, Canada H9S 3J6

Sean St. George, Contact
Ph: (514)631-1394
Free: 800-361-2657
Fax: (514)631-6258

★3543★
Amitie Autochtone Hors Reserve Quebec
81 rue Eddy
Hull, PQ, Canada J8X 2W3
Monique, Contact
Ph: (819)778-0141
Fax: (819)778-6431

★3544★
Native Alliance of Quebec Inc.
2 Brodeur St.
Hull, PQ, Canada J8Y 2P6
Rheal Boudrias, Pres.
Also Known As: Alliance Autochtone du Quebec.
Ph: (819)770-7763
Fax: (819)770-6070

★3545★
Avataq Cultural Institute, Inc.
Inukjuak, PQ, Canada J0M 1M0
Johnny Epoo, Pres.
Ph: (819)254-8919
Fax: (819)254-8148

★3546★
Kanien'Kehaka Raotitiohkwa Cultural Centre
Box 1988
Kahnawake, PQ, Canada J0L 1B0
Jessica Hill, Exec.Dir.
Ph: (514)638-0880
Fax: (514)638-0920

★3547★
Quebec Indian Rights for Indian Women
PO Box 614
Kahnawake, PQ, Canada J0L 1B0
Mary Two-Axe Earley, Contact
Ph: (514)632-6304

★3548★
Centre d'Amitie de La Tuque
334 St. Joseph
La Tuque, PQ, Canada G9X 3P3
Roseanne Larouche, Exec.Dir.
Ph: (819)523-6121

★3549★
Makivik Corporation
650 32nd Ave.
Lachine, PQ, Canada H8T 3K5
Also Known As: Societe Makivik.
Ph: (514)634-8091

★3550★
Centre d'Amitie Autochtone de Quebec
234 St. Louis St.
Loretteville, PQ, Canada G2B 1L4
Joscelin Grolehuit, Exec.Dir.
Ph: (418)843-5818
Fax: (418)843-5960

★3551★
James Bay Cree Communications Society
75 Riverside
Mistassini Lake, PQ, Canada G0W 1C0
Dianne Reid, Sec.
Ph: (418)923-3191
Fax: (418)923-2088

★3552★
Association des Femmes Autochtones du Quebec
1450 City Councillors, Ste. 440
Montreal, PQ, Canada H3A 2E5
Michel Rouleau, Pres.
Ph: (514)844-9168
Fax: (514)844-2108

★3553★
Grand Council of the Crees
Montreal Regional Office
1 Place Ville Marie, Ste. 3438
Montreal, PQ, Canada H3B 3N6
Ph: (514)861-5837
Fax: (514)861-0760

★3554★
Native Friendship Centre
3730 Cote des Neiges Rd.
Montreal, PQ, Canada H3H 1V6
Ida Williams, Exec.Dir.
Ph: (514)937-5338
Fax: (514)937-4437

★3555★
Quebec Native Women's Association
1450 City Councillors, Ste. 440   Ph: (514)844-0314
Montreal, PQ, Canada H3A 2E5   Fax: (514)844-2108
Michele Rouleau, Pres.

★3556★
Grand Council of the Crees
Quebec City Regional Office
425 St. Amable, Ste. 145   Ph: (418)525-4565
Quebec City, PQ, Canada G1R 5E4   Fax: (418)525-7351

★3557★
Institut Educatif et Culturel Attikamek-Montagnais
Village Huron
40 Francois Gros-Louis St., No.7   Ph: (418)843-0258
Quebec City, PQ, Canada G0A 4V0   Fax: (418)843-7313

★3558★
Restigouche Institute of Cultural Education
Restigouche Indian Band
PO Box 298   Ph: (418)788-2904
Restigouche, PQ, Canada G0C 2R0   Fax: (418)788-2058
Rodney Labillios, Dir.

★3559★
Centre d'Entraide et d'Amitie de Senneterre
910 10th Ave., C.P. 1769   Ph: (819)737-2324
Senneterre, PQ, Canada J0Y 2M0   Fax: (819)737-8311
Louis Bordeleau, Exec.Dir.

★3560★
Centre d'Entraide Autochtone de Val D'Or
1011 6th St.   Ph: (819)825-6857
Val D'Or, PQ, Canada J9P 3W4   Fax: (819)805-7515
Edith Cloutier, Exec.Dir.

★3561★
Tewegan Communications Society
351 Central Ave.
Val D'Or, PQ, Canada J9P 1P6   Ph: (819)825-5192
Charley Anichinapeo, Pres.

★3562★
Conseil Attikamek-Montagnais
80 Boulevard Bastien
Village des Hurons, PQ, Canada G0A   Ph: (418)842-0277
4V0   Fax: (418)842-9458
Rene Simon, Pres.

★3563★
Le Regroupement des Centres d'Amitie Autochone du Quebec
30 rue de L'Ours
Village des Hurons, PQ, Canada G0A   Ph: (418)842-6354
1L4   Fax: (418)842-9795

★3564★
Les Artisans Indiens du Quebec
840 Max Gros-Louis St.
Village des Hurons, PQ, Canada G0A   Ph: (418)845-2150
4V0   Fax: (418)845-9633
Jean Picard, Gen.Dir.

★3565★
Nation Huronne-Wendat
Cultural/Educational Centre
255 Place Chef Michel Lebeau
Village des Hurons, PQ, Canada G0A   Ph: (418)843-3767
4V0   Fax: (418)842-1108
M. Regent Sioui, Dir.

★3566★
Regroupement des Centres d'Amitie Autochtone du Quebec
30 rue de l'Ours
Village des Hurons, PQ, Canada G0A   Ph: (418)842-6354
1L4   Fax: (418)842-9795
Raymond Ditard, Coord.

★3567★
Societe de Communications-Atikamekw Montagnais
80 boul. Bastien 329
Village des Hurons (Wendake), PQ,   Ph: (418)843-3873
Canada G0A 4V0   Fax: (418)845-9774
Ghislain Picard, Contact

★3568★
Secretariat of First Nations of Quebec
430 Koska   Ph: (418)842-5020
Wendake, PQ, Canada G0A 4V0   Fax: (418)842-2660
Gislin Picard, Contact

—————————— **Saskatchewan** ——————————

★3569★
Buffalo Narrows Friendship Centre
PO Box 189   Ph: (306)235-4633
Buffalo Narrows, SK, Canada S0M 0J0   Fax: (306)235-4544
Cecile Shatilla, Exec.Dir.

★3570★
Moose Mountain Friendship Centre
Main St.
PO Box 207   Ph: (306)453-2425
Caryle, SK, Canada S0C 0R0   Fax: (306)453-6777
Almer Standing-Ready, Exec.Dir.

★3571★
Native Council of Saskatchewan
PO Box 278
Cumberland House, SK, Canada S0E 0S0   Ph: (306)888-2149
Harvey Young, Pres.

★3572★
Qu'Appelle Valley Friendship Centre
PO Box 240   Ph: (306)332-5616
Fort Qu'Appelle, SK, Canada S0G 1S0   Fax: (306)332-5091
J. Peter Dubois, Exec.Dir.

★3573★
Kikinahk Friendship Centre, Inc.
320 Boardman St.
Box 254   Ph: (306)425-2051
La Ronge, SK, Canada S0J 1L0   Fax: (306)425-3559
Norm Bovier, Exec.Dir.

★3574★
La Roche Friendship Centre
PO Box 254   Ph: (306)425-2051
La Ronge, SK, Canada S0J 1L0   Fax: (306)425-3359
Norm Bouvier, Exec.Dir.

★3575★
Northwest Friendship Centre
PO Box 1780   Ph: (306)236-3766
Meadow Lake, SK, Canada S0M 1V0   Fax: (306)236-5451
Gladys Joseph, Exec.Dir.

★3576★
Moose Jaw Native Friendship Centre
42 High St., E.   Ph: (306)693-6966
Moose Jaw, SK, Canada S6H OB8   Fax: (306)692-3509
Barry Kennedy, Exec.Dir.

★3577★
Battlefords Indian and Metis Friendship Centre
11501 8th Ave.
Box 667   Ph: (306)445-8216
North Battleford, SK, Canada S9A 2Y9   Fax: (306)445-6863
Barb Heisler, Exec.Dir.

★3578★
Aboriginal Women's Council of Saskatchewan
1311 Central, Ste. 326   Ph: (306)763-6005
Prince Albert, SK, Canada S6V 4W2   Fax: (306)922-6034
Lil Sanderson, Contact

★3579★
Federation of Saskatchewan Indian Nations
1100 1st Ave., E.   Ph: (306)764-3411
Prince Albert, SK, Canada S6V 2A7   Fax: (306)763-3255
Alma Roy, Contact

★3580★
Indian and Metis Friendship Centre
1409 1st Ave., E.
Box 2197   Ph: (306)764-3431
Prince Albert, SK, Canada S6V 6Z1   Fax: (306)763-3205
Roberta Burns, Exec.Dir.

★3581★
Aboriginal Friendship Centre of Saskatchewan (AECS)
1440 Scarth St.   Ph: (306)525-5459
Regina, SK, Canada S4R 2E9   Fax: (306)525-3005
Sharon Ironstar, Pres.

★3582★
Regina Friendship Centre
1440 Scarth St.   Ph: (306)525-5459
Regina, SK, Canada S4R 2E9   Fax: (306)525-3005
Dona Racette, Exec.Dir.

★3583★
Metis National Council
2600 8th St. E., Ste. 290A   Ph: (306)373-8855
Saskatoon, SK, Canada S7H 0V7   Fax: (306)373-3755
Ron Rivard, Exec.Dir.

★3584★
Metis Society of Saskatchewan Inc.
1249 8 St. E.   Ph: (306)343-8285
Saskatoon, SK, Canada S7H 0S5   Fax: (306)343-0171
Gerald Morin, Pres.

★3585★
Native Law Centre
University of Saskatchewan
141 Diefenbaker Centre   Ph: (306)966-6189
Saskatoon, SK, Canada S7N 0W0   Fax: (306)966-8517
Dan Purich, Dir.

★3586★
Saskatchewan Archaeological Society
816 1st Ave. N., No. 5   Ph: (306)664-4124
Saskatoon, SK, Canada S7K 1Y3   Fax: (306)665-1928
Tim Jones, Dir.

★3587★
Saskatchewan Indian Cultural Centre
120 33rd St., E.   Ph: (306)244-1146
Saskatoon, SK, Canada S7K 0S2   Fax: (306)665-6520
Linda Pelley-Landrie, Dir.

★3588★
Saskatchewan Native Communications Corporation
173 2nd Ave., S., Ste. 2026   Ph: (306)663-2253
Saskatoon, SK, Canada S7K 1K6   Fax: (306)664-8851

★3589★
Saskatchewan People First Council
101440 2nd Ave. N.
Saskatoon, SK, Canada S7J 3L1   Ph: (306)653-0508

★3590★
Saskatoon Indian and Metis Friendship Centre
168 Wall St.   Ph: (306)244-0174
Saskatoon, SK, Canada S7K 1N4   Fax: (306)664-2536
Maurice Blondeau, Exec.Dir.

★3591★
Saskatoon Indian and Metis Friendship Centre
168 Wall St.
Saskatoon, SK, Canada S7K 1N4   Ph: (306)244-0174

★3592★
Yorkton Friendship Centre
283 Myrtle Ave.   Ph: (306)782-2822
Yorkton, SK, Canada S3N 1R5   Fax: (306)782-6662
Ivan Cote, Exec.Dir.

─────────────── Yukon ───────────────

★3593★
Council for Yukon Indians
22 Nisutlin Dr.   Ph: (403)667-7631
Whitehorse, YT, Canada Y1A 2S5   Fax: (403)668-6577
Judy Gingell, Chair

★3594★
Council for Yukon Indians
11 Nisutlin Dr.   Ph: (403)667-7631
Whitehorse, YT, Canada Y1A 3S4   Fax: (403)668-6577
Judy Gingell, Chairman

★3595★
Northern Native Broadcasting of Yukon (NNBY)
4228A 4th Ave.
Whitehorse, YT, Canada Y1A 1K1   Ph: (403)688-6629

★3596★
Skookum Jim Friendship Centre
3159 3rd Ave.   Ph: (403)668-4465
Whitehorse, YT, Canada Y1A 1G1   Fax: (403)667-6303
Art Stevenson, Exec.Dir.

★3597★
Ye-Sa-To Communications Society
22 Nisutlin Dr.
Whitehorse, YT, Canada Y1A 3S5   Ph: (403)667-7636
Elizabeth Jackson, Pres.

★3598★
Yukon Indian Arts and Crafts Co-Operative Limited
4230 4th Ave.   Ph: (403)668-5955
Whitehorse, YT, Canada Y1A 1K1   Fax: (403)668-6466
Brenda Knutson, Spokesperson

★3599★
Yukon Indian Cultural-Education Society Resource Center
Council for Yukon Indians
11 Nisutlin Dr.   Ph: (403)667-7631
Whitehorse, YT, Canada Y1A 3S4   Fax: (403)668-6577
Judy Gingell, Chairperson

★3600★
Yukon Indian Women's Association
22 Nisutlin Dr.   Ph: (403)667-6162
Whitehorse, YT, Canada Y1A 3S5   Fax: (403)668-6577
Nina Bolton, Pres.

Federal Government Agencies

★3601★
Canada—Department of Health and Welfare
Medical Services
Indian and Northern Health Services
Ottawa, ON, Canada K1A 0L3   Ph: (613)952-9616
                                      Fax: (613)957-9969

★3602★
Canada—Department of Indian Affairs and Northern Development (DIAND)
Les Terrasses de la Chaudiere   Ph: (819)997-0002
Ottawa, ON, Canada K1A 0H4   Fax: (819)997-1587
Honorable Tom Siddon, Minister
Also Known As: Ministere des Affaires Indiennes et du Nord Canadien.

★3603★
Canada—Department of Indian Affairs and Northern Development
Inuit Cultural and Linguistic Section
Ottawa, ON, Canada K1A 0H4   Ph: (819)997-0811

★3604★
Canada—Department of the Secretary of State
Native Citizens' Directorate
Ottawa, ON, Canada K1A 0M5   Ph: (819)994-3874
                                      Fax: (819)953-2673

★3605★
Canada—Indian Claims Commission
255 Albert St., Ste. 200
PO Box 1750, Sta. B   Ph: (613)943-2737
Ottawa, ON, Canada K1P 1A2   Fax: (613)943-0157
Harry S. LaForme, Chief Commissioner
Also Known As: Commission des Revendications des Indiens.

State/Provincial & Local Government Agencies

Alberta

★3606★
Canada—Department of Indian Affairs and Northern Development
Alberta Regional Office
Canada Pl., 6th Fl.
9700 Jasper Ave.   Ph: (403)495-2773
Edmonton, AB, Canada T5J 4G2   Fax: (403)495-4088

★3607★
Canada—Department of Indian Affairs and Northern Development
Alberta Regional Office
Fort McMurray Service Centre
9913 Biggs Ave., 2nd Fl.   Ph: (403)790-3010
Fort McMurray, AB, Canada T9H 1S2   Fax: (403)791-3010

★3608★
Canada—Department of Indian Affairs and Northern Development
Alberta Regional Office
Fort Vermilion Service Centre
PO Box 720   Ph: (403)926-3741
High Level, AB, Canada T0H 1Z0   Fax: (403)926-2966

★3609★
Canada—Department of Indian Affairs and Northern Development
Alberta Regional Office
Lethbridge District
220 3rd Ave., S., Ste. 330
Lethbridge, AB, Canada T1J 0G9   Ph: (403)382-3111

★3610★
Canada—Department of Indian Affairs and Northern Development
Alberta Regional Office
St. Paul Service Centre
4713 50th St.
PO Box 850   Ph: (403)645-3313
Saint Paul, AB, Canada T0A 3A0   Fax: (403)645-5774

★3611★
Canada—Department of Indian Affairs and Northern Development
Alberta Regional Office
Southern Alberta District
Harry Hays Bldg.
220 4th Ave. SE   Ph: (403)292-5901
Calgary, AB, Canada T2P 3K3   Fax: (403)292-6903

British Columbia

★3612★
Canada—Department of Indian Affairs and Northern Development
British Columbia Regional Office
1550 Alberni St., Ste. 300   Ph: (604)666-5121
Vancouver, BC, Canada V6G 3C5   Fax: (604)666-2546

★3613★
Canada—Department of Indian Affairs and Northern Development
British Columbia Regional Office
Northwestern British Columbia Field Office
3219 Eby St.   Ph: (604)638-4115
Terrace, BC, Canada V8G 4R3   Fax: (604)638-0400

★3614★
Canada—Department of Indian Affairs and Northern Development
British Columbia Regional Office
Prince George Field Office
280 Victoria St., Ste. 209   Ph: (604)561-5121
Prince George, BC, Canada V2L 4X3   Fax: (604)561-5418

★3615★
Canada—Department of Indian Affairs and Northern Development
British Columbia Regional Office
Vancouver Island Field Office
60 Front St., Ste. 401   Ph: (604)754-0355
Nanaimo, BC, Canada V9R 5H8   Fax: (604)754-0247

Manitoba

★3616★
Canada—Department of Indian Affairs and Northern Development
Manitoba Regional Office
275 Portage Ave., Rm. 1100
Winnipeg, MB, Canada R3B 3A3
Ph: (204)983-2474
Fax: (204)983-0861

★3617★
Canada—Department of Indian Affairs and Northern Development
Manitoba Regional Office
Thompson Area Advisory Centre
306-83 Churchill Dr.
Thompson, MB, Canada R8N 0L6
Ph: (204)778-8324
Fax: (204)677-7018

Northwest Territories

★3618★
Canada—Department of Indian Affairs and Northern Development
Northwest Territories Regional Office
4919 50th St.
PO Box 1500
Yellowknife, NT, Canada X1A 2R3
Ph: (403)920-8283
Fax: (403)873-5763

Nova Scotia

★3619★
Canada—Department of Indian Affairs and Northern Development
Atlantic Regional Office
40 Havelock St.
PO Box 160
Amherst, NS, Canada B4H 3Z3
Ph: (902)667-3818
Fax: (902)667-9947

Ontario

★3620★
Canada—Department of Indian Affairs and Northern Development
Ontario Regional Office
25 St. Clair Ave., E.
Toronto, ON, Canada M4T 1M2
Ph: (416)973-6201
Fax: (416)973-6472

★3621★
Canada—Department of Indian Affairs and Northern Development
Ontario Regional Office
Sioux Lookout District
45 Prince St.
PO Box 369
Sioux Lookout, ON, Canada P0V 2T0
Ph: (807)737-2800
Fax: (807)737-1706

★3622★
Canada—Department of Indian Affairs and Northern Development
Ontario Regional Office
Southern Ontario District
58 Dalhousie St., 3rd Fl.
PO Box 1960
Brantford, ON, Canada N3T 5W5
Ph: (519)754-0323
Fax: (519)754-0693

★3623★
Canada—Department of Indian Affairs and Northern Development
Ontario Regional Office
Sudbury District
1760 Regent St., S.
Sudbury, ON, Canada P3E 3Z8
Ph: (705)522-5100

★3624★
Canada—Department of Indian Affairs and Northern Development
Ontario Regional Office
Western Ontario District
905 Victoria Ave., E.
Thunder Bay, ON, Canada P7C 1B3
Ph: (807)623-3534

★3625★
Ontario Ministry of Citizenship
Native Community Branch
77 Bloor St. W, 5th Fl.
Toronto, ON, Canada M7A 2R9
Ph: (416)965-5003
Fax: (416)324-6774

Quebec

★3626★
Canada—Department of Indian Affairs and Northern Development
Quebec Regional Office
320 rue St.-Joseph, E.
PO Box 3725
Saint Roch, PQ, Canada G1K 7Y2
Ph: (418)648-3270
Fax: (418)648-2266

Saskatchewan

★3627★
Canada—Department of Indian Affairs and Northern Development
Saskatchewan Regional Office
2110 Hamilton St.
Regina, SK, Canada S4P 4K4
Ph: (306)780-5945
Fax: (306)780-5733

★3628★
Canada—Department of Indian Affairs and Northern Development
Saskatchewan Regional Office
North Central Saskatchewan District
3601 5th Ave., E.
PO Box 5500
Prince Albert, SK, Canada S6V 7V6
Ph: (306)953-8522
Fax: (306)953-8648

★3629★
Canada—Department of Indian Affairs and Northern Development
Saskatchewan Regional Office
Northwest Saskatchewan District
PO Box 280
Meadow Lake, SK, Canada S0M 1V0
Ph: (306)236-4472
Fax: (306)236-3288

★3630★
Canada—Department of Indian Affairs and Northern Development
Saskatchewan Regional Office
Reginal Counseling Centre
2054 Broad St.
Regina, SK, Canada S4P 1Y3
Ph: (306)780-5360

★3631★
Canada—Department of Indian Affairs and Northern Development
Saskatchewan Regional Office
Saskatoon Counseling Centre
101 22nd St., E., Rm. 201   Ph: (306)975-4800
Saskatoon, SK, Canada S7K 0E1   Fax: (306)975-4771

★3632★
Canada—Department of Indian Affairs and Northern Development
Saskatchewan Regional Office
Southern Saskatchewan District
PO Box 760   Ph: (306)332-5643
Fort Qu'Appelle, SK, Canada S0G 1S0   Fax: (306)332-6019

─────────── **Yukon** ───────────

★3633★
Canada—Department of Indian Affairs and Northern Development
Yukon Regional Office
200 Range Rd.
PO Box 4100   Ph: (403)667-3344
Whitehorse, YT, Canada Y1A 3S9   Fax: (403)668-4148

Library Collections

★3634★
British Columbia Ministry of Tourism & Culture
Fort Steele Heritage Town
Research Library
Fort Steele, BC, Canada V0B 1N0   Ph: (604)489-3351
        Fax: (604)489-2624
Ken Zurosky, Cur.

Subjects: East Kootenay and British Columbia history, 19th century material culture, Kootenay Indians, mining. **Special Collections:** Archives of personal papers, business papers, and diaries (800 feet). **Holdings:** 8000 books; 20,000 photographs; 130 audiotapes (interviews and historical readings); 500 microforms; 650 manuscripts. **Formerly:** British Columbia Ministry of Municipal Affairs, Recreation & Culture. **Remarks:** Library's main focus is on Southeastern British Columbia, 1860-1930.

★3635★
Campbell River Museum & Archives
Reference Library
1235 Island Hwy.   Ph: (604)287-3103
Campbell River, BC, Canada V9W 2C7   Fax: (604)286-6490

Subjects: History - Northern Vancouver Island, Northwest Coast native Indian culture and history. **Special Collections:** Native culture; local diaries and memorabilia. **Holdings:** 1300 books; 200 oral history tapes; archival documents; videotapes.

★3636★
Canada—Department of Indian Affairs and Northern Development
Departmental Library
Ottawa, ON, Canada K1A 0H4   Ph: (819)997-0811
        Fax: (819)953-5491
Sue Hanley, Dept.Libn.

Subjects: Native lands, revenues, trusts, economic development, and self-government; Canadian North; Canadian history and exploration; Indian and Inuit culture, education, and housing. **Special Collections:** Arctic and rare book collection. **Holdings:** 51,000 titles in 200,000 volumes; 20,000 bound periodical volumes; 3500 special government documents; 3000 reels of microfilm; 15 drawers of microfiche; Canadian native and northern newspapers. **Remarks:** Library located at Terrasses de la Chaudiere, Hull, PQ.

★3637★
Canada—Department of Indian Affairs and Northern Development
Regional Library
1100-275 Portage Ave., 8th Fl.   Ph: (204)983-4928
Winnipeg, MB, Canada R3B 3A3   Fax: (204)983-7820
Sandi Krynski, Libn.

Subjects: Indian history and issues. **Special Collections:** Newspaper clipping files by subject, issues and band names. **Holdings:** 2000 books; government documents. **Also Known As:** Department of Indian & Northern Development.

★3638★
CEGEP de l'Abitibi-Temiscamingue
Bibliotheque
425 College Blvd.
Box 8000   Ph: (819)762-0931
Rouyn-Noranda, PQ, Canada J9X 5M5   Fax: (819)762-3815
Serge Allard, Dir.

Subjects: Northwest Quebec (Abitibi-Temiscamingue). **Holdings:** 64,091 books. **Remarks:** CEGEP is an acronym for College d'Enseignement General et Professionel.

★3639★
Gabriel Dumont Institute of Native Studies and Applied Research
Library
121 Broadway Ave.   Ph: (306)522-5691
Regina, SK, Canada S4N 0Z6   Fax: (306)565-0809
John Murray, Coord.

Subjects: Metis and aboriginal studies and education, Metis. **Special Collections:** Aboriginal History Archives. **Holdings:** 30,000 books. **Remarks:** Branch libraries are maintained in the following cities throughout Saskatchewan: Prince Albert, Saskatoon, Regina, Ile a la Crosse.

★3640★
Glenbow-Alberta Institute
Library & Archives
130 9th Ave., S.E.   Ph: (403)264-8300
Calgary, AB, Canada T2G 0P3   Fax: (403)265-9769
Leonard J. Gottselig, Chf.Libn.

Subjects: Western Canada, Canadian Arctic, Indians of North America, fur trade, missionaries, local history, Canadian art. **Special Collections:** Dewdney papers; J.J. Bowlen papers; George Coote papers; Sir F.W.G. Haultain papers. **Holdings:** 80,000 books; 3000 bound periodical volumes; 12 million pages of manuscripts; 4000 reels of microfilm; 48 VF drawers of newspapers clippings; 30 VF drawers of trade catalogs; 2000 Western Canadian political pamphlets and leaflets; 100 motion picture films; 500,000 photographs; 4000 tape recordings.

★3641★
Huronia Historical Parks
Resource Centre
P.O. Box 160   Ph: (705)526-7838
Midland, ON, Canada L4R 4K8   Fax: (705)526-9193
Sandra Saddy, Libn.

Subjects: New France to 1660; Jesuit missions in North America; Huron Indians in the 17th century; British naval and military establishments in Penetanguishene; archeology. **Holdings:** 7000 books; 50 bound periodical volumes; 2500 photocopied articles; 4 drawers of manuscripts; 10 boxes of archival records; 1000 maps; 3200 pictures; 3000 slides; 250 microforms. **Formerly:** Its Information Services Department.

★3642★
Manitoba Indian Cultural Education Centre
Peoples Library
119 Sutherland Ave.   Ph: (204)942-0228
Winnipeg, MB, Canada R2W 3C9   Fax: (204)947-6564
V.J. Chalmers, Libn.

Subjects: Native peoples. **Holdings:** 4500 books; 2000 vertical files; 100 kits; 60 books of clippings; 47 films; 67 videotapes; 67 cassettes of Indian music; 24 tapes; 8 slide presentations.

★3643★
Metropolitan Toronto Reference Library
Languages and Literature Department
789 Yonge St.
Toronto, ON, Canada M4W 2G8   Ph: (416)393-7010
Jaswinder Gundara, Mgr.

Subjects: Literature of the English-speaking world; literary history and criticism; journalism; linguistics; language and literature materials in languages other than English. **Special Collections:** North American Indian and Eskimo linguistics (1132 volumes); Canadiana Ethnica; English as a second language collections; Arthur Conan Doyle Collection; Maria Chapdelaine Collection; Russelas Collection. **Holdings:** 281,004 books; 14,427 bound periodical volumes; 12,645 language and spoken word phonograph records, tapes, cassettes; 7649 VF folders; 7299 other cataloged items. **Remarks:** Most staff members are language specialists, with 30-40 languages represented.

★3644★
Nanaimo & District Museum Society
Nanaimo Centennial Museum
Archives
100 Cameron Rd.
Nanaimo, BC, Canada V9R 2X1   Ph: (604)753-1821

Subjects: History - local Native Canadian groups, coal mining, Nanaimo area, fishing and logging industries. **Special Collections:** Local historical photographs; diorama depicting traditional Native life style; restored and fully furnished miner's cottage; extensive Chinese artifact collection. **Holdings:** 1000 volumes; 8000 photographs; 150 maps; 8000 archival materials.

★3645★
National Indian Brotherhood
Assembly of First Nations
Resource Centre
47 Clarence St., 3rd Fl.   Ph: (613)236-0673
Ottawa, ON, Canada K1N 9K1   Fax: (613)237-5306
Cindy Peltier

Subjects: First nations government, land claims, constitutional status, aboriginal rights. **Holdings:** 10,000 books; 4000 documents on microfiche.

★3646★
National Library of Canada
Reference and Information Services Division
Official Publications
395 Wellington St.   Ph: (613)996-7452
Ottawa, ON, Canada K1A 0N4   Fax: (613)943-1112
Betty Deavy, Govt. & Law Spec.

Special Collections: Depository for Canadian Federal and Provincial publications; includes Canadian Indian Rights Collection (historical, parliamentary, legal, socioeconomic documentation on native claims from Canada, United States, Australia, New Zealand). **Holdings:** 2 million government documents in hardcopy and 2 million in microform from Canada, foreign countries, international governmental organizations.

★3647★
National Library of Canada
Special Collections
395 Wellington St.   Ph: (613)996-1318
Ottawa, ON, Canada K1A 0N4   Fax: (613)996-4424
Claude LeMoire, Hd.Cur.

Special Collections: Rare Canadiana including native-language materials and Canadian limited editions and livres d'artistes; Jacob M. Lowy Collection (rare Hebraica and Judaica); Saul Hayes Collection of Hebraic manuscripts and Microforms; Literary Manuscript Collection (manuscripts and papers of Canadian authors and organizations including small literary presses, private presses, the book arts, and illustrations of Canadian children's literature). **Holdings:** 25,000 items. **Formerly:** Its Rare Book Division.

★3648★
Northwest Territory Canadian & French Heritage
Center
Minnesota Genealogical Society Library
1101 W. 7th St.
Saint Paul, MN 55102   Ph: (612)222-6929
Ozzie Thompson, Libn.

Subjects: Quebec, Canada, Canadians in the U.S., Metis Indians. **Holdings:** 2000 books; 100 bound periodical volumes; 1600 microforms; 10 manuscripts; 3 AV programs.

★3649★
Nova Scotia Human Rights Commission
Library
P.O. Box 2221   Ph: (902)424-4111
Halifax, NS, Canada B3J 3C4   Fax: (902)424-0596
May Lui, Pub.Educ.Off.

Subjects: Civil rights. **Special Collections:** Multiculturalism; women; aboriginal people, and other visible minorities; disability; racism; human rights. **Holdings:** 3244 books; 26 bound periodical volumes; 1261 reports; case decisions in braille and on audio cassette.

★3650★
Ontario Ministry of Tourism and Recreation
Old Fort William
Resource Library
Vicker's Heights Post Office   Ph: (807)577-8461
Thunder Bay, ON, Canada P0T 2Z0   Fax: (807)475-8037
Shawn J. Allaire, Lib.Techn.

Subjects: North American fur trade history and society, North West Company, Ojibway Indians, early 19th century trades and technology, material culture. **Special Collections:** National Heritage Limited (200 transfer cases of primary, secondary, pictorial data); Fort William Archaeological Project (400 files; 20 boxes of subject cards); interpreted buildings (41 kits of specialized data). **Holdings:** 4000 books; 700 documents; 20 VF drawers; 100 reels of microfilm.

★3651★
Prince of Wales Northern Heritage Centre
Library
Yellowknife, NT, Canada X1A 2L9   Ph: (403)873-7177
Carolynn Kobelka, Libn.   Fax: (403)873-0205

Subjects: History of the Northwest Territories, archeology, Arctic exploration, heritage resource management, native cultures of the Northwest Territories. **Special Collections:** Admiral Sir Leopold M'Clintock and Rear Admiral Noel Wright Collections (600 19th century imprints of Arctic exploration). **Holdings:** 7000 books; federal and provincial government publications; microfilm; microfiche; reprints. **Formerly:** Its Northwest Territories Archives.

★3652★
Saskatchewan Indian Federated College
Library
University of Regina
127 College W.
Regina, SK, Canada S4S 0A2   Ph: (306)584-8333
Phyllis G. Lerat, Libn.

Subjects: Indian studies; art; band administration; health careers; Indian education; management; economics; Indian languages, linguistics, and literature. **Special Collections:** Extension collection; RG 10 series; Eeniwuk collection. **Holdings:** 15,000 books; 533 bound periodical volumes; 20 VF drawers; 38 VF drawers of clippings, pamphlets, reports; 24 drawers of microfilm/microfiche; 250 videotapes.

★3653★
Saskatchewan Indian Federated College
Saskatoon Campus Library
310 20th St., E.   Ph: (306)931-1825
Saskatoon, SK, Canada S7K 0A7   Fax: (306)665-0175
Phyllis G. Lerat, Hd.Libn.

Subjects: North American Indian studies, social work, and art. **Holdings:** 4782 books; 28 bound periodical volumes; 30 videotapes; 12 VF drawers.

★3654★
Saskatchewan Provincial Library
1352 Winnipeg St.   Ph: (306)787-2976
Regina, SK, Canada S4P 3V7   Fax: (306)787-8866
Gloria Materi, A/Prov.Libn.

Subjects: Library science, Canada and Saskatchewan documents, general reference. **Special Collections:** Multicultural Collection (26 languages; 66,600 titles); Native Collection (4000 titles); large print and talking books (8400 titles). **Holdings:** 200,000 volumes; 5900 cassettes and tapes; 5000 phonograph records.

★3655★
University of Alberta
Humanities and Social Sciences Library
Bruce Peel Special Collections Library
Rutherford South   Ph: (403)492-5998
Edmonton, AB, Canada T6G 2J4   Fax: (403)492-4327
John Charles, Spec.Coll.Libn./Hd.

Subjects: Western Canadiana; prairie provinces; English literature, 1600-1940; Canadian drama; European drama, 17th-18th centuries; California history; European history, 1500-1900; book arts. **Special Collections:** Includes Gregory Javitch Collection on North and South American Indians (emphasis on treaties, warfare, language, and ceremonial dances); 900 volumes. **Holdings:** 85,000 volumes; 14,250 volumes of University of Alberta dissertations and theses; 48 volumes of diaries and typescripts on Alberta early settlers and local history.

★3656★
University of Alberta
Legal Resource Centre
Library
Faculty of Extension   Ph: (403)492-5732
10049 81st Ave.   Free: 800-232-1961
Edmonton, AB, Canada T6E 1W7   Fax: (403)492-1857
Elaine Hutchinson, Libn.

Subjects: Law for the layperson, criminal law, public legal education, family and juvenile law, business law, native rights. **Special Collections:** Pamphlets (3000 titles). **Holdings:** 30,000 books and AV programs.

★3657★
University College of Cape Breton
Beaton Institute
Eachdraidh Archives
Box 5300   Ph: (902)539-5300
Sydney, NS, Canada B1P 6L2   Fax: (902)562-0119
Dr. R.J. Morgan, Dir.

Subjects: Cape Breton Island - history, labor history, Gaelic literature, folklore, political history, industrial history; traditional Scottish music of Cape Breton Island; genealogy. **Special Collections:** John Parker Nautical Collection (8.7 meters); Gaelic and Scottish collection (3000 volumes); political papers; Micmac Indian, Acadian, and other ethnic collections (manuscripts; audio- and videotapes). **Holdings:** 5000 books; 200 bound periodical volumes; 300 unbound reports; 50,000 photographs; 1000 maps; 200 meters of manuscripts; 5 VF drawers of clippings; 600 reels of microfilm; 200 large scrapbooks; 3500 tapes; 600 slides; 50 videotapes.

★3658★
University of New Brunswick
Education Resource Centre
D'Avray Hall
PO Box 7500   Ph: (506)453-3516
Fredericton, NB, Canada E3B 5H5   Fax: (506)453-4596
Andrew Pope, Hd.

Subjects: Education, home economics. **Special Collections:** Micmac-Maliseet Institute (1070 volumes); Children's Literature Collection (2112 volumes). **Holdings:** 38,526 books; 3855 bound periodical volumes; 427,538 microfiche; 28 VF drawers of pamphlets; 17,449 AV and instructional programs.

★3659★
University of Saskatchewan
Native Law Centre
Library
159 Diefenbaker Centre   Ph: (306)966-6195
Saskatoon, SK, Canada S7N 0W0   Fax: (306)966-8517
Mary Tastad, Libn.

Subjects: Law, native studies. **Special Collections:** Mackenzie Valley Pipeline Inquiry (archival materials); Canadian native rights cases (reported and unreported, relating to aboriginal, treaty, and Indian Act issues). **Holdings:** 3000 books; cases.

★3660★
University of Sudbury
Jesuit Archives
Sudbury, ON, Canada P3E 2C6   Ph: (705)673-5661
Robert Toupin, S.J., Prof. of Hist.

Subjects: French-Canadian and Catholic institutions in the Sudbury area, Manitoulin Island, Indians, Jesuit missionaries in Northern Ontario, Ste. Anne parish, St. Ignace/Sault Ste. Marie parish, French education in Ontario, Manitoulin Ojibway missions, Detroit and Windsor 18th century missions among the French and Hurons, Thunder Bay missions. **Special Collections:** Societe historique du Nouvel-Ontario (85 volumes); College du Sacre-Coeur Archives; papers of Romanet, Racette, and Hurtubise (10 boxes each). **Holdings:** 350 books; 200 bound periodical volumes; 150 pamphlets; 18 cassettes; 60 maps; 300 photographic portraits; 60 photograph albums; 450 boxes of archival material. **Remarks:** Most of the holdings are in French.

★3661★
University of Sudbury
Library
Sudbury, ON, Canada P3E 2C6   Ph: (705)673-5661
Olga Beaulieu, Dir. of Lib.   Fax: (705)673-4912

Subjects: Religion, philosophy, Native studies, folklore. **Holdings:** 40,000 books; 4600 bound periodical volumes. **Also Known As:** Universite de Sudbury.

★3662★
Winnipeg Art Gallery
Clara Lander Library
300 Memorial Blvd.   Ph: (204)786-6641
Winnipeg, MB, Canada R3C 1V1   Fax: (204)788-4998

Subjects: History of art and painting, drawing, sculpture, ceramics, prints, architecture, antiques and photography. **Special Collections:** Canadiana; Inuit art. **Holdings:** 22,000 books; 720 bound periodical volumes; 8500 exhibition catalogs; 844 reports; 800 vertical files; 7000 folders of biographies of artists; 136 binders of archives.

Museum Collections

--- Alberta ---

★3663★
Medicine Hat Museum and Art Gallery
1302 Montfort Cir. SW
Medicine Hat, AB, Canada T1A 5E6   Ph: (403)527-6266
Description: Collections include Indian artifacts.

British Columbia

★3664★
Alert Bay Library/Museum
199 Fir St.
Alert Bay, BC, Canada B0N 1A0   Ph: (604)974-5721
Description: Contains Kwakiutl and local history artifacts.

★3665★
Campbell River Museum and Archives
1235 Island Hwy.
Campbell Island, BC, Canada V9W 2C7   Ph: (604)287-3103
Description: Displays artifacts crafted by Indians of Northern Vancouver Island, principally Kwakiutl, Nuu-cha-nulth, and Salishan.

★3666★
'Ksan Indian Village
Box 326
Hazelton, BC, Canada B0J 1Y0   Ph: (604)842-5544
Description: A Gitksan Indian village consisting of seven tribal houses.

★3667★
Kwagiulth Museum and Cultural Centre
Box 8
Quathiaski Cove, BC, Canada V0P 1N0   Ph: (604)285-3733
Description: Displays items used in potlatch, a ceremonial feast of the Indians of the Northwest. The collection includes masks, rattles, whistles, head and neck rings, and various other headgear, and photographs of traditional Kwakiutl villages at the turn of the century.

★3668★
Museum of Northern British Columbia
PO Box 669
Prince Rupert, BC, Canada B8J 3S1   Ph: (604)624-3207
Description: Contains objects from the Northwest coast Indian culture. Reconstructed models, maps, graphic displays, and an ethnological collection explain pioneer history and the lifestyles of the coastal Indian groups from prehistoric times through their first contact with explorers. A modern Indian carving shed is on the museum grounds.

★3669★
U'Mista Cultural Centre
Box 253
Alert Bay, BC, Canada B0N 1A0   Ph: (604)974-5403
Description: Displays a collection of masks, cedar baskets, copper items, and other artifacts from Indian Potlatches.

Manitoba

★3670★
Eskimo Museum
La Verendrye St.
Box 10
Churchill, MB, Canada R0B 0E0   Ph: (204)675-2030
Description: Displays artifacts and exhibits featuring contemporary and historic eskimo culture. Kayaks from the pre-Dorset period dating back to 2000 B.C., a collection of Cree and Chipewyah Indian art, and Eskimo carvings are also displayed.

Northwest Territories

★3671★
Northern Life Museum
110 King St.
Box 420
Fort Smith, NT, Canada X0E 0P0   Ph: (403)872-2859
Description: Collections include Indian artifacts, and Inuit tools and artifacts.

★3672★
Nunatta Sunaqutangit
Box 605
Iqaluit, NT, Canada S0A 0H0
Description: Exhibits include a collection of Inuit sculpture and displays of local artifacts.

Ontario

★3673★
Art Gallery of Windsor
445 Riverside Dr. W.
Windsor, ON, Canada N9A 6T8   Ph: (519)258-7111
Description: Maintains an Inuit gallery which includes carvings.

★3674★
Canadian Museum of Civilization
100 Laurier St.
Ottawa, ON, Canada J8X 4H2   Ph: (819)776-7000
Description: Exhibits illustrate Canada's history, prehistory, periods of migration, and native settlement.

★3675★
Huron Indian Village
Box 638
Midland, ON, Canada L4R 4P4   Ph: (705)526-2844
Description: A reconstructed village that interprets 16th-century life of the Huron Indians of the region.

★3676★
Museum of Indian Archaeology and Lawson
   Prehistoric Village
Lawson-Jury Bldg.
1600 Attawandaron Rd.
London, ON, Canada N6G 3M6   Ph: (519)473-1360
Description: Depicts 11,000 years of Indian habitation in southwestern Ontario. Includes an excavation site and exhibits arranged according to five periods of development.

★3677★
North American Indian Travel College
The Living Museum
RR 3
Cornwall Island, ON, Canada K6H 5R7   Ph: (613)932-9452
Description: A re-created village consisting of traditional buildings of the Cree, Ojibway, and Iroquois tribes. Depicts Indian lifestyles typical of the early 18th-century; museum contains cultural artifacts.

★3678★
Ska-Nah-Doht Indian Village
Longwoods Rd. Conservation Area
Hwy. 2
London, ON, Canada N0L 1W0   Ph: (519)264-2420
Description: A re-created village depicting the Iroquois culture in southwestern Ontario about the year 1000. Offers a slide show and displays devoted to conservation and Indian artifacts.

★3679★
Thunder Bay Art Gallery
1080 Keewatin St.
PO Box 1193
Thunder Bay, ON, Canada P7C 4X9   Ph: (807)577-6427
Description: Collections include Indian artifacts, and contemoprary Indian art.

★3680★
The Turtle: Native American Center for the Living Arts
25 Rainbow Blvd.
Niagra Falls, ON, Canada
Description: Collections focus on American Indian heritage, culture, symbols, and art.

★3681★
Woodland Indian Cultural Education Centre
184 Mohawk St.
PO Box 1506
Brantford, ON, Canada N3T 5V6   Ph: (519)759-2650
Description: Exhibits include artifacts, art, clothing, and the Indian Hall of Fame, which commemorates the contributions of 21 individuals.

─────────── **Quebec** ───────────

★3682★
Abenakis Museum
Rte. 226
Odanak, PQ, Canada J0G 1H0   Ph: (514)568-2600
Description: Displays relate the history of the Abenaki tribe of Odanak.

★3683★
Amerindien and Inuit Museum of Godbout
134 Rd. Pascal-Comeau
Godbout, PQ, Canada G0H 1G0   Ph: (418)568-7724
Description: Collections include recent Indian and Inuit sculpture and artifacts exhibited in connection with small pottery. Visitors can observe native artists at work.

─────────── **Saskatchewan** ───────────

★3684★
Allen Sapp Gallery
100th St.
North Battleford, SK, Canada S9A 2Y1   Ph: (306)445-3304
Description: Allen Sapp, a nationally known Cree artist, depicts the culture of his people and the day to day events of life on the Red Pheasant Reserve.

★3685★
Regina Plains Museum
1801 Scarth St.
Regina, SK, Canada S4P 2G9   Ph: (306)352-0844
Description: Collections include exhibits on the Plains Indian culture, the Metis pilgrimage, and the Riel rebellion.

Research Centers

★3686★
Igloolik Research Centre
Science Institute of the Northwest Territories
PO Box 210
Igloolik, NT, Canada X0A 0L0   Ph: (819)934-8836
John MacDonald, Coord.
Research Activities and Fields: Inuit culture and linguistics. Assists government, university, and industrial scientists' research in a wide variety of disciplines related to northern science. Provides complete laboratory facilities and acts as a base from which scientific field parties can be mounted and supported. **Formerly:** Eastern Arctic Scientific Resource Centre.

★3687★
McGill University
McGill Subarctic Research Station
PO Box 790
Schefferville, PQ, Canada G0G 2T0   Ph: (418)585-2489
Dr. T. Moore, Scientific Dir.
Research Activities and Fields: Subarctic environment, including studies on snow, ice, permafrost, hydrology, caribou ecology, entomology, geology, Naskapi land use and hunting, peatlands, phytosociology, phenology, subarctic vegetation, snowcover, snowmelt, geomorphology, periglacial processes, meteorology, climatology, biological productivity, limnology, soils, stringbog and muskeg, plant ecology, acid rain, demography, social sciences, and Canadian Indians. **Publications:** *McGill Subarctic Research Papers* (one to two per year). **Formerly:** McGill Subarctic Research Laboratory (1977).

★3688★
Memorial University of Newfoundland
Archaeology Unit
Elizabeth Ave.
Saint John's, NF, Canada A1C 5S7   Ph: (709)737-8869
J.A. Tuck, Dir.
Research Activities and Fields: Archeology, with emphasis on the sixteenth century whaling communities in Labrador, sixteenth and seventeenth century English colonies in Newfoundland, prehistoric Eskimo and Indian occupations of Newfoundland and Labrador, and ethnoarcheological studies in Mexico. Also studies the prehistory of the Maritime Provinces and occasionally undertakes international expeditions, including sites in Sri Lanka. **Publications:** *Reports in Archeology.*

★3689★
Museum of Indian Archaeology
Lawson-Jury Bldg.
1600 Attawandaron Rd.
London, ON, Canada N6G 3M6   Ph: (519)473-1360
Dr. William D. Finlayson, Dir. General
Research Activities and Fields: Prehistoric and historic archeology of Southwestern Ontario, including excavation, restoration, and interpretation of a prehistoric Neutral village. Develops a system of computer programs to process archeological materials. **Publications:** *Museum Notes; Bulletins* (occasionally); *Research Reports; Newsletter* (quarterly). **Formerly:** Museum of Indian Archaeology and Pioneer Life (1978).

★3690★
University of Western Ontario
Centre for Research and Teaching of Canadian Native Languages
Dept. of Anthropology
London, ON, Canada N6A 5C2   Ph: (519)661-3430
Prof. Margaret E. Seguin, Dir.
Research Activities and Fields: Canadian native languages, languages of Ontario, and government policy on native languages. **Publications:** Monograph Series.

Education Programs & Services

Community Colleges

★3691★
Red Crow Community College
PO Box 1258
Cardston, AB, Canada T0K 0K0
Ph: (403)737-3966
Fax: (403)737-2361
Marie Smallface Marule, Pres.

★3692★
Saskatchewan Indian Federated College
University of Regina
Rm. 118, College West
Regina, SK, Canada S4S 0A2
Ph: (306)779-6209
Fax: (306)584-0955
Dr. Eber Hampton, Pres.

Studies Programs

Four-Year Programs

★3693★
Brandon University
Native Studies Program
Brandon, MB, Canada R7A 6A9
Ph: (204)727-9640
Free: 800-852-2704

Faye Douglas, Dir. of Adm.

★3694★
Laurentian University
Native Studies Program
Sudbury, ON, Canada P3E 2C6
Ph: (705)675-1151
Free: 800-461-4030

Matthew Brennan, Asst. Registrar

★3695★
St. Thomas University
Native Studies Program
Fredericton, NB, Canada E3B 5G3
Ph: (506)452-7700
Fr. John Jennings, Asst. Registrar

★3696★
University of Lethbridge
Native Studies Program
Lethbridge, AB, Canada T1K 3M4
Ph: (403)329-2758
Marilyn Withage, Dir. of Adm. & Recruitment

★3697★
University of Regina
Native Studies Program
Regina, SK, Canada S4S 0A2
Ph: (306)585-4591
Donna Schwandt, Asst. Registrar/Admissions & Awards

★3698★
University of Saskatchewan
Native Studies Program
Saskatoon, SK, Canada S7N 0W0
Ph: (306)966-6718
E.B. Farnham, Dir. of Adm.

★3699★
University of Toronto
Native Studies Program
Toronto, ON, Canada M5S 1A1
Ph: (416)978-6125
Beverly Nicholson, Exec. Asst. to the Dir. of Adm.

Graduate Programs

★3700★
Trent University
Native Studies Program
Peterborough, ON, Canada K9J 7B8
Ph: (705)748-1215
Alan P Saxby, Registrar/Dir. of Adm

★3701★
University of Regina
Interdisciplinary Studies Program
Regina, SK, Canada S4S 0A2
Ph: (306)585-4161
Dr. D.M. Secoy, Assoc. Dean
Remarks: Program includes Indian Studies.

Scholarships, Fellowships, & Loans

★3702★
Petro-Canada Education Awards for Native Students
Petro-Canada Inc.
PO Box 2844
Calgary, AB, Canada T2P 3E3

Study Level: Undergraduate. **Award Type:** Award. **Applicant Eligibility:** Candidates must be of Canadian or Inuit ancestry who are pursuing studies in disciplines applicable to the oil and gas industry. **Funds Available:** A number of awards valued up to $5,000 are available. **Contact:** Native Development Advisor.

Print & Broadcast Media

Directories

★3703★
Arrowfax National Aboriginal Directory
Arrowfax Inc.
202-286 Smith St.
Winnipeg, MB, Canada R3C 1K5
Ph: (204)942-3533

Covers: 12,000 Canadian Aboriginal communities, professional services, and social and professional organizations. **Entries Include:** Name, address, phone, fax. **Pages (approx.):** 400. **Frequency:** Annual; updated quarterly. **Price:** $20 (Canadian).

★3704★
Bead Forum Archeology
Society of Bead Researchers
Canadian Parks Service
1600 Liverpool Ct.
Ottawa, ON, Canada K1A 0H3
Ph: (613)990-4814

Frequency: Semiannual. **Price:** $15.00 per year.

★3705★
Native American Directory: Alaska, Canada, United States
National Native American Cooperative
Box 1000
San Carlos, AZ 85550-1000
Ph: (602)622-4900

Covers: Native American performing arts groups, craft materials suppliers, stores and galleries, Indian-owned motels and resorts; tribal offices, museums, and cultural centers; associations, schools; newspapers, radio and television programs and stations operated, owned, or specifically for Native Americans; calendar of events, including officially sanctioned powwows, conventions, arts and crafts shows, all-Indian rodeos, and Navajo rug auctions. **Entries Include:** Generally, organization or company name, address, descriptive comments, dates (for shows or events). **Pages**

(approx.): 335. **Frequency:** Irregular; previous edition 1982; latest edition March 1992. **Price:** $44.95, plus $3.00 shipping.

——————— **Journals & Magazines** ———————

★3706★
Canadian Journal of Native Education
University of Alberta
Department of Educational Foundation
5-109 Education N.
Edmonton, AB, Canada T6G 2G5
Ph: (403)492-2769
Fax: (403)492-0762
First Published: 1973. **Frequency:** 2/yr. **Formerly:** *Indian Ed.*

★3707★
Canadian Native Law Reporter
University of Saskatcehwan
Native Law Centre
Diefenbaker Centre
Saskatoon, SK, Canada 27N OWO
Ph: (306)966-6189
Fax: (306)966-8517
First Published: 1977. **Frequency:** Quarterly. **ISSN:** 0225-2279.

★3708★
Dannzha
Ye Sato Communications Society
22 Nisutlin Dr.
Whitehorse, YT, Canada Y1A 3S5
Ph: (403)667-2775
Description: Magazine covering Yukon Indian interests and issues. **First Published:** 1973. **Frequency:** 6x/yr. **Subscription:** $11.10 Yukon; $15 out of province; $20 other countries. **ISSN:** 0883-3837.

★3709★
Indian Life
Intertribal Christian Communications
PO Box 3765, Sta. B
Winnipeg, MB, Canada R2W 3R6
Ph: (204)661-9333
Description: A non-denominational Christian magazine addressing the social, cultural, and spiritual needs of North American Indians. **First Published:** November 1979. **Frequency:** 6x/yr. **Subscription:** $7. **ISSN:** 0226-9317.

★3710★
Saskatchewan Indian Federated College Journal
Saskatchewan Indian Federated College
University of Regina
127 College W.
Regina, SK, Canada S4S 0A2
Ph: (306)779-6235
Fax: (306)584-0955
Description: Reports on issues of interest to professionals involved with Native Americans. Also available in Cree and Ojibway. **Frequency:** Semiannual.

——————— **Newsletters** ———————

★3711★
Alliance Autochtone du Quebec
Native Alliance of Quebec
21 Brodeur
Hull, PQ, Canada J8X 2P6
Ph: (819)770-7763
Fax: (819)770-6070

★3712★
Mal-I-Mic-News
New Brunswick Aboriginal Peoples Council
320 St. Mary's St.
Fredericton, NB, Canada E3A 2S4
Ph: (506)458-8422
Description: Provides off reserve aboriginal people with information on functions, workshops, and job opportunities at the Council. Also provides articles on land claims, education as well as human interest stories. **First Published:** 1972. **Frequency:** Monthly. **Price:** Included in membership; $12/yr. for nonmembers.

★3713★
Native Issues
Native Peoples Support Group of
  Newfoundland and Labrador
Box 961, Sta. C
Saint John's, NF, Canada A1C 5M3
First Published: 1979. **Frequency:** Irregular. **Former Title(s):** *Indian and Inuit Supporter.*

★3714★
Native Voice
Native Brotherhood of British Columbia
1755 E. Hasting St., No. 200
Vancouver, BC, Canada V5L 1T1
Ph: (604)255-3137
Fax: (604)255-0955
Frequency: Bimonthly. **ISSN:** 0028-0542.

★3715★
The Pailsade Post
Museum of Indian Archaeology
1600 Attawandaron Rd.
London, ON, Canada N6G 3M6
Ph: (519)473-1360
Fax: (519)473-1363
Description: Focuses on archaeological findings and the Museum's exhibits, activities, and special events. **First Published:** 1979. **Price:** Included in membership; $10/yr. for nonmembers, Canada. **ISSN:** 0826-9971. **Former Title(s):** *Museum of Indian Archaeology–Newsletter*, December 1984.

★3716★
The Phoenix
Canadian Alliance in Solidarity With the
  Native People
PO Box 574, Sta. P
Toronto, ON, Canada M5R 2S7
Ph: (416)972-1573
Description: Covers native issues, history, and culture. Promotes cultural education. **First Published:** 1978. **Frequency:** Quarterly. **Price:** Included in membership.

★3717★
Sagitawa Friendship Centre—Newsletter
Sagitawa Frienship Centre
10108-100 Ave.
PO Box 5083
Peace River, AB, Canada T8S 1R7
Ph: (403)624-2443
Fax: (403)624-2728
Description: Presents news of the Centre, which is a focal point of activities and information pertaining to Native Canadians. **Frequency:** Quarterly. **Price:** Included in membership; $2/yr. for nonmembers, Canada.

★3718★
Unity
Association of Iroquois and Allied Indians
R.R. 2
Southwold, ON, Canada N0L 2G0
Frequency: Quarterly. **Former Title(s):** *Strength in Unity.*

——————— **Newspapers** ———————

★3719★
Micmac News
Native Communication Society of Nova
  Scotia
PO Box 344
Sydney, NS, Canada B1P 6H2
Ph: (902)539-0045
Description: Newspaper providing provincial coverage. **First Published:** 1969. **Frequency:** Monthly. **Subscription:** $20; $25 outside Canada.

★3720★
New Breed
Saskatchewan Native Communications
   Corp.
173-2nd Ave., S., Ste. 202
Saskatoon, SK, Canada S7K 1K6   Ph: (306)653-2253
Description: Newspaper (tabloid) for Metis and non-status Indians of Saskatchewan (English and Cree). **First Published:** 1969. **Frequency:** Monthly. **Subscription:** $24.

★3721★
Nunatsiaq News
Nunatext Publishing Corp.
Box 8
Iqaluit, NT, Canada X0A 0H0   Ph: (819)979-5357
Description: Community newspaper (English and Inuktitut). **First Published:** 1972. **Frequency:** Weekly (Fri.). **Subscription:** $25; $75 first class. **ISSN:** 0702-7915

★3722★
Windspeaker
15001 112th Ave.   Ph: (403)455-2700
Edmonton, AB, Canada Y6M 2V6   Fax: (403)452-1428
Frequency: Biweekly.

Radio Stations

★3723★
CFWE-FM
PO Box 2250   Ph: (403)623-3333
Lac La Biche, AB, Canada T0A 2C0   Fax: (403)623-3302
Frequency: 89.9. **Format:** Country. Produces the "Native Perspective" program. **Owner:** Aboriginal Multi-Media Society of Alberta; 15001 112th Ave., Edmonton, AB, Canada, T5M 2Y0.

★3724★
CHON-FM
4228 4th Ave.   Ph: (403)668-6629
Whitehorse, YT, Canada Y1A 1K1   Fax: (403)668-6612
Frequency: 98.1. **Format:** Country; Adult Contemporary; Rock. **Owner:** Northern Native Broadcasting, Yukon.

★3725★
CKNM-FM
4910-49th St.
PO Box 1919
Yellowknife, NT, Canada X1A 2P4   Ph: (403)920-2277
Frequency: 101.9. **Format:** Talk; Ethnic (Native Language); News; Country; Contemporary Country. **Owner:** Native Communication Society.

★3726★
CKQN-FM
Baker Lake, NT, Canada X0C 0A0   Ph: (819)793-2962
Frequency: 99.3. **Network Affiliation:** Canadian Broadcasting Corporation (CBC)/Societe Radio-Canada (SRC). **Format:** Ethnic (Eskimo, Inuit). **Owner:** Qamani'tuap Naalautaa Society.

★3727★
WRN-FM
16 5th Ave.
PO Box 1180   Ph: (807)737-2951
Sioux Lookout, ON, Canada P0V 2T0   Fax: (807)737-3224
Frequency: 89.1. **Format:** News. **Owner:** Wawatay Native Communications Society.

Publishers

★3728★
Bill Hanson Consulting
310 Garrison Crescent
Saskatoon, SK, Canada S7H 2Z8   Ph: (306)374-0288
Description: Publishes a handbook on programming for aboriginal people. Reaches market through direct mail and telephone sales. Annual Sales: $5000. **Number of New Titles:** 1989 - 1; Total Titles in Print - 1. **Selected Titles:** *Dual Realities-Dual Strategies* by Bill Hanson. **Principal Officials and Managers:** Bill Hanson, Manager and Publisher.

★3729★
Council for Yukon Indians
22 Nisutlin Dr.
Whitehorse, YT, Canada Y1A 3S5   Ph: (403)667-7631
Description: Negotiates with the Government of Canada and plans for the implementation, in the Yukon Territory, of a Land Claims Settlement that reflects the needs and aspirations of those Indian people with aboriginal rights in the Yukon Territory. Reaches market through public meetings. **Subjects:** The Yukon Indian people, their culture, language, their land. **Selected Titles:** *Together Today for Our Children Tomorrow* by the Yukon Indian People; *My Stories Are My Wealth* by Angela Sidney, Kitty Smith, and Rachel Dawson; *Stories from Fort Selkirk as Told by Our Elders* by Pearl Silas and Betty Joe; *How to Tan Hides in the Native Way* by Gertie Tom. **Principal Officials and Managers:** Judy Gingell, Chairor; Rose-Marie Blair-Smith, Dayle MacDonald, Vice-Chairors.

★3730★
Gabriel Dumont Institute of Native Studies and
   Applied Research
121 Broadway Ave., E.
Regina, SK, Canada S4N 0Z6   Ph: (306)522-5691
Description: Publishes on the native history and culture of Saskatchewan. Offers video and audio cassettes and the periodical, *Journal of Indigenous Studies*. Reaches market through direct mail. **Number of New Titles:** 1992 (est.) - 3; Total Titles in Print - 21. **Selected Titles:** *Metis Development and the Canadian West, Flags of the Metis*, both by Calvin Racette; *Home from the Hill, 1885: Metis Rebellion or Government Conspiracy*, both by Don McLean; *A Metis Wedding* by Christal Barber; *The Flower Beadwork People* by Sherry Farrell-Racette. **Principal Officials and Managers:** Christopher LaFontaine, Executive Director; Max Morin, Chairor; Noble Shanks, Vice-Chairor.

★3731★
Good Medicine Books (GMB)
PO Box 844
Skookumchuck, BC, Canada V0B 2E0   Ph: (212)685-8848
Description: Publishes on Native American culture, history, and natural lifestyles; also publishes on railroad and western history. Offers videotapes, audio cassettes, and cards and calendars on the Canadian railways. Reaches market through direct mail and reviews. **Number of New Titles:** 1989 - 4, 1990 - 3; Total Titles in Print - 10. **Selected Titles:** *Traditional Dress, Canadian Railway Scenes. Nos. 1-3, Teachings of Nature*, all by Adolf Hungry Wolf; *Canadian Railway Stories* by Okam Hungry Wolf; *Indian Tribes of the Northern Rockies, Blackfoot Craftworker's Handbook*, both by Adolf and Beverly Hungry Wolf. **Principal Officials and Managers:** Beverly Hungry Wolf, Publisher.

★3732★
Iroqrafts Ltd.
RR 2, Ohsweken
Six Nations Reserve, ON, Canada N0A 1M0 Ph: (416)765-4206

Description: Publishes titles of importance in the history and culture of the Iroquois peoples and of other North American Indians. Reaches market through direct mail. **Number of New Titles:** 1990 - 1; Total Titles in Print - 19. **Selected Titles:** *The Code of Handsome Lake the Seneca Prophet* by A. C. Parker; *Costume of the Iroquois* by R. Gabor; *Iroquois Crafts* by A. Lyford; *Wampum Belts* by R.

Fadden; *Iroquois Women: An Anthology* edited by W. G. Spittal; *Scalping and Torture: Warfare Practices among North American Indians.* **Principal Officials and Managers:** W. G. Spittal, President and Manager.

★3733★
Metis Association of the Northwest Territories
PO Box 1375
Yellowknife, NT, Canada X1A 2P1   Ph: (403)873-3505
Description: Publishes on the history and culture of the northern Metis. Offers a newsletter. **Selected Titles:** *Our Metis Heritage* edited by Joanne Overvold. **Principal Officials and Managers:** Gary Bohnet, President; Joyce Pittman, Executive Director; Gordon Lennie, David Krutko, Vice-Presidents.

★3734★
Namaka Community Historical Committee
RR 1
Strathmore, AB, Canada T0S 3H0   Ph: (403)934-4515
Description: Publishes Indian community history to help outsiders understand the native people and their customs. Presently inactive. **Subjects:** Family history, Blackfoot history. **Total Titles in Print:** 1. **Selected Titles:** *Trails to Little Corner.* **Principal Officials and Managers:** Marguerite Watson, Editor; Ann Scheer, Assistant Editor; Ed Theissen, Finance Manager.

★3735★
North American Indian Traveling College
RR 3
Cornwall Island, ON, Canada K6H 5R7   Ph: (613)932-9452
Description: Publishes on the culture and history of Native Americans. Reaches market through direct mail. **Selected Titles:** *Contributions Coloring Book; Splint Basketry; Legends of Our Nations; Traditional Teachings; Mohawk Coloring Book; Coloring Book of Our Nations.*

★3736★
Ojibway-Cree Cultural Centre
84 Elm St. S.
Timmins, ON, Canada P4N 1W6   Ph: (705)267-7911
Description: Involved in developing native-oriented materials including videotapes for elementary classroom use. Concerned both with the historical as well as the contemporary aspect of Canada's native peoples. Offers cassette tapes, posters, a coloring book, and teacher's manuals. Reaches market through direct mail. **Number of New Titles:** 1989 - 1; Total Titles in Print - 3. **Selected Titles:** *The Metis, The Seasons,* both by B. Karp; *Let's Sing Hymns; Nisnawbe-Aski Nation History Workbook and Teacher's Guide; What Do You Have in Your Canoe Teacher's Manual; What Do You Have in Your Canoe* (cassette). **Principal Officials and Managers:** Esther Wesley, Executive Director; Diane Cyr, Bookkeeper.

★3737★
Pemmican Publications Inc.
412 McGregor St.
Winnipeg, MB, Canada R2W 4X5   Ph: (204)589-4351
Description: Specializes in work about, by, and for Metis people, including history, social studies, fiction, short stories, etc. Accepts unsolicited manuscripts. Reaches market through commission representatives, direct mail, and trade sales. **Number of New Titles:** 1989 - 5, 1990 - 6, 1991 (est.) - 10; Total Titles in Print - 48. **Selected Titles:** *Eagle Feather* by Ferguson Plain; *In Search of April Raintree* by Beatrice Culleton; *Brothers in Arms* by Jordan Wheeler; *Honour the Sun* by Ruby Slipperjack; *Where the Rivers Meet* by Don Sawyer; *Our Bit of Truth* edited by Agnes Grant. **Principal Officials and Managers:** Sue MacLean, Administrator; Stan Manoakeesick, Promotion and Marketing; Virginia Maracle, Managing Editor.

★3738★
Secwepemc Cultural Education Society
345 Yellowhead Hwy.
Kamloops, BC, Canada V2H 1H1   Ph: (604)374-0616
Description: Publishes books either written by or about Shuswap people. Offers social studies curriculum, oral histories, supplementary teaching resources, children stories, Shuswap language materials, and periodicals. Also offers slides, a newspaper,

maps, games, teaching kits, calendars, posters, art prints, cassette tapes, and cards. Reaches market through direct mail, telephone sales, and trade sales. **Subjects:** Native Indians. **Total Titles in Print:** 19. **Selected Titles:** *Donna Meets Coyote Student Book, Donna Meets Coyote Teacher Guide,* both by Don Sawyer; *We Are the Shuswap Student Book* by Heather Smith Siska; *We Are the Shuswap Teacher Guide* by Vicki Mulligan; *Shuswap Cultural Series* (7 booklets) by Marie Matthew and Mable Caron. **Principal Officials and Managers:** Ron Ignace, President; Terry Morgan, Vice-President; Muriel Sasakamoose, Executive Director; Lorraine Lebourdais, Secretary-Treasurer; Dodie Manuel, Publications and Curriculum Coordinator.

★3739★
Skelep Publishing
345 Yellowhead Hwy.
Kamloops, BC, Canada V2H 1H1   Ph: (604)374-0616
Description: Publishes materials to preserve and record Shuswap language, history, and culture. Offers cassette tapes, slides, and video cassettes. Accepts unsolicited manuscripts on the Shuswap culture. Reaches market through direct mail and trade sales. **Total Titles in Print:** 2. **Selected Titles:** *Donna Meets Coyote* by Don Sawyer; *We Are the Shuswap* by Heather Smith Siska; *Shuswap Cultural Series; Shuswap Language Series.* **Principal Officials and Managers:** Clarence Jule T., President; Ron Ignace, Vice-President; Terry Morgan, Treasurer.

★3740★
Theytus Books Ltd.
PO Box 218
Penticton, BC, Canada V2A 6K3   Ph: (604)493-7181
Description: Publishes native Indian and curriculum development materials, especially locally developed material. Accepts unsolicited manuscripts; include a self-addressed, stamped envelope. Reaches market through commission representatives, direct mail, trade sales, Raincoast Book Distribution Ltd., and John Coutts Library Services. **Number of New Titles:** 1989 - 2, 1990 - 2, 1991 (est.) - 5; Total Titles in Print - 35. **Selected Titles:** *Okanagan Sources* edited by Jean Webber; *Slash* by Jeannette Armstrong; *Renewal Book I & II* by Barbara Smith; *Forgotten Soldiers* by Fred Gaffen; *Major John Richardson* (short stories) edited by David Beasley; *Seventh Generation: Contemporary Native Writing* edited by Heather Hodgson. **Principal Officials and Managers:** Greg Young-Ing, Manager.

★3741★
Thunder Bay Art Gallery
PO Box 1193
Thunder Bay, ON, Canada P7C 4X9   Ph: (807)577-6427
Description: A public art gallery specializing in contemporary Indian art. Publications consist of catalogs produced for exhibitions. Offers *Imprint,* a quarterly newsletter. Reaches market through direct mail and trade sales. **Number of New Titles:** 1989 - 4, 1990 - 5, 1991 (est.) - 4; Total Titles in Print - 36. **Selected Titles:** *Altered Egos: The Multimedia Work of Carl Beam* by Elizabeth McLuhan and Roz Vanderburg; *Woodlands: Contemporary Art of the Anishabe, Markle: The Painter and His Models,* both by Carol Podedworny; *From Periphery to Centre: The Art of Susan and Krista Point* by Joanne P. Danford; *Frances Anne Hopkins* by Janet Clark and Robert Stacey; *Stardusters: New Works by Jane Ash Poitras, Pierre Sioui, Joane Cardinal-Schubert, Ed Poitras* by Gary Mainprize. **Principal Officials and Managers:** Sharon Godwin, Director; Janet Clark, Curator; Christopher Morden, President, Board of Directors; Gail Fikis, Registrar.

★3742★
University of New Brunswick
Micmac-Maliseet Institute
Fredericton, NB, Canada E3B 6E3   Ph: (506)453-4840
Description: Publishes Indian studies and local history. Reaches market through direct mail and reviews. **Number of New Titles:** 1989 - 2, 1990 - 1; Total Titles in Print - 12. **Selected Titles:** *The Julian Tribe, Miramichi Papers,* both by W. D. Hamilton; *Memories of a Micmac Life* by J. Richard McEwan; *The Wampum Records* by Robert M. Leavitt and David A. Francis. **Principal Officials and Managers:** W. D. Hamilton, Director.

★3743★
University of Saskatchewan
Native Law Centre
141 Diefenbaker Centre
Saskatoon, SK, Canada S7N 0W0　　Ph: (306)966-6189
Description: Undertakes and supports independent research into legal problems and topics affecting native people. The Centre publishes one quarterly legal periodical, and publishes a series of books, papers, and research reports. Reaches market through direct mail. **Number of New Titles:** 1989 - 2, 1990 - 3, 1991 (est.) - 3; Total Titles in Print - 35. **Selected Titles:** *Aboriginal Peoples and Section 25 of the Canadian Charter of Rights and Freedoms* by Bruce H. Wildsmith; *In the Best Interest of the Metis Child* by Clem Chartier; *The Taking of Indian Lands in Canada: Consent or Coercion* by Darlene Johnston; *Indian Reserves and Aboriginal Lands in Canada: A Homeland* by Richard H. Bartlett; *Manitoba's Metis Settlement Scheme of 1870* by Paul L.A.H. Chartrand. **Principal Officials and Managers:** Donald J. Purich, Director; Zandra MacEachern, Editor and Publications Manager; Ruth Thompson, Professional Researcher.

★3744★
X-Press
3905 W. 12th Ave.
Vancouver, BC, Canada V6R 2P1　　Ph: (604)224-0886
Subjects: Inuit (Eskimo) games. **Selected Titles:** *Inuit Eskimo Games, Bks. 1-3*, all by F. H. Eger. **Principal Officials and Managers:** F. H. Eger, Editor.

Videos

★3745★
....And The Word Was God
Video Out
1102 Homer St.
Vancouver, BC, Canada V6B 2X6　　Ph: (604)688-4336
Description: A poetic narrative video focusing on the Cree-speaking natives of northern Saskatchewan. **Release Date:** 1987. **Length:** 28 mins. **Format:** Beta, VHS, 3/4″ U-matic Cassette.

★3746★
Augusta
Phoenix/BFA Films
468 Park Ave., S.　　　　　　　Ph: (212)684-5910
New York, NY 10016　　　　　　Free: 800-221-1274
Description: A portrait of an 88-year-old woman, born a daughter of a Shuswap chief in Canada. She lives today in Cariboo country of British Columbia without running water or electricity. Augusta lost her status as an Indian in 1903, when she married a white man. **Release Date:** 1978. **Length:** 17 mins. **Format:** Beta, VHS, 3/4″ U-matic Cassette.

★3747★
The Ballad of Crowfoot
CRM/McGraw-Hill Films
674 Via de la Valle
PO Box 641
Del Mar, CA 92014
Description: This program is a graphic history of the Canadian West, filmed by Indians who wanted to reflect the traditions, attitudes, and problems of their own people. **Release Date:** 1972. **Length:** 10 mins. **Format:** Beta, VHS, 3/4″ U-matic Cassette.

★3748★
Beavertail Snowshoes
Trust for Native American Cultures &
　Crafts
PO Box 142
Greenville, NH 0348　　　　　　Ph: (603)878-2944
Description: A look at the construction of beavertail snowshoes by the Eastern Cree Indians of Mistassini Lake, Quebec. **Release Date:** 1990. **Length:** 40 mins. **Format:** Beta, VHS, 3/4″ U-matic Cassette.

★3749★
Building an Algonquin Birchbark Canoe
Trust for Native American Cultures &
　Crafts
PO Box 142
Greenville, NH 0348　　　　　　Ph: (603)878-2944
Description: The endangered art of canoe building is demonstrated by a pair of elderly Algonquin Indians in Maniwaki, Quebec. **Release Date:** 1990. **Length:** 54 mins. **Format:** Beta, VHS, 3/4″ U-matic Cassette.

★3750★
Canada's Original Peoples: Then and Now
Native American Public Broadcasting
　Consortium
PO Box 86111
1800 N. 33rd St.
Lincoln, NE 68501　　　　　　　Ph: (402)472-3522
Description: A tour of the Indian artifacts in the Royal Ontario Museum and the history they indicate. **Release Date:** 1977. **Length:** 20 mins. **Format:** VHS, 3/4″ U-matic Cassette, 1″ Broadcast Type ″C″, 2″ Quadraplex Open Reel.

★3751★
Circle of the Sun
National Film Board of Canada
1251 Avenue of the Americas, 16th Fl.
New York, NY 10020-1173　　　Ph: (212)586-5131
Description: The Spectacle of the Sun Dance is demonstrated by the Blood Indians of Alberta, as the young generation breaks ties with their people to fit into the changing society. **Release Date:** 1960. **Length:** 29 mins. **Format:** Beta, VHS, 3/4″ U-matic Cassette.

★3752★
Completing Our Circle
CRM/McGraw-Hill Films
674 Via de la Valle
PO Box 641
Del Mar, CA 92014
Description: The traditions of the Plains and West Coast Indians, the Inuit, and the first Europeans and settlers in Western Canada are shown in this program. Their art and craftsmanship are presented as a way to express both individual identity and oneness with other men. **Release Date:** 1978. **Length:** 27 mins. **Format:** Beta, VHS, 3/4″ U-matic Cassette.

★3753★
Concerned Aboriginal Women
Video Out
1102 Homer St.
Vancouver, BC, Canada V6B 2X6　　Ph: (604)688-4336
Description: A moving documentary about the occupation by native women of the federal Indian and Northern Affairs office in Vancouver, British Columbia. **Release Date:** 1981. **Length:** 60 mins. **Format:** Beta, VHS, 3/4″ U-matic Cassette.

★3754★
Cree Hunters of Mistassini
National Film Board of Canada
1251 Avenue of the Americas, 16th Fl.
New York, NY 10020-1173　　　Ph: (212)586-5131
Description: The Cree Indians of northern Quebec live with the land in a way that reflects not only a set of ecological principles and religious beliefs, but an entire way of life that they are afraid of losing. **Release Date:** 1974. **Length:** 58 mins. **Format:** Beta, VHS, 3/4″ U-matic Cassette.

★3755★
Daughters of the Country
National Film Board of Canada
1251 Avenue of the Americas, 16th Fl.
New York, NY 10020-1173　　　Ph: (212)586-5131
Description: This series examines the prejudices Canadians have had against native North Americans in four different periods in time,

focusing on four women. **Release Date:** 1986. **Length:** 57 mins. **Format:** Beta, VHS, 3/4″ U-matic Cassette.

★3756★
Doctor, Lawyer, Indian Chief
National Film Board of Canada
1251 Avenue of the Americas, 16th Fl.
New York, NY 10020-1173   Ph: (212)586-5131
Description: This film documents the achievements of five Native American Canadian women who have overcome problems and prejudices to attain a variety of positions, including one who is an Indian Chief. **Release Date:** 1986. **Length:** 29 mins. **Format:** Beta, VHS, 3/4″ U-matic Cassette.

★3757★
How to Build An Igloo
National Film Board of Canada
1251 Avenue of the Americas, 16th Fl.
New York, NY 10020-1173   Ph: (212)586-5131
Description: A demonstration of igloo building in Canada's far north. **Release Date:** 1987. **Length:** 18 mins. **Format:** Beta, VHS, 3/4″ U-matic Cassette.

★3758★
Indian Hide Tanning
Trust for Native American Cultures &
   Crafts
PO Box 142
Greenville, NH 0348   Ph: (603)878-2944
Description: Eastern Cree Indians of Mistassini, Quebec demonstrate the methods used in the tanning of moose and caribou hides. The hides are then used to make moccasins, mittens, and snowshoes. **Release Date:** 1990. **Length:** 38 mins. **Format:** Beta, VHS, 3/4″ U-matic Cassette.

★3759★
John Cat
National Film Board of Canada
1251 Avenue of the Americas, 16th Fl.
New York, NY 10020-1173   Ph: (212)586-5131
Description: Based on a story by W.P. Kinsella, this drama concerns the violence and prejudice that two young Canadian Indians encounter. **Release Date:** 1987. **Length:** 24 mins. **Format:** Beta, VHS, 3/4″ U-matic Cassette.

★3760★
Joshua's Soapstone Carving
Coronet/MTI Film & Video   Ph: (708)940-1260
108 Wilmot Rd.   Free: 800-621-2131
Deerfield, IL 60015   Fax: (708)940-3640
Description: Inuit culture is explored as this film shows the carving craft of young Joshua Qumaluk. **Release Date:** 1982. **Length:** 25 mins. **Format:** Beta, VHS, 3/4″ U-matic Cassette, Other than listed.

★3761★
Keep the Circle Strong
Cinema Guild
1697 Broadway   Ph: (212)246-5522
New York, NY 10019   Fax: (212)246-5525
Description: Mike Auger is a Canadian Cree Indian who traveled to Bolivia to work with the Amayra Indians. In the process, he rediscovered his own cultural roots, and came to terms with some of the anger and confusion he experienced as a young man. **Release Date:** 1990. **Length:** 28 mins. **Format:** VHS.

★3762★
The Last Days of Okak
National Film Board of Canada
1251 Avenue of the Americas, 16th Fl.
New York, NY 10020-1173   Ph: (212)586-5131
Description: A documentary about the plague of Spanish influenza that wiped out an Inuit settlement on the Northern Labrador coast. **Release Date:** 1987. **Length:** 24 mins. **Format:** Beta, VHS, 3/4″ U-matic Cassette.

★3763★
Legends and Life of the Inuit
National Film Board of Canada
1251 Avenue of the Americas, 16th Fl.
New York, NY 10020-1173   Ph: (212)586-5131
Description: Five folktales from this Native American community are presented. **Release Date:** 1987. **Length:** 58 mins. **Format:** Beta, VHS, 3/4″ U-matic Cassette.

★3764★
Magic in the Sky
National Film Board of Canada
1251 Avenue of the Americas, 16th Fl.
New York, NY 10020-1173   Ph: (212)586-5131
Description: This program looks at the impact of television on Arctic Eskimos. **Release Date:** 1983. **Length:** 57 mins. **Format:** Beta, VHS, 3/4″ U-matic Cassette.

★3765★
Mariculture: The Promise of the Sea
Video Out
1102 Homer St.
Vancouver, BC, Canada V6B 2X6   Ph: (604)688-4336
Description: This program looks at an Indian community involved in a mariculture project. **Release Date:** 1981. **Length:** 21 mins. **Format:** Beta, VHS, 3/4″ U-matic Cassette.

★3766★
National Native Artists' Symposium
Video Out
1102 Homer St.
Vancouver, BC, Canada V6B 2X6   Ph: (604)688-4336
Description: The gathering of Indian artists from across Canada at this symposium is documented. **Release Date:** 1983. **Length:** 59 mins. **Format:** Beta, VHS, 3/4″ U-matic Cassette.

★3767★
North of 60 Degrees: Destiny Uncertain
Native American Public Broadcasting
   Consortium
PO Box 86111
1800 N. 33rd St.
Lincoln, NE 68501   Ph: (402)472-3522
Description: A series that examines the Canadian wilderness both as it is now and as it was known to Indians in the past. **Release Date:** 1983. **Length:** 29 mins. **Format:** VHS, 3/4″ U-matic Cassette, 1″ Broadcast Type "C", 2″ Quadraplex Open Reel.

★3768★
Potlatch People
Cinema Guild
1697 Broadway   Ph: (212)246-5522
New York, NY 10019   Fax: (212)246-5525
Description: The attempts to preserve the culture of the Pacific Northwest Indian are vividly presented in scenes of excavations underway in British Columbia and at museums where many of the prized artifacts are now on display. **Release Date:** 1976. **Length:** 26 mins. **Format:** 3/4″ U-matic Cassette, Other than listed.

★3769★
Rendezvous Canada, 1606
National Film Board of Canada
1251 Avenue of the Americas, 16th Fl.
New York, NY 10020-1173   Ph: (212)586-5131
Description: This film examines the clash of cultures between the natives and the European settlers in Canada around 1606, and the influences that each culture had on the other. **Release Date:** 1988. **Length:** 29 mins. **Format:** Beta, VHS, 3/4″ U-matic Cassette.

★3770★
Richard's Totem Pole (Canada)
Coronet/MTI Film & Video   Ph: (708)940-1260
108 Wilmot Rd.   Free: 800-621-2131
Deerfield, IL 60015   Fax: (708)940-3640
Description: A 16-year-old Gitskan Indian living in British Columbia helps his father carve a 30-foot totem pole. He learns about his heritage and culture while working on it. Part of the "World Cultures and Youth" series. **Release Date:** 1981. **Length:** 25 mins. **Format:** Beta, VHS, 3/4″ U-matic Cassette, Other than listed.

★3771★
Standing Alone
National Film Board of Canada
1251 Avenue of the Americas, 16th Fl.
New York, NY 10020-1173   Ph: (212)586-5131
Description: The story of Pete Standing Alone, a Blood Indian who, as a young man was more at home in the white man's culture than in his own. After becoming a father, he re-enters Indian society. **Release Date:** 1987. **Length:** 58 mins. **Format:** Beta, VHS, 3/4″ U-matic Cassette.

★3772★
Tales of Wesakachak
Native American Public Broadcasting
  Consortium
PO Box 86111
1800 N. 33rd St.
Lincoln, NE 68501   Ph: (402)472-3522
Description: This series for children relates orally conveyed Canadian Creek folktales. **Release Date:** 1984. **Length:** 15 mins. **Format:** VHS, 3/4″ U-matic Cassette, 1″ Broadcast Type "C", 2″ Quadraplex Open Reel.

★3773★
Telling Our Story
University of Calgary Dept. of
  Communications Media
2500 University Dr. NW   Ph: (403)220-3709
Calgary, AB, Canada T2N 1N4   Fax: (403)282-4497
Description: Northern Alberta Indians discover and share their cultural heritage through innovative drama presentations. **Release Date:** 1983. **Length:** 20 mins. **Format:** Beta, VHS, 3/4″ U-matic Cassette, 1″ Broadcast Type "C".

★3774★
White Justice
Cinema Guild
1697 Broadway   Ph: (212)246-5522
New York, NY 10019   Fax: (212)246-5525
Description: The Canadian Criminal Justice system and its effect on the Inuits of northern Quebec is examined, particularly the clash of white and native cultures. **Release Date:** 1987. **Length:** 57 mins. **Format:** Beta, VHS, 3/4″ U-matic Cassette.

★3775★
Women Within Two Cultures
Women in Focus
849 Beatty St.
Vancouver, BC, Canada V6B 2M6   Ph: (604)872-2250
Description: The influences of white settlers on the British Columbia West Coast Indian women is depicted in this program. **Release Date:** 1976. **Length:** 30 mins. **Format:** 3/4″ U-matic Cassette, Other than listed.

★3776★
You Are on Indian Land
National Film Board of Canada
1251 Avenue of the Americas, 16th Fl.
New York, NY 10020-1173   Ph: (212)586-5131
Description: This film documents the 1969 demonstration by Mohawk Indians of the St. Regis Reserve on the international bridge between Canada and the United States near Cornwall, Ontario. **Release Date:** 1987. **Length:** 37 mins. **Format:** Beta, VHS, 3/4″ U-matic Cassette.

General Resources

National Organizations

★3777★
A Better Chance (ABC)
419 Boylston St.
Boston, MA 02116   Ph: (617)421-0950
Judith B. Griffin, Pres.

Description: Identifies, recruits, and places academically talented and motivated minority students into leading independent secondary schools and selected public schools. Students receive need-based financial assistance from member schools. Prepares students to attend selective colleges and universities and encourages their aspirations to assume positions of responsibility and leadership in American society. Conducts research and provides technical assistance on expanded educational opportunities for minority group students in secondary and higher education. Bestows awards; maintains statistical files and biographical archives. **Founded:** 1963. **State Groups:** 22. **Publications:** *Abecedarian*, 2/year. Newsletter. • *Annual Report.* • *Letters to Member Schools*, annual. • Also publishes brochure. **Formerly:** Independent Schools Talent Search Program.

★3778★
Alliance of Minority Women for Business and Political Development
c/o Brenda Alford
Brassman Research
PO Box 13933
Silver Spring, MD 20911-3933   Ph: (301)565-0258
Brenda Alford, Pres.

Description: Minority women who own businesses in industries including manufacturing, construction, service, finance, insurance, real estate, retail trade, wholesale trade, transportation, and public utilities. Objectives are to unite minority women entrepreneurs and to encourage joint ventures and information exchange for political influence. **Founded:** 1982. **Members:** 650. **Formerly:** (1982) Task Force on Black Women Business Owners.

★3779★
American Civil Liberties Union (ACLU)
132 W. 43rd St.
New York, NY 10036   Ph: (212)944-9800
Ira Glasser, Exec.Dir.

Description: Champions the rights set forth in the Bill of Rights of the U.S. Constitution: freedom of speech, press, assembly, and religion; due process of law and fair trial; equality before the law regardless of race, color, sexual orientation, national origin, political opinion, or religious belief. Activities include litigation, advocacy, and public education. Maintains library of more than 3000 volumes. Sponsors litigation projects on topics such as women's rights, gay and lesbian rights, and children's rights. **Founded:** 1920. **Members:** 375,000. **State Groups:** 125. **Local Groups:** 200. **Publications:** *Civil Liberties*, quarterly. • *Civil Liberties Alert*, monthly. • Also publishes policy statements, handbooks, reprints, and pamphlets.

★3780★
American Civil Liberties Union Foundation (ACLUF)
132 W. 43rd St.
New York, NY 10036   Ph: (212)944-9800
Ira Glasser, Exec.Dir.

Description: Established as the tax-exempt arm of the American Civil Liberties Union (see separate entry). Purposes are legal defense, research, and public education on behalf of civil liberties including freedom of speech, press, and other First Amendment rights. Sponsors projects on topics such as children's rights, capital punishment, censorship, women's rights, immigration, prisoners' rights, national security, voting rights, and equal employment opportunity. Conducts research and public education projects to enable citizens to know and assert their rights. Seeks funds to protect liberty guaranteed by the Bill of Rights and the Constitution. **Founded:** 1966. **Regional Groups:** 2. **State Groups:** 81. **Publications:** *Annual Report.* • *Civil Liberties*, quarterly. Newsletter covering the legal defense, research, and public education projects of the foundation. Includes legislative news. • *First Principles*, monthly. **Formerly:** (1969) Roger Baldwin Foundation of ACLU.

★3781★
American Friends Service Committee (AFSC)
1501 Cherry St.
Philadelphia, PA 19102   Ph: (215)241-7000
Asia A. Bennett, Exec.Sec.

Description: Founded by and related to the Religious Society of Friends (Quakers) but supported and staffed by individuals sharing basic values regardless of religious affiliation. Attempts to relieve human suffering and find new approaches to world peace and social justice through nonviolence. Work in 22 countries includes development and refugee relief, peace education, and community organizing. Sponsors off-the-record seminars around the world to build better international understanding. Conducts programs with U.S. communities on the problems of minority groups such as housing, employment, and denial of legal rights. Maintains Washington, DC office to present AFSC experience and perspectives to policymakers. Seeks to build informed public resistance to militarism and the military-industrial complex. A co-recipient of the Nobel Peace Prize. Programs are multiracial, nondenominational, and international. **Founded:** 1917. **Regional Groups:** 9. **Publications:** *Annual Report.* • *Quaker Service Bulletin*, semiannual. Newsletter.

★3782★
Center for Third World Organizing (CTWO)
3861 Martin Luther King Jr. Way
Oakland, CA 94609   Ph: (415)654-9601
Gary Delgado, Dir.

Description: Provides training, issue analyses, and research to low-income minority organizations including welfare, immigrant, and Native American rights groups. Monitors and reports on incidents of discrimination against people of color. Sponsors Minority Activist Apprenticeship Program, which works to develop minority organizers and leaders for minority communities. Sponsors seminars on issues affecting minorities. Maintains speakers' bureau; operates placement service. Compiles statistics. **Founded:** 1980. **State Groups:** 6. **Local Groups:** 200. **Publications:** *Directory of Church Funding Sources*, periodic. • *Issue Pac*, quarterly. • *Minority Trendsetter*, quarterly. • Also publishes *Surviving America: What You're Entitled to and How to Get It*, *Images of Color: A Guide to Media from and for Asian, Black, Latino and Native American Communities*, occasional papers series, guides, and manuals.

★3783★
Citizens' Commission on Civil Rights (CCCR)
2000 M St. NW, Ste. 400
Washington, DC 20036   Ph: (202)659-5565
Dr. Arthur Flemming, Chm.

Description: Bipartisan former federal cabinet officials concerned with achieving the goal of equality of opportunity. Objectives are to: monitor the federal government's enforcement of laws barring discrimination on the basis of race, sex, religion, ethnic background, age, or handicap; foster public understanding of civil rights issues; formulate constructive policy recommendations. **Founded:** 1982. **Members:** 16. **Publications:** *Lost Opportunities*, *One Nation Indivisible: The Civil Rights Challenge For the 1990s*, *Barriers to Registration and Voting: An Agenda for Reform*, and reports on fair housing, busing and the Brown Decision, and affirmative action; provides press releases.

★3784★
Department of Civil Rights, AFL-CIO
815 16th St. NW
Washington, DC 20006   Ph: (202)637-5270
Richard Womack, Dir.

Description: Staff arm of the AFL-CIO Civil Rights Committee. Serves as official liaison with women's and civil rights organizations and government agencies working in the field of equal opportunity; helps to implement state and federal laws and AFL-CIO civil rights policies; aids affiliates in the development of affirmative programs to expand opportunities for minorities and women; prepares and disseminates special materials on civil rights; speaks at union and civil rights institutes, conferences, and conventions; helps affiliates resolve complaints involving unions under Title VII of the 1964 Civil Rights Act and Executive Order 11246. **Founded:** 1955. **Publications:** *AFL-CIO and Civil Rights*, biennial.

★3785★
Minority Business Enterprise Legal Defense and Education Fund (MBELDEF)
220 I St. NE, Ste. 280
Washington, DC 20002   Ph: (202)543-0040
Anthony W. Robinson, Pres.

Description: Minority businesspersons united to defend, enhance, and expand minority business. Acts as advocate and legal representative for the minority business community, offering legal representation in matters of national or regional importance. **Founded:** 1980. **Members:** 2000. **Publications:** *MBE Vanguard*, quarterly. Newsletter.

★3786★
National Action Council for Minorities in Engineering (NACME)
3 W. 35th St.
New York, NY 10001   Ph: (212)279-2626
    Fax: (212)629-5178
George Campbell Jr., Pres.

Description: Seeks to increase the number of African American, Hispanic, and Native American students enrolled in and graduating from engineering schools. Offers incentive grants to engineering schools to recruit and provide financial assistance to increasing numbers of minority students. Works with local, regional, and national support organizations to motivate and encourage precollege students to engage in engineering careers. Conducts educational and research programs; operates project to assist engineering schools in improving the retention and graduation rates of minority students. Maintains speakers' bureau; bestows awards; compiles statistics. **Founded:** 1980. **Publications:** *Annual Report*. • *Directory of Pre-College and University Minority Engineering Programs*, periodic. • *Financial Aid Unscrambled: A Guide for Minority Engineering Students*, biennial. • *NACME News*, 3/year. Newsletter for educators, counselors, and program directors who participate in minority engineering education. • *NACME Statistical Report*, biennial. • Also publishes *Gearing Up: How to Start a Pre-College Minority Program* and books.

★3787★
National Association of Minority Women in Business (NAMWIB)
906 Grand Ave., Ste. 200
Kansas City, MO 64106   Ph: (816)421-3335
Inez Kaiser, Pres.

Description: Minority women in business ownership and management positions; college students. Serves as a network for the exchange of ideas and information on business opportunities for minority women in the public and private sectors. Conducts research and educational programs, as well as workshops, conferences, seminars, and luncheons. Maintains speakers' bureau, hall of fame, and placement service; compiles statistics; bestows awards to women who have made significant contributions to the field. **Founded:** 1972. **Members:** 5000. **Publications:** *Today*, bimonthly. Newsletter. • Also publishes brochures.

★3788★
National Catholic Conference for Interracial Justice (NCCIJ)
3033 4th St. NE
Washington, DC 20017-1102   Ph: (202)529-6480
Jerome B. Ernst, Exec.Dir.

Description: Catholic organization working for interracial justice and social concerns in America. Initiates programs within and outside the Catholic church to end discrimination in community development, education, and employment. **Founded:** 1959. **Members:** 1151. **State Groups:** 4. **Publications:** *Commitment*, quarterly. Newsletter. • Also publishes *LASER: Creating Unity in Diversity* (book), *Workshops on Racism* (manual), *Pentecost: A Feast for all Peoples*, *Martin Luther King Jr. Holiday Celebration Packet*, and pamphlets.

★3789★
National Committee on Pay Equity (NCPE)
1126 16th St. NW, Rm. 411
Washington, DC 20036   Ph: (202)331-7343
Claudia E. Wayne, Exec.Dir.

Description: Individuals (220) and organizations (140) such as women's groups, labor unions, professional associations, minority and civil rights groups, and governmental and educational groups. Educates the public about the historical, legal, and economic bases for pay inequities between men and women and white people and people of color. Sponsors speakers' bureau; acts as an information clearinghouse on pay equity activities. **Founded:** 1979. **Members:** 360. **State Groups:** 5. **Publications:** *Newsnotes*, 2-4/year. Newsletter; includes international news, federal legislation updates, and litigation reports. • Also publishes *Pay Equity Activity in the Public Sector, 1979-1989*, *Pay Equity: An Issue of Race, Ethnicity, and Sex*, *Briefing Paper: The Wage Gap*, *Bargaining for Pay Equity: A Strategy Manual*, *Pay Equity Makes Good Business Sense*, and *Pay Equity Bibliography and Resource Listing*. **Formerly:** (1980) National Pay Equity Committee.

★3790★
National Council for Culture and Art (NCCA)
1600 Broadway, Ste. 611C
New York, NY 10019   Ph: (212)757-7933
Robert H. LaPrince Ph.D., Exec.Dir. and Pres.

Description: Artists, civic and business leaders, professional performers, and visual arts organizations. Purpose is to provide exposure and employment opportunities for rural Americans, disabled Americans, and other minorities including blacks, Hispanics, American Indians, and European-Americans. Sponsors arts programs and spring and fall concert series. Operates Opening Night, a cable television show. Bestows annual Monarch Award and President's Award, and sponsors annual Monarch Scholarship Program. Offers children's and placement services; conducts charitable program; maintains hall of fame. Plans to conduct Minority Playwrights Forum, Dance Festival U.S.A., Vocal and Instrumental Competition, Film and Video Festival, and Concerts U.S.A. **Founded:** 1980. **Members:** 1500. **Publications:** *Monarch Herald*, quarterly. Newsletter.

★3791★
National Institute for Women of Color
1301 20th St. NW, Ste. 702   Ph: (202)296-2661
Washington, DC 20036   Fax: (202)296-8140
Sharon Parker, Bd.Chm.

Description: Aim to: enhance the strengthens of diversity; promote educational and economic equity for Black, Hispanic, Asian-American, Pacific-Islander, American Indian, and Alaskan Native women. Focuses on mutual concerns and needs, bringing together women who have traditionally been isolated. **Founded:** 1981. **Publications:** *Brown Papers*, *NIWC Network News*, bibliographies, bulletins, fact sheets, and other related resources.

★3792★
National Minority Business Council (NMBC)
235 E. 42nd St.
New York, NY 10017   Ph: (212)573-2385
John F. Robinson, CEO & Pres.

Description: Minority businesses in all areas of industry and commerce. Seeks to increase profitability by developing marketing, sales, and management skills in minority businesses. Acts as an informational source for the national minority business community. Programs include: a legal services plan that provides free legal services to members in such areas as sales contracts, copyrights, estate planning, and investment agreement; a business referral service that develops potential customer leads; an international trade assistance program that provides technical assistance in developing foreign markets; an executive banking program that teaches members how to package a business loan for bank approval; a procurement outreach program for minority and women business owners. Conducts continuing management education and provides assistance in teaching youth the free enterprise system. Bestows awards. **Founded:** 1972. **Members:** 400. **State Groups:** 8. **Publications:** *Corporate Minority Vendor Directory*, annual. • *Corporate Purchasing Directory*, annual. • *NMBC Business Report*, bimonthly. • *NMBC Corporate Purchasing Directory*, periodic.

★3793★
National Minority Supplier Development Council (NMSDC)
15 W. 39th St., 9th Fl.
New York, NY 10018   Ph: (212)944-2430
Harriet Michel, Pres.

Description: Minority businesspersons, corporations, government agencies, and other organizations who are members of regional purchasing councils or who have agreed to participate in the program. Program provides, exclusively for educational purposes, consultative, advisory, and informational services and technical resources to corporations, minority businesses, and regional and local minority purchasing councils. These services include purchasing, marketing, industrial, and managerial operations. Conducts sales training programs for minority entrepreneurs, and buyer training program for corporate minority purchasing programs. Bestows awards; compiles statistics. **Founded:** 1972. **Members:** 160. **Regional Groups:** 45. **State Groups:** 10. **Publications:** *Minority Supplier News*, 6/year. • *Minority Vendor Directory*, periodic. • *National Minority Supplier Development Council–Annual Report*. Reports financial data of the organization. **Formerly:** (1980) National Minority Purchasing Council.

★3794★
National Network of Minority Women in Science
c/o American Association for the
    Advancement of Science
Directorate for Educ. and Human
    Resource Programs
1333 H St. NW   Ph: (202)326-6682
Washington, DC 20005   Fax: (202)371-9526
Audrey Daniels, National Coord.

Description: Asian, Black, Mexican American, Native American, and Puerto Rican women involved in science related professions; other interested persons. Promotes the advancement of minority women in science fields and the improvement of the science and mathematics education and career awareness of minorities. Supports public policies and programs in science and technology that benefit minorities. Compiles statistics; serves as clearinghouse for identifying minority women scientists. Offers writing and conference presentations, seminars, and workshops on minority women in science and local career conference for students. **Founded:** 1978. **Members:** 400.

★3795★
Quality Education for Minorities Network (QEM)
1818 N St. NW, Ste. 350
Washington, DC 20036   Ph: (202)659-1818
Shirley M. McBay, Pres.

Description: Created to implement the plan developed by the QEM Project to improve education at all levels for American Indians, African Americans, Mexican Americans, Native Alaskans, and Puerto Ricans. Believes minorities are underserved by the educational system and thus disproportionately lack the skills needed to participate effectively in a society increasingly based on high technology. Plans to: cooperate with school systems, communities, universities, and public and private sector institutions to insure that minorities in the U.S. have equal access to educational opportunities; facilitate networking and coordination among institutions and organizations involved in the education of minorities; maintain research programs; assist local schools in implementing minority education programs, especially those dealing with science and mathematics. **Founded:** 1987. **Publications:** *QEM Update*, quarterly. **Formerly:** (1990) Quality Education for Minorities Project.

Regional, State/Provincial, & Local Organizations

—————— Alabama ——————

★3796★
Mobile Minority Business Development Center
801 Executive Park Dr., Ste. 102
Mobile, AL 36606   Ph: (205)471-5165

★3797★
American Civil Liberties Union (ACLU)
Alabama Affiliate
PO Box 447
Montgomery, AL 36101   Ph: (205)262-0304
Olivia Turner, Dir.

★3798★
Montgomery Minority Business Development Center
770 S. McDonough St., Ste. 207
Montgomery, AL 36104   Ph: (205)834-7598

───────── **Alaska** ─────────

★3799★
Alaska Minority Business Development Center
1577 C St. Plaza, Ste. 200
Anchorage, AK 99501   Ph: (907)274-5400

───────── **Arizona** ─────────

★3800★
American Civil Liberties Union (ACLU)
Arizona Affiliate
PO Box 17148
Phoenix, AZ 85011   Ph: (602)650-1967
Louis L. Rhodes, Dir.

★3801★
Phoenix Minority Business Development Center
432 N. 44th St., Ste. 354
Phoenix, AZ 85008   Ph: (602)225-0740

★3802★
Tucson Minority Business Development Center
181 W. Broadway
Tucson, AZ 85702-0180   Ph: (602)629-9744

───────── **Arkansas** ─────────

★3803★
American Civil Liberties Union (ACLU)
Arkansas Affiliate
103 W. Capitol, No. 1120   Ph: (501)374-2660
Little Rock, AR 72201   Fax: (501)379-2842
Joseph L. Jacoboson, Dir.

★3804★
Little Rock Minority Business Development Center
1 Riverfront Pl., Ste. 415
North Little Rock, AR 72114   Ph: (501)372-7312

───────── **California** ─────────

★3805★
Bakersfield Minority Business Development Center
218 South H St., Ste. 103
Bakersfield, CA 93304   Ph: (805)837-0291

★3806★
Riverside Minority Business Development Center
1016 Cooley Dr., Ste. F
Colton, CA 92324   Ph: (714)824-9695

★3807★
Fresno Minority Business Development Center
2010 N. Fine, Ste. 103
Fresno, CA 93727   Ph: (209)252-7551

★3808★
American Civil Liberties Union (ACLU)
Southern California Affiliate
1616 Beverly Blvd.   Ph: (213)977-9500
Los Angeles, CA 90026   Fax: (213)250-3919
Ramona Ripston, Dir.

★3809★
Los Angeles Minority Business Development Center
911 Wilshire Blvd., Ste. 1700
Los Angeles, CA 90017   Ph: (213)488-9322

★3810★
San Francisco/Oakland Minority Business Development Center
1000 Broadway, Ste. 270
Oakland, CA 94607   Ph: (415)465-6756

★3811★
Oxnard Minority Business Development Center
451 W. 5th St.
Oxnard, CA 93030   Ph: (805)483-1123

★3812★
Sacramento Minority Business Development Center
1779 Tribute Rd., Ste. J
Sacramento, CA 95815   Ph: (916)920-2251

★3813★
Salinas Minority Business Development Center
14 Maple St., Ste. D
Salinas, CA 93901   Ph: (408)422-8825

★3814★
American Civil Liberties Union (ACLU)
San Diego Affiliate
1202 Kettner Blvd., No. 6200   Ph: (619)232-2121
San Diego, CA 92101   Fax: (619)232-0036
Linda Hills, Dir.

★3815★
San Diego Minority Business Development Center
6495 Alvarado Ct., Ste. 106
San Diego, CA 92120   Ph: (619)594-3684

★3816★
American Civil Liberties Union (ACLU)
Northern California Affiliate
1663 Mission St., No. 460
San Francisco, CA 94103   Ph: (415)621-2488
Dorothy M. Ehrlich, Dir.

★3817★
San Francisco/Oakland Minority Business Development Center
1 California St., Ste. 2100
San Francsico, CA 94111   Ph: (415)989-2920

★3818★
San Jose Minority Business Development Center
150 Almaden Blvd., Ste. 600
San Jose, CA 95150   Ph: (408)275-9000

★3819★
Anaheim Minority Business Development Center
6 Hutton Center Dr., Ste. 1050
Santa Ana, CA 92707   Ph: (714)434-0444

★3820★
Santa Barbara Minority Business Development Center
4141 State St., Ste. B-4
Santa Barbara, CA 93110   Ph: (805)964-1136

★3821★
Stockton Minority Business Development Center
5361 N. Pershing Ave., Ste. A-1
Stockton, CA 95207   Ph: (209)477-2098

Colorado

★3822★
American Civil Liberties Union (ACLU)
Colorado Affiliate
815 E. 22nd Ave.　　　　Ph: (303)861-2258
Denver, CO 80205　　　Fax: (303)861-2269
James Joy, Dir.

★3823★
American Civil Liberties Union (ACLU)
Mountain States Regional Office
Bldg. 2, Ste. 262
6825 E. Tennessee Ave.　　Ph: (303)321-4828
Denver, CO 80224　　　Fax: (303)321-4851
Dorothy Davidson, Dir.

★3824★
Denver Minority Business Development Center
3003 Arapaho, Ste. 202
Denver, CO 80205　　　Ph: (303)296-5590

Connecticut

★3825★
American Civil Liberties Union (ACLU)
Connecticut Affiliate
32 Grand St.　　　　　Ph: (203)247-9823
Hartford, CT 06106　　Fax: (203)728-0287
William Olds, Exec.Dir.

★3826★
Connecticut Minority Business Development Center
410 Asylum St., Ste. 243
Hartford, CT 06103　　　Ph: (203)246-5371

Delaware

★3827★
American Civil Liberties Union (ACLU)
Delaware Affiliate
702 King St., No. 600A　　Ph: (302)654-3966
Wilmington, DE 19801　　Fax: (302)654-3689
Judith Mellen, Dir.

District of Columbia

★3828★
American Civil Liberties Union (ACLU)
National Capital Area Affiliate
1400 20th St. NW, No. 119　Ph: (202)457-0800
Washington, DC 20036　　Fax: (202)452-1868
Mary Jane DeFrank, Exec.Dir.

★3829★
Washington Minority Business Development Center
1133 15th St., NW, Ste. 1120
Washington, DC 20005　　Ph: (202)785-2886

Florida

★3830★
Jacksonville Minority Business Development Center
333 N. Laura St., Ste. 465
Jacksonville, FL 32202-3508　Ph: (904)353-3826

★3831★
American Civil Liberties Union (ACLU)
Florida Affiliate
225 NE 34th St., No. 102　　Ph: (505)576-2336
Miami, FL 33137　　　　Fax: (305)576-1106
Robyn Blumner, Dir.

★3832★
Miami/Ft. Lauderdale Minority Business Development Center
1200 NW 78th Ave., Ste. 301
Miami, FL 33126　　　　Ph: (305)591-7355

★3833★
Orlando Minority Business Development Center
132 E. Colonial Dr., Ste. 211
Orlando, FL 32801　　　Ph: (407)422-6234

★3834★
West Palm Beach Minority Business Development Center
2001 Broadway, Ste. 301
Riveria Beach, FL 33404　　Ph: (407)393-2530

★3835★
Tampa/St. Petersburg Minority Business Development Center
4601 W. Kennedy Blvd., Ste. 200
Tampa, FL 33609　　　　Ph: (813)289-8824

Georgia

★3836★
American Civil Liberties Union (ACLU)
Georgia Affiliate
233 Mitchell St. SW, No. 200　Ph: (404)523-5398
Atlanta, GA 30303　　　Fax: (404)577-0181
Teresa Nelson, Dir.

★3837★
American Civil Liberties Union (ACLU)
Southern Regional Office
44 Forsyth St. NW, Ste. 202　Ph: (404)523-2721
Atlanta, GA 30303　　　Fax: (404)653-0331
Laughlin McDonald, Dir.

★3838★
Atlanta Minority Business Development Center
75 Piedmont Ave., NE, Ste. 256
Atlanta, GA 30303　　　Ph: (404)586-0973

★3839★
Augusta Minority Business Development Center
1208 Laney Walker Blvd.
Augusta, GA 30901-2796　　Ph: (404)722-0994

★3840★
Columbus Minority Business Development Center
1214 1st Ave., Ste. 430
Columbus, GA 31902-1696　Ph: (404)324-4253

★3841★
Savannah Minority Business Development Center
31 W. Congress St., Ste. 201
Savannah, GA 331401　　　Ph: (912)236-6708

———— Hawaii ————

★3842★
American Civil Liberties Union (ACLU)
Hawaii Affiliate
PO Box 3410
Honolulu, HI 96801
Vanessa Y. Chong, Dir.
Ph: (808)545-1722
Fax: (808)545-2993

★3843★
Honolulu Minority Business Development Center
1001 Bishop St., Ste. 2900
Honolulu, HI 96813
Ph: (808)531-6232

———— Idaho ————

★3844★
American Civil Liberties Union (ACLU)
Idaho Affiliate
PO Box 1897
Boise, ID 83701
Jack Van Valkenburg, Dir.
Ph: (208)344-5243
Fax: (208)345-8274

———— Illinois ————

★3845★
American Civil Liberties Union (ACLU)
Illinois Affiliate
20 E. Jackson Blvd., Ste. 1600
Chicago, IL 60604
Jay Miller, Dir.
Ph: (312)427-7330
Fax: (312)427-9315

★3846★
Chicago Minority Business Development Center, No. 1
35 E. Wacker Dr., Ste. 790
Chicago, IL 60601
Ph: (312)977-9190

★3847★
Chicago Minority Business Development Center, No. 2
700 One Prudential Plaza
Chicago, IL 60601
Ph: (312)565-4710

———— Indiana ————

★3848★
Gary Minority Business Development Center
567 Broadway
Gary, IN 46402
Ph: (219)883-5802

★3849★
Indianapolis Minority Business Development Center
617 Indiana Ave., Ste. 319
Indianapolis, IN 46202
Ph: (317)685-0055

———— Iowa ————

★3850★
American Civil Liberties Union (ACLU)
Iowa Affiliate
446 Insurance Exchange Bldg.
Des Moines, IA 50309
Cryss D. Farley, Dir.
Ph: (515)243-3576

———— Kentucky ————

★3851★
American Civil Liberties Union (ACLU)
Kentucky Affiliate
425 W. Muhammad Ali Blvd., Ste. 230
Louisville, KY 40202
Everett Hoffman, Dir.
Ph: (502)581-1181
Fax: (502)589-9687

★3852★
Louisville Minority Business Development Center
611 W. Main St., 4th Fl.
Louisville, KY 40202
Ph: (502)589-7603

———— Louisiana ————

★3853★
Baton Rouge Minority Business Development Center
2036 Wooddale Blvd., Ste. D
Baton Rouge, LA 70806
Ph: (504)924-0186

★3854★
Shreveport Minority Business Development Center
820 Jordan St., Ste. 105
Shreveport, LA 71101
Ph: (318)226-4931

———— Maine ————

★3855★
American Civil Liberties Union (ACLU)
Maine Affiliate
97A Exchange St.
Portland, ME 04101
Sally Sutton, Dir.
Ph: (207)774-8087
Fax: (207)774-5444

———— Maryland ————

★3856★
American Civil Liberties Union (ACLU)
Maryland Affiliate
2219 St. Paul St.
Baltimore, MD 21218
Stuart Comstock-Gay, Dir.
Ph: (301)889-8555
Fax: (301)366-7838

★3857★
Baltimore Minority Business Development Center
2901 Druid Park Dr., Ste. 201
Baltimore, MD 21215
Ph: (301)383-2214

———— Massachusetts ————

★3858★
American Civil Liberties Union (ACLU)
Massachusetts Affiliate
19 Temple Pl.
Boston, MA 02111
John Roberts, Dir.
Ph: (617)482-3170
Fax: (617)451-0009

★3859★
Boston Minority Business Development Center
985 Commonwealth Ave., Rm. 201
Boston, MA 02215
Ph: (617)353-7060

Michigan

★3860★
American Civil Liberties Union (ACLU)
Michigan Affiliate
1249 Washington Blvd., Ste. 2910
Detroit, MI 48226-1822
Howard Simon, Dir.
Ph: (313)961-4662
Fax: (313)961-9005

★3861★
Detroit Minority Business Development Center
26913 Northwestern Hwy., Ste. 400
Southfield, MI 48034
Ph: (313)262-1950

Minnesota

★3862★
American Civil Liberties Union (ACLU)
Minnesota Affiliate
1021 W. Broadway
Minneapolis, MN 55411
William Roath, Dir.
Ph: (612)522-2423

★3863★
Minneapolis Minority Business Development Center
2021 E. Hennepin Ave., Ste. LL 35
Minneapolis, MN 55413
Ph: (612)331-5576

Mississippi

★3864★
American Civil Liberties Union (ACLU)
Mississippi Affiliate
921 N. Congress St.
Jackson, MS 39202
Deirdre Janney, Exec.Dir.
Ph: (601)355-6464
Fax: (601)353-7260

★3865★
Jackson Minority Business Development Center
5285 Galaxie Dr., Ste. A
Jackson, MS 39206
Ph: (601)362-2260

Missouri

★3866★
American Civil Liberties Union (ACLU)
Kansas/Western Missouri Affiliate
201 Wyandotte St., No. 209
Kansas City, MO 64105
Dick Kurtenbach, Dir.
Ph: (816)421-4449

★3867★
Kansas City Minority Business Development Center
1101 Walnut St., Ste. 1600
Kansas City, MO 81647-1150
Ph: (816)471-1520

★3868★
American Civil Liberties Union (ACLU)
Eastern Missouri Affiliate
4557 LacLede Ave.
Saint Louis, MO 63108
Joyce Armstrong, Dir.
Ph: (314)361-2111
Fax: (314)361-3135

★3869★
St. Louis Minority Business Development Center
500 Washington Ave., Ste. 1200
Saint Louis, MO 63101
Ph: (314)621-6232

Montana

★3870★
American Civil Liberties Union (ACLU)
Montana Affiliate
PO Box 3012
Billings, MT 59103
Scott Crichton, Dir.
Ph: (406)248-1086
Fax: (406)248-7763

Nebraska

★3871★
American Civil Liberties Union (ACLU)
Nebraska Affiliate
PO Box 81455
Lincoln, NE 68501
Bill Schatz, Dir.
Ph: (402)476-8091
Fax: (402)476-8135

Nevada

★3872★
American Civil Liberties Union (ACLU)
Nevada Affiliate
325 S. 3rd St., No. 25
Las Vegas, NV 89101
Chan Kendrick, Dir.
Ph: (702)366-1226

★3873★
Las Vegas Minority Business Development Center
1830 E. Sahara, Ste. 310A
Las Vegas, NV 89104
Ph: (702)369-2339

New York

★3874★
New Brunswick Minority Business Development Center
100 Jersey Ave., Bldg. D, Ste. 3
New Brunswick, NY 08901
Ph: (908)249-5511

New Jersey

★3875★
Newark Minority Business Development Center
60 Park Place, Ste. 1404
Newark, NJ 07102
Ph: (201)623-7712

New Mexico

★3876★
Albuquerque Minority Business Development Center
718 Central SW
Albuquerque, NM 87102
Ph: (505)843-7114

★3877★
American Civil Liberties Union (ACLU)
New Mexico Affiliate
PO Box 80915
Albuquerque, NM 87108
Grace W. Williams, Dir.
Ph: (505)266-5915
Fax: (505)266-5916

───────────── **New York** ─────────────

★3878★
Bronx Minority Business Development Center
2027 Williamsbridge Rd.
Bronx, NY 10461   Ph: (212)824-1563

★3879★
Brooklyn Minority Business Development Center
16 Court St., Rm. 1903
Brooklyn, NY 11201   Ph: (718)522-5880

★3880★
Williamsburg/Brooklyn Minority Business Development Center
12 Heywood St.
Brooklyn, NY 11211   Ph: (718)522-5620

★3881★
Buffalo Minority Business Development Center
570 E. Delvan Ave.
Buffalo, NY 14211   Ph: (716)895-2218

★3882★
Queens Minority Business Development Center
110-29 Horace Harding Expy.
Corona, NY 11368   Ph: (718)699-2400

★3883★
Nassau/Suffolk Minority Business Development Center
150 Broad Hollow Rd., Ste. 304
Melville, NY 11747   Ph: (516)549-5454

★3884★
American Civil Liberties Union (ACLU)
New York Affiliate
132 W. 43rd St., 2nd Fl.   Ph: (212)382-0557
New York, NY 10036   Fax: (212)354-2583
Norman Siegel, Dir.

★3885★
Harlem Minority Business Development Center
2090 Adam Clayton Powell Blvd., Rm. 604
New York, NY 10027   Ph: (212)749-8604

★3886★
Manhattan Minority Business Development Center
51 Madison Ave., Ste. 2212
New York, NY 10010   Ph: (212)779-4360

★3887★
Rochester Minority Business Development Center
350 North St.
Rochester, NY 14604   Ph: (716)232-6120

───────────── **North Carolina** ─────────────

★3888★
Charlotte Minority Business Development Center
700 E. Stonewall St., Ste. 360
Charlotte, NC 28236   Ph: (704)334-7522

───────────── **South Carolina** ─────────────

★3889★
Fayetteville Minority Business Development Center
114-1/2 Anderson St.
Fayetteville, SC 28302   Ph: (919)483-7513

───────────── **North Carolina** ─────────────

★3890★
Raleigh/Durham Minority Business Development Center
817 New Bern Ave., Ste. 8
Raleigh, NC 27601   Ph: (919)833-6122

───────────── **Ohio** ─────────────

★3891★
Cleveland Minority Business Development Center
6200 Frank Rd., NW
Canton, OH 44720-7299   Ph: (216)494-6170

★3892★
Cincinnati Minority Business Development Center
113 W. 4th St., Ste. 600
Cincinnati, OH 45202   Ph: (513)381-4770

★3893★
American Civil Liberties Union (ACLU)
Ohio Affiliate
1223 W. 6th St., 2nd Fl.
Cleveland, OH 44113   Ph: (216)781-6276
Christine Link, Dir.

★3894★
American Civil Liberties Union (ACLU)
Ohio Affiliate
Cleveland Chapter
1223 W. 6th St., 2nd Fl.
Cleveland, OH 44113   Ph: (216)781-6276
Loretta Mikolaj, Dir.

★3895★
Cleveland Minority Business Development Center
601 Lakeside, Ste. 335
Cleveland, OH 44114   Ph: (216)664-4150

───────────── **Oklahoma** ─────────────

★3896★
American Civil Liberties Union (ACLU)
Oklahoma Affiliate
1411 Classen, Ste. 318
Oklahoma City, OK 73106   Ph: (405)524-8511
Joann Bell, Dir.

★3897★
Oklahoma City Minority Business Development Center
1500 NE 4th St., Ste. 101
Oklahoma City, OK 73117   Ph: (405)235-0430

★3898★
Tulsa Minority Business Development Center
240 E. Apache St.
Tulsa, OK 74106   Ph: (918)592-1995

───────────── **Oregon** ─────────────

★3899★
American Civil Liberties Union (ACLU)
Oregon Affiliate
705 Board of Trade Bldg.
310 SW 4th Ave.
Portland, OR 97204   Ph: (503)227-3186
Ms. Stevie Remington, Dir.

★3900★
Portland Minority Business Development Center
8959 SW Barbur Blvd., Ste. 102
Portland, OR 97219   Ph: (503)245-9253

─────────── Pennsylvania ───────────

★3901★
American Civil Liberties Union (ACLU)
Pennsylvania Affiliate
PO Box 1161   Ph: (215)923-4357
Philadelphia, PA 19105-1161   Fax: (215)592-1343
Deborah Leavy, Dir.

★3902★
Philadelphia Minority Business Development Center
125 N. 8th St., 4th Fl.
Philadelphia, PA 19106   Ph: (215)629-9841

★3903★
Pittsburgh Minority Business Development Center
9 Parkway Center, Ste. 250
Pittsburgh, PA 15220   Ph: (412)921-1155

★3904★
American Civil Liberties Union (ACLU)
Pennsylvania Affiliate
Pittsburgh Chapter
237 Oakland Ave.   Ph: (412)681-7736
Pittsburh, PA 15213   Fax: (412)681-8707
Marion Damick, Dir.

─────────── Puerto Rico ───────────

★3905★
San Juan Minority Business Development Center
122 Eleanor Roosevelt Ave.
Hato Rey, PR 00918   Ph: (809)753-8484

★3906★
Mayaguez Minority Business Development Center
70 W. Mendez Bigo
PO Box 3146 Marina Sta.
Mayaguez, PR 00709   Ph: (809)833-7783

★3907★
Ponce Minority Business Development Center
19 Salud St.
Ponce, PR 00731   Ph: (809)840-8100

─────────── Rhode Island ───────────

★3908★
American Civil Liberties Union (ACLU)
Rhode Island Affiliate
212 Union St., Rm. 211
Providence, RI 02903   Ph: (401)831-7171
Steve Brown, Dir.

─────────── South Carolina ───────────

★3909★
Charleston Minority Business Development Center
701 E. Bay St., Ste. 1539
Charleston, SC 29403   Ph: (803)724-3477

★3910★
American Civil Liberties Union (ACLU)
South Carolina Affiliate
Middleberg Plaza, Ste. 104
2712 Middleburg Dr.
Columbia, SC 29204   Ph: (803)799-5151
Steven Bates, Dir.

★3911★
Columbia Minority Business Development Center
2711 Middleburg Dr., Ste. 114
Columbia, SC 29204   Ph: (803)256-0528

★3912★
Greenville/Spartanburg Minority Business Development
  Center
300 University Ridge, Ste. 200
Greenville, SC 29601   Ph: (803)271-8753

─────────── Tennessee ───────────

★3913★
Memphis Minority Business Development Center
5 N. 3rd St., Ste. 2000
Memphis, TN 38103   Ph: (901)527-2298

★3914★
American Civil Liberties Union (ACLU)
Tenessee Affiliate
PO Box 120160   Ph: (615)320-7142
Nashville, TN 37212   Fax: (615)320-7260
Hedy Weinberg, Dir.

★3915★
Nashville Minority Business Development Center
404 J. Robertson Pkwy., Ste. 1920
Nashville, TN 37219   Ph: (615)255-0432

─────────── Texas ───────────

★3916★
Austin Minority Business Development Center
301 Congress Ave., Ste. 1020
Austin, TX 78701   Ph: (512)476-9700

★3917★
Beaumont Minority Business Development Center
550 Fannin, Ste. 106A
Beaumont, TX 77701   Ph: (409)835-1377

★3918★
Brownsville Minority Business Development Center
2100 Boca Chica, Ste. 301
Brownsville, TX 78521-2265   Ph: (512)546-3400

★3919★
Corpus Christi Minority Business Development Center
3649 Leopard, Ste. 514
Corpus Christi, TX 78404

★3920★
American Civil Liberties Union (ACLU)
Texas Affiliate
Dallas Chapter
PO Box 215135
Dallas, TX 75221   Ph: (214)823-1555
Joe Cook, Dir.

★3921★
Dallas Minority Business Development Center
5445 Ross Ave., Ste. 800
Dallas, TX 75202　　　　Ph: (214)855-7373

★3922★
El Paso Minority Business Development Center
1312-A E. Rio Grande St.
El Paso, TX 79902　　　　Ph: (915)544-2700

★3923★
American Civil Liberties Union (ACLU)
Houston Chapter Affiliate
1236 W. Gray
Houston, TX 77009　　　　Ph: (713)524-5925
Helen M. Gros, Dir.

★3924★
Houston Minority Business Development Center
1200 Smith St., Ste. 2800
Houston, TX 77002　　　　Ph: (713)650-3831

★3925★
Laredo Minority Business Development Center
777 Calle Del Norte, No. 2
Laredo, TX 78401　　　　Ph: (512)725-5177

★3926★
Lubbock/Midland-Odessa Minority Business
　Development Center
1220 Broadway, Ste. 509
Lubbock, TX 79401　　　　Ph: (806)762-6232

★3927★
McAllen Minority Business Development Center
1701 W. Bus. Hwy. 83, Ste. 1108
McAllen, TX 78501　　　　Ph: (512)687-5224

★3928★
San Antonio Minority Business Development Center
UTSA, Hemisphere Tower
San Antonio, TX 78285　　　　Ph: (512)224-1945

─────────── **Utah** ───────────

★3929★
American Civil Liberties Union (ACLU)
Utah Affiliate
Boston Bldg.
9 Exchange Pl., Ste. 701
Salt Lake City, UT 84111　　　　Ph: (801)521-9289
Michele Parish, Dir.

★3930★
Salt Lake City Minority Business Development Center
350 E. 500 So., Ste. 101
Salt Lake City, UT 84111　　　　Ph: (801)328-8181

─────────── **Vermont** ───────────

★3931★
American Civil Liberties Union (ACLU)
Vermont Affiliate
PO Box 810
Montepelier, VT 05601　　　　Ph: (802)223-6304
Leslie Williams, Dir.

─────────── **Virgin Islands** ───────────

★3932★
Virgin Islands Minority Business Development Center
35 King St. Christensted
Saint Croix, VI 00820　　　　Ph: (809)773-6334

★3933★
Virgin Islands Minority Business Development Center
81-AB Kronprindens Gade, 3rd Fl.
PO Box 838
Saint Thomas, VI 00804　　　　Ph: (809)774-7215

─────────── **Virginia** ───────────

★3934★
Newport News Minority Business Development Center
6060 Jefferson Ave., Ste. 6016
Newport News, VA 23605　　　　Ph: (804)245-8743

★3935★
Norfolk Minority Business Development Center
355 Crawford Pkwy., Ste. 608
Portsmouth, VA 23701　　　　Ph: (804)399-0888

★3936★
Richmond Minority Business Development Center
3805 Cutshaw Ave., Ste. 402
Richmond, VA 23230　　　　Ph: (804)355-4000

─────────── **Washington** ───────────

★3937★
American Civil Liberties Union (ACLU)
Washington Affiliate
705 2nd Ave., Rm. 300
Seattle, WA 98104　　　　Ph: (206)624-2180
Kathleen Taylor, Dir.

★3938★
Seattle Minority Business Development Center
155 NE 100th Ave., Ste. 401
Seattle, WA 98125　　　　Ph: (206)525-5617

─────────── **West Virginia** ───────────

★3939★
American Civil Liberties Union (ACLU)
West Virginia Affiliate
PO Box 3952
Charleston, WV 25339-3952　　　　Ph: (304)345-9246

─────────── **Wisconsin** ───────────

★3940★
American Civil Liberties Union (ACLU)
Wisconsin Affiliate
207 E. Buffalo St., No. 325　　　　Ph: (414)272-4032
Milwaukee, WI 53202　　　　Fax: (414)272-0182
Eunice Edgar, Dir.

★3941★
Milwaukee Minority Business Development Center
3929 N. Humboltd Blvd.
Milwaukee, WI 53212　　　　Ph: (414)332-6268

───── **Wyoming** ─────

★3942★
American Civil Liberties Union (ACLU)
Wyoming Affiliate
PO Box A
Laramie, WY 82070 Ph: (307)745-4515
Laurie Seidenberg, Dir.

Federal Government Agencies

★3943★
U.S. Commission on Civil Rights
1121 Vermont Ave. NW
Washington, DC 20425 Ph: (202)523-5571
Arthur A. Fletcher, Chairman

★3944★
U.S. Commission on Civil Rights
Central Regional Office
Old Federal Bldg.
911 Walnut St. Ph: (816)426-5253
Kansas City, MO 64106 Fax: (816)426-2233
Melvin Jenkins, Dir.

Territory Includes: Alabama, Arkansas, Iowa, Kansas, Louisiana, Mississippi, Missouri, and Nebraska.

★3945★
U.S. Commission on Civil Rights
Eastern Regional Office
1121 Vermont Ave. NW Ph: (202)523-5264
Washington, DC 20425 Fax: (202)376-1163
John I. Binkley, Dir.

Territory Includes: Connecticut, Delaware, District of Columbia, Maine, Maryland, Massachusetts, New Hampshire, New Jersey, New York, Pennsylvania, Rhode Island, Vermont, Virginia, and West Virginia.

★3946★
U.S. Commission on Civil Rights
Midwestern Regional Office
175 W. Jackson St. Ph: (312)353-8311
Chicago, IL 60604 Fax: (312)353-8324
Constance D. Davis, Dir.

Territory Includes: Illinois, Indiana, Michigan, Minnesota, Ohio, and Wisconsin.

★3947★
U.S. Commission on Civil Rights
Rocky Mountain Regional Office
Federal Office Bldg.
1961 Stout St.
PO Drawer 3585 Ph: (303)844-6716
Denver, CO 80924 Fax: (303)844-6721
William Muldrow, Dir.

Territory Includes: Colorado, Montana, North Dakota, South Dakota, Utah, and Wyoming.

★3948★
U.S. Commission on Civil Rights
Southern Regional Office
101 Marietta St.
Atlanta, GA 30303 Ph: (404)730-2476
Bobby Doctor, Dir.

Territory Includes: Florida, Georgia, Kentucky, North Carolina, South Carolina, and Tennessee.

★3949★
U.S. Commission on Civil Rights
Western Regional Office
3660 Wilshire Blvd. Ph: (213)894-3437
Los Angeles, CA 90010 Fax: (213)894-0508
Philip Montez, Dir.

Territory Includes: Alaska, Arizona, California, Hawaii, Idaho, Nevada, New Mexico, Oklahoma, Oregon, Texas, and Washington.

★3950★
U.S. Department of Agriculture
Office of Small and Disadvantaged Business
Utilization
14th St. & Independence Ave. SW
Washington, DC 20250 Ph: (202)720-7117
James House, Assoc.Dir.

★3951★
U.S. Department of Commerce
Bureau of the Census
Population Division
Racial Statistics Branch
Federal Office Bldg., Rm. 2335
3 Silver Hill and Suitland Rds.
Suitland, MD 20746 Ph: (301)763-7572
Roderick Harrison, Chief

★3952★
U.S. Department of Commerce
Economic Development Administration
Civil Rights Office of Program Support
Compliance Renew Division
14th St. & Constitution Ave. NW, Rm.
7221
Washington, DC 20230 Ph: (202)377-5575
David E. Lasky, Chief

★3953★
U.S. Department of Commerce
Minority Business Development Agency
Herbert Hoover Bldg.
14th St. & Constitution Ave. NW
Washington, DC 20230 Ph: (202)377-5061
Joe Lira, Dir.

★3954★
U.S. Department of Commerce
Minority Business Development Agency
Atlanta Region
401 W. Peachtree St. NW, Ste. 1930
Atlanta, GA 30308-3516 Ph: (404)730-3300
Carlton L. Eccles, Reg.Dir.

Territory Includes: Alabama, Florida, Georgia, Kentucky, Mississippi, North Carolina, South Carolina, and Tennessee.

★3955★
U.S. Department of Commerce
Minority Business Development Agency
Chicago Region
55 E. Monroe St., Ste. 1440
Chicago, IL 60603 Ph: (312)353-0182
David Vega, Reg.Dir.

Territory Includes: Illinois, Indiana, Iowa, Kansas, Michigan, Minnesota, Missouri, Nebraska, Ohio, and Wisconsin.

★3956★
U.S. Department of Commerce
Minority Business Development Agency
Dallas Region
1100 Commerce St., Rm. 7-B23
Dallas, TX 75242   Ph: (214)767-8001
Melda C. Cabrera, Reg.Dir.
Territory Includes: Arkansas, Colorado, Louisiana, Montana, New Mexico, North Dakota, Oklahoma, South Dakota, Texas, Utah, and Wyoming.

★3957★
U.S. Department of Commerce
Minority Business Development Agency
New York Region
26 Federal Plaza, Rm. 3720
New York, NY 10278   Ph: (212)264-3262
John F. Iglehart, Reg.Dir.
Territory Includes: Connecticut, Maine, Massachusetts, New Hampshire, New Jersey, New York, Puerto Rico, Rhode Island, Vermont, and the Virgin Islands.

★3958★
U.S. Department of Commerce
Minority Business Development Agency
San Francisco Region
221 Main St., Rm. 1280
San Francisco, CA 94105   Ph: (415)744-3001
Xavier Mena, Reg.Dir.
Territory Includes: Alaska, American Samoa, Arizona, California, Hawaii, Idaho, Nevada, Oregon, and Washington.

★3959★
U.S. Department of Commerce
Minority Business Development Agency
Washington, DC Region
Herbert Clark Hoover Bldg.
14th St. & Constitution Ave. NW
Washington, DC 20230   Ph: (202)377-8275
Georgina Sanchez, Reg.Dir.
Territory Includes: Delaware, District of Columbia, Maryland, Pennsylvania, Virginia, and West Virginia.

★3960★
U.S. Department of Commerce
Office of Civil Rights
14th St. & Constitution Ave. NW, Rm. 6010
Washington, DC 20230   Ph: (202)377-3940
Gerald R. Lucas, Dir.

★3961★
U.S. Department of Commerce
Office of Small and Disadvantaged Business Utilization
14th St. & Constitution Ave. NW, Rm. 6411
Washington, DC 20230   Ph: (202)377-3387
James P. Maruca, Dir.

★3962★
U.S. Department of Education
Assistant Secretary for Postsecondary Education
Higher Education Programs
Minorities and Women
Regional Office Bldg., Rm. 3915
7th & D Sts. SW
Washington, DC 20202   Ph: (202)708-5656
William C. Young, Liason Officer

★3963★
U.S. Department of Education
Civil Rights Office
Region I, Boston
McCormack Post Office & Courthouse, Rm. 222
Boston, MA 02109-4557   Ph: (617)223-9667
Thomas Habino, Reg.Dir.
Territory Includes: Connecticut, Maine, Massachusetts, New Hampshire, Rhode Island, and Vermont.

★3964★
U.S. Department of Education
Civil Rights Office
Region II, New York
26 Federal Plaza, Rm. 36-118
New York, NY 10278   Ph: (212)264-4633
Paula Kuebler, Reg.Dir.
Territory Includes: New Jersey, New York, Puerto Rico, and the Virgin Islands.

★3965★
U.S. Department of Education
Civil Rights Office
Region III, Philadelphia
3535 Market St., Rm. 6300
Philadelphia, PA 19104-3326   Ph: (215)596-6787
Dr. Robert Smallwood, Reg.Dir.
Territory Includes: Delaware, District of Columbia, Maryland, Pennsylvania, Virginia, and West Virginia.

★3966★
U.S. Department of Education
Civil Rights Office
Region IV, Atlanta
101 Marietta Tower Bldg.
Atlanta, GA 30323   Ph: (404)331-2954
Archie B. Meyer Sr., Reg.Dir.
Territory Includes: Alabama, Florida, Georgia, Kentucky, Mississippi, North Carolina, South Carolina, and Tennessee.

★3967★
U.S. Department of Education
Civil Rights Office
Region V, Chicago
401 S. State St.
Chicago, IL 60605   Ph: (312)886-3456
Kenneth Mines, Reg.Dir.
Territory Includes: Illinois, Indiana, Michigan, Minnesota, Ohio, and Wisconsin.

★3968★
U.S. Department of Education
Civil Rights Office
Region VI, Dallas
1200 Main Tower Bldg., 22nd Fl.
Dallas, TX 75202   Ph: (214)767-3959
Taylor D. August, Reg.Dir.
Territory Includes: Arkansas, Louisiana, New Mexico, Oklahoma, and Texas.

★3969★
U.S. Department of Education
Civil Rights Office
Region VII, Kansas City
10220 N. Executive Hills Blvd.
Kansas City, MO 61453   Ph: (816)891-8026
Territory Includes: Iowa, Kansas, Missouri, and Nebraska.

★3970★
U.S. Department of Education
Civil Rights Office
Region VIII, Denver
1961 Stout, Rm. 342
Denver, CO 80294　　　　　　Ph: (303)844-5695
Cathy H. Lewis, Reg.Dir.

Territory Includes: Colorado, Montana, North Dakota, South Dakota, Utah, and Washington.

★3971★
U.S. Department of Education
Civil Rights Office
Region IX, San Francisco
221 Main St.
San Francisco, CA 94105-1925　　Ph: (415)227-8040
John E. Palomino, Reg.Dir.

Territory Includes: American Samoa, Arizona, California, Guam, Hawaii, Nevada, and the Pacific Islands.

★3972★
U.S. Department of Education
Civil Rights Office
Region X, Seattle
915 2nd Ave., Rm. 3362
Seattle, WA 98174-1099　　　　Ph: (206)553-6811
Gary Jackson, Reg.Dir.

Territory Includes: Alaska, Idaho, Oregon, and Washington.

★3973★
U.S. Department of Education
Office of the Secretary
Assistant Secretary for Civil Rights
330 C St. SW, Rm. 5000
Washington, DC 20202　　　　　Ph: (202)732-1213
Michael L. Williams, Asst.Sec.

★3974★
U.S. Department of Education
Office of Small and Disadvantaged Business
　Utilization
400 Maryland Ave. SW, Rm. 3120
Washington, DC 20202　　　　　Ph: (202)708-9820
Daniel L. Levin, Dir.

★3975★
U.S. Department of Energy
Office of Minority Economic Impact
Forrestal Bldg.
1000 Independence Ave. SW, Rm. 5B-110
Washington, DC 20585　　　　　Ph: (202)586-8383
Melva Wray, Dir.

★3976★
U.S. Department of Energy
Office of Small and Disadvantaged Business
　Utilization
Forrestal Bldg.
1000 Independence Ave. SW, Rm. 905
Washington, DC 20585　　　　　Ph: (202)254-5583
Leo V. Miranda, Dir.

★3977★
U.S. Department of Health and Human Services
Administration for Children and Families
Head Start Bureau
American Indian Program Branch
PO Box 1182
Washington, DC 20013　　　　　Ph: (202)245-0437
James Kolb, Dir.

★3978★
U.S. Department of Health and Human Services
Assistant Secretary for Management and Budget
Office of Management and Acquisition
Office of Equal Employment Opportunity
330 Independence Ave. SW, Rm. 4317
Washington, DC 20201　　　　　Ph: (202)619-1564
Barbara Aulenbach, Dir.

★3979★
U.S. Department of Health and Human Services
Civil Rights Office
200 Independence Ave. SW, Rm. 5400
Washington, DC 20201　　　　　Ph: (202)619-0403
Edward Mercado, Dir.

★3980★
U.S. Department of Health and Human Services
Civil Rights Office
Equal Employment Opportunity/Affirmative Action
300 Independence Ave. SW, Rm. 5400
Washington, DC 20201　　　　　Ph: (202)619-0585
Mary Martin, Coord.

★3981★
U.S. Department of Health and Human Services
Civil Rights Office
Region I, Boston
2100 J.F.K. Federal Bldg.
Boston, MA 02203　　　　　　　Ph: (617)565-1340
Caroline Chang, Man.

★3982★
U.S. Department of Health and Human Services
Civil Rights Office
Region II, New York
J.K. Javtis Federal Bldg., Ste. 3835
New York, NY 10278　　　　　　Ph: (212)264-3313
Frank Cedo, Man.

★3983★
U.S. Department of Health and Human Services
Civil Rights Office
Region III, Philadelphia
Gateway Bldg.
PO Box 13716
Philadelphia, PA 19101　　　　　Ph: (215)596-1262
Paul Cushing, Man.

★3984★
U.S. Department of Health and Human Services
Civil Rights Office
Region IV, Atlanta
101 Marietta Tower
Atlanta, GA 30323　　　　　　　Ph: (404)331-2779
Maria A. Chretien, Man.

★3985★
U.S. Department of Health and Human Services
Civil Rights Office
Region V, Chicago
105 W. Adams
Chicago, IL 60603　　　　　　　Ph: (312)886-2359
Charlotte Irons, Man.

★3986★
U.S. Department of Health and Human Services
Civil Rights Office
Region VI, Dallas
1200 Main Tower Bldg.
Dallas, TX 75202　　　　　　　Ph: (214)767-4056
Davis A. Sanders, Man.

★3987★
U.S. Department of Health and Human Services
Civil Rights Office
Region VII, Kansas City
601 E. 12th St.
Kansas City, MO 64106   Ph: (816)426-7277
John Halverson, Man.

★3988★
U.S. Department of Health and Human Services
Civil Rights Office
Region VIII, Denver
1961 Stout St.
Denver, CO 80294   Ph: (303)844-2024
Vada Kyle-Holmes, Man.

★3989★
U.S. Department of Health and Human Services
Civil Rights Office
Region IX, San Francisco
50 United Nations Plaza
San Francisco, CA 94102   Ph: (415)556-8586
Virginia Apodaca, Man.

★3990★
U.S. Department of Health and Human Services
Civil Rights Office
Region X, Seattle
2201 6th Ave.
Mail Stop RX-11
Seattle, WA 98121   Ph: (206)442-0473
Carmen Rockwell, Man.

★3991★
U.S. Department of Health and Human Services
Public Health Service
Centers for Disease Control
Minority Health
1600 Clifton Rd. NE, Rm. 2122
Atlanta, GA 30333   Ph: (404)639-3703
Rueben Warren, Asst.Dir.

★3992★
U.S. Department of Housing and Urban Development
Assistant Secretary for Fair Housing and Equal
  Opportunity
451 7th St. SW, Rm. 5700
Washington, DC 20410   Ph: (202)708-4242
Gordon H. Mansfield, Asst. Sec.

★3993★
U.S. Department of Housing and Urban Development
Office of Fair Housing and Equal Opportunity
Region I, Boston
O'Neill Federal Bldg., Rm. 309
10 Causeway St.
Boston, MA 02222   Ph: (617)565-5304
Robert W. Laplante, Dir.

★3994★
U.S. Department of Housing and Urban Development
Office of Fair Housing and Equal Opportunity
Region II, New York
26 Federal Plaza
New York, NY 10278   Ph: (212)264-1290
Stanley Seidenfeld, Dir.

★3995★
U.S. Department of Housing and Urban Development
Office of Fair Housing and Equal Opportunity
Region III, Philadelphia
Liberty Sq. Bldg.
105 S. 7th St.
Philadelphia, PA 19106   Ph: (215)597-2338
Barry C. Anderson, Dir.

★3996★
U.S. Department of Housing and Urban Development
Office of Fair Housing and Equal Opportunity
Region IV, Atlanta
75 Spring St. SW
Atlanta, GA 30303   Ph: (404)331-5140
Kathelene Coughlin, Dir.

★3997★
U.S. Department of Housing and Urban Development
Office of Fair Housing and Equal Opportunity
Region V, Chicago
77 W. Jackson
Chicago, IL 60606   Ph: (312)353-7776
Thomas Higginbothan, Dir.

★3998★
U.S. Department of Housing and Urban Development
Office of Fair Housing and Equal Opportunity
Region VI, Fort Worth
PO Box 2905
Fort Worth, TX 76113   Ph: (817)885-5491
John E. Wright, Dir.

★3999★
U.S. Department of Housing and Urban Development
Office of Fair Housing and Equal Opportunity
Region VII, Kansas City
400 State Ave.
Kansas City, MO 66101   Ph: (913)236-3958
Floyd May, Dir.

★4000★
U.S. Department of Housing and Urban Development
Office of Fair Housing and Equal Opportunity
Region VIII, Denver
1405 Curtis St.
Denver, CO 80202   Ph: (303)844-4751
Lloyd R. Miller, Dir.

★4001★
U.S. Department of Housing and Urban Development
Office of Fair Housing and Equal Opportunity
Region IX, San Francisco
450 Golden Gate Ave.
PO Box 36003
San Francisco, CA 94102   Ph: (415)556-6826
LaVera Gillespie, Dir.

★4002★
U.S. Department of Housing and Urban Development
Office of Fair Housing and Equal Opportunity
Region X, Seattle
1321 2nd Ave.
Mailstop 10-E
Seattle, WA 98101   Ph: (206)553-0226
James Brown, Dir.

★4003★
U.S. Department of Housing and Urban Development
Office of Small and Disadvantaged Business
Utilization
Minority Business
451 7th St. SW
Washington, DC 20410   Ph: (202)708-3350
Clarence White, Dir.

★4004★
U.S. Department of the Interior
Office of Equal Opportunity
C St. between 18th & 19th St. NW, Rm.
  1324
Washington, DC 20240   Ph: (202)208-5693
Carmen R. Maymi, Dir.

★4005★
U.S. Department of the Interior
Office of Small and Disadvantaged Business
Utilization
C St. between 18th & 19th Sts. NW, Rm.
  2759
Washington, DC 20240   Ph: (202)208-8493
Kenneth Kelly, Dir.

★4006★
U.S. Department of Justice
Civil Rights Division
10th St. & Constitution Ave. NW, Rm.
  5643
Washington, DC 20530   Ph: (202)514-2151
John R. Dunne, Asst. Attorney General

★4007★
U.S. Department of Labor
Assistant Secretary for Administration and
  Management
Directorate of Civil Rights
200 Constitution Ave. NW
Washington, DC 20210   Ph: (202)523-8927
Annabelle T. Lockhart, Dir.

★4008★
U.S. Department of Labor
Assistant Secretary for Administration and
  Management
Office of Equal Employment Opportunity and
  Affirmative Action
200 Constitution Ave. NW
Washington, DC 20210   Ph: (202)523-6362
Andre C. Whisenton, Chief

★4009★
U.S. Department of Labor
Civil Rights Office
Region I, Boston
J.F.K. Federal Bldg.
Boston, MA 02203   Ph: (617)565-2011
Jane Daugherty, Dir.

★4010★
U.S. Department of Labor
Civil Rights Office
Region II, New York
201 Varick St.
New York, NY 10014   Ph: (212)337-2218
Charles Mason, Dir.

★4011★
U.S. Department of Labor
Civil Rights Office
Region III, Philadelphia
3535 Market St., Rm. 14120
Philadelphia, PA 19104   Ph: (215)596-6751
Jerome Hines, Dir.

★4012★
U.S. Department of Labor
Civil Rights Office
Region IV, Atlanta
1371 Peachtree St. NE
Atlanta, GA 30367   Ph: (404)347-2195
Alice Ahlers, Dir.

★4013★
U.S. Department of Labor
Civil Rights Office
Region V, Chicago
230 S. Dearborn St.
Chicago, IL 60604   Ph: (312)353-4670
Herb Roth, Dir.

★4014★
U.S. Department of Labor
Civil Rights Office
Region VI, Dallas
Federal Bldg., Rm. 735
525 Griffin St.
Dallas, TX 75202   Ph: (214)767-4136
Jim Lyke, Dir.

★4015★
U.S. Department of Labor
Civil Rights Office
Region VII, Kansas City
911 Walnut St.
Kansas City, MO 64106   Ph: (816)426-6171
Donna Porter, Dir.

★4016★
U.S. Department of Labor
Civil Rights Office
Region VIII, Denver
c/o Region VII
911 Walnut St.
Kansas City, MO 64106   Ph: (816)426-3891
Donna Porter, Dir.

★4017★
U.S. Department of Labor
Civil Rights Office
Region IX, San Francisco
71 Stevenson St.
San Francisco, CA 94105   Ph: (415)744-6683
Lee Makapagal, Dir.

★4018★
U.S. Department of Labor
Civil Rights Office
Region X, Seattle
1111 3rd Ave., Rm. 920
Seattle, WA 98101   Ph: (206)535-2767

★4019★
U.S. Department of Labor
Office of Small and Disadvantaged Business
  Utilization
200 Constitution Ave. NW
Washington, DC 20210   Ph: (202)523-9148
William T. Alexander, Dir.

★4020★
U.S. Department of State
Office of Small and Disadvantaged Business
  Utilization
1701 N. Fort Myer Dr., Rm. 633
Rosslyn, VA 22209   Ph: (703)875-6824
Durie N. White, Dir.

★4021★
U.S. Department of Transportation
Coast Guard, United States
Office of Acquisition
Contract Support Division for Small and Minority
  Business
2100 2nd St. SW, Rm. 2400
Washington, DC 20590   Ph: (202)267-2499
Dan Sturdivant, Branch Chief

★4022★
U.S. Department of Transportation
Coast Guard, United States
Office of Civil Rights
2100 2nd St. SW, Rm. 2400
Washington, DC 20590   Ph: (202)267-1562
Walter R. Somerville, Chief

★4023★
U.S. Department of Transportation
Federal Highway Administration
Office of Civil Rights
400 7th St. SW, Rm. 4132
Washington, DC 20590   Ph: (202)366-0693
Edward W. Morris Jr., Div.Chief

★4024★
U.S. Department of Transportation
Office of Small and Disadvantaged Business
  Utilization
Minority Business Resource Center
400 7th St. SW, Rm. 9410
Washington, DC 20590   Ph: (202)366-2852
Joe Capuano, Chief

★4025★
U.S. Equal Employment Opportunity Commission
1801 L St. NW
Washington, DC 20507   Ph: (202)634-4001
Evan J. Kemp, Dir.

★4026★
U.S. Equal Employment Opportunity Commission
Atlanta District
75 Piedmont Ave. NE, Ste. 1100   Ph: (404)331-6093
Atlanta, GA 30335   Fax: (404)331-6093
Chris Roggerson, Dir.
Territory Includes: Georgia.

★4027★
U.S. Equal Employment Opportunity Commission
Baltimore District
111 Market Pl., Ste. 4000   Ph: (410)962-3932
Baltimore, MD 21202   Fax: (410)962-4270
Issie L. Jenkins, Dir.
Territory Includes: Maryland and Virginia.

★4028★
U.S. Equal Employment Opportunity Commission
Birmingham District
1900 3rd Ave., N.   Ph: (205)731-0083
Birmingham, AL 35203   Fax: (205)731-2101
Warren A. Bullock, Dir.
Territory Includes: Alabama and Mississippi.

★4029★
U.S. Equal Employment Opportunity Commission
Charlotte District
5500 Central Ave.   Ph: (704)567-7100
Charlotte, NC 28212   Fax: (704)567-7192
Marsha Drane, Dir.
Territory Includes: North Carolina and South Carolina.

★4030★
U.S. Equal Employment Opportunity Commission
Chicago District
536 S. Clark St., Rm. 930-A   Ph: (312)353-2713
Chicago, IL 60605   Fax: (312)353-7355
Jack Rowe, Dir.
Territory Includes: Northern Illinois.

★4031★
U.S. Equal Employment Opportunity Commission
Cleveland District
1375 Euclid Ave., Rm. 600   Ph: (216)522-2001
Cleveland, OH 44115   Fax: (216)522-7395
Harold Ferguson, Dir.
Territory Includes: Ohio.

★4032★
U.S. Equal Employment Opportunity Commission
Dallas District
8303 Elmbrook Dr., 2nd Fl.   Ph: (214)767-7015
Dallas, TX 75247   Fax: (214)767-7959
Jacqueline Bradley, Dir.
Territory Includes: Oklahoma and Northern Texas.

★4033★
U.S. Equal Employment Opportunity Commission
Denver District
1845 Sherman St.   Ph: (303)866-1300
Denver, CO 80203   Fax: (303)866-1085
Francisco J. Flores, Dir.
Territory Includes: Colorado, Montana, Nebraska, North Dakota, South Dakota, and Wyoming.

★4034★
U.S. Equal Employment Opportunity Commission
Detroit District
477 Michigan Ave., Rm. 1540   Ph: (313)226-7636
Detroit, MI 48226   Fax: (313)226-2778
A. William Schukar, Dir.
Territory Includes: Michigan.

★4035★
U.S. Equal Employment Opportunity Commission
Houston District
1919 Smith St., 7th Fl.   Ph: (713)653-3320
Houston, TX 77002   Fax: (713)653-3381
Harriet J. Ehrlich, Dir.
Territory Includes: Central Texas.

★4036★
U.S. Equal Employment Opportunity Commission
Indianapolis District
46 E. Ohio St., Rm. 456   Ph: (317)226-7210
Indianapolis, IN 46204   Fax: (317)226-7953
Thomas Hadfield, Dir.
Territory Includes: Indiana and Louisville, Kentucky.

★4037★
U.S. Equal Employment Opportunity Commission
Los Angeles District
3660 Wilshire Blvd., 5th Fl.   Ph: (213)251-7278
Los Angeles, CA 90010   Fax: (213)251-7800
Dorthy Porter, Dir.
Territory Includes: Southern California and Nevada.

★4038★
U.S. Equal Employment Opportunity Commission
Memphis District
1407 Union Ave.   Ph: (901)722-2617
Memphis, TN 38104   Fax: (901)521-2602
Walter Grabon, Dir.

Territory Includes: Kentucky (except Louisville) and Tennessee.

★4039★
U.S. Equal Employment Opportunity Commission
Miami District
1 NE 1st St., 6th Fl.   Ph: (305)536-4491
Miami, FL 33132   Fax: (305)536-4011
Frederico Costales, Dir.

Territory Includes: Florida and the Panama Canal Zone.

★4040★
U.S. Equal Employment Opportunity Commission
Milwaukee District
310 W. Wisconsin Ave., Ste. 800   Ph: (414)291-1111
Milwaukee, WI 53203   Fax: (414)291-4133
Chester V. Bailey, Dir.

Territory Includes: Iowa, Minnesota, and Wisconsin.

★4041★
U.S. Equal Employment Opportunity Commission
New Orleans District
701 Loyola Ave., Ste. 600   Ph: (504)589-2329
New Orleans, LA 70113   Fax: (504)589-6861
Patricia F. Bivins, Dir.

Territory Includes: Arkansas and Louisiana.

★4042★
U.S. Equal Employment Opportunity Commission
New York District
90 Church St., Rm. 1501   Ph: (212)264-7161
New York, NY 10007   Fax: (212)264-3135
Spencer H. Lewis, Dir.

Territory Includes: Connecticut, Maine, Massachusetts, New Hampshire, New York, Puerto Rico, Rhode Island, Vermont, and the Virgin Islands.

★4043★
U.S. Equal Employment Opportunity Commission
Philadelphia District
1421 Cherry St., 10th Fl.   Ph: (215)597-9350
Philadelphia, PA 94103   Fax: (215)597-4073
Johnny J. Butler, Dir.

Territory Includes: Delaware, New Jersey, Pennsylvania, and West Virginia.

★4044★
U.S. Equal Employment Opportunity Commission
Phoenix District
4520 N. Central Ave.   Ph: (602)640-5000
Phoenix, AZ 85012   Fax: (602)640-2489
Charles Burtner, Dir.

Territory Includes: Arizona, New Mexico, and Utah.

★4045★
U.S. Equal Employment Opportunity Commission
St. Louis District
625 Euclid St.   Ph: (314)425-6523
Saint Louis, MO 63108   Fax: (314)425-6105
Lynn Brunner, Dir.

Territory Includes: Kansas and Missouri.

★4046★
U.S. Equal Employment Opportunity Commission
San Antonio District
5410 Fredericksburg Rd., Ste. 200   Ph: (512)229-4810
San Antonio, TX 78229   Fax: (512)229-4806
Pedro Esquivel, Dir.

Territory Includes: Southern Texas.

★4047★
U.S. Equal Employment Opportunity Commission
San Francisco District
901 Market St., Ste. 500   Ph: (415)744-6500
San Francisco, CA 94103   Fax: (415)744-6009
Paula Montanez, Dir.

Territory Includes: American Samoa, Northern Caliornia, Commonwealth of the Northern Mariana Islands, Guam, Hawaii, and Wake Island.

★4048★
U.S. Equal Employment Opportunity Commission
Seattle District
2815 2nd Ave.   Ph: (206)553-0968
Seattle, WA 98121   Fax: (206)553-1308
Jeanette Leino, Dir.

Territory Includes: Alaska, Idaho, Oregon, and Washington.

★4049★
U.S. Equal Employment Opportunity Commission
Washington Field Office
1400 L St. NW, Ste. 200   Ph: (202)275-6365
Washington, DC 20005   Fax: (202)275-6834
Susan Reilly, Dir.

Territory Includes: District of Columbia.

★4050★
U.S. General Accounting Office
Civil Rights Office
441 G St. NW, Rm. 3027
Washington, DC 20001   Ph: (202)275-6388
Nilda Aponte, Dir.

★4051★
U.S. Information Agency
Bureau of Management
Office of Equal Employment Opportunity and Civil Rights
301 4th St. SW, Rm. 365
Washington, DC 20547   Ph: (202)619-5151
Marilyn B. Thompson, Dir.

★4052★
U.S. National Aeronautics and Space Administration
Office of Equal Opportunity Programs
Discrimination Complaints Division
400 Maryland Ave. SW
Washington, DC 20546   Ph: (202)453-2180
Oceola S. Hall, Dir.

★4053★
U.S. National Aeronautics and Space Administration
Office of Small and Disadvantaged Business Utilization
Minority Businesses Advisor
400 Maryland Ave. SW
Washington, DC 20546   Ph: (202)453-2088
Rae C. Martel, Dir.

★4054★
U.S. Office of Personnel Management
Office of Equal Employment Opportunity
1900 E. St. NW, Rm. 5457
Washington, DC 20415   Ph: (202)606-2460
Teresa Alzamora del Rio, Asst.Dir.

★4055★
U.S. Small Business Administration
Minority Small Business and Capital Ownership
  Development
409 3rd St.
Washington, DC 20416   Ph: (202)205-6410
Judith A. Watts, Assoc.Adm.

★4056★
U.S. Small Business Administration
Minority Small Business and Capital Ownership
  Development
Region I, Boston
155 Federal St., 9th Fl.
Boston, MA 02110   Ph: (617)223-2036
Samuel W. Brown, Asst.Adm.

★4057★
U.S. Small Business Administration
Minority Small Business and Capital Ownership
  Development
Region II, New York
26 Federal Plaza, Rm. 3108
New York, NY 10278   Ph: (212)264-1046
Francesco Marrero, Asst.Adm.

★4058★
U.S. Small Business Administration
Minority Small Business and Capital Ownership
  Development
Region III, Philadelphia
475 Allendale Rd., Ste. 201
King of Prussia, PA 19406   Ph: (215)962-3758
Delores Ellis, Asst.Adm.

★4059★
U.S. Small Business Administration
Minority Small Business and Capital Ownership
  Development
Region IV, Atlanta
1375 Peachtree St. NE
Atlanta, GA 30367   Ph: (404)347-4089
Isaiah Washington, Asst.Adm.

★4060★
U.S. Small Business Administration
Minority Small Business and Capital Ownership
  Development
Region V, Chicago
230 S. Dearborn St., Rm. 510
Chicago, IL 60604   Ph: (312)353-6847
Gary Peele, Asst.Adm.

★4061★
U.S. Small Business Administration
Minority Small Business and Capital Ownership
  Development
Region VI, Dallas
8625 King George Dr., Bldg. C
Dallas, TX 75235   Ph: (214)767-7631
Lavan Alexander, Asst.Adm.

★4062★
U.S. Small Business Administration
Minority Small Business and Capital Ownership
  Development
Region VII, Kansas City
911 Walnut St., 13th Fl.
Kansas City, MO 64106   Ph: (816)426-3516
Art Seibert, Asst.Adm.

★4063★
U.S. Small Business Administration
Minority Small Business and Capital Ownership
  Development
Region VIII, Denver
999 18th St., Ste. 701
Denver, CO 80202   Ph: (303)294-7076
Gerald Martinez, Asst.Adm.

★4064★
U.S. Small Business Administration
Minority Small Business and Capital Ownership
  Development
Region IX, San Francisco
71 Stevenson St., 20th Fl.
San Francisco, CA 94102   Ph: (415)774-6429
R. Stephen Bangs, Asst.Adm.

★4065★
U.S. Small Business Administration
Minority Small Business and Capital Ownership
  Development
Region X, Seattle
2615 4th Ave., Ste. 440
Seattle, WA 98121   Ph: (206)442-0391
Carol Colpitts, Asst.Adm.

★4066★
U.S. Smithsonian Institute
Office of Equal Employment and Minority Affairs
955 L'Enfant Plaza North, SW
Washington, DC 20560   Ph: (202)287-3487
Robert L. Osborne, Dir.

Federal Domestic Assistance Programs

★4067★
U.S. Department of Commerce
Economic Development Administration
Economic Development—Grants for Public Works and
  Development Facilities
Public Works Division
Herbert C. Hoover Bldg., Rm. H7326
Washington, DC 20230   Ph: (202)377-5265
David L. McIlwain, Dir.

Catalog Number: 11.300. **Objectives:** To promote long-term economic development and assist in the public works and development facilities needed to initiate and encourage the creation or retention of permanent jobs in the private sector in areas experiencing severe economic distress. **Applicant Eligibility:** States, cities, counties, and other political subdivisions, Indian tribes, the Federated States of Micronesia, the Republic of the Marshall Islands, Commonwealths and territories of the U.S. flag, and private or public nonprofit organizations or associations representing a redevelopment area or a designated Economic Development Center are eligible to receive grants. **Types of Assistance:** Project grants. **Beneficiary Eligibility:** Unemployed or underemployed persons and/or members of low-income families.

★4068★
U.S. Department of Commerce
Economic Development Administration
**Economic Development—Support for Planning
  Organizations**
Herbert C. Hoover Bldg., Rm. H7203
Washington, DC 20230   Ph: (202)377-2873
Luis F. Bueso, Dir. of Planning

Catalog Number: 11.302. **Objectives:** To assist in providing
administrative aid to multi-county districts, redevelopment areas and
Indian tribes to establish and maintain economic development
planning and implementation capability and thereby promote
effective utilization of resources in the creation of full-time
permanent jobs for the unemployed and the underemployed in areas
of high distress. **Applicant Eligibility:** (1) Public bodies and other
nonprofit organizations representing groups of State-delineated and
EDA-approved adjoining counties, which include at least one area
designated as a redevelopment area by the Secretary of Commerce
and one or more growth centers not over 250,000 population; (2)
Indian Tribes; and (3) counties designated as redevelopment areas
or nonprofit organizations representing redevelopment areas or
parts of such areas. **Types of Assistance:** Project Grants.
Beneficiary Eligibility: Areas or substantial and persistent
unemployment and residents (particularly unemployed and low
income persons) of those areas.

★4069★
U.S. Department of Commerce
Minority Business Development Agency
Minority Business Development Centers
Office of Program Development
14th & Constitution Ave. NW, Rm. 5096
Washington, DC 20230   Ph: (202)377-0940
Georgina Sanchez, Dir.

Catalog Number: 11.800. **Objectives:** To provide business
development services for a minimal fee to minority firms and
individuals interested in entering, expanding or improving their
efforts in the marketplace. Minority business development center
operators provide a wide range of services to clients, from initial
consultations to the identification and resolution of specific business
problems. **Applicant Eligibility:** No restrictions. **Types of
Assistance:** Project grants (cooperative agreements). **Beneficiary
Eligibility:** Recipient is to provide assistance to minority-owned
businesses or minorities interested in starting a business.

★4070★
U.S. Department of Commerce
Minority Business Development Agency
Minority Business Resource Development
Office of Program Development
14th & Constitution Ave. NW, Rm. 5096
Washington, DC 20230   Ph: (202)377-0940
Georgina Sanchez, Dir.

Catalog Number: 11.802. **Objectives:** The resource development
activity provides for the indirect business assistance program
conducted by MBDA. These programs encourage minority business
development by identifying and developing private markets and
capital sources; decreasing minority dependence on government
programs; expanding business information and business services
through trade associations; promoting and supporting the
mobilization of resources of Federal agencies and State and local
governments at the local level; and assisting minorities in entering
new and growing markets. **Applicant Eligibility:** Restricted to
established business, industry, professional, and trade associations,
and chambers of commerce. **Types of Assistance:** Project grants
(cooperative agreements). **Beneficiary Eligibility:** Restricted to
established business, industry, professional, and trade associations,
and chambers of commerce.

★4071★
U.S. Department of Education
**Office of Assistant Secretary for Elementary and
  Secondary Education**
**Desegregation Assistance, Civil Rights Training, and
  Advisory Service**
Division of Discretionary Grants
400 Maryland Ave. SW
Washington, DC 20202   Ph: (202)401-0360
Sylvia Wright, Contact

Catalog Number: 84.004. **Objectives:** To provide technical
assistance and training services to school districts to cope with
educational problems occasioned by race, sex, and national origin
desegregation. **Applicant Eligibility:** State educational agencies,
desgregation assistance centers, any private nonprofit organizations
or any public agency (other than SEA or school board). **Types of
Assistance:** Project grants. **Beneficiary Eligibility:** Educational
personnel and elementary and secondary students in local school
districts will benefit.

★4072★
U.S. Department of Education
**Office of Assistant Secretary for Elementary and
  Secondary Education**
Magnet Schools Assistance in Desegregating Districts
Division of Discretionary Grants
400 Maryland Ave. SW, Rm. 2040
Washington, DC 20202-6440   Ph: (202)401-0360
Sylvia Wright, Contact

Catalog Number: 84.165. **Objectives:** To provide grants to eligible
local educational agencies for use in magnet schools that are part of
approved desegregation plans and that are designed to bring
together students from different social, economic, racial, and ethnic
backgrounds. **Applicant Eligibility:** Educational agencies. **Types of
Assistance:** Project grants. **Beneficiary Eligibility:** Educational
agencies.

★4073★
U.S. Department of Education
**Office of Assistant Secretary for Postsecondary
  Education**
**Grants to Institutions to Encourage Minority
  Participation in Graduate Education**
Division of Higher Education Incentive
  Programs
Washington, DC 20202   Ph: (202)708-9393
Walter T. Lewis, Contact

Catalog Number: 84.202. **Objectives:** To provide grants to
institutions of higher education to enable them to identify talented
undergraduate students that demonstrate financial need and are
from minority groups underrepresented in graduate education.
Applicant Eligibility: Accredited institutions of higher education.
Types of Assistance: Project grants. **Beneficiary Eligibility:**
Institutions receiving the awards will provide direct fellowship aid to
graduate students accepted and approved by the institution.

★4074★
U.S. Department of Education
**Office of Assistant Secretary for Postsecondary
  Education**
Minority Science Improvement
Division of Higher Education Incentive
  Programs
Washington, DC 20202   Ph: (202)708-9393
Argelia Velez-Rodriguez, Contact

Catalog Number: 84.120. **Objectives:** (1) To assist institutions
improve the quality of preparation of their students for graduate
work or careers in physical and social science; (2) to improve access
of undergraduate minority students to careers in the physical and
social sciences, mathematics and engineering; (3) to improve access
for precollege minority students to careers in physical and social
science and engineering through precollege enrichment programs
conducted through eligible colleges and universities; and (4) to
improve the capability of predominantly minority institutions for self-
assessment, management and evaluation of their physical and social

science programs and dissemination of their results. **Applicant Eligibility:** Private and public accredited two- and four-year institutions of higher education whose enrollments are predominantly (50% or more) American Indian, Alaskan Native, Black, Hispanic, Pacific Islander, or any combination of these or other disadvantaged ethnic minorities who are underrepresented in science and engineering. Proposals may also be submitted by professional scientific societies, and all nonprofit accredited colleges and universities. **Types of Assistance:** Project grants. **Beneficiary Eligibility:** Same as above; also nonprofit science-oriented societies, and all nonprofit accredited colleges and universities.

★4075★
U.S. Department of Education
Office of Assistant Secretary for Postsecondary
  Education
Upward Bound
Division of Student Services
Education Outreach Branch
400 Maryland Ave. SW, Rm. 3060
Washington, DC 20202-5334   Ph: (202)708-4804
Goldia Hogdon, Contact

Catalog Number: 84.047. **Objectives:** To generate skills and motivation necessary for success in education beyond high school among low-income and potential first-generation college students and veterans. **Applicant Eligibility:** Institutions of higher education, public and private agencies and organizations, and in exceptional cases, secondary schools. **Types of Assistance:** Project grants. **Beneficiary Eligibility:** Low-income individuals and potential first-generation college students who have a need for academic support in order to successfully pursue a program of postsecondary education. Two-thirds of the participants must be low-income individuals who are potential first generation college students. The remaining participants must be either low-income individuals or potential first generation college students. Except for veterans, who can be served regardless of age, project participants must be between 13 and 19 years old, have completed the eighth grade, but who have not entered the twelfth grade (exceptions allowed).

★4076★
U.S. Department of Energy
Office of Minority Economic Impact
Management and Technical Assistance for Minority
  Business Enterprise
1000 Independence Ave. SW
Washington, DC 20585   Ph: (202)586-1594
Sterling Nichols, Contact

Catalog Number: 81.082. **Objectives:** To support increased participation of minority business enterprises (MBE's) in the Department of Energy's high technology research and development contracting activities. **Applicant Eligibility:** Minority businesses. **Types of Assistance:** Advisory services and counseling. **Beneficiary Eligibility:** Minority businesses wanting to do business with the Department of Energy.

★4077★
U.S. Department of Energy
Office of Minority Economic Impact
Minority Honors Training and Industrial Assistance
  Program
1000 Independence Ave. SW
Washington, DC 29585   Ph: (202)896-1593
Isiah O. Sewell, Contact

Catalog Number: 81.084. **Objectives:** To provide scholarship funding to financially needy minority honor students pursuing training in energy-related technologies and to develop linkages with energy industries. **Applicant Eligibility:** Limited to minority honors students students attending institutions offering degree programs in at least four energy-related areas of study. **Types of Assistance:** Project grants. **Beneficiary Eligibility:** Financially needy minority honor students will benefit.

★4078★
U.S. Department of Energy
Office of Minority Economic Impact
Minority Math Science Leadership Development
  Recognition
1000 Independence Ave. SW, Rm. 5B-110
Washington, DC 20585   Ph: (202)586-1593
Isiah O. Sewell, Contact

Catalog Number: 81.099. **Objectives:** To demonstrate clear leadership in promoting or encouraging minority students to pursue studies and careers in math/science related fields. **Applicant Eligibility:** Educational institutions, states, private nonprofit institutions/organizations. **Types of Assistance:** Project grants. **Beneficiary Eligibility:** Any organizations that promote or encourage minority students and groups.

★4079★
U.S. Department of Energy
Office of Minority Economic Impact
National Minority Energy Information Clearinghouse
1000 Independence Ave. SW
Washington, DC 20585   Ph: (202)586-5876
Effie A. Young, Contact

Catalog Number: 81.085. **Objectives:** To develop and disseminate information related to energy programs that impact minorities, minority business enterprises, minority educational institutions and other appropriate minority organizations. **Applicant Eligibility:** No restrictions. **Types of Assistance:** Dissemination of technical information. **Beneficiary Eligibility:** Scholars and members of organizations doing energy-related research and minority business enterprises.

★4080★
U.S. Department of Energy
Office of Minority Impact
Office of Minority Impact Loans
1000 Independence Ave. SW
Washington, DC 20585   Ph: (202)856-1594
Joe Easton, Contact

Catalog Number: 81.063. **Objectives:** To provide direct loans to minority business enterprises to assist them in financing bid or proposal preparation costs they would incur in pursuing Department of Energy work, enabling such MBEs to participate in Department of Energy research, development, demonstration, and contract activities. **Applicant Eligibility:** A firm, including sole proprietorship, corporation, association, or partnership, which is at least 50% owned or controlled by a member of a minority or group of members of a minority. Control means direct or indirect posession of the power to direct or cause the direction of management and policies, whether through the ownership of voting securities, by contact or otherwise. **Types of Assistance:** Direct loans. **Beneficiary Eligibility:** Minority business enterprises.

★4081★
U.S. Department of Health and Human Services
Office of the Secretary
Civil Rights Compliance Activities
330 Independence Ave. SW
Washington, DC 20201   Ph: (202)619-0671

Catalog Number: 93.001. **Objectives:** To eliminate unlawful discrimination and ensure equal opportunities for beneficiaries and potential beneficiaries of Federal financial assistance provided by the Department of Health and Human Services (HHS), as well as to eliminate unlawful discrimination against those involved in programs and activities conducted by HHS on the basis of any individual's handicap(s). The Office for Civil Rights (OCR) enforces various civil rights laws and regulations that prohibit discrimination on a variety of bases including race, color, national origin, handicaps, and age. OCR also enforces the community services assurance under which health care facilities assisted by the Hill-Burton Act must provide health care services to all persons residing in the service area without discrimination. Finally, OCR enforces the nondiscrimination provisions enacted under the health care and other block grants administered by the Department, and nondiscrimination provisions of the Family Violence Prevention and Services Act, which prohibit discrimination on all of the bases listed above, as well as sex and religion. **Applicant Eligibility:** Anyone who believes he or she has been discriminated against and recipients of Federal financial assistance who desire technical assistance and information for the purpose of assuring their compliance with nondiscrimination laws. **Types of Assistance:** Investigation of complaints; dissemination of technical information. **Beneficiary Eligibility:** Individuals subject to discrimination and recipients who require technical assistance and information.

★4082★
U.S. Department of Health and Human Services
Public Health Service
Community Coalition Intervention Demonstration
Projects to Support Health and Human Service
Needs for Minority Males
Office of Minority Health
200 Independence Ave. SW, Rm. 118F
Washington, DC 20201-0001   Ph: (202)245-7065
Howard Kelley, Dir.

Catalog Number: 93.910. **Objectives:** To demonstrate ways to improve health and human services to minority males at high risk of (1) health problems such as alcohol, tobacco, or other chemical dependency; homicide, suicide, and unintentional injuries; or human immunodeficiency virus (HIV) infection and sexually-transmitted diseases; mental health problems, and (2) social problems such as unemployment, undereducation, poor social development, homelessness, family dysfunction, child abuse and neglect, delinquency, criminal backgrounds, teenage pregnancy and fatherhood. **Applicant Eligibility:** Public and private nonprofit organizations. **Types of Assistance:** Project grants. **Beneficiary Eligibility:** Minority male population at high risk for health and human service problems.

★4083★
U.S. Department of Health and Human Services
Public Health Service
Health Resources and Services Administration
Scholarships for Health Professions Students from
Disadvantaged Backgrounds
Division of Student Services
5600 Fishers Ln., Rm. 8-34
Rockville, MD 20857   Ph: (301)443-4776
Bruce Baggett, Contact

Catalog Number: 93.25. **Objectives:** To make funds available for grants to schools of medicine, nursing, osteopathic medicine, dentistry, pharmacy, podiatric medicine, optometry, veterinary medicine, allied health, or public health, or schools that offer graduate programs in clinical psychology for the purpose of assisting such schools in providing scholarships to individuals from disadvantaged backgrounds who are enrolled (or accepted for enrollment) as full-time students in the schools. **Applicant Eligibility:** Accredited public or private nonprofit schools of medicine. **Types of Assistance:** Project grants. **Beneficiary Eligibility:** Students who are (1) citizens, U.S. nationals, aliens lawfully admitted for permanent residency in the U.S., or citizens of the Commonwealth of the Northern Mariana Islands, the Trust Territory of the Pacific Islands, or citizens of the Republic of Marshall Islands, and the Federated States of Micronesia.

★4084★
U.S. Department of Health and Human Services
Public Health Service
National Institutes of Health
Minority Biomedical Research Support
National Institute of General Medical
Science
5333 Westbard Ave.
Bethesda, MD 20892   Ph: (301)496-6745
Dr. Ciriaco Gonzales, Dir.

Catalog Number: 93.375. **Objectives:** To address the lack of representation of minorities in biomedical research by increasing the pool of minorities pursuing research careers. **Applicant Eligibility:** Four-year colleges, universities, and health profession schools with over 50% minority enrollment; four-year institutions with significant, but not necessarily over 50% enrollment, provided they have a history of encouragement and assistance to minorities; two-year colleges with 50% minority enrollment. **Types of Assistance:**

Project grants. **Beneficiary Eligibility:** Minority students and faculty, and investigators at eligible institutions.

★4085★
U.S. Department of Health and Human Services
Public Health Service
Office of the Assistant Secretary for Health
Minority AIDS and Related Risk Factors
Education/Prevention Grants
Office of Minority Health
Rockwall II Bldg., Ste. 1102
5515 Security Ln.
Rockville, MD 20852   Ph: (301)443-9870
Georgia Buggs R.N., Contact

Catalog Number: 93.160. **Objectives:** To demonstrate that minority community-based organizations and minority institutions can effectively develop and implement human immunodeficiency virus (HIV) infection education and prevention strategies, using innovative approaches to prevent and reduce HIV transmission among minority populations. **Applicant Eligibility:** Private nonprofit and for-profit minority community-based organizations and national minority organizations. **Types of Assistance:** Project grants. **Beneficiary Eligibility:** Members of the four major minority groups: Asian and Pacific Islanders, Blacks, Hispanics, Native Americans, or any subgroup of these.

★4086★
U.S. Department of Health and Human Services
Public Health Service
Office of the Assistant Secretary for Health
Minority Community Health Coalition Demonstration
Office of Minority Health
Rockwall II Bldg., Ste. 1102
5515 Security Ln.
Rockville, MD 20852   Ph: (301)443-4761
Joan S. Jacobs, Contact

Catalog Number: 93.137. **Objectives:** To demonstrate that coalitions of local community organizations can be formed to effectively promote health and effect disease risk factors within minority populations, through unique and innovative methods of modifying the behavioral and environmental factors involved. **Applicant Eligibility:** Public organizations, private nonprofit organizations, and for-profit organizations. **Types of Assistance:** Project grants. **Beneficiary Eligibility:** Members of the four major minority groups: Asian/Pacific Islanders, Blacks, Hispanics, American Indians, or a subgroup of any of these groups.

★4087★
U.S. Department of Housing and Urban Development
Assistant Secretary for Fair Housing and Equal
Opportunity
Equal Opportunity in Housing
451 7th St. SW
Washington, DC 20410   Ph: (202)708-4252

Catalog Number: 14.400. **Objectives:** To provide fair housing throughout the United States; to create an administrative enforcement system which is subject to judicial review. **Applicant Eligibility:** Any individual aggrieved by a discriminatory housing practice because of race, color, religion, sex, or national origin may file a complaint with the Department of Housing and Urban Development. Litigation may be initiated by the individual aggrieved and under certain conditions by the Attorney General. **Types of Assistance:** Investigation of complaints. **Beneficiary Eligibility:** Individuals.

★4088★
U.S. Department of Housing and Urban Development
Assistant Secretary for Fair Housing and Equal
Opportunity
Fair Housing Assistance Program—State and Local
451 7th St. SW
Washington, DC 20410   Ph: (202)708-3215

Catalog Number: 14.401. **Objectives:** To provide to those state and local agencies to whom HUD must refer Title VIII complaints both the incentive and the resources required to develop an effective work force to handle complaints, provide technical assistance, training, and other fair housing projects to assure that HUD referred complaints are properly and efficiently handled. **Applicant Eligibility:** State and local governments administering state and local fair housing laws and ordinances which have been recognized by HUD as providing sustantially equivalent rights and remedies as those provided by Title VIII of the Civil Rights Act of 1968, and which have executed formal Memoranda of Understanding with HUD to process Title VIII complaints. **Types of Assistance:** Project grants (cooperative agreements). **Beneficiary Eligibility:** Any person or group of persons aggrieved by a discriminatory housing practice because of race, color, religion, sex, or national origin.

★4089★
U.S. Department of Housing and Urban Development
Assistant Secretary for Fair Housing and Equal
  Opportunity
Non-Discrimination in the Community Development
  Block Grant Program
451 7th St. SW
Washington, DC 20410   Ph: (202)708-2904
Peter Kaplan, Contact

Catalog Number: 14.406. **Objectives:** Section 109 of Title I of the Housing and Community Development Act of 1974, as amended prohibits discrimination in Community Development Block Grant Programs on the basis of race, color, national origin, sex, handicap, and age. **Applicant Eligibility:** Any individual feeling aggrieved because of an alleged discriminatory action in a Title I program on the basis of race, color, national origin, handicap, or age may file a complaint with the Department of Housing and Urban Development. **Types of Assistance:** Investigation of complaints. **Beneficiary Eligibility:** Aggrieved individuals.

★4090★
U.S. Department of Housing and Urban Development
Assistant Secretary for Fair Housing and Equal
  Opportunity
Non-Discrimination in Federally Assisted Programs
451 7th St. SW
Washington, DC 20410   Ph: (202)708-2904
Peter Kaplan, Contact

Catalog Number: 14.405. **Objectives:** Title VI of The Civil Rights Act of 1964 prohibits discrimination on the basis of race, color, or national origin in federally assisted programs. **Applicant Eligibility:** Any individual feeling aggrieved because of an alleged discriminatory action on the basis of race, color, or national origin may file a complaint with the Department of Housing and Urban Development. **Types of Assistance:** Investigation of complaints. **Beneficiary Eligibility:** Aggrieved individuals.

★4091★
U.S. Department of Justice
Civil Rights Division
Educational Opportunities Litigation Section
Desegregation of Public Education
10th & Constitution Ave. NW
Washington, DC 20530   Ph: (202)514-4092
Amy Casner, Contact

Catalog Number: 16.100. **Objectives:** To secure equal educational opportunity for persons regardless of race, color, religion, sex, or national origin. **Applicant Eligibility:** Parent or group of parents in the case of public schools. An individual or his parents in the case of a public college. **Types of Assistance:** Provision of specialized services. **Beneficiary Eligibility:** Same as applicant eligibility.

★4092★
U.S. Department of Justice
Civil Rights Division
Employment Litigation Section
Equal Employment Opportunity
10th & Constitution Ave. NW
Washington, DC 20530   Ph: (202)514-3831
Amy Casner, Contact

Catalog Number: 16.101. **Objectives:** To enforce Federal laws providing equal employment opportunities for all without regard to race, religion, national origin or sex, and where authorized, handicap

condition. **Applicant Eligibility:** All persons. **Types of Assistance:** Provision of specialized services. **Beneficiary Eligibility:** All persons.

★4093★
U.S. Department of Justice
Civil Rights Division
Housing & Civil Enforcement Section
Fair Housing and Equal Credit Opportunity
10th & Constitution Ave. NW
Washington, DC 20530   Ph: (202)514-4713
Amy Casner, Contact

Catalog Number: 16.103. **Objectives:** To provide freedom from discrimination on the basis of race, color, religion, sex or national origin in connection with the sale, rental, and financing of housing and other related activities. (Fair Housing Act). The Equal Credit Opportunity Act (ECOA) prohibits discrimination in credit transactions on the basis of race, color, religion, national origin, sex, marital status, or age (provided the applicant has the capacity to contract,) because all or a part of the applicant's income is derived from a public assistance program, or because the applicant has in good faith exercised any right under the Consumer Credit Protection Act. **Applicant Eligibility:** All persons. **Types of Assistance:** Provision of specialized services. **Beneficiary Eligibility:** All persons.

★4094★
U.S. Department of Justice
Civil Rights Division
Voting Section
Protection of Voting Rights
10th & Constitution Ave. NW
Washington, DC 20530   Ph: (202)307-6292
Amy Casner, Contact

Catalog Number: 16.104. **Objectives:** To provide protection of an individual's right to register and vote in all local, state, and federal elections without discrimination on account of race, color, membership in a language minority group, or age; to assure the rights of persons who are disabled or are unable to read or write to receive assistance in voting for a person of their choice, to assure the right to vote in federal elections to U.S. citizens residing overseas, and to assure access to registration and voting to the elderly and handicapped. **Applicant Eligibility:** All U.S. citizens of voting age. **Types of Assistance:** Provision of specialized services. **Beneficiary Eligibility:** Same as applicant eligibility.

★4095★
U.S. Department of Justice
Community Relations Service
Washington, DC 20530   Ph: (301)492-5929
Flores Hughes, Dir.

Catalog Number: 16.200. **Objectives:** To assist communities in resolving disputes, disagreeements, and difficulties arising from discrimination based on race, color, or national origin. **Applicant Eligibility:** Any person, group, community, or state or local governmental unit that seeks to alleviate tensions related to race, color, or national origin may be considered for CRS assistance. **Types of Assistance:** Provision of specialized services. **Beneficiary Eligibility:** Same as applicant eligibility.

★4096★
U.S. Department of Labor
Employment Standards Administration
Non-Discrimination and Affirmative Action by Federal
  Contractors and Federally Assisted Construction
  Contractors
200 Constitution Ave. NW
Washington, DC 20210   Ph: (202)523-6191
Carl M. Dominquez, Dir.

Catalog Number: 17.301. **Objectives:** To assure non-discrimination and affirmative action in employment by covered federal contractors, including Federal construction contractors, and federally assisted construction contractors. **Applicant Eligibility:** Complaints against Federal contractors and federally assisted construction contractors which allege class-type discrimination on the basis of race, sex, religion, or national origin may be filed. **Types of Assistance:** Dissemination of technical information and investigation of complaints. **Beneficiary Eligibility:** Employees, former employees, or applicants with a government contractor or federally involved contractor, including construction contractors.

★4097★
U.S. Equal Employment Opportunity Commission
Employment Discrimination—Private Bar Program
1801 L St. NW, Rm. 80521
Washington, DC 20507   Ph: (202)663-4862
Johnnie L. Johnson Jr., Sr. Trial Attorney

Catalog Number: 30.005. **Objectives:** (a) To assist aggrieved individuals who have obtained notices of rights to sue in contacting members of the private bar, (b) to provide technical assistance to aggrieved parties and their attorneys in Title VII, Equal Pay and Age Discriminiation in Employment Act cases, (c) to establish the attorney referral mechanism; and (d) to coordinate the strategies of the private bar with those of the Commission. **Applicant Eligibility:** Any individual who has received a notice of right to sue from the Commission. **Types of Assistance:** Provision of specialized services. **Beneficiary Eligibility:** Same as applicant eligibility.

★4098★
U.S. Equal Employment Opportunity Commission
Employment Discrimination—State and Local
 Antidiscrimination Contracts
Program Development & Coordination
 Division
Systematic Investigation & Individual
 Compliance Programs
1801 L St. NW, Rm. 8058
Washington, DC 20507   Ph: (202)663-4866
Winston Robertson, Chief

Catalog Number: 30.002. **Objectives:** To assist EEOC in the enforcement of Title VII of the Civil Rights Act of 1964, as amended, and of the Age Discrimination in Employment Act of 1967 by investigating and resolving charges of employment discrimination based on race, color, religion, sex, national origin, or age. **Applicant Eligibility:** Offical state and local government agencies charged with the administration and enforcement of fair employment practices laws. **Types of Assistance:** Direct payments for specified use. **Beneficiary Eligibility:** Employees, potential employees, and former employees covered by Title VII of the Civil Rights Act o 1964 as amended, or the Age Discrimination in Employment Act of 1967.

★4099★
U.S. Equal Employment Opportunity Commission
Employment Discrimination—Title VII of the Civil
 Rights Act of 1964
Office of Communications & Legislative
 Affairs
Public Information Unit
1801 L St. NW
Washington, DC 20507   Free: 800-872-3362

Catalog Number: 30.001. **Objectives:** To provide for enforcement of the Federal prohibition against employment discrimination in the private and public sector based on race, color, religion, sex, or national origin. **Applicant Eligibility:** Any aggrieved individual or individuals, labor union, association, legal representative, or unincorporated organization, filing on behalf of an aggrieved individual who have reason to believe that an unlawful employment practice within the meaning of Title VII, as amended, has beem committed by an employer with more than 15 employees, employment agency, labor organization, or joint labor-management committee. **Types of Assistance:** Investigation of complaints. **Beneficiary Eligibility:** Potential employees, employees and former employees of the named respondents in a charge who have been subject to unlawful employment practices.

★4100★
U.S. Small Business Administration
Minority Business Development
Office of AA/MSBDCOD
409 3rd St. SW
Washington, DC 20416   Ph: (202)205-6410

Catalog Number: 59.006. **Objectives:** To foster business ownership by individuals who are both socially and economically disadvantaged; and to promote the competitive viability of such firms

by providing such available contract, financial, technical, and managerial assistance as may be necessary to become independent and self-sustaining in a normal competitive environment. **Applicant Eligibility:** Qualification as a socially and economically disadvantaged person on the basis of clear and convincing evidence. **Types of Assistance:** Provision of specialized services. **Beneficiary Eligibility:** Socially and economically disadvantaged individuals.

★4101★
U.S. Small Business Administration
Office of Minority Small Business and Capital
 Ownership Development
Management and Technical Assistance for Socially
 and Economically Disadvantaged Business
409 3rd St. SW
Washington, DC 20416   Ph: (202)205-6423

Catalog Number: 59.007. **Objectives:** To provide management and technical assistance through qualified individuals, public or private organizations to existing or potential businesses which are economically and socially disadvantaged or which are located in areas of high concentration of unemployment; or are participants in activities authorized by Sections 7(i), 7(j) and 8(a) of the Small Business Act. **Applicant Eligibility:** State and local governments, educational institutions, public or private organizations that have the capability to provide the necessary assistance. **Types of Assistance:** Project grants (cooperative agreements). **Beneficiary Eligibility:** Businesses or potential businesses which are economically and socially disadvantaged, or participants in the 8(a) program.

State/Provincial & Local Government Agencies

Alabama

★4102★
Alabama Attorney General
Civil Rights Division
11 S. Union St.
Montgomery, AL 36130   Ph: (205)242-7300
Milt Belcher, Dir.

★4103★
Alabama Department of Human Resources
Civil Rights & Equal Employment Opportunity Office
50 N. Ripley St.
Montgomery, AL 36130-1801   Ph: (205)242-1550
Sylvester Smith, Dir.

★4104★
Alabama Department of Public Health
Division of Primary Care and Minority Health
434 Monroe St.
Montgomery, AL 36130-1701   Ph: (205)242-2807
Sharon Rose, Dir.

Alaska

★4105★
Alaska Office of the Governor
Equal Employment Opportunity Office
PO Box AE
Juneau, AK 99811   Ph: (907)465-3570
Michael McKennet, Dir.

★4106★
Alaska Office of the Governor
Human Rights Commission
800 A St., Ste. 202
Anchorage, AK 99501-3628   Ph: (907)276-7474
Paula Haley, Exec.Dir.

──────────── **Arizona** ────────────

★4107★
Arizona Attorney General
Civil Rights Division
1275 W. Washington
Phoenix, AZ 85007   Ph: (602)542-5263
Philip A. Austin, Dir.

★4108★
Arizona Department of Administration
Affirmative Action Office
State Capitol, WW, Rm. 104
1700 W. Washington
Phoenix, AZ 85007   Ph: (602)542-3711
Brenda J. Smith, Dir.

★4109★
Arizona Department of Health Services
Affirmative Action Office
1740 W. Adams
Phoenix, AZ 85007   Ph: (602)542-1030
David Goldberg, Dir.

★4110★
Phoenix Economic Security Department
Equal Employment Opportunity Office
550 W. Washington St.
Phoenix, AZ 85003   Ph: (602)262-7716

★4111★
Phoenix Equal Opportunity Department
Affirmative Action Section
Minority Business Enterprise Program
550 W. Washington
Phoenix, AZ 85003   Ph: (602)262-6790

★4112★
Phoenix Equal Opportunity Department
Community Relations Committee
Fair Housing Services
550 W. Washington St.
Phoenix, AZ 85003   Ph: (602)495-5289

★4113★
Tucson Human Relations Division
Civil Rights Investigations
Affirmative Action Section
110 E. Pennington
PO Box 27210
Tucson, AZ 85726   Ph: (602)791-4593
Robert McKnight, Dir.

★4114★
Tucson Human Relations Division
Minority Business Enterprise
110 E. Pennington
Tucson, AZ 85726   Ph: (602)791-4593
Wayne Casper, Dir.

──────────── **Arkansas** ────────────

★4115★
Arkansas Corrections Department
Equal Employment Opportunity Grievance Office
PO Box 8707
Pine Bluff, AR 71611   Ph: (501)247-1800
Jane Manning, Dir.

★4116★
Arkansas Education Department
Affirmative Action Section
Bldg. 4, Capitol Mall
Little Rock, AR 72201-1071   Ph: (501)682-4210
Fred Dawson, Dir.

★4117★
Arkansas Industrial Development Commission
Minority Business Division
1 Capitol Mall
Little Rock, AR 72201   Ph: (501)682-5060
James Hall, Dir.

──────────── **California** ────────────

★4118★
California Community Colleges
Civil Rights Office
1107 9th St., Ste. 600
Sacramento, CA 95814   Ph: (916)327-5491
Nancy Davenport, Dir.

★4119★
California Education Department
Affirmative Action Office
PO Box 944272
Sacramento, CA 94244-2720   Ph: (916)322-9636
Sharon Felix, Dir.

★4120★
California Education Department
Ethnic Advisory Councils
PO Box 944272
Sacramento, CA 94244-2720   Ph: (916)324-9063
Eva Fong, Dir.

★4121★
California Fair Employment and Housing Department
Sacramento Office
2014 T St., Ste. 210
Sacramento, CA 95814   Ph: (916)739-4616
Dorinda Henderson, Dir.

★4122★
California Fair Employment and Housing Department
San Diego Office
110 W. C St., Rm. 1702
San Diego, CA 92101   Ph: (619)237-7405

★4123★
California Fair Employment and Housing Department
San Francisco Office
1390 Market St., Ste. 410
San Francisco, CA 94102   Ph: (415)557-2005

★4124★
California Health and Welfare Agency
Employment Development Department
Equal Employment Opportunity Office
800 Capitol Mall
PO Box 826880
Sacramento, CA 94280-0001   Ph: (916)445-7777
Roberto Gracia, Dir.

★4125★
California Health and Welfare Agency
Mental Health Department
Human Rights Division
1600 9th St., Rm. 151
Sacramento, CA 95814   Ph: (916)323-9163
Roberto Lozano, Dir.

★4126★
California Justice Department
Affirmative Action and Civil Rights Office
1515 K St., Ste. 511
PO Box 944255
Sacramento, CA 94244   Ph: (916)324-5482
Aisha Martin-Walton, Dir.

★4127★
California Parks and Recreation Department
Cooperating Associations & Minority Community
   Development Division
PO Box 942896
Sacramento, CA 94296-0001   Ph: (916)445-2358
Daniel Abeyta, Dir.

★4128★
California State and Consumer Services Agency
Fair Employment and Housing Department
2014 T St., Ste. 210
Sacramento, CA 95814   Ph: (916)739-4616
Dorinda Henderson, Dir.

★4129★
California State and Consumer Services Agency
Small and Minority Business Office
1808 14th St., Ste. 100
Sacramento, CA 95814   Ph: (916)322-1847
Alice Flissinger, Chief

★4130★
California State and Consumer Services Agency
State Personnel Board
Affirmative Action and Merit Oversight Division
PO Box 944201
Sacramento, CA 94244-2010   Ph: (916)322-1436
Laura Aguilera, Dir.

★4131★
Los Angeles Affirmative Action Compliance Office
500 W. Temple St., Rm. 780
Los Angeles, CA 90012   Ph: (213)974-1088

★4132★
San Diego Equal Opportunity Management Office
1600 Pacific Hwy., Rm. 208
San Diego, CA 92101   Ph: (619)531-5819

Colorado

★4133★
Colorado Regulatory Agencies Department
Civil Rights Division
1560 Broadway, Ste. 1550
Denver, CO 80202   Ph: (303)894-7505
Jack Lang y Marquez, Dir.

Connecticut

★4134★
Connecticut Children and Youth Services Department
Affirmative Action Division
170 Sigourney St.
Hartford, CT 06105   Ph: (203)566-8689
Ann Mikulak, Dir.

★4135★
Connecticut Economic Development Department
Small Business, Women in Business, & Minority
   Affairs Division
865 Brook St.
Rocky Hill, CT 06167-3405   Ph: (203)258-4269
Les Twible, Dir.

★4136★
Connecticut Human Rights and Opportunities
   Commission
90 Washington St.
Hartford, CT 06106   Ph: (203)566-4895
Lewis Martin, Dir.

Delaware

★4137★
Delaware Community Affairs Department
Human Relations Division
820 N. French St., 4th Fl.
Wilmington, DE 19801   Ph: (302)571-3485
Andrew J. Turner Jr., Dir.

★4138★
Delaware Labor Department
Industrial Affairs Division
Discrimination Review Board
820 N. French St.
Wilmington, DE 19801   Ph: (302)577-2877
John F. Kirk Jr., Dir.

★4139★
Delaware Transportation Department
Equal Employment Opportunity and Civil Rights Office
Transportation Administration Bldg.
PO Box 778
Dover, DE 19903   Ph: (302)739-4359
Willie Jones, Dir.

District of Columbia

★4140★
District of Columbia Arts and Humanities Commission
Human Rights Commission
1350 Pennsylvania Ave. NW, Rm. 202
Washington, DC 20004   Ph: (202)727-0656
Patricia Grace Smith, Chair

★4141★
District of Columbia Arts and Humanities Commission
Human Rights and Minority Business Development
  Office
2000 14th St. NW
Washington, DC 20009   Ph: (202)939-8740
Margie Utley, Dir.

─────────── Florida ───────────

★4142★
Florida Administration Department
Human Relations Commission
325 John Knox Rd.
Tallahassee, FL 32399-1570   Ph: (904)488-7082
Ronald McElrath, Dir.

★4143★
Florida Commerce Department
Small & Minority Business Office
Collins Bldg., Ste. 536
Tallahassee, FL 32399-2000   Ph: (904)487-4698
Laurise Thompson, Dir.

★4144★
Florida Health and Rehabilitative Services Department
Civil Rights Office
1317 Winewood Blvd.
Tallahassee, FL 32399-0700   Ph: (904)487-1901
Melvin Herring, Dir.

★4145★
Florida Health and Rehabilitative Services Department
Human Rights Advocacy Department
1317 Winewood Blvd.
Tallahassee, FL 32399-0700   Ph: (904)488-6173
Rowe Hinton, Dir.

★4146★
Florida Labor and Employment Security Department
Civil Rights Office
Hartman Bldg.
2012 Capitol Circle SE
Tallahassee, FL 32399-2152   Ph: (904)488-5905
Vicky Johnson, Dir.

★4147★
Hillsborough County Equal Opportunity Office
412 Madison, Ste. 913
Tampa, FL 33602   Ph: (813)272-5969
Cretta Johnson, Dir.

★4148★
Jacksonville Purchasing Department
Minority Business Coordinator
220 E. Bay St., Rm. 301
Jacksonville, FL 32202   Ph: (904)630-1165
Connell Heyward, Dir.

★4149★
Orange County Equal Employment Opportunity Office
55 E. Livingston, 2nd Fl.
PO Box 1393
Orlando, FL 32802-1393   Ph: (407)836-5675

★4150★
Orange County Fair Housing Office
City Hall
400 S. Orange Ave.
Orlando, FL 32801   Ph: (407)836-4242

★4151★
Orange County Minority and Women Business
  Enterprise
55 E. Livingston, 2nd Fl.
PO Box 1393
Orlando, FL 32802-1393   Ph: (407)836-7317

★4152★
Tampa Administration Department
Equal Employment Opportunity Office
306 E. Jackson St.
Tampa, FL 33602   Ph: (813)223-8192

─────────── Georgia ───────────

★4153★
Georgia Fair Employment Practices Office
156 Trinity Ave. SW, Ste. 208
Atlanta, GA 30303   Ph: (404)656-1736
Carla A. Ford, Admin.

─────────── Hawaii ───────────

★4154★
Hawaii Health Department
Affirmative Action Office
PO Box 3378
Honolulu, HI 96801   Ph: (808)548-8760
Gerald Ohta, Dir.

★4155★
Hawaii Labor and Industrial Relations Department
Equal Employment Opportunity Office
830 Punchbowl St.
Honolulu, HI 96813   Ph: (808)548-4533
Alice Hong, Dir.

★4156★
Hawaii Office of the Governor
Affirmative Action Coordinator
Pioneer Plaza
900 Fort St. Mall, Rm. 1540
Honolulu, HI 96813   Ph: (808)548-3432

─────────── Idaho ───────────

★4157★
Idaho Human Rights Commission
450 W. State St.
Boise, ID 83720   Ph: (208)334-2873
Marilyn T. Shuler, Dir.

─────────── Illinois ───────────

★4158★
Illinois Board of Education
Program Development and Intervention
Office of Urban and Ethnic Education
188 W. Randolph St.
Chicago, IL 60601   Ph: (312)814-3606
Joe Frattaroli, Dir.

★4159★
Illinois Central Management Services Department
Minority and Female Business Enterprises Office
715 William Stratton Bldg.
Springfield, IL 62706   Ph: (217)814-4190
Sharon Matthews, Dir.

★4160★
Illinois Commerce and Community Affairs Department
Equal Employment Opportunity and Affirmative Action
Office
620 E. Adams
Springfield, IL 62701   Ph: (217)785-7360
Victoria Benn, Dir.

★4161★
Illinois Employment Security Department
Equal Employment Opportunity/Affirmative Action
Office
401 S. State St.
Chicago, IL 60605   Ph: (312)793-4305
Juliette Hurtz, Dir.

★4162★
Illinois Human Rights Department
100 W. Randolph, Ste. 10-100
Chicago, IL 60601   Ph: (312)814-6245
Rosemary Bombela, Dir.

★4163★
Illinois Revenue Department
Equal Employment Opportunity Office
101 W. Jefferson
Springfield, IL 62708   Ph: (217)782-4708
Sherry Meady, Dir.

★4164★
Illinois Secretary of State
Affirmative Action Officer
213 Capitol Bldg.
Springfield, IL 62756   Ph: (217)782-3405

──────────── **Indiana** ────────────

★4165★
Indiana Administration Department
Minority Business Development Division
402 W. Washington St., Rm. W479
Indianapolis, IN 46204   Ph: (317)232-3061
Gary Gibson, Dir.

★4166★
Indiana Civil Rights Commission
32 E. Washington St., Ste. 900
Indianapolis, IN 46204   Ph: (317)232-2612
Alpha Blackburn, Chair

★4167★
Indiana Employment and Training Services Department
Equal Employment Opportunity and Compliance
Secretary
10 N. Senate Ave., Rm. 103
Indianapolis, IN 46204   Ph: (317)232-7482
David Shaheed, Dir.

★4168★
Indiana State Board of Health
Bureau of Family Health Services
Interagency Council on Black and Minority Health
1330 W. Michigan St., Rm. 232
Indianapolis, IN 46206   Ph: (317)633-0683
Valarie Rochester, Minority Health Consultant

★4169★
Indianapolis Equal Opportunity Division
129 E. Market St., Ste. 300
Indianapolis, IN 46204   Ph: (317)236-5262
Robert Ransom, Dir.

──────────── **Iowa** ────────────

★4170★
Iowa Attorney General
Civil Rights Division
Hoover State Office Bldg., 2nd Fl.
Des Moines, IA 50319   Ph: (515)281-4121
Teresa Baustian, Dir.

★4171★
Iowa Civil Rights Commission
Grimes Bldg.
211 E. Maple St.
Des Moines, IA 50319   Ph: (515)281-4121
Ione G. Shadduck, Exec.Dir.

★4172★
Iowa Human Rights Department
Lucas State Office Bldg.
321 12th St.
Des Moines, IA 50319   Ph: (515)281-5960
Almo Hawkins, Dir.

★4173★
Iowa Human Services Department
Equal Opportunity and Affirmative Action Bureau
Hoover State Office Bldg.
Des Moines, IA 50319-0114   Ph: (515)281-6090
Barb Oliver Hall, Dir.

──────────── **Kansas** ────────────

★4174★
Kansas Administration Department
Equal Employment Opportunity Division
State Capitol, Rm. 263E
Topeka, KS 66612   Ph: (913)296-4278
Clyde Howard, Dir.

★4175★
Kansas Civil Rights Commission
900 SW Jackson St., Ste. 851S
Topeka, KS 66612-1258   Ph: (913)296-3206
Roger Lovett, Exec.Dir.

★4176★
Kansas Commerce Department
Minority Business Office
400 SW 8th St., 5th Fl.
Topeka, KS 66603   Ph: (913)296-2954
Tony Augusto, Dir.

★4177★
Kansas Corrections Department
Equal Employment Opportunity Office
900 SW Jackson St., No. 400
Topeka, KS 66612-1284   Ph: (913)296-4495
Alice Stutz, Dir.

★4178★
Kansas Human Resources Department
Equal Employment Opportunity Office
401 Topeka Ave.
Topeka, KS 66603   Ph: (913)296-5233
Hobart Hayes, Dir.

★4179★
Kansas Social and Rehabilitation Services Department
Civil Rights/Equal Employment Opportunity Office
Docking State Office Bldg.
Topeka, KS 66612   Ph: (913)296-4766
Gene Wilson, Dir.

─────────── **Kentucky** ───────────

★4180★
Kentucky Economic Development Cabinet
Minority Business Development Commisssion
Capitol Plaza Tower, 24th Fl.
Frankfort, KY 40601   Ph: (502)564-2064
Floyd C. Taylor, Dir.

★4181★
Kentucky Human Rights Commission
832 Capitol Plaza Tower
Frankfort, KY 40601   Ph: (502)564-3550
Leonard W. Clark, Exec.Dir.

★4182★
Kentucky Human Rights Commission
Louisville Office
332 W. Broadway
PO Box 69
Louisville, KY 40201   Ph: (502)588-4024
John Kelsey, Compliance Dir.

★4183★
Kentucky Justice Cabinet
Minority Recruitment Division
417 High St.
Frankfort, KY 40601   Ph: (502)564-6712
Jane Driskell, Dir.

★4184★
Kentucky Public Instruction Department
Equal Employment Opportunity Division
Capitol Plaza Tower
Frankfort, KY 40601   Ph: (502)564-6916
Wendy Poore, Dir.

★4185★
Kentucky Transportation Cabinet
Minority Affairs and Equal Employment Opportunity
   Office
State Office Bldg.
Frankfort, KY 40622   Ph: (502)564-3601
Bill Colfield, Dir.

─────────── **Louisiana** ───────────

★4186★
Kenner Office of the Mayor
Minority Affairs
2000 18th St.
Kenner, LA 70062   Ph: (504)468-7295
Joseph James, Dir.

★4187★
Louisiana Office of the Governor
Minority Business Development Office
PO Box 94185
Baton Rouge, LA 70804   Ph: (504)342-5373
Angelisa Harris, Exec.Dir.

★4188★
Louisiana Social Services Department
Civil Rights Division
PO Box 3776
Baton Rouge, LA 70821-1532   Ph: (504)342-1532
George Clark, Dir.

★4189★
New Orleans Human Resources Department
Policy and Planning Office
Administrative Unit for Human Rights
City Hall, Rm. 1W-06
1300 Perdido St.
New Orleans, LA 70112   Ph: (504)565-7120
Tommie Lockhart, Dir.

─────────── **Maine** ───────────

★4190★
Maine Human Rights Commission
Statehouse Sta. 51
Augusta, ME 04333   Ph: (207)289-2326
Patricia Ryan, Exec.Dir.

★4191★
Maine Transportation Department
Equal Opportunity Secretary
Statehouse Sta. 16
Augusta, ME 04333-0016   Ph: (207)289-3576
Jane Gilbert, Dir.

─────────── **Maryland** ───────────

★4192★
Baltimore City Housing Authority
Fair Housing and Equal Opportunity Division
417 E. Fayette St.
Baltimore, MD 21202   Ph: (301)396-3246
Dr. Robert Hearn, Commissioner

★4193★
Maryland Economic and Employment Development
   Department
Equal Employment Opportunity Office
217 E. Redwood St., Ste. 1123
Baltimore, MD 21202   Ph: (301)333-6626
Dale Webb, Dir.

★4194★
Maryland Education Department
Equal Opportunity Office
200 W. Baltimore St.
Baltimore, MD 21201   Ph: (301)333-2228
Woodrow Grant, Dir.

★4195★
Maryland Higher Education Commission
Equal Educational Division
Jeffrey Bldg.
16 Francis St.
Annapolis, MD 21401   Ph: (301)974-2971

★4196★
Maryland Housing and Community Development
   Department
Equal Employment Opportunity Office
100 Community Pl.
Crownsville, MD 21032   Ph: (301)974-3103
Tina Wells, Dir.

★4197★
Maryland Human Relations Commission
20 E. Franklin St.
Baltimore, MD 21202   Ph: (301)333-1715
Jennifer Burdick, Exec.Dir.

★4198★
Maryland Human Resources Department
Equal Opportunity Division
311 W. Saratoga St.
Baltimore, MD 21201   Ph: (301)333-0350
Harry Hamrick, Dir.

★4199★
Maryland Personnel Department
Equal Opportunity Officer
301 W. Preston St.
Baltimore, MD 21201   Ph: (301)225-4792
Celeste Morgan, Dir.

——————— **Massachusetts** ———————

★4200★
Arlington Civil Rights Committee
c/o Ruth Ann Putnam
116 Winchester Rd.
Arlington, MA 02174   Ph: (614)646-3387
Ruth Ann Putnam, Pres.

★4201★
Boston Fair Housing Ofice
Boston City Hall, Rm. 966
Boston, MA 02201   Ph: (617)725-4408

★4202★
Boston Office of Personnel Development
Affirmative Action Program
1 City Hall Sq.
City Hall Plaza, Rm. 612
Boston, MA 02108   Ph: (617)725-3361
Roscoe Marvis, Dir.

★4203★
Cambridge Affirmative Action Office
795 Massachusetts Ave.
Cambridge, MA 02139   Ph: (617)349-4332

★4204★
Massachusetts Administration and Finance Executive
  Office
Affirmative Action Central Regional Office
City Hall
455 Main St.
Worcester, MA 01608   Ph: (508)799-1186

★4205★
Massachusetts Administration and Finance Executive
  Office
Affirmative Action Office
1 Ashburton Pl., Rm. 303
Boston, MA 02108   Ph: (617)727-7441
Linda Lynn-Weaver, Dir.

★4206★
Massachusetts Administration and Finance Executive
  Office
Boston Commission Against Discrimination
1 Ashburton Pl., 6th Fl.
Boston, MA 02108   Ph: (617)727-3990

★4207★
Massachusetts Administration and Finance Executive
  Office
Personnel Administration Department
Equal Employment Practices Office
1 Ashburton Pl., Rm. 213
Boston, MA 02108   Ph: (617)727-3777
Eugene H. Rooney Jr., Dir.

★4208★
Massachusetts Administration and Finance Executive
  Office
Revenue Department
Affirmative Action Bureau
100 Cambridge St., Rm. 806
Boston, MA 02204   Ph: (617)727-0193
Virginia Johnson, Dir.

★4209★
Massachusetts Administration and Finance Executive
  Office
Springfield Commission Against Discrimination
145 State St., Rm. 506
Springfield, MA 01103   Ph: (413)739-2145
Alan Cassella, Mgr.

★4210★
Massachusetts Attorney General
Civil Rights and Civil Liberties Division
1 Ashburton Pl., Rm. 2010
Boston, MA 02108   Ph: (617)727-2200
Richard Cole, Dir.

★4211★
Massachusetts Bay Transportation Authority
Affirmative Action and Equal Employment Opportunity
  Division
10 Park Plaza, Rm. 3910
Boston, MA 02116   Ph: (617)722-3305
Herb Hentz, Dir.

★4212★
Massachusetts Commission Against Discrimination
1 Ashburton Pl.
Boston, MA 02108   Ph: (617)727-3990

★4213★
Massachusetts Department of Education
Equal Employment Opportunity Office
1385 Hancock St.
Quincy, MA 02169   Ph: (617)770-7530
Charles Glenn, Dir.

★4214★
Massachusetts Economic Affairs Executive Office
Minority Business Development Division
100 Cambridge St., 13th Fl.
Boston, MA 02202   Ph: (617)727-3220
Mukiya Baker-Gomez, Dir.

★4215★
Massachusetts Human Services Executive Office
Corrections Department
Affirmative Action Office
100 Cambridge St.
Boston, MA 02202   Ph: (617)727-1238
Carole Montalto, Dir.

★4216★
Massachusetts Minority Business Development
  Division
100 Cambridge St., 13th Fl.
Boston, MA 02114   Ph: (617)727-3220
Jose Perez, Asst.Sec.

───────── Michigan ─────────

★4217★
Michigan Agriculture Department
Affirmative Action Office
PO Box 30017
Lansing, MI 48909   Ph: (517)373-9264
Sandra Yonker, Dir.

★4218★
Michigan Attorney General
Civil Rights Division
PO Box 30212
Lansing, MI 48909   Ph: (517)256-2557
Robert Willis, Dir.

★4219★
Michigan Civil Rights Department
303 W. Kalamazoo, 4th Fl.
Lansing, MI 48913   Ph: (517)335-3165
John Roy Castillo, Dir.

★4220★
Michigan Civil Rights Department
Minority/Women Business Certification
State Plaza Bldg.
1200 6th Ave.
Detroit, MI 48226   Ph: (313)335-3165
Winifred Avery, Dir.

★4221★
Michigan Civil Service Department
Equal Employment Opportunity/Affirmative Action
  Office
Box 30002
Lansing, MI 48909   Ph: (517)373-2961
Mary Pollock, Dir.

★4222★
Michigan Education Department
Minority Equity Office
Ottawa Street Office Bldg., S. Tower
600 W. Allegan
PO Box 30008
Lansing, MI 48909   Ph: (517)334-6275
Earl Nelson, Dir.

★4223★
Michigan Natural Resources Department
Equal Employment Opportunity Office
Box 30028
Lansing, MI 48909   Ph: (517)335-1582
Cordree McConnell, Dir.

★4224★
Michigan Public Health Department
Office of Minority Health
3500 N. Logan St.
Box 30035
Lansing, MI 48909   Ph: (517)335-9287
Cheryl Anderson-Small, Chief

★4225★
Michigan Social Services Department
Affirmative Action Office
235 S. Grand Ave.
Box 30037
Lansing, MI 48909   Ph: (517)373-8520
James Newsom, Dir.

★4226★
Michigan Transportation Department
Equal Employment Opportunity Office
Box 30050
Lansing, MI 48909   Ph: (517)373-6732
Charles E. Ford, Dir.

───────── Minnesota ─────────

★4227★
Minneapolis Civil Rights Department
City Hall, Rm. 239
350 S. 5th St.
Minneapolis, MN 55415   Ph: (612)673-3012

★4228★
Minneapolis Community Development Agency
Women/Minority Business Enterprise
331 2nd Ave. S., Ste. 600
Minneapolis, MN 55401   Ph: (612)348-7161

★4229★
Minnesota Attorney General
Human Rights Division
State Capitol Bldg., Rm. 102
75 Constitution Ave.
Saint Paul, MN 55155   Ph: (612)296-9417
Richard Varco, Dir.

★4230★
Minnesota Education Department
Affirmative Action Office
Capitol Square Bldg.
550 Cedar St.
Saint Paul, MN 55101   Ph: (612)296-0342

★4231★
Minnesota Employee Relations Department
Equal Opportunity Division
520 Lafayette Rd., 3rd Fl.
Saint Paul, MN 55155   Ph: (612)296-8272
Elsa Vega-Perez, Dir.

★4232★
Minnesota Housing Finance Agency
Fair Housing and Equal Opportunity Division
400 Sibley St., Rm. 300
Saint Paul, MN 55101   Ph: (612)296-9825
Charles Williams, Dir.

★4233★
Minnesota Human Rights Department
500 Bremer Tower
7th Pl. & Minnesota
Saint Paul, MN 55101   Ph: (612)296-5665
Pamela B. Kelly, Commissioner

★4234★
Minnesota Human Rights Department
Equal Employment Opportunity Commission Office
500 Bremer Tower
7th Pl. & Minnesota
Saint Paul, MN 55101   Ph: (612)296-9061
Karen Ferguson, Dir.

★4235★
Minnesota Human Services Department
Affirmative Action Office
444 Lafayette Rd.
Saint Paul, MN 55155   Ph: (612)296-3510
Mary Jean Anderson, Dir.

★4236★
Minnesota Human Services Department
Civil Rights Office
444 Lafayette Rd.
Saint Paul, MN 55155   Ph: (612)296-4638
Roberto Reyna, Dir.

★4237★
Minnesota Jobs and Training Department
Affirmative Action Office
390 N. Robert St.
Saint Paul, MN 55101   Ph: (612)296-1823
Linda Sloan, Dir.

———————— **Missouri** ————————

★4238★
Missouri Administration Office
Affirmative Action Office
PO Box 809
Jefferson City, MO 65102   Ph: (314)751-1856
Jacqueline Lester, Dir.

★4239★
Missouri Administration Office
Minority Business Development Commission
PO Box 809
Jefferson City, MO 65102   Ph: (314)751-2249
Mark Miller, Dir.

★4240★
Missouri Department of Health
Office of Minority Health
1738 E. Elm St.
PO Box 570
Jefferson City, MO 65102   Ph: (314)751-6064
Jacquelin Horton, Chief

★4241★
Missouri Housing Development Commission
Human Rights Commission
3770 Broadway
Kansas City, MO 64111   Ph: (816)756-4126

★4242★
Missouri Labor and Industrial Relations Department
Human Rights Commission
3315 W. Truman Blvd.
Jefferson City, MO 65109   Ph: (314)751-3325
Alvin A. Plummer, Exec.Dir.

★4243★
St. Louis Civil Rights Enforcement Agency
Civil Courts Bldg., 10 N.
Saint Louis, MO 63101   Ph: (314)622-3301

———————— **Montana** ————————

★4244★
Montana Commissioner of Higher Education
Minority Achievement Division
33 S. Last Chance Gulch
Helena, MT 59620   Ph: (406)444-6570
Ellen Swaney, Dir.

★4245★
Montana Labor and Industry Department
Human Rights Division
PO Box 1728
Helena, MT 59624   Ph: (406)444-2884
Ann MacIntyre, Dir.

★4246★
Montana Transportation Department
Civil Rights Bureau
2701 Prospect Ave.
Helena, MT 59620   Ph: (406)444-6333
Ray Brown, Dir.

———————— **Nebraska** ————————

★4247★
Nebraska Equal Opportunity Commission
PO Box 94934
Lincoln, NE 68509   Ph: (402)471-2024
Lawrence R. Myers, Exec.Dir.

★4248★
Nebraska Labor Department
Equal Employment Opportunity/Civil Rights Division
PO Box 94600
Lincoln, NE 68509   Ph: (402)471-9926
Lois Rohla, Dir.

———————— **Nevada** ————————

★4249★
Nevada Equal Rights Commission
1515 E. Tropicana Ave., Ste. 590
Las Vegas, NV 89109   Ph: (702)486-7161
Delia E. Martinez, Exec.Dir.

———————— **New Hampshire** ————————

★4250★
New Hampshire Human Rights Commission
163 Louden Rd.
Concord, NH 03301   Ph: (603)271-2767
Raymond S. Perry Jr., Exec.Dir.

———————— **New Jersey** ————————

★4251★
New Jersey Commerce and Economic Development
  Department
Small, Minority, and Women-Owned Business
  Development Office
Minority Business Enterprise
20 W. State St., CN 820
Trenton, NJ 08625-0820   Ph: (609)292-0500

★4252★
New Jersey Community Affairs Department
Affirmative Action Office
101 S. Broad St., CN 800
Trenton, NJ 08625-0800   Ph: (609)292-6830
Gloria Taylor, Dir.

★4253★
New Jersey Higher Education Department
Affirmative Action/Equal Opportunity Office
20 W. State St., CN 542
Trenton, NJ 08625-0542   Ph: (609)292-0781
Laurence Howell, Dir.

★4254★
New Jersey Law and Public Safety Department
Civil Rights Division
1100 Raymond Blvd., Rm. 400
Newark, NJ 07102-0860   Ph: (201)648-2700
C. Gregory Stewart, Dir.

★4255★
New Jersey Law and Public Safety Department
Civil Rights Division
Asbury Park Office
601 Bangs Ave.
Asbury Park, NJ 07712   Ph: (908)988-5550

★4256★
New Jersey Law and Public Safety Department
Civil Rights Division
Atlantic City Office
1548 Atlantic Ave.
Atlantic City, NJ 08401   Ph: (609)441-3100

★4257★
New Jersey Law and Public Safety Department
Civil Rights Division
Camden Office
Camden State Office Bldg.
101 Haddon Ave., 1st Fl.
Camden, NJ 08103   Ph: (609)757-2850

★4258★
New Jersey Law and Public Safety Department
Civil Rights Division
Newark Office
1100 Raymond Blvd., Rm. 400
Newark, NJ 07102-0860   Ph: (201)648-2700
C. Gregory Stewart, Dir.

★4259★
New Jersey Law and Public Safety Department
Civil Rights Division
Paterson Office
369 Broadway
Paterson, NJ 07522   Ph: (201)977-4500

★4260★
New Jersey Law and Public Safety Department
Civil Rights Division
Trenton Office
383 W. State St.
Trenton, NJ 08625   Ph: (609)292-7992

★4261★
New Jersey Personnel Department
Equal Employment Opportunity/Affirmative Action
  Division
44 S. Clinton Ave.
Trenton, NJ 08625   Ph: (609)777-0919
S. Howard Woodson, Dir.

★4262★
New Jersey State Department
Office of Ethnic Affairs
State House, CN 300
Trenton, NJ 08625   Ph: (609)984-7145
Juhan Simonson, Dir.

★4263★
New Jersey Transit Corporation
Civil Rights Division
PO Box 10009
Newark, NJ 07101   Ph: (201)643-4323
Alvin Stokes, Dir.

New Mexico

★4264★
Albuquerque Affirmative Action Office
Minority Business Enterprises
PO Box 1293
Albuquerque, NM 87103   Ph: (505)768-3540

★4265★
New Mexico Labor Department
Human Rights Division
1596 Pacheco St.
Santa Fe, NM 87501   Ph: (505)827-6838
Lenton Malry, Exec.Dir.

New York

★4266★
Manhattan Human Relations Commission
Community Relations Office
52 Duane St.
Manhattan, NY 10007   Ph: (212)306-7500
Benjamin Tucker, Dir.

★4267★
New York Agriculture and Markets Department
Affirmative Action Program
Capital Plaza
1 Winners Circle
Albany, NY 12235   Ph: (518)457-2737
James Burnes, Dir.

★4268★
New York Alcoholism and Alcohol Abuse Division
Affirmative Action Bureau
194 Washington Ave.
Albany, NY 12210   Ph: (518)474-5418
Henry Gonzales, Dir.

★4269★
New York Cultural Education Office
Cultural Education Center, Rm. 10A 33
Albany, NY 12230   Ph: (518)474-5976
Carole F. Huxley, Deputy Commissioner

★4270★
New York Department for the Aging
Senior Citizen Information and Referral
Minority Affairs
280 Broadway, Rm. 212
New York, NY 10007   Ph: (212)577-0847

★4271★
New York Division of Human Rights
Albany Regional Office
State Office Bldg.
PO Box 7063
Albany, NY 12225   Ph: (518)474-2705
Carol Praylor, Dir.

★4272★
New York Division of Human Rights
Binghamton Regional Office
State Office Bldg. Annex
164 Hawley St.
Binghamton, NY 13901   Ph: (607)773-7713
John H. Peterson, Dir.

★4273★
New York Division of Human Rights
Brooklyn/Staten Island Regional Office
555 Hanson Pl.
Brooklyn, NY 11217   Ph: (718)260-2856
Susanna Moquette, Reg.Coord.

★4274★
New York Division of Human Rights
Buffalo Regional Office
65 Court St., Ste. 506
Buffalo, NY 14202   Ph: (716)847-7632
Richard E. Clark, Dir.

★4275★
New York Division of Human Rights
Nassau County Regional Office
100 Main St.
Hempstead, NY 11550   Ph: (516)538-1360
Ralph Seskine, Dir.

★4276★
New York Division of Human Rights
New York City/Lower Manhattan Regional Office
55 W. 125th St.
New York, NY 10027   Ph: (212)870-8790
Margarita Rosa, Dir.

★4277★
New York Division of Human Rights
Rochester Regional Office
259 Monroe Ave.
Rochester, NY 14607   Ph: (716)238-8250
Forrest Cummings, Dir.

★4278★
New York Division of Human Rights
Suffolk County Regional Office
State Office Bldg.
Veterans Memorial Hwy.
Hauppauge, NY 11788   Ph: (516)360-6434
Vera Parisi, Dir.

★4279★
New York Division of Human Rights
Syracuse Regional Office
100 New St.
Syracuse, NY 13202   Ph: (315)428-4633
Walter Byrne, Dir.

★4280★
New York Division of Human Rights
White Plains Regional Office
30 Glenn St.
White Plains, NY 10603   Ph: (914)949-4394
John A. Lind, Dir.

★4281★
New York Economic Development Department
Minority and Women's Business Division
1515 Broadway, 51st Fl.
New York, NY 10036   Ph: (212)827-6181
Angela Cabrera, Asst. Deputy Commissioner

★4282★
New York Education Department
Affirmative Action Office
Education Bldg.
Washington Ave.
Albany, NY 12234   Ph: (518)474-1265
Steven Earle, Dir.

★4283★
New York Housing and Urban Development
Department
Fair Housing and Equal Opportunity Division
New York City Regional Office
26 Federal Plaza
Manhattan, NY 10278   Ph: (212)264-1290

★4284★
New York Human Rights Commission
Brooklyn Technical Assistance Unit
1368 Fulton St., 3rd Fl.
Brooklyn, NY 11216   Ph: (718)230-3600

★4285★
New York Human Rights Department
55 W. 125th St.
New York, NY 10027   Ph: (212)870-8790
Margarita Rose, Commissioner

★4286★
New York Labor Department
Affirmative Action Programs Division
State Campus, Bldg. 12
Albany, NY 12240   Ph: (518)457-2736
William Vance, Dir.

★4287★
New York Law Department
Civil Rights Bureau
120 Broadway
New York, NY 10271   Ph: (212)341-2240
Sanford Cohen, Dir.

★4288★
New York Mental Health Office
Affirmative Action Division
44 Holland Ave.
Albany, NY 12229   Ph: (518)474-7950

★4289★
New York Minority and Women's Business
Development Office
Empire State Plaza, Box 2072
Albany, NY 12220   Ph: (518)474-6342
Joseph Baez, Dir.

★4290★
New York Taxation and Finance Department
Affirmative Action Office
State Campus, Bldg. 9
Albany, NY 12227   Ph: (518)457-3286
Keith Kissee, Dir.

★4291★
New York Transportation Department
Equal Opportunity & Compliance Office
State Campus, Bldg. 5
Albany, NY 12232   Ph: (518)457-1134
Howard Sheffey, Dir.

─────────── **North Carolina** ───────────

★4292★
North Carolina Insurance Department
Regulatory Services Division
Minority Assistance Program
Box 26387
Raleigh, NC 27611   Ph: (919)733-4048
Ronnie Moore, Dir.

★4293★
North Carolina Office of the Governor
Human Relations Council
121 W. Jones St.
Raleigh, NC 27603   Ph: (919)733-7996
Jim Stowe, Dir.

★4294★
North Carolina Office of the Governor
Minority Affairs Special Assistant
116 W. Jones St.
Raleigh, NC 27603-8001   Ph: (919)733-5811
James K. Polk, Dir.

★4295★
North Carolina State Personnel Office
Equal Employment Opportunity Services Division
116 W. Jones St.
Raleigh, NC 27603-8004   Ph: (919)733-0205
Nelly Riley, Dir.

─────────── **North Dakota** ───────────

★4296★
North Dakota Labor Department
Equal Employment Opportunity Division
600 East Blvd.
Bismarck, ND 58505   Ph: (701)224-2665
John E. Lynch, Dir.

★4297★
North Dakota Transportation Department
Civil Rights Office
600 East Blvd.
Bismarck, ND 58505-0700   Ph: (701)224-2576
Deb Igoe, Dir.

─────────── **Ohio** ───────────

★4298★
Cleveland Human Services Department
Office of Human Resources
Equal Employment Opportunity Division
30 E. Broad St., 32nd Fl.
Columbus, OH 43266-0423   Ph: (614)466-2455

★4299★
Ohio Administrative Services Department
Equal Employment Opportunity Division
65 E. State St., 8th Fl.
Columbus, OH 43266   Ph: (614)466-8380
Booker T. Tall, Deputy Dir.

★4300★
Ohio Attorney General
Civil Rights Section
50 W. Broad St.
Columbus, OH 43215   Ph: (614)466-7900
Sherrie Passmore, Chief

★4301★
Ohio Civil Rights Commission
Columbus Chapter
220 Parsons Ave.
Columbus, OH 43206-0543   Ph: (614)466-2785
Joseph Carmichaels, Exec.Dir.

★4302★
Ohio Commerce Department
Equal Employment Opportunity Office
77 S. High St., 23rd Fl.
Columbus, OH 43266-0544   Ph: (614)466-3636
Joyce Frazier, Dir.

★4303★
Ohio Commission on Minority Health
77 S. High St., Ste. 745
Columbus, OH 43266-0377   Ph: (614)466-4000
Cheryl Boyce, Exec.Dir.

★4304★
Ohio Department of Human Services
Minority Family Preservation & Prevention Services
  Office
30 E. Broad St.
Columbus, OH 43266-0423   Ph: (614)466-2306
Fran Frazier, Dir.

★4305★
Ohio Development Department
Minority Business Development Office
77 S. High St.
Box 1001
Columbus, OH 43266-0101   Ph: (614)466-5700
Harvey Norton Jr., Dir.

★4306★
Ohio Development Department
Minority Development Finance Commission
77 S. High St.
Box 1001
Columbus, OH 43266-0101   Ph: (614)644-7708
Richard Crockett, Dir.

★4307★
Ohio Education Department
Equal Employment Opportunity Division
65 S. Front St.
Columbus, OH 43266-0308   Ph: (614)466-3304
Hazel Flowers, Dir.

★4308★
Ohio Employment Services Bureau
Affirmative Action Office
145 S. Front St.
Columbus, OH 43216   Ph: (614)481-5797

★4309★
Ohio Industrial Relations Department
Equal Employment Opportunity Office
2323 W. 5th Ave.
PO Box 825
Columbus, OH 43266-0567   Ph: (614)644-2229
Lynnette Riley, Dir.

★4310★
Ohio Natural Resources Department
Equal Employment Opportunity
Fountain Square
Columbus, OH 43224-1387   Ph: (614)265-6872
Phyllis Hart, Dir.

★4311★
Ohio Rehabilitation Services Commission
Equal Employment Opportunity Office
4656 Heaton Rd.
Columbus, OH 43229   Ph: (614)438-1434
Gregory Pringle, Dir.

Oklahoma

★4312★
Oklahoma Education Department
Human Relations Services
2500 N. Lincoln Blvd.
Oklahoma City, OK 73105   Ph: (405)521-2841
Annette Murphy, Dir.

★4313★
Oklahoma Education Department
Multicultural Education Section
2500 N. Lincoln Blvd.
Oklahoma City, OK 73105   Ph: (405)521-3196
Glenda Barrett, Dir.

★4314★
Oklahoma Employment Security Commission
Equal Employment Opportunity Office
2401 N. Lincoln Blvd.
Oklahoma City, OK 73105   Ph: (405)557-7255
Barbara Williams, Dir.

★4315★
Oklahoma Health Department
Affirmative Action Division
1000 NE 10th St.
PO Box 53551
Oklahoma City, OK 73152   Ph: (405)271-4171
Charles Smith, Dir.

★4316★
Oklahoma Human Rights Commission
2101 N. Lincoln Blvd., Rm. 480
Oklahoma City, OK 73105   Ph: (405)521-3441
Ronald L. Johnson, Dir.

★4317★
Oklahoma Human Services Department
Affirmative Action Division
PO Box 25352
Oklahoma City, OK 73125   Ph: (405)521-3491
Kim Jones-Shelton, Dir.

Oregon

★4318★
Oregon Department of Human Resources
Affirmative Action Unit
417 Public Service Bldg.
Salem, OR 97310   Ph: (503)378-3687
Linda Topping, Personnel Officer

★4319★
Oregon Department of Human Resources
Health Division
Minority Health Section
State Office Bldg., Rm. 502
Portland, OR 97201   Ph: (503)299-5446
Barbara Taylor, Minority Health Consultant

★4320★
Oregon Labor and Industries Bureau
Civil Rights Division
1400 SE 5th Ave. Ste. 409
Portland, OR 97201   Ph: (503)229-6600
Raleigh Lewis, Admin.

★4321★
Oregon Office of the Governor
Affirmative Action Director
State Capitol Bldg., Rm. 254
Salem, OR 97310   Ph: (503)378-5336
Jeanne Pai, Dir.

★4322★
Oregon Transportation Department
Civil Rights Section
105 Transportation Bldg.
Salem, OR 97310   Ph: (503)378-8077
Bill Hayden, Dir.

Pennsylvania

★4323★
Pennsylvania Attorney General
Civil Rights Enforcement Division
Strawberry Sq., 16th Fl.
Harrisburg, PA 17120   Ph: (717)787-0822
Paul E. Waters, Dir.

★4324★
Pennsylvania Commerce Department
Bureau of Minority Business Development
1400 Spring Garden St., Rm. 1712
Philadelphia, PA 19130   Ph: (215)560-3236
Karim A. Nalik, Reg.Rep.

★4325★
Pennsylvania Commerce Department
Minority Business Development Authority
433 Forum Bldg.
Harrisburg, PA 17120   Ph: (717)783-1127
Aquid Sabur, Dir.

★4326★
Pennsylvania Corrections Department
Affirmative Action Office
PO Box 598
Camp Hill, PA 17011   Ph: (717)975-4906
Eugene Smith, Dir.

★4327★
Pennsylvania General Services Department
Minority Construction Information Center
210 S. Bouquet St.
Pittsburgh, PA 15213   Ph: (412)565-2365

★4328★
Pennsylvania General Services Department
Minority Development Office
N. Office Bldg., Rm. 515
Harrisburg, PA 17125   Ph: (717)787-7629
Brenda Blake, Dir.

★4329★
Pennsylvania Human Relations Commission
PO Box 3145
Harrisburg, PA 17105   Ph: (717)787-4410
Homer Floyd, Exec.Dir.

★4330★
Pennsylvania Human Relations Commission
Harrisburg Regional Office
Uptown Shopping Center
2971E N. 7th St.
Harrisburg, PA 17110   Ph: (717)787-9780
Howard L. Tucker Jr., Reg.Dir.

★4331★
Pennsylvania Human Relations Commission
Philadelphia Regional Office
711 State Office Bldg.
1400 Spring Garden St.
Philadelphia, PA 19130   Ph: (215)560-2496
Sandra Holman Bacote, Reg.Dir.

★4332★
Pennsylvania Human Relations Commission
Pittsburgh Regional Office
State Office Bldg., Ste. 1100
300 Liberty Ave.
Pittsburgh, PA 15222   Ph: (412)565-5395
George A. Simmons, Reg.Dir.

★4333★
Pennsylvania Labor and Industry Department
Affirmative Action Office
Labor & Industry Bldg.
Harrisburg, PA 17120   Ph: (717)787-1182
Tom Webster, Dir.

★4334★
Pennsylvania Office of the Governor
Administration Office
Affirmative Action Bureau
207 Finance Bldg.
Harrisburg, PA 17120   Ph: (717)783-1130
Richard James, Dir.

★4335★
Pennsylvania Public Welfare Department
Affirmative Action Office
PO Box 2675
Harrisburg, PA 17105   Ph: (717)787-3336
Mary Majors, Dir.

——————— **Rhode Island** ———————

★4336★
Rhode Island Administration Department
Equal Opportunity Office
1 Capitol Hill
Providence, RI 02908   Ph: (401)277-3090
A. Vincent Igliozzi, Dir.

★4337★
Rhode Island Employment and Training Department
Equal Opportunity Office
101 Friendship St.
Providence, RI 02903   Ph: (401)277-3713
Veronica Whittle, Dir.

★4338★
Rhode Island Human Rights Commission
10 Abbott Park Pl.
Providence, RI 02903-3768   Ph: (401)277-2661
Marguerita Beaubien, Chair

★4339★
Rhode Island Transportation Department
External Equal Employment Opportunity Division
210 State Office Bldg.
Providence, RI 02903   Ph: (401)277-3260
Phillip Kydd, Dir.

——————— **South Carolina** ———————

★4340★
South Carolina Department of Health and
** Environmental Control**
Office of Minority Health
c/o Division of Maternal Health
2600 Bull St.
Columbia, SC 29201   Ph: (803)737-4000
Gardenia Ruff, Dir.

★4341★
South Carolina Highways and Public Transportation
** Department**
Equal Employment Opportunity Office
PO Box 191
Columbia, SC 29202   Ph: (803)737-1372
Benjamin F. Byrd, Dir.

★4342★
South Carolina Human Affairs Commission
PO Box 11009
Columbia, SC 29211   Ph: (803)253-6336
James E. Clyburn, Commissioner

——————— **South Dakota** ———————

★4343★
South Dakota Commerce and Regulations Department
Human Rights Division
State Capitol
910 E. Sioux
Pierre, SD 57501   Ph: (605)773-4493
Beth Pay, Dir.

★4344★
South Dakota Education and Cultural Affairs
** Department**
700 Governors Dr.
Pierre, SD 57501-2291   Ph: (605)773-3134
Dr. John A. Bonaiuto, Sec.

★4345★
South Dakota Education and Cultural Affairs
** Department**
Equal Employment Opportunity Office
700 Governors Dr.
Pierre, SD 57501-2291   Ph: (605)773-3219
Pat Stewart, Dir.

★4346★
South Dakota Personnel Bureau
Equal Employment Opportunity
500 E. Capitol
Pierre, SD 57501   Ph: (605)773-4919
Douglas Decker, Dir.

——————— **Tennessee** ———————

★4347★
Tennessee Department of Economic and Community
** Development**
Minority Business Enterprise Division
320 6th Ave. N., 8th Fl.
Nashville, TN 37243-0405   Ph: (615)741-2545
John Birdsong, Dir.

★4348★
Tennessee Human Rights Commission
226 Capitol Blvd., Ste. 602
Nashville, TN 37243-0745   Ph: (615)741-5825
Warren Moore, Exec.Dir.

Texas

★4349★
Houston Affirmative Action Office
500 Jefferson
Houston, TX 77002   Ph: (713)658-3800

★4350★
Houston Housing and Community Development Office
Fair Housing Section
601 Sawyer St., 4th Fl.
Houston, TX 77007-7511   Ph: (713)868-8480
Annie R. Hall, Admin.

★4351★
Texas Employment Commission
Equal Employment Opportunity Division
101 E. 15th St.
Austin, TX 78778   Ph: (512)463-2320
David Laurel, Dir.

★4352★
Texas Higher Education Coordinating Board
Equal Employment Opportunity Planning Division
PO Box 12788
Austin, TX 78711   Ph: (512)483-6100
Elaine P. Adams, Dir.

★4353★
Texas Historical Commission
Austin Office
1511 Colorado St.
Austin, TX 78701   Ph: (512)463-6100
Curtis Tunnell, Exec.Dir.

★4354★
Texas Human Rights Commission
Austin Office
PO Box 13493, Capitol Sta.
Austin, TX 78711   Ph: (512)837-8534
Frank Thompson, Commissioner

★4355★
Texas Human Services Department
Civil Rights Section
701 W. 51st St.
Box 2960
Austin, TX 78769   Ph: (512)450-3630
George Johnson, Dir.

Utah

★4356★
Utah Department of Health
Division of Community Health Services
Ethnic Minority Health Committee Program
288 North 1460 West
PO Box 16660
Salt Lake City, UT 84116-0660   Ph: (801)538-6305
Mary Ellen Warstler, Coord.

★4357★
Utah Industrial Commission
Anti-Discrimination Division
PO Box 510910
Salt Lake City, UT 84151-0910   Ph: (801)530-6921
John Medina, Dir.

Vermont

★4358★
Vermont Human Rights Commission
PO Box 997
Montpelier, VT 05601   Ph: (802)828-2480
Susan Sussman, Exec.Dir.

Virginia

★4359★
Virginia Administration Office
Personnel and Training Department
Equal Employment Opportunity Services
Monroe Bldg.
101 N. 14th St.
Richmond, VA 23219   Ph: (804)225-3303
George Gardner, Dir.

★4360★
Virginia Commerce Department
Fair Housing Office
3600 W. Broad St.
Richmond, VA 23230   Ph: (804)367-8530
Susan Scovill, Dir.

★4361★
Virginia Department of Health
Office of Human Resource Management
Equal Employment Opportunity Division
109 Governor St., Rm. 400
Richmond, VA 23219   Ph: (804)225-4059
Vaughn M. Cunningham, Dir.

★4362★
Virginia Department of Social Services
Civil Rights Coordinator
8007 Discovery Dr.
Richmond, VA 23229-8699   Ph: (804)662-9236
Brenda Macklin, Dir.

★4363★
Virginia Economic Development
Minority Business Enterprises
200-202 N. 9th St. Office Bldg., 11th Fl.
Richmond, VA 23219   Ph: (804)786-5560
Esther Vassar, Dir.

★4364★
Virginia Employment Commission
Equal Employment Opportunity Office
703 E. Main St.
Richmond, VA 23219   Ph: (804)786-3025
John McNeil, Dir.

★4365★
Virginia Human Rights Council
Washington Bldg.
1100 Bank St.
Richmond, VA 23219   Ph: (804)225-2438

Washington

★4366★
King County Affirmative Action Office
Minority/Women's Business Enterprise
406 S. Water
Olympia, WA 98504   Ph: (206)753-9693
James Medina, Dir.

★4367★
King County Office of Civil Rights and Compliance
Fair Employment Office
King County Courthouse, Rm. E224
516 3rd Ave.
Seattle, WA 98104-2312   Ph: (206)296-7594

★4368★
King County Office of Civil Rights and Compliance
Fair Housing Office
King County Courthouse, Rm. E224
516 3rd Ave.
Seattle, WA 98104-2312   Ph: (206)296-7652

★4369★
King County Office of Human Resource Management
Affirmative Action Department
King County Administration Bldg., Rm. 214
500 4th Ave.
Seattle, WA 98104   Ph: (206)296-7340

★4370★
King Office of County Civil Rights and Compliance
King County Courthouse
516 3rd Ave.
Seattle, WA 98104-2312   Ph: (206)296-7592

★4371★
Washington Department of Personnel
Workforce Diversity Program
PO Box 1789, FE-11
Olympia, WA 98507   Ph: (206)753-3758
Roy Standifer, Prog.Admin.

★4372★
Washington Human Rights Commission
711 S. Capitol Way, FJ41
Olympia, WA 98504   Ph: (206)753-6770
Kathryn Friedt, Exec.Dir.

★4373★
Washington Human Rights Commission
Seattle Office
1511 3rd Ave., Ste. 921
Seattle, WA 98101   Ph: (206)464-6500
Kathryn Friedt, Exec.Dir.

★4374★
Washington Human Rights Commission
Spokane Office
W. 905 Riverside, Ste. 416
Spokane, WA 99201   Ph: (509)456-4473

★4375★
Washington Human Rights Commission
Yakima Office
32 N. 3rd St., Ste. 441
Yakima, WA 98901   Ph: (509)575-2772

★4376★
Washington Social and Health Services Department
Equal Opportunity Office
OB-44
Olympia, WA 98504   Ph: (206)753-4070
Dan Lundsford, Dir.

West Virginia

★4377★
West Virginia Attorney General
Civil Rights Deputy Attorney General
State Capitol 26 E.
Charleston, WV 25305   Ph: (304)348-0246
Mary C. Buckmelter, Dir.

★4378★
West Virginia Commerce, Labor, and Environmental
  Resources Department
Minority and Small Business Development Agency
1500 Virginia St., E.
Charleston, WV 25301   Ph: (304)348-2960
Eloise Jack, Dir.

★4379★
West Virginia Human Rights Commission
1321 Plaza, E., Rm. 104-106
Charleston, WV 25301   Ph: (304)348-2616
Quewannocoii C. Stephens, Exec.Dir.

Wisconsin

★4380★
Wisconsin Employment Relations Department
Affirmative Action Division
PO Box 7855
Madison, WI 53707-7855   Ph: (608)266-3017
Arley Gonnering, Dir.

★4381★
Wisconsin Health and Social Services Department
Affirmative Action/Civil Rights Office
PO Box 7850
Madison, WI 53707   Ph: (608)266-3465
Georgina Taylor, Dir.

★4382★
Wisconsin Industry, Labor, and Human Relations
  Department
Equal Rights Division
PO Box 8928
Madison, WI 53708   Ph: (608)266-0946
Sheehan Donoghue, Admin.

Wyoming

★4383★
Wyoming Department of Labor
Labor Standards/Fair Employment Division
Herschler Bldg., 2nd Fl., E.
Cheyenne, WY 82002   Ph: (307)777-6381
Dave Simonton, Dir.

Library Collections

★4384★
Kansas State University
Farrell Library
Minority Resource Research Center
Manhattan, KS 66506　　　Ph: (913)532-7453
　　　　　　　　　　　　　　Fax: (913)532-6144

Antonia Pigno, Dir.

Subjects: African-American history and literature, American ethnic studies, Kansas minority groups, Native American archeology, 20th century Native American sociology, Chicano studies. **Special Collections:** American Ethnic Studies (100 titles); Kansas State Minority Programs (125 titles). **Holdings:** 5000 volumes; 147 microfiche; 388 reels of microfilm; 15 VF drawers of reports; 4 VF drawers of archives; 732 AV programs.

★4385★
Queens College of City University of New York
Ethnic Materials Information Exchange
Graduate School of Lib. & Info. Studies
NSF 300
65-30 Kissena Blvd.　　　　Ph: (718)997-3790
Flushing, NY 11367　　　　Fax: (718)793-8049
David Cohen, Prog.Dir.

Subjects: Ethnic studies resources, minority groups in America, multicultural librarianship. **Holdings:** 2000 volumes; 40 filmstrips; 10 tapes; 250 pamphlets; curriculum materials; vertical file of clippings for each group and information area.

★4386★
State Historical Society of Wisconsin
Library
816 State St.　　　　　　　Ph: (608)264-6534
Madison, WI 53706-1482　　Fax: (608)262-4711
R. David Myers, Dir.

Subjects: History - American, Canadian, state, local, labor, U.S. church; radical/reform movements and groups in the U.S. and Canada; ethnic and minority groups in North America; genealogy; women's history; military history; religious history. **Holdings:** 2.8 million items. **Remarks:** FAX: (608)264-6520. This library is a U.S. Federal Government regional depository, a Wisconsin State official depository, and a Canadian Federal Government selective depository for government publications.

★4387★
U.S. Equal Employment Opportunity Commission
Library
1801 L St., N.W., Rm. 6502　　Ph: (202)663-4630
Washington, DC 20507　　　　Fax: (202)663-4629
Susan D. Taylor, Lib.Dir.

Subjects: Employment discrimination, minorities, women, aged, handicapped, testing, labor law, civil rights. **Special Collections:** Equal Employment Opportunity Commission Publications. **Holdings:** 25,000 books. **Also Known As:** EEOC.

★4388★
Western Interstate Commission for Higher Education
Library
Drawer P
Boulder, CO 80301　　　　　Ph: (303)541-0285
Eileen Conway, Cons.Dir.

Subjects: Higher education, mental health and human services, nursing, minority education. **Holdings:** 7000 books and documents; 1000 volumes of unbound periodicals; 2000 documents on microfiche.

Research Centers

★4389★
Columbia University
ERIC Clearinghouse on Urban Education
Institute for Urban and Minority Education
Teachers College
Box 40
New York, NY 10027　　　　Ph: (212)678-3433
Dr. Erwin Flaxman, Dir.

Research Activities and Fields: Information collection and dissemination regarding urban education, with an aim to better serve the populations in urban school districts, including education of minorities, women, immigrants, and refugees. **Publications:** Monographs; Fact Sheets; Urban Diversity Series; Trends and Issues Series; ERIC/CUE Digests. Enters documents into ERIC educational database, indexed in published volumes of Resources in Education and Current Index to Journals in Education. **Formerly:** ERIC Clearinghouse for the Urban Disadvantaged; IUME/ERIC Clearinghouse on Urban Education.

★4390★
University of Oklahoma
Center for Research on Multi-Ethnic Education
601 Elm Ave., Rm. 146
Norman, OK 73019-0315　　Ph: (405)325-4529
Prof. Wanda Ward, Dir.

Research Activities and Fields: Needs of and opportunities for minorities in education and the nature of minority participation in education and the workforce. Activities focus on higher education, including minority graduate education, effect of various admission standards upon minority student access, factors affecting academic success and the cultural identity of minority students on college and university campuses, and minority faculty career development. **Publications:** Cultural Diversity (newsletter). **Formerly:** Center for Research on Minority Education.

★4391★
University of Pennsylvania
Institute for Research on Higher Education
4200 Pine St., 5th Fl.
Philadelphia, PA 19104-4090　Ph: (215)898-4585
Dr. Robert Zemsky, Dir.

Research Activities and Fields: Enrollment planning, demographic research, and minority participation in higher education. Also conducts collegiate curriculum analysis, strategic planning, postsecondary education finance studies, and research on institutional decision making. **Publications:** Policy Perspectives (quarterly).

Scholarships, Fellowships, & Loans

★4392★
AACP-AFPE Gateway Scholarships for Minorities
American Foundation for Pharmaceutical
　Education
618 Somerset St.
PO Box 7126
North Plainfield, NJ 07060　　Ph: (201)561-8077

Study Level: Graduate. **Award Type:** Scholarship. **Purpose:** To encourage minority undergraduates in pharmacy colleges to continue their education and pursue a Ph.D. in one of the pharmaceutical sciences. **Applicant Eligibility:** Applicants must have participated in the American Association of Colleges of Pharmacy (AACP) Undergraduate Research Participation Program for Minorities. Candidates must be U.S. citizens or permanent residents and demonstrate proof of acceptance into a graduate program leading to a Ph.D. degree in any pharmaceutical discipline. **Selection Criteria:** Selection by the AFPE Boards of Grants. **Funds Available:** Four scholarhips at $5,000 each funded through a grant from

AGLAXO, Inc. are available. **Applicant Details:** Applicants must send the following information: letter providing a summary of research conducted as a recipient of the Research Participation Program award , additional research experience gained while a pharmacy undergraduate, and reasons for wishing to earn a Ph.D. degree; letter of recommendation from the pharmacy college/school dean; name of the graduate school applicant has been accepted into and the major area of study to be undertaken, e.g. pharmaceutics, pharmacy administration, pharmaceutical chemistry, etc; transcript of all completed pharmacy course work; list of special honors, awards, accomplishments in high school and pharmacy college reflecting achievement and an ability to succeed in graduate school. **Application Deadline:** All information must be received by AFPE by July 1. Recipients will be notified by August 1. Award will be provided anytime after September 1 and after confirmation that the student is enrolled in a graduate program for the Ph.D.

★4393★
AAUW Focus Professions Fellowships
American Association of University Women
Educational Foundation
1111 16th St., NW
Washington, DC 20006   Ph: (202)728-7603
     Fax: (202)872-1425

Study Level: Graduate. **Award Type:** Fellowship. **Applicant Eligibility:** Awarded to minority women who are citizens or permanent residents of the United States and who are graduate professional degree candidates completing their final year of study in the fellowship year in the fields of business administration, law, or medicine. No restrictions exist on the age of the applicant or place of study (among accredited U.S. institutions). **Selection Criteria:** Special consideration will be given to applicants who demonstrate professional promise in innovative or neglected areas of research and/or practice, public interest concerns, or those specialties in which women remain underrepresented. **Funds Available:** Fellowships stipends range from $5,000 to $9,500 for full-time study. **Applicant Details:** Applications available August 1 - December 1 (except M.B.A.); August 1 - December 15 (M.B.A. only). **Application Deadline:** December 15; February 1 (M.B.A. only).

★4394★
ABF Summer Research Fellowships in Law and Social Science for Minority Undergraduate Students
American Bar Foundation
750 N. Lake Shore Dr.
Chicago, IL 60611

Study Level: Undergraduate. **Award Type:** Fellowship. **Purpose:** To acquaint undergraduate minority students with research in the field of law and social science. **Applicant Eligibility:** Applicants must be citizens or permanent residents of the United States. They must be American Indians, Blacks, Mexicans, or Puerto Ricans. Candidates should have completed at least the sophomore year of college and must not have received a bachelor's degree by the time the fellowship begins. Applicants must have a grade point average of at least 3.0 on a 4.0 scale and be moving toward an academic major in one of the social science disciplines. **Funds Available:** Four summer fellowships are awarded. The fellowship lasts 10 weeks and pays a stipend of $3,300. **Contact:** Summer Research Fellowships for Minority Undergraduates. **Applicant Details:** A formal application must be submitted, along with a personal statement, official transcripts, and one letter of reference from a faculty member familiar with the student's work. **Application Deadline:** March 1. Recipients are announced by April 15.

★4395★
ADHA Minority Scholarship Program
American Dental Hygienists' Association
    Institute
Institute for Oral Health
444 N. Michigan Ave., Ste. 3400   Ph: (312)440-8944
Chicago, IL 60611   Fax: (312)440-8929

Study Level: Undergraduate. **Award Type:** Scholarship. **Purpose:** Minority scholarships provide financial assistance for minority groups currently underrepresented in the dental hygiene program. **Applicant Eligibility:** Applicants must be members of minority groups including Native Americans, African-Americans, Hispanics, and Asians, or males. Male applicants are not required to be members of minority groups. Applicants must have completed a minimum of one year in a dental hygiene curriculum. They must have a minimum grade point average of 3.0 on a 4.0 scale for the time they have been enrolled in a dental hygiene curriculum. Applicants must be full time students during the academic year for which they are applying. Candidates must be able to document financial need of at least $1,500. **Funds Available:** Funds for financial assistance are limited because they consist of donations and grants from various sources. **Applicant Details:** A formal application must be filed. Upon request, a Scholarship Application Packet is sent to interested candidates. **Application Deadline:** Completed packets and all other application materials must be filed by May 1. All applicants are notified in September whether or not they have been selected as recipients.

★4396★
AEJ Summer Internships for Minorities
Institute for Education in Journalism
New York University
Institute of Afro-American Affairs
289 Mercer St., Ste. 601   Ph: (212)998-2130
New York, NY 10003   Fax: (212)995-4040

Study Level: Undergraduate. **Award Type:** Internship. **Applicant Eligibility:** The program is for undergraduates; preference is for full-time juniors or full-time seniors going on to graduate schools. The students' credentials must reflect an interest in journalism. Students must be members of a minority group, e.g., Black, Puerto Rican, American Indian, Mexican American, Eskimo, or Aleut. **Funds Available:** As an AEJ intern, the candidate is placed for 10 weeks in an entry level position with news publications, primarily in the New York/New Jersey area. As a full-time writer the minimum stipend is $200 a week for a 35-hour week. **Applicant Details:** Formal application requires information about the applicant's reasons for pursuing a career in journalism; what he/she would like to gain from the internship; an autobiographical essay of less than 500 words; college transcript; samples of work; resume; and two recommendations. **Application Deadline:** Application must be filed by mid-December.

★4397★
AFDH Dental Scholarships for Minority Students
American Fund for Dental Health
211 E. Chicago Ave., Ste. 820   Ph: (312)787-6270
Chicago, IL 60611   Fax: (312)787-9114

Study Level: Doctorate. **Award Type:** Scholarship. **Purpose:** The American Fund for Dental Health recognizes the fact that the cost of a dental education has prevented many promising students from disadvantaged minorities from considering dentistry as a career. It is also acutely aware of the need for many more dentists to provide basic dental care for all Americans. In 1968, the AFDH received a three-year challenge grant from the W.K. Kellogg Foundation to establish a dental scholarship program for Black students. Since then the program has been expanded to include students from three aditional minority groups. **Applicant Eligibility:** Candidates must be United States citizens from a minority group which is currently under-represented in the dental profession, i.e., African Americans, Hispanics, Blacks, Native Americans and Puerto Ricans. Only minority students who are entering their first year of dental school are eligible. **Selection Criteria:** Candidates are considered on the basis of their academic records, financial need, and character. While scholastic achievement is important, any student with an interest in dentistry is encouraged to apply. **Funds Available:** Up to $1,000 is awarded for first year dental school only. Scholarships are intended to be used for school expenses and living costs. Grants will not be made to anyone receiving a full scholarship from another source. **Contact:** Financial Aid Office, or Student Affairs Office of dental school candidate plans to attend. **Applicant Details:** Each candidate must submit a formal application, transcripts and college records, and a financial aid form. Each applicant must arrange for two persons to send letters of reference addressing the candidate's character, personality, and academic ability. No application is considered unless it is completely filled out and accompanied by required supporting documents. **Application Deadline:** May 1. Recipients are announced in July.

★4398★
AHA Minority Scientist Development Award
American Heart Association
National Center
7320 Greenville Ave.
Dallas, TX 75231

Study Level: Postdoctorate. **Award Type:** Grant. **Purpose:** To assist promising minority scientists in the early stages of research careers and minority clinical faculty seeking basic research training to develop independent research programs. These five-year awards combine rigorous full-time training in a highly qualified preceptor's laboratory for two years, and project support for three years of independent research. **Applicant Eligibility:** Applicants must hold an M.D., Ph.D., D.O., or equivalent degree, and must be members of ethnic groups underrepresented in the field of cardiovascular research. Underrepresented minority investigators are defined as persons who are Black, Hispanic, Native American, or Pacific Islander. Candidates must have between two and five years of relevant postdoctoral experience. Those having attained the rank of Assistant Professor and clinical faculty wishing to resume or embark upon research careers are eligible to apply if this criterion is met. Applicants must demonstrate a strong commitment to a career of investigative science. At the time of application, candidates must be citizens or permanent residents of the United States. Student and exchange visas are not acceptable. **Selection Criteria:** Factors which enter into the committee's judgement include: probability of recruiting a potential investigator who otherwise might not establish an independent research program; applicant's need for research training; qualifications and commitment of the preceptor; growth potential for the applicant implicit in the preceptorship; scientific merit of the studies proposed for the preceptorship; estimate of the potential of the applicant; and institutional commitment. The initiation of independent research will be based upon: a detailed account of the work done during the preceptorship; an evaluation of the candidate's potential as an independent investigator by the preceptor; a detailed plan of the work to be undertaken in the sponsoring institution; and possibly an interview with a member of the Research Committee. **Funds Available:** Total salary paid to awardee will be determined by the awardee's department head and/or institutional sponsor. The Association's annual portion of the total stipend will not exceed $40,000 in the first year of the award. $1,000 incremental increases will be given annually thereafter during the term of the award. No indirect costs are provided. After satisfactory completion of the preceptorship, an Initiation Grant of $33,000 plus 10 percent overhead will be provided to the awardee for initiation of independent research at the sponsoring institution. Moving expenses, up to $2,500 each way, may be provided if justified, if the preceptor's laboratory is more than 50 miles from the sponsoring institution. **Applicant Details:** Applicants must furnish a specific plan for the development of an independent research program. Statements and commitments are required from three participants in that plan: the applicant, a sponsor at the applicant's institution, and a research preceptor. Applicants without home institutions must identify a facility where they will conduct independent research by the end of the preceptorship period. A sponsor at such a facility must also be identified by this time. **Application Deadline:** June 1; award activation July of the following year.

★4399★
AICPA Scholarships for Minority Undergraduate Accounting Majors
American Institute of Certified Public
    Accountants
1211 Avenue of the Americas
New York, NY 10036-8775

Study Level: Undergraduate. **Award Type:** Scholarship. **Applicant Eligibility:** Applicant must be a minority student who is an undergraduate accounting major, and a United States citizen or permanent resident. **Funds Available:** The maximum individual scholarship is $2,000 for an academic year. More than five hundred scholarships may be awarded annually. Scholarships may be renewed if recipients are making satisfactory progress toward completing their degree; reapplication forms and transcripts must be submitted. **Contact:** Manager, Minority Recruitment, Ms. Sharon L. Donahue, CPA. **Applicant Details:** Application forms call for information on personal background, individual and family financial needs, academic background, expected college expenses and income from other sources. A current transcript of all academic

grades must also be submitted. The application must be signed by the responsible financial aid officer of the student's college or university. **Application Deadline:** Applications must be filed by July 1 for consideration of scholarships for the full academic year or fall semester and by December 1 for the spring semester.

★4400★
Albert W. Dent Scholarship
American College of Healthcare Executives
    Foundation
840 N. Lake Shore Dr.
Chicago, IL 60611

Study Level: Graduate. **Award Type:** Scholarship. **Purpose:** To provide financial aid and increase the enrollment of minority and physically disabled students in healthcare management graduate programs and to encourage them to obtain middle- and upper-level positions in healthcare management. **Applicant Eligibility:** Candidates are Student Associates in good standing in the American College of Healthcare Executives. They must be either minority or physically disabled undergraduate students who either have been accepted for full-time study for the fall term in a healthcare management graduate program accredited by the Accrediting Commission on Education for Health Services Administration or who are enrolled full-time and are in good academic standing in an accredited graduate program in healthcare management. Candidates must be United States or Canadian citizens. Previous recipients are not eligible. Financial need must be demonstrated. **Funds Available:** Each scholarship is $3,000, and the number awarded varies from year to year. **Application Deadline:** Completed applications must be filed between January 1 and March 31.

★4401★
American Psychological Association Minority Fellowship in Neuroscience
American Psychological Association
1200 17th St., NW
Washington, DC 20036   Ph: (202)995-7600

Study Level: Doctorate. **Award Type:** Fellowship. **Purpose:** To increase the number of ethnic minority students who are trained at the doctorate level in the neuroscience field. **Applicant Eligibility:** Must be American citizens or permanent visa residents including, but not limited to, those who are Black, Hispanic, American Indian, Alaskan Native, Asian American, and Pacific Islanders, and those who show an interest in and commitment to careers in neuroscience research. This program is open to students beginning study leading to the doctoral degree in neuroscience as listed in the *Society for Neuroscience Training Programs in North America* handbook. New students must gain admission to a graduate prgram and express a commitment to neuroscience research. **Selection Criteria:** Based on scholarship, research potential, research experience, commitment to research career in neuroscience, writing ability, and financial need. **Funds Available:** $8,500 for twelve months; cost-sharing arrangements with unversities often include full tuition scholarships and additional stipends. Students can receive up to three years of funding, contingent upon their continued good standing in the school's graduate program and the availability of funding. **Contact:** Dr. James Jones or Ernesto A. Guerra. **Applicant Details:** Write or phone for application form. **Application Deadline:** January 15; announcements are made in March.

★4402★
American Psychological Association Minority Fellowships in Psychology-Clinical Training
American Psychological Association
1200 17th St., NW
Washington, DC 20036   Ph: (202)995-7600

Study Level: Doctorate. **Award Type:** Fellowship. **Purpose:** To increase the number of ethnic minority students who are trained in psychology at the doctorate level. The ultimate goal of the program is that upon completion of training, these persons will provide services in their respective ethnic minority communities as clinicians or will conduct research that will increase the base of knowledge related to ethnic minority mental health issues. **Applicant Eligibility:** Must be American citizens or permanent visa residents including, but not limited to, those who are Black, Hispanic, American Indian, Alaskan Native, Asian American, and Pacific Islanders, and those who show an interest in and commitment to careers in mental health, research, and/or services relevant to ethnic and racial minority groups. This program is open to students beginning or continuing study leading to the doctoral degree in psychology; students must be enrolled in a training program that is APA accredited. New students must gain admission to a graduate program and express a commitment to research, delivery of clinical services, and involvement in minority issues in mental health and behavioral sciences. **Selection Criteria:** Based on clinical and/or research potential, scholarship, writing ability, ethnic minority identification, knowledge of broad issues in psychology, professional commitment, and financial aid. **Funds Available:** $8,500 for twelve months; cost-sharing arrangments with universities often include full tuition scholarships and additional stipends. Fellowship is an annual award that may be extended up to three years contingent on satisfactory academic progress. **Contact:** Dr. James M. Jones, Director or Ernesto A. Guerra, Officer. **Applicant Details:** Call or write for application form beginning in August. **Application Deadline:** January 15.

★4403★
American Psychological Association Minority Fellowships in Psychology-Research Training
American Psychological Association
1200 17th St., NW
Washington, DC 20036   Ph: (202)995-7600
Study Level: Doctorate. **Award Type:** Fellowship. **Purpose:** To increase the number of ethnic minority students who are trained in psychology at the doctorate level. The ultimate goal of the program is that upon completion of training, these persons will conduct research that will increase the base of knowledge related to ethnic minority mental health issues. **Applicant Eligibility:** Must be American citizens or permanent visa residents including, but not limited to, those who are Black, Hispanic, American Indian, Alaskan Native, Asian American, and Pacific Islanders, and those who show an interest in and commitment to careers in mental health, research, and/or services relevant to ethnic and racial minority groups. This program is open to students beginning or continuing study leading to the doctoral degree in psychology and students must be enrolled in a training program that is APA accredited. New students must gain admission to a graduate program and express a commitment to research, delivery of clinical services, and involvement in minority issues in mental health and behavioral sciences. **Selection Criteria:** Based on research potential, scholarship, writing ability, ethnic minority identification, knowledge of broad issues in psychology, professional commitment, and financial aid. **Funds Available:** $8,500 for twelve months; cost-sharing arrangments with universities often include full tuition scholarships and additional stipends. Fellowship is an annual award that may be extended for up to three years contingent on satisfactory academic progress. **Contact:** Dr. James M. Jones, Director or Ernesto A. Guerra, Officer. **Applicant Details:** Call or write for application form beginning in August. **Application Deadline:** January 15.

★4404★
ANPAF Minority Fellowships
American Newspaper Publishers
    Association Foundation
The Newspaper Center
Box 17407
Dulles Airport   Ph: (703)648-1000
Washington, DC 20041   Fax: (703)620-1265
Study Level: Professional Development. **Award Type:** Fellowship. **Purpose:** To widen opportunities for racial and ethnic minority professionals to enter into or advance in newspaper management. **Selection Criteria:** Based on supervisors' recommendations and panel's belief that the applicants are candidates for advancement into newspaper management. **Funds Available:** Thirty fellowships cover seminar and workshop registration fees, travel, meals, and hotel expenses. Fifteen winners are selected in winter and fifteen more in the summer. **Contact:** Leslie Thomas, Minority Affairs. **Applicant Details:** Newspaper executives are asked to nominate candidates who demonstrate managerial potential. Self-nomination, with a supervisor's recommendation, also is encouraged. Application must be submitted. **Application Deadline:** December 6.

★4405★
APA Planning Fellowships
American Planning Association
1776 Massachusetts Ave., NW
Washington, DC 20036   Ph: (202)872-0611
Study Level: Graduate. **Award Type:** Fellowship. **Applicant Eligibility:** Applicants must be citizens of the United States or Canada and must be members of African-American, Hispanic, or Native American minority groups. Candidates must be enrolled or accepted for enrollment as first and second year students in a graduate planning program that has been accredited by the Planning Accreditation Board. **Selection Criteria:** Preference is given to full-time schedules. **Funds Available:** Several fellowships ranging from $1,000 to $4,000 are awarded annually. One-half of the award is paid to the school in September; the second half in January, contingent upon a written report from the school stating that the student is still enrolled and doing satisfactory work. Recipients of first year Fellowships may reapply for the second year. **Contact:** APA Planning Fellowship Program. **Applicant Details:** The application must include a letter of nomination from a professor or school official unless self-nominated. A maximum of two other letters of recommendation may be submitted to enhance the application. A two to five page statement by the applicant describing how his or her graduate education will be applied to career goals and why the student has chosen planning as a career as well as a resume must also be provided. Transcripts of all previous collegiate and graduate work must be sent directly from the office of the registrar. The following materials must be also submitted: an APA financial aid application form; a notarized statement of financial independence; a photocopy of the university's acceptance letter for graduate study in planning; and written verification from the university's financial officer or copies of a school publication indicating the average cost of one academic year of graduate school. **Application Deadline:** May 15. Awards decisions are made by mid-June.

★4406★
APA Undergraduate Minority Scholarships
American Planning Association
1776 Massachusetts Ave., NW
Washington, DC 20036   Ph: (202)872-0611
Study Level: Undergraduate. **Award Type:** Scholarship. **Purpose:** To recognize outstanding minority undergraduate planning programs in the United States. **Applicant Eligibility:** Must be students in their second or third year of study. **Selection Criteria:** Based on academic merit, leadership potential, and evidence of responsible citizenship. An advisory board consisting of seven members of the American Planning Association will screen the applications. **Applicant Details:** Application will ask for: grade point average; participation in university activities, participion in community, city, state and/or national activities; involvement in minority community affairs; and career objectives. Applicants must also submit a brief essay, copy of college transcript, and at least two letters of recommendations. Applications will be distributed to both degree and non-degree planning programs that offered curricula programs. **Application Deadline:** May 15.

★4407★
ASC Fellowship for Ethnic Minorities
The American Society of Criminology
1314 Kinnear Rd., Ste. 212   Ph: (614)292-9207
Columbus, OH 43212   Fax: (614)292-6767
Study Level: Doctorate. **Award Type:** Fellowship. **Purpose:** To encourage minority students to enter the field of criminology. **Applicant Eligibility:** Applicants should be minority students, especially African Americans, Hispanics, Native Americans, and Asian Americans. They need not be members of The American Society of Criminology. The winner must be accepted in a program of doctoral studies in criminology or criminal justice. Individuals studying in social sciences or public policy are encouraged to apply. **Funds Available:** The ASC offers a one year fellowship for $12,000. **Applicant Details:** Applicants must provide: an up-to-date curricum vita; evidence of academic excellence (e.g., copies of undergraduate and/or graduate transcripts); three letters of reference; and a letter or statement describing career plans, salient experiences, and the nature of the applicant's interest in criminology or criminal justice, as well as an indication of race/ethnicity and of need and prospects for financial assistance for graduate study. Application materials should

be sent to Sarah Hall, Administrator, American Society of Criminology. **Application Deadline:** June 1.

★4408★
AT&T Bell Laboratories Cooperative Research
 Fellowships for Minorities
AT&T Bell Laboratories
Special Programs
Crawfords Corner Rd., Rm. 1E-209   Ph: (908)949-4301
Holmdel, NJ 07733-1988   Fax: (908)949-6800

Study Level: Graduate. **Award Type:** Fellowship. **Purpose:** To identify and develop scientific and engineering research ability among members of underrepresented minority groups, and to increase their representation in the sciences and engineering. **Applicant Eligibility:** Applicants must be members of underrepresented minority groups (Black Americans, Native American Indians, and Hispanics) who are graduate students in programs leading to doctoral degrees in the following disciplines: chemistry, chemical engineering, communications science, computer science/engineering, electrical engineering, information science, materials science, mathematics, mechanical engineering, operations research, physics, and statistics. Awards are made only to U.S. citizens or permanent residents, and who are admitted to full-time study in a graduate program agreed to by AT&T Bell Laboratories. **Selection Criteria:** Candidates are selected on the basis of scholastic attainment in their field of specialization, and other evidence of their ability and potential as research scientists. A personal interview with AT&T Bell Laboratories scientists and engineers is arranged to select an appropriate summer mentor. **Funds Available:** Nine to 12 fellowships are awarded annually. The fellowship provides full tuition, an annual stipend of $13,200 (paid bi-monthly September through May), books, fees, and related travel expenses. Fellowship recipients may not accept any other fellowship support. Fellowships may be renewed on a yearly basis for four years, contingent upon satisfactory progress toward the doctoral degree. If needed the fellowship will be renewed after four years subject to an annual review by the CRFP committee. Fellowship holders are invited to resume employment at AT&T Bell Laboratories during subsequent summers, but may elect to continue supervised university study or research; fellowship support would be continued (with the exception of the living stipend). During periods of summer employment, fellowship holders receive salaries commensurate with those earned by employees at approximately the same level of training. **Applicant Details:** Applications should include: a completed application form; official transcripts of grades from all undergraduate schools attended; a statement of interest; letters of recommendation from college professors who can evaluate the applicant's scientific aptitude and potential for research (additional letters of recommendation are also invited); Graduate Record Examination scores on the Aptitude Test and the appropriate Advanced Test (scores are required and should be submitted by listing on the GRE registration form Institution Code R2041-2-00, AT&T Bell Laboratories). **Application Deadline:** Applications and all supporting documentation, preferably in one package, must be received by January 15.

★4409★
Aura E. Severinghaus Award
National Medical Fellowships, Inc.
254 W. 31st St., 7th Fl.
New York, NY 10001

Study Level: Doctorate. **Award Type:** Scholarship. **Applicant Eligibility:** Candidates must be Black Americans, mainland Puerto Ricans, Mexican-Americans, and American Indians who are enrolled in accredited schools of allopathic or osteopathic medicine in the United States and who are United States citizens. **Selection Criteria:** Severinghaus Award is for a student at Columbia University College of Physicians and Surgeons who has academic excellence and leadership. **Funds Available:** One-renewable Severinghaus Award of $2000 is awarded annually. **Applicant Details:** Application by nomination by the committee of faculty at Columbia University College of Physicians and Surgeons only. **Application Deadline:** Nominations requested in September.

★4410★
Baxter Foundation Scholarships
National Medical Fellowships, Inc.
254 W. 31st St., 7th Fl.
New York, NY 10001

Study Level: Doctorate. **Award Type:** Scholarship. **Applicant Eligibility:** Candidates must be Black Americans, mainland Puerto Ricans, Mexican-Americans, and American Indians who are enrolled in accredited schools of allopathic or osteopathic medicine in the United States and who are United States citizens. Baxter Scholarship applicants are second-year students who have previously received NMF financial assistance and have outstanding academic achievement. **Funds Available:** Two non-renewable Baxter Scholarships of $2500 each are awarded annually. **Applicant Details:** Applications by Dean's nomination only. **Application Deadline:** Nominations requested in September.

★4411★
CIC Predoctoral Fellowship
Committee on Institutional Cooperation
 (CIC)
Kirkwood Hall
Indiana University   Ph: (812)855-0822
Bloomington, IN 47405   Fax: (812)855-9943

Study Level: Doctorate; Graduate. **Award Type:** Fellowship. **Purpose:** To increase minority representation in areas of study leading toward the Ph.D., and to increase minority presence on "Big Ten" campuses. **Applicant Eligibility:** Applicants should hold a bachelors degree from an accredited institution. To be eligible for the fellowship, applicants should be admitted into an approved masters or doctorate program leading to a Ph.D. **Selection Criteria:** Selections are based entirely upon merit as demonstrated on the application and supporting materials. **Funds Available:** CIC awards 10, 4-year fellowships to minority candidates in the humanities and 25, 5-year fellowships to minority candidates in the social sciences. The award amount for the 1990-91 school year was full tuition waiver plus a $9,000 stipend. **Contact:** Dr. Ronald R. Smith, Director, CIC. **Applicant Details:** Students can apply to graduate study at any of the "Big Ten" universities through CIC by submitting the fellowship/graduate admission application. They are required to provide three letters of recommendation, all official transcripts, GRE scores, and a statement of purpose. Inquiries about specific fields covered by the fellowship should be directed to the CIC office. **Application Deadline:** January 1.

★4412★
Corporate Sponsored Scholarships for Minority
 Undergraduate Physics Majors
American Physical Society
335 E. 45th St.
New York, NY 10017-3483   Ph: (212)682-7341

Study Level: Undergraduate. **Award Type:** Scholarship. **Purpose:** To increase significantly the level of underrepresented minority participation in physics in this country. **Applicant Eligibility:** Any Black, Hispanic, or American Indian U.S. citizen who is majoring or plans to major in physics and who is a high school senior, or college freshman or sophomore is eligible. **Selection Criteria:** A Selection Committee of the APS Committee on Minorities in Phyics and appointed by the AOS President will select the scholarship recipients and match the recipient with an available scholarship from a host corporate sponsor. The Selection committee will provide an accomplished physicist as a mentor for each scholarship recipient. **Funds Available:** $2,000 for tuition, room, or board, and $500 awarded to each college or university physics department that hosts one or more APS minority undergraduate scholars. The scholarship may be renewed one time. It is the intention of the Selection Committee to give approximately half the awards to students in institutions with historically or predominantly Black, Hispanic, or American Indian enrollment. **Contact:** APS Minorities Scholarship Program. **Applicant Details:** Applicants must submit completed application form, with a personal statement. Three completed reference forms and a copy of applicant's high school and/or college transcripts should be mailed directly to the APS office. ACT, SAT, and any other scholastic aptitude test scores must be sent directly to the APS office, by the testing service. **Application Deadline:** February 25.

★4413★
Cox Minority Journalism Scholarship
Cox Newspapers
Minority Journalism Scholarship
PO Box 4689
Atlanta, GA 30302
Study Level: Undergraduate. **Award Type:** Scholarship. **Applicant Eligibility:** Must be graduating high school seniors in need of financial assistance, who are racial minorities from the public schools of the Atlanta, Georgia area. They must have at least a B average and an interest in journalism. The recipient will attend either Georgia State University or one of the colleges in the Atlanta University Center. The recipient must major or minor in journalism. **Funds Available:** All education expenses will be paid for four years of college, including room, board, books and tuition. Only one student will be awarded a scholarship each year. **Contact:** Mrs. Alexis Scott Reeves. **Application Deadline:** April 30.

★4414★
Detroit Free Press Minority Journalism Scholarship
Detroit Free Press
Publishers Office
321 W. Lafayette Blvd.   Ph: 800-678-6400
Detroit, MI 48226   Fax: (313)222-8874
Study Level: Undergraduate. **Award Type:** Scholarship. **Purpose:** To encourage outstanding minorities to enter journalism. **Applicant Eligibility:** Black, Asian, Hispanic and Native American high school seniors in the Free Press circulation area who plan to become writers, editors, or photojournalists and to attend a four-year college majoring in journalism or related field. A 3.0 cumulative average is mandatory. **Selection Criteria:** Based on grades, essay (on why student wants to become a journalist), extracurricular activities (particularly those related to journalism) and recommendations from high school. Finalists are interviewed in person. **Funds Available:** First place winners (2) win $1,000, second place winner receives $750. First place winners automatically compete for three $20,000 scholarships offered nationally by Knight Ridder, Inc. **Contact:** Louise Reid Ritchie. **Applicant Details:** Application form must be accompanied by 3-5 page essay, high school transcript, two letters of recommendation from students' school, and copy of ACT or SAT scores. **Application Deadline:** January 6.

★4415★
Doctoral Fellowships in Sociology
American Sociological Association
Minority Fellowship Program
1722 N St., NW
Washington, DC 20036
Study Level: Doctorate. **Award Type:** Fellowship. **Purpose:** The program's purpose is to contribute to the development of sociology by recruiting individuals who will add differing orientations and creativity to the field. Persons who can approach research on mental health issues relating to minorities from an indigenous perspective are sought. **Applicant Eligibility:** Candidates must be American citizens or permanent visa residents from minority backgrounds. Applicants include but are not limited to persons who are Black, Latino-Hispanic (Chicano, Cuban, Puerto Rican), American Indian, Asian American (Chinese, Japanese, Korean), and Pacific Islanders (Filipino, Samoan, Hawaiian, Guamanian). Candidates may be beginning or continuing study in sociology departments. New students must qualify for acceptance at accredited institutions of higher learning and indicate a commitment to teaching, research, and service careers on the sociological aspects of mental health issues. Recipients are expected, upon completion of their program, to engage in behavioral research or teaching for a period equal to the period of support beyond 12 months. **Selection Criteria:** Financial need and potential for success in graduate studies are considered. **Funds Available:** Depending upon the availability of funds, approximately ten fellowships a year are awarded. Maximum stipend is $8,800. Arrangements are made with the universities for payment of tuition. A limited number of awards to support dissertation research are also provided. **Applicant Details:** Official transcripts for each college and university attended are required. Three references, at least two of whom must have taught the applicant, must be supplied. An essay of not more than three double-spaced pages must include a statement of career goals and aspirations, anticipated date of receipt of doctorate, and how the candidate thinks the attainment of the Ph.D. relates to his/her goals. **Application**

Deadline: A formal application and all supporting materials must be received by January 15th; recipients are announced by April 15th.

★4416★
Dow Jones Newspaper Fund Minority Reporting
   Scholarships
The Dow Jones Newspaper Fund
PO Box 300
Princeton, NJ 08543-0300   Ph: (609)452-2820
Study Level: Undergraduate. **Award Type:** Scholarship. **Applicant Eligibility:** Must be a college minority sophomore who completes a reporting internship during the summer at the end of their sophomore year. **Selection Criteria:** Scholarship recipients will be judged on the writing they did during their internship, an essay, and recommendation from their supervisor. **Funds Available:** 20 scholarships of $1,000 each. **Applicant Details:** Students must be nominated by their newspaper supervisors. Details will be availabe at the beginning of December. Applications will be available between March 1 and August 15. **Application Deadline:** September 1.

★4417★
Edward D. Stone Jr. and Associates Minority
   Scholarship
Landscape Architecture Foundation
4401 Connecticut Ave., NW, Ste. 500
Washington, DC 20008   Ph: (202)686-2752
Study Level: Undergraduate. **Award Type:** Scholarship. **Purpose:** To help continue the education of students entering their final years of undergraduate study in landscape architecture. **Applicant Eligibility:** Must be a minority student in the final years of his/her study. **Funds Available:** Two $1,000 scholarships are awarded. **Applicant Details:** Applications consist of the following: a typed, double-spaced 500-word essay; between four and eight 35mm color slides neatly arranged in a plastic folder or three to five 8x10 black and white or color photographs which demonstrate the student's best work; two letters of recommendation; a completed application form; and a completed Financial Aid Form. **Application Deadline:** May 15.

★4418★
Flemmie P. Kittrell Fellowship for Minorities
American Home Economics Association
  Foundation
1555 King St.
Alexandria, VA 22314   Ph: (703)706-4600
Study Level: Graduate. **Award Type:** Fellowship. **Applicant Eligibility:** This fellowship is available to members of minority groups in the United States and to home economists from developing countries. Applicants must be members of the American Home Economics Association and be United States citizens, permanent residents of the United States, or foreign nationals who wish to study home economics in the United States. Candidates must have completed at least one year of professional home economics experience (which may include a graduate assistantship, traineeship, or internship) by the beginning of the year for which the award is granted. In addition, candidates must show clearly defined plans for full-time graduate study during the award period. Exceptions in qualification requirements may be made for applicants from countries which offer little or no college training in home economics. The recipient of this fellowship must submit an annual progress report to the Foundation, and upon completing the required investigation or study, must submit its title, date of completion, and the location where a written report is available. **Selection Criteria:** Applicants are evaluated on the basis of the following criteria: scholarship and special aptitudes for advanced study; proposed research problems or areas; educational and/or professional experiences; professional and personal characteristics; and professional contributions to home economics. **Funds Available:** One award of $3,000. **Applicant Details:** An application fee ($10 for AHEA members, $30 for nonmembers) must accompany each request for fellowship materials. International students living outside the United States at the time of application are not assessed an application fee. Six copies of the application must be filed. **Application Deadline:** January 15; recipient is notified in April.

★4419★
Ford Foundation Dissertation Fellowships for Minorities
National Academy of Sciences
National Research Council
2101 Constitution Ave.
Washington, DC 20418   Ph: (202)334-2860

Study Level: Doctorate. **Award Type:** Fellowship. **Purpose:** To increase the presence of underrepresented minorities on the nation's college and university faculties by offering doctoral fellowships to members of those groups. Fellowships can be used for study in research-based doctoral programs in the behavioral and social sciences, humanities, engineering, mathematics, physical sciences, and biological sciences, as well as for interdisciplinary programs comprised of two or more eligible disciplines. **Applicant Eligibility:** Applicants must be U.S. citizens or nationals at the time of application and must be members of one of the following minority groups: Alaskan Natives (Eskimo or Aleut), Native American Indians, Black or African Americans, Mexican Americans or Chicanos, native Pacific Islanders (Polynesian or Micronesian), and Puerto Ricans. Students must have finished all required course work and examinations except for the defense of the dissertation. They must be admitted to degree candidacy by January 13 and expect to complete the dissertation during the academic year. **Selection Criteria:** Achievement and ability as determined via academic records, letters of recommendation, the suitability of the proposed institution for the plan of study, and the applicants's ability to present a well-written, thoughtfully prepared application. **Funds Available:** Approximately 20 fellowships are awarded annually. Tenure is from 9 to 12 months; stipends of $18,000 are disbursed through the sponsoring institution. **Applicant Details:** Application materials are available in September from the Fellowship Office of the NRC. Applications are comprised of two parts. Completed applications must be submitted along with the following: verification of doctoral degree status; abstract of dissertation prospectus; official copies of all undergraduate and graduate transcripts; at least two reference reports, one of which must be from applicant's dissertation advisor; description of previous research experience; and proposed plan for completion of doctoral degree. Also required for the second part of the application process are two additional reference reports; a resume; and a working dissertation bibliography. **Application Deadline:** November.

★4420★
Ford Foundation Postdoctoral Fellowships for Minorities
National Academy of Sciences
National Research Council
2101 Constitution Ave.
Washington, DC 20418   Ph: (202)334-2860

Study Level: Doctorate. **Award Type:** Fellowship. **Purpose:** To assist young teacher-scholars who are members of underrepresented minorities and who are either preparing for, or already engaged in college or university teaching and research to achieve greater recognition in their respective fields and develop professional associations. Fellowships can be used for study in research-based doctoral programs in the behavioral and social sciences, humanities, engineering, mathematics, physical sciences, and biological sciences, as well as for interdisciplinary programs comprised of two or more eligible disciplines. Research must be conducted at an institution other than their home institution and may include universities, museums, libraries, government or national laboratories, privately sponsored nonprofit institutes, government chartered nonprofit research organizations, and centers for advanced study. **Applicant Eligibility:** Applicants must be U.S. citizens or nationals at the time of application and must be members of one of the following minority groups: Alaskan Natives (Eskimo or Aleut), Native American Indians, Black or African Americans, Mexican Americans or Chicanos, native Pacific Islanders (Polynesian or Micronesian), and Puerto Ricans. They must have earned the Ph.D. or Sc.D. degree by the January application date and must be engaged in or planning a teaching and research career. **Selection Criteria:** Applications are evaluated for achievement and ability as measured by academic records, letters of recommendation, and evidence of competence as a teacher. Also considered is the quality of the proposed plan of study or research, the appropriateness of the proposed fellowship activities and choice of institution, and the anticipated growth that will occur as a result of the fellowship. **Funds Available:** Approximately 25 fellowships are awarded annually, each

with a 9 to 12 month tenure. Fellowships include a stipend of $25,000, a cost of research allowance of $2,000 and a post-fellowship grant-in-aid of $2,500 for research expenditures. **Applicant Details:** Application materials are available in September from the Fellowship Office of the NRC. In addition to completed applications, the following is required: a proposed plan of study or research; curriculum vitae that includes publications, and courses taught in the last five years, and teaching load; undergraduate and graduate transcripts; one-page abstract of doctoral dissertation; reference reports, one of which should be from the applicant's department chair, division chair, or dean; and a letter from the proposed fellowship institution endorsing the applicant's prospective affiliation. **Application Deadline:** January.

★4421★
Ford Foundation Predoctoral Fellowships for Minorities
National Academy of Sciences
National Research Council
2101 Constitution Ave.
Washington, DC 20418   Ph: (202)334-2860

Study Level: Doctorate. **Award Type:** Fellowship. **Purpose:** To increase the presence of underrepresented minorities on the nation's college and university faculties by offering doctoral fellowships to members of those groups. Fellowships can be used for study in research-based doctoral programs in the behavioral and social sciences, humanities, engineering, mathematics, physical sciences, and biological sciences, as well as for interdisciplinary programs comprised of two or more eligible disciplines. **Applicant Eligibility:** Applicants must be U.S. citizens or nationals at the time of application and must be members of one of the following minority groups: Alaskan Natives (Eskimo or Aleut), Native American Indians, Black or African Americans, Mexican Americans or Chicanos, native Pacific Islanders (Polynesian or Micronesian), and Puerto Ricans. Students must be at or near the beginning of their graduate study and plan to work toward the Ph.D. or Sc.D. degree; persons holding a doctoral degree earned at any time in any field are not eligible to apply. Applicants must have taken the GRE (Graduate Record Examinations) General Test. **Selection Criteria:** Fellowships are awarded to candidates who have demonstrated superior scholarship and who show the greatest promise for future achievement as scholars, researchers, and teachers in institutions of higher education. Applications are evaluated for achievement and ability as measured by academic records, letters of recommendation, suitability of proposed institution for the graduate study plan, and applicants's ability to present a well-written, thoughtfully prepared application. **Funds Available:** Approximately 55 fellowships are awarded annually, each including an annual stipend of $11,500 for each of three years; an annual institutional grant of $6,000 to the fellowship institution in lieu of tuition and fees is also awarded. Continuation of fellowship support for second and third years is contingent upon satisfactory progress toward the Ph.D. or Sc.D. degree. **Applicant Details:** Application materials are available in September from the Fellowship Office of the NRC. Applications are comprised of two parts. Completed applications must be submitted along with the following: GRE General Test scores; official copies of all undergraduate and graduate transcripts; at least two reference reports, one of which must be from a faculty member in the applicant's major academic field; and a proposed plan of graduate study. Also required at the second stage of the application process are course reports from which the applicant's GPA is derived; official transcript of any work completed during the current Fall term; two additional reference reports; description of previous research experience; and resume. **Application Deadline:** November.

★4422★
Franklin C. McLean Award
National Medical Fellowships, Inc.
254 W. 31st St., 7th Fl.
New York, NY 10001

Study Level: Doctorate. **Award Type:** Scholarship. **Applicant Eligibility:** Candidates must be Black Americans, mainland Puerto Ricans, Mexican-Americans, and American Indians who are enrolled in accredited schools of allopathic or osteopathic medicine in the United States and who are United States citizens. McLean Awards are for senior medical students in recognition of outstanding academic achievement, leadership, and community service. **Applicant Details:** After students have received acceptance from at least one medical school, they are urged to request National Medical Scholarship applications. They should also obtain information about the additional special funds listed above that the National Medical Fellowships, Inc. administers so that they may apply for those for which they are also eligible. Scholarship applications for NMF Scholarships become available in March. **Application Deadline:** New applicants must submit their applications by August 31; renewals are due by April 30.

★4423★
GE Foundation Minority Student Scholarships
General Electric Foundation
Fairfield, CT 06431

Study Level: Undergraduate. **Award Type:** Scholarship. **Purpose:** To assist minority engineering and business students. **Selection Criteria:** GE Foundation does not provide scholarships directly to individuals. Awards are made to universities and organizations which then select the individuals. **Funds Available:** $1,000,000 in funds available.

★4424★
GEM Master's Fellowships
National Consortium for Graduate Degrees
  for Minorities in Engineering and Science
PO Box 537   Ph: (219)287-1097
Notre Dame, IN 46556   Fax: (219)287-1486

Study Level: Graduate. **Award Type:** Fellowship. **Purpose:** To provide opportunities for ethnic minority students to obtain a master's degree in engineering through a program of paid summer engineering internships and financial aid. **Applicant Eligibility:** Candidate must be an American citizen and belong to one of the ethnic groups underrepresented in engineering: American Indian, Black American, Mexican-American, or Puerto Rican. At the time of application the student must have attained at least junior year status in an accredited engineering discipline. Individuals currently in their senior year or who have received a B.S. degree in engineering are encouraged to apply. They must have an undergraduate record which indicates the ability to pursue graduate studies in engineering. **Funds Available:** Graduate fellowships pay tuition, fees, and a stipend of $6,000 per graduate academic year. The summer internship brings the total award value to between $20,000 and $40,000, depending upon academic class, summer employer, and graduate school involved. **Applicant Details:** Applications are available August 15 of each year. Awards are made by February 1 of the following year. **Application Deadline:** December 1.

★4425★
GEM Ph.D. Engineering Fellowships
National Consortium for Graduate Degrees
  for Minorities in Engineering and Science
PO Box 537   Ph: (219)287-1097
Notre Dame, IN 46556   Fax: (219)287-1486

Study Level: Doctorate. **Award Type:** Fellowship. **Purpose:** To provide opportunities for ethnic minority students to obtain a doctoral degree in engineering through a program of paid tuition, fees, and a stipend. **Applicant Eligibility:** Candidates must be American citizens and belong to one of the ethnic groups underrepresented in engineering: American Indian, Black American, Mexican-American, or Puerto Rican. They must be applicants to the Ph.D. engineering component and must have, or be in the process of obtaining, a master's degree. The academic records of applicants to all programs must indicate the ability to pursue doctoral studies in engineering. **Funds Available:** Graduate fellowships are awarded that pay tuition, fees, and a stipend of $12,000 per calendar year. The total award value is between $60,000 and $100,000, depending upon the graduate school involved. **Applicant Details:** Applications are available August 15 of each year. Awards are made by February 1 of the following year. **Application Deadline:** December 1.

★4426★
GEM Ph.D. Science Fellowships
National Consortium for Graduate Degrees
  for Minorities in Engineering and Science
PO Box 537   Ph: (219)287-1097
Notre Dame, IN 46556   Fax: (219)287-1486

Study Level: Doctorate. **Award Type:** Fellowship. **Purpose:** To provide opportunities for ethnic minority students to obtain a Ph.D. degree in the natural sciences through a program of paid summer internship and financial aid. **Applicant Eligibility:** Candidates must

be American citizens and belong to one of the ethnic groups underrepresented in engineering: American Indian, Black American, Mexican-American, or Puerto Rican. At the time of application, they should have a minimum academic status of junior year enrollment in an accredited science discipline. Their general undergraduate record should indicate an ability to pursue doctoral studies in the natural sciences. **Funds Available:** Graduate fellowships pay tuition, fees, and a stipend of $12,000 per calendar year. The summer internship brings the total award value to between $60,000 and $100,000, depending upon academic class, summer employer, and graduate school involved. **Applicant Details:** Applications are available August 15 of each year. Awards are made by February 1 of the following year. **Application Deadline:** December 1.

★4427★
George A. Strait Minority Stipend
American Association of Law Libraries
53 W. Jackson Blvd., Ste. 940   Ph: (312)939-4764
Chicago, IL 60604   Fax: (312)431-1097

Study Level: Graduate. **Award Type:** Scholarship. **Applicant Eligibility:** Candidate must be a member of a minority group (as defined by current guidelines of the United States Government) who are college graduates, college seniors, or matriculated graduate library school students and who have an interest in law librarianship. They must be working toward an advanced degree that will further their law/library career. Applicants must be citizens of the United States or Canada or submit evidence of becoming naturalized at the beginning of the award period. A definite interest and aptitude for law library work and financial need are required. **Selection Criteria:** Preference is given to those with previous service in law librarianship. **Funds Available:** The stipend is $3500 a year. **Contact:** Scholarships Committee. **Application Deadline:** April 1.

★4428★
Golden State Minority Foundation Scholarships
Golden State Minority Foundation
1999 W. Adams Blvd.
Los Angeles, CA 90018

Study Level: Undergraduate. **Award Type:** Scholarship. **Applicant Eligibility:** Applicants must attend school in or be a resident of California or Michigan, study business, be a qualified minority (African-American, Hispanic, Native American, or other underrespresented minority), have minimum 3.0 GPA, be a U.S. citizen or legal resident, be of at least junior standing (60 units of college credit), work not more than 20 hours per week, and have full-time status at an accredited four-year college or university. **Applicant Details:** Applications are on file at most schools' financial aid offices or can be obtained by sending a self-addressed stamped envelope.

★4429★
HANA Scholarships
The United Methodist Church
Office of Loans and Scholarships
General Board of Higher Education and
  Ministry
PO Box 871
Nashville, TN 37202   Ph: (615)340-7344

Study Level: Graduate; Undergraduate. **Award Type:** Scholarship. **Applicant Eligibility:** Applicants must be Hispanic, Asian or Native American; an active member of the United Methodist Church for at least one year; a United States citizen or permanent resident; and be able to establish financial need. Candidates for the HANA may be graduate or undergraduate (junior or senior) students who are seeking to develop leadership in higher education and the HANA communities. **Funds Available:** The maximum HANA Scholarships are $1000 for undergraduates and $3000 for graduates. **Applicant Details:** Applications for HANA Scholarships may be requested between January 1 and March 15. **Application Deadline:** April 1.

★4430★
HRSA-BHP MARC Honors Undergraduate Research Training Awards
Health Resources and Services
  Administration
Bureau of Health Professions
Parklawn Bldg., Rm. 8-38
5600 Fishers Ln.
Rockville, MD 20857
Study Level: Graduate. **Award Type:** Award. **Purpose:** To help prepare minority students for careers in biomedical research and to increase the number of minorities successfully completing Ph.D. in biomedical research. **Applicant Eligibility:** Must be third or fourth year undergraduate honor students in a college or university whose enrollment is drawn substantially from ethnic minority groups. **Selection Criteria:** Based on potential for success in biomedical sciences and demonstration of intent to enter graduate programs leading to a Ph.D. **Funds Available:** Each school will give five to ten awards for tuition and stipend. Travel expenses to one national meeting closely related to the project may be included. **Contact:** United State Health and Human Services, National Institute of Health, National Institute of General Medical Sciences, Westwood Bldg., Rm. 9A18, Bethesda, MD, 20892. **Application Deadline:** January 10, May 10 or September 10.

★4431★
Hugh J. Andersen Memorial Scholarships
National Medical Fellowships, Inc.
254 W. 31st St., 7th Fl.
New York, NY 10001
Study Level: Doctorate. **Award Type:** Scholarship. **Applicant Eligibility:** Candidates must be Black Americans, mainland Puerto Ricans, Mexican-Americans, and American Indians who are enrolled in accredited schools of allopathic or osteopathic medicine in the United States and who are United States citizens. National Medical Fund Scholarships are for students enrolled in the first or second year of medical school. Andersen Scholarship candidates must attend Minnesota medical schools and exhibit outstanding leadership, community service, and financial need. Minnesota residents attending out-of-state schools are also eligible. **Funds Available:** Up to 7 new Andersen Scholarships are awarded annually; they are renewable and range from $2500 to $4000. **Applicant Details:** Applications by Dean's nomination only. **Application Deadline:** Nominations requested in October.

★4432★
IBM Minority Fellowships
International Business Machines
T.J. Watson Research Center
PO Box 218
Yorktown Heights, NY 10598
Study Level: Graduate. **Award Type:** Fellowship. **Purpose:** To assist universities in training graduate students in areas of central interest to the electronics industry. **Applicant Eligibility:** Applicants must be minority graduate students in the following fields: computer science; electrical engineering; mechanical engineering; mathematics; physics; manufacturing engineering; industrial engineering; materials science; chemistry; chemical engineering. **Selection Criteria:** Academic excellence; relevance to ongoing research in the electronics industry. **Funds Available:** 15 fellowships are awarded. Duration of award is one year. **Application Deadline:** February 1.

★4433★
Iowa Minority Academic Grants for Economic Success
Iowa College Student Aid Commission
914 Grand Ave.   Ph: (515)281-3501
Des Moines, IA 50309   Fax: (515)242-5996
Study Level: Undergraduate. **Award Type:** Grant. **Purpose:** To assist needy Iowa minority students attending an eligible Iowa private college or state university. **Selection Criteria:** Financial need, with priority given to the neediest applicants and those holding college-bond vouchers. **Applicant Details:** Applicants must follow the same application procedures as stated for all Iowa-sponsored grants. Students attending one of the three state universities should contact the financial aid administrator at the institution to determine

the application procedures. **Application Deadline:** Applications must be received by April 22 to be given first priority.

★4434★
Irving Graef Memorial Scholarship
National Medical Fellowships, Inc.
254 W. 31st St., 7th Fl.
New York, NY 10001
Study Level: Doctorate. **Award Type:** Scholarship. **Applicant Eligibility:** Candidates must be Black Americans, mainland Puerto Ricans, Mexican-Americans, and American Indians who are enrolled in accredited schools of allopathic or osteopathic medicine in the United States and who are United States citizens. The Graef Scholarship is for third year medical students who have previously received NMF financial assistance and demonstrated academic achievement, leadership, and community service. **Funds Available:** One new Graef Scholarship is awarded annually. Stipend is $2,000 and is renewable. **Application Deadline:** Contact Special Programs, National Medical Fellowships, Inc. for deadline.

★4435★
James H. Robinson Memorial Prizes
National Medical Fellowships, Inc.
254 W. 31st St., 7th Fl.
New York, NY 10001
Study Level: Doctorate. **Award Type:** Scholarship. **Applicant Eligibility:** Candidates must be Black Americans, mainland Puerto Ricans, Mexican-Americans, and American Indians who are enrolled in accredited schools of allopathic or osteopathic medicine in the United States and who are United States citizens. Robinson prizes given to senior medical for outstanding achievement in surgery. **Funds Available:** Two non-renewable Robinson Awards of $500 each are awarded annually. **Contact:** Special Programs. **Applicant Details:** Students apply by dean's nomination. **Application Deadline:** Nominations requested in January.

★4436★
Jimmy A. Young Memorial Scholarships
American Respiratory Care Foundation
11030 Ables Lane   Ph: (214)243-8892
Dallas, TX 75229   Fax: (214)484-2720
Study Level: Undergraduate. **Award Type:** Scholarship. **Purpose:** To assist minority students in respiratory therapy programs based on academic achievement. Applicants must be United States citizens or submit a copy of their immigrant visa. They must be members of minority groups, which include American Indians, Asian or Pacific Islanders, Black-Americans, Spanish-Americans, and Mexican-Americans. They must provide evidence of enrollment in an AMA-approved respiratory care program. Candidates must have a minimum grade point average of 3.0 on a 4.0 scale. **Funds Available:** One scholarship of $1,000 is awarded annually. **Contact:** Ann Smith, Scholarships/Grants. **Applicant Details:** Candidates must submit official transcripts of grades, two letters of recommendation from the program director and medical director that verifies the applicant is deserving and a member of a designated minority group. A budget must be submitted. An original essay on some facet of respiratory care is also required. **Application Deadline:** Applications are accepted between April 1 and June 1. Scholarships are awarded by September 1.

★4437★
KNTV Minority Scholarship
KNTV Television
645 Park Ave.
San Jose, CA 95110
Study Level: Undergraduate. **Award Type:** Scholarship. **Applicant Eligibility:** Students must be either Black, Hispanic, Asian/Pacific Islander , or American Indian. They must be residents of either Santa Clara, Santa Cruz, Monterey, or San Benito Counties. The award is contingent on the acceptability of student for admission to an accredited California four-year college or university. The major should be television production or journalism or a related field (marketing, public relations, advertising, graphics, or engineering with demonstrated interest in television). Students must have one full year of undergraduate work remaining and must carry a minimum of 12 semester units during each semester of the 1991-92 school year. **Selection Criteria:** These scholarships are given to students with

financial need who demonstrate interest and potential in the field of television production and television journalism. **Funds Available:** Two $750 scholarships will be awarded. **Applicant Details:** Contact KNTV for applications. **Application Deadline:** April.

★4438★
Leonard M. Perryman Communications Scholarship for Ethnic Minority Students
United Methodist Communications
475 Riverside Dr., Ste. 1901
New York, NY 10115

Study Level: Undergraduate. **Award Type:** Scholarship. **Applicant Eligibility:** The scholarship is for college juniors or seniors who are members of an ethnic minority. The students must have an intention to pursue a career in religious communication in an accredited institution of higher education. Applicant must be a U.S. citizen. **Selection Criteria:** The applicants are judged on five criteria: Christian commitment and involvement in the life of the church; academic achievement as revealed by transcripts, grade point averages, and certain letters of reference; journalistic experience and/or evidence or journalistic talent; clarity of purpose in plans and goals for the future; and potential professional usefulness as a journalist in the field of religion. **Funds Available:** The scholarship is $1000. Half of the award will be paid in August or September after the recipient is enrolled in an undergraduate program in an accredited school or department of journalism in the United States, and the remainder of the grant will be paid in December. There are no grants for summer sessions. **Contact:** The Scholarship Committee. **Applicant Details:** A formal application must be submitted. Three letters of recommendation are required: one from the applicant's local church pastor or a denominational official; one from the chairperson of the department in which the candidate is majoring as an undergraduate; and an employer for whom the applicant has worked as a journalist. If any of these are not available, a letter from a knowledgeable person related to journalism may be substituted. All letters of recommendation should be sent by the writer directly to New York. An official transcript from the institution of higher learning that the applicant is attending must be submitted, along with the transcripts from any previously attended colleges or universities. These should be mailed from the school directly to New York. A statement of not more than 500 words about the candidate's interest in religious journalism must be submitted. No more than three examples of the applicant's journalistic work are required (if requested in writing, these materials will be returned after the Committee has completed its work). The applicant should also send a recent black and white glossy photograph, preferably head and shoulders, suitable for publicity use should the applicant win the award. **Application Deadline:** February 1.

★4439★
LITA/OCLC Minority Scholarship in Library and Information Science
American Library Association
Library and Information Technology
  Association
50 E. Huron St.   Ph: (312)944-6780
Chicago, IL 60611   Fax: (312)440-9374

Study Level: Graduate. **Award Type:** Scholarship. **Purpose:** To encourage a qualified student, with a strong commitment to the use of automation in libraries, to enter library automation. **Applicant Eligibility:** Applicants must be members of principal minority groups. Applicants must be master's students. **Funds Available:** $2,500.

★4440★
Louise Giles Minority Scholarship
American Library Association
Office for Library Personnel Resources
50 E. Huron St.
Chicago, IL 60611   Ph: (312)944-6780

Study Level: Graduate. **Award Type:** Scholarship. **Purpose:** To permit a worthy minority student to begin an MLS degree at an ALA-accredited program. **Applicant Eligibility:** Applicants must be members of a minority group, and must be U.S. or Canadian citizens. **Funds Available:** $3,000.

★4441★
Martin Luther King, Jr. Memorial Scholarships
California Teachers Association
1705 Murchison Dr.
PO Box 921
Burlingame, CA 94011-1400   Ph: (415)697-1400

Study Level: Graduate. **Award Type:** Scholarship. **Purpose:** To provide scholarship aid for graduate studies to qualifying racial and ethnic minorities. **Applicant Eligibility:** Minority applicants should be one or more of the following: active CTA members; dependent children of active CTA members; dependent children of deceased CTA members; or student CTA members. **Funds Available:** Scholarships vary each year depending on the amount of contributions and on the financial need of individual applicants. **Applicant Details:** Applications are available in January of each year. They may be obtained by contacting the CTA Human Rights Department in Burlingame or any CTA Regional Resource Center Office. **Application Deadline:** March 15.

★4442★
Minority Advertising Internships
American Association of Advertising
  Agencies
666 Third Ave.
New York, NY 10017

Study Level: Undergraduate. **Award Type:** Internship. **Purpose:** The Program, a ten week (June-August) summer experience in Chicago, Detroit, Los Angeles, San Francisco and New York, is designed to provide student interns with a realistic job experience in an advertising agency and to help prepare a student for an entry-level professional position in advertising. Advertising agencies also gain an opportunity to identify talented minority students with an interest in advertising. **Applicant Eligibility:** Applicants must be racial minority students in an undergraduate or graduate program who will have completed at least their junior year by the summer for which they are applying. They must plan to return to school in the fall to complete their studies. There are no restrictions in major or concentration. **Funds Available:** Undergraduates receive a salary of $250 per week for a ten week internship. A higher salary is set for graduate students. Sixty percent of dormitory housing and transportation expenses are paid for students who do not live in the cities where they are placed. **Contact:** Minority Advertising Intern Program. **Applicant Details:** Candidates must submit an application form, undergraduate school transcript, letters of recommendation from a professor and a previous employer, and other supporting material, e.g., sample art work. Initial screening is conducted by the A.A.A.A. Equal Employment Opportunities Committee. Semi-finalists are interviewed by the participating agencies. **Application Deadline:** January 15.

★4443★
Minority Student Scholarships in Earth, Space, and Marine Sciences
American Geological Institute   Ph: (703)379-2480
4220 King St.   Free: 800-336-4764
Alexandria, VA 22302-1507   Fax: (703)379-7563

Study Level: Graduate; Undergraduate. **Award Type:** Scholarship. **Applicant Eligibility:** The scholarships are open to graduate and undergraduate students in earth, space, and marine sciences, and Earth science education. Eligible are members of Black, Native American and Hispanic ethnic groups, who are United States citizens. **Selection Criteria:** Geoscience students, particularly marine science students who are enrolled in or applying to accredited institutions and who have good academic records are urged to apply. **Funds Available:** Approximately 80 scholarships each ranging from $500-$10,000 are awarded annually. **Contact:** Director of Education, American Geophysical Institute, 4220 King St., Alexandria, VA 22302; (703)379-2480. **Applicant Details:** These fellowships are a cooperative program of the American Geophysical Union, the American Geological Institute's Minority Participation Program and the NOAA Sea Grant Program. **Application Deadline:** Completed applications must be filed by February 1.

★4444★
MLA Scholarship for Minority Students
Medical Library Association
6 North Michigan Ave., Ste. 300
Chicago, IL 60602

Study Level: Graduate. **Award Type:** Scholarship. **Purpose:** Scholarships are part of the Medical Library Association's effort to encourage candidates showing excellence in scholarship and potential for accomplishment in health sciences librarianship. **Applicant Eligibility:** Applicants must be minority students entering an ALA accredited graduate library school or having at least one-half of his or her academic requirements to complete during the year following the granting of the scholarship. Competition is open only to citizens of or those having permanent resident status in the United States or Canada. Previous winners of MLA Scholarships or the MLA Scholarships for Minority Students are ineligible. Minority group is defined as Black, Hispanic, Asian, Native American or Pacific Islander American. **Funds Available:** One scholarship of $2,000 is awarded annually. Funds are disbursed in four equal installments over the course of a year. **Contact:** Professional Development Department. **Applicant Details:** Applicants must submit a formal application form, three letters of reference, official transcripts, and a statement of career objectives. **Application Deadline:** Applications are due by February 1.

★4445★
NACA Multi-Cultural Scholarship
National Association for Campus Activities
Educational Foundation
13 Harbison Way   Ph: (803)732-6222
Columbia, SC 29212-3401   Fax: (803)749-1047

Study Level: Professional Development. **Award Type:** Scholarship. **Purpose:** To increase the participation of ethnic minorities in the field of campus activities by providing economic assistance to qualified minority group members to allow attendance at NACA-sponsored training workshops, regional conferences or national conventions. **Applicant Eligibility:** Applicants must be identified as members of Black, Latino, Native American, Pacific Islander, or Asian-American ethnic minority groups who are interested in training in campus activities. **Funds Available:** Up to three scholarships are available for registration to NACA-sponsored training workshops, regional conferences and national conventions. Travel is not included. **Applicant Details:** In addition to a completed application form, candidates must submit documentation attesting to minority status, financial need and intention to engage in campus activities for at least one year following the workshop for which a scholarship is being sought. At least one letter of recommendation is required from a person well-acquainted with the applicant's campus involvements. Also needed is a statement of future goals in this field. **Application Deadline:** Applications must be filed by May 1.

★4446★
National FFA Foundation Minority Scholarships
National FFA Foundation
310 N. Midvale Blvd.
PO Box 5117   Ph: (608)238-4222
Madison, WI 53705-0117   Fax: (608)238-6350

Study Level: Undergraduate. **Award Type:** Scholarship. **Applicant Eligibility:** Applicants must be FFA members planning to pursue a college degree in any area of agriculture. Applicants must represent a minority ethnic group (American Indian or Alaskan Native, Asian or Pacific Islander, Black, or Hispanic). FFA members from any state, Puerto Rico, the Virgin Islands, or the District of Columbia are eligible. **Funds Available:** Four scholarships of $10,000 each and two scholarships of $5,000 each. Winners of the $10,000 scholarship shall provide documentation of college expenses (tuition, books, room and board) to the National FFA in order to receive allotment of funds. Winners must maintain full-time student status and a C average (2.0 GPA) or above (on a 4.0 GPA scale). A copy of quarter, trimester, or semester grades will be sent to the National FFA. **Applicant Details:** Application material is available from the FFA. **Application Deadline:** Applications must be postmarked no later than March 1.

★4447★
Newsday Scholarship in Communications for Minorities
Newsday
Long Island, NY 11747   Ph: (516)454-2183

Study Level: Undergraduate. **Award Type:** Scholarship. **Purpose:** To provide financial assistance to minority students from Nassau and Suffolk counties. **Applicant Eligibility:** Applicant must be graduating from high school in Queens, Nassau, or Suffolk County, New York, must be interested in communications, and must intend to enroll in a 4-year college in one of the above mentioned counties. **Funds Available:** Full tuition is provided for one year and may be renewed for up to 3 years if student maintains a 3.0 GPA and remains interested in communications. **Application Deadline:** March.

★4448★
NIH Postdoctoral Fellowship Awards for Minority Students
National Institute of General Medical
Sciences   Ph: (301)496-7260
Bethesda, MD 20892   Fax: (301)402-0019

Study Level: Doctorate. **Award Type:** Fellowship. **Purpose:** To make fellowships available to minority undergraduates, including the many students who have participated in other NIH programs preparing them for careers in research. **Applicant Eligibility:** Applicant must be currently enrolled in a Ph.D. or M.D./Ph.D. graduate program in the biomedical sciences, or he/she must have been accepted by and agreed to enroll in such a graduate program the following academic year. **Selection Criteria:** Selection is based upon academic records and research experience which will be evaluated for scientific merit and training potential as well as originality of proposed research. **Funds Available:** In 1991, approximately $1.5 million is available for 50 to 75 anticipated fellowship awards. **Contact:** Dr. John C. Norvelle, Westwood Building, Room 907. **Applicant Details:** Fellowship application PHS 416-1 should be used when applying. It is available through the Office of Grants Inquiries, Division of Research Grants, National Institutes of Health, Westwood Building, Room 449, Bethesda, MD 20892. **Application Deadline:** September 10.

★4449★
NSF Minority Graduate Fellowships
National Science Foundation
2101 Constitution Ave.
Washington, DC 20418   Ph: (202)357-9498

Study Level: Doctorate; Graduate. **Award Type:** Fellowship. **Purpose:** To increase the number of practicing scientists and engineers who are members of ethnic minority groups that traditionally have been underrepresented in the advanced levels of the science and engineering talent pool. The NSF awards Graduate Fellowships for study and research in the sciences or in engineering leading to master's or doctoral degrees in the mathematical, physical, biological, engineering, and social sciences, and in the history and philosophy of science. NSF also grants fellowships for study toward a research-based Ph.D. in science education that requires a science competence comparable to that for Ph.D. candidates in those disciplines. Fellowships are intended for students at or near the beginning of their graduate study in science or engineering. **Applicant Eligibility:** Applicants must be citizens or nationals of the U.S. and members of ethnic minority groups, including American Indian, Black American, Native Alaskan (Eskimo or Aleut), or Native Pacific Islander (Polynesian or Micronesian). They must have, by the begining of the Fall term of the application year, completed no more than 30 semester hours, 45 quarter hours, or the equivalent of graduate study in the science and engineering fields since completion of their last baccalaureate degree in science or engineering. Applicants who have earned any type of medical degree are not eligible. **Selection Criteria:** Ability and special aptitude for advanced training in science or engineering as judged by academic records, recommendations regarding applicant's qualifications, and GRE scores. **Funds Available:** Fellowships for a three-year tenure (usable over a five-year period). Stipends for 12 months periods are $13,5000 (prorated monthly at $1,125 for lesser periods). Additionally, cost-of-education allowances of $6,000 per fellow are awarded to sponsoring institutions, as well as a special international research travel allowance for Fellows who qualify. **Contact:** The Fellowship Office, National Research Council, 2101 Constitution Ave., Washington, DC 20418; (202) 334-2872. **Applicant Details:** In addition to completed applications (comprised of two parts), candidates are required to provide a proposed plan of study/research, description of previous research experience, course reports and academic transcripts, reference reports, and GRE scores. **Application Deadline:** Part 1 of the application is due in early November; part 2 in early December.

★4450★
NSF Minority Graduate Fellowships for Women
National Science Foundation
2101 Constitution Ave.
Washington, DC 20418   Ph: (202)357-9498
Study Level: Doctorate; Graduate. **Award Type:** Fellowship. **Purpose:** To increase the number of practicing female scientists and engineers who are members of ethnic minority groups that traditionally have been underrepresented in the advanced levels of the Nation's engineering talent pool. NSF annually awards 15 fellowships to support graduate studies in engineering leading to master's or doctoral degrees. Fellowships are intended for students at or near the beginning of their graduate study in engineering. **Applicant Eligibility:** Applicants must be female citizens or nationals of the U.S. and members of minority groups underrepresented in the advanced levels of the U.S. engineering pool. Such groups currently include American Indian, Black, Hispanic, Native Alaskan (Eskimo or Aleut), and Native Pacific Islander (Polynesian or Micronesian). They must have, by the beginning of the Fall term of the application year, completed no more than 30 semester hours, 45 quarter hours, or the equivalent of graduate study in the science and engineering fields since completion of their last baccalaureate degree in science or engineering. Applicants who have earned any type of medical degree are not eligible. **Selection Criteria:** Ability and special aptitude for advanced training in science or engineering as judged by considering academic records, recommendations regarding applicant's qualifications, and GRE scores. **Funds Available:** Fellowships for a three-year tenure (usable over a five-year period). Stipends for 12 month periods are $13,5000 (prorated monthly at $1,125 for lesser periods). Additionally, cost-of-education allowances of $6,000 per fellow are awarded to sponsoring institutions, as well as a special international research travel allowance for Fellows who qualify. **Contact:** The Fellowship Office, National Research Council, 2101 Constitution Ave., Washington, DC 20418; (202)334-2872. **Applicant Details:** In addition to completed applications (comprised of two parts), candidates are required to provide a proposed plan of study/research, description of previous research experience, course reports and academic transcripts, reference reports, and GRE scores. **Application Deadline:** Part 1 of the application is due in early November; part 2 in early December.

★4451★
Presbyterian Church Racial/Ethnic Leadership Supplemental Grants
Presbyterian Church (U.S.A.)
Office of Financial Aid for Studies
100 Witherspoon St.
Louisville, KY 40202-1396   Ph: (502)569-5745
Study Level: Graduate. **Award Type:** Grant. **Applicant Eligibility:** Candidates must be U.S. citizens, members of the Presbyterian Church (U.S.A.) under care of a presbytery for a church occupation, and be enrolled at least half-time in a prescribed program of study approved by their presbytery. Applicants must be Asian, Black, Hispanic or Native American. **Funds Available:** Under normal circumstances, the maximum grant is $1,000 for a one year period. **Contact:** Office of Financial Aid for Studies. **Applicant Details:** Applicants should contact the Financial Aid Officer at their seminary or other institution of study who will make recommendations to the Office of Financial Aid for Studies.

★4452★
Presbyterian Church Student Opportunity Scholarships
Presbyterian Church (U.S.A.)
Office of Financial Aid for Studies
100 Witherspoon St.
Louisville, KY 40202-1396   Ph: (502)569-5745
Study Level: Undergraduate. **Award Type:** Scholarship. **Purpose:** Student Opportunity Scholarships have been established for young persons of limited opportunities from ethnic minority groups. **Applicant Eligibility:** Applicants must be Asian, Black, Hispanic, Native American and members of the Presbyterian Church (U.S.A.).

Candidates must be entering college as incoming full-time freshmen and must have applied to the college for financial aid. They must be U.S. citizens or permanent residents. **Funds Available:** Scholarships range from $100 to $1,400 and are individually determined based on financial need and funds available. They may be renewed during a student's undergraduate years depending upon continued financial need and satisfactory academic progress. **Contact:** Student Opportunity Scholarships. **Application Deadline:** April 1 of the candidate's senior year in high school.

★4453★
REC Educational Grant
Racine Environment Committee Educational
     Fund
310 5th St., Rm. 101
Racine, WI 53403   Ph: (414)631-5600
Study Level: Undergraduate. **Award Type:** Grant. **Purpose:** To provide financial assistance to low-income, minority students in order for them to attend a college or university. **Applicant Eligibility:** Applicant must be a minority member, resident of the city of Racine, and show financial need. **Funds Available:** Funds vary. **Contact:** Mary Day. **Applicant Details:** Application is available upon request. **Application Deadline:** June 30 for the first semester; October 31 for the second semester.

★4454★
SLA Affirmative Action Scholarships
Special Libraries Association
1700 Eighteenth St. NW
Washington, DC 20009   Ph: (202)234-4700
Study Level: Graduate. **Award Type:** Scholarship. **Purpose:** To assist graduate students attain a master's degree in librarianship at a recognized school of library or information science. **Applicant Eligibility:** Applicants must be members of a minority group (Black, Hispanic, Asian or Pacific Islander, or American Indian or Alaskan Native). **Selection Criteria:** Preference is given to applicants who display an aptitude for and interest in special library work. Extra consideration is given to members of SLA and to persons who have worked in and for special libraries. **Funds Available:** Number and value of scholarships depend on the availability of funds. Students may receive only one SLA scholarship during their graduate library school career. **Contact:** SLA Scholarship Committee. **Applicant Details:** Candidates must submit the following: completed application form; evidence of financial need; statement (500 to 1,000 words) describing experience in special libraries and expected contribution to special librarianship; and a statement of provisional acceptance by a recognized library school or information science program. Matriculated school applicants must submit an official transcript of their library school record to date. Applicants must also arrange to have reference letters sent directly to SLA from three persons not related to applicant. **Application Deadline:** October 31. Reference letters must be received by SLA by November 6. Scholarship winners are notified in May. Official announcement and presentation is made at the Association's Annual Conference in June.

★4455★
SOCHE/PGA Scholarship
Southwestern Ohio Council for Higher
     Education
2900 Acosta St., Ste. 141
Dayton, OH 45420
Study Level: Undergraduate. **Award Type:** Scholarship. **Purpose:** To Assist minority students who have enrolled in one of the Council institutions. **Selection Criteria:** Recipients are selected on a needs basis by the Financial Aid Officers of SOCHE.

★4456★
Society of Actuaries/Casualty Actuarial Society Scholarships for Minority Students
Society of Actuaries
475 N. Martingale Rd., Ste. 800
Schaumburg, IL 60173   Ph: (708)706-3500
Study Level: Undergraduate. **Award Type:** Scholarship. **Purpose:** The scholarship program is designed to aid minority students interested in pursuing actuarial careers. **Applicant Eligibility:** Candidates must be members of a minority group (i.e., Black,

Hispanic, Asian, or Native North American). They must be either U.S. citizens or have permanent resident visas. Candidates must be admitted to a college or university offering either a program in Actuarial Science or courses which will serve to prepare the student for an actuarial career. All applicants must have demonstrated mathematical ability and evidence some understanding of the field. Applicants must have taken Exam 100 of the Actuarial Examinations, the Scholastic Aptitude Test (SAT), or the ACT. **Selection Criteria:** Scholarships are awarded on the basis of individual merit and financial need. **Funds Available:** The number and amount of the scholarships are determined by a committee of members of the Society of Actuaries and the Casualty Actuarial Society. The number and amount of the awards vary from year to year. **Contact:** High school guidance department, college chairman of mathematics department, or the Society of Actuaries. **Applicant Details:** Applicants must submit the Financial Aid Form (FAF) to the College Scholarship Service (CSS) of the College Board not later than March 31 and give CSS permission to forward information to the Society. Applicants must also submit two nomination forms, completed by their instructors or academic advisors. **Application Deadline:** May 1.

★4457★
**Tennessee Community College Education Recruitment
  Scholarship**
Tennessee Student Assistance Corporation
Parkway Towers, Ste. 1950
404 James Robertson Pkwy.
Nashville, TN 37219-5097   Ph: (615)741-1346
Study Level: Undergraduate. **Award Type:** Scholarship. **Purpose:** To attract members of Tennessee minorities into teacher education programs at Tennessee community colleges. **Applicant Eligibility:** Applicants must be U.S. citizens and Tennessee residents. They must be freshmen enrolled full-time in an eligible Tennessee community college. The courses that they are enrolled in full-time must be documented to be transferable to a teacher education program at a senior institution. The receiving community college cannot enroll more than ten awardees per academic year and must have a transfer agreement in place with a senior institution that has a state-approved teacher education program. **Funds Available:** $2,000 per academic year, renewable for a second year. **Applicant Details:** Applications are available through TSAC.

★4458★
Tennessee Teaching Fellowships
Tennessee Student Assistance Corporation
Parkway Towers, Ste. 1950
404 James Robertson Pkwy.
Nashville, TN 37219-5097   Ph: (615)741-1346
Study Level: Undergraduate. **Award Type:** Scholarship Loan. **Purpose:** To encourage qualified minority students to enter the teaching profession. **Applicant Eligibility:** Only entering freshmen who are minority Tennesseans are eligible for first-time awards. To be considered, they must have earned at least a 3.5 GPA in high school through the seventh semester level, and either have scored at least an 18 on the ACT or 780 on the SAT or be in the top 25 percent of their high school graduating class. They must be U.S. citizens and agree in writing to teach at the K-12 level in a Tennessee public school upon college graduation. **Funds Available:** $5,000 for each year eligible. $20,000 maximum. Those who fail to fill the obligation by teaching must repay the award balance plus 12 percent interest. **Contact:** Program Administrator at TSAC. **Applicant Details:** Application forms will be sent to Tennessee high schools only if awards are to be made in a given year (funds must be made available by the state legislature).

★4459★
**Texas State Scholarship Program for Ethnic
  Recruitment**
Texas Higher Education Coordinating
  Board
PO Box 12788
Capitol Station
Austin, TX 78711-2788   Ph: (512)462-6325
Study Level: Undergraduate. **Award Type:** Scholarship. **Applicant Eligibility:** Applicant must be a resident minority student enrolling for the first time either as freshmen or new transfer student and whose ethnic group comprises less than 40 percent of the enrollment at a particular school. Entering freshmen must score at least 800 on the SAT or at least 18 on the ACT, and transfer students must have a GPA of at least 2.75. **Selection Criteria:** A judgement of financial need by the financial aid director at the institution and recommendations of the admissions officer or minority affairs officer help determine eligibility for the scholarship. **Funds Available:** One time awards range from $500 to $1,000. **Applicant Details:** Interested students should contact the financial aid director at the public senior college.

★4460★
United Methodist Ethnic Scholarships
The United Methodist Church
Office of Loans and Scholarships
General Board of Higher Education and
  Ministry
PO Box 871
Nashville, TN 37202   Ph: (615)340-7344
Study Level: Undergraduate. **Award Type:** Scholarship. **Applicant Eligibility:** Applicants must be Hispanic, Asian or Native American; an active member of the United Methodist Church for at least one year; a United States citizen or permanent resident; be able to establish financial need. Candidates for the Ethnic Scholarships must be full-time undergraduates at an accredited college. **Funds Available:** Ethnic Scholarships vary from $100-$1000. **Applicant Details:** Applications for Ethnic Minority Scholarships may be requested between January and April. **Application Deadline:** May 1.

★4461★
**U.S. Central Intelligence Agency
Undergraduate Scholarship**
Central Intelligence Agency
Office of Student Programs
Dept. S, Rm. 4N2OJ
Washington, DC 20013   Ph: (703)482-7303
Study Level: Undergraduate. **Award Type:** Internship; Scholarship. **Purpose:** To give financial assistance to disabled or minority undergraduates who wish to complete postsecondary education and gain experience at the CIA. **Applicant Eligibility:** Applicants must be minority or disabled, must have 3.0 GPA, and must major in engineering, computer science, mathematics, physics, cartography, imagery science, Russian, Chinese, or Japanese. **Funds Available:** Five or more scholarships/internships are awarded each year and provide tuition; summer internships provide competitive salaries. **Application Deadline:** January.

★4462★
**U.S. Smithsonian Institute
Minority Fellowships**
Smithsonian Institution
Office of Fellowships and Grants
955 L'Enfant Plaza, Ste. 7300
Washington, DC 20560   Ph: (202)287-3271
Study Level: Graduate; Undergraduate. **Award Type:** Internship. **Applicant Eligibility:** Applicants must be minority undergraduate or graduate students. **Funds Available:** Internships carry a cash stipend and a travel allowance.

★4463★
Virgil Hawkins Fellows Scholarships
Florida Department of Education
Office of Student Financial Assistance
1344 Florida Education Center
Tallahassee, FL 32399-0400   Ph: (904)487-0049
Study Level: Graduate. **Award Type:** Scholarship. **Purpose:** Provides financial assistance to first-year minority law students. **Applicant Eligibility:** Applicants must: be a member of an ethnic group that was by law and custom previously denied access to a law school at a predominately white institution in Florida; meet the registration requirements of the Selective Service Administration; be admitted to the law school at Florida State University or the University of Florida; and be recommended by the law school dean. A renewal applicant must continue studies toward completion of a Juris Doctor degree, be considered to be in good standing by the law school, and be recommended by the law school dean for continuation of the scholarship. **Funds Available:** $5,000 per academic year or as specified in the General Appropriations Act for a

maximum of six semesters. Scholarships are limited to 10 new awards each at Florida State University and the University of Florida. **Contact:** The Dean of the Law School at Florida State University, 425 W. Jefferson St., Tallahassee, FL 32306, or at the University of Florida, 164 Holland Law Center, Gainesville, FL 32611.

★4464★
William and Charlotte Cadbury Awards
National Medical Fellowships, Inc.
254 W. 31st St., 7th Fl.
New York, NY 10001

Study Level: Doctorate. **Award Type:** Scholarship. **Applicant Eligibility:** Candidates are Black Americans, mainland Puerto Ricans, Mexican-Americans, and American Indians who are enrolled in accredited schools of allopathic or osteopathic medicine in the United States and who are United States citizens. Cadbury Award candidates are senior medical students who have exhibited superior scholastic achievement and leadership. **Funds Available:** One Cadbury Award of $2000 is awarded annually. **Applicant Details:** Applications by Dean's nomination only. **Application Deadline:** Nominations requested in October.

★4465★
Wisconsin Minority Retention Grants
Wisconsin Higher Education Aids Board
131 W. Wilson St.
PO Box 7885
Madison, WI 53707   Ph: (608)266-0888

Study Level: Undergraduate. **Award Type:** Grant. **Purpose:** To provide financial assistance to Black, Hispanic, and Native American students, and students who were admitted to the United States after December 31, 1975, and who are either a former citizen of Laos, Vietnam, or Cambodia or whose ancestor was a citizen of Laos, Vietnam, or Cambodia. The goal of the Grant is to improve the rate of retention and graduation.

★4466★
Wisconsin Minority Teacher Loans
Wisconsin Higher Education Aids Board
131 W. Wilson St.
PO Box 7885
Madison, WI 53707   Ph: (608)266-0888

Study Level: Undergraduate. **Award Type:** Loan. **Applicant Eligibility:** Must be Wisconsin resident minority students attending private colleges or universities in Wisconsin who are in their junior or senior year majoring in education. **Funds Available:** Recipients may borrow up to $2,500 per academic year for a total of $5,000. Loans are forgiven when the borrower is employed as a teacher in an eligible Wisconsin school district. For each year so employed, 25 percent of the amount borrowed is forgiven. **Applicant Details:** Interested students should contact the financial aid office of the school at which they are enrolled.

★4467★
Woodrow Wilson Program in Public Policy and
 International Affairs Junior Year Summer Institutes
Woodrow Wilson National Fellowship
 Foundation
PO Box 642   Ph: (609)924-4713
Princeton, NJ 08542   Fax: (609)497-9064

Study Level: Undergraduate. **Award Type:** Other. **Applicant Eligibility:** Must have completed the junior year in college and have at least one full semester of coursework left before graduation. Must be U.S. citizens or permanent residents and members of minority groups historically underrepresented in public policy and international careers, especially African Americans, Hispanics, Native Americans, Asian Americans, and Alaska Natives. No particular major is required. Students must, however, demonstrate strong interest in public policy and internationl affairs. **Applicant Details:** Write for current information. Applications are made directly to the summer institutes at participating universities. **Application Deadline:** March 15.

Print & Broadcast Media

Directories

★4468★
Affirmative Action Register
Affirmative Action, Inc.
8356 Olive Blvd.
Saint Louis, MO 63132   Ph: (314)991-1335

Covers: In each issue, about 300 positions at a professional level (most requiring advanced study) available to females, minorities, veterans, and the handicapped; listings are advertisements placed by employers with affirmative action programs. **Entries Include:** Company or organization name, address, contact name; description of position including title, requirements, duties, application procedure, salary, etc. **Pages (approx.):** 50. **Frequency:** Monthly. **Price:** $1.50 per issue; distributed free to female, minority and handicapped candidate sources. **ISSN:** 0146-2113.

★4469★
Directory of Financial Aids for Minorities
Reference Service Press
1100 Industrial Rd., Ste. 9
San Carlos, CA 94070   Ph: (415)594-0743

Covers: Over 2,000 financial aid programs and awards available to members of minority groups; includes scholarships, fellowships, loans, grants, awards, and internships; state government agencies with related information. **Entries Include:** Program title, sponsor name, address, phone, eligibility requirements, purpose, duration, application deadline, financial data, etc. **Pages (approx.):** 600. **Frequency:** Biennial, January of odd years. **Price:** $49.50, plus $4.00 shipping.

★4470★
Directory of Minority Arts Organizations
Civil Rights Division
National Endowment for the Arts
1100 Pennsylvania Ave., N.W., Rm. 812
Washington, DC 20506   Ph: (202)682-5454

Covers: Almost 1,000 performing groups, presenters, galleries, art and media centers, literary organizations, and community centers with significant arts programming which have leadership and constituency that is predominantly Asian-American, Black, Hispanic, Native American, or multi-racial. **Entries Include:** Organization name, address, phone, name and title of contact, description of activities. **Pages (approx.):** 120. **Frequency:** Irregular; previous edition 1982; latest edition February 1987. **Price:** Free.

★4471★
Directory of Special Programs for Minority Group
 Members: Career Information Services, Employment
 Skills Banks, Financial Aid Sources
Garrett Park Press
Box 190F
Garrett Park, MD 20896   Ph: (301)946-2553

Covers: About 2,000 private and governmental agencies offering financial aid, employment assistance, and career guidance programs for minorities. **Entries Include:** Organization or agency name, address, phone, contact name, type of organization, purpose, description of services and activities in the equal opportunity employment area. **Pages (approx.):** 350. **Frequency:** Irregular; latest edition 1990. **Price:** $27.00, payment with order; $30.00, billed.

★4472★

Educating Tomorrow's Engineers: A Guide to Precollege Minority Engineering Programs

National Action Council for Minorities in
  Engineering
3 W. 35th St.
New York, NY 10001-2281   Ph: (212)279-2626

Covers: More than 100 precollege engineering programs for minority students. **Entries Include:** Program name, address, phone, names and titles of key officials, description of activities. **Pages (approx.):** 146. **Frequency:** Irregular; latest edition 1990. **Price:** $12.00.

★4473★

Financial Aid for Minorities in...

Garrett Park Press
Box 190F
Garrett Park, MD 20896   Ph: (301)946-2553

Covers: In 6 volumes, sources of financial aid for minorities. Volume 1 covers health occupations; volume 2 covers business and law; volume 3 covers education; volume 4 covers engineering and science; volume 5 covers journalism and mass communications; volume 6 covers financial aid for students with any major. **Entries Include:** Organization, institution, or agency name, address, type of assistance, amounts available, application deadline and procedures. **Pages (approx.):** 80 per volume. **Frequency:** Irregular; latest edition 1991. **Price:** $4.95 per volume; $25.00 per set; postpaid.

★4474★

Financial Aid Unscrambled: A Guide for Minority Engineering Students

National Action Council for Miniorities in
  Engineering
3 W. 35th St.
New York, NY 10001   Ph: (212)279-2626

Covers: Over 80 state financial aid and Guaranteed Student Loan (GSL) offices; over 40 private grants and scholarships; and 10 publications on financial aid for African American, Hispanic, and Native American engineering students. **Entries Include:** For state financial aid or GSL offices Program name, address, phone. For private grants and scholarships Program name, description, requirements, deadline, sponsor name, address, phone. For publications Title, publisher name, address, phone. **Pages (approx.):** 24. **Frequency:** Biennial, even years. **Price:** $1.00.

★4475★

Guide to Multicultural Resources

Praxis Publications, Inc.
2215 Atwood Ave.
Madison, WI 53704   Ph: (608)244-5633

Covers: Over 4,000 minority and multicultural organizations and associations involved with the Asian, Black, Hispanic, and Native American communities. **Entries Include:** Organization name, address, phone, contact names, description of organization, information or publications available, whether willing to network with other groups. **Pages (approx.):** 500. **Frequency:** Biennial, January of odd years. **Price:** $63.00.

★4476★

Guide to Obtaining Minority Business Directories

Try Us Resources, Inc.
2105 Central Ave. NE
Minneapolis, MN 55418   Ph: (612)781-6819

Covers: About 115 organizations that publish directories of minority businesses; includes local directories covering commercial, industrial, professional, and/or retail business in all lines, and directories of wider geographical scope that tend to cover single lines of business. **Entries Include:** Publisher or source name, address, phone, type of publication, date of publication. **Pages (approx.):** 35. **Frequency:** Annual, January. **Price:** $10.00, plus $1.00 shipping. **Former Title(s):** *Guide to Minority Business Directories.*

★4477★

Guide to Prehistoric Ruins of the Southwest

Pruett Publishing Company
2928 Pearl St.
Boulder, CO 80301   Ph: (303)449-4919

Covers: Over 200 archeological sites in Arizona, New Mexico, Utah and Colorado. **Entries Include:** Site name, location, size, features and description of site, names of excavators or sponsoring organization, discoveries, whether accessible to the handicapped, active parts of site. **Pages (approx.):** 208. **Frequency:** Irregular; previous edition August 1981; latest edition May 1989. **Price:** $12.95, plus $2.00 shipping; payment with order.

★4478★

Higher Education Opportunities for Minorities and Women: Annotated Selections

U.S. Office of Postsecondary Education
400 Maryland Ave., Rm. 3915
Washington, DC 20202-5151   Ph: (202)708-9180

Covers: Programs of public and private organizations and state and federal government agencies that offer loans, scholarships, and fellowship opportunities for women and minorities. **Entries Include:** Organization name, address, brief description of program. **Pages (approx.):** 143. **Frequency:** Biennial, odd years. **Price:** $5.00. **Former Title(s):** *Selected List of Postsecondary Education Opportunities for Minorities and Women.*

★4479★

How and Where to Research Your Ethnic-American Cultural Heritage

Robert D. Reed
PO Box 2008
Saratoga, CA 95070   Ph: (408)866-6303

Covers: Historical societies, cultural institutes, libraries, archives, publishers, and other sources for genealogical research into German, Russian, Native American, Polish, Black, Japanese, Jewish, Irish, Mexican, Italian, Chinese, and Scandinavian backgrounds; 12 separate volumes cover each ethnic group. Institution name, address, phone. **Pages (approx.):** 30. **Frequency:** Most volumes first published 1979; new edition expected 1993. **Price:** $3.50, plus $1.00 shipping per volume.

★4480★

Minorities and Women: A List of Major Organizations in Librarianship

American Library Association (ALA)
50 E. Huron St.
Chicago, IL 60611   Ph: (312)280-4277

Covers: About 10 minority and women librarian organizations. **Entries Include:** Organization name, address, phone, names and titles of key personnel, publications. **Frequency:** Annual, summer. **Price:** Free.

★4481★

Minority Business Development Agency Directory of Regional & District Offices and Funded Organizations

U.S. Minority Business Development
  Agency
*Washington, DC 20230   Ph: (202)377-2414

Covers: About 10 regional and district offices of the Minority Business Development Agency; approximately 110 agency-funded minority business development centers which offer business services for a nominal fee to current and prospective minority business operators. **Entries Include:** For regional offices Office name, address, phone, states served, director name. For district offices Office address and phone, names of district officers. For development centers Center name, address, phone, project director name. **Pages (approx.):** 15. **Price:** Free.

★4482★
Minority Health Resources Directory
ANROW Publishing
5515 Security Ln., Ste. 510
Rockville, MD 20852   Ph: (301)231-9241

Covers: 360 federal government programs and agencies, organizations, and foundations offering health services and products to minority group members. **Entries Include:** Name, address, phone, description, activities for minorities, publications and other communications, meetings and conferences. **Pages (approx.):** 355. **Frequency:** Published 1991. **Price:** $50.00, plus $6.95 shipping.

★4483★
Minority Organizations: A National Directory
Garrett Park Press
Box 190F
Garrett Park, MD 20896   Ph: (301)946-2553

Covers: Over 7,700 groups composed of or intended to serve members of minority groups, including Alaska Natives, American Indians, Blacks, Hispanics, and Asian Americans. **Entries Include:** Organization name, address, description of activities, purpose, publications, etc. **Pages (approx.):** 690. **Frequency:** Irregular; previous edition 1987; latest edition 1992. **Price:** $36.00, payment with order; $40.00, billed.

★4484★
Minority Student Enrollments in Higher Education: A Guide to Institutions with...Asian, Black, Hispanic, and Native American Students
Garrett Park Press
Box 190F
Garrett Park, MD 20896   Ph: (301)946-2553

Covers: About 500 colleges and universities at which one or more minority (Asian, Black, Hispanic, or Native American) constitutes at least 20% of the student body. **Entries Include:** Institution name, address, phone, total enrollment, highest level of degree offered, partial list of major programs offered, minority groups representing at least one-fifth of the total enrollment. **Pages (approx.):** 80. **Frequency:** First edition 1987; latest edition 1988. **Price:** $14.00, payment with order; $15.00, billed.

★4485★
Minority Student Opportunities in United States Medical Schools
Association of American Medical Colleges (AAMC)
2450 N St. NW
Washington, DC 20037-1126   Ph: (202)828-0400

Covers: Programs for minority group students at nearly 130 medical schools. **Entries Include:** Name of school, name of parent institution, if applicable, address, phone, name of contact; descriptions of recruitment, admissions, financial aid, and academic assistance programs for the minority student; statistical table on minority admissions and enrollment. **Pages (approx.):** 325. **Frequency:** Biennial, August of even years. **Price:** $7.50, plus $2.50 shipping; payment must accompany order.

★4486★
NACME Students' Guide to Engineering Schools
National Action Council for Minorities in Education (NACME)
3 W. 35th St.
New York, NY 10001   Ph: (212)279-2626

Covers: Engineering colleges and universities in the United States with at least one curriculum accredited by the Accreditation Board for Engineering and Technology. **Entries Include:** Institution name, location, financial data, outline of admission dates and requirements, minority enrollment, engineering curricula offered, description of program, and support activities. **Pages (approx.):** 45. **Frequency:** Irregular; latest edition 1988, new edition expected late 1992. **Price:** $10.00 per 30 copies; $25.00 per 100.

★4487★
National Directory of Minority-Owned Business Firms
Business Research Services, Inc.
4201 Connecticut Ave. NW, Ste. 610
Washington, DC 20008   Ph: (202)364-6473

Covers: Over 35,000 minority-owned businesses. **Entries Include:** Company name, address, phone, name and title of contact, minority group, certification status, date founded, number of employees, description of products or services, sales volume government contracting experience, references. **Pages (approx.):** 1,350. **Frequency:** Biennial; previous edition 1990; latest edition January 1992. **Price:** $225.00, plus $5.00 shipping. **ISSN:** 0886-3881.

★4488★
Try Us: National Minority Business Directory
Try Us Resources, Inc.
2105 Central Ave. NE
Minneapolis, MN 55418   Ph: (612)781-6819

Covers: Over 6,000 minority-owned companies capable of supplying their goods and services on national or regional levels. **Entries Include:** Company name, address, phone, name of principal executive, number of employees, date established, trade and brand names, financial keys, products or services, names of three customers, certification status, minority identification, gross sales. **Pages (approx.):** 500. **Frequency:** Annual, January. **Price:** $45.00.

★4489★
Venture Capital Directory
Forum Publishing Co.
383 E. Main St.
Centerport, NY 11721   Ph: (516)754-5000

Covers: Over 500 members of the Small Business Administration and the Small Business Investment Company that provide funding for small and minority businesses. **Entries Include:** Company name, address, phone, names and titles of key personnel, geographical area served, financial data, branch office or subsidiary names, description of services and projects. **Pages (approx.):** 50. **Frequency:** Annual, February. **Price:** $12.95.

Journals & Magazines

★4490★
Aim—America's Intercultural Magazine
Aim Publications
7308 S. Eberhart Ave.
Chicago, IL 60619   Ph: (312)874-6184

Subtitle: Aim Quarterly. **Description:** Magazine promoting intercultural awareness and understanding in America. **First Published:** 1974. **Frequency:** Quarterly. **Subscription:** $10.

★4491★
The Americas
Academy of American Franciscan History
The Catholic University of America
B-17 Gibbons Hall
620 Michigan Ave.,NE
Washington, DC 20064   Ph: (202)319-5890

Subtitle: Inter-American Cultural History. **Description:** Journal on international-American culture and history. **First Published:** 1944. **Frequency:** 4x/yr. **Subscription:** $28; $49 institutions; $17 Pan-American. $15 single issue. **ISSN:** 0003-1615.

★4492★
Collage
221 Riverside Dr., Ste. 11
Ottawa, ON, Canada K1H 7X2   Ph: (403)281-0674

Description: Multicultural magazine. **First Published:** 1984. **Frequency:** Monthly. **Subscription:** $17.50.

★4493★
Cultural Survival Quarterly
Cultural Survival, Inc.
11 Divinity Ave.
Cambridge, MA 02138   Ph: (617)495-2562
Description: Magazine for general public and policy makers intended to stimulate action for ethnic minorities. **First Published:** 1976. **Frequency:** Quarterly. **Subscription:** $25. $3 single issue. **ISSN:** 0740-3291.

★4494★
Horizons Interculturels
Intercultural Institute of Montreal
4917 St-Urbain
Montreal, PQ, Canada H2T 2W1   Ph: (514)288-7229
Description: Intercultural magazine. **First Published:** 1985. **Subscription:** $12, $17 outside Canada. **ISSN:** 0827-1569.

★4495★
Interculture
Intercultual Institute of Montreal
4917 St-Urbain
Montreal, PQ, Canada H2T 2W1   Ph: (514)288-7229
Description: Journal covering cross-cultural themes. **First Published:** 1968. **Frequency:** Quarterly. **Subscription:** $22 individual; $35 institutions; $4.25 single issue. **ISSN:** 0828-797X (English); 0172-1571 (French).

★4496★
PHYLON
Atlanta University
223 James P. Brawley Dr. SW
Atlanta, GA 30314   Ph: (404)880-8680
Description: Race and culture review magazine. **First Published:** 1940. **Frequency:** Quarterly. **Subscription:** $14; $24 institutions.

★4497★
Skipping Stones
PO Box 3939
Eugene, OR 97403-0939
Subtitle: A Multicultural Children's Quarterly. **Description:** International magazine containing original literature, visual art, entertainment, and reviews by and for children. Includes writings in languages other than English. Focuses on ecological, cultural and linguistic richness. **First Published:** 1988. **Frequency:** Quarterly. **Subscription:** Free to qualified subscribers; $15; $20 institutions; $25 airmail. $5 single issue. **ISSN:** 0899-529X.

Newsletters

★4498★
AAAA News
American Association for Affirmative Action
11 E. Hubbard St., Ste. 200
Chicago, IL 60611   Ph: (312)329-2512
Description: Reports on Association news and activities as well as pertinent civil rights legislation and Equal Employment Opportunity Commission (EEOC) decisions. **Price:** Included in membership. **ISSN:** 0896-8217.

★4499★
Las Palabras
Millicent Rogers Museum
PO Box A
Taos, NM 87571   Ph: (505)758-2462
Description: Supports the Museum's purpose, which is to support "the collection and interpretation of the art, history, and culture of the Native American, Hispanic, and Anglo peoples of the Southwest, focusing on Taos and northern New Mexico." Provides in-depth information on exhibits and collections, and museum news. Includes a calendar of events. **First Published:** January 1980. **Frequency:** Quarterly. **Price:** Included in membership.

★4500★
Museum of the Great Plains Newsletter
Institute of the Great Plains
Elmer Thomas Park
601 Ferris
PO Box 68
Lawton, OK 73502   Ph: (405)581-3460
Description: Reports on the exhibits, educational programming, museum activities, and archival collections of the Museum, which is concerned with the history, archeology, and natural history of the Great Plains of North America. **First Published:** 1977. **Frequency:** Annually. **Price:** Included in subscription to the Great Plains Journal.

★4501★
Order of the Indian Wars—Communique
Order of the Indian Wars
PO Box 7401   Ph: (501)225-3996
Little Rock, AR 72217   Fax: (501)225-5167
Description: Centers on the study and dissemination of information on America's frontier conflicts, with interest in both sides of the conflicts that occurred in the early years of this country. Concerned about the preservation of important military sites of the Indian Wars. **First Published:** August 1979. **Frequency:** Monthly. **Price:** $20/yr. for members. **Also Known As:** *OIW Communique*.

★4502★
The Piegan Storyteller
James Willard Schultz Society
135 Wildwood Dr.
New Bern, NC 28562   Ph: (919)637-5985
Description: Focuses on J.W. Schultz, author of western children's books. Also discusses Montana history and Blackfeet Indians. **First Published:** January 1976. **Frequency:** Quarterly. **Price:** $10/yr., U.S. and Canada; $15 elsewhere.

★4503★
'Round Robbins
The Friends of the Robbins Museum
Massachusetts Archaeological Society
PO Box 700
Middleborough, MA 02346-0700   Ph: (508)947-9005
Description: Concerned with the preservation and study of Massachusetts' archaeological heritage; supports the Robbins Museum. Presents information on artifacts collected, volunteers, and Native American culture. **Price:** Included in membership.

Publishers

★4504★
American Committee to Advance the Study of Petroglyphs and Pictographs
PO Box 158
Shepherdstown, WV 25443-0158   Ph: (304)876-9431
Description: Publishes occasional papers and a journal; offers consultant services. Distributes for Editons Sureste, S.A. (Mexico). Reaches market through direct mail. **Subjects:** Archaeology, rock art, Native American studies, anthropology. **Total Titles in Print:** 2. **Selected Titles:** *Occasional Papers, Vol. 1* by Martineau et al. **Principal Officials and Managers:** Joseph J. Snyder, Executive Secretary and Editor; Benjamin K. Swartz, Jr., President; James L. Swauger, Vice-President.

★4505★
Bear & Co., Inc.
506 Agua Fria St.
PO Drawer 2860
Santa Fe, NM 87501   Ph: (505)983-5968
Description: Publishes books "to celebrate and heal the Earth." Reaches market through direct mail, trade sales, and wholesalers. **Subjects:** Personal and social transformation, spirituality, native American studies. **Number of New Titles:** 1990 - 10, 1991 - 11,

1992 (est.) - 11; Total Titles in Print - 78. **Selected Titles:** *Vibrational Medicine: New Choices for Healing Ourselves* by Richard Gerber; *Medicine Cards: The Discovery of Power through the Ways of Animals* by Jamie Sams and David Carson; *Profiles in Wisdom: Nature Elders Speak about the Earth* by Steven McFadden; *Sacred Places: How the Living Earth Seeks Our Friendship* by James Swan; *Light: Medicine of the Future* by Dr. Jacob Liberman; *Liquid Light of Sex: Understanding Your Key Life Passages* by Barbara Hand Clow. **Principal Officials and Managers:** Gerald C. Clow President; Barbara Hand Clow, Executive Vice-President; Charlotte A. Romero, Secretary; Diane Winters, Treasurer.

★4506★
Blue Bird Publishing
1713 E. Broadway, No. 306
Tempe, AZ 85282   Ph: (602)968-4088

Description: Publishes educational material for libraries about home schooling, social issus, parenting, and American Indian cultural items. Accepts unsolicited manuscripts. Reaches market through commission representatives, direct mail, Baker & Taylor, Quality Books, Inc., Pacific Pipeline, and Spring Arbor Distributors. **Number of New Titles:** 1990 - 6, 1991 (est.) - 6; Total Titles in Print - 14. **Principal Officials and Managers:** Cheryl Gorder, Owner and President.

★4507★
Butterfly Books Ltd.
PO Box 294
Maple Creek, SK, Canada S0N 1N0   Ph: (204)947-0719

Description: Originated as publishing division of Walter P. Stewart Consultant Ltd. Publishes on photo-journalism, Canada, and North American Indians; offers the magazine *Photo-Essai.* **Selected Titles:** *The Town of Maple Creek, Saskatchewan; The City of Regina, Saskatchewan; The Growth of Western Canada Nationalism,* all by W. Stewart; *My Name Is Piapot: The Biography of Chief Piapot, Plains Cree (1816-1908); Eagle Feathers in the Dust; G-5.* **Principal Officials and Managers:** W. P. Stewart, President.

★4508★
Costano Books
PO Box 355
Petaluma, CA 94953   Ph: (707)762-4848

Description: Publishes on North American Indians, lighthouses, and maritime books. Reaches market through direct mail, commission representatives, reviews, telephone sales, direct mail, and major small press wholesalers and distributors. **Subjects:** Native Americans, maritime history, lighthouses, travel. **Number of New Titles:** 1989 - 1; Total Titles in Print - 3. **Selected Titles:** *North American Indian Travel Guide; Lighthouses and Lightboats on the Redwood Coast; Lighthouses of San Francisco Bay; Guardians of the Golden Gate.* **Principal Officials and Managers:** Dan Lacewell, Manager; Torrey Pine, Secretary.

★4509★
Council on Interracial Books for Children, Inc.
1841 Broadway
New York, NY 10023   Ph: (212)757-5339

Description: Publishes "to identify--and more recently to counteract--racism, sexism, and other anti-human values in children's learning materials and in society." Offers books, maps, filmstrips, catalogs, and booklists. Reaches market through direct mail. **Total Titles in Print:** 30. **Selected Titles:** *Embers: Stories for a Changing World; Guidelines for Selecting Bias-Free Textbooks and Storybooks; Stereotypes, Distortions and Omissions in U.S. History Textbooks; Violence, the Ku Klux Klan and the Struggle for Equality; Chronicles of American Indian Protest; Unlearning "Indian" Stereotypes,* all by the CIBC. **Principal Officials and Managers:** Melba Kgositsile, Executive Director.

★4510★
Cultural Survival, Inc.
53A Church St.
Cambridge, MA 02138   Ph: (617)495-2562

Description: A human rights organization dedicated to assisting indigenous people and ethnic minorities in increasing their autonomy and ability to adapt to development efforts. Publishes occasional research papers and special reports on these topics. Offers t-shirts, calendars, slides, and notecards. Distributes for Minority Rights Group (England), Anti-Slavery Society (England), ZED Press (England), International Work Group for Indigenous Affairs (Denmark), CEDI (Brazil), and Consumer Association of Penang (Malaysia). Reaches market through direct mail and trade sales. **Subjects:** Human rights, economic development, social anthropology. **Number of New Titles:** 1990 - 1. **Selected Titles:** *Politics and the Ethiopian Famine* by Jason Clay and Bonnie Holcomb; *American Indian Societies, Strategies of Cultural Survival in American Indian Society* both by Duane Champagne; *Indigenous People and Tropical Forests* by Jason Clay; *Report from the Frontier* by Julian Burger; *Settlements of Hope* by Ann Forbes. **Principal Officials and Managers:** David Maybury-Lewis, President; Jason Clay, Director of Research and Editor; Theodore Macdonald, Director of Projects; Pam Solo, Executive Director; Domique Irvine, Program Director.

★4511★
Denver Art Museum
100 W. 14th Ave. Pkwy.
Denver, CO 80204   Ph: (303)640-2765

Description: Publishes educational and scholarly materials about permanent collections and temporary exhibitions. Reaches market through University of Washington Press. **Subjects:** Art. **Number of New Titles:** 1989 - 2, 1990 - 2, 1991 (est.) - 2; Total Titles in Print - 22. **Selected Titles:** *Native American Art in the Denver Art Museum* by Richard Conn. **Principal Officials and Managers:** Marlene Chambers, Director of Publications; Beth Bazar, Publications Assistant; Mary H. Junda, Graphic Designer; Mary Jane Butler, Bookshop Manager.

★4512★
Don M. Chase
916 Colorado St.
Santa Rosa, CA 95405   Ph: (707)823-7670

Description: Publishes paperbound and velo-bound items of local western history and Indians. Some are first or limited editions that are numbered and signed. Reaches market through direct mail and wholesalers. Presently inactive. **Subjects:** California, Western Americana, Native Americans, church history, mountain men. **Total Titles in Print:** 7. **Selected Titles:** *A Road Past His Door, They Came This Way: Highroad to the Goldrush,* both by Don M. Chase; *Pack Saddles and Rolling Wheels* by Marjory Helms and Don Chase; *They Pushed Back the Forest* by Doris Chase; *Basket-Maker Artists* by Carl Purdy, Clara McNaughton, and Don M. Chase; *Jedediah Strong Smith* by Patrick and Don M. Chase. **Principal Officials and Managers:** Don M. Chase, Proprietor.

★4513★
Douglas County Planning Department
Courthouse Annex No. 2
205 SE Jackson St.
Roseburg, OR 97470   Ph: (503)440-4289

Description: Publishes a scholarly history of Douglas County and the surrounding area based on source material about Indian-white relations and the role of the federal government in the county's history. Reaches market through direct mail and Oregon Pacific Books. **Total Titles in Print:** 1. **Selected Titles:** *Land of the Umpqua* by Stephen Dow Beckham. **Principal Officials and Managers:** Keith L. Cubic, Planning Director.

★4514★
Eager Beaver Books
1230 SW Park Ave.
Portland, OR 97205   Ph: (503)222-1741

Description: Publishes Northwest regional fiction and nonfiction for juvenile readers. Also offers T-shirts. Accepts unsolicited manuscripts. Reaches market through direct mail, trade sales, and wholesalers. **Number of New Titles:** 1990 - 2, 1991 (est.) - 1; Total Titles in Print - 2. **Selected Titles:** *Chief Sarah: Sarah Winnemucca's Fight for Indian Rights* by Dorthy Nafus Morrison; *Treasure Mountain* by Evelyn Sibley Tampman. **Principal Officials and Managers:** Bruce Taylor Hamilton, Director; Virginia M. Linnman, Sales and Marketing Manager.

★4515★
Friends of Malatesta, Inc.
PO Box 937
Ellsworth, ME 04605 Ph: (207)667-8569

Subjects: Poetry, native Americans, anarchism. **Principal Officials and Managers:** Robert S. Dickens, Secretary.

★4516★
Hancock House Publishers Ltd.
19313 Zero Ave.
Surrey, BC, Canada V3S 5J9 Ph: (604)538-1114

Description: Publishes fieldguides, northern biographies, and books on Native Americans. Accepts unsolicited manuscripts; send self-addressed, stamped envelope. Distributes for Bellerophon. U.S. address: 1431 Harrison Ave., Blaine, WA 98230. Reaches market through commission representatives, direct mail, and wholesalers. **Number of New Titles:** 1989 - 20, 1990 - 15, 1991 (est.) - 15; Total Titles in Print - 120. **Selected Titles:** *The Incredible Eskimo* by Raymond DeCoccol; *Tidepool and Reef* by Rick Harbo; *Birds of BC* by David Hancock; *Ruffles on My Longjohns* by Isabel Edwards; *My Heart Soars* by Chief Dan George and Helmut Hirschau; *Northwest Gardener's Almanac* by Bill VanDerzalm. **Principal Officials and Managers:** David Hancock, Editor-in-Chief.

★4517★
Heidelberg Graphics
1116 Wendy Way
Chico, CA 95926 Ph: (916)342-6582

Description: Promotes contemporary creative writing, literature for and about authors, and multicultural expression. Offers consulting to self-published authors. **Subjects:** Fiction, poetry, biography, Native Americans, graphic art. **Number of New Titles:** 1990 - 3, 1991 - 3, 1992 (est.) - 3; Total Titles in Print - 15. **Selected Titles:** *The Face of Poetry* by LaVerne Clark and Mary MacArthur; *Focus 101* by LaVerne Clark; *Riding the Tiger's Back: A Footnote to the Assassination of JFK* by Phillip Hemenway; *Greyhounding This America* by Maurice Kenny; *The Outfielder* by H. R. Coursen; *Year of the Native American* (calendar). **Principal Officials and Managers:** Larry S. Jackson, Owner.

★4518★
Impresora Sahuaro
7575 Sendero de Juana
Tucson, AZ 85718 Ph: (602)297-3089

Subjects: Minority education, books about American Indians for children. **Selected Titles:** *The Education of a Black Muslim; Self Guide to Linguistics; Anthropology and Educational Administration* by R. Barnhardt et al. **Principal Officials and Managers:** John H. Chilcott, Managing Editor.

★4519★
KC Publications
PO Box 14883
Las Vegas, NV 89114 Ph: (702)731-3123

Description: Publishes on national parks and Indian culture, especially Southwestern Indians. Offers calendars. Reaches market through direct mail and trade sales. **Number of New Titles:** 1989 - 5; Total Titles in Print - 75. **Selected Titles:** *Yellowstone; Zion in Pictures; Grand Canyon; Story behind the Scenery; Southwest Indian Arts and Crafts; National Park Service.* **Principal Officials and Managers:** K. C. DenDooven, Publisher; Gary H. Nicholson, President; Michael LaBaire, Marketing Director.

★4520★
Lantern Books
Rte. 1, Box 104
Farwell, MN 56327 Ph: (612)283-5876

Description: Publishes regional general interest books concentrating on the Upper Midwest. Some titles used in North Dakota schools. Also offers audiotape versions of several titles. Reaches market through direct mail, trade sales, and wholesalers. **Subjects:** Regional titles. **Number of New Titles:** 1989 - 2; Total Titles in Print - 8. **Selected Titles:** *Indians of the Upper Midwest, The Tiger-Lily Years, With the Wind at My Back: Recollections and Reflections, Flickertail Stories, Gopher Trails for Papa, Story of the Peace Garden State,* all

by Erling Nicolai Rolfsrud. **Principal Officials and Managers:** Erling N. Rolfsrud, Publisher.

★4521★
Legacy House, Inc.
PO Box 786
Orofino, ID 83544 Ph: (208)476-5632

Description: "Preserves and publishes American folktales and oral history." Reaches market through direct mail, commission representatives, and trade sales. **Number of New Titles:** 1989 - 2, 1990 - 1, 1991 (est.) - 2; Total Titles in Print - 5. **Selected Titles:** *Great-Grandfather in the Honey Tree* by Sam and Zoa Swayne; *Thunder Chaser, Do Them No Harm,* both by Zoa Swayne; *Tee-Ga's Story: A Cougar's Autobiography* by Jim and Ot-Ne-We Swayne. **Principal Officials and Managers:** Samuel F. Swayne, President; Zoa L. Swayne, Secretary.

★4522★
Minor Heron Press
PO Box 2615
Taos, NM 87571 Ph: (505)758-0081

Description: Publishes Southwest regional fiction, poetry, belle lettres including bilingual material in Native American languages, English, and Spanish-English. Also produces an art poster and videotape. Presently inactive. **Total Titles in Print:** 1. **Selected Titles:** *Ornithology* by Peter Rabbit. **Principal Officials and Managers:** Anne MacNaughton, Peter Douthit, Editorial Board.

★4523★
National Lawyers Guild
55 Avenue of the Americas
New York, NY 10013 Ph: (212)966-5000

Subjects: Affirmative action, criminal law, civil liberties, immigration, labor law. **Selected Titles:** *Representation of Witnesses Before Grand Juries; Immigration Defense Manual; Police Misconduct Lititgation Manual; Rethinking Indian Law; Employee and Union Member Guide to Labor Law; Sexual Orientation and the Law.* **Principal Officials and Managers:** Haywood Burns, President; Barbara Dudley, Executive Secretary.

★4524★
Petereins Press
PO Box 10446
Glendale, CA 91209 Ph: (212)344-1660

Description: Established with the aim of publishing books on Chicano studies, Native American history, and on the Southwest. **Subjects:** Philosophy, religion, history. **Number of New Titles:** 1992 (est.) - 2; Total Titles in Print - 3. **Selected Titles:** *Republican Protestantism in Aztlan* by E. C. Orozco. **Principal Officials and Managers:** H. L. Petereins, Vice-President and Publisher; Eric K. Dollinger, Sales, Marketing Manager.

★4525★
Pine Cone Publishers
2251 Ross Ln.
Medford, OR 97501 Ph: (503)773-3892

Subjects: Regional Americana, nature. **Selected Titles:** *The Indian History of the Modoc War* by Jeff C. Riddle; *Among the Shoshones* by Elijah N. Wilson; *Wildflower Trails of the Pacific Northwest, Tunnel 13,* both by Art Chipman; *A Bride on the Bozeman Trail* by Francis D. Haines, Jr. **Principal Officials and Managers:** Art Chipman, Publisher; Mary M. Chipman, Assistant.

★4526★
Proof Press
PO Box 1256
Berkeley, CA 94701 Ph: (415)521-8741

Subjects: Social studies, North American Indians. **Selected Titles:** *The Native Americans; American Women: 1607 to the Present; Money in America: Its History and Its Uses,* all by Polly and John Zane. **Principal Officials and Managers:** Polly Zane, John Zane, Partners.

★4527★
Ross and Haines Old Books Co.
167 N. Snelling Ave.
Saint Paul, MN 55104   Ph: (612)647-1471
Subjects: Americana, American Indians, regional and military history. **Selected Titles:** *Chippewa Music* by Frances Densmore; *Life and Adventures of James P. Beckwourth* by T. D. Bonner; *Chronicles of the Yellowstone* by E. S. Topping; *The Marvelous Country* by Samuel W. Cozzens; *Tales of the Northwest* by Wm. Joseph Snelling; *Death of a Business: The Red Wing Pottery* by Richard S. Gillmer. **Principal Officials and Managers:** S. B. Anderson, President.

★4528★
R.V. Greeves Art Gallery
53 North Fork Rd.
PO Box 428
Fort Washakie, WY 82514   Ph: (307)332-3557
Description: Publishes a photographic essay documenting the process of sculpting and casting a bronze monument to the North American Plains Indians. Reaches market through direct mail, reviews, telephone sales, and Baker & Taylor. **Subjects:** Art, sculpture, American Indians. **Selected Titles:** *The Unknown: A Monument* by *R.V. Greeves* text by John Running. **Principal Officials and Managers:** R. V. Greeves, Owner; Carolyn Hebb, Director.

★4529★
Shorey Publications
1411 1st Ave., Ste. 200
Seattle, WA 98101   Ph: (206)624-0221
Description: Publishes facsimile reprints of older, hard-to-find books on Northwest history, Indian history, mining and gold prospecting, and how-to titles. Also produces reprints of maps. Distributed by Pacific Pipeline. Reaches market through direct mail. **Total Titles in Print:** 225. **Selected Titles:** *Early Days in Oregon* by George W. Riddle; *Handbook for Gold Prospectors in Washington* by Wayne S. Moen and Marshall T. Huntting; *The Pacific Northwest: Oregon and Washington Territory; The Whitman Massacre*, both by Matilda S. Delaney; *The Ghost Dance Religion: Smohalla and His Doctrine*. **Principal Officials and Managers:** John W. Todd, Jr., Owner; Jim Todd, Manager.

★4530★
Survival News Service
PO Box 41834
Los Angeles, CA 90041   Ph: (213)255-9502
Description: Publishes on practical survival skills, American Indians, and spirituality. Also offers the monthly *Blue Rose Journal* and audio cassettes. Accepts unsolicited manuscripts. Distributes for Dover, Word Foundations, DeVrys, and others. Reaches market through direct mail. **Number of New Titles:** 1991 - 8, 1992 (est.) - 8. **Selected Titles:** *Guide to Wild Foods* by Christopher Nyerges; *The Old Ways* by Waubliain and Woodenturtle; *What Causes Gas* by Dolores Mitler Nyerges; *History and Use of Carob*. **Principal Officials and Managers:** Christopher Nyerges, Director.

★4531★
Sweetlight Books
16625 Heitman Rd.
Cottonwood, CA 96022-9305   Ph: (602)567-7208
Description: Publishes books "for people who love the earth." Accepts unsolicited manuscripts with a self-addressed, stamped envelope. Reaches market through direct mail and wholesalers. **Subjects:** Anthropology, Indians, natural history. **Number of New Titles:** 1989 - 1, 1990 - 1; Total Titles in Print - 6. **Selected Titles:** *Not for Innocent Ears* by Ruby Modesto and Guy Mount; *The Peyote Book, Lady Ocean, How Steelhead Lost His Stripes, Coyote's Big Penis*, all by Guy Mount; *Canyon deChelly* by Conger Beasley Jr. **Principal Officials and Managers:** Guy Mount, Publisher and Editor; Jeanette Mount, Assistant Editor.

★4532★
Tahoma Publications/Tahoma Research Service
PO Box 44306
Tacoma, WA 98444   Ph: (206)537-7877
Description: Publishes a history of Fort Nisqually from both a British and an Indian point of view. Reaches market through direct mail. **Total Titles in Print:** 2. **Selected Titles:** *Fort Nisqually: A Documented History of Indian and British Interaction, They Walked Before: The Indians of Washington State*, by Cecelia Svinth Carpenter. **Principal Officials and Managers:** Cecelia Carpenter.

★4533★
Trees Co. Press
49 Van Buren Way
San Francisco, CA 94131   Ph: (415)334-8352
Description: Publishes on Native Americans and chemistry. Reaches market through direct mail and distributors, including BookPeople and Publishers Group West. **Total Titles in Print:** 2. **Selected Titles:** *Earth Is Our Mother: Guide to California Indians, Elementary Chemistry: Study Guide and Lab Manual*, both by Dolan Eargle. **Principal Officials and Managers:** Dolan Eargle, Director; Nadyne Gray, Assistant Director.

★4534★
University of Arizona
University of Arizona Press
1230 N. Park Ave., Ste. 102
Tucson, AZ 85719   Ph: (602)621-1441
Subjects: Arizona, American West, natural history, anthropology, archaeology, space sciences, American Indians, women's studies. **Number of New Titles:** 1989 - 48, 1990 - 43, 1991 (est.) - 47; Total Titles in Print - 481. **Selected Titles:** *Desert Solitaire* by Edward Abbey; *Musui's Story: The Autobiography of a Takagawa Samurai* by Katsu Kokichi; *Beyond the Aspen Grove* by Ann Zwinger; *Navajo Textiles* by Nancy Blomberg; *Quaternary Extinctions* by Paul Martin; *Metorite Craters* by Kathleen Mark. **Principal Officials and Managers:** Stephen Cox, Director; Joanne O'Hare, Senior Editor; Charlotte Tilson, Marketing Manager.

★4535★
University of Idaho
University of Idaho Press
16 Brink Hall
Moscow, ID 83843   Ph: (208)885-6245
Description: Publishes scholarly books on regional studies, Americana, natural history, ethics and human values, anthropology, and American Indians. Accepts unsolicited manuscripts with self-addressed, stamped envelope. Distributes for Idaho Geological Survey Press and Idaho State Historical Society Press. Reaches market through direct mail, trade sales, and wholesalers. **Number of New Titles:** 1990 - 8, 1991 - 9, 1992 (est.) - 10; Total Titles in Print - 75. **Selected Titles:** *Ethics and Agriculture: An Anthology of Current Issues in World Context* by Charles V. Blatz; *Bonanza Rich: Lifestyles of the Western Mining Entrepreneurs* by Richard H. Peterson; *Powers Which We Do Not Know: The Gods and Spirits of the Inuit* by Daniel Merkur; *Mandan Social and Ceremonial Organization* by Alfred W. Bowers; *Lives of the Saints in Southeast Idaho: An Introduction to Mormon Pioneer Life Story Writing* by Susan Hendricks Swetnam; *Interpreting Local Culture and History* edited by J. Sanford Rikoon and Judith Austin. **Principal Officials and Managers:** Karla Fromm, Production and Design Manager; Mitzi Grupp Boyd, Sales, Marketing, Customer Service Manager; Peg Harvey-Marose, Order Fulfillment.

★4536★
University of Massachusetts, Amherst
Horace Mann Bond Center for Equal Education
University Library 2220
School of Education
Amherst, MA 01003   Ph: (413)545-0327
Description: Publishes magazines, pamphlets, and books dealing with the education of minorities. **Selected Titles:** *The Indian in American History; A Bibliography: Education of Poor and Minority Children; Black Education in South Africa; Inequality and Racism on U.S. Campuses; Worlds of Children* by Helen and Harold Friedman. **Principal Officials and Managers:** Jeffrey W. Eiseman, Editor.

★4537★
Watson & Dwyer Publishing Ltd.
232 Academy Rd.
Winnipeg, MB, Canada R3M 0E7   Ph: (204)284-0985
Description: Publishes social history of the fur trade and Northwest and Arctic regions. Also covers native art and social history of the Inuit and Indian. Accepts unsolicited manuscripts. Reaches market through commission representatives and direct mail. **Number of New Titles:** 1989 - 2, 1990 - 3; Total Titles in Print - 14. **Selected Titles:** *The Home Children* by Phyllis Harrison; *Many Tender Ties: Women in Fur Society* by Sylvia Van Kirk; *Inuit Art: An Anthology* by Alma Houston; *Trader Tripper Trapper* by Sydney Augustus Keighley; *Manager's Tale* by Hugh Mackay Ross; *Across the Keewatin Trefields* by Christian Leden. **Principal Officials and Managers:** Helen Burgess, President; Helen Cheung, Office Manager.

★4538★
Westernlore Press
Box 35305
Tucson, AZ 85740   Ph: (602)297-5491
Description: Publishes historical books on the western United States and on Native Americans. Reaches market through trade sales, library jobbers, and direct mail. **Selected Titles:** *The Tenderfoot Bandits* by Paula Reed and Grover Ted Tate; *Ocean of Bitter Dreams: Maritime Relations between China and the United States, 1850-1915* by Robert J. Schwendinger; *Harold Bell Wright: Storyteller to America* by Lawrence V. Tagg; *Ghost Dance Messiah: The Jack Wilson Story* by Paul D. Bailey; *Shady Ladies of the West* by Ronald Dean Miller; *Indian Slave Trade in the Southwest* by L. R. Bailey.

Videos

★4539★
The ABA Commission on Minorities and Judicial Administration Division
American Bar Association
Commission on Public Understanding
  About the Law
750 N. Lakeshore Dr.
Chicago, IL 60611   Ph: (312)988-5000
Description: Issues of prejudice in the courtroom are discussed. **Release Date:** 1988. **Length:** 15 mins. **Format:** Beta, VHS, 3/4″ U-matic Cassette.

★4540★
Alice Elliott
University of California at Berkeley
  Extension Media Center
2176 Shattuck Ave.
Berkeley, CA 94704   Ph: (510)642-0460
Description: The artist who makes Indian-style baskets is profiled. **Release Date:** 1977. **Length:** 45 mins. **Format:** VHS, 3/4″ U-matic Cassette.

★4541★
And Justice for Some
Downtown Community TV Center
87 Lafayette St.
New York, NY 10013   Ph: (212)966-4510
Description: This documentary examines the unfairness of the justice system towards minorities. **Release Date:** 1983. **Length:** 7 mins. **Format:** 1/2″ Reel-EIAJ, 3/4″ U-matic Cassette, Other than listed.

★4542★
Are People All the Same?
Pyramid Film & Video
Box 1048   Ph: (310)828-7577
2801 Colorado Ave.   Free: 800-421-2304
Santa Monica, CA 90406   Fax: (310)453-9083
Description: This part of the "Who We Are" series features live action and animation showing children the meaning of race and the uniqueness of each and every person. **Release Date:** 1977. **Length:** 9 mins. **Format:** Beta, VHS, 3/4″ U-matic Cassette.

★4543★
Combating Racism
Chinese for Affirmative Action
17 Walter Lum Pl.
San Francisco, CA 94108   Ph: (415)982-0801
Description: In this program various community representatives from San Francisco are interviewed as to what can be done to combat racism. Among those interviewed were Leaonard Carter, George Tamsak, Mack Hall, Shone Martinez, John Chinn, and Margaret Cruz. **Release Date:** 1973. **Length:** 30 mins. **Format:** 1/2″ Reel-EIAJ.

★4544★
Equal Opportunity
Barr Films
12801 Schabarum Ave.   Ph: (818)338-7878
PO Box 7878   Free: 800-234-7878
Irwindale, CA 91706-7878   Fax: (818)814-2672
Description: This program explores the meaning of equal opportunity within the context of affirmative action, racial discrimination, past discrimination, union contracts, seniority, fairness and the Bill of Rights. **Release Date:** 1983. **Length:** 22 mins. **Format:** Beta, VHS, 3/4″ U-matic Cassette.

★4545★
Mental Health Needs of Minority Children
Social Psychiatry Research Institute
150 E. 69th St.
New York, NY 10021   Ph: (212)628-4800
Description: This program describes the special problems of minority groups, blacks, Hispanics and native Americans, with an emphasis on preventive work with children in school settings so as to avoid the continued high incidence of neurosis and psychoses in this population. **Release Date:** 1981. **Length:** 50 mins. **Format:** 1/2″ Reel-EIAJ, 3/4″ U-matic Cassette.

★4546★
Minorities in Journalism: Making a Difference
PBS Video
1320 Braddock Pl.
Alexandria, VA 22314-1698   Ph: (703)739-5380
Description: A look at how minority students can enter and get ahead in the various branches of journalism - print, radio, and TV. **Release Date:** 1989. **Length:** 25 mins. **Format:** VHS, 3/4″ U-matic Cassette.

★4547★
Opportunities in Criminal Justice
William Greaves Productions
80 8th Ave., Ste. 1701
New York, NY 10011   Ph: (212)206-1213
Description: The wide variety of career opportunities available to women and minorities in the criminal justice system. **Release Date:** 1978. **Length:** 25 mins. **Format:** Beta, VHS. **Credits:** Narrated by: Bill Cosby.

★4548★
Prejudice: A Lesson to Forget
American Educational Films
3807 Dickerson Rd.
Nashville, TN 37207   Free: 800-822-5678
Description: An interview with people who exhibit unconscious prejudices against minorities. **Release Date:** 1973. **Length:** 17 mins.

Format: Beta, VHS, 3/4″ U-matic Cassette. **Credits:** Narrated by: Joseph Campanella.

★4549★
Prejudice: Causes, Consequences, Cures
CRM/McGraw-Hill Films
674 Via de la Valle
PO Box 641
Del Mar, CA 92014
Description: This program focuses on research findings and their implications for dealing with prejudice against women and racial, national, and ethnic groups. **Release Date:** 1974. **Length:** 24 mins. **Format:** Beta, VHS, 3/4″ U-matic Cassette.

★4550★
The Prejudice Film
Motivational Media
12001 Ventura Pl., No. 202   Ph: (818)508-6553
Studio City, CA 91604   Free: 800-331-8454
Description: The historical background of contemporary forms of prejudice are examined in this program. **Release Date:** 1984. **Length:** 28 mins. **Format:** Beta, VHS, 3/4″ U-matic Cassette. **Credits:** Narrated by: David Hartman.

★4551★
Racism and Minority Groups: Part 1
University of Washington Instructional
  Media Services
Kane Hall, DG-10
Seattle, WA 98195   Ph: (206)543-9909
Description: Each of the major racial minorities is presented in historic and current respective and members of each group respond to the series' presentations. Programs available individually. **Release Date:** 1973. **Length:** 30 mins. **Format:** 3/4″ U-matic Cassette.

★4552★
Racism and Minority Groups: Part 2
University of Washington Instructional
  Media Services
Kane Hall, DG-10
Seattle, WA 98195   Ph: (206)543-9909
Description: These programs are a continuation of ''Racism and Minority Groups 1.'' Programs are available individually. **Release Date:** 1973. **Length:** 30 mins. **Format:** 3/4″ U-matic Cassette.

★4553★
Storm of Strangers
Films, Inc.
5547 N. Ravenswood Ave.   Ph: (312)878-2600
Chicago, IL 60640-1199   Free: 800-323-4222
Description: This series introduces America's ethnic and racial minorities to each other. **Release Date:** 1983. **Length:** 29 mins. **Format:** Beta, VHS, 3/4″ U-matic Cassette.

★4554★
What Color Is Skin
Pyramid Film & Video
Box 1048   Ph: (310)828-7577
2801 Colorado Ave.   Free: 800-421-2304
Santa Monica, CA 90406   Fax: (310)453-9083
Description: This part of the ''Who We Are'' series combines live action and animation to show that individual skin coloring is determined by the amount of melanin in the skin. **Release Date:** 1977. **Length:** 9 mins. **Format:** Beta, VHS, 3/4″ U-matic Cassette.

Master Name and Keyword Index

The alphabetical Master Name and Keyword Index provides access to all entries included in NAID, as well as former or alternate names which appear within its text. The index also provides access to entries via inversions on significant keywords appearing in an entry name. Index references are to book entry numbers rather than page numbers. Entry numbers appear in **boldface** type if the reference is to the unit for which information is provided in NAID and in lightface if the reference is to a program, former, or alternate name included within the text of the cited entry.

Aleut Owned-and-Operated Arts and Crafts Businesses; Source Directory of Indian, Eskimo, and **1618, 2522**
Aleutian Pribiloff Island Association **2424**
Alexander Indian Band **2763**
Alexandria Band **2923**
Alexis Creek Indian Band **2814**
Alexis Indian Band **2749**
Algaaciq; Native Village of **2363**
Algonquin Birchbark Canoe; Building an **3749**
Algonquins of Barriere Lake Indian Band **3199**
Algonquins of Golden Lake Band **3086**
Alice Elliott **4540**
Aliuk: Eskimo in Two Worlds; Matthew **2573**
Alkali Indian Band **2962**
All Indian Pueblo Council **328**
Allakaket Traditional Council **2195**
Allen County Historical Society • Elizabeth M. MacDonell Memorial Library **789**
Allen Sapp Gallery **3684**
Alliance Autochtone du Quebec **3544, 3711**
Alliance of Minority Women for Business and Political Development **3778**
Alliance Tribal Council **3360**
Alliance of Tribal Nations **3387**
Allied Indian & Metis Society **3388**
Aloha Publishing **2713**
Alta-Northwest Territories Native Band; Fitz/Smith— **3040**
Alturas Rancheria **23**
ALU LIKE, Inc. **2590**
    Hawaii Island Center **2602**
        Kailua-Kona Annex **2625**
        Kamuela Annex **2626**
    Kauai Island Center **2632**
    Maui Island Center **2639**
    Molokai Island Center **2629**
    Ohau Island Center **2606**
ALU LIKE, Inc. Business Development Center **2605**
Amarillo Public Library • Local History Collection **790**
Ambler Traditional Council **2196**
The American as Artist: A Portrait of Bob Penn **1818**
American Association on Indian Affairs **354**
American Civil Liberties Union **3779**
    Alabama Affiliate **3797**
    Arizona Affiliate **3800**
    Arkansas Affiliate **3803**
    Colorado Affiliate **3822**
    Connecticut Affiliate **3825**
    Delaware Affiliate **3827**
    Eastern Missouri Affiliate **3868**
    Florida Affiliate **3831**
    Georgia Affiliate **3836**
    Hawaii Affiliate **3842**
    Houston Chapter Affiliate **3923**
    Idaho Affiliate **3844**
    Illinois Affiliate **3845**
    Iowa Affiliate **3850**
    Kansas/Western Missouri Affiliate **3866**
    Kentucky Affiliate **3851**
    Maine Affiliate **3855**
    Maryland Affiliate **3856**
    Massachusetts Affiliate **3858**
    Michigan Affiliate **3860**
    Minnesota Affiliate **3862**
    Mississippi Affiliate **3864**
    Montana Affiliate **3870**
    Mountain States Regional Office **3823**
    National Capital Area Affiliate **3828**
    Nebraska Affiliate **3871**
    Nevada Affiliate **3872**
    New Mexico Affiliate **3877**
    New York Affiliate **3884**
    Northern California Affiliate **3816**
    Ohio Affiliate **3893**
        Cleveland Chapter **3894**
    Oklahoma Affiliate **3896**
    Oregon Affiliate **3899**
    Pennsylvania Affiliate **3901**
        Pittsburgh Chapter **3904**
    Rhode Island Affiliate **3908**
    San Diego Affiliate **3814**
    South Carolina Affiliate **3910**

    Southern California Affiliate **3808**
    Southern Regional Office **3837**
    Tenessee Affiliate **3914**
    Texas Affiliate • Dallas Chapter **3920**
    Utah Affiliate **3929**
    Vermont Affiliate **3931**
    Washington Affiliate **3937**
    West Virginia Affiliate **3939**
    Wisconsin Affiliate **3940**
    Wyoming Affiliate **3942**
American Civil Liberties Union Foundation **3780**
American Committee to Advance the Study of Petroglyphs and Pictographs **4504**
American Friends Service Committee **3781**
American Horse School **1462**
The American Indian **1819**
American Indian Affairs; Association on **354**
American Indian After the White Man Came **1820**
American Indian and Alaska Native Periodicals Project **350, 2409**
American Indian and Alaska Native Support Program • School of Public Health • University of Hawaii at Honolulu **1578, 2509**
American Indian and Alaska Native Traders Directory **1602, 2517**
American Indian Archaeological Institute **329, 1048, 1183, 1729**
    Library **791**
American Indian Archival Material: A Guide to Holdings in the Southeast **1603**
American Indian Art Magazine **1623**
American Indian Artists: Part I **1821**
American Indian Artists: Part II **1822**
American Indian Basketry Magazine **1624**
American Indian Basketry and Other Native Arts **1730**
American Indian Before the White Man **1823**
American Indian Bible College • Dorothy Cummings Memorial Library **792**
American Indian Center [Chicago, IL] **483**
American Indian Center [Saint Louis, MO] **513**
American Indian Center • American Indian Service Corporation **482**
American Indian Center of Arkansas **447**
American Indian Center of Central California **448**
American Indian Center; Lansing North **500**
American Indian; A Century of Silence...Problems of the **1868**
American Indian Chamber of Commerce **576**
American Indian Collection: Geronimo and the Apache Resistance **1824**
American Indian Collection: Myths and Moundbuilders **1825**
American Indian Collection: Seasons of the Navajo **1826**
American Indian Collection: Spirit of Crazy Horse **1827**
American Indian Collection: Winds of Change—A Matter of Promises **1828**
American Indian College Fund **330**
American Indian Community Center **585**
The American Indian Community House **540**
American Indian Council on Alcoholism **589**
American Indian Council of Architects and Engineers **331**
American Indian Council of Central California **449**
American Indian Culture Center Journal **1625**
American Indian Culture Research Center **332**
    Museum **1159**
American Indian Culture and Research Journal **1625**
American Indian Development Association **333**
American Indian Education: A Directory of Organizations and Activities in American Indian Education **1604**
American Indian Education Center **467**
American Indian Education Policy Center • Pennsylvania State University **1199**
American Indian Free Clinic **450**
American Indian Friendship House **474**
American Indian Fund **354**
American Indian Fund; National Congress of **352**
American Indian Graduate Center **334**
American Indian Health Care Association **335**
American Indian Health Service **484**
American Indian Heritage Foundation **336**
American Indian Higher Education Consortium **337**
American Indian Historical Society **338**
American Indian Index **1605, 2518**
American Indian Influence on the United States **1829**

Civil Liberties Union; American **3779** (continued)
  Idaho Affiliate **3844**
  Illinois Affiliate **3845**
  Iowa Affiliate **3850**
  Kansas/Western Missouri Affiliate **3866**
  Kentucky Affiliate **3851**
  Maine Affiliate **3855**
  Maryland Affiliate **3856**
  Massachusetts Affiliate **3858**
  Michigan Affiliate **3860**
  Minnesota Affiliate **3862**
  Mississippi Affiliate **3864**
  Montana Affiliate **3870**
  Mountain States Regional Office **3823**
  National Capital Area Affiliate **3828**
  Nebraska Affiliate **3871**
  Nevada Affiliate **3872**
  New Mexico Affiliate **3877**
  New York Affiliate **3884**
  Northern California Affiliate **3816**
  Ohio Affiliate **3893**
    Cleveland Chapter **3894**
  Oklahoma Affiliate **3896**
  Oregon Affiliate **3899**
  Pennsylvania Affiliate **3901**
    Pittsburgh Chapter **3904**
  Rhode Island Affiliate **3908**
  San Diego Affiliate **3814**
  South Carolina Affiliate **3910**
  Southern California Affiliate **3808**
  Southern Regional Office **3837**
  Tenessee Affiliate **3914**
  Texas Affiliate • Dallas Chapter **3920**
  Utah Affiliate **3929**
  Vermont Affiliate **3931**
  Washington Affiliate **3937**
  West Virginia Affiliate **3939**
  Wisconsin Affiliate **3940**
  Wyoming Affiliate **3942**
Civil Liberties Union Foundation; American **3780**
Civil Rights Bureau
  Montana Transportation Department **4246**
  New York Law Department **4287**
Civil Rights; Citizens' Commission on **3783**
Civil Rights and Civil Liberties Division • Massachusetts Attorney General **4210**
Civil Rights Commission; Indiana **4166**
Civil Rights Commission; Iowa **4171**
Civil Rights Commission; Kansas **4175**
Civil Rights Committee; Arlington **4200**
Civil Rights Compliance Activities • Office of the Secretary • U.S. Department of Health and Human Services **4081**
Civil Rights and Compliance; King Office of County **4370**
Civil Rights Coordinator • Virginia Department of Social Services **4362**
Civil Rights Department; Michigan **4219**
  Minority/Women Business Certification **4220**
Civil Rights Department; Minneapolis **4227**
Civil Rights Deputy Attorney General • West Virginia Attorney General **4377**
Civil Rights Division
  Alabama Attorney General **4102**
  Arizona Attorney General **4107**
  Colorado Regulatory Agencies Department **4133**
  Iowa Attorney General **4170**
  Louisiana Social Services Department **4188**
  Michigan Attorney General **4218**
  New Jersey Law and Public Safety Department **4254**
  New Jersey Transit Corporation **4263**
  Oregon Labor and Industries Bureau **4320**
  U.S. Department of Justice **4006**
Civil Rights Division; Equal Employment Opportunity/ • Nebraska Labor Department **4248**
Civil Rights Enforcement Agency; St. Louis **4243**
Civil Rights Enforcement Division • Pennsylvania Attorney General **4323**
Civil Rights & Equal Employment Opportunity Office
  Alabama Department of Human Resources **4103**
  Kansas Social and Rehabilitation Services Department **4179**

Civil Rights Office
  California Community Colleges **4118**
  Florida Health and Rehabilitative Services Department **4144**
  Florida Labor and Employment Security Department **4146**
  Minnesota Human Services Department **4236**
  North Dakota Transportation Department **4297**
  U.S. Department of Health and Human Services **3979**
  U.S. General Accounting Office **4050**
Civil Rights Office; Affirmative Action and
  California Justice Department **4126**
  Wisconsin Health and Social Services Department **4381**
Civil Rights Office; Equal Employment Opportunity and • Delaware Transportation Department **4139**
Civil Rights Section
  Ohio Attorney General **4300**
  Oregon Transportation Department **4322**
  Texas Human Services Department **4355**
Civil Rights Training, and Advisory Service; Desegregation Assistance, • Office of Assistant Secretary for Elementary and Secondary Education • U.S. Department of Education **4071**
Civil Rights; U.S. Commission on **3943**
  Central Regional Office **3944**
  Eastern Regional Office **3945**
  Midwestern Regional Office **3946**
  Rocky Mountain Regional Office **3947**
  Southern Regional Office **3948**
  Western Regional Office **3949**
Civilization; Canadian Museum of **3674**
Civilized Tribes **1874**
CKNM-FM **3725**
CKQN-FM **3726**
Clack Museum; H. Earl **1096**
Clapp Library; Margaret • Special Collections • Wellesley College **1004**
Clara Lander Library • Winnipeg Art Gallery **3662**
Clark's Point; Native Village of **2230**
Clausen Memorial Museum **2474**
Clearinghouse on Rural Education and Small Schools; ERIC **1187, 2492**
  Library **824, 2461**
Clearinghouse on Urban Education; ERIC • Columbia University **4389**
Clerks Association; National American Indian Court **388**
Cleveland American Indian Center **552**
Cleveland Chapter • Ohio Affiliate • American Civil Liberties Union **3894**
Cleveland Human Services Department • Office of Human Resources • Equal Employment Opportunity Division **4298**
Cleveland Minority Business Development Center [Canton, OH] **3891**
Cleveland Minority Business Development Center [Cleveland, OH] **3895**
Click Relander Collection • Reference Department • Yakima Valley Regional Library **1013**
Cliff Dwellings Museum; Manitou **1044**
Cline Library • Special Collections and Archives Department • Northern Arizona University **905**
Clouded Land **1875**
Cloverdale Rancheria **41**
Clues to Ancient Indian Life **1876**
Coalition for Indian Education **359**
Coast Indian Community of the Resighini Rancheria **67**
Cochise Visitor Center and Museum **1019**
Cochiti; Pueblo of **197**
Cockburn Island Band **3158**
Cocopah Tribal Council **15**
Cocopah Tribe • Head Start Program **1216**
Coeur D'Alene Tribal Council **125**
  Head Start Program **1236**
Coeur D'Alene Tribal School **1376**
Cold Lake First Nations Band **2751**
Cold Springs Rancheria **105**
Coldwater Indian Band **2884**
Colgate University • Native American Studies Program **1540**
Collage **4492**
College of Eastern Utah • Prehistoric Museum **1171**
College Fund; American Indian **330**
College Journal; Saskatchewan Indian Federated **3710**
College of the Redwoods • Native American Studies Program **1523**

Grand Lac Victoria; Bande indienne du **3187**
Grand Mound History Center; Minnesota Historical
  Society's **1089**
Grand Portage National Monument • Library • U.S. National
  Park Service **963**
Grand Portage Reservation Business Committee **150**
    Head Start Program **1244**
Grand Rapids First Nation Band **2990**
Grand Rapids Inter-Tribal Council **497**
Grand Traverse Band of Ottawa and Chippewa Tribes
    Head Start Program **1240**
    Tribal Council **143**
Grand Village of the Natchez Indians **1091**
Grande Prairie Friendship Centre **3334**
Grande Ronde Tribal Council; Confederated Tribes of the **267**
Grassy Narrows First Nation Band **3087**
Grayling; Organized Village of **2262**
Greasewood Boarding School **1332**
Great American Indian Heroes **1928**
Great Falls Indian Education Center **518**
The Great Movie Massacre **1929**
Great Plains; Museum of the **1150, 1193**
Great Plains Newsletter; *Museum of the* **4500**
Great Plains Studies; Center for • University of Nebraska,
  Lincoln **984**
Great Spirit Within the Hole **1930**
Greatland Graphics **2534**
Greenville Rancheria **89**
Greenville/Spartanburg Minority Business Development
  Center **3912**
Greeves Art Gallery; R.V. **4528**
Greyhills High School **1333**
Grindstone Bluff Museum • Library **839**
Grindstone Rancheria **48**
Grouard Indian Band **2752**
Group Hunting on the Spring Ice, Parts I-III **2563**
Guide to Minority Business Directories **4476**
Guide to Multicultural Resources **4475**
Guide to Obtaining Minority Business Directories **4476**
Guide to Prehistoric Ruins of the Southwest **4477**
Guilford Native American Association **547**
Gulkana Village Council **2254**
Gull Bay Indian Band **3051**
Gwa'sala-'Nakwaxda'xw Indian Band **2909**
Gwitchin Indian Band; Vuntut **3292**
H. Earl Clack Museum **1096**
Haa Shagoon **2564**
*Had You Lived Then: Life in the Woodlands Before the White
  Man Came* **1931**
Hagwilget Indian Band **2897**
Haida Central Council; Tlingit and • Head Start Program **2506**
Haida Indian Tribes of Alaska; Central Council of the Tlingit
  and **2277**
Halalt Indian Band **2811**
Halau Hula O Mililani **2635**
Halau Mohala Ilima **2623**
Hale Kako'o Punana Leo/Hilo **2679**
Hale Kako'o Punana Leo/Honolulu **2680**
Hale Naua III Society of Hawaiian Art **2598**
Hale Ola Ho'opakolea, Inc. **2636**
Halfway River Indian Band **2966**
Hall of Fame for Famous American Indians; National **1152**
Hamilton; Native Village of **2297**
Hamilton Regional Indian Centre **3489**
Hampshire College • Native American Studies Program **1548**
HANA Scholarships **4429**
Hancock House Publishers Ltd. **4516**
Hannahville Indian Community Council **145**
Hannahville Indian School **1384**
Harlem Minority Business Development Center **3885**
Harold McCracken Research Library **1188**
Harold S. Colton Memorial Library • Museum of Northern
  Arizona **886**
Harrison Western Research Center; Michael and Margaret B. •
  University of California, Davis **977**
Harry M. Trowbridge Research Library • Wyandotte County
  Historical Society and Museum **1010**
Hartley Bay Indian Band **2842**
Hartwick College • Stevens-German Library • Special
  Collections **840**

Harwell Goodwin Davis Library • Special Collections • Samford
  University **926**
Haskell Indian Alcohol Education and Prevention Program **486**
Haskell Indian Junior College **1497**
Hatchet Lake Indian Band **3283**
Hauberg Indian Museum **1065**
Haudensaunee: Way of the Longhouse **1932**
Havasupai School **1334**
Havasupai Tribal Council **16, 1766**
    Head Start Program **1219**
Hawaii Accounting and General Services Department • King
  Kamehameha Celebration Commission **2654**
Hawaii Affiliate • American Civil Liberties Union **3842**
Hawaii Children's Museum **2666**
Hawaii Community Foundation • Irving A. Singer
  Foundation **2608**
Hawaii Computer Training Center **2590**
Hawaii Cultural Research Foundation **2609**
Hawaii Culture and the Arts Foundation **2655**
Hawaii; Daughters of **2607**
Hawaii Foundations; Historic **2612**
Hawaii Health Department
    Affirmative Action Office **4154**
    Health Resources Administration • Office of Hawaiian
      Health **2656**
Hawaii Labor and Industrial Relations Department • Equal
  Employment Opportunity Office **4155**
Hawaii Nei; Ka Imi Naauao O **2628**
Hawaii Office of the Governor • Affirmative Action
  Coordinator **4156**
Hawaii Seahorse Press **2719**
Hawaii Stitchery and Fibre Art Guild **2610**
Hawaiian Advisory Council; Native **2594**
Hawaiian Affairs; Office of • State of Hawaii **2658**
Hawaiian Art; Hale Naua III Society of **2598**
Hawaiian Band; Royal **2620**
Hawaiian Canoe Racing Association **2611**
Hawaiian Children; Center for Gifted and Talented Native •
  University of Hawaii at Hilo **2597**
Hawaiian Club; Wakinikona **2643**
Hawaiian Drug-Free Schools and Communities Program;
  Native **2681**
Hawaiian Health Professions Scholarship Program; Native **2681**
Hawaiian Heritage; State Council on **2621**
Hawaiian Higher Education Program; Native **2681**
Hawaiian Home Lands Department **2657**
Hawaiian Library Project; Native **2595**
Hawaiian Model Curriculum Development; Native • Kamehameha
  Elementary Education Program • U.S. Department of
  Education • Office of the Assistant Secretary for Elementary
  and Secondary Education **2646**
Hawaiian Natives; Library Services for Indian Tribes and •
  Office of Assistant Secretary for Educational Research and
  Improvement • U.S. Department of Education **636, 2645**
Hawaiian People; Congress of the **2591**
Hawaiian Studies Institute **2681**
Hawaiian Substance Abuse Prevention Project; Native **2590**
Hawaiian Vocational Education Program; Native **2596**
Hawaiian Water Resources Control Project; Native **2594**
Hay River Indian Band **3042**
Head Start Program
    Association of Village Council Presidents **2499**
    Bad River Tribal Council **1314**
    Blackfeet Tribal Business Council **1250**
    Bois Forte Reservation Business Committee **1242**
    Caddo Tribe **1280**
    Central Tribes of the Shawnee Area, Inc. **1281**
    Chehalis Tribal Business Council **1301**
    Cherokee Nation of Oklahoma **1282**
    Cheyenne-Arapaho Tribes of Oklahoma **1283**
    Cheyenne River Sioux Tribal Council **1294**
    Chickasaw Nation of Oklahoma **1284**
    Choctaw Nation of Oklahoma **1285**
    Cocopah Tribe **1216**
    Coeur D'Alene Tribal Council **1236**
    Colorado River Indian Tribes **1217**
    Colville Confederated Tribes **1302**
    Confederated Salish and Kootenai Tribes **1251**
    Confederated Tribes of Siletz Indians **1292**
    Confederated Tribes of Warm Springs **1293**
    Cook Inlet Tribal Council **2501**

Hui No Ke Ola Pono **2640**
   Hana Office **2600**
Hula O Mililani; Halau **2635**
Hulihee Palace **2667**
Human Affairs Commission; South Carolina **4342**
Human Development; Dine Center for **1195**
Human Relations Commission • Florida Administration
   Department **4142**
Human Relations Commission; Manhattan • Community
   Relations Office **4266**
Human Relations Commission; Maryland **4197**
Human Relations Council • North Carolina Office of the
   Governor **4293**
Human Relations Division • Delaware Community Affairs
   Department **4137**
Human Relations Services • Oklahoma Education
   Department **4312**
Human Rights Advocacy Department • Florida Health and
   Rehabilitative Services Department **4145**
Human Rights Commission
   Alaska Office of the Governor **4106**
   District of Columbia Arts and Humanities
     Commission **4140**
   Missouri Housing Development Commission **4241**
   Missouri Labor and Industrial Relations Department **4242**
Human Rights Commission; Idaho **4157**
Human Rights Commission; Kentucky **4181**
   Louisville Office **4182**
Human Rights Commission; Maine **4190**
Human Rights Commission; New Hampshire **4250**
Human Rights Commission; Rhode Island **4338**
Human Rights Commission; Tennessee **4348**
Human Rights Commission; Vermont **4358**
Human Rights Commission; West Virginia **4379**
Human Rights Council; Virginia **4365**
Human Rights Department; Illinois **4162**
Human Rights Department; Iowa **4172**
Human Rights Department; Minnesota **4233**
   Equal Employment Opportunity Commission Office **4234**
Human Rights Department; New York **4285**
Human Rights Division
   Mental Health Department • California Health and Welfare
     Agency **4125**
   Minnesota Attorney General **4229**
   Montana Labor and Industry Department **4245**
   New Mexico Labor Department **4265**
   South Dakota Commerce and Regulations
     Department **4343**
Human Rights and Minority Business Development Office •
   District of Columbia Arts and Humanities Commission **4141**
Human Rights; New York Division of
   Rochester Regional Office **4277**
   Suffolk County Regional Office **4278**
   Syracuse Regional Office **4279**
   White Plains Regional Office **4280**
Human Rights and Opportunities Commission;
   Connecticut **4136**
Humboldt State University • Center for Indian Community
   Development **1189**
Hunter Library • Special Collections • Western Carolina
   University **1006**
Hunters; Iowa's Ancient **1982**
Hunters Point Boarding School **1339**
Hunters of the Seal **2567**
Huntington Free Library • Museum of the American Indian •
   Library **844**
Hupa Indian White Deerskin Dance **1955**
Huron Indian Village **3675**
Huronia Historical Parks • Resource Centre **3641**
Huronne-Wendat; Bande indienne de la Nation **3210**
Huronne-Wendat; Nation **3565**
Huslia Village Council **2270**
Huteetl: A Koyukon Memorial Potlatch **2568**
Hydaburg Cooperative Association **2271**
I Am Different From My Brother: Dakota Name-Giving **1956**
I Will Fight No More Forever **1957**
IBM Minority Fellowships **4432**
Ichana **1662**
I.D. Weeks Library • Richardson Archives • University of South
   Dakota **996**
Idaho Affiliate • American Civil Liberties Union **3844**

Idaho Education Department • Adult Education and Indian
   Education **699**
Idaho Heritage Museum **1060**
Idaho Human Rights Commission **4157**
Igiugig Village Center **2272**
Igloo; How to Build An **3757**
Iglooik: Peter's Story; Easter in **2550**
Iglooik Research Centre **3686**
IHS Health Professions Pre-Graduate Scholarships **1584, 2512**
IHS Health Professions Preparatory Scholarships **1585, 2513**
Iisaw: Hopi Coyote Stories **1958**
Iliamna; Native Village of **2274**
Illinois Affiliate • American Civil Liberties Union **3845**
Illinois Board of Education • Program Development and
   Intervention • Office of Urban and Ethnic Education **4158**
Illinois Central Management Services Department • Minority and
   Female Business Enterprises Office **4159**
Illinois Commerce and Community Affairs Department • Equal
   Employment Opportunity and Affirmative Action Office **4160**
Illinois Employment Security Department • Equal Employment
   Opportunity/Affirmative Action Office **4161**
Illinois Human Rights Department **4162**
Illinois Revenue Department • Equal Employment Opportunity
   Office **4163**
Illinois Secretary of State • Affirmative Action Officer **4164**
Illinois State Historical Library **845**
Images of Indians **1959**
Impresora Sahuaro **4518**
In Quest of a Vision **1960**
In Search of the First Americans **1961**
In the White Man's Image **1962**
Inaja and Cosmit Band of Mission Indians **88**
Independent Schools Talent Search Program **3777**
Indian Action Council of Northwestern California **456**
Indian Activities Association; National **394**
Indian Affairs **1663**
Indian Affairs; American Association on **354**
Indian Affairs; Associated Committee of Friends on **353**
Indian Affairs; Association on American **354, 1737**
Indian Affairs; Colorado Commission on **692**
Indian Affairs Commission; Alabama **671**
Indian Affairs Commission; Arizona **673**
Indian Affairs Commission; Michigan **706**
Indian Affairs Commission; North Carolina **745**
Indian Affairs Commission; North Dakota **747**
Indian Affairs Commission; Oklahoma **755**
Indian Affairs Commisssion; Maryland **704**
Indian Affairs Coordinator • Virginia Department of Human
   Resources **778**
Indian Affairs Council; Connecticut • Connecticut Department of
   Environmental Protection **695**
Indian Affairs Council; Florida **696**
Indian Affairs Council; Minnesota **709**
Indian Affairs Division • Office of the Solicitor • U.S.
   Department of the Interior **628**
Indian Affairs Division; Utah **777**
Indian Affairs; Massachusetts **705**
Indian Affairs; Montana Governor's Office of **715**
Indian Affairs; Nebraska Commission on **723**
Indian Affairs; New York State Department of **742**
Indian Affairs and Northern Development; Canada—Department
   of **3602**
   Alberta Regional Office **3606**
     Fort McMurray Service Centre **3607**
     Fort Vermilion Service Centre **3608**
     Lethbridge District **3609**
     St. Paul Service Centre **3610**
     Southern Alberta District **3611**
   Atlantic Regional Office **3619**
   British Columbia Regional Office **3612**
     Northwestern British Columbia Field Office **3613**
     Prince George Field Office **3614**
     Vancouver Island Field Office **3615**
   Departmental Library **3636**
   Inuit Cultural and Linguistic Section **3603**
   Manitoba Regional Office **3616**
     Thompson Area Advisory Centre **3617**
   Northwest Territories Regional Office **3618**
   Ontario Regional Office **3620**
     Sioux Lookout District **3621**
     Southern Ontario District **3622**

Indian Band; Cat Lake **3064**
Indian Band; Cayoose Creek **2872**
Indian Band; Champagne/Aishihik **3290**
Indian Band; Chapleau Ojibway **3067**
Indian Band; Chawathil **2845**
Indian Band; Cheam **2929**
Indian Band; Chehalis **2777**
Indian Band; Chemainus **2867**
Indian Band; Cheslatta Carrier Nation **2797**
Indian Band; Chippewas of Georgina Island **3159**
Indian Band; Chippewas of Kettle & Stony Point **3078**
Indian Band; Chippewas of Nawash **3172**
Indian Band; Chippewas of Rama First Nation **3139**
Indian Band; Chippewas of Sarnia **3145**
Indian Band; Chisasibi **3180**
Indian Band; Coldwater **2884**
Indian Band; Columbia Lake **2965**
Indian Band; Comox **2820**
Indian Band; Constance Lake **3063**
Indian Band; Coquitlam **2908**
Indian Band; Cote **3241**
Indian Band; Couchiching **3080**
Indian Band; Cowessess **3221**
Indian Band; Cowichan **2827**
Indian Band; Crane River **2976**
Indian Band; Cree **2741**
Indian Band; Cross Lake **2977**
Indian Band; Cumberland House **3229**
Indian Band; Curve Lake **3070**
Indian Band; Dakota Plains **3011**
Indian Band; Dakota Tipi **3012**
Indian Band; Dalles **3096**
Indian Band; Dauphin River **2992**
Indian Band; Dawson **3289**
Indian Band; Day Star **3265**
Indian Band; Dease River **2807**
Indian Band; Deer Lake **3072**
Indian Band; Ditidaht **2904**
Indian Band; Dog Rib Rae **3037**
Indian Band; Doig River **2928**
Indian Band; Dokis **3111**
Indian Band; Douglas [Harrison Hot Springs, BC, Canada] **2841**
Indian Band; Driftpile **2738**
Indian Band; Duncan's **2733**
Indian Band; Eagle Lake **3076**
Indian Band; Eastmain **3181**
Indian Band; Ebb and Flow **2980**
Indian Band; Ehattesaht **2803**
Indian Band; Enoch **2774**
Indian Band; Ermineskin **2755**
Indian Band; Esquimalt **2958**
Indian Band; Fairford **2984**
Indian Band; Fisher River **2998**
Indian Band; Fishing Lake **3280**
Indian Band; Flying Dust **3254**
Indian Band; Flying Post **3121**
Indian Band; Fond du Lac **3234**
Indian Band; Fort Alexander **2985**
Indian Band; Fort Chipewyan **2742**
Indian Band; Fort Churchill **3023**
Indian Band; Fort Franklin **3031**
Indian Band; Fort George **2916**
Indian Band; Fort Good Hope **3032**
Indian Band; Fort Liard **3033**
Indian Band; Fort McKay **2743**
Indian Band; Fort McMurray **2744**
Indian Band; Fort Nelson **2831**
Indian Band; Fort Norman **3035**
Indian Band; Fort Providence **3036**
Indian Band; Fort Resolution **3038**
Indian Band; Fort Severn **3084**
Indian Band; Fort Simpson **3039**
Indian Band; Fort William **3163**
Indian Band; Fort Wrigley **3041**
Indian Band; Fountain **2873**
Indian Band; Fox Lake **2986**
Indian Band; Frog Lake **2747**
Indian Band; Gamblers **2971**
Indian Band; Garden Hill First Nation **2997**
Indian Band; Gibson **3054**

Indian Band; Gitanmaax **2843**
Indian Band; Gitlakdamix **2896**
Indian Band; Gitsegukla **2944**
Indian Band; Gitwangak **2863**
Indian Band; Gitwinksihlkw **2836**
Indian Band; God's Lake **2988**
Indian Band; God's River **2989**
Indian Band; Gordon **3266**
Indian Band; Grouard **2752**
Indian Band; Gull Bay **3051**
Indian Band; Gwa'sala-'Nakwaxda'xw **2909**
Indian Band; Hagwilget **2897**
Indian Band; Halalt **2811**
Indian Band; Halfway River **2966**
Indian Band; Hartley Bay **2842**
Indian Band; Hatchet Lake **3283**
Indian Band; Hay River **3042**
Indian Band; Heart Lake **2762**
Indian Band; Heiltsuk **2960**
Indian Band; Henvey Inlet **3130**
Indian Band; Hesquiaht **2950**
Indian Band; High Bar **2875**
Indian Band; Hollow Water **3026**
Indian Band; Homalco **2804**
Indian Band; Horse Lake **2759**
Indian Band; Ingenika **2918**
Indian Band; Iskut **2852**
Indian Band; Island Lake **3251**
Indian Band; Islington **3171**
Indian Band; Jackhead **2978**
Indian Band; James Smith **3255**
Indian Band; Janvier **2745**
Indian Band; John Smith **3219**
Indian Band; Joseph Bighead **3263**
Indian Band; Kahkewistahaw **3222**
Indian Band; Kamloops **2853**
Indian Band; Kanaka Bar **2876**
Indian Band; Kanesatake **3196**
Indian Band; Kasabonika **3090**
Indian Band; Katzie **2903**
Indian Band; Kawacatoose **3267**
Indian Band; Kee-Way-Win **3143**
Indian Band; Keeseekoose **3242**
Indian Band; Keeseekoowenin **2982**
Indian Band; Kehewin **2731**
Indian Band; Key **3257**
Indian Band; Kincolith **2858**
Indian Band; Kingfisher Lake **3099**
Indian Band; Kinistin **3277**
Indian Band; Kipawa **3208**
Indian Band; Kispiox **2860**
Indian Band; Kitamaat **2861**
Indian Band; Kitasoo **2865**
Indian Band; Kitigan Zibi Anishinabeg **3188**
Indian Band; Kitkatla **2862**
Indian Band; Kitselas **2948**
Indian Band; Kitsumkalum **2949**
Indian Band; Kitwancool **2864**
Indian Band; Klahoose **2945**
Indian Band; Kluskus **2924**
Indian Band; Kwa-Wa-Aineuk **2912**
Indian Band; Kwakiutl **2910**
Indian Band; Kwanlin Dun **3298**
Indian Band; Kwaw-Kwaw-A-Pilt **2815**
Indian Band; Kwiakah **2805**
Indian Band; Kwicksutaineuk-Ah-Kwaw-Ah-Mish **2940**
Indian Band; Kyuquot **2866**
Indian Band; Lac La Croix **3081**
Indian Band; Lac La Ronge **3245**
Indian Band; Lac des Milles Lacs **3165**
Indian Band; Lac Seul **3100**
Indian Band; Lakahahmen **2825**
Indian Band; Lakalzap **2839**
Indian Band; Lake Babine **2798**
Indian Band; Lake Manitoba **3025**
Indian Band; Lake St. Martin **2993**
Indian Band; Langley **2830**
Indian Band; Lansdowne House **3132**
Indian Band; Lax-Kw-alaams **2914**
Indian Band; Lillooet **2874**
Indian Band; Little Black Bear **3239**

Minority Business Development Center; New Brunswick **3874**
Minority Business Development Center; Newark **3875**
Minority Business Development Center; Newport News **3934**
Minority Business Development Center; Norfolk **3935**
Minority Business Development Center; Oklahoma City **3897**
Minority Business Development Center; Orlando **3833**
Minority Business Development Center; Oxnard **3811**
Minority Business Development Center; Philadelphia **3902**
Minority Business Development Center; Phoenix **3801**
Minority Business Development Center; Pittsburgh **3903**
Minority Business Development Center; Ponce **3907**
Minority Business Development Center; Portland **3900**
Minority Business Development Center; Queens **3882**
Minority Business Development Center; Raleigh/Durham **3890**
Minority Business Development Center; Richmond **3936**
Minority Business Development Center; Riverside **3806**
Minority Business Development Center; Rochester **3887**
Minority Business Development Center; Sacramento **3812**
Minority Business Development Center; St. Louis **3869**
Minority Business Development Center; Salinas **3813**
Minority Business Development Center; Salt Lake City **3930**
Minority Business Development Center; San Antonio **3928**
Minority Business Development Center; San Diego **3815**
Minority Business Development Center; San Francisco/Oakland [Oakland, CA] **3810**
Minority Business Development Center; San Francisco/Oakland [San Francisco, CA] **3817**
Minority Business Development Center; San Jose **3818**
Minority Business Development Center; San Juan **3905**
Minority Business Development Center; Santa Barbara **3820**
Minority Business Development Center; Savannah **3841**
Minority Business Development Center; Seattle **3938**
Minority Business Development Center; Shreveport **3854**
Minority Business Development Center; Stockton **3821**
Minority Business Development Center; Tampa/St. Petersburg **3835**
Minority Business Development Center; Tucson **3802**
Minority Business Development Center; Tulsa **3898**
Minority Business Development Center; Virgin Islands [Saint Croix, VI] **3932**
Minority Business Development Center; Virgin Islands [Saint Thomas, VI] **3933**
Minority Business Development Center; Washington **3829**
Minority Business Development Center; West Palm Beach **3834**
Minority Business Development Center; Williamsburg/Brooklyn **3880**
Minority Business Development Centers • Minority Business Development Agency • U.S. Department of Commerce **4069**
Minority Business Development Commission • Missouri Administration Office **4239**
Minority Business Development Commisssion • Kentucky Economic Development Cabinet **4180**
Minority Business Development Division
   Indiana Administration Department **4165**
   Massachusetts Economic Affairs Executive Office **4214**
Minority Business Development Division; Massachusetts **4216**
Minority Business Development Office
   Louisiana Office of the Governor **4187**
   Ohio Development Department **4305**
Minority Business Development Office; Human Rights and • District of Columbia Arts and Humanities Commission **4141**
Minority Business Directories; Guide to **4476**
Minority Business Directories; Guide to Obtaining **4476**
Minority Business Directory; Try Us: National **4488**
Minority Business Division • Arkansas Industrial Development Commission **4117**
Minority Business Enterprise
   Small, Minority, and Women-Owned Business Development Office • New Jersey Commerce and Economic Development Department **4251**
   Tucson Human Relations Division **4114**
Minority Business Enterprise Division • Tennessee Department of Economic and Community Development **4347**
Minority Business Enterprise Legal Defense and Education Fund **3785**
Minority Business Enterprise Program • Affirmative Action Section • Phoenix Equal Opportunity Department **4111**
Minority Business Enterprises
   Albuquerque Affirmative Action Office **4264**
   Virginia Economic Development **4363**

Minority Business Office • Kansas Commerce Department **4176**
Minority Business Resource Center • Office of Small and Disadvantaged Business Utilization • U.S. Department of Transportation **4024**
Minority Business Resource Development • Minority Business Development Agency • U.S. Department of Commerce **4070**
Minority Businesses Advisor • Office of Small and Disadvantaged Business Utilization • U.S. National Aeronautics and Space Administration **4053**
Minority Children; Mental Health Needs of **4545**
Minority Community Health Coalition Demonstration • Office of the Assistant Secretary for Health • Public Health Service • U.S. Department of Health and Human Services **4086**
Minority Construction Information Center • Pennsylvania General Services Department **4327**
Minority Development Finance Commission • Ohio Development Department **4306**
Minority Development Office • Pennsylvania General Services Department **4328**
Minority Education; Center for Research on **4390**
Minority Energy Information Clearinghouse; National • Office of Minority Economic Impact • U.S. Department of Energy **4079**
Minority Engineering Programs; Educating Tomorrow's Engineers: A Guide to Precollege **4472**
Minority Engineering Students; Financial Aid Unscrambled: A Guide for **4474**
Minority Equity Office • Michigan Education Department **4222**
Minority Family Preservation & Prevention Services Office • Ohio Department of Human Services **4304**
Minority Fellowship in Neuroscience; American Psychological Association **4401**
Minority Fellowships • U.S. Smithsonian Institute **4462**
Minority Fellowships; ANPAF **4404**
Minority Fellowships; IBM **4432**
Minority Fellowships in Psychology-Clinical Training; American Psychological Association **4402**
Minority Fellowships in Psychology-Research Training; American Psychological Association **4403**
Minority and Female Business Enterprises Office • Illinois Central Management Services Department **4159**
Minority Foundation Scholarships; Golden State **4428**
Minority Graduate Fellowships; NSF **4449**
Minority Graduate Fellowships for Women; NSF **4450**
Minority Group Members: Career Information Services, Employment Skills Banks, Financial Aid Sources; Directory of Special Programs for **4471**
Minority Health • Centers for Disease Control • Public Health Service • U.S. Department of Health and Human Services **3991**
Minority Health; Ohio Commission on **4303**
Minority Health Resources Directory **4482**
Minority Health Section • Health Division • Oregon Department of Human Resources **4319**
Minority Honors Training and Industrial Assistance Program • Office of Minority Economic Impact • U.S. Department of Energy **4077**
Minority Journalism Scholarship; Cox **4413**
Minority Journalism Scholarship; Detroit Free Press **4414**
Minority Math Science Leadership Development Recognition • Office of Minority Economic Impact • U.S. Department of Energy **4078**
Minority Organizations: A National Directory **4483**
Minority-Owned Business Firms; National Directory of **4487**
Minority Purchasing Council; National **3793**
Minority Recruitment Division • Kentucky Justice Cabinet **4183**
Minority Reporting Scholarships; Dow Jones Newspaper Fund **4416**
Minority Resource Research Center • Farrell Library • Kansas State University **4384**
Minority Retention Grants; Wisconsin **4465**
Minority Scholarship; Edward D. Stone Jr. and Associates **4417**
Minority Scholarship; KNTV **4437**
Minority Scholarship in Library and Information Science; LITA/OCLC **4439**
Minority Scholarship; Louise Giles **4440**
Minority Scholarship Program; ADHA **4395**
Minority Scholarships; APA Undergraduate **4406**
Minority Scholarships; National FFA Foundation **4446**

Minority Science Improvement • Office of Assistant Secretary for Postsecondary Education • U.S. Department of Education **4074**
Minority Scientist Development Award; AHA **4398**
Minority and Small Business Development Agency • West Virginia Commerce, Labor, and Environmental Resources Department **4378**
Minority Stipend; George A. Strait **4427**
Minority Student Enrollments in Higher Education: A Guide to Institutions with...Asian, Black, Hispanic, and Native American Students **4484**
Minority Student Opportunities in United States Medical Schools **4485**
Minority Student Scholarships in Earth, Space, and Marine Sciences **4443**
Minority Student Scholarships; GE Foundation **4423**
Minority Students; AFDH Dental Scholarships for **4397**
Minority Students; Leonard M. Perryman Communications Scholarship for Ethnic **4438**
Minority Students; MLA Scholarship for **4444**
Minority Students; NIH Postdoctoral Fellowship Awards for **4448**
Minority Students; Society of Actuaries/Casualty Actuarial Society Scholarships for **4456**
Minority Supplier Development Council; National **3793**
Minority Teacher Loans; Wisconsin **4466**
Minority Undergraduate Accounting Majors; AICPA Scholarships for **4399**
Minority Undergraduate Physics Majors; Corporate Sponsored Scholarships for **4412**
Minority Undergraduate Students; ABF Summer Research Fellowships in Law and Social Science for **4394**
Minority/Women Business Certification • Michigan Civil Rights Department **4220**
Minority and Women Business Enterprise; Orange County **4151**
Minority Women in Business; National Association of **3787**
Minority Women for Business and Political Development; Alliance of **3778**
Minority Women in Science; National Network of **3794**
Minority and Women's Business Development Office; New York **4289**
Minority and Women's Business Division • New York Economic Development Department **4281**
Minority/Women's Business Enterprise • King County Affirmative Action Office **4366**
Minority Youth: Adam **2018**
Minot State University • Memorial Library **878**
Minto Life; Songs In **2580**
Minto Village Council **2318**
Miss Indian America **2019**
Miss Indian U.S. Scholarship; National **1591**
Missanabie Cree **3148**
Mission Houses Museum **2673**
Mission Indian Friendship Centre **3368**
Mission Indians; Cahuilla Band of **24**
Mission Indians; Campo Band of **36**
Mission Indians; Cuyapaipe Band of **85**
Mission Indians; Inaja and Cosmit Band of **88**
Mission Indians; La Jolla Band of **111**
Mission Indians; La Posta Band of **69**
Mission Indians; Los Coyotes Band of **114**
Mission Indians; Mesa Grande Band of **96**
Mission Indians; Morongo Band of **27**
Mission Indians; Pala Band of **81**
Mission Indians; Pauma Band of **84**
Mission Indians; Pechanga Band of **103**
Mission Indians; Rincon Band of **112**
Mission Indians; San Manuel Band of **59**
Mission Indians; Santa Ynez Band of **95**
Mission Indians; Santa Ysabel Band of **97**
Mission Indians; Soboba Band of **94**
Mission Indians; Torres-Martinez Band of **104**
Mission Indians; Twenty Nine Palms Band of **83**
Mission Museum; Iowa, Sac and Fox Presbyterian **1073**
Missions; Bureau of Catholic Indian **357, 2411**
Mississauga Indian Band **3060**
Mississaugas of the Credit Band **3088**
Mississippi Affiliate • American Civil Liberties Union **3864**
Mississippi Band of Choctaw Indians **159**
     Head Start Program **1249**
Missoula Indian Alcohol and Drug Service **522**

Missoula Indian Center **523**
Missouri Administration Office
     Affirmative Action Office **4238**
     Minority Business Development Commission **4239**
Missouri Affiliate; Kansas/Western • American Civil Liberties Union **3866**
Missouri Department of Health • Office of Minority Health **4240**
Missouri Historical Society
     Archives **879**
     Library **880**
Missouri Housing Development Commission • Human Rights Commission **4241**
Missouri Indian Center; Southwest **514**
Missouri Labor and Industrial Relations Department • Human Rights Commission **4242**
Missouri Tribal Council; Sac and Fox of **129**
Missouri Tribe; TOE • Head Start Program **1291**
Missouria Tribal Council; Otoe- **254**
Mistassini; Cree Hunters of **3754**
Mistawasis Indian Band **3246**
Mistissini Indian Band **3179**
Mistress Madeleine **2020**
Mitchell Indian Museum • Library • Kendall College **856**
The Mitchell Indian Museum at Kendall College **1066, 2489**
MLA Scholarship for Minority Students **4444**
Moanalua Gardens Foundation **2674**
Moapa Business Council **186**
Moberly Indian Band; West **2891**
Mobert Indian Band; Pic **3110**
Mobile Minority Business Development Center **3796**
Mobile; Museums of the City of • Museum Reference Library **888**
Moencopi Day School **1350**
Mohave-Apache Community Council (Fort McDowell) **3**
Mohave Museum of History and Arts **1024**
Mohave Tribal Council; Fort **76**
Mohawk Council Chiefs; St. Regis **217**
Mohawk Tribe; St. Regis • Head Start Program **1273**
Mohawks of Akwesasne Indian Band **3069**
Mohawks of the Bay of Quinte Indian Band **3073**
Mohawks of Kahnawake **3183**
Monacan JTPA Consortium; Mattaponi- Pamunkey- **579**
Monroe County Library System • General George Armstrong Custer Collection **881**
Montagnais des Escoumins; Bande indienne des **3186**
Montagnais du Lac St. Jean **3197**
Montagnais de Natashquan; Bande indienne des **3192**
Montagnais de Pakua Shipi Indian Band **3202**
Montagnais de la Romaine; Bande indienne **3184**
Montagnais de Schefferville **3205**
Montagnais; Societe de Communications-Atikamekw **3567**
Montagnais de Uashat et Maliotenam; Bande indienne des **3207**
Montana Affiliate • American Civil Liberties Union **3870**
Montana Commerce Department • Indian Affairs **714**
Montana Commissioner of Higher Education • Minority Achievement Division **4244**
Montana Council for Indian Education **363**
Montana Governor's Office of Indian Affairs **715**
Montana Historical Society • Library/Archives **882**
Montana Indian Band **2757**
Montana Indian Manufacturers Network **520**
Montana Labor and Industry Department • Human Rights Division **4245**
Montana Museum; Central **1093**
Montana State University • Center for Native American Studies **1192**
Montana Transportation Department • Civil Rights Bureau **4246**
Montana United Indian Association **521**
Montclair Art Museum • Le Brun Library **883**
Montgomery Minority Business Development Center **3798**
Montreal Lake Indian Band **3256**
Montreal Regional Office • Grand Council of the Crees **3553**
Monument; Coronado State **1107**
Monument; Effigy Mounds National **1070**
Monument; Mound City Group National **1138**
Monument Valley: Navajo Homeland **2021**
Moon Drum **2022**
Moore's Slough Native Village; Bill **2302**
Mooretown Rancheria **80**

Ruins of the Southwest; Guide to Prehistoric **4477**
Rumsey Rancheria **34**
Run, Appaloosa, Run **2111**
The Runaway **2112**
Running on the Edge of the Rainbow: Laguna Stories and Poems **2113**
Rural America Initatives, Inc. • Head Start Program **1299**
Rural and Native Education • Alaska Education Department **2451**
Russian Mission; Native Village of **2361**
Rutgers University • Minority Advancement Program • North American Indian Studies Program **1571**
R.V. Greeves Art Gallery **4528**
Saanich Cultural Education Centre **3356**
Sabewaing Indian Museum **1084**
Sac and Fox of Missouri Tribal Council **129**
Sac and Fox of Oklahoma Business Committee **257**
Sac and Fox Presbyterian Mission Museum; Iowa, **1073**
Sac and Fox Settlement School **1378**
Sac and Fox Tribal Council **126**
Sacajawea **2114**
Sachigo Lake Indian Band **3142**
Sacramento Minority Business Development Center **3812**
Sacramento Urban Indian Health Project **472**
Sacred Ground: The North American Indian's Relationship to the Land **2115**
Saddle Lake Band • Goodfish Lake Group **2750**
Saddle Lake Cultural Education Program **3350**
Saddle Lake Indian Band • Saddle Lake Group **2770**
Safford-Thatcher Stakes • Family History Center • Church of Jesus Christ of Latter-Day Saints **812**
Saginaw Chippewa Tribal Council **141**
Saginaw Inter-Tribal Association, Inc. **501**
Sagitawa Friendship Centre **3346**
Sagitawa Friendship Centre—Newsletter **3717**
Sagkeeng Cultural Centre, Inc. **3412**
St. Augustine Center for American Indians **485**
St. Croix Council **320**
St. Francis Indian School **1480**
St. George Island Village Council **2362**
St. John's Native Friendship Centre **3452**
St. Joseph Museum • Library **925**
St. Louis Civil Rights Enforcement Agency **4243**
St. Louis Minority Business Development Center **3869**
St. Martin Indian Band; Lake **2993**
St. Mary's Indian Band **2821**
St. Michael; Native Village of **2365**
St. Paul Indian Education; South **511**
St. Paul Island; Aleut Community of **2366**
St. Petersburg Minority Business Development Center; Tampa/ **3835**
St. Regis Mohawk Council Chiefs **217**
St. Regis Mohawk Tribe • Head Start Program **1273**
St. Stevens Indian School **1494**
St. Theresa Point Indian Band **3016**
St. Thomas University • Native Studies Program **3695**
Sakimay Indian Band **3240**
Salamatof; Native Village of **2287**
Salinas Minority Business Development Center **3813**
Salish Kootenai College **1505**
    Native American Studies Program **1533**
Salish and Kootenai Tribes; Confederated
    Head Start Program **1251**
    Tribal Council **166**
Salt Lake City Minority Business Development Center **3930**
Salt River Day School **1360**
Salt River Pima-Maricopa Indian Community Council **13**
    Head Start Program **1225**
Samahquam Indian Band **2890**
Sambaa K'e Dene Indian Band **3048**
Samford University • Harwell Goodwin Davis Library • Special Collections **926**
Samson Indian Band **2758**
Samuel K. Fox Museum **2478**
San Antonio Minority Business Development Center **3928**
San Antonio Museum Association • Ellen Schultz Quillin Memorial Library **927**
San Carlos Apache Tribe • Head Start Program **1226**
San Carlos Tribal Council **12**
San Diego Affiliate • American Civil Liberties Union **3814**
San Diego American Indian Health Clinic **473**

San Diego Equal Opportunity Management Office **4132**
San Diego Minority Business Development Center **3815**
San Diego Museum of Man • Scientific Library **928**
San Diego Public Library • Special Collections • Wangenheim Room **929**
San Diego State University • Native American Studies Program **1555**
San Felipe; Pueblo of **206**
    Head Start Program **1269**
    San Felipe School **1426**
San Felipe School • Pueblo of San Felipe **1426**
San Francisco/Oakland Minority Business Development Center [Oakland, CA] **3810**
San Francisco/Oakland Minority Business Development Center [San Francsico, CA] **3817**
San Francisco State University • School of Ethnic Studies • American Indian Studies Program **1572**
San Ildefonso Day School **1427**
San Ildefonso; Maria! Indian Pottery of **2011**
San Ildefonso; Pueblo of **211**
San Jose, Inc.; Indian Center of **475**
San Jose Minority Business Development Center **3818**
San Juan County Archaeological Research Center & Library **930**
San Juan Day School **1428**
San Juan Minority Business Development Center **3905**
San Juan; Pueblo of **207**
San Juan Southern Paiute Council **17**
San Luis Archaeological and Historic Site **1053**
San Manuel Band of Mission Indians **59**
San Pasqual General Council **113**
San Simon School **1361**
Sananguagat: Inuit Masterworks **2579**
Sand Point; Village of **2367**
Sandia; Pueblo of **195**
Sandoval Indian Pueblos, Inc.; Five **535**
    Head Start Program **1262**
Sandpoint Indian Band **3164**
Sandy Bay Indian Band **3001**
Sandy Lake Indian Band **3144**
Sanostee Day School **1429**
Santa Ana; Pueblo of **196**
Santa Barbara City College • Native American Studies Program **1534**
Santa Barbara Minority Business Development Center **3820**
Santa Barbara Museum of Natural History **1201**
    Library **931**
Santa Clara Day School **1430**
Santa Clara; Pueblo of **199**
Santa Fe Indian School **1431**
Santa Rosa Boarding School **1362**
Santa Rosa Junior College • Jesse Peter Native American Art Museum **1039**
Santa Rosa Ranch School **1363**
Santa Rosa Rancheria **71**
Santa Rosa Reservation **58**
Santa Ynez Band of Mission Indians **95**
Santa Ysabel Band of Mission Indians **97**
Sante Fe Indian School **381, 2413**
Santee Sioux Tribal Council **169**
    Head Start Program **1258**
Santo Domingo; Pueblo of **213**
Santo Domingo Tribe • Head Start Program **1271**
Sappujjijit Friendship Centre **3465**
Sara Hightower Regional Library • Special Collections **932**
(Sarcee); Tsuu T'Ina Nation **2735**
Sarnia Indian Band; Chippewas of **3145**
Saskatchewan; Aboriginal Friendship Centre of **3581**
Saskatchewan; Aboriginal Women's Council of **3578**
Saskatchewan Archaeological Society **3586**
Saskatchewan Inc.; Metis Society of **3584**
Saskatchewan Indian Cultural Centre **3587**
Saskatchewan Indian Federated College **3692**
    Library **3652**
    Saskatoon Campus Library **3653**
Saskatchewan Indian Federated College Journal **3710**
Saskatchewan Indian Nations; Federation of **3579**
Saskatchewan Native Communications Corporation **3588**
Saskatchewan; Native Council of **3571**
Saskatchewan People First Council **3589**
Saskatchewan Provincial Library **3654**

U.S. Department of the Interior   (continued)
    Bureau of Indian Affairs   **611**   (continued)
            Warm Springs Agency   **768**
            Western Navajo Agency   **685**
            Western Nevada Agency   **727**
            Wewoka Agency   **764**
            Wind River Agency   **787**
            Winnebago Agency   **724**
            Yakima Agency   **784**
            Yankton Agency   **775**
            Zuni Agency   **740**
        Indian Arts and Crafts Board   **627**
            Indian Arts and Crafts Development   **667, 2449**
            Library   **950, 2467**
        Law Branch Library   **951**
        Museum   **1051, 2488**
        Natural Resources Library   **952**
        Office of Equal Opportunity   **4004**
        Office of Small and Disadvantaged Business
            Utilization   **4005**
        Office of the Solicitor • Indian Affairs Division   **628**
        Policy, Management and Budget • Board of Indian
            Appeals   **629**
U.S. Department of Justice
    Civil Rights Division   **4006**
        Educational Opportunities Litigation Section •
            Desegregation of Public Education   **4091**
        Employment Litigation Section • Equal Employment
            Opportunity   **4092**
        Housing & Civil Enforcement Section • Fair Housing
            and Equal Credit Opportunity   **4093**
        Voting Section • Protection of Voting Rights   **4094**
    Community Relations Service   **4095**
    Environment and Natural Resources Branch Library   **953**
    Office for Victims of Crime • Office of Justice Programs •
        Children's Justice Act for Native American Indian
        Tribes   **668**
U.S. Department of Labor
    Assistant Secretary for Administration and Management
        Directorate of Civil Rights   **4007**
        Office of Equal Employment Opportunity and
            Affirmative Action   **4008**
    Civil Rights Office
        Region I, Boston   **4009**
        Region II, New York   **4010**
        Region III, Philadelphia   **4011**
        Region IV, Atlanta   **4012**
        Region V, Chicago   **4013**
        Region VI, Dallas   **4014**
        Region VII, Kansas City   **4015**
        Region VIII, Denver   **4016**
        Region IX, San Francisco   **4017**
        Region X, Seattle   **4018**
    Employment Standards Administration • Non-Discrimination
        and Affirmative Action by Federal Contractors and
        Federally Assisted Construction Contractors   **4096**
    Employment and Training Administration • Division of Indian
        and Native American Programs • Native American
        Employment and Training Programs   **669, 2450, 2653**
    Office of Small and Disadvantaged Business
        Utilization   **4019**
U.S. Department of State • Office of Small and Disadvantaged
    Business Utilization   **4020**
U.S. Department of Transportation
    Coast Guard, United States
        Office of Acquisition • Contract Support Division for
            Small and Minority Business   **4021**
        Office of Civil Rights   **4022**
    Federal Highway Administration • Office of Civil
        Rights   **4023**
    Office of Small and Disadvantaged Business Utilization •
        Minority Business Resource Center   **4024**
U.S. Equal Employment Opportunity Commission   **4025**
    Atlanta District   **4026**
    Baltimore District   **4027**
    Birmingham District   **4028**
    Charlotte District   **4029**
    Chicago District   **4030**
    Cleveland District   **4031**
    Dallas District   **4032**
    Denver District   **4033**
    Detroit District   **4034**
    Employment Discrimination—Private Bar Program   **4097**
    Employment Discrimination Project Grants—Indian
        Tribes   **670**
    Employment Discrimination—State and Local
        Antidiscrimination Contracts   **4098**
    Employment Discrimination—Title VII of the Civil Rights Act
        of 1964   **4099**
    Houston District   **4035**
    Indianapolis District   **4036**
    Library   **4387**
    Los Angeles District   **4037**
    Memphis District   **4038**
    Miami District   **4039**
    Milwaukee District   **4040**
    New Orleans District   **4041**
    New York District   **4042**
    Philadelphia District   **4043**
    Phoenix District   **4044**
    St. Louis District   **4045**
    San Antonio District   **4046**
    San Francisco District   **4047**
    Seattle District   **4048**
    Washington Field Office   **4049**
U.S. Executive Office of the President
    Office of Management and Budget
        Indian Education   **630**
        Indian Employment and Training Programs   **631**
        Indian Health   **632**
        Indian Programs   **633**
U.S. General Accounting Office • Civil Rights Office   **4050**
U.S. Information Agency • Bureau of Management • Office of
    Equal Employment Opportunity and Civil Rights   **4051**
U.S. Library of Congress
    American Folklife Center   **954**
    General Reading Rooms Division • Microform Reading
        Room Section   **955**
    Rare Book and Special Collections Division   **2662**
U.S. National Aeronautics and Space Administration
    Office of Equal Opportunity Programs • Discrimination
        Complaints Division   **4052**
    Office of Small and Disadvantaged Business Utilization •
        Minority Businesses Advisor   **4053**
U.S. National Park Service
    Big Hole National Battlefield • Library   **956**
    Bighorn Canyon National Recreation Area • Library   **957**
    Custer Battlefield National Monument • Library   **958**
    Fort Laramie National Historic Site • Library   **959**
    Fort Larned National Historic Site • Library   **960**
    Gila Cliff Dwellings National Monument • Visitor Center
        Library   **961**
    Glacier National Park • George C. Ruhle Library   **962**
    Grand Portage National Monument • Library   **963**
    Lava Beds National Monument • Library   **964**
    Mound City Group National Monument • Library   **965**
    Natchez Trace Parkway • Library & Visitor Center   **966**
    Nez Perce National Historical Park • Library   **967**
    Olympic National Park • Pioneer Memorial Museum •
        Library   **968**
    Pipestone National Monument • Library & Archives   **969**
    Point Reyes National Seashore • Library   **970**
    Pu'uhonau o Honaunau National Historical Park •
        Library   **2663**
    Sitka National Historical Park • Library   **2468**
    Southwest Regional Office • Library   **971**
U.S. Office of Personnel Management • Office of Equal
    Employment Opportunity   **4054**
U.S. Small Business Administration
    Minority Business Development   **4100**
    Minority Small Business and Capital Ownership
        Development   **4055**
        Region I, Boston   **4056**
        Region II, New York   **4057**
        Region III, Philadelphia   **4058**
        Region IV, Atlanta   **4059**
        Region V, Chicago   **4060**
        Region VI, Dallas   **4061**
        Region VII, Kansas City   **4062**
        Region VIII, Denver   **4063**
        Region IX, San Francisco   **4064**
        Region X, Seattle   **4065**

Urban Indian Council; National **407, 2421**
Urban Indian Health Project **443**
Urban Indians **2166**
Urban Indians; Nevada **532**
User-Friendly Press **2542**
Utah Affiliate • American Civil Liberties Union **3929**
Utah Department of Health • Division of Community Health
  Services • Ethnic Minority Health Committee Program **4356**
Utah Indian Affairs Division **777**
Utah Industrial Commission • Anti-Discrimination Division **4357**
Utah Navajo Development Council **577**
Utah State Historical Society • Library **1002**
Utah State University • Native American Studies Program **1567**
Utah; Tribal Council of Paiute Indian Tribe of **285**
Ute Indian Cultural Center; Southern **1046**
Ute Indian Museum **1047**
Ute Indian Tribe • Head Start Program **1300**
Ute Mountain Ute Tribe
    Head Start Program **1233**
    Tribal Council **117**
Ute Tribal Council; Southern **116**
    Head Start Program **1232**
Ute Tribal Museum **1173**
Ute Tribe; Ute Mountain
    Head Start Program **1233**
    Tribal Council **117**
Uts'itishtaan'i **1692**
Val D'Or; Centre d'Entraide Autochtone de **3560**
Valley Native Friendship Centre Society **3361**
Valley River Indian Band **3019**
Vancouver Indian Centre Society **3399**
Vaughan Library/LRC; John • Special Collections and Archives •
  Northeastern Oklahoma State University **903**
Venetie Village Council **2204**
Venture Capital Directory **4489**
Vermont Affiliate • American Civil Liberties Union **3931**
Vermont Human Rights Commission **4358**
Veterans Inter-Tribal Association; Vietnam Era **433**
Victoria Native Friendship Centre **3400**
Viejas Tribal Council **22**
Vietnam Era Veterans Inter-Tribal Association **433**
Viger Indian Band **3203**
Village of Alakanuk **2192**
Village of Aniak **2201**
Village of Atmautluak **2206**
Village of Chuathbaluk **2226**
Village Council of Port Heiden **2354**
Village of Crooked Creek **2235**
Village of Kotlik **2303**
Village of Lower Kalskag **2280**
Village of Mary's Igloo **2389**
Village of Nelson Lagoon **2231**
Village of Old Harbor **2342**
Village of Ouzinkie **2344**
Village of Perryville **2346**
Village of Pilot Point **2348**
Village of Red Devil **2359**
Village of Sand Point **2367**
Village of Sleetmute **2378**
Village of Solomon **2379**
Village of Stoney River **2383**
Village of (Upper) Kalskag **2281**
Vine Deloria, Jr.; A Conversation with **1883**
Virgil Hawkins Fellows Scholarships **4463**
Virgin Islands Minority Business Development Center [Saint
  Croix, VI] **3932**
Virgin Islands Minority Business Development Center [Saint
  Thomas, VI] **3933**
Virginia Administration Office • Personnel and Training
  Department • Equal Employment Opportunity Services **4359**
Virginia Commerce Department • Fair Housing Office **4360**
Virginia Department of Health • Office of Human Resource
  Management • Equal Employment Opportunity Division **4361**
Virginia Department of Human Resources • Indian Affairs
  Coordinator **778**
Virginia Department of Social Services • Civil Rights
  Coordinator **4362**
Virginia Economic Development • Minority Business
  Enterprises **4363**
Virginia Employment Commission • Equal Employment
  Opportunity Office **4364**

Virginia Human Rights Council **4365**
Visitation Center; Acoma Tourist and **1102**
Vocational Education Program; Native Hawaiian **2596**
Voice of Alberta Native Women's Society **3354**
Vowell Band; Glen **2844**
Vuntut Gwitchin Indian Band **3292**
Wa He Lut Indian School **1490**
Wabauskang Indian Band **3098**
Wabigoon Lake Ojibway Nation **3075**
Wahgoshig Band **3108**
Wahnapitae Indian Band **3166**
Wahpeton Indian Band **3264**
Wahpeton Indian Boarding School **1454**
Wahpeton Sioux Tribal Council; Sisseton- **281**
Waianae Coast Culture and Arts Society **2638**
Waiau Elementary School **2694**
Wainwright Traditional Council **2401**
The Wake **2167**
Wakinikona Hawaiian Club **2643**
Wales; Native Village of **2402**
Walker River Paiute Tribal Council **190**
Walker Wildlife and Indian Artifacts Museum **1090**
Walking with Grandfather **2168**
Walking in a Sacred Manner **2169**
Walnut Canyon National Monument **1031**
Walpole Island Indian Band **3167**
Wampanoag Tribal Council of Gay Head **138**
Wanbli Ho **1630**
Wapekeka Indian Band **3050**
War Lake Indian Band **2996**
Warm Springs; Confederated Tribes of • Head Start
  Program **1293**
Warm Springs Tribal Council **271**
Warpaint and Wigs **2170**
Warriors **2171**
Wars—Communique; Order of the Indian **4501**
Wars; Order of the Indian **421**
Wasagamack Indian Band **3027**
WASG-AM **1724**
Washagamis Bay Indian Band **3093**
Washington Affiliate • American Civil Liberties Union **3937**
Washington, DC Region • Minority Business Development
  Agency • U.S. Department of Commerce **3959**
Washington Department of Personnel • Workforce Diversity
  Program **4371**
Washington Human Rights Commission **4372**
    Seattle Office **4373**
    Spokane Office **4374**
    Yakima Office **4375**
Washington Indian Affairs **785**
Washington Minority Business Development Center **3829**
Washington Social and Health Services Department • Equal
  Opportunity Office **4376**
Washington State Indian Education Association **580**
Washington State University • Native American Studies
  Program **1568**
Washoe County Law Library **1003**
Washoe Tribal Council **181**
Waskaganish Band **3211**
Waswanipi Indian Band **3212**
Water Is So Clear That a Blind Man Could See **2172**
Water Resources Control Project; Native Hawaiian **2594**
Waterhen Indian Band **3020**
Waterhen Lake Indian Band **3281**
Watkinson Library • Trinity College **948**
Watson & Dwyer Publishing Ltd. **4537**
Wawakapewin Indian Band **3058**
Wawatay Communications Society **3519**
Way of Our Fathers **2173**
Waywayseecappo First Nation Treaty Four—1874 **3015**
We Are One: A Series **2174**
We Are a River Flowing **2175**
(We Someone, The Hopi); Itam Hakim Hopiit **1986**
A Weave of Time **2176**
Weaving; The Art of Navajo **1846**
The WEB **1693**
Webber Resource Center: Native Cultures of the Americas •
  Field Museum of Natural History **827**
Webequi Indian Band **3135**
The Wedding of Palo **2586**

124414